A Word About ERTS-1 Imagery

This amazing Earth Resources Technology Satellite image represents what your eye could see from 570 miles high. It is a synthesis of many images made between July and October of 1972 on what is known as MSS, Band 5 (Multiple Channel Scanner System, Red Band.) The scale is about 1 inch to 32 miles. The images were made at various times to obtain clear weather in all of the region being scanned. This mosaic represents at least 34 different images with their edges meticulously matched. It requires about 30 days for a skilled cartographer to assemble such a mosaic. The large metropolitan areas appear lighter than the surrounding countryside because of the larger quantities of infrared given off by stone and concrete; and we have photographically enhanced that portion of the State that is our subject. Your eye can see the surprisingly clear definition of Puget Sound, rivers, lakes, mountains and islands. And, with a magnifying glass, you can even see the stack smoke from some Port Townsend pulp mills.

Operation of ERTS-1 is a function of the National Aeronautics and Space Administration. They provided this imagery for use by the Soil Conservation Service, U.S. Department of Agriculture, for land use study.

Spokane

Columbia River

Yakima

Snake River

GODDARD SPACE FLIGHT CENTER

ERTS
EARTH RESOURCES TECHNOLOGY SATELLITE-1
IMAGERY 0.6 TO 0.7 MICROMETER BAND
JULY 25 TO OCTOBER 3, 1972

CONSERVATION SERVICE

THE WET SIDE OF THE MOUNTAINS

THE WET SIDE OF THE MOUNTAINS

(OR PROWLING WESTERN WASHINGTON)

BY BILL SPEIDEL

Seattle, Washington
Nettle Creek Publishing Company 1974

FIRST EDITION

CIP Library of Congress Cataloging in Publication Data

Speidel, William C.   1912-

   The wet side of the mountains.

   Bibliography: p.
   Includes index.
   1. Washington (State)—Description and Travel—1951—
   —Guide—books.
     I. Title. II. Title: Prowling western Washington.

F.889.3.S65   917.97/04/4   74-83445
ISBN 0-914890-01-8

International Standard Book Number 0-914890-01-8

Library of Congress Catalog Card Number 74-83445

Copyright © 1974 by William C. Speidel

Nettle Creek Publishing Company
108 South Jackson Street
Seattle, Washington 98104

Printed in the United States of America
by Banta West, Inc., Sparks, Nevada

THIRTEEN DOLLARS AND FIFTY CENTS

To Gunnar Larsen
who had a bright
idea on aluminum
conduit
Bill Seidel
2/20/75

A Word About "Who" . . .

To Shirley and Lou
And the rest of the crew
For what do you see
And how do you do?

Also by Bill Speidel
You Can't Eat Mt. Rainier
Be My Guest in the Pacific Northwest
You Still Can't Eat Mt. Rainier!
Sons of the Profits (Seattle Story 1851 - 1901)

A Word About Contents

Regional Tour Maps

Simplified City Maps

REGION ONE
CLALLAM AND JEFFERSON COUNTIES

A Word About Region I

When one of the young men researching the Olympic Peninsula for this book returned to the office, he said in awestruck tones, "Do you realize they let trees grow old and *die* — and never make a *dime* off of them?"

He was referring, of course, to the biggest thing on the Peninsula, the Olympic National Park. It's as big as the state of Rhode Island with a border around it. Author Murray Morgan hit the nail on the head when he called his book about it *The Last Wilderness*. The idea is to provide a heritage to the American people of a wilderness as untouched by human hands as you can get.

And they've been fighting about it here . . . and in Olympia . . . and in Washington, D.C. ever since that great naturalist, John Muir, suggested a century ago that if we didn't call a halt to things some place, there wouldn't be any forests left. Generally, the fight has been along political lines with the Republicans saying, "Yeah, but does it have to be as big as Rhode Island!" and the Democrats retorting with, "Who ever heard of a *little* ocean?"

They don't have "keep off the grass" signs as such, but there's a great National Park Service cliche that gives you the general idea. And with the multitudes who show up, their reaction is understandable: "The American people are loving the Park to death." (With their big feet.)

You can look at the wonders . . . and enjoy the stimulating lectures and walks conducted by naturalist rangers at certain locations during the summer time . . .

But don't touch . . . and above all, don't take!

One of the big features of the Park, incidentally, is that it has the largest remaining herd of the species of animal called the "Roosevelt Elk." That was in honor of the Republican Roosevelt, who turned over big acreage for these animals a couple of days before he left the White House permanently. (It should be noted that while it was a Republican who paved the way for the Park, he was behaving like a Democrat at the time he did it.) It was shortly after the turn of the century when some guys had figured out a wrinkle of killing elk off for their teeth — which were sold, of course, to the Benevolent and Protective Order of Elks at a time when men's watches had fobs instead of wrists.

The National Foresters, on the other hand, are the poor bastards between the evil lumber barons and the pure conservationists. The National Parks and Forests are refinements of the National Reserves which were to safeguard watersheds and insure a permanent supply of timber. While you can only fish — and perhaps spit — in the Park, you can do lots of things in a National Forest. You can mine in them and build reclamation and power projects in them and let people and even sheep walk on grass in them.

The Olympic National Forest is about three-quarters the size of the Park. It sort of surrounds the Park like a buffer state to absorb the shock of civilization.

About 50% of the people living around the Park think it's greater than the invention of sliced bread. The other 50% is made up of the people our

1

young man talked with. The two groups are still fighting although the Park has existed since June 29, 1933.

Between the National Forest and the Park, the Federal Government owns over 50% of Region 1.

In the minds of local businessmen, the controversy boils down to who's going to make the bucks out of those woods.

And the Republicans are on shaky ground. The number of tourists visiting the Park is up from about 90,000 thirty years ago, to over 2,000,000. Every tourist is worth 20 bucks to the local merchants.

That tourism is a lot like prostitution. . . .

You sell it and you still got it.

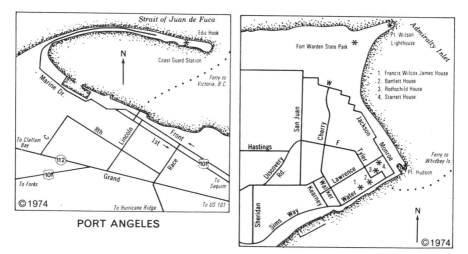

PORT ANGELES

PORT TOWNSEND

Port Angeles Tour 1 — In and Around the City (Map II)

This is a split-level harbor town looking north over 17 wet miles of the Strait of Juan de Fuca to Victoria, B.C. Business district slopes to the waterfront with residences enjoying a panoramic vista from up above. As the major urban area in Region 1, it's home base for our tours around here. Best view of the city is from Ediz Hook, which creates the harbor. Especially good on a moonlit night when the rugged Olympics form an ethereal backdrop for the warm lights of the city.

Port Angeles — (Pop. 16,450. Elev. Sea level to 99.) — Clallam County Seat and U.S. Port of Entry. Frankly, Port Angeles is the metropolis of the Olympic Peninsula. It's a major accommodations center for people taking the Olympic Loop trip, or pausing before boarding the Victoria ferry. Summer visitors add 7,000 to the hotel-motel population and it's wise to make advance reservations.

Everybody in town knows that Ediz Hook, some 3½ miles long, is the second largest sandspit in the world and you haven't really seen Port Angeles until you've seen it from Ediz Hook.

The history of Port Angeles is a colorful one. For instance, during the Civil War, one of the local guys sympathized with President Abraham Lincoln, but felt compelled to add, "However, you could lose, you know — and then what would you do for a capital of the United States of America?"

Lincoln was pretty busy at the time, but he did agree that the history books possibly could read: "North Loses!" Not knowing he was talking to Victor Smith, the "Father" of all Port Angeles real estate promoters, Lincoln asked if he had any suggestions for a second-string capital.

"Well," Smith said, "There's this place out on the west coast. It's about as far away from your present trouble as you can get. It's a dandy spot . . . . "

And that's when he said the magic words.

He said, "It's in a great harbor, behind Ediz Hook . . . and Ediz Hook is part of the second largest sandspit in the world."

Lincoln figured that a good place for the capital of the United States would be behind the second largest sandspit in the world. So he named Port Angeles the "Second National City." Well, how could you get better advertising than that for selling real estate? So Smith came racing home and told everybody around town the big news.

And all ten of 'em thought it was just great.

One of the problems is that Smith died before he told the folks how he had pronounced the name of the Hook — which is contracted from an Indian name — when he talked with Lincoln. And ever since, half the people have pronounced it "eediz" and the other half "ed-is." He also neglected to bring the folks up to date on which was the largest sandspit in the world . . . but then, nobody in Port Angeles really cares.

Port Angeles was, is and probably always will be the most aggressive town on the Olympic Peninsula. They got a gunboat and aimed some guns at the guys in Port Townsend and, with this kind of intellectual persuasion, removed the customs records and made Port Angeles the Port of Entry to the United States on the theory they had this protected harbor behind Ediz Hook. And they got a ferry going to Victoria, and a pulp mill and the Coast Guard Air Station located there — all on account of Ediz Hook.

You can take a drive out on this important hunk of land. In addition to a superb view of the town, you get a real feel of what the 3½ mile Hook does for the harbor, because the waves on the outside are hurling themselves with casual abandon against the stuff that's been piled there to keep the rough water out. Then on the other side are the calm waters of the harbor and this splendid view of Port Angeles and the Olympic Mountains.

You feel close to the whole operation because the road on top of the Hook is only 14 feet above the water.

But back to the bootstrap aspects of Port Angeles.

In her book, *The Untamed Olympics*, Ruby El Hult notes one of the giant steps taken by the residents of the city: "that of hydroelectric power. The moving force behind this forward step was Thomas T. Aldwell, pioneer realtor, who boiled the problem down to a simple creed: 'Industry was what was really needed and back of industry was power.' He had homesteaded a natural power site on the lower Elwha River . . . in 1890. Having spent years acquiring adjacent land, by 1910 he was ready to put his dream into reality. . . . They organized the Olympic Power Company."

So they built a dam on the Elwha, west of town, and Mr. Aldwell wrote himself an autobiography entitled, *Conquering the Last Frontier.*

Well, not quite, as you will see.

There's still a little conquering going on.

Among the conquerors, in addition to Mr. Aldwell, were the residents of a high bluff, which is also west of the Hook. That cliff kept sloughing off, and the people thought, "You know, one of these days a house or two could come tumbling down that cliff . . . and that's quite a drop. . . ."

So they got the Corps of Engineers of the U.S. Army to dump some riprap at the bottom of the cliff.

The idea was to cut that slough stuff. And it did. But that was only the beginning.

On Monday, June 22, 1970, there was an item in the Port Angeles Daily News with the heading, "Violent Wave Takes Out Part of Ediz Hook Road Sunday. . . ." The news story noted that one lane of the road on the Hook had been taken out and the Army Engineers would make a study of the problem and meanwhile, city authorities would do anything possible about solving the problem "short of spending money. . . ."

Short of spending money.

Dr. Alyn C. Duxbury, of the University of Washington School of Oceanography, explained to us about hooks and things. He noted that Ediz and Dungeness Hooks (or spits) have over the centuries migrated up and down the coast with total disregard for the fact that Port Angeles is (1) The Second National City, (2) Port of Entry to the United States for about 2,500 ships a year,

(3) The Seat of Clallam County, (4) Landing for the Black Ball Ferry to Victoria, (5) Location of two of the biggest industries on the Peninsula, Crown Zellerbach and ITT Rayonier, (6) Site of the Coast Guard Air Station which rescues all kinds of people every year and (7) home base of the Puget Sound Pilots' Association.

The Doctor noted that a hook is in equilibrium when the rate of erosion and the rate of a new supply of materials is in balance. But that dam and stopping the sloughing off of those cliffs changed the balance. And the Hook started changing. It doesn't care how many entrances it has or where it's located along the coast.

"You got to feed hooks," Dr. Duxbury pointed out.

Mr. Aldwell had gotten his power company going; and the folks with the view property had arranged to have their homes protected against a sudden, if you'll excuse the expression, "drop" in price. But these necessary arrangements eventually got the Hook off its regular feed. . . .

And Ediz Hook started to come unhooked.

This *was* a revolting development to the Port Angeles Chamber of Commerce . . . and several other people.

The other things were nice. . . . But lose the harbor? My God!

So they had meetings and decided that regardless of how you pronounce the word, somebody better get busy with the care and feeding of Ediz Hook before the whole operation went down the Strait.

Estimated costs of doing something about the Hook ranged from $5- to $20-million, and one of the alternatives suggested by the Army Engineers included the removal of Mr. Aldwell's dam. The $5-million method of saving the Hook, which finally was agreed upon, involved providing 344,000 tons of armor rock and 108,000 cubic yards of gravel and cobbles as a blanket for the revetment.

But then they had to feed that beach annually with about 13,000 cubic yards of what was referred to in a report called Ediz Hook Beach Erosion Control as "artificial beach nourishment." The Plan got its final stamp of approval on May 7, 1973. This stuff is to be stockpiled in sort of a one-acre snack bar near the base of the Hook and replaced from time to time as the Hook is fed.

Now all they've got to do is get this material from some place else — and hope the place they get it from doesn't start some other kind of a chain reaction.

Meanwhile, Ruby El Hult was right about *The Untamed Olympics* . . . and Mr. Aldwell must be looking up or down from his eternal abode and saying, "I guess I goofed when I called the book, *Conquering the Last Frontier!*"

◄►

Prowling Port Angeles

At the tip of the spit is *U.S. Coast Guard Air Station, Port Angeles,* which maintains administrative and operational control of all Coast Guard units in the Olympic Peninsula. It rescues about 1,400 people annually. One man had drifted 54 miles out to sea in a storm and had been gone for 3½ days, which usually means for good, but they brought him back alive. At one point, Indians in Neah Bay thought a Coast Guard helicopter was a flying saucer and tried to shoot it down. And at another time when weather prohibited flying normal routes, it flew an emergency mission ten feet above the ground along a twisting logging road at Lake Ozette. Pilot reported it was like flying in a coke bottle. Visitors are welcome, but it is necessary to make arrangements ahead of time for a tour of the base.

A lot of people get their kicks out of watching the huge ocean-going ships anchored in the harbor. Others get a certain satisfaction from watching them load the Black Ball Ferry for Victoria.

One of the most spectacular views in the entire area is yours for a visit to *Ocean View Cemetery*, west of town and secretly coveted by every real estate promoter around. Further poking around should take you to *Lincoln Park,* a heavily wooded area with picnic tables and playground equipment, and an authentic Indian Longhouse featuring artifacts of the Clallam Indians.

While *Crown Zellerbach* company is vital here, you will read considerably more about it when you arrive at Camas in Region 6. Here in Port Angeles "Crown Z's" *huge turbine wheel* weighing 16 tons is the drawing card you'll find out about from the Chamber of Commerce . . . and the cafeteria is the plus factor you'll get from us. You have to drive past it to get to Ediz Hook, and you ought to drive by in the morning for ham n' eggs and hot cakes, and there are few places that offer better coffee. It's there primarily for the millworkers, but the public is welcome, and the chances are you can find a parking place in and among huge rolls of paper. Call about tours of the plant, or check the Chamber of Commerce.

A little later on, you'll read something about the "bark" of the hemlock, but what's going on here at *ITT Rayonier* (nèe Peninsula Plywood) is the "bite," because Rainier, which became Rayonier, which became ITT Rayonier, was the first in the state of Washington to prove the truth of that Ralph Waldo Emerson quote, "A weed is a plant whose virtue has not yet been discovered." And Russell M. Pickens, formerly DuPont scientist, was the man who figured out that the hemlock — our State tree — no longer was the so-called "weed of the forest." Prior to 1932, hemlock was used for paper pulp only. But Mr. Pickens figured out a way to dissolve the pure cellulose portion of the hemlock, which today is used in the tires you drove here on, the film you're taking your pictures with and any number of other accouterments of our civilization.

With Mr. Pickens' discovery, the Rainier Pulp and Paper Company started making rayon, which turned out to be a product important enough to become the tail that wagged the dog and the company changed its name to *Rayon*-ier, from a new substance that was hotter than a $2 pistol, back before the World War II.

There was a problem here. The company was young and struggling. It only had slim pickin's for Pickens, but would he gamble with them and take a "leetle" stock instead? He would and did, and when it became Rayonier, he was more than reasonably assured that it would not be necessary for him to go on relief during his waning years — and that's exactly the way it turned out. He did not die in a poorhouse.

Rayonier didn't eagerly fly into the new concepts of ecology. For a while there, the attitude was, "We'll do anything you can force us to do in court." But somewhere along the line, they got the message and at the moment, they're blowing $150,000,000 ($45,000,000 in Washington State) in air and water pollution control. In a sulfite mill like this one in Port Angeles, which produces a purer pulp but dumps its effluent in the water, the State Department of Ecology requires removal of 80% of the sulfite liquor discharged in the water and they figure that with all the construction going on at the plant in 1974, they will have removed 85%.

The mill produces 500 tons of cellulose paper daily . . . a $5,000,000 annual payroll for 450 people here and $500,000 in state, county and local taxes.

The raw material, the mill bites into small pieces and then chews up into pulp, comes from 370,000 acres of managed forest land in Clallam, Jefferson, Grays Harbor and Pacific Counties. There is another mill at Hoquiam and a research center at Shelton . . . together with sorting yards at Crane Creek (near Amanda Park off 101) and at Forks. Tours at the Port Angeles mill have been discontinued until the present new construction is completed in 1975, but still are available at Hoquiam.

Uncommon shopping – Hottest items are Wilma Madison's botanically authentic ceramic mushrooms — all collector's items and some museum pieces; try any specialty shops in the region. In Port Angeles, these include *Grebin's*, E. Front . . . *Skylight Gallery*, a tasteful shop on E. 1st . . . *The Tourist Trap*, N. Laurel . . . *Noah's Ark*, W. 1st. We also like *Mart Second Hand Store*, W. 8th St. (with a picture of a hand after "Second") . . . *Poor Bill's* on 101 West . . . *Burke's*, 101 East, rents it, whatever it is, including camping equipment, seven days a week . . . *Swain's General Store*, E. 1st, is just that, open seven days.

A word about eating – Enroute to Ediz Hook is *Clarke's Clam Shack*, Marine Drive, unpretentious eatery with excellent seafood . . . *Crown Zellerbach Cafeteria*, good for breakfast and local color. Local consensus of best restaurants: *Harrington's*, N. Laurel . . . *Traylor's Seafood*, 101 East . . . *Haguewood's*, N. Lincoln, and *Aggie's*, E. Front. *Rayonier's* counterpart cafeteria to "Crown Z" also open to public. *Goldie's*, Front, and *Birney's*, 1st, open 24 hours. A great piece of local Americana is the *M & C Taverne*, W. Front, and its outspoken owner, Cleo McLennon. She does a big business with local folk and foreign and domestic sailors. Lots of turn-of-the-century memorabilia, good homemade dill pickles. (We like that "e" on taverne.)

A word about sleeping – On a peninsula trip, your safest bet is Port Angeles for an overnight stop. It has the greatest number and variety of motels — the Olympic Peninsula Directory includes 16 places. Most luxurious are *Bayshore*, N. Lincoln, and *Royal Victoria*, E. 1st; *Aggie's*, E. Front, is by far best known and biggest. For a free directory, write the Olympic Peninsula Travel Association, P.O. Box 625, Port Angeles 98362 or pick one up at the Washington State Ferry Terminal in Seattle.

Annual affairs – *Skin Diving Meet and Octopus Grab* in March (some of the world's biggest octopi grow in these waters) . . . *Arts in Action*, third weekend in July . . . *Clallam County Fair* in August . . . *Derby Days*, including a Labor Day water ski race from Port Angeles to Victoria, B.C. and back . . . *Junior Salmon Derby*, the weekend after Labor Day, in which about 1,000 youngsters participate.

For further information – Chamber of Commerce, 1217 E. First; phone, 452-2363. Director Dorothy Munkeby is a fountainhead of information about the Peninsula.

Port Angeles Tour 2 — Hurricane Ridge (Map II)

This is a "must," especially on a clear day. The drive to mile-high Hurricane Ridge in the Olympic National Park winds fairly steeply up through dense timber. The occasional breath-taking views looking down on the Strait and Vancouver Island or into sheer canyon walls give you a distinctly "top-of-the-world" feeling as you climb. Then you're in an Alpine setting, virtually eyeball-to-eyeball with jagged mountain ridges. There's a lodge building, nature trails, picnic areas and the chance for a close-up of Mount Olympus from the snow-patched meadows of Obstruction Point. Winter viewing great, too, but access sometimes limited.

Start at the *Pioneer Memorial Museum* in Port Angeles where the Park Service has a relief map of the whole Park along with a slide presentation, an extensive collection of literature for free and for sale, exhibits of flora and fauna and a full-sized replica of an 1890 log cabin. (It is interesting to note that the cabin was constructed by a Port Angeles High School carpentry class.) Among the literature here look for Ruth Kirk's very valuable books: *Exploring the Olympic Peninsula*, and *The Olympic Seashore*. There also is an auditorium for lectures, a reference study collection, offices of the Park Staff and, last but not least — restrooms. Adjacent to the information center is the *Thomas T. Aldwell Environmental Study Area*, named after the man who built that dam on the Elwha River. It is a sample of virgin forest that has been preserved inside the city limits. Paths encompass the area which give you a couple of samples of virgin trees and then go on through showing the impact of man on the forest. In this era of instant everything, it's a fast way of getting the "feel" of what happens to forests. A reporter for the Port Angeles Daily News, which publishes a splendid Annual Summer Supplement, caught the feel of this section rather succinctly with the following: "Here is an aura of excitement, mystery, peace, and a place to learn to live in harmony with our environment. . . ."

Now you're ready to head for Hurricane Ridge some 17 miles away. The Port Angeles Chamber of Commerce notes that it's 35 minutes from "sea level to ski level." The drive is open all summer and on weekends after the snow flies.

◄►

About five miles out of Port Angeles as you head up Highway 111 to Heart O' The Hills, you'll come to a small neighborhood around a little body of water called Lake Dawn where they had a "border" incident in 1950 that shook the Public Information Officer of the Olympic National Park to the soles of his socks.

A number of years back, Oscar Nelson and his wife Eloise figured they could make a buck off their property by turning it into a residential subdivision. They could put a dam across Ennis Creek and create a man-made body of water which they could call Lake Dawn and not only have a view but fresh waterfront property.

This was an especially neat idea in that the government was getting going on access to Hurricane Ridge. The folks would be within commuting distance of their work on the newly improved road and it could be something more than a summer colony.

There was a little confusion at the time over whether this subdivision was in the Park or in the private sector on the other side of the border. The park people like to keep things pretty pure and they wouldn't sail for this kind of a real estate sale . . . not changing the course of Nature to make a lake, anyway.

Well, the Nelsons did their thing and the folks bought the land and they put in the roads and the waterfront houses and all like that. Then, on February 26, 1950, the folks woke up in the morning and looked out. . . .

And Lake Dawn was gone!

The story in the Port Angeles Daily News the next day started out with, "Lake Dawn is in the Strait of Juan de Fuca today, and behind the Olympic Highway fill over Ennis Creek is a jam of driftwood that would make a logger's mouth water. . . ." The story further noted that one of the houses built along the creek, but below the dam, was dislodged from its moorings by the flash flood caused when the dam went out and "shivered to pieces against a county bridge."

Well, things were a mess for a while, physically and legally. But now the dam and lake are back. And the alert Public Relations Officer for the Park got it noted in the original story that this kind of thing happened on the private, not the Park side, of the border.

◆

Now that you're about to excursion over the border into the *Olympic National Park*, let's pause for an over-view of this magnificent chunk of U.S. Here it is in a nutshell.

Of the 1.5 million acres of federally owned forest land on the Olympic Peninsula, about 60% is in the Park, which is surrounded by and divided by the National Forest. The Park is in two major parts, the Mountains — not considered a part of the coast range, but a unique hunk of mountains of its own — and the Seashore, and has 3 major features: Hurricane Ridge — a riot of mountainscapes with Mt. Olympus fittingly in the center; the Rain Forest, and fifty miles of seashore.

There are three approachable sides to the Park, each completely different: *East*, from sea level up river valleys looking up into the mountains; *North*, a high ridge from which you look across into the mountains and the *West*, the seashore and rain forest areas.

There are 13 "arrow" roads you can take leading into the Park. Where the roads end, the trails begin. You return by the road you entered on. There are 3 places where U.S. 101 goes through the Park: Lake Crescent, Ruby Beach-Kalaloch and, briefly, at Lake Quinault. The two lake locations have traditional National-Park-type lodges.

Hurricane Ridge — (Elev. 5,757 feet) — The "Mile High" panorama. It's perfectly safe, but you may or may not enjoy the road, depending on how you like heights. Between June 1 and September 10, Port Angeles *Gray Line buses* have three regularly scheduled tours to various parts of the Park, and Hurricane Ridge is included. While Park Superintendent Roger A. Allin is not promoting the Gray Line, he wishes that more of the 2,000,000 people who visit the Park annually would do so by bus.

If the wind's blowing you won't wonder why they called it "Hurricane" Ridge. Several million people have experienced the feeling of being on top of the world from this point as they view the cold magnificence of this mountainous earthscape. Winter viewing is fantastic! Summer offers naturalist walks and talks. Best bet for masses of wild-flowers — two middle weeks in July.

Less than one percent of the United States remains free of the inroads of commercial activities. This fragment that you're looking at is a gigantic amphitheater of the Olympic National Park . . . a piece of original America. Mount Olympus, the highest peak in the Park and the one from which the Park got its name, helps set the tone.

Man's urge to explore it came in the 1880's. In 1885, a group from the 14th Infantry under Lieutenant Joseph P. O'Neil cut a trail past Mount Angeles to Hurricane Ridge and probably went to the headwaters of Lillian River, which is directly below the Lodge. O'Neil was hot to trot on further explorations, but before he could get moving, a bright young city editor of *The Seattle Press* instigated what turned out to be the "Press Expedition" into the Olympics starting in December of 1889.

The 27-year-old city editor who got the exploration bit going, turns out to be none other than the venerable Edmond S. Meany, who not only has a mountain in the Olympics named after him, but a Seattle school and a hall on the University of Washington campus. Meany suggested in a news story that "There is a fine opportunity to acquire fame by unveiling the mystery which wraps the land encircled by the snowcapped Olympic Range."

At the time, they thought the mountains completely encircled a hidden valley that might even be subject to colonization. Anyway, a former hunter, Indian fighter and arctic explorer by the name of James H. Christie headed a party of half-a-dozen who started up the Elwha River in December with the notion of being on hand to explore the valley.

Six months later, they emerged from the mountains at Lake Quinault with a whole bunch of information, maps, pictures and like that, having blazed a trail through the Olympics. . . .

And what was even more delightful to Meany, they had beaten the U.S. Army to the punch and got themselves a nice scoop.

Bailey Range, which is immediately southwest of Hurricane Ridge is named for William H. Bailey, publisher of the paper which financed the Christie expedition.

◆

You'll probably want to pack a lunch and find the picnic spot about a mile from the Lodge where you can peacefully sit and appreciate the beauty these men originally explored. There's a great alpine flower display at the right time of the year (including 8 varieties of flowering plants found nowhere else) and unbelievable views of the inner Olympics. And you might spot a Roosevelt elk or a big "black" bear. (Black bears elsewhere may be brown or even cinnamon-colored — but here they're only black.)

For the somewhat more adventuresome, the view of Mount Olympus from Obstruction Point is so spectacular they went to all the trouble of building a highway to it . . . and providing a picnic ground en route there. Carry your own water. Obstruction elevation is 6,400 feet. Great high country view. Closed in winter.

Return to Port Angeles the way you came.

A word about eating – In the Lodge there's a lunch counter, curio shop, restrooms.

Port Angeles Tour 3 — Sequim, Dungeness, Port Townsend, Port Ludlow, Quilcene, Brinnon (Map II)

This is the driest, sunniest tour. Altogether, this area presents a kind of "variety package" of a pleasant, low-key nature.

You start along the land shelf between the Strait and the mountains, veering off for a cliff-top marine drive and the beach at Dungeness Spit. Then through pastoral farmlands around Sequim's "banana belt" to Discovery Bay, the wooded Quimper Peninsula, and past the wild rhododendrons to Port Townsend, site of a fine collection of Victorian houses. Then a quiet coastal road to old mill town, Port Ludlow, with its new luxury resort, and off cross-country to Hood Canal and Quilcene, home of our best oysters. Nearby, the chance for the view from Mt. Walker's summit and a stop at a state shellfish laboratory. On past steep, forested hills to Brinnon and a sidetrip into Dosewallips Falls before returning to Port Angeles.

Not far east of Ediz Hook, or Spit, is Dungeness Spit (pronounced "Dunj," not "Dung"). Off of Dungeness Spit is Graveyard Spit. We kind of hate to say this, but they're all within "spitting" distance of one another. Dungeness originally was named by Capt. Vancouver because it resembled a spot in his native England. The name spread from the spit to the crab to the harbor to the river to the town. Dungeness was the larger town until 1934 when Highway 101 came through and Sequim, pronounced, of course, "Skwim," became the dominant center. Our tour map shows another route into the Dungeness Valley if you like, but easiest is using Sequim as the gateway.

Sequim — (Pop. 1,560. Elev. 209.) — Looks from the highway as though it were about the same size as Port Angeles, but is only about one-tenth as big. It's sort of the shopping center for Dungeness. Both of them are on a shelf about 200 feet high that juts out to a point in the Strait. And what they lack in size they make up for in pride. There is no way of passing through this part of the earth without learning that in the welter of wetness around it, the Sequim-Dungeness Valley is in the driest spot north of Los Angeles. If you were a crow, for instance, you would only have to fly 40 miles southwest to the Hoh River Valley to take a bath in nearly 10 times as much rain as they've got in Sequim. It's 16 versus 140 inches.

The Sequim-Dungeness Valley Chamber of Commerce makes the point that this is the heart of the "Sunshine Belt." (The others involved don't make as big a thing about it, but the "belt" extends to Port Townsend, Chimacum and parts of Whidbey, Camano, Lopez and San Juan Islands). They also tell you here that this is the "Retirement Capital of the Northwest." In recent years, it certainly has proved to be that. You'll find more sophistication among the older generation here than any place west of New York City. They love to have the water all around them, but prefer having it fall on somebody else.

When we heard about the Irrigation Festival, at first we thought it was a gag concocted by the Chamber of Commerce to advertise the idea that this is the banana belt. But it's a for-real celebration dating back to 1896 when they completed the first of nine irrigation ditches which feed water from the Dungeness River to some 25,000 acres of land that was previously arid in the summer.

They sent the first fellow who suggested this to the bughouse, but by 1895 everybody was crazy about the idea.

The engineer who surveyed the project took part of his pay in potatoes. Somebody else hauled logs. Another made them into lumber for the first flume. Others donated nails, time, muscle. And they worked through the winter. Mrs. James W. Grant prepared the noonday dinners for the men building the flume.

Everybody in the valley assembled for a picnic on the big day, May 1, 1896. Long wooden tables were set up under the trees and were loaded with hams, roasts, chickens, salads, homemade breads, butter pies, cakes, cookies, doughnuts and all kinds of pickles and jellies. A plowed furrow led across the prairie from the picnic grounds to the newly installed headgate. The day was clear and beautiful. Local historian Virginia Keeting wrote, "The headgate was lifted and water made its way along the ditch. Charles Scherer walked backward in the ditch pulling a shovel and a stream of water touched the edge of the picnic grounds. . . ."

The consensus beforehand had been the guys who thought up the project were out of their minds, on the grounds "you couldn't make water run uphill." The statement was true, of course. But they had their levels on wrong.

Mrs. Keeting points out that on that important day in May, "Mrs. Grant, at whose dinner table the project started, stood with tears in her eyes as the muddy waters trickled slowly through the prairie dust. . . ."

All on the "Wet" side of the mountains.

Prowling Dungeness Valley

There is a unique pastoral charm to the area which the residents deeply appreciate — as you will feel, especially as you proceed north of Sequim to Dungeness and away from the beaten track of 101.

Dungeness, itself, isn't even a wide spot in the road. It consists of *Cramer's General Store* where everybody knows everybody else and they sell groceries, boots and oyster knives . . . that kind of a place. Wooden floors and high shelves. About 6 miles away, a little old red 1889 schoolhouse has been repainted a smart buff color and made into a Community Hall that's used for "occasions."

Occasions include the Christmas season when "Women of the Dungeness" doll it all up as a *Christmas House*. People come from all over and love it. Every year there is a different theme, which is carried out in every room of the schoolhouse and in costumes and food.

The Community Hall which is on the State Register of Historic Places is largely "women's work" although they allow the men in to lift things. They've retained the flavor of the old two-story schoolhouse with its flagpole and bell cupola whilst adding the conveniences necessary for meetings. One evidence of sophistication lies in the fact they don't charge monthly dues. You just pay a buck when they have a function. On that kind of a no-commitment basis, they get a lot of topflight speakers and big attendance. Moneywise, it comes out about the same.

After considerable effort, including the purchase of several hundred acres of land, the county has provided access to the *Dungeness Spit* for car cushion travelers. Overnight camping and pedestrians only are allowed on the spit and its offshoot, Graveyard Spit, named for an Indian massacre at that spot. This also is a wildlife refuge, closed to people some of the time.

If you don't have the urge to go down the hill, *Marine View Drive* is all that the name implies. Down on the beach you can see oysters shucked at the *Dungeness Oyster Farm.* You can also catch octopus and crab in this area, if you know how. (See *"Footloose Around Puget Sound"* for hike on spit.)

"Footloose Around Puget Sound" is a handy book by Janice Krenmayr who has been described as a diligent reporter with a feel for nature. Certainly there is something of Sacajawea and Lewis and Clark in a little woman who personally takes 150 hikes (many of them twice) to get 100 of them down on paper. And how many women would venture into the wilds alone or accompanied only by a 13-year-old dog, Smokey?

"Footloose," as we will be referring to it from time to time in this volume, provides detailed information, maps and photographs for walks on beaches, lowlands and foothills in the area described by the title.

The volume, which was re-walked, re-researched and presumably re-indexed in 1973, has been brought out by The Mountaineers of Seattle. In the introduction, that organization quoted some state statistics showing that in 1970 there were some 60 million "people-occasions" when residents of our state went bicycling for pleasure, 44 million when they went driving for the fun of it, 32 million nonrequired walking trips.

The Wet Side is aimed at "Car-Cushion Travelers," so our line of inquiry ends for the most part in a parking lot some place. However, some of our readers may still be capable of walking anywhere from the 10 yards to the 10 miles encompassed by Mrs. Krenmayr's excellent research. She opined that unlike Sacajawea, she had to put it all down on paper. The walking was pure pleasure and the writing 99% perspiration.

You can own both her pleasure and perspiration all bound in 222 pages by applying $4.95 plus tax to the cash register of almost any bookstore in the Puget Sound area . . . and at the same time extend the scope of our book to byways we don't cover.

Further inland at Dungeness is the *Lloyd Beebe Olympic Game Farm* which raises wild and domestic animals for what it officially lists as "research purposes." It's primarily to breed and preserve endangered species from all over the world, but locally it's famous for providing animals for Walt Disney pictures. You see tigers, leopards, bears, jaguars, cougars and their cubs, and a 10-foot Kodiak Grizzly. Kids will be fascinated. Guided tours 10 a.m. to dusk in summer, 12 and 4 p.m. weekdays and noon-5 p.m. weekends in winter. No cameras allowed, both to protect the animals and the film copyrights.

This is great strawberry, raspberry, avocado, tree seed and mint growing country . . . and with luck you can see white geese doing the mint farmer's weeding for him. In some berry farms, U-pick.

Uncommon Shopping – Highlight of the Dungeness area is a visit to *Henderson House Art Gallery* in the Old Henderson House restored by Bill Sullivan. Offers work of local artists and craftsmen including Sullivan's book of photos of the Peninsula, *Shadow of Goose Wing*, with poems by Michael Lieb. Among crafts is superlative creative stitchery by Leah Wright, who lives down the road a piece. In Sequim is the *House of Oddiments*; 3 miles west are *House of Art and Driftwood Cache, Velma's Antiques and Collectibles, Yesteryear House Antiques* . . . and on Sequim Road, going toward the mountains, is *Cedarbrook Herb Farm*, for scented geraniums, elephant garlic, French shallots and such.

A word about eating – Most popular is *The Three Crabs*, offering Dungeness crab and other seafood, lots of local color . . . *Dungeness Inn* at the Golf and Country Club is poshy, with French and Italian menu.

A word about sleeping – Two small motel-resorts in Dungeness overlook the Strait: *Dungeness Bay Resort* and *Juan de Fuca Motel*, nothing fancy but the view . . . Fancy is the *Dungeness Inn's* condominium units featuring stained wood and wide windows with view of golf course . . . a few miles east at Sequim Bay is *Silver Sands Resort and Marina*, on the water, and a favorite of actor John Wayne.

Annual affairs – *The Christmas House* of Dungeness in December . . . the *Irrigation Festival*, second weekend in May.

For further information – Sequim Chamber of Commerce, Highway 101; phone, 683-6191.

Gardiner — Jack and Marjorie Lynch have an interesting thing going here. Gardiner wasn't even a wide spot in the road until they came along with a bunch of wolves, bought a 40-acre tract and called it *Loboland*. Most of the animals are the famous "Lobos," but there are others in the interesting collection. The wolves don't mind posing for pictures and they don't mind biting off your fingers if you push them through the chain link fences. You not only get a closeup look at this famous, endangered species, but a lot of fascinating information in the lectures conducted from 10 a.m. until dusk daily. Small charge.

Continue east on 101 and down the hill to the head of Discovery Bay.

A word about eating & sleeping – *Discovery Bay Lodge* on the water, offers a pleasant restaurant and a cocktail lounge called the Bay Room with the bar from The Rose Room in the old Butler Hotel, Pioneer Square, Seattle. Operating while it's still being built, it offers some motel rooms out over the water.

We've caught lots of Dungeness crab bare-handed down in the tideflats in our day, and might good eating they were. But that was 20 years ago. There may be people somewhere doing it now, but we are not among them. The way to get a good, big fat Dungeness crab today is not via Dungeness Bay from which they derived their name. It's in the middle of a storm in deep water off the coast of Washington or British Columbia — and that'a a little deep for anybody's "waders." An easier bet is the *crab stand* at the bend in the road at Discovery Bay. Make sure they have never been frozen. *Discovery Bay Tavern* offers steamed clams with its beer, on 101 near crab stand.

Heading left on Highway 20 you follow Discovery Bay for a while and then take off cross-country to . . .

Port Townsend — (Pop. 5,241. Elev. Sea level to 80.) It's away up here on a point where ships turn the corner from the Strait of Juan de Fuca into Puget Sound. At one time the folks who lived here thought their town would become the hub of the state . . . a little later on they worried about not even being on the rim of the wheel. And today, it's the most colorful vestige of the Victorian era in the United States.

Port Townsend was the only town in the Puget Sound area that didn't start out with a sawmill. It was a Port of Entry to the United States, and for a while, it looked like it might become the San Francisco of the Pacific Northwest. In his book, *Steep Trails*, John Muir captured the feeling of the place in the 1880's with . . . "all vessels stop here, and they make a lively show about the wharves and in the bay. The winds stir the flags of every nation. Curious groups of people may often be seen, English, French, Spanish, Portuguese, Scandinavians, Germans, Greeks, Moors, Japanese and Chinese of every rank and station and style of dress and behavior. . . ."

In order to understand Port Townsend you must be aware that to every town on the Sound, the possibility of becoming the Pittsburgh of the West was the *raison d'être*. Washington's governor, John R. Rogers, exuberantly proclaimed in the 1890's that land within a 200-mile radius of Mt. Rainier held the greatest industrial potential of any piece of geography on earth. There was supposed to be an enormous copper deposit in nearby Iron Mountain. Capitalists from Seattle and San Francisco thought enough of the iron ore potential at Chimacum to build an immense steel mill at nearby Irondale. The military marked Port Townsend as one corner of the triangular defenses of Puget Sound. At one point lots on Water Street, downtown, sold for $500 a front foot. There were 3 streetcar lines and 6 banks. And with a population of 5,000, the townspeople dug up a railroad subsidy of $100,000. Incredible!

Efforts like that are hard to forget, and only recently has the final quietus been placed on the abiding concept that what's good for Pittsburgh is good for Port Townsend.

It was called the Key City, and a lot of wealthy, sophisticated people from around the globe bet their bucks that this was going to be *the* place and they were going to be *the* elite residents. It showed up in the construction of more than 200 homes reflecting the period when Victoria Regina was "Queen of the United Kingdom of Britain and Ireland, and Empress of India," and the "sun never sets on the British Empire." Whether it was for real estate investment or retirement, the folks built well and vied with one another for ostentation, on a beautiful hill at the end of Quimper Peninsula, with sweeping views of the water.

Then the copper and iron and the railroad petered out, and almost overnight, a town designed for a population of 20,000 plummeted to 3,500. The mansions were vacated or turned into boarding houses, some of them little better than slum housing. If the town had been a mere 70 air miles to the west in the Rain Forest, Nature would have rotted and destroyed the wooden buildings. But the dry weather preserved them as a cohesive unit, unmarred by a business district in a setting that still retains the beauty that caused the construction in the first place.

◆

It's easy to understand why the buildings were erected and how they were preserved, but the real modern miracle lies in the quality of the restoration that has been taking place without the benefit of any government ukase. And the catalyst for that is Mary Johnson who was 64 years old when the metamorphosis got under way.

In 1961, Mary Johnson and her dentist husband, Robert, completed the restoration of a home built in 1880 by Frank A. Bartlett and his wife, Lela, at the end of the street overlooking the water from the bluff. The Bartletts were members of the social "400." It's a two-story house with a mansard roof and painted in a soft light blue. It may be seen, but not entered, because like so many of the fine homes in the town, it is privately occupied.

Mary's efforts on what was largely considered an old hulk of a house were viewed with amusement and amazement by many of the townspeople, and the emphasis was on the latter when the Johnsons were given the Historic Preservation Award by the Seattle Chapter of the American Institute of Architects in 1961.

Mrs. Johnson, who back-pedals fast when you try and hand her credit for Port Townsend's restoration movement, suggested that she didn't really do the Bartlett House restoration job herself. She was just the instrument of Lela Seavey Bartlett's ghost who had fretted around the decaying premises for over half a century and proved to be an indomitable taskmaster.

It's impossible to run all of the names of the people who were part of the Port Townsend restoration that was just waiting to happen. Most of them were women. But one man, Frank Kilham, deserves honorable mention. He was the house painter who "did" the Bartlett home under contract with the Johnsons. He was a man with an instinctive feel for this kind of thing and has had an important influence on subsequent exterior work done to these houses.

The unbelievable part of this restoration is that some 200 different people, all with their own individual ideas, standards and economic conditions, are coming up with a compatible whole.

Mary said it another way and with beautiful simplicity: "They saw what could be done — and came up to quality."

To Mary, the real magic was wrought by the Port Townsend Summer School of the Arts. It was the lodestone for the kind of people, young and old, who loved and wanted to recreate Victorian homes. "I had a burning desire to bring in that school," Mary said. "And it had to meet standards of (1.) full-fledged professors from the University of Washington, and (2.) courses for which people got full-fledged University credits."

The word came back she could have her school if she dug up a $2,400 subsidy from a community that wasn't at all sure how to spell "Art," let alone "Culture." There wasn't a buck to be made in either!

"They might as well have asked for $24,000,000," she anguished. And her "blessed" husband came through with, "If you feel that strongly about it, I'll underwrite it."

So came Summer School . . . summer theatre . . . art . . . culture . . . people . . . and year-round restoration — and money for the merchants.

Queried about how Mary did it, *Port Townsend Leader* newsman, Frank Garrett said, "She's gracious, accommodating, honest . . . . Hell, you've got your own thesaurus. You look up the words!" Garrett said he had seen Mary persuade people who previously had announced they were flatly opposed to what she wanted them to do.

Said Mary, "You might not believe this, but basically I'm a very shy person. I can understand why people lack confidence in themselves. But I can see talents in them they don't know they have. I begin pointing out their talents to them and pretty soon, they're using them . . . . "

Prowling Port Townsend

This is a 2 level town, clearly divided. At the base of a high bluff is the main street of downtown — Water Street — where most businesses are located. "Uptown" is up on top of the bluff and is generally view and residential.

A great approach to the town is on the State Ferry from Whidbey Island, which clearly shows why old sailing captains retired from the sea to Port Townsend.

There's an easily obtained tour map of Port Townsend showing places of interest and giving a little biography of each, but here are some highlights:

The Rothschild House, now a State Park, was built in 1868 by "Baron" D.C.H. Rothschild, owner of the Kentucky Store which sold everything from "needles to anchors" and was the biggest mercantile establishment in town. Rothschild was a Baron in the sense that a Kentuckian is a "Colonel." But he was a member of the Rothschild family, however distant, at a time when it provided England with the money to buy controlling interest in the brand new Suez Canal. And he provided Port Townsend with something a grubby little sawmill town like Seattle didn't have — Class!

The Rothschild garden was famous. It had 17 varieties of peonies, lilacs, and old-fashioned roses (one of them dating back to 1700). And as a personal project, Mr. and Mrs. Chester Flint replanted the garden exactly as it had been, once State Parks and Recreation restored the house.

The Starrett House, a gem because it's such a horror . . . early "Carpenter Gothic" . . . built in 1885 by George E. Starrett, a building contractor who helped a lot of the Joneses keep up with the other Joneses during that competitive house building period. So naturally it had to be more rococo than the rest. The present owner, Trudy Ericksen, exercised cosmic humor when she painted it entirely white — with no additional trim. How else would you cover a wedding cake at the top of a hill? Incidentally, you can tour it for a small fee or eat brunch or dinner there Fridays through Sundays most of the year.

The Francis Wilcox James House, Washington St. Bill Eaton, the present owner, spent the first year after he had bought it with nightmares about what he had gotten himself into. It had been a badly abused building and he took it on after it had reached the depths of a Harlem slum structure. Now, with some 10,000 hours of his own labor later, he's made it the pride of Port Townsend. It has been restored with tender loving care, and filled with antiques which Bill and his late wife collected all around the country for this purpose. And you can have the experience of living there. You can even spend the first night of your marriage in the honeymoon suite. There also are other overnight accommodations and a continental breakfast, but you'd better make your reservations in advance.

All three of the above homes are on both the National and State Registers of Historic Places . . . as are other places in and around Port Townsend.

If Victorian buildings are your bag, keep your eyes open for the $5 Victorian Home Tour in September or October. You're past the tourist peak. It's easier to find some place to stay on the Peninsula or in town. And your chances of good weather are very good. About 200 homes show small signs indicating the original owners, but you can't read them driving by.

Poking-around projects include four parks: *Fort Worden*, (a State Registered Historic Place), an 1890-ish park which once was a Fort of national importance and is now in the process of becoming a major cultural center, (a locomotive on display here was buried 75 years ago in order to get rid of it, and recently was discovered under a building being torn down) . . . *Chetzemoka*, designed for strolling and picnicking and striking view of the strait . . . *Fort Townsend*, a wooded area sloping to the beach, laid out as the Fort once was . . . *Fort Flagler*, on Marrowstone Island, overlooks water and back to Port Townsend, and has a wonderful spit running out from it. You can walk the beach all the way from downtown Point Hudson to the *Point Wilson Lighthouse*; visiting hours are from 1 to 4 p.m. Then there's the *County Courthouse* with the four-way clock tower which you can climb and view from the inside . . . the 1891 *City Hall* . . . *Jefferson County Museum and Library* in City Hall, with pioneer exhibits, Indian artifacts and jail where Jack London once was incarcerated . . . and the 1890 *Post Office* and *Customs Building*, Washington St. Note Indian carvings over the entrance. See *Footloose* (page 136) for a good town walking tour.

Union Dock is reviving the waterfront life. Unused for years at the foot of Taylor St., this huge pier is now a fish-buying station and marina where fishing boats come to unload tuna, salmon, and bottom fish. The Virginia V and other excursion boats visit regularly; Navy ships tie up.

Uncommon shopping – *Jean Sprague*, Fillmore St., on the bluff, has most complete collection of antiques and is in one of the restored houses . . . across the street is the *Loft*, in a restored building but with a smaller antique collection . . . also on the hill are the *Jack and Jill Children's Shop*, Lawrence St., with *Grandma Lillie's* upstairs, a gift shop of mostly Scandinavian things where your purchase is wrapped in the comic pages.

On Water Street are the *Green Eyeshade*, clothing boutique, arts, crafts, imports . . . the *Post Lantern "B"* where you get the pungent odor of brass polish used by the owner, Ed Beeth, on the wealth of brass antiques of every size and description (and if you want a critical, outspoken appraisal of anything, anything in the world, Ed will provide it) . . . *Hewitt's* and *Brown Bag* on the west side of the street has handmade jewelry in one-half of the store, and yarn and rug making materials in the other half. *Port Townsend Art Gallery* (our favorite spot) is in an old bank restored by Mary Johnson after it's true character had been buried beneath ersatz modern materials and turned into a tavern. What a day it was when they ripped off phony walls and found brick beneath and windows facing the Bay . . . Frank and Edna Smith own it now and purvey books, art and antiques. Frank's a retired Navy submarine captain and great restorationist who quickly became C of C prexy and then Mayor, a significant indication that the town has swung completely behind restoration . . . *Greensleeves Plant Parlor* is owned by a young plant lover who sells plants and unusual planters, and makes housecalls complete with black bag and first aid kit.

A word about eating – *The Farmhouse*, North Beach (a real one outside of town on a bluff overlooking the water), where John and Dorothy Conway provend the finest food on the Peninsula . . . a sophisticated blend of international gourmet cookery that would compete with the best anywhere, usually open weekends only and reservations essential . . . *Hadlock House* at nearby Hadlock, a local favorite . . . *The Surf*, foot of Taylor, inexpensive, fun dockside spot joyfully patronized by the sailing fraternity . . . and, of course, the *Starrett House,* Clay St. . . . *Waterfront Cafe,* on Water St. through entrance of Hewitt's and Brown Bag, a delightful balcony restaurant overlooking the water, specializing in soups, sandwiches, homemade desserts, all pretty casual . . . *Water St. Delicatessen* has delectables to eat there or carry home . . . *Spendthrift Tavern* on Water St. is an attractive place that's good for viewing the "locals" . . . nearby on Discovery Bay, *Chevy Chase Golf Club* makes a special thing of their Sunday breakfasts; the interesting nearby building once was "Saint's Rest," a historic country inn.

A word about sleeping – The classic *James House,* Washington St., is outstanding.

Annual affairs – *Rhododendron Festival*, 3rd weekend in May. (Highway 101 may have by-passed Port Townsend, but God provided her with one of the richest crops of our native flower, and the appendix road which leads to town is called *Rhododendron Lane.*) *Jefferson County Fair* in August . . . and the previously mentioned *Victorian Home Tour* in September or October.

For further information – Chamber of Commerce, 2139 Sims Way; phone, 385-2722.

Continuing on this tour, you turn left toward Hadlock, Indian and Marrowstone Islands, past Irondale and along the coast route to Port Ludlow. Trees obscure the view most of the time, but you get a wonderful shot at Mats Harbor through a clearing.. It's a very short trip over good highway.

Port Ludlow — (Elev. Sea level to 100.) — If you have the bucks or can lay your hands on them, you should arrange to spend some living time at the *Admiralty* here. The Pope & Talbot people, who did it, had the money to do it right . . . and they did. It's quietly sophisticated Northwest contemporary architecture — all stained wood, decks and overhanging rooflines set in a handsome landscape; some remnants of original orchards blend with lots of use of grass and rocks and curving roads. You can stay at one of the condominiums, which have from 1 to 4 bedrooms and kitchens . . . plus community beach club . . . swimming pool . . . tennis . . . squash . . . billiards . . . sailboats.

There even is an informational highway sign reading, "Caution, Adults At Play."

Old Cyrus Walker, the big local boss of Pope and Talbot's earlier years, would have screamed at the amount of money the company spent putting this complex together — and he'd have walked every stick of lumber in the place through the mill to make sure it was the best of its kind for the doing of it.

He was a man who had it in his head that one day the seemingly inexhaustible timber supply in the Pacific Northwest would be depleted, and the company which had the most timberlands — and kept them after they had been logged — would be the company that lasted. So he bought the logs with which to feed the mills from somebody else. And he bought timberlands to hold for Pope & Talbot mills to cut after everybody else had run out.

His first great buys were from the Reverend Mr. Daniel H. Bagley of Seattle who had sale of school lands for University purposes. Walker bought the choicest parcels on Puget Sound for $1.50 an acre. When possible, he paid for land with greenbacks that were worth maybe 70 cents on the dollar. But he bought 15,260 acres first, at the $1.50, and paid Bagley $22,130 — which was more than two-thirds of the amount it took to get the University of Washington underway, making Walker sort of the "Godfather" of the University.

He bought an additional 17,398 acres from veterans, paying them cash for the 160 acres apiece, they could buy for $200 worth of military "scrip." Later on, he bought land on an "arrangement" basis from individuals who filed on it under the Timber and Stone Act by declaring they were citizens or intending to become citizens and thus could take up claims on 160 acres, provided the land was of no use for agricultural purposes.

They say about him that he never let sailors staking the claims assigned to them for that purpose go further than a mile inland from the Sound for fear they would get lost in the woods. The fact is he had them buy the land near the water because it was cheaper to log.

He bought timberlands with the verve and attention to detail given to the selection of a wedding dress — by the bride's mother.

Before they reined him to a halt, he'd bought 186,000 acres, making Pope & Talbot the biggest holders of timberland on the Wet Side of the Mountains. (When some 92,000 acres of it was sold in the 1920's, the 10% down payment by the purchasers was roughly the equivalent of what Walker had paid for the whole 186,000 acres in the first place. It later was repossessed by Pope & Talbot for nonpayment . . . another case of selling it and still having it.)

Walker didn't get around to marrying until he was 58 years old — and then it was to Emily Pope, the boss' daughter. And that's when he moved to and dwelled in the finest mansion around. You can see a photograph of it when you visit Port Ludlow.

As early as 1868, when Seattle still was a sawmill town with a population of 1,000, hanging on by the skin of its teeth along with the other little sawmill towns on the Sound, Walker bet on the come, bought extensively in that village, and became a key figure in making Seattle the major Pacific Northwest city.

Some of the Seattle property he bought . . . and logged . . . and held for later subdividing was in a location presently called Broadmoor . . . one of the most exclusive places to live in Seattle. On behalf of the company, according to C.T. Conover in *Mirrors of Seattle*, he also bought and logged and held what today is known as Washington Park — 320 acres along Lake Washington — for $224, including the virgin timber.

But that wasn't the best buy . . .

There was the bit of land he bought in West Seattle.

Conover, who was in the real estate business himself and ought to have known, wrote, "The company would purchase nothing that was not timbered . . . so frequently (it) picked up fractions for a song adjoining the company's holdings. One little piece in West Seattle (was) . . . acquired for 28 cents . . . ."

Cyrus Walker was offered $10,000 for that hunk of property . . .

And he turned the offer down!

When he died in Seattle in 1913 he was the richest man in the State.

◆

A word about eating – *The Harbor Master Restaurant*, at the Admiralty, dining with sophistication and an intimate harbor view.

A word about sleeping – *Admiralty Inn*, the most luxurious and tasteful condominium accommodations on the Olympic Peninsula; call ahead for reservations. Expensive but worth it . . . marina, nearby golf.

Leaving Port Ludlow by means of the southwest route, you can avoid both 101 and 104 and cut across fairly low rolling country to Center, passing up the head of Dabob Bay which doesn't have all that much to see and head for Quilcene, the furthest point south to which tracks for the hopeful Port Townsend and Southern Railroad once were built.

Quilcene — (Pop. Nom. Elev. 30) — In a book called *The Wet Side of the Mountains*, you might anticipate that a certain amount of space would be dedicated to the subject of water. And with Puget Sound playing the major role it does in the lives of most of us, you logically could figure that the Sound would come up as an entity, and also the creatures that live in it — like oysters, for instance.

Ah, they're the ones!

In addition to having been known historically as the world's greatest gourmet marine food, they have a way of telling us how well mankind is doing with his environment. They're barometers of civilization. Given the right conditions, they multiply with a multiplicity that puts the famous fertility of the rabbit to shame. When they do, mankind *always* believes they are there in such profusion that nothing he can do to them ever will deplete the supply.

And the advent of big-time civilization always wipes them out.

But in Puget Sound, and most especially in Hood Canal, Nature has not as yet sent man to the foot of the class. Here at Quilcene and down at the Washington State Shellfish Laboratory at Point Whitney, and across the water from us at Dabob Bay is oyster country *non pareil*. This is the mother lode of the future of oystering on the west coast of our country, which to all practical purposes here is the State of Washington.

Here, God has given us another chance . . .

And "chance" is the key word.

Nearly half a century ago, a high-flying promoter by the name of Gerard T. Mogan, about whom you will read more when you reach our Willapa Bay comments, became about the millionth novice in the history of the world who thought he had oystering all figured out. Like all of his predecessors, he also thought he was the first to do so. In the late 1920's and early '30's, he was making such a bundle selling oyster lands in Willapa Bay, you wouldn't believe it. By the time Mogan came along, we had overharvested our native Olympia oysters to a point close to extinction. (It should be noted in passing that this was well before the pulp mills came along to administer the *coup de grace*. We, the people, had done most of our "natives" in before the big bad wolf of the oyster growers' world even started snapping his jaws.)

Then we got a reprieve in the form of a new species of oyster from Japan that was hardier and could better withstand the onslaught of increased human population . . . and especially it multiplied and prospered in Willapa Bay where Mogan was doing his thing. He figured that all you had to do was drop a couple of boxes of Japanese oyster seed in what looked like a likely spot — and presto, chango! — instant oysters. So, he went around Puget Sound dropping boxes of oyster seed in likely places.

Nothing appeared to have happened from the boxes he had dropped in Quilcene and Dabob Bays and he went on to bigger and better things — more specifically, the farming of whales, using submarines that had been surplused from World War I, a venture that never came to fruition. At the time he did this, he happened to owe some money to a business associate by the name of Ray C. Canterbury. He unloaded his "worthless" oyster land in Quilcene Bay on Canterbury instead of cash.

The Canterbury family has been making a nice living in the oyster business off of that land ever since — and they have never had to import any more seed from Japan.

Some years ago, Peter Canlis, who is one of the real geniuses in the restaurant business, took a personal taste-testing tour of the Pacific Northwest, seeking in every bay and inlet the best-tasting oyster in the realm . . .

And Canlis found it here, in the "Quilcenes."

You, too, can sample this delectable animal by taking the Linger Longer Road to the *Canterbury Oyster Farms*, where you can buy Quilcenes shucked or unshucked and in various sizes. We recommend the smallest size of shucked oysters. We also advise you that they have a more pronounced marine taste than any others, with the possible exception of the native Olympias. We happen to like that flavor very much, but some people might wish to rinse them off before eating them — raw, of course.

It is well to remember that despite some use of the name "Quilcene" in advertising oysters throughout the Pacific Northwest, the only bonafide oysters marketed from Quilcene Bay come from this oyster farm and are sold under the Canterbury label.

If you can't take time for this visit, you can find Canterbury Oysters at Canlis' in Seattle, naturally . . . also at Starrett House, Hudson Point, and Hadlock House in Port Townsend . . . Halfway House in Brinnon . . . Freddie Steele's at Westport . . . Olympic Hotel, Rainier Club, Sea-Tac Motor Inn and the Mirabeau restaurant in Seattle.

Dabob Bay, which is over the hump of Bolton Peninsula directly east of here, is the great seed oyster bed on the U.S. side of the Pacific Northwest. It is possible — just barely possible — that enough seed oysters can be raised here to at least partially liberate us from what in the past has been total dependence on Japan for the seed that makes our present oyster supply possible. You can find out more about that when you visit the State shellfish lab which is a few miles down the pike on this tour.

A word about eating – Try the *Quilcene Cafe* for their homemade soups and pies. Three times a year, in February, April and November the Presbyterian Church, Lion's Clubs and Community Club, respectively, man the place with volunteers and the proceeds are turned over to their organizations. The help may not be as efficient as normally, but these are the big events of the year here and everyone has a great time pitching in. Call ahead for the specific days.

Heading south out of Quilcene you will come to *Mount Walker* and the opportunity for a side driving trip to the top that will provide you with a sweeping view of Hood Canal . . . maybe even Seattle on a clear day.

You also will find it profitable to take a side road to *Whitney Point State Shellfish Laboratory*. It's a nice drive through the woods to splendid view of Quilcene and Dabob Bays. The Lab has parking, and is visitable 8-4, weekdays. It was here they figured out there were 200,000,000 geoducks in Puget Sound and that it was a harvestable crop of a marine delicacy that surpasses the flavor of abalone.

In 1967, Ron Westley, the chief marine biologist here, did a paper entitled "The Oyster Producing Potential of Puget Sound" that ought to be food for thought for all of us. The first thing to remember is that oysters shortcut travel up the food chain by converting the chemical nutrients of the water directly into edible food without the necessity of big fish eating little fish until the former reach our dinner tables.

In our oyster farms, we produce about 800 pounds of oyster meats to the acre. Westley figured that by utilizing raft culture of oysters like they do in Japan, we could up that to 32,000 pounds per acre! And if we did this in just 28% of Puget Sound, we could raise 6 billion pounds of oyster meats annually. This is the equivalent of the total annual U.S. Fisheries production — including all species of fish. At the present wholesale price of oysters (50¢ a pound), we could get $3,000,000,000 worth of oysters alone annually from Puget Sound.

That's 80% more money every year than was brought in by the Klondike and Nome gold rushes combined in 10 years . . . and exceeds the total sales of the Boeing Company in its best year to date.

◆

Uncommon shopping – About a hundred feet south of the Whitney Point road off of Highway 101 is a gas station . . . and *Mrs. Ethel Hjelvik's General Store*, which is a general store in the tradition of the early 1900's. So if you need anything from a loaf of bread and a pound of butter to a mouse trap or a pair of rubber boots, the chances are it's stacked in there somewhere.

At Brinnon and the mouth of the Dosewallips River, you'll encounter the great, grassy, wide open *Dosewallips State Park*. Approximately 14 miles up the river is yet another entrance to the Olympic National Park, with a couple of waterfalls nearby. By driving an additional mile or so (in the summer), you can drive to the Dosewallips campground and ranger station at an elevation of 1,640 feet. It's a rural, winding drive along the river in a generally sharply "V" shaped valley.

A word about eating – While you can buy oysters almost anywhere along the canal, there's a "shrimp" stop for you 2 miles south of Brinnon and past the *Geoduck Tavern*, which serves good sausage with its beer. It's on the left or water side of the highway going south and if you don't look sharp you are liable to miss it. Between April and October, there should be a handmade sign reading "Fresh Shrimp." The rest of the year, there's a gunnysack hanging over the sign. In the cafe, Bob and Alene Haley vend homemade bread, and pie made from the small wild, succulent blackberries that grow nearby, and offer a delightful perspective of Pleasant Harbor, which is a jade green appendix off the canal.

And the venerable Floyd Chapman, who is perhaps the last remaining "Shrimp Man" of a once prolific shrimp fishery on Puget Sound, cooks and sells those wonderful, tiny shrimp in the shell by the side of the road. Chapman, 66 years old and a self-confessed "Jack-of-all-trades," functions in a boat that looks like a shrimp boat ought to look and goes "ka chug, ka chug," like a shrimp boat ought to go. He has white hair, a white stubble of a beard, a blunt round face and an Irish accent.

He looks like a shrimp man ought to look.

When he bought his boat, Mrs. Chapman informed him it looked like the devil . . . so he called it the "Imp-A-Satan." He has 30 shrimp nets, takes up 15 of them a day during the season, and chugs home with between 40 and 100 pounds of shrimp. With a little bit of luck you'll be there early enough in the day to buy some. With even more luck you might be on hand at the little float when he comes chugging in.

Within 4 hours of the time he lands, the gunnysack has been flipped over on top of the shrimp sign, indicating he's sold out for the day.

As you head south from Pleasant Harbor on down to the Hamma Hamma River, you'll be skirting Hood Canal on one side and mountains rising precipitously on the other. Don't count on making a million miles an hour. The road has some curves and some state patrolmen.

(For purposes of organizing the material, we have stopped this expedition here. So you're either ready to go on to another section, or return to Port Angeles . . . this time following 101, back through Quilcene where you turn left instead of returning on the road that brought you to 101 in the first place.)

Port Angeles Tour 4 — Joyce, Clallam Bay, Neah Bay, Lake Ozette (Map III)

This takes you to the farthest-away northwestern point in the conterminous (a perfectly good word — you don't have to look it up) United States. The remote spot is Cape Flattery, with its famed view of the wild, wave-crashing beauty of Tatoosh Island. You won't find Conrad Hilton and his minions — or anybody else's minions — on hand with a fancy welcome mat on this tour. The road doesn't rate any brags even from the Highway Dept. You will, however, meet logging truck drivers who seem to treat it like it was a super freeway, plus lots of campers bearing people who like to fish for salmon, and at one point meet a remote, independent Indian tribe, the Makahs, to whom this has been home since long before your grandfather, or George Washington's was born. Your route varies from passing forest to windblown seascape, and you wind up at a wilderness lake near a current archaelogical dig of considerable significance.

A few miles out of Port Angeles you will cross the canyon of the Elwha River on a one-way bridge that has backseat drivers sort of clutching and grabbing at one another. Early in the game they tried bridging over down nearer the beach but the spring floods wiped them out. Your route continues past forested areas broken intermittently by homesteads or very small towns.

Joyce — (Pop. Nom. Elev. 90) — is the first wide spot you pass through. Here, with cosmic simplification, is a symbol of the impact that the Olympic National Park and National Forest has had on civilization . . . a no-fooling, bonafide *log railroad depot*, marking the last stand of the railroad barons.

On Washington's Birthday, 1897, President Grover Cleveland signed his name to a document that turned 2,168,320 acres of the Olympic Peninsula into a Forest Reserve — to the intense horror of lumber barons everywhere. This was one of the most heavily timbered areas in the entire country.

Henry Gannett, Chief Geographer for the U.S. Geological Survey, initiated a program in the following year that would result in a Geological Survey Report published in 1902 under the title "Forest Conditions in the Olympic Reserve, Washington."

The gist of the report was there were 81 billion(!) feet of uncut, merchantable timber on the Olympic Peninsula.

The railroad barons got busy.

Author Ruby El Hult notes that by 1907 "pure pandemonium" had broken out on the Olympic Peninsula. She quoted one engineer as saying, "I don't know and no one knows how many railroads are going to be built." It looked like two for sure, three as a probability and four as a possibility. The Union Pacific and the Northern Pacific had survey crews vying for the "passes" (just like the old days on transcontinental lines) between Grays Harbor and Port Angeles. The Port Angeles paper smugly noted that, "Everyone in Port Angeles realizes that three railroads are bound for this place. To enjoy the trade and commerce of the Peninsula they must build to Port Angeles."

Nobody really believed the federal government could do them out of all the beautiful money that was to made here. Besides, they had a Republican as President, not one of those dumb Democrats.

But they reckoned without the entree that Washington State Congressman W. E. Humphrey had with President Theodore Roosevelt. That, together with the President's interest in animal life, turned the trick. On March 2, 1909, Humphrey got to a Roosevelt who'd been on the receiving end of a lot of pressure from both sides on this front for quite a while . . . and Roosevelt had made up his mind.

"Prepare your order and I'll sign it," Roosevelt snapped. Humphrey did and, as previously mentioned, Roosevelt did. The latter signed a document proclaiming the Mount Olympus National Monument of 610,560 acres in the heart of the Olympic National Forest. And nobody's allowed to chop up a National Monument!

◆

That was the real end of the "railroadization" of the Olympic Peninsula. The Milwaukee Road functions here today, but it's strictly a local proposition that barges railroad cars to Seattle from Port Townsend. The logging trucks you see are coming primarily from stands in the National Forest, where logging is permitted on a sustained yield basis. And if you should see a big balloon with some logs hanging from it away up in the air, it's not a mirage, it's the Japanese experimenting with a new method of logging. The balloons can handle 25,000 pounds of logs apiece.

A word about eating – Here's one of the few eateries on 112 — hence named *"Atlasta Burger!"* Also wild blackberry pie and coffee by a potbelly stove. Free coffee, at *Maddock's Grocery* . . . cluttered but fun . . . campers tout (and tote) their bacon.

Agate and *Crescent Beaches*, north of Joyce are adjacent to an enormous knoll that today is part of *Salt Creek County Park*, but once was a military reservation and has emplacements for 16″ gun battery, only one this size north of San Francisco. They say it could be turned into a fort in a matter of 24 hours. It's only about 8 miles across the Strait to Canada at this point. *Tongue Point* on the west of the knoll is a favored spot for Port Angeles people who are showing visitors around. Its rocks and tidepools make it a fascinating beach at low tide.

In the early 1890's the Port Crescent Improvement Company decided Crescent Bay would be the terminus of the transcontinental railroad. It platted a town, named 7 of its streets after 7 presidents, and on June 11, 1891 started construction of a breakwater that was to be 600 feet wide and 3,000 feet long. The theory was they could blow up an annoying reef in their way that extends from Clam to Tongue Point.

But they couldn't, and everybody, including the folks who had bought the town lots, went belly-up.

◆

Clallam Bay — (Pop. Nom. Elev. Sea level.) — Boom time came to Clallam Bay at the turn of the century when the California Tanning Company selected this spot for its only extract factory on the west coast.

In the extraction business, they once cut down hemlock trees, which abound in this region, solely for the bark and threw away the wood. The factory here was enormous, employing more than 200 men, and prosperity came with a capital "P" to the bay. The 30 to 40 barrels of extract produced daily were the finest in the world.

But with prosperity came problems.

There was *East* Clallam Bay and *West* Clallam Bay, and in spite of the fact that a monumental mailing confusion resulted, neither of these independent entities would change its name to accommodate the other. And for a time there was a merry mixup of mail to the two places.

Then they lowered the boom on the Clallam Bay boom. After more than 2,000 years, somebody came up with a new process for making tanning fluid.

Hemlock juice was out.

By 1900 the extract factory went out of business. And there was so little mail it didn't matter. What did matter to the men thrown out of work was some means of making a living.

This may come as a matter of astonishment to the people whose main purpose in Clallam Bay today is that of catching a fish, but prior to the debacle of the factory, salmon fishing was barely a secondary consideration here. With the factory closure they turned to it in desperation to keep from starving. They made their own spoons and stealing another guy's spoon was a lynching offense like horse-thievery in the Western movies. The San Juan Packing Company stationed a barge in the bay to buy the daily catch. And the pay was great . . . two-bits a fish, regardless of the size. On the other hand, a guy could catch as many as 30 fish weighing in excess of 12 pounds each in an hour's time if they were running . . .

Oh yes, the question of the mail and the two Clallams.

The Goodyear Lumber Company owners, who brought their mill into the bay in 1907, finally got so frustrated with the right mail going to the wrong town, that they knocked folks on the head, circulated a petition, and in 1920 West Clallam became *Sekiu.*

———◆———

Uncommon shopping – *Clallam Custom Cannery* open May to October, watch them canning, buy canned seafood, Indian crafts . . . watch Dave Forlines carve totem poles.

En route to Neah Bay the road parallels the Strait, with an occasional view across the water to Vancouver Island.

Neah Bay — (Pop. Nom. Elev. 10.) — As the most recent representative of our civilization to visit the village of Neah Bay, which is wholly owned and operated by the Makah Indian tribe, it is highly probable that you will reach some value judgments based on similar experiences in other villages of comparable size in our country. And before you do, it might be wise to contemplate the story of the White Easter Bunny.

We made the mistake one long Easter weekend of taking a rented camper to the coast at Neah Bay. In addition to being rained on unmercifully, we attempted the road to Shi Shi Beach . . . lost our spare tire and wheel in the mud and were thankfully warming ourselves over bowls of chili and steaming up a Neah Bay cafe with our wet clothes, when the Easter Bunny came in and draped itself over a counter stool for a cup of hot coffee. The Easter Bunny seemed a little incongruous in an Indian village — it was an Indian girl in full costume with cotton tail and big pink ears, wearing horned-rimmed glasses — but nobody in the place except us thought anything of it.

Here's a group of people that knows how to go along with the gag, be it Easter or any quaint custom. If the Bureau of Indian Affairs frowns on Potlatches but lets you do the same thing and call it Christmas, so be it. If a new pestilence calling itself "Civilization" moves in and decimates half of your population with smallpox, it's no different than a visit from those tough tribes up north . . . a village-swallowing mud slide . . . or an eruption of Mount Rainier. Survival is the ultimate goal, and if you're a member of the tribe, you adapt.

We whites have burglarized their forests of their "Gods-given" clear cedar trees and their streams of protein-producing salmon, and imposed our standards on them at gunpoint. We've even tried to con them into working 50 weeks a year with a two-week vacation instead of doing it the other way around — which was a system under which they out-lived the late Roman Empire, let alone our wasteful brand of civilization. They were doing their thing for at least 5,000 years with the spear as the ultimate weapon. We're only 200 years away from the Industrial Revolution, and already we've produced the atom bomb which could knock off every interesting target in America, with the possible exception of Neah Bay.

They have a simple solution to problems like an impassable road to Shi Shi Beach . . .

They don't go.

They've survived the Ice Age . . . the Stone Age . . . the Bronze Age . . . the Steel Age and the Machine Age. There's no reason to suppose they won't survive the Garb Age.

While there no longer is a Washburn connected with *Washburn's* at Neah Bay, it still is the most consecutive and venerable mercantile establishment in the village, having started with Wilbur Wright Washburn in 1902.

Mrs. Miriam Elizabeth Washburn brought out highlights of the operation in the Clallam County history book, *Jimmy Come Lately*, including the fact that in the old days it was common for Indian girls to buy calico at the store which would be seen as dresses at the dance that night. At one time, the store carried maybe 900 Indian baskets, the full price of which was credited to the ladies who had made them. Washburns served as postmasters for over half a century and the store remained open 12 hours a day or longer, "except for Christmas when they tried to close by one in the afternoon." Until 1958, when the Makah Tribal Council granted a 25-year lease, the land lease had to be renegotiated every year. The Indian gals don't make many baskets these days. They can make more money as maids in the motels.

Perhaps the most touching example of the esteem in which the Washburn family was held came after a fire on February 26, 1962 in which the store burned to the ground with a loss in excess of $100,000. Mrs. Washburn reported: "After much deliberation and a great display of affection shown by the community through a Potlatch given for the Washburns, they decided to rebuild . . ."

Uncommon shopping – Neah Bay offers the largest selection of Indian baskets and shell jewelry on the Peninsula. There is a museum at the *Indian Center* and a display of Indian artifacts at the *Elementary School*. Also there's *David Butler Custom Canning Company and Gift Shop* for canned sturgeon, octopus, lingcod, red snapper . . . *Ora's Gift Shop* for genuine Makah Indian crafted items, and all of the best local gossip . . . *Harold Ides* at Sooes River for Indian baskets made by Mrs. Ides.

Cape Flattery — The chances are that unless you are a fisherman you'll be going to Neah Bay with the notion of standing on the most northwest point of land in the "lower 48" — and that's what they're expecting you to do. En route you'll see decaying logs so big they couldn't be removed with the equipment they had in the old days. There's a good parking lot, an interesting, albeit often muddy, path to an excellent viewpoint with tight coves and dashing waves underfoot, sheer rock walls pocked with large coves. Nearby are Hole-in-the-Wall Cove and Look-Through-Rock Arch.

Half a mile offshore is *Tatoosh Island* where a light has warned ships since 1857. Coast Guard families live on the island and man the light today, and receive weekly mail and supplies lifted from a boat by an overhanging crane up perpendicular rock cliffs.

It is possible that you might wish to drive as far south as Shi Shi Beach, about 10 miles away, either to view the wreckage of the *"General Meigs"* or to look at the *Point of the Arches*. But, unless you have four-wheel drive, and it's summer and it isn't raining, you shouldn't even think of driving it. Then you should think about it until the thought goes away, or at the very least consult the local authorities. They may have done you the favor of blocking it off. The Indians are pretty casual about this sort of thing, so be warned.

Annual affairs – *Makah Days* last week in August. The Makahs celebrate receiving American citizenship a few years ago; parade, raising of the flag, salmon baked in traditional style, bone game. Inquire at Makah Indian Tribal Council Office, Neah Bay or phone 645-2205.

For further information – Write Washburn's, Neah Bay, phone 645-2211.

To get to Lake Ozette you'll have to leave Neah Bay on the same road you came in on, turning south 2 miles before you reach Sekiu. Your 21-mile drive skirts the Hoko River and climbs gradually through thick timber and past an occasional farm.

Lake Ozette is generally billed (but sometimes disputed) as the largest "natural" lake in the State. Despite a few settlements along its shores, it has retained much of its wilderness spell.

Things can get a little confusing for fishermen here because the west shore of the lake is in the Olympic National Park and no fishing license is required. In the rest of the lake, State fishing licenses prevail. It also is possible to catch either State or Federal fish on the Ozette River.

The fish know which they are and tell the fishermen, but unfortunately they lisp and the "F" and the "S" sound similar. In the old days a lot of fishermen got caught with a Federal fish when they thought they had a State fish and it caused a lot of trouble.

Now it's all very simple.

The Federal government fish are branded with an "F," and those belonging to the State bear the initial "S."

◆

A 3-mile Indian Village Trail leaves the end of the road for the ocean
beaches. (For a dime you can get a booklet telling all about them.)

The Trail ends at *Cape Alava*, the westernmost point of the south 48
states, a broad, sandy beach with offshore islands. Nearby is the famous
Washington State University Archaeological Excavation. The "dig" is about a
mile long and a quarter of a mile wide and they have come up with an
impressive 80,000 bones — four-fifths of which came from seals. There's a
boardwalk all the way on the trail to the dig.

About the time Johann Gutenberg was printing the first bible and
Christopher Columbus was doing his thing about America, a bank of very fine
clay slid over an Indian village that already was several thousand years old. The
clay completely sealed off the air and perfectly preserved household objects
and other evidences of living conditions . . . making it possible to reconstruct
the Indian life-style of the time. The objects removed will be housed in a
yet-to-be-built museum on the Makah Reservation at Neah Bay instead of being
carted off to some museum in England or New York. There are regular tours of
the dig scheduled in the summer and at other times if someone official happens
to be on hand. Students working there are friendly about discussing the project,
too. Check with the park ranger at Port Angeles or Lake Ozette.

If you have the motivation, the rain gear and the rubber boots, you can
go out from Indian Village Trail, south 3 miles along the beach to Sand Point
and triangulate yourself another 3 miles back to the Ranger Station. This is part
of the Olympic National Park seashore we mentioned earlier. It also is a
National Wildlife Refuge, and if you're lucky you may see bear or raccoons
foraging on the beach, or seals and sea lions on Ozette Island. The total journey
is about 9.3 miles.

We love the candor of the guy who wrote the Park Service brochure on
the outdoor accommodations here. He said, "Trail shelters are available on a
first-come, first-served basis and probably will be occupied when you
arrive . . ."

From here, if you're going back to Port Angeles, you will save your
driving arm some if you cut south 6 miles east of Clallam Bay and take the Burnt
Mountain Road to Sappho and U.S. 101.

Otherwise you can go south on 101 at Sappho, and pick up the latter part
of Tour 5 in this Region.

Port Angeles Tour 5 — Lake Crescent, La Push, Forks, Kalaloch, Lake Quinault (Map III)

Here's where you get a real feel of the forest primeval the first white settlers experienced when they arrived in the Pacific Northwest. It's an area of dense hemlock, with periodic flashes of superb scenery. The street lights are few and far between, with the most at Forks. You follow the Elwha and Soleduck River valleys into mountainous hot springs areas, admire the beautiful Swiss-Alps-type setting of Lake Crescent, pursue the Soleduck River to La Push and the Hoh, Quinault and/or Queets River valleys into the shadowy fantasyland of the world's only coniferous Rain Forest, and experience an exhilarating, rugged coastline. Most of this trip you're in tree-farmed National Forest, with occasional spectacular side trips into the National Park and one to a picturesque Indian Village on the ocean.

Head west on highway 101 and 9 miles later you can make a scenic side trip up the Elwha River Valley into the National Park.

Olympic Hot Springs — Good paved road climbs steeply to the hot springs, which are at an elevation of 2,200 ft. There are 21 of them — discovered in September, 1892, 9 years after a volcano on the Indonesian Island of Krakatoa had thrown nearly 5 cubic miles of rock fragments into the air, and generally made everybody nervous. Andrew Jacobsen, the discoverer of the springs, thought the mountain was about to blow and got the hell out of there. They remained "lost" for 15 years.

Three men rediscovered the hot springs on June 25, 1907.

Temperatures ranged from lukewarm to 138 degrees Fahrenheit. The 3 hunters fashioned a tub out of a hollow cedar log, flumed water in and took baths.

People were pretty hot for hot springs in those days. The water was supposed to cure everything from clap to constipation and they hiked in the 11 miles you'll be driving . . . sometimes staying for 2 or 3 weeks. The owners of the springs got so good at making smooth, comfortable tubs out of cedar, that people tried to buy them instead of the baths.

By 1920, they had quite a resort going there, advertising they had 800 electric lights, and telephones. Cab fare from Port Angeles was $3.75. Lodge rates were $28 a week, including baths. In 1940, as seems inevitable with resorts on the Peninsula, the place burned down. It was rebuilt and shortly after came under the Park Service. Civilization's loss, Nature's gain.

In 1955, the National Park Service decided that the smelly hot springs water in the pool should be replaced with chlorinated and heated freshwater from the "crick." But the folks didn't get the same kick out of this water as they did out of the real stuff and business was cut in half.

Now the Park Service is letting the whole operation return to Nature, with interpretive information about the Springs posted.

◄►

Lake Crescent — About 18 miles west of Port Angeles on 101, gets star billing as the biggest lake in the Olympic National Park and an especially high regard from a young Swiss friend, who opined it looked "just like home!" The lake lies wholly inside the park and is edged by mountains rising to as much as 5,300 feet. The lake, itself, is 579 feet above sea level and is 600 feet deep, putting its bottom below sea level.

It's just west of much smaller Lake Sutherland, which lies entirely outside of the park.

Often referred to as the "Jewel of the Olympics," Crescent is the spot where the Park Service braces itself for the heaviest onslaught of civilization, because it's the easiest place in the Park for people in automobiles to reach. You can "happen" on this lake — while in most of the rest of the Park you must go there on purpose.

Highway 101 follows a road literally chiseled out of the mountains which descend precipitously down from enormous heights. The Park Service has arranged to give you parking at spots where you can get splendid views from both the east and west sides.

The Lake also is famed for its fighting trout, which at one time grew to weights of up to 35 pounds. Admiral Lester Anthony Beardslee, who took some Navy ships into Port Townsend at the turn of the century, sent a sample of the trout to the Smithsonian Institute which named it the Beardslee after the admiral. It also is called Crescenti Trout.

Storm King Visitor Center — (579 feet.) — For good lake views, 3 miles from the park boundary, named after a nearby mountain. Summer only. *Marymere Falls Nature Trail* open year-round takes off from the parking lot. Half a mile farther is the *Lake Crescent Ranger Station* for handy information. *Fairholm Ranger Station* on the north shore is open in summer, with summer walks and talks by ranger naturalists.

A word about eating and sleeping – Near Park entrance: *Lake Crescent Lodge*, a classic "park lodge" and *Fairholm Resort*, both good with great views of the lake, dining rooms, cocktail lounges . . . Fairholm open year-round. *Lake Crescent Log Cabin Resort*, a quiet spot at Piedmont on north side of lake. Write or call via Port Angeles.

You won't need formal clothes in any of these spots. Under Park Service philosophy, the least civilization is the best civilization.

Soleduck River Valley and Sol Duc Hot Springs — Why they spell the hot springs without an "e" in the middle or a "k" at the end like the river never has been explained satisfactorily to us, but that's the way it is, and probably at the bottom of the pile there's a clerical error some place. Same pronunciation, though — "sol-duck."

This is your next change to get up into the National Park. It's 12 miles of good road from 101 up through the pretty Soleduck River Valley into scenic mountain country, at an elevation of 1,679 ft. There's a ranger station and summer walks and talks, and a quarter mile beyond, the hot springs and today's modest hot springs resort.

In this remote spot you'll find it hard to believe that earlier in this century this was the site of an amazing amount of elegance and activity.

In the summer of 1903, lumber baron Mike Earles' doctor informed him that unless he could take the mineral baths at Carlsbad, Czechoslovakia, he would die. And upon further consideration of the problem, the doctor opined that even if he left the office immediately — that very day — and headed for Europe, he would die before he could get to Carlsbad . . .

Bad news for Mike Earles.

Having heard of Sol Duc Hot Springs and their therapeutic qualities, Earles plunged into them in August of that year with a desire born of desperation. Gulping the stuff like it was going out of style and immersing himself in it, he came out in a couple of weeks a well man.

And, man, was he sold on Sol Duc Hot Springs!

He promptly attempted to buy them, but one Theodore Moritz, the original white man to file a claim on them wouldn't sell. So Earles had to wait until Moritz died. And in 1909, he was able to buy the property from Moritz' heirs.

It must be remembered the existence of hot springs created many European towns like Carlsbad. Wiesbaden, Germany, with its mineral springs, had been an international watering place since the Romans discovered them in 83 A.D. A whole city has been built around their springs. White Sulphur Springs, West Virginia, which had been the summer White House for Presidents Van Buren, Tyler and Fillmore, had finally gotten itself incorporated the year Earles bought Sol Duc. And while White Sulphur was no Wiesbaden, the Chamber of Commerce there knew it had a good thing going. Anyway such springs had big reputations in those days.

According to Clallam County historian Patty May Hassel, Earles determined to build the hot springs as a "monument for the good of humanity," although it should be noted in all fairness that Earles usually managed to make a buck whenever he gave humanity a helping hand.

The articles of incorporation for the Sol Duc Hot Springs Company state that it was formed to: "build and operate hotels, sanitariums, and bathing establishments, at the hot springs in Clallam County, or at any other place; to distill, bottle and to sell natural and mineral waters; to build, operate and maintain electric and steam railroads and steamboats; to establish and maintain wagon and toll roads . . . operate stage lines . . . sawmills . . . logging operations . . . ."

In 1910, 200 men went to work on the job of constructing a road from Fairholm, and on building a hotel that was a monument to the timber industry in which Earles had made his fortune. It took 2,000,000 feet of lumber and 750,000 shingles to build the four-story structure with rustic log facade, and 165 rooms, each with an outside view, hot and cold running water, steam heat and a free bottle of Sol Duc Hot Springs mineral water (also available by the case).

The decor was done by Frederick and Nelson, so you know it had to be first class. The lobby had massive white columns, the walls were covered with burlap, the upper half a golden brown and the lower half a dark green, separated by a molding of white. The ceilings and window casings were painted white with gold trim, together with the pillars. The dining room was separated from the lobby by swinging portieres and large screens. The 2 rooms together were half a block long and 40 feet wide.

The cook was a gentleman by the name of Bill Lenoir. He came from France and he could cook, so they felt they could legitimately advertise him as a "French Chef." There was sterling silver service in the dining room and as many as 23 maids who catered to guests who came from far and wide and dressed for dinner, usually staying at least 2 weeks. In its peak year there were nearly 10,000 guests.

Above all else, Mr. Earles' pride and joy was an organ placed in a music mezzanine above the lobby. Large doors opened from the lobby on 3 sides and the organist could saturate the entire area with the sound of music.

The formal grand opening was on May 15, 1912.

Four years and 11 days later, chimney sparks fanned by a strong wind hit those 750,000 shingles and spread to the other buildings. In 3 hours, the whole thing was only a memory.

But it went out with a flourish.

It was in the tradition of Nero and old Rome. Early in the proceedings, the automatic organ was motivated to music by some mysterious influence. And until it was consumed by the flames, 3 hours later, the holocaust was accompanied by the sonorous, full-throated and dismal cadence of Beethoven's "Funeral March."

◆

As you will see when you get here, the Park Service couldn't care less about another Wiesbaden or White Sulfur Springs.

A word about eating and sleeping – Today's *Sol Duc Resort, National Park Concession, Inc.* offers simple fare: motel, cabins, dining room, coffee shop, cocktails, groceries, fishing supplies and hot mineral swimming pools. Open April to October. Call or write via Port Angeles.

Returning to 101 and heading west, you're following the valley of the Soleduck River through massive forests.

Sappho — In the old days, when it was a major break in the mail run from Clallam or Pysht to Forks and La Push, the hotel at Sappho was known as the Halfway House, which is something you might have in mind in order to appreciate the local humor provided by the following: Mayor J. M. Goodwin, who operates *Goodies Tavern* at Sappho, advertises his place as a "dump halfway between San Francisco and Anchorage, Alaska — left side of the road." He also notes that the population of Sappho is less than 3,000,000. The tavern has enough interesting stuff lying around to be worth a stop and a beer. Goodwin, who is 81 years young at this writing, notes that his tavern also serves as a bomb shelter. He's mayor of this wide spot in the road . . . also "Undertaker, Sheriff, Constable, Judge, and part-time posthole digger for the P.U.D."

◆

These are the most prolific western hemlock forests in the world. More than 75% of the total cut of hemlock in the United States is this western species, with Washington and Oregon supplying 95% of the cut. And an equally high percentage of that cut comes from a so-called fog belt extending in from the ocean some 20 to 30 miles in a strip that runs from the Strait of Juan de Fuca south through Oregon. "Fog drip" adds as much as 26% to annual precipitation in this strip.

Also called the hemlock fir, the tree grows upwards of 200 feet high and up to 10 feet in diameter. Timbers up to 24 inches square and as high as a two-story building have come from these forests, and it's somewhat incredible to contemplate the fact that prior to 1900, they were cut down to supply bark used in tanning, and the tanbark used for performances in a circus someplace. After 1900 when the fellas discovered that with chrome salts instead of tanbark they could tan leather in days instead of weeks, hemlock became the previously mentioned "weed." Today it is used as structural and finished lumber, plywood and most importantly, pulp chips.

It grows in the fog belt along with spruce and you can tell it by the fact that the top of the tree always tips in a graceful curve. The needles are dark green on top and whitish underneath and the branches form lacy patterns, which may be why it is the official tree of the state of Washington.

It also is murder to split — if you've ever assayed into that experience with sledge and wedge and the notion that you can use it in your local friendly fireplace . . . .

But that, too, is a characteristic tangled toughness that can be found inside the beautiful green facade of the Evergreen State.

Something you also will experience in this valley is the tangy and refreshing odor of cut cedar. There are a lot of shake mills — sort of family affairs. You might check with the Chambers of Commerce in either Port Angeles or Forks for one that likes visitors. These have some of the last vestiges of clear cedar in the Pacific Northwest.

About 2 miles before you reach Forks, you make a right turn to La Push, Mora and Rialto Beach, for a most scenic side trip into more of the seashore strip of the Olympic National Park. About 7 miles in, you come to a branch in the road. One leg takes you to La Push and the other to Mora and Rialto. This is a place of decision, because once you get to the mouth of the river, you can't get across without a dunking, or without coming back here.

A few hundred feet left of the bridge over the Soleduck is an enormous pool about 200 feet wide and 50 feet deep. It is here that the Soleduck and Bogachiel rivers converge to form the Quillayute River. Six miles long, it's the shortest river in the State (about 2 miles shorter than the Snohomish) and the Indian derivation of the name is "river without a head."

In March and April gray whales migrate north to the Bering Sea from Mexico — and again in the fall, off the coast. Sometimes they come inshore within yards of the beach.

Mora-Rialto Beach — Mora's about 4 miles from the junction and Rialto Beach is a couple miles farther. There's *Mora Picnic and Campground* at Mora and summer nature walks and talks at Rialto, one of the few beaches you drive right up to. You can walk out on a glorious long sandspit backed by the Quillayute River and a view of La Push . . . on the ocean side, walk to James Island at low tide.

La Push — A Quileute Indian village with offshore seascapes that have probably inspired more art work on the part of northwest painters than any other except Mt. Rainier. A fishing fleet ties up here, and Indians in dugout canoes fish for salmon and smelt in season . . . .

And the wind blows. This is great "kite" country. Lots of beach to play with and no running necessary to get your kite in the air.

In this territory you get another one of those quirks that makes it hard for people to win spelling bees. A la "Sol Duc — Soleduck," it's Quileute Indians . . . but Quillayute River.

A word about eating – *Butts Cafe*, overlooking the harbor and Indian fishing fleet, April through September. You really should do most of your own cooking which you can at "our" motel because that will give you an excuse to go to the *La Push Grocery*, a proper general store.

A word about sleeping – We like *La Push Ocean Park* best. Also there is *Shoreline Resort*. Both have housekeeping rooms, are open year-around. Call or write via La Push.

Forks — (Pop. 1,713. Elev. 375.) — You will like Forks. It's civilization again, with hospitable people who will know better than you the subconscious emotional trauma you are undergoing when you reach this small outpost. Plan to linger a while because there's a lot more wilderness to come before you reach Aberdeen and Hoquiam.

Our friend Jack Dolstad, who heads up the Student Conservation Association, a program under which city kids volunteer to build trails and shelters and that sort of thing in the Olympic National Park, gives us a clue to what is happening to you. Some of the kids from the metropolitan centers just eat up life in the wild. But others encounter a fear in the great silences that drives them right up one of the trees. There have been circumstances where tough kids from the Asphalt Jungle in New York were so frightened they had to be sent home after a couple days of it.

◀

The folks in Forks have a better feel for the tenuous hold our civilization has over the wilderness, because they live with it year in and year out. They obtained some of their best insight into the old cigarette ad philosophy that "Nature in the raw is seldom mild" — when wild fire hit Forks beginning early in the morning of September 10, 1951. Clallam County historian Genevieve Miller provides a dramatic description of the holocaust that happened on this day and demonstrated how much the lives of the people in this area depend upon the vagaries of Nature. It was a wild fire that nearly wiped out Forks.

Creating its own draft, it raced through the dry woods, sometimes leaping 2 miles in one gulping jump. It traveled 8 miles in 2½ hours . . . 17 miles in 8 hours. Some 269 persons were evacuated from the town. There were 450 men fighting the fire, including fire equipment from Port Angeles. People fled to Port Angeles, to Aberdeen and to the Quillayute Naval Air Base a little northeast of La Push.

Some of the vivid sights and sounds are portrayed by Miller in the following: "By 2:30 p.m. nervous residents heard sound-equipped trucks blaring forth the warning, that there remained only twenty minutes to get past the fire which had reached the Olympic Highway on the north side of town . . . . The roaring fury, aided by the draft it created as it raced along, cut a mile-wide swath . . . . Air observers were unable to get close because of downdrafts . . . street lights automatically turned on . . . . Cars with headlights on collided with deer and other terrified wild animals almost invisible in the gray dimness . . . . At 2:50 p.m. State Highway Patrol Sergeant Cliff Arden officially ordered Forks evacuated . . . ."

Nature's score in that fire was 28 houses . . . 4 garages . . . a mill . . . a ranch house . . . 3 barns . . . countless pieces of logging equipment and 33,000 acres of forest land.

A carelessly flung match started it.

A fire border along the southern edge of Forks, plus a miraculous change in the wind and a light rain, saved Forks, but 575,000,000 board feet of timber were lost. Afterwards, they bulldozed a 27-mile fire trail around the area. It took 3 years to salvage what was left. The entire 60 square miles of the burn has been reseeded, but you can get some kind of a feel of what it was all about by driving a few miles northeast of town on the Calawah Sitkum road and looking at the evidence which still remains.

Forks lists itself as the "Steelhead Capital of the World" and the "Home of the Bald Eagle Totems." It's at the "forks" of the Calawah, Bogachiel and Soleduck Rivers. The first settler there lived in a hollow stump when he arrived. And they never will forget that the second guy who showed up had just turned down an opportunity to buy 40 acres of what is now downtown Seattle for $400 . . . settling here instead.

A word about eating – *Pay 'N Save Coffee Shop* has the best cook in town and lavish banana splits. Like every cafe in Forks, they do lunches to go (necessity for loggers) . . . *Antlers* for local color and "where it's at" . . . *Vagabond Cafe and Pebble Room* to catch local flavor (drop in here 4-6 a.m. for loggers, in seemingly identical blue and white striped shirts, cut-short jeans, and suspenders, eating breakfast and picking up lunches), open 24 hours, 7 days a week . . . *Slather's Smoked Salmon Cafe* features seafood, including salmon from their own smokehouse.

A word about sleeping – Best place is *Forks Motel* with 48 units and a swimming pool.

And for a real taste of civilization, try the local movie house, the Olympic Theatre. The seats are not brand new.

Annual affairs – An *Old-Fashioned Fourth of July* with pie and watermelon-eating contests, a parade, races and fireworks.

For further information – KVAC Radio Station, P.O. Box 450; phone 374-5130.

Hoh River Valley and Rain Forest — The 19-mile drive up to the *Hoh River Visitor Center* seems a lot farther going than coming, but it's by far and away the easiest method for car-cushion travelers to experience a portion of the Rain Forest. You'll be driving about 6 miles within the National Park and the elevation is 578 feet so while you may be using the steering wheel some, following the river upstream, it's not a tough climb. You go through some farmlands and the homestead type of thing en route. The *museum* at the center and 2 *nature trails* at the end afford glimpses of moss-draped vegetation, clear streams and possibly a glimpse of Roosevelt elk. These are short, well-kept trails, like less than a mile . . . a capsule of the Rain Forest. The museum tells the Rain Forest story. Naturalist walks and talks in the summer.

This is the only coniferous rain forest in the world. It is the most awesome remnant virgin forest in the United States. Nothing else in the world compares to this green and padded region where nature fills every cubic inch with growth. Moss-heavy branches of hemlock, spruce, fir and vine maple blot out the sky and allow only thin filters of sunlight to penetrate. Underneath, moss and ferns carpet the forest floor softly.

You should mark this experience down as a must.

It also is where the folks take off if they're going to climb Mt. Olympus—the highest peak and almost dead center of the Olympics, befitting it's name. Incidentally, 65% of the drainage from this mountain runs off in the Hoh, one of the biggest—if not the biggest—river in the Olympics.

A mile past the Hoh Rain Forest road and just across the Hoh River, a road goes off west to the Clearwater River sustained yield forest mentioned in Region 2, Tour 5. The road returns to 101 a few miles inland from Queets.

Ruby Beach to Kalaloch (pronounced "Clay lock")—About 25 miles south of Forks, Highway 101 re-enters the National Park at Ruby Beach. If you can resist the temptation to drive a little bit north to Oil City, which has no oil and is not a city (years ago they thought they were going to get both but didn't), you can instead treat yourself to one of the most spectacular ocean views on earth. At Ruby Beach down a cliff path about 300 yards long to the beach, there is wild beauty to feel and sea arches to contempate. This is a good place to remember the fact that of the 1,700 miles of the Pacific Coast of the United States, only 300 is available for the public to use. South of Ruby Beach is a short spur road about a third of a mile inland to where you can see the *World's Largest Western Red Cedar Tree.* You can take pictures of it or buy them on a postcard almost anywhere.

At Kalaloch is the *Kalaloch Ranger Station* where you can find out about clamming, smelting, tides and the nice paths that lead to the beach along this area. In case you don't feel "up" to "down" at Ruby Beach, the drop is only about 20 feet at Kalaloch instead of Ruby's 300 yards. In the summer, rangers conduct walks and talks. Migrating whales are often seen off this beach in spring and fall. Driftwood, which is lavish here, is an exclusive northwest specialty. It's of *local* origin — something rarely found on Atlantic beaches.

A word about eating and sleeping – *Kalaloch Beach Ocean Village & Kalaloch Lodge*—Open all year on one of Washington's finest ocean beaches. . . . Superior accommodations in the Lodge, good housekeeping cottages, two-story hotel unit, general store. Dining room has a great ocean view, cocktails. Quinault salmon is specialty; home-cooked food. Route 1, Clearwater or telephone 962-2372.

South of Kalaloch the road crosses the Queets River. From this bridge you might see Indians pulling salmon into their canoes from gill nets set in the river. Seven miles further the *Queets River Valley* goes into the *Queets Rain Forest* area.

Back on Highway 101, you leave the coast and take off for the tall timber land, going around the Quinault Indian Reservation. As you will note further down on your map, going around the Reservation is not the most obvious scenic and direct route along the coast. For years, some maps have shown a dotted line labeled "under construction" along the coastline. At one time, the State even got so far as building a bridge across the Quinault River. Locally, it's referred to as the Julia Butler Hansen Memorial Bridge, in honor of our congresswoman who was chairman of the Roads and Bridges Committee in the State House of Representatives at the time it was built.

It cost $500,000.

But the Indians, annoyed with our track record for messing up the landscape, won't let us use it . . . .

Lake Quinault — One part Quinault Indian Reservation, one part Olympic National Park, one part Quinault Recreation Area — is the furthest inland point of the Olympic Loop trip. It also borders the Indian reservation, largest on the Peninsula, whose residents supply most of the Quinault salmon and rainbow trout served hereabouts. Roads encircle the lake to ascend into the ranger station and return a short distance to cross a bridge and go up the *Quinault River Valley* through a dense stand of trees to its furthest ranger stations and return. Both roads have car-cushion views of an exceptionally beautiful rain forest.

To us the most interesting adventure attainable at Lake Quinault is the 35-mile ride to the mouth of the river. Make arrangements well ahead of time — especially during the summer season when the Indians are for the most part employed elsewhere. Mostly this is for fishermen, but "civilians" are doing it, too. The canoes, hewn from huge cedar trees, are about 24 feet long and a yard wide, and in the hands of an expert are quite seaworthy . . . . Check at Amanda Park or Quinault Lodge, or write Tribal Affairs Council at Taholah. Trip takes about 4 hours with a couple of beer stops. You furnish the beer.

A word about eating and sleeping – The Lake is big tourist objective and has a lot of accommodations: *Lake Quinault Lodge* is a fine classic lodge structure with windows looking out to the Lake . . . has comfortable rooms and an excellent dining room; *Rain Forest Motel, Amanda Park Motel and O'Connor's Lochaerie* are good. Write or call via Lake Quinault or Amanda Park respectively.

If you are continuing south on 101 to the North Beaches, there is a shortcut right to Moclips 6 miles out of Amanda Park.

REGION TWO
GRAYS HARBOR AND PACIFIC COUNTIES

A Word About Region II

The biggest clue to the economic character of southwest Washington comes to us in the name of its library system — *Timberland Regional Libraries* — which serve Grays Harbor, Pacific, Lewis, Thurston and Mason Counties. In the heart of it all — Montesano, Elma and McCleary — they even have a Timberland Telephone Company.

Timberlands are big in Region II, which centers around Washington's only major ocean harbors — Grays and Willapa.

Once you get south of the Olympic National Forest, 74% of all the land is owned by private individuals and companies in the lumber business. The trees you see along the highway are the fringes of the most prolific and intensively managed Douglas fir forests in the world, and Douglas fir has furnished wood for more homes than any other tree in the history of mankind. There are some 15 million acres of it in Oregon and Washington.

From the standpoint of the car-cushion traveler, this is one of the most fantastic parts of our evergreen playground. It's a remote natural area of surf-crashed shoreline with nearby recently logged, sturdy second or third growth timber. But it is second only to Seattle Center as the most often attended recreation facility in the State . . . and excellent roads have been built to accommodate the nearly 4 million people who come here annually.

You will be visiting three different colorful and dramatic ocean beaches — Olympic, Twin Harbor and Long Beaches . . . have a chance at digging or at least tasting the delectable and unique razor clam . . . see 2 — (count 'em) 2 — "Salmon Capitals of the World!" . . . find a major Dungeness crab port . . . and look over the biggest oyster-producing area of the State.

Your tours will take you past desolate migratory bird sanctuaries to the wild meeting of the mighty Columbia River and the crashing Pacific Ocean.

But most of all you will witness the miracle of modern commercial forestry.

One forester likened the new breed of trees to present-day professional basketball teams when he said, "They had to grow players 7 feet tall before they began to make any real money."

They not only had to grow the trees tall, but also had to grow them evenly and fast — like gargantuan fields of green grain.

The commercial companies are a little lax about posting signs along the edge of the road informing passing motorists about what's going on, but the State Department of Natural Resources is not. And there are a couple of places where you can get a good feel of managed forests.

One is a trip through the Capitol Forest which leaves the Aberdeen-Olympia freeway via the Rock Candy Mountain exit to Bordeaux. This winds through 100,000 acres of reforestation and comes out in the Mima Mound country and the Weyerhaeuser seed plant and nursery near Rochester. Another is near the north edge of the Quinault Indian Reservation, as mentioned in Tour 5 of this Region II section.

Failing either of these, the back roads from Cosmopolis to Raymond or Montesano are in first-class condition and give you the feel of forest farming. While you're doing it, a point to remember is that from time to time (including as late as 1973) Congress contemplates the possibility of banning this kind of forestry management ... via a federal prohibition against clearcutting,a practice which is like mowing your lawn except that it's on a grander scale. Looks like the forests have been ruined forever when they're first cut, but they come back stronger than ever after clearcutting.

Inasmuch as either yours or your neighbor's job is based on clearcutting timber, it should be of more than casual interest to you that all of the forests you're passing through have been clearcut anywhere up to 3 times in the past century.

Responding to the thought that National Parks are visited by a lot of tourists because forests are untouched by human hands and tourism is like prostitution, one forester commented,

"We sell it and we've still got it, too . . .

"And *we* pay taxes on it!"

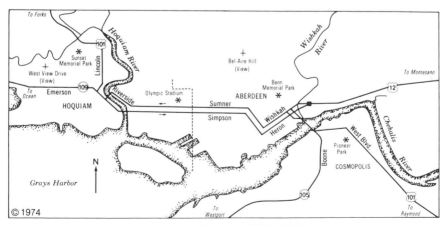

ABERDEEN-HOQUIAM-COSMOPOLIS

Aberdeen-Hoquiam Tour 1 — In and Around the Cities; Cosmopolis (Map IV)

Y̲ou get 3-for-1 here, because these three waterside towns virtually flow into one another. Both Aberdeen, lying at the confluence of the Chehalis and Wishkah Rivers, and Hoquiam, on deep water at the mouth of the Hoquiam River, are similar in layout, with industry along the harbor and residences on northerly bluffs. In Hoquiam, particularly, the hill houses tend to have glassed-in entry ways as protection against "horizontal" rainstorms coming in from the west. Cosmopolis, on the banks of the lower Chehalis River, links to Aberdeen as does Hoquiam, with a continuity of streets. To residents of all 3 towns, the rumble of logging trucks is the familiar sound, and mills emitting environmentally controlled smoke, and piles of logs reached practically into the horizon, are the familiar sights. Fishing fleets, canneries, lighthouses and clear-day views to the Pacific Ocean add to the panorama. And stretching upward behind all this are those forested mountains and hills that make this spot one of the great lumbering meccas of the nation.

Aberdeen — (Pop. 18,489. Elev. 10.) — While "Stinkin' Water, Washington" has kind of a euphonious ring to it, it's not exactly the kind of a return address you'd like on your business envelopes. So it's a good thing for posterity that Mrs. J. B. Stewart wrote that letter to the editor back in 1884. Mrs. Stewart was one of the demure ladies of the Victorian pattern at the time when the men came up with the brilliant idea of platting a town at the confluence of the Wishkah and Chehalis Rivers and naming it Wishkah, which is the Indian word for "Stinkin' Waters."

In a word, Mrs. Stewart thought the idea was stinkin'.

But liberated women hadn't been invented at the time, and she was not about to burn her bra and carry a placard around in front of the town's most important citizen, Samuel Benn. So she wrote a letter to the editor of the Portland Oregonian suggesting that inasmuch as the leading industry in town was the Aberdeen Packing Company, named in honor of the famous salmon center in Scotland, this name might well be pasted over the name Wishkah on the town plat. She neglected to mention that both she and her father had been born in Aberdeen. The guys in the packing company, who could see the advertising value of the name, flipped over the idea. Since they were the biggest taxpayers in town, Mr. Benn did his own version of a backward handspring when they suggested this idea to him. There was the added value that the Gaelic word for Aberdeen meant "meeting of two rivers" and they had two rivers.

A little later on, when he met Mrs. Stewart on the road, Benn announced that he'd had a great idea and was changing the name of the plat from Wishkah to Aberdeen, and Mrs. Stewart demurely responded with the 1884 version of, "How clever of you!"

It is impossible to resist pointing out some of the other amazing ideas that have cropped up in the twin cities of Aberdeen and Hoquiam on Grays Harbor — like two earlier day efforts at letting the world know they manufacture a lot of plywood in the area. Hoquiam hit it first with a plywood postcard cutout of a foot and naming it a "broad foot." Not to be outdone, the Aberdeen

Chamber of Commerce countered with a plywood cutout of a hand and labeled it a "glad hand."

The hottest historical item in Aberdeen is a 71-year-old steam fire engine which the city bought brand new on October 4, 1902 for $6,200 (including Grant roller bearings, wheels and freight charges).

This venerable piece of equipment doesn't get fired up very often these days, but Mayor Walt Failor gets up a head of steam every time he thinks about it, and it's caused a lot of ire fire in the city council chambers . . . along with "Ol' Tige," an antique hand pumper.

Slightly over a year after it was purchased with pride, the pumper distinguished itself in kind of a perverse way that has pursued its career ever since. At 9 o'clock in the morning of October 16, 1903 an overheated stove started a fire in a rooming house a couple of doors away from the fire station. According to the newspaper account 3 days after the blaze, the new pumper not only failed to get up a head of steam in time to quench the fire at the start, they barely got it out of the fire station before the station was burned to the ground.

Then, adding to the spectacular features of the occasion, coals dropping from the firebox of the engine caused the flames to spread far and wide in their race to the river. The next day the *Aberdeen Herald* described the holocaust as "Aberdeen's Great Baptism of Fire!" When detractors of the engine suggest that it didn't help much by spreading coals over tinder-dry sawdust streets in the town's hour of greatest need, the stout defenders point to the final comment in the first fire story, "The HERALD feels safe in saying that from the wooden town, built on sawdust, will arise the real city of Aberdeen, a manufacturing and commercial city of the first class."

In 1914, the engine was sold to Henry McCleary for his privately owned town and 30 years later when the Simpson Timber Company took over McCleary, it gave the engine to Joe Malinowski, who was associated with the Aberdeen Water Department practically forever and was the father of the Wynooche Dam, which you will read about in good time.

Phran (like tele"ph"one) White, 50 and feisty, is Joe's daughter.

For years, Phran and her father fought for proper recognition of this important piece of machinery, to the extent that when the town built a new fire station in the mid-1960's a display room was designed for it in the new building . . . and that's when the fun began.

Mayor Failor figured it would please a lot more people as a star of the Washington State Fire Service Historical Museum at Seattle Center, and that's where it was shipped.

This did not warm the cockles of Phran's heart, and in the campaign of 1967, she turned to with a will in the Second Ward and got out enough votes to insure Failor's defeat at the polls. This failed to please Failor. On October 24, 1967, before he left office, the *Aberdeen Daily World* reported that the two were traveling on a "collision course" in an upcoming City Council meeting. And in spite of Mrs. White's argument that the folks in Seattle were planning to make a coin-operated slot machine out of her baby, the Council voted to leave the engine in Seattle.

Phran was still at it a year later, noting that the engine had blown its pipes in disgust at the treatment accorded it in the big city, and City Councilman Roger Pierce of the Fifth Ward was moved to say, "Mrs. White, we've got enough problems without having to worry about a couple of old relics. If that equipment belongs to your Dad, then I'll vote to give it back to him."

But Phran wanted the engine on public display in the space provided for it in the new fire station, and by this time she had longtime Mayor Ed Lundgren back in the head man's job. Together, they got a one-way ticket back to Aberdeen for the fire engine and Old Tiger for the Loggers' Playday Parade on September 7, 1968.

This is where the wicket got sticky, however.

The fire station hadn't been built big enough for the fire engine.

Meanwhile, Mayor Lundgren had died. Mayor Failor had been re-elected in his place and things looked bad for Phran, the fire engine and Ol' Tige, in that order.

The story has a happy ending, though . . . .

Before he died, Mayor Lundgren had coughed up $10,000 out of his own personal funds so Phran's Mini Museum could be included when they remodeled the old car barns.

If you want to check out another long-term argument in this area, inquire about the spelling of the name of the river on which the Wynooche impoundment dam has been built.

The Wynooche River — so named because it's crooked — originates in that portion of the Olympic Mountains which has the greatest rainfall in the United States. It takes an irregular course south to the Chehalis River a little west of Montesano.

Back at the turn of the century, when the white folks first were settling down in the area, their interpretation of the Indian pronunciation was "Wynooche," The Federal Work Projects Administration financed a book entitled *Washington, A Guide to the Evergreen State*, a writer's project published in 1941 with meticulous attention to detail, and it went along with a single "e" at the end. And to this day, the county's largest newspaper, the *Aberdeen Daily World*, reflecting local opinion, sticks with one "e."

But government officialdom is hot for the double "ee" at the end, like Wenatchee.

The problem reached crisis proportions in 1967 when a contract came through from the U.S. Corps of Engineers for the construction of a dam on the river. Somebody in City Hall carefully eliminated all of the second "e's." The document was formally signed with news media in attendance taking pictures and all that.

Then a few weeks later, the contract came back from Washington, D.C. with an ultimatum:

No "ee," no dam!

The city succumbed and added the second "e," but a locally produced postcard of the ground-breaking ceremony spelled it with one "e." And unless some bureaucrat gets his hand in and changes it, you'll find one "e" when you're crossing over the bridge in one direction at Montesano — and two "ee's" going the other way.

Cosmopolis — (Pop. 1,600. Elev. 9.) — There's a rather delightful story about the ingenuity of the Town Fathers in solving a problem some years ago when the second story of the Town Hall was rented out as a dance floor in order to augment the town's income. Those were the days when loggers danced in their caulked boots to keep from skidding around when they'd been doing a little drinking. It may not have been rock 'n roll, but these were heavy-footed guys whose boots rocked the city government building to its foundation. They also were tough guys — too tough to be evicted. So the Town Fathers, as good politicians, took the easy route out.

They simply voted to remove the top story of the structure. Exit ballroom . . . enter 1-story Town Hall.

The *Weyerhaeuser Plant* in Cosmopolis is located at the spot where Governor Isaac Stevens signed peace treaties with the Indians in 1855. It is still possible to see the layout of the campground at the foot of F Street including all of the space between the river and the City Hall. The actual spot, they say, where the Governor had a big table on which to place the treaty papers now is the location of the overflow standpipe for effluent from the mill . . . .

A product considerably cleaner than the deal we gave the Indians.

Approximately 200 truckloads of logs a day arrive at the Weyerhaeuser sorting yard in Cosmopolis, which is some kind of a clue to the amount of business they do.

Prowling Aberdeen and Cosmopolis

For a *scenic overview* of Aberdeen, go up Broadway to 12th and wind up the hill on Bel Aire Avenue. Many fine homes from the pioneer era still exist in the Broadway area. There also is a great view of the town from the campus of Grays Harbor Community College across the Chehalis River in south Aberdeen.

As is the case with port towns, there are many foreign ships and here they literally loom above you in the town's "front yard." A lot of them like to have visitors to break the monotony. The *Port Office* , 421 W. State, can direct you to them and help you find your way around the docks. An enormous number of logs are shipped to Japan from here and the loading operation is something to behold.

The *Aberdeen Public Library,* part of the Timberland system, is a handsome new klinker brick building in the center of town with a magnificent brass owl sculpture by well-known San Francisco sculptor Beniamino Bufano. The Library is a major center for community events and its art gallery displays change every 6 weeks. Incidentally, Rosalie Spellman, the librarian, is married to the librarian for the Community College, so the two libraries are referred to locally as "His" and "Hers."

Parks include *Samuel Benn Park* – old, with formal rose gardens and grassy, sloping terrain, picnic tables, site of the annual Easter egg hunt and sometimes band concerts; *Stewart Park*, a primitive wilderness park with an occasional bear, and nature study trails; *Zelasko Park*, a downtown entrance park on the site of the Samuel Benn homestead, with 30-ft. wood sculptures of a logger and a bobcat, a World War I memorial doughboy and cannon, plus flowering cherry trees.

To visit the plants of *Weyerhaeuser Pulp Mill*, Cosmopolis, and *Evans Products*, plywood, Port Dock, Aberdeen, call ahead for tour schedules, or check Chamber of Commerce. See how modern techniques have upped use of forest products 50% above 20 years ago without cutting one more tree.

And to see *Phran White's Mini Museum*, take the truck route to Hoquiam and drive to the site of the old Grays Harbor Railroad and Light Company — presently housing the electrical and water department shops — at West Heron and Monroe.

Uncommon shopping – The *Freeque Boutique*, So. H St., is a way-out place with barn-siding-and-shingle interior, and macrame, earrings, what-not, all locally handcrafted . . . the *Scott-Craft Candle Shop*, So. H St., unconventional candles, mostly by owner . . . *Eaton's Bookstall* on Heron St. for old books, records, posters . . . *Book Carnival*, E. Wishkah St., marvelous paperbacks, Northwest and children's books (beware of the back room) . . . *Simonson's Coffee and Gift Shop*, Market St., coffees, teas, gifts for the home . . . *Carney's Coin Castle & Museum*, W. Heron St., a museum of Grays Harbor past, including wooden money and souvenir programs . . . . Under a sign "Corner Store, Fountain, Sundries" is a genuine old-time drug store, W. 1st St. Cosmopolis. Faded yellow false-front building, oak fountain counter with 7 stools, malted milk shakers, metal cash register . . . and they're just celebrating 50 years in business.

There are 11 regional *antique shops* in southwest Washington. The trick is to find one and then obtain from it a map and list of the others. They're spread around Aberdeen, Hoquaim, South Bend, Grayland, Montesano, Oakville, Olympia and Shelton.

Old Theatre Gallery, E. Heron St., run by enthusiastic Patt Pearson, and full of discoveries like the Indian art by John and Barbara Hoover, whose works are collector's items . . . old *Weir Theatre*, in same building, a classic, small theatre for 200, authentically restored, and reopened the summer of 1973, reflecting regional theatre. Off-stage, is the *Louis Benanto Studio*, workshop of an eastern sculptor lured to the Harbor by the trees which he sculpts . . . *Florence Bailey*, home studio 608 W. 3rd, is nationally famed for oils, watercolors, sculpture.

A word about eating – Real "find" is *Wirta's*, F St., hiding behind an old wooden door (with difficult handle), serving Finnish food in a country where there are a lot of Finns to judge its excellence . . . *Wirta Bar* on corner, an unchanging character spot and long a "bank" for Scandinavians who didn't trust modern banking . . . *Bridges'*, G St., with rough cedar shake and cascara bark dividers, good fish dishes . . . locals like the *New China Cafe* for tasty Chinese fare . . . *Duffy's*, Simpson Ave., is open 24-hours for all kinds of seafood, huge crab salads . . . and there's *Swaneze*, Wishkah St., ice cream parlor in high-ceilinged old building with Gay Nineties decor; features weekly ethnic menu . . . The *Nordic*, good coffee shop and restaurant at motel across Chehalis River on Highway 105 below college . . . *Ali Baba*, tavern with pizza, young people and loud music ... *Hansen's,* cheerful breakfast spot with Swedish pancakes ... for adventuresome, *707 Restaurant and Bar* across the Chehalis River on Hwy. 101 — local color and "over-heards," and don't miss larger-than-life-size portrait of one of the owners over bar ... *Lawanna's Tea Room,* in Cosmopolis, W. 1st St., small lunch, pastry-gift shop with homemade blackberry pie, German chocolate cake, chicken salad, sandwiches, ice cream.

A word about sleeping — Highly thought of are the new *Nordic* on Hwy. 105 by the college, and the newer *Olympic Inn* on W. Heron St.; reservations usually needed.

Annual affairs — *Rhododendron Annual Show* in spring ... *Rose Annual Show* in June ... *Outdoor Art Show,* last Saturday in July ... *Rain Fair* – third weekend in August (month of normally one inch of rain), mammoth parade, arts and crafts festival, booths, street dances, talent show ... *Annual Flea Market* — in fall ... *AAUW Book Sale* in November. *Art Show* of Grays Harbor Art League, first weekends of December.

For further information — Grays Harbor Chamber of Commerce, 2704 Sumner Ave., Aberdeen, 98520, or phone 532-1924.

Hoquiam — (Pop. 10,430. Elev. 10.) — As the half ended in a football game between Hoquiam and Aberdeen HighSchools at Electric Park, which was approximately on the dividing line between the two cities back at the time of World War I, a Hoquiam minister announced in loud tones, "I'm a man before I'm a minister!"

He then socked Goodbar Jones, Aberdeen real estate man, on the nose.

That started the festivities. And, as usual, the second half was late because they had to clear the field of fighting spectators before the game could proceed.

In those days there were no confining grandstands like there are today, and violently opinionated spectators mingled among themselves on the sidelines. But the sentiments haven't changed much in thehalf-century or more since. And that's why Hoquiam, (which has lagged behind Aberdeen in population for the past 40 years by about 8,000 people) and Aberdeen never have effected the obvious economies of a merger. Somewhere in the distant past they buried their differences long enough to have the major east-west streets like Cherry, Sumner, Simpson and Bay run continuously past the dividing line between the two cities at Myrtle Street. And they have formed the Grays Harbor Chamber of Commerce to serve the two cities — making sure in advance that the building which houses the Chamber was no more than half a block inside of Aberdeen. There also is a Port of Grays Harbor, which serves not only these two cities, but Cosmopolis and Westport as well, all of which are on the 90-square-mile Harbor.

Old Timer John Forbes put it this way, "You can work reasonably and effectively for consolidation 51 weeks of the year ... and be making good progress. Then they blow it all to hell on the week of the Thanksgiving Game."

And the thing that the folks in each town are thankful for when the nation recognizes this as a day in which to give thanks, is that they are not residents of the other town.

Forbes, who is not without opinions, himself, suggests that if a good marksman with a shotgun selectively knocked off between 10 and 20 people on either side of Myrtle Street, the matter of consolidating the two towns would become relatively simple. Meanwhile, Forbes has long since given up.

The most current contretemps between these rival municipal entities concerns the matter of how much industrial water is necessary for the future economic development of the Harbor. Headed by Aberdeen, the cities of Cosmopolis and Montesano together with Grays Harbor County and the Port and Public Utility District Number One, went along with the federal government in the construction of a dam to impound a lot of water for industrial purposes.

But not Hoquiam. No, indeed!

Hoquiam held out on the grounds it had all the water it needed either for now or in the foreseeable future. So if you want to get into an argument in Grays Harbor, just take a firm position one way or another on this question . . . .

Prowling Hoquiam

Coming into Hoquiam you'll see that the residential area on th hills above provides a good opportunity to view the main part of town. And there is a splendid view from the *Sunset Memorial Park Cemetery.*

Star historical attraction in town is the *Hoquiam Castle,* which is on the National Register of Historic Places. It is high on the hillside with a spectacular view of the city, harbor, and Pacific Ocean. Built in 1897 by lumber baron Robert Lytle, it has 20 rooms, turrets and period furniture. It has been beautifully restored by the Robert Watson family which lives in it, but opens it by appointment in the winter time and from 11 to 5 p.m. in the summer. There's a small fee.

At *Olympic Stadium,* built during the depression with W.P.A. funds, there is a playfield, tennis courts, picnic tables and in the back area, there are trails.

You might be able to catch a performance at the *Driftwood Playhouse* on "B" Street — 15 years the outlet for adult dramatic experience in Hoquiam.

You also can visit *ITT Rayonier,* pulp and paper; call ahead for tour schedule, or check Chamber of Commerce.

Uncommon shopping — *Walton Butts home-studio,* 160 Circle Drive; protégé of the late, well-known Northwest artist and Hoquiam resident, Elton Bennett, Butts designs and sells calendars, Christmas and note cards of beach, Puget Sound and gulls . . . *Marie's Handicrafts,* 7th St., *Junque Shoppe,* 8th Street, and *Olde Tyme Antique Shop* on Simpson Ave., for antiques.

A word about eating — *Chuck's Hideaway,* Lincoln St., upstairs for view up and down the Hoquiam River . . . *Colonial West,* doesn't look like it, but it's kind of wild — filled with antiques, fireplaces (one room has seven); extensive menu and features oysters . . . *Stone's,* a family restaurant, features home cooking, peanut butter pie . . . *Patty's Ice Cream Parlor,* homemade ice cream.

A word about sleeping – *Gunderson, Stoken,* and *Burgess Motels* are regarded as good.

Annual affairs — YMCA *Book Sale* in spring . . . Hoquiam Timberland Public Library *Pet Show* in August . . . *Loggers' Playday* in early September; ax-throwing, power saw bucking, speed climbing, choker setting, tree topping, Beer Keg Put, parade, booths . . . YMCA *Bazaar* in November, selling handmade items, food.

For further information — Grays Harbor Chamber of Commerce, 2704 Sumner Ave., Aberdeen, 98520 or phone 532-1924.

◄━━

Aberdeen-Hoquiam Tour 2 — Ocean Shores, Ocean City, Copalis Beach, Pacific Beach, Moclips, Taholah (Map IV)

It is a practical impossibility to participate in this part of the country without seeing signs commanding you to visit Ocean Shores, one of the most amazing real estate developments ever to hit our State. If you've read a book called *Lady On The Beach*, which is about the normal habitués and sons of habitués on the North Beach out of Aberdeen and Hoquiam, you can imagine the astonishment with which this Hollywood production was greeted by the natives. Promoted by one of the State's former Attorneys General and Actress Ginny Simms, this significant spectacular occupies the wind-ridden sandspit that forms the north entrance to Grays Harbor. It kind of engulfs the Oyehut State Game Range at the end of the spit. You get there via an ancient settlement called Hogan's Corner. At Hogan's Corner you can either go south to Ocean Shores or north to the rest of the Olympic Beaches at Ocean City, Copalis Beach, Pacific Beach, Moclips and the Quinault Indian Reservation . . . places indigenous to the land where "the wild wind raves, the tide runs high . . . . " The Ocean Shores people selected a location directly across the road from a spare and weatherbeaten village with a name we always have loved — *Oyehut*. Oyehut has been there for centuries and huddles humbly against the landscape, graying and unadorned. But we mean to tell you how to get to Ocean Shores. Head south at Hogan's Corner, and then turn left at the Oyehut Grocery Store. You can't miss it.

Ocean Shores — (Pop. 918. Elev. 10.) — Makes an unabashed play for the convention dollar. Incorporated in 1970, it notes that it's the most westerly incorporated city in the continental United States, and there are more bright lights here than in all of the rest of the towns on the North Beach put together. It advertises 600 hotel-motel rooms ranging from modest to the posh, a golf course and the Ocean Shores Inn which seats 1,400 and has a night club atmosphere and big time acts from around the country to go with it, plus an open, seemingly endless gray sand beach sloping to the surf. Development of the area was made physically possible because the north jetty protecting the entrance to Grays Harbor enlarged the sandspit . . . and made practicable for subdivision by the construction of a system of canals. It's an enormous project that's a long way from reaching its full potential as a population center, as you will see from the vacant lots.

The town's most colorful character is Robert N. Ward, councilman and publisher of the local paper.

As the professional public relations man for Ocean Shores during the heyday of its promotional activities, he did more to draw attention to this development than any human being on earth. One tribute to his genius is "Undiscovery Day." On April 27, 1792, George Vancouver failed to discover Ocean Shores. He sailed right past. So every midnight of that day now, there's a general exodus from the local bar to the beach where the folks holler out, "Hey, George!"

The one that has provided the town with continuing worldwide publicity, however, is the "February Fog Festival" where they hold the "North American Midwinter Wading Championship." People wade out in the surf to a post about a hundred yards away, while 4,000 to 5,000 others sit around on wet logs and with vast amusement watch the waders perform their remarkable feats.

Aided by Mr. Ward's agile imagination, the press has had a field day with this event, because in most of the years that it's been held, the Fog Festival has been spoiled by good weather. And Ward has garnered great headlines like, "Clement Weather Batters Fog Festival!" But Ward solved that one . . . he issues "Sun" checks. At this writing, Mr. Ward is attempting to figure out how to provide his city with the latest innovation he found in Portland — a bail bondsman who gives Green Stamps.

Prowling North Beach

As we mentioned in the introduction, the North Beach is divided into two separate entities, Ocean Shores, which has not as yet been whipped into line by the edge of the ocean, and the others which have been there a lot longer for the most part and cling to the landscape sort of hoping that "Nature In The Raw" won't notice them and knock 'em down.

Speaking of Nature brings us to the fact that the *razor clam* is the big attraction for most people down here. As it is, this unique marine delicacy is fought for by some 300,000 persons annually. And if the Washington State Department of Fisheries hadn't joined forces with The Lord in protecting them, they would have become an extinct species years ago. As it is, the Department doesn't let you dig them during the summer months and The Lord takes care of them during most of the winter months by providing minus tides in the middle of the night. To all practical purposes, you can dig clams from about March until about mid-June . . . at which time you and 49,999 other people will be after them on every "clam" tide.

Happily, the Indians, who have barred us and our beer cans and our plastic containers from their part of the North Beach (from Moclips north), supply the restaurants and canneries around and about with enough razor clams for us to taste them chowdered, frittered and fried and to buy them canned (which you can't do at your corner grocer anymore).

The Indians also supply the restaurateurs with Quinault salmon and rainbow trout. The only tragedy is that most of the restaurants around here don't know what to do with them once they get them in the kitchen, with a couple of notable exceptions.

Nevertheless, you probably will insist, as we do, on going after some clams, and here are some thoughts on that front: Wear warm clothes! Take along thermos jugs of hot coffee or any other beverage that seems apropos and doesn't spoil your aim with the shovels — colloquially called "clam guns." Get to the beach at least an hour in advance of low tide or you'll find yourself in a traffic jam that shames Fourth Avenue in Seattle at 5 o'clock on a Friday night. And get your "clam tide" reservations at your favorite motel about a year in advance.

For your edification and enlightenment, the two prime seasons in the motels are July and February . . . July because a lot of people who don't know about ocean beaches converge there then and are disappointed to learn that when it's sunny inland it's foggy here . . . and February because that's when knowledgeable people you have your best chance of a storm. There's no more dramatic sight on earth than the wild surf trying to beat the beach to death during a storm. Nor is there any better time for beachcombing than after that storm.

The contrast with the bleak vigor of the surroundings is a part of the richness to be enjoyed. You will see brave pretensions on the beach, but death and destruction never are distant. Danger is inherent in every wave . . .

Like here is a small sad paragraph which appeared in the *Seattle Post-Intelligencer* on Monday, November 27, 1972: "In Grays Harbor County, two Bremerton girls . . . both 14 — were killed Saturday when a large log, hit by a wave, rolled on them at a Taholah beach, sheriff's deputies said . . . ."

The biting edge of the beach is impartially merciless, and sudden death is around for the unwary. The bones of stalwart ships bear mute testimony . . . and the tragedies in the continuing records of the Coast Guard Rescue Stations along the beaches. It's a thought that never should be far from your mind. Deeds of heroism also are legend and here is one of them.

The British iron bark "Ferndale," seeking to enter the mouth of the Columbia River on January 29, 1892 went ashore 15 miles north of the entrance to Grays Harbor at 9 o'clock in the morning, with a crew of 23 men on board.

While her husband and others went elsewhere for help as the ship was breaking up, a young mother by the name of Mrs. Edward White was horrified to see the waves roll the apparently lifeless body of a sailor on the beach. Before the next wave could snatch him back, she rolled him to safety and started artificial resuscitation. By the time he was revived, another man's form appeared in the surf and she pulled him to safety. And that's when she saw the third man riding in on the crest of a wave.

All alone, Mrs. White waded out to meet him. When the wave bearing the man came crushing in, his body dashed against hers, rolling over and over again beneath the water. But she lost neither presence of mind nor her grasp on a handful of his hair. The undertow seized her legs with fearful force, but she was familiar with the water and braced herself against it once her feet touched ground.

He was a big man — and unconscious — but she didn't let go . . . and finally dragged him to safety. As his consciousness returned, he thought she was an Indian intent on harming him and attacked her, but when she spoke, he stopped.

The British Government gave Mrs. White an award of 25 pounds sterling. Some people in Portland added $250 and a medal for heroism.

The three men she got her hands on survived. The other 20 members of the crew drowned.

Not all of the warnings that should be heeded about this area are as serious as that one. Every year some automobiles, as they say on the beach, "get water in the engine."

If you're stuck in the sand on an outgoing tide, you have a chance of digging yourself out if you don't panic. The trick is to have a shovel in the car and make gradual ramps up for all four wheels — preferably with planks as surfaces. And don't gun the engine while you're at it.

If it's an incoming tide, get a tow truck now!

A good illustrative picture in this connection appeared some years ago in *The Aberdeen World*. It showed a Volkswagen half covered by the tide with a caption reading, "Some Volks never learn."

All of this is why, percentagewise, there are more tow trucks listed in the yellow pages of the beach phone books than in most places.

The trick is to drive where other people have made tracks in the middle and damp sand . . . not on the wet sand of the clam beds and not on the dry sand above. As a further motivation, there's a stiff fine for driving on the clam beds.

Our route now introduces you to the North Beach towns in the order of their appearance: Ocean City . . . Copalis Beach . . . Pacific Beach . . . and Moclips. They cover an overall distance of 15 miles from Hogan's Corner. They're all at sea level and none of them is listed by the Association of Washington Cities as an urban area and all of them have access roads to the beach. The highway between them is very good, albeit slow, when there's a clam tide. And all of them are worth prowling, regardless of where you have planted your body for the night. Once you're there, you find yourself thinking nothing of driving the entire distance maybe for one meal or to visit one particular shop. The ocean roars impartially for everybody and the razor clam is the main topic of conversation everywhere. It's the only place on earth where a clam is King.

Uncommon shopping — There are lots of pottery, craft shops, galleries in all styles and sizes on the beach. Of the lot, four of them are worth a trip to the beach all by themselves: The *Cove Gallery* near Iron Springs, with artist-owner David Waller there on weekends in winter . . . the *Sandpiper*, south of Pacific Beach, with potter-owner Betty Winders there all the time, specializes in crafts only by local residents plus indigenous plants in small berry cartons . . . *Bluffhouse*, Moclips, artist Uldine Burgon and her watercolors and prints and a fantastic view of the ocean (please call ahead) . . . and *Les Winningham's*, 3 blocks east of Tradewinds, Moclips, featuring polished burl table tops from local cedar and maple. Also there is the unusual *Grey Goose* pottery, Ocean City, with Larry Cush resident potter in a real "toonerville" shack behind an ice cream drive-in . . . *Fox's Grocery*, Pacific Beach, owes a lot of its character to Connie Fox . . . the *Oyehut Grocery* is completely "local" . . . *Sea Chest* at Ocean Crest has a collection of northwest books, plus western crafts, Mexico to Alaska.

A word about eating – *Ocean Crest Dinner House* at Moclips and

Surf and Sand at Copalis get whole-hearted nods . . . the former for elegance, superb view, and Quinault salmon, trout and the like cooked at the table (reservations a necessity); the latter because it does more with fresh seafood than any other restaurant, like clam and eggs for breakfast, or fresh crab sandwich and chowder for lunch — not classy but they serve good plain seafood and are on the beach . . . *Ocean Shores Inn* has a coffee shop and night-club-type dining with entertainment, at Ocean Shores . . . *Tradewinds* at Moclips does a south seas thing in its view restaurant.

A word about sleeping – *Ocean Crest* at Moclips, with fireplaces and indoor pool . . . *Beachwood* at Copalis, separate cottages around a pool are attractive and fit the terrain . . . *Grey Gull* and *Canterbury Inn* at Ocean Shores are condominiums, if you like city living planted at the beach . . . we particularly like *Sandpiper*, 2 miles south of Pacific Beach. They have ocean front cottages and a handsome new Beach House of 8 well designed units . . . very much in keeping with the beach.

But the one we flip over and have flipped over for 30 years is *Iron Springs Resort*. This, to our notion, is what a beach resort is all about. It consists of a series of cottages, set apart from one another among the trees above a stream on a hillside . . . each cottage with a view of and within hearing distance of the roar of the surf. Nothing fancy, but fireplaces, kitchens and easy access to the beach either on foot or by car — if you don't mind driving through the shallow part of the stream to get there. It's about 3 miles north of Copalis and you'll know it from the large lifeboat stationed upside down at the entrance. You'll need a reservation at any of these good lodging places, but even more so because of people like us who have made a particular spot a lifetime habit.

Annual affairs – *Fog Festival* in February at Ocean Shores, *Indian Canoe Races* up the Quinault River on Memorial Day . . . *Annual Taholah Days*, Fourth of July . . . *Olympic North Beach Art Show* at Moclips, Copalis, Ocean City and Ocean Shores in August.

For further information — Olympic North Beach Chamber of Commerce, Copalis Beach, 98535.

Quinault Indian Reservation — You are welcome to drive north of Moclips into the Quinault Indian Reservation for a spectacular cliff-top view at Point Grenville, and to visit the village at Taholah, and also to attend their annual celebrations on Memorial Day and July 4.

However, you will encounter something refreshingly different here that has caused astonishment, chagrin, anger and pure delight — depending upon your point of view — when you enter the reservation. To begin with, there's a sign alerting you to the fact that by your tacit consent you are entering the legal jurisdiction of the tribe. Their laws are about the same as those in the rest of the state, but by this announcement they are telling you they will arrest and prosecute you if you disobey the rules. This isn't something they thought up overnight, either. A lot of your predecessors driving to the reservation brought it on the rest of us — and we had it coming. And that's why non-Indians no longer can utilize the beach here.

You might like to pre-arrange a trip up the Quinault River in an Indian canoe and for details on this see the Lake Quinault section Tour 5, Region 1.

Uncommon shopping — The *Quinault Indian Reservation Arts and Crafts Shop* offers excellent examples of Indian arts and crafts for the collector.

Annual affairs — Memorial Day and July 4.

For further information — Call the Quinault Tribal Affairs Council, Taholah, 276-4445.

At the end of this tour, if you're returning to Aberdeen, pick up Highway 101 via Copalis Crossing for the faster trip back.

If you're going north to our Region 1 area, there's a good new road from Moclips direct to Lake Quinault.

◄—

Aberdeen-Hoquiam Tour 3 — Westport, Grayland, North Cove, Tokeland (Map IV)

The tang of salt air is with you most of the way on this coastal route which touches on the State's two great harbors and the Twin Harbor Beaches on the Pacific Ocean. As you parallel the southern shore of Grays Harbor, you can pause to visit a cranberry processing plant and then go on past marshes and quiet tidelands to Westport, one of our self-proclaimed "Salmon Capitals of the World." It's a hive of fishing activity out on a sandy spit, with northeast views to the Olympic Mountains. Then south through a schizophrenic State Park, part woods and part sand dune, into the State's cranberry-growing area. As you start around the north side of Willapa Bay, you can take a spur road to the water and faded Tokeland, once a crowded fishing resort. Then through logged-off timber lands skirting the Bay, which is edged with broad mud flats at low tide. At Raymond you pick up Highway 101 for a return through alder groves and unspoiled natural beauty.

Markham, twelve miles out of Aberdeen, is where Johns River flows into the harbor, and the chances are you can see them shucking oysters at an oyster farm and buy yourself a pint or two if you like. These oysters are much milder than the ones you'll find along Hood Canal and farther to the north. Their flavor is akin to that of the eastern oyster . . . and, as usual, we suggest that you buy Cocktails or Yearlings. They cost about twice as much as the Small oyster. But a Small oyster in west coast parlance is gigantic.

Also at Markham is the *Ocean Spray Cranberry Processing Plant.* There are something like 1,100 acres of cranberries in the State of Washington, of which some 600 acres are in and around the area west of here. Tours can be scheduled if you call a day or so in advance . . . or you can peek through the windows and see the juice assembly line.

At 15 miles you come to a wide spot in the road once referred to in literature published by the Northern Pacific Railroad as "OCOSTA! The ocean terminus of the Northern Pacific Railroad and Coast City of Washington and the Great Northwest, etc. . . . The future City of Grays Harbor and Commercial Metropolis of the Big Woods and the Pacific Coast."

Pretty big title. Pretty small town.

Next along the bay is a former whaling station bearing the name Bay City. Away back in 1850, a young army lieutenant named Ulysses S. Grant did a survey which ended in a recommendation that a canal be built from this location through Willapa Harbor and on down to the Columbia River. It's been a dream of navigation interests and a nightmare to the cranberry growers, oyster farmers and ecologists ever since. By 1935, the idea seemed close enough to reality that the *Daily Olympian* ran a half-page sketch of the proposed route which would be connected from Puget Sound to Black Lake, west of Olympia, by a series of locks and then into the Chehalis River at Oakville.

For years the State Canal Commission struggled with the problem, pointing with pride to the fact that such a project would make it possible to go by inland waterways from Lewiston, Idaho to Juneau, Alaska. Hope for progress got a little dim on June 30, 1970, when Governor Daniel J. Evans ended the existence of the Commission by vetoing an appropriation of $44,000 for its continuance.

Your next important landmark is the Cohassett Beach Telephone Company, which is at what is known as the Westport "Y." This is where you take a right turn to Westport.

Westport — (Pop. 1,364. Elev. Sea level.) — They're terribly enthusiastic here about a fish-loving New York taxi driver who described Westport as "the place Seattle is near to."

For that matter, they're just terribly enthusiastic in Westport.

Prior to 1950, it was described as sort of a sleepy, little, wind-swept town on a sandy arm tipped by Point Chehalis with a main street bordered on by some small wooden store buildings together with some modest summer homes shaded by fir and shore pine trees. The summer population was about 272. Today, Westport is reborn and modestly admits to being the "Salmon Fishing Capital of the World."

By 1930 the cut-and-get-out system of logging ended. The county had peaked in population and was starting down hill. Most people figured Grays Harbor was finished.

Then in 1950, somebody got the bright idea of selling "excitement."

The most exciting thing they had in quantity was salmon, or more definitively, the catching of salmon.

The Port of Grays Harbor owned a chunk of land north of bucolic little Westport, and with the aid of the U.S. Army Engineers, the Port set about creating a fishing machine which amateurs could crank.

There really are two Westports: the little old Westport of 40 years ago, and the Westport centered around the fishing basin. Because it owned the land, the Port set about creating a model business district . . . and the "business" was Amateur Salmon Fishing. Buildings were subjected to zoning and construction codes. There are scenic drives around the base. There's a "small fry fishing float" where youngsters can try their luck. There's parking for thousands of cars. Where they broke precedent the most realistically was with a policy of allowing fishermen and nonfishermen alike to tromp the moorage floats and look at the fishing boats.

These are the stars of the show, and a lot of excitement accrues during the summer afternoons when the boats come in with their catch and the landlubbers who've been poking around all day in the shops gravitate to the center of activity.

In and around Westport there now are 4 taverns, one of them delightfully called the "Local Tavern." There are 5 canneries and an equal number of barber shops and beauty salons . . . 8 gift shops . . . 11 grocery stores . . . 16 trailer parks . . . 20 restaurants and drive-ins . . . 60 hotels, motels and condominiums, and a fishing fleet of 700 sea-going charter and commercial fishing boats, with a value of $5,000,000. And there's a waiting list for berths.

The assessed valuation of Westport has gone up 192% in the past decade — about 4 times that of the next highest real estate worth in the county.

In 1971, amateur fishermen brought in an estimated 900 TONS of salmon . . . . If you figure the average fish at 10 pounds a piece, it means that the noncommercial fishermen who got all those hair cuts . . . drank all that beer . . . bought all of those gifts and groceries . . . ate at all those restaurants . . . and stayed at all those hotels, motels and trailer parks, landed something over 180,000 salmon. The fishing cost was something like $20 a day plus equipment rentals.

For many of them, it was a lifetime "first" in excitement.

For others, it's an addiction.

The commercial fishermen — and there are 3 out of 5 of them on the Westport City Council at the moment — view this invasion of their privacy and economics with a somewhat jaundiced eye.

Salmon fishing, however, isn't the only excitement that ever has been visited upon Westport. There was, for example, the Indian War of 1859. Desperate for steamboat transportation on the Chehalis River, the settlers of the Harbor persuaded Captain Tom Wright to put his 115-foot stern-wheeler, "Enterprise," into service. The "Enterprise," which had made as much as $25,000 on a single trip on the Fraser River, nearly sank off Cape Flattery as Captain Wright was bringing her down the coast. Then she sank 3 times while he was trying to get her to the head of navigation on the Chehalis.

Once there, some settlers charged him $50 for what he considered to be about 5 bucks worth of butter and eggs, and he determined to quit the Chehalis forever.

Wright, who was a man with verve and imagination, was awakened by a bar room brawl between some Indians and some whites when he got back to the Harbor. He went back upstream again, nosed his boat into a sandbar and tromped on to Olympia where he persuaded Territorial Governor Richard Gholson, a militaristic southerner who shortly thereafter returned to Kentucky to participate in the Civil War, that there was an Indian insurrection.

The Governor established a "Fort" at Point Chehalis (now Westport), and Wright made himself a few bucks transporting soldiers and supplies to and from Olympia for a year before the State concluded the threat of an Indian uprising was less than critical and cut him off at the pockets.

So he took his trade elsewhere.

The area also proved more rather than less exciting to a young couple who had gone to spoon in the dune west of town on a Friday evening, March 27, 1964. It was a lovely, moonlit night and they enjoyed themselves until they returned to the beach to pick up their car and found it gone. They were quite excited when they hiked into the sheriff's office and reported the car stolen.

It was stolen all right.

By the tsunami wave generated by the Alaska earthquake of that date.

Prowling Westport

One of the more interesting drives for us car-cushion travelers is out on the *south jetty* which juts spectacularly like a long finger into the Pacific Ocean. The right-of-way has to be kept open so that huge, off-highway trucks can be barged to the Bay side and use the special road to transport the tremendous rocks needed in repairing the jetty.

The jetty last was rebuilt in 1965-66 by the Umpqua Valley Navigation Company.

They underbid the next lowest bidder by $1,000,000!

They didn't lose their shirts, either. It just happened they had recently acquired the kind of machinery needed for this kind of work for another job in Oregon and didn't have to transport it as far as the other bidders.

The *Westport Lighthouse*, which recently has been declared surplus by the Coast Guard, also makes interesting prowling. This was the site of an early day lifeboat launching station.

The 210 acres around the lighthouse are being made into a State Park.

You don't have to go salmon fishing at Westport. There's good fishing . . . beachcombing . . . clam digging . . . surfing and, well — sitting . . . like out of the wind in the sand dunes.

Uncommon shopping — The *Basket shop,* on the main pier, touristy but interesting . . . *Coley's Fish Market* for smoked salmon and fresh crab. "Fresh?" the clerk replied when we asked. "It was shook out today!" *House of Holly* – being Holly Hollenbeck art and craft gallery . . . *Barton Bazaar* for new and used antiques in old Westport . . . also *Terrell's Antiques* . . . *Bottle and Ball,* if you prefer to avoid the gamble of beachcombing . . . *King Salmon, Inc., Pt. Chehalis Packers, Washington Crab Producers, Mary's Smokehouse* for seafood ready to be taken or shipped out . . . the *Seafood Market* at the "Y."

A word about eating — The delightful thing here is that they not only have fresh seafood but they know how to prepare it for the dinner table. *Sourdough Lil's* is famous . . . and *Freddie Steele's,* which serves Canterbury oysters . . . . Others that come recommended locally are the *Islander, Continental House, Dave's Ocean Galley,* all with good viewing . . . the *Colonial* where the commercial fishermen gather to swap yarns and *Dee's Cafe.*

A word about sleeping — There are accommodations for every taste and pocketbook, however the enormous *Canterbury West* with 110 units, and the *Islander,* which is right on the docks, are best, and the *Frank L. Motel* and *Sportsman* are good ones.

Annual affairs — *Blessing of the Fleet,* April 15, marching bands, floats, wreaths on the water — "the works," on opening of fishing season . . . *Driftwood Show,* weekend after St. Patrick's Day . . . *Westport Fishing Derby,* weekend of July 4 . . . *Westport Charter Association Fishing Derby,* late August.

For further information — Westport-Grayland Chamber of Commerce, Box 306, Westport, 98595. Phone 268-8122 or 268-7456.

If you don't know what sand dunes are, you're surely going to find out if you pause at all by taking any road west and south of Westport, especially if you see some numbers marking it, like 105. You also could have by-passed Westport altogether if sand dunes, etc., were your objective, back there at the "Y" in the road where the telephone company is the major landmark.

The dunes and a wide assortment of places to stay are on the beach side of the highway. The tourist accommodations are nestled behind a large dune which slopes down on the west to an area of smaller dunes and beachgrass for several hundred yards before you get to the driftwood and the long ocean flats.

Grayland — (Pop. Nom. Elev. Sea level.) — It was settled primarily by Finnish people in the first quarter of the present century. Mostly, they came by the beach, to work the peat bogs into cranberry bogs. This involved back-breaking handwork with a "scalping hoe." They had to strip the rich vegetation from the peat, leaving it bare so cranberries could be planted. And then they had to guard the berries against all of the myriad of pests who like cranberries as well if not better than us car-cushion travelers. They dug clams and worked in the mills in Aberdeen to augment their income until the bogs became self-sufficient. It was a mighty hard life and took the industrious and independent Finns to beat the rap. Today it's not as solidly Finnish as it once was in the area, but pretty solid with cranberries.

If you turn east of the South Mercantile store in Grayland and then south at the Smith Anderson Road, you'll be heading through the main *cranberry bog area.* They harvest the berries around October 1, and it's possible that some of the places will let you pick some for yourself. Each house is set primly in its little corner of its rectangular bog . . . and if you look closely you may find a lot of them have been built from Number One clear lumber. This happenstance resulted when a shipload of lumber hit the beach by mistake a few years ago. It was awfully good lumber which the beach combers — locally called "honkers" (from a slang word for heavy boots, or marine feet) — swooped down on when the load hit the sand.

For a view, turn east on the road just south of the Grayland Grocery and go straight back and up the hill, and on the left there's a vacant lot where you can get a panoramic view of the area from the jetty on the north to the cranberry bogs and the ocean.

Uncommon shopping – *Driftwood Gift Shop* for Elton Bennett prints, glassware, etc., in an attractive building . . . *Ed's Beach Shoppe,* for his fine driftwood sculpture and candles, pottery, shells, rocks, leather goods, macrame — by many other craftsmen; a bit touristy but fun . . . *Cabin 4,* exceptionally good antiques . . . *Presto's Trading Post,* new and used merchandise . . . *Treasure Chest,* antiques . . . *Ivonen's Home Market,* 2 blocks east of No. 105 in cranberry bogs, a small grocery store and meat market, is highly recommended locally, especially for cuts of meat.

A word about beer — Some long-forgotten soul with a deep sense of humor named the *"Local" Tavern*. In the 1959 Columbus Day storm, the liberty ship "Lapari" landed on the beach a few yards away with her prow pointed at the Local Tavern, causing some local wag to note the crew must have been mighty eager for a beer. At low tide they could walk all the way around the ship, but the "Salvage Chief," a tug with a mighty reputation around these parts, was able to pull her off intact . . . presumably after the crew had had a couple beers.

A word about eating – *The Clamdigger's Haven,* for breakfast after digging clams . . . *The Dunes,* identified by 5-ft. wooden razor clam and sign pointing to the beach, has eclectic decor of mounted animals, exotic plants, beach curiosities, pictures, antiques, surrounding old oak furniture and lace-edged table linens . . . unusual menu, ocean view, excellent cooking by LaRene Morrison and lively conversation with John Morrison.

When Highway 105 makes its left turn inland at North Cove on Cape Shoalwater, you are getting your first sight of one of the most enigmatic bodies of water in the State. At the moment, it's named *Willapa Bay,* after an extinct Indian tribe. On a blustery Saturday afternoon in July nearly two centuries ago, and with considerably more discretion than valor, Lieutenant John Meares of the British Navy poked around outside of the harbor you are approaching and finally concluded that a pretty good name for it was Shoalwater Bay. Four years later, his report on the Bay became general public knowledge and in 1852, one James Alden, Captain of the steamer "Active" of the United States Coast Survey, prowled the area. Treating the Bay with the same prudence accorded it by Meares, Alden concluded that Shoalwater was about as good a name for it as you could get.

Historian James G. Swan sailed into the harbor the same year that Captain Alden poked around and there's nothing in Swan's report that dissuaded anybody from making the name permanent. In his book, *The Northwest Coast*, published in 1857, Swan tells of entering the Bay aboard the brig "Oriental."

The passengers were pretty excited when a heavy sea stove in the cabin window and when they saw that the Columbia River discolored the sea for a distance of 60 miles around its mouth. Swan noted a huge quantity of water running from the river and carrying with it enormous logs, boards, chips and sawdust.

The boat beat back and forth in front of the entrance for 3 days. On November 28th, they ventured close for another look and Swan wrote: A heavy sea was breaking on the bar and no opening presented itself to us. Russell (Charles J. W.), who as acting pilot, felt afraid to venture, and wished to stand off; but by the time he made up his mind, we had neared the entrance, so that it was impossible for us to turn to the windward, and the only alternative was to go ashore or go into the harbor. . . ."

They had two guys at the wheel, two on the foreyard as lookouts, one heaving the lead and a bunch of sailors at the braces. Swan pointed out that the breakers were very high and foamed and roared and dashed about them in "a most terrific manner."

Like a chip on the wave, they passed into the harbor without shipping a drop of water — on that trip.

Anyway, it was Shoalwater.

Then somebody got a map of the State of Washington. They cut in half and ran the western half in the 1891 souvenir edition of the *South Bend Journal*. On the map there was a projected railroad line that ran due west of Yakima and south of Mt. Tacoma through Chehalis and bang into South Bend on the Willapa River which goes into the Bay. It was labeled the Pacific Coast Branch of the Northern Pacific R.R. The map was an advertisement of the South Bend Land Company and informed the reader that he was looking at "The Gateway of a Commercial Empire!"

The editorial columns stated that "grit, faith and energy" were the "magic" that built cities. (It should be noted in passing that all of Western Washington at the time was loaded with "magic" cities.) The paper opined, for example, that South Bend was no worse than a place on the Neva River in Russia called St. Petersburg . . . and all it took was grit, faith and energy on the part of Peter The Great to forge a remarkable city out of the swamps. (That's Leningrad these days.) Of course if there had been somebody in South Bend with the same political clout as Peter The Great, they might have pulled it off, too.

In the absence of Peter, however, they did have a tugboat captain by the name of A. T. Stream and the newspaper milked him for all he was worth. Captain Stream reported that he had been towing vessels in and out of the harbors in these parts for 8 years and boats were as "safe at the wharves of South Bend as they would be in the docks of London. . . ."

He neglected to mention the bit about crossing the bar, however.

Well, with all this safety going around about the harbor, and the prospects of soon-to-be metropolitan status equaling that of St. Petersburg, it seemed foolish to leave their harbor with a lead balloon around its neck like the name Shoalwater. There was no way of preventing the Brobdingnagian forces in South Bend from changing the name of the Bay, and with the Indian tribe being extinct and all, there wouldn't be any opposition generated on that front.

It seemed obvious that all they had to do to prove they had an easy entrance to their city was change the name of the Bay from Shoalwater to Willapa . . . .

There have been one or two people since who have wondered whether or not the new name made any dent in the characteristics of the shoals which gave the bay its name in the first place.

For instance, there was this lighthouse erected at the North Cove entrance to the bay somewhat over a century ago.

It was a grand old landmark until 1941 when the sea came along and reclaimed the sand it was sitting on, marking finis to that navigational aid . . . and leaving as the chief resident of the area where the lighthouse had stood a gentleman by the name of Houston S. Summers. His home doubled as post office after the Coast Guard had retreated before the onslaught of the sea.

In 1955, even the redoubtable Mr. Summers and his wife determined that discretion was the better part of valor and moved their home three-quarters of a mile inland . . . which was a good thing, because their former homesite now is under water.

Meanwhile, the State of Washington constructed Highway 105 maybe a mile or so inside the coastline and to the north of the Summers' home. But the currents of Shoalwater, pardon, Willapa Bay had not as yet ceased to function in what Summers considered to be a totally unreasonable manner. They kept chewing away at the land.

A bunch of scientists did things like carbon tests of logs lodged in the bluffs way to the north of the existing shoreline and opined they had been deposited there maybe only a couple hundred years ago and Nature might have decided that now was the time to put some more driftwood on those bluffs.

This made the Washington State Highway Department kind of nervous so they bought some land a little farther north for a right-of-way just in case. . .

Summers had another thought.

He and some of the neighbors scrounged around the county for the carcasses of abandoned automobiles which they dumped in the path of the waves. It was a grand way of getting rid of eyesores along the highway, but the water said, "You gotta be kidding!" and ate 'em up. So the folks persuaded the County to spend $15,000 dumping rock in and among the old cars . . . and Mr. Summers personally hauled 450 loads of rock — at 5 yards to the crack — and dumped them into the beach.

In the meantime, about three-quarters of the three-quarters of a mile that Summers had put between himself and the beach had been swallowed by the currents.

The Highway Department sat nervously on the possible expenditure of the $575,000 that would be necessary to change the roadbed. When would the cycle of the current change?

The day after they moved the highway . . . or the day before?

When Summers located his present home in 1955, it was nearly a mile from the shoreline. The water has been eroding away the land for a decade at a rate of 140 to 200 feet a year. Today, the Summers have waterfront property. So, if you're driving past their home, keep a weather eye out for it on the south side of the highway.

It might not be there when you arrive.

Come to think of it, the highway may not even be there.

The Corps of Engineers did a study to determine the feasibility of trying to do anything with the Bay and in August of 1972 came up with some informative material on the subject, which went back to congress: since 1887, the entrance channel has moved north 11,700 feet; some 3,000 acres, 30 homes and businesses have been wiped out along with the Grange Hall and a public school; the Coast Guard lighthouse has been relocated twice; an additional 765 acres with another 29 homes is being threatened; the State presently is blowing the half million relocating highway 105; a body of water equal to the normal daily flow of the Mississippi River flows in and out of the channel 4 times a day, doing all kinds of crazy things with the bottom.

Today's pilots treat the Bay with the same respect accorded it by Meares. The Twin Harbor Pilots' Association will not attempt to negotiate the entrance at night or with a deep sea vessel loaded to more than a third of its capacity.

The U.S. Fish and Wildlife Service opines that even a single modification could set up a chain reaction that could affect the entire ecosystem and raise cain with bird sanctuaries and oysters.

Of the possible alternatives of what to do, the Corps listed "nothing" as number one, i.e., "discontinue maintenance of the existing navigational channel. . . ."

But what about the Port of Willapa Harbor?

Between 1964 and 1971, the average annual cost of dredging the channel was $599,000. And in 1972, the total number of deep sea ships which had used the channel was 26. So for the dredging alone, the cost per ship was over $23,000. Add to that the cost of taking each ship some place like Grays Harbor to complete the loading — $6,000. So in 1972, it cost $29,000 per ship to transport 23 loads of logs and 3 of lumber out of the harbor.

Willapa is the biggest ocean bay we've got in the State . . . but when the tide's out, 50 of its 110 square miles are in exposed tideflats. It also seems unlikely that South Bend still has a shot at being the western terminus of the Northern Pacific.

It looks like the Bay has won and we ought to change its name back to Shoalwater.

Tokeland — Continuing past North Cove and the Summers' house, if it's still there, you go around the end of the bay to Toke Point and the small community of Tokeland, both of them named after an Indian chief, although it really should have been named after his wife, Suis, who was the brains of the outfit. Chief Toke was only one of her 7 husbands and she surely sounds a lot more interesting than he does.

Suis was by no means the only bright member of the Willapa tribe, however. During World War II in France, Stanley Charlie figured one out that drove the intelligence section of the German war machine right out of its collective mind.

Until Stanley came wandering happily down the pike, with an idea for the suggestion box, the Germans had broken every code the allies could concoct.

His new code: Chinook Jargon.

At Tokeland, you'll find a sheltered harbor for swimming and scuba diving, a marina, and a Coast Guard Life Saving Station — and a nostalgic hulk of an old resort hotel.

Uncommon shopping — Worth the trip is a visit to *Nelson Crab, Inc.* producers and distributors of Sea Products, very fancy marine delicacies. They're not set up for visitors but during the summer and on winter weekends, you can buy from their small retail store . . . at the entrance to the point, on the Shoalwater Indian Reservation is a *Smoke Shop* operated by the Indians where you can buy cigarettes at bargain rates if the State still has been unable to make our local sales tax stick.

A word about eating and sleeping — Like many other good quotes in the Pacific Northwest, the one about "when the tide is out, the table's set," has been attibuted to a lot of different people. And the progenitors of *Kindred's Tokeland Hotel* are among them. Anyway the venerable hotel at Tokeland got its start as a home in 1885, was added on to from time to time until it had 30 rooms, and you can stay there in the summer today if you've a mind to. It's a plain, two-story building with a lot of background built in when Tokeland was supposed to replace Coney Island as a major place in the United States. Happily it never made it and trundles on au natural in a placid part of the world community. Meals also served, but you'd better check in advance. Other and more modern accommodations are to be found at the *Tradewinds Motel* and the *Oceanside* and *Toke Point* Resorts. You also, and this is a totally delightful thought, can rent a bonafide Indian tepee to camp in overnight for only 4 bucks.

For further information — call Westport-Grayland Chamber of Commerce (see Westport).

We pass Raymond on this tour and take Highway 101 back to Grays Harbor, about 18 miles of winding, but good, road through second or third growth forest to the "Y" where you take a left turn through Cosmopolis to Aberdeen.

Aberdeen-Hoquiam Tour 4 — Raymond, South Bend Chinook, Ilwaco, Long Beach Peninsula (Map IV)

Here you're really involved with a number of the "wets" that bless the Wet Side of our Mountains — rivers from small to formidable, bays from quiet to treacherous, and ocean that gives us land to enjoy and is just as likely to start chewing it away. Starting on the Willapa River Delta, you have the lumbering center, Raymond, which needs bridges at both sides of town. Then nostalgic South Bend — named because the river did, and now noted for its oyster-growing industry. On through a state park overlooking vast mudflats at low tide, an old fishing village, then down through alder and evergreen hillsides to a historic Lewis and Clark area along the Columbia River — a river so powerful you can see a remarkable "hump" of water where it fights the force of the ocean. Then Ilwaco, sport fishermen's haven and our other "Salmon Capital of the World!" and up the Long Beach Peninsula. Barely a mile wide, but there's 28 miles of spacious-feeling sandy beach to drive, fish or clam on among modest beach towns, and on which to discover an outstanding rhododendron nursery, a large cranberry farm, and an undeveloped wildlife refuge area. Then down the quieter, Bay side and off for a look at a State Fisheries Oyster Lab, and a haven for the migratory fowl who like the marshy, mudflats-wetness of the area.

Raymond — (Pop. 3,130. Elev. 11.) — It is one of the ironies of life that the towns of Raymond and South Bend have two railroad freight lines, not just the one they thought 80 years ago they were going to get and become a great metropolis like St. Petersburg. They're strategically located in about 800,000 acres of the most richly productive timberlands in the world and the headquarters of one of the biggest oyster producing firms in the United States. . . .

But they have neither railroad nor bus passenger service.

A decade ago a dozen or more steamship companies served the port, but with hazardous navigation conditions like inadequate channel depths, an unprotected harbor entrance and a bar that scares the hell out of navigators, only one deep draft shipping company services the harbor now . . . and environmentalists are in full cry to have the Bay, as one of maybe 5 major unpolluted estuaries in the United States and her possessions, preserved as intact as possible.

The Weyerhaeuser Company, which provides the greatest payroll by all odds here can function without the port facility . . . and the operation of the port rests in very tentative hands in Washington, D.C. at this moment. The fact mentioned earlier that only 23 shiploads of logs and 3 of lumber left the port in 1972 is not helpful to the future outlook of the town as a thriving port.

But tourists in ever-increasing numbers are finding their way along a beautiful drive west across the Willapa Hills from Centralia-Chehalis and on almost a straight shot south through heavily wooded country from Cosmopolis. Raymond is a major gateway to the Bay and west to Tokeland and Westport. It is in the delta of the Willapa River, and about a third larger than its twin city, South Bend.

Prowling Raymond

If there are members of the younger generation aboard, this isn't a bad place for a "station break." There's a large supermarket with comic books, bakery goods and fresh vegetables along with a wide assortment of service stations. The Department of Game has stocked a *rainbow trout pond* for juveniles . . .

And there's *George Bales' Pond.*

Water power runs a windmill and water wheel which in turn bring a number of wooden figures into action. Two men are boxing, a lady scrubs clothes, boats are bobbing in the water and a log monster lurks in the pond. To see them, take the bridge over the Willapa River, on the north side of town, go left on the Westport Road about 2 miles to the airport road, then right about 1 mile.

Weyerhaeuser has tours but call for schedule or check with Raymond Chamber of Commerce.

You might like to make a side trip out of Raymond on Highway 6 going toward Chehalis. Two miles out is the site of Willie Keil's grave. Willie, who was going to head up a wagon train and start a "sect" settlement out here, died before they got underway. His sentimental father brought him anyway — pickled in alcohol, in a hearse that headed up the wagon train. That was one wagon train which had no problem with the Indians.

About a dozen miles past Menlo down Highway 6 you encounter the little towns of LeBam and Frances, worth detouring for, to take in the annual "S-schwingfest," which occurs about July 4th. Between the two towns is *Swiss Park*, owned by the Lewis-Pacific County Swiss Association. The fest includes 2 days of Swiss-style wrestling, copious beer-drinking, flag-throwing, stone-throwing and yodeling and general camaraderie in the new Swiss Hall in the evening. Very colorful, very popular event. As an aside, LeBam is "Mabel" spelled backwards. Mabel was the first baby born in this community. Nearby Frances was named for the daughter of a N.P. official.

A word about eating — Locals eat at the cheerful, busy *Bridges Inn*, *Tradewinds Restaurant* in the Willapa Hotel, and *China Clipper . . . Burger Barge* is just that, a nice looking drive-in or eat-in perched on the south fork of the Willapa River.

Annual affairs — Many *crab feeds* put on by local organizations and you'd have to check for dates. *Willapa Bulb and Flower Society Show*, early April. *Pacific County Fair* in August at Menlo, 5 miles east on Highway 6.

For further information — Raymond Chamber of Commerce, 434 N. 3rd; phone 942-2456.

South Bend — (Pop. 1,800. Elev. 11.) — You will be charmed by the historic nostalgia present everywhere in this town which got its name, not surprisingly, from the fact that the Willapa River makes a bend south at this spot, on its way into Willapa Bay about 5 miles west. The town is very much "of" the river with small boats chugging around the waterfront. It's the seat of Pacific County and has a quaint old courthouse on the hill.

By far and away the most important industry here is the Coast Oyster

Company, sort of the "Weyerhaeuser" of the oyster producers. It is owned by British Columbia Packers, one of the biggest fish-packing companies in the world.

There always are problems in growing oysters and at the moment the biggest one is that of obtaining seed. In the past half-century, billions of baby oysters were bought in Japan to stock the oyster estuaries of the Pacific Northwest, including Canada. Some bays, like Dabob in Hood Canal and Pendrell Sound in British Columbia, have frequent commercial "sets" that are caught on the shells which you see piled around and about. Biologists alert the industry when conditions are right and the old shells, strung on wire, are dropped in the waters to catch the spat. But the most reliable sets have been in Japan where, in 1956 for instance, Pacific Northwest oystermen bought 101,000 cases of seed (with around 20,000 baby oysters to the case).

In 1973, our oystermen were only able to buy 7,000 cases. France, which probably is the greatest oyster-eating country in the world, was in Japan bidding against us and raising the price of seed from what once was $4 or $5 a case to $28. To top that off, the French then had to air freight them home . . . bringing the total cost of landing them in France to $74 a case! They still bought almost $9,000,000 worth, hoping to restock their sagging oyster supply.

The French bought 120,000 cases in Japan in 1973, but predictions were at this writing that the total set in Japan wouldn't reach a third of that figure in 1974. Protein-wise, things are tough all over, and Japan is no exception.

Coast Oyster is able to take advantage of sets in both Dabob and Pendrell, and additionally is experimenting with raising oysters from seed under laboratory conditions in Nahcotta.

In a South Bend Chamber of Commerce brochure, it is noted that this city is the Oyster Capital of the West. The brochure goes on to state, "a writer once described Willapa Harbor as the 'ugly sister of Northwest waterways,' because it is mostly mudflat when the tide is low enough. Ugly like $2 million worth of oysters annually, with a capital value of private beds at more than $30 million!" (About 15,000 acres of the bay are privately owned . . . with about 10,000 acres in actual oyster production.)

The Chamber brochure also pointed out that planting and harvesting are done with sophisticated machinery, and the processing plants have the most modern equipment.

It is worth your effort to visit the plant during the opening (oysters, that is) hours, where you'll quickly find that the most effective modern shucking equipment is several pairs of human hands. The speed with which they shuck those oysters is astonishing but it's costly. About 40% of the cost of the oysters in the jar you buy lies in the shucking operation . . . all of which brings us to the story of the Pacific Northwest Oyster Growers' Association and Battelle Northwest.

As you may know, Battelle Memorial Institute is a global organization with some 6,500 scientist, engineers and supporting personnel. They work on everything from the construction of atom bombs to artificial heart implantation. The oyster guys figured if anybody could figure out how to open an oyster mechanically it would be Battelle. About 6 years ago, Battelle agreed to undertake the project. The trick was to open them without cooking them. (A real oyster connoisseur likes his raw.)

Two years after they started, Battelle made a progress report. They had tried ultrasonic vibration . . . explosive decompression . . . electric shock . . . blow torches . . . carbon dioxide, and cryogenic freezing . . . all to no avail.

So then they decided to try microwave heating. Up to 15 seconds nothing happened.

At 20 seconds the oyster blew up all over the oven. . . .

So Battelle has gone back to the drawing board . . . and a good pair of hands are the only effective openers we've got.

Prowling South Bend

It's kind of fun to prowl the streets of South Bend, look at th old railroad station, and note that the backs of many buildings on Robert Bush Drive are stilted in the River. One of the sights is the barber still plying his trade amidst the ornate woodwork, old chairs and under the light of a bare bulb.

There's a nice museum *(Pacific County Historical Society Museum)* on a corner of the main street, located in what at one time was a drugstore . . . with pressed tin ceiling and lots of memorabilia of the past. Curator of the museum and chief historian of the county is Ruth Dixon . . . a goldmine of information about the town's colorful past.

Tours are available at *Coast Oyster Company,* and nearby *Bendiksen Oyster Company.* Call to arrange or check South Bend Chamber of Commerce.

Uncommon Shopping — *Gradmaw's Attic,* an interesting clutter of old glass, primitives, furniture . . . *Crafty Hand* for contemporary pottery and art wares . . . *South Bend Bakery,* an old-fashioned family bakery — and get there early or you're out of luck.

A word about eating and sleeping – *H & H. Cafe & Motel* for oyster stew, homemade pie and best sleeping accommodations in the area . . . *Boondocks Cafe,* hanging over the river at the end of a street, has a great view . . . *The Hut,* used brick and wood exterior, makes a point of pizza — also breakfasts.

Annual affairs — Liveliest festivities occur over *Labor Day,* three days of parades, carnivals, log-rolling, fireworks, water show — annual highlight is kids blowing whistle on old (used 1880-1951) steam donkey engine, by supermarket.

For further information — South Bend Chamber of Commerce, W. 1st and Alder; phone, 875-5231.

Bruceport State Park — This park along Highway 101 is worth stopping at even if you have only a few minutes. It's a beautiful forested spot overlooking the remarkable body of water you're traveling around. And historically, this is where the local folks had their first fight. There's something about the Bay that's conducive to battles royal and one way or another they've been at them for nearly 125 years. Anyway this is where the action was and there's a historical marker telling you what it was all about — well almost . . . .

When the white man first showed up in the middle of the last century, Shoalwater Bay was to all practical purposes an enormous, gold mine of oyster reefs. Thanks to a small pox epidemic induced by the whites, the number of Indians who had been dining here for thousands of years was way down. Oysters were an internationally famous delicacy at the time. Depletion of the oyster supply in France had caused a national emergency in which Napoleon III pressed the leading biologist in that country into service to try and solve the problem. The Whistling Oyster was England's most famous tavern. The Baltimore and Ohio railroad was speeding express oyster trains of 150 cars a day out of Baltimore.

That was the background when the previously mentioned Charles J. W. Russell, a Baron Munchausen kind of character with a deep sense of his own importance, showed up. He always, for instance, used his first name and both initials. And generally, he did things that annoyed other people. For instance, in wet country like this, the Indians were buried in canoes in trees and frequently became mummified. It was not uncommon for the settlers to burn the mummies, which was bad enough, but Russell packed one up and sent it to a sideshow in San Francisco. He was an impressionable young man who bought town lot number 130 in Baker City, an imaginary metropolis on Baker Bay concocted by Elijah White, Methodist minister-turned-real-estate-promoter. When that folded, young Charlie crossed the portage to Shoalwater Bay where he found an "infinite" supply of oysters. Of supreme significance is the fact that Mr. Russell was from Virginia and knew the value of oysters.

But even he must have been dumbfounded when the first champagne bucket full of our native oysters, iced and in their shells, brought a price of $24 in a fancy restaurant in San Francisco. The 49'er gold rush was at its height in that city then and a lot of the guys had more gold than good sense. But that added up to $96 a bushel!

Another fact also added up. There were some other men in San Francisco besides Russell who knew the value of oysters. A group of them decided to enter competition with Russell and came to Willapa Bay in the schooner "Robert Bruce." They were from Maryland. And the guys from Virginia and Maryland were not getting along at all well in those days. There's an article by John Kohler in the November 1, 1958 issue of *The Saturday Evening Post* on the subject.

The heading on the article is, "They've been fighting for 173 years." Some of the stories about the Chesapeake Bay oyster wars stand your hair on end. At one point the authorities fished 3 skeletons from the Potomac. Their necks were chained together and their heads bashed in. At another time, an armada of 75 oyster boats staged an armed raid on somebody else's oyster beds . . . a government patrol boat deliberately rammed a pirate boat, trapping and drowning 11 men who were below deck. (Even today, when our state has but three biologists who are trying to do their thing and also patrol the oyster beds in Willapa Bay, there are 120 policemen with helicopters and fast boats trying to keep order in Chesapeake Bay.) Kohler concluded his article with, "and so the hardy oystermen who consider the bottom to be their God-given heritage, not subject to man-made laws, go their defiant, bellicose ways. . . ."

The story you'll read on the historical marker at Bruceport County Park about the early oystermen here is that a "mad" cook attempted to eliminate the "Bruce Boys" by drugging them and setting fire to their boat, the "Robert Bruce."

In a pig's eye!

That incident was the Chesapeake Bay oyster wars brought to Shoal-water Bay. And the chief suspect even today is the late Charles J. W. Russell of Virginia who probably hired the cook to do the Bruce Boys in.

As you continue south on Highway 101, consider detouring west across the Palix River for a little side trip on Dike Road.

Bay Center — (Pop. Nom. Elev. Sea level.) — Strictly speaking, this should be called "Approximately-one-third-of-the-Bay" Center, but that's a little cumbersome, and didn't fit in with what the folks who started the place probably thought was going to be a metropolis that showed the rest of the Bay people what for. The town's about the size of a square city block cut by lanes into 4 smaller ones, but it has its interesting facets.

Prowling Bay Center

If you're trying to get the "feel" of the Bay, this is yet another spot for the experience . . . good enough that the State put a park here. It's *Bush Pacific Pioneer State Park*, and gives you a good spot for picnicking and viewing the scenery. You'll have a good chance of finding gillnetters and crab trappers, or at least their trappings, at *Palix River Oyster Dock.* Or maybe a couple of guys with a recently caught sturgeon, an animal that looks like it's right out of a prehistoric animal coloring book. It would be worthwhile to check locally for the time the fishermen come in to unload at the docks each morning. You are welcome to be there and admire the catch, the still Bay, and the sight of the little boats putting in with the results of their night's work.

You'll note a sign, "Bay Center Mariculture," and while this is not open to the public you might like to know that it, too, is trying to meet the oyster crisis of the world by producing seed under laboratory conditions. It's the work of a couple of biologists from the University of Washington who couldn't stay there when the action in their field was down here. You'll note the inevitable oyster shells piled around and turning white under the weather.

A word about eating — *The Penguin Inn* sells home-cooking and Willapa Bay oysters. There's also a tavern, and a general store where you can buy a copy of the sturgeon you saw on the dock — but cut up and put in a nice can.

Annual affairs — The Methodist Church annually holds a well-known *seafood dinner* at Bay Center about May 15th . . . every kind of sea fare but lobster, prepared every possible way.

From the standpoint of some human beings, this part of Highway 101 is pretty desolate country with copious quantities of water in, around and coming down on it. There are a lot of logging trucks and many evidences of fishing and oystering on the highway, but the bright lights are few and far between. At Johnson's Landing you can go south to the Columbia River or west on 101 to the Long Beach Peninsula, and on this tour, we're taking the first choice to unfold the drama of the mighty clash of river and ocean.

Highway 4 coming in from Longview intersects 401 in a marsh-filled valley. We take 401 and cross the Naselle River.

Naselle — (Pop. Nom. Elev. 130.) — You might like stopping here to look into a shop, *Fishermen & Wives*, just what the name implies. Half the shop purveys fishing equipment and the other half has a charming selection of gifts intriguing to women. Shop owned by an attractive young lady recently moved here from Port Townsend . . . a move which provides her with a lot more water than she had before. The rainfall is 16 inches up there, 145 inches annually here. Of particular interest are chests and tables carved by a local craftsman.

Highway 401 emerges at the widest spot on the Columbia along the Lewis & Clark Trail. Astoria is directly across the river and connected to Washington by the Megler-Astoria bridge. Just past the bridge is a tunnel from which you emerge at an interesting park.

Fort Columbia State Park — stands on Chinook Point here about 6 miles from the mouth of the Columbia. It's on a spur that juts into the river between Chinook and Megler. The peak, 840 feet above the river on Scarboro Hill, is a conspicuous landmark and major feature of the park and is on the State and National Registers of Historic Places, because it was a Lewis and Clark campsite. The old army post, established shortly after the Civil War, never had any enemy foolish enough to brave the entrance to the Columbia and was dedicated as Fort Columbia Historical State Park in 1951. There are gun emplacements, an interpretive center, contemporary art gallery, a gift shop and museum. Summer hours of 10 to 5 seven days a week, comfortable picnic facilities and a breath-taking view. The park is a game sanctuary.

Chinook — This was once the richest per capita town in the state (when salmon canning was big on the river) and was named for the Indian tribe of traders whose jargon was the universal language. About 300 people live here in this town on flat terrain with its early-beach-community look. There are number of interesting turn-of-the-century homes which feature "fish-scale" shingles. Residents say they have more sun and less fog than at Ilwaco or Long Beach. There's a strong community loyalty, although someone at the Chinook Packing Company opined that "In Chinook, you can buy herring, gas, day-old bread, and beer."

Prowling Chinook

One of the chief features is a *moorage basin* for about 300 commercial and sports fishing boats, together with a boat launch. *Pacific County Chinook Park* is on the beach with a partial screen of trees dividing campsites from driftwood and sand. There still are pilings in the river from the old fish trap days. At nearby McGowan is the frequently pictured *St. Mary's Catholic Church*. This landmark for fishermen on the river was a gift to the Diocese by Patrick James McGowan, one of the important early pioneers. Just west of the church is a small *day park and rest area*, marking another spot where Lewis and Clark camped.

◆

For an unusual tour, look for signs leading to *Sea Resources*. In 1968, a group of local men joined with Ted Hallway in the incorporation of an organization called Sea Resources. The idea was to teach the young people of the community about the fish that made the whole place famous.

The Tyee Lumber Company gave an important piece of land to the project. Weyerhaeuser and Crown Zellerbach dropped several thousand dollars into the pot and the federal government plunked up $20,000 . . . but mostly it was the enthusiasm of the local citizens who pushed it through. The Ocean Beach and Naselle-Grays River School districts created a vocational school designed to train high school students in the fishing industry . . . thus qualifying them for jobs on charter or commercial fishing boats, and providing them with valuable stepping-stone experience if they wished to go on into higher education in oceanography and fishing.

During the 540 hours of instruction, both classroom and on-the-job training are offered in such areas as the relationship of the physical environment, spawning, care of eggs, record keeping, maintenance of rearing ponds, fish food and ship handling and navigation.

As a first step in the school, everybody in town turned to and helped clean up an abandoned fish hatchery just east of town on the Chinook River and built the necessary buildings. There's a big sign telling you where to visit the operation, but to us, the big story is this: The kids released baby chum salmon in 1970 after hatching them from eggs . . . .

Last year 200 of these salmon came swimming upstream again as grown fish . . . and the hatchery they came to, although abandoned nearly 40 years ago, was the first fish hatchery ever built in the State of Washington.

Uncommon shopping — To buy fresh and fresh-canned crab and salmon, *Chinook Packing Company* . . . smoked and canned fish at the *Chinook Custom Cannery.*

Your route now takes you to the south end of the peninsula.

Ilwaco — (Pop. 510. Elev. Sea level.) — This is the southwest-most town in the state. The town got its pleasure-resortish reputation back at the turn of the century when the Ilwaco Railway and Navigation Company ran an excursion train from here north to Nahcotta, a distance of 17 miles. The headlands on the west protect the town from the fury of the Pacific, and for more than a century, its harbor has been a haven for fishing boats. Closure of the fish traps on the river in 1935 was a savage blow to the economy.

But in the last decade Ilwaco has been making the most of the fact that it is located nearer salmon fishing grounds than Westport, and has entered into a lively competition with that town over which is the "Salmon Fishing Capital of the World!" (The words must be accompanied by an exclamation point.) Ilwaco has a moorage basin for 900 fishing boats as compared to Westport's 700, and the accommodation resources of both towns are strained when the fish are running.

The State Department of Fisheries wisely takes no position on which of these towns actually is the "Salmon Fishing Capital of the World!" The fact is that from the time the fishing season opens on April 15 until it closes on October 15 a lot of people catch several hundred tons of salmon on boats based in the moorage basins of these towns.

In their 1972 summer tabloid, the *Ilwaco Observer* based its claim to being in the Sport Salmon Fishing Capital of the World on the fact that individual salmon fishermen out of their port caught 1.74 salmon while those out of Westport caught a mere 1.42 fish each.

A mere 32/100th of a fish doesn't seem like much . . . .

But then Mark Spitz won seven gold medals in the 1971 Olympics . . . and he was only a couple of seconds ahead of the other guys.

Prowling Ilwaco

The *marina* is a good place to browse and listen to the fishermen's yarns, especially from April to October, and particularly when the fishing boats are coming in with their catch. In *Fort Canby State Park,* you can climb a hill and see the World War I gun emplacements. There's good swimming at *Waikiki Beach* in the summer and unlicensed fishing on the 2 mile jetty with fresh-water fish on one side and saltwater fish on the other . . . fantastic views plus lighthouses at *North Head* and *Cape Disappointment,* accessible by short and easy trails. Good "free" driftwood hunting on *Benson Beach.*

The *Cape Disappointment Coast Guard Station* is the country's only motor lifeboat training school and they get their training in the surf of what frequently is called the most dangerous coastline in the United States. It also often is called "Calamity Corner." Last year, the Coast Guard answered 782 calls; of these, 120 would otherwise have proved fatal. The worst calls are in winter. The very worst was in 1961 when a 150-mile-an-hour gale caught and sank a Coast Guard cutter with the resultant loss of four lives. If you want to get the feel of how the Columbia River meets the sea as an adversary and literally see it, take the walk along the North Jetty with somebody. You can also see what the sea does to the enormous boulders of the jetty — and you can visit the lighthouse.

Uncommon shopping – *What Next Shop* for junk and antiques . . . *Ice Palace,* an old-fashioned butcher and good meats connected with small grocery store . . . *Captain Nelson's Seafood,* delicatessen-cannery.

A word about eating – *Red's Restaurant.* "Everyone" gathers at Red's in Ilwaco, local color and buffet breakfast starting at 4 a.m. . . . *Al's* on the Port Dock views the fishing fleet; favorite hangout for fishermen.

A word about beer – *Sea Hag Tavern* is where they tell the biggest fish stories.

Long Beach Peninsula — It is reflective that two men of more than incidental intelligence are among those who have selected for their homes this tenuous piece of ground that shifts and turns and stays alive between two powerful forces, the Columbia River and the Pacific Ocean.

One of the men is the Pacific Northwest's most famous artist-in-residence, Kenneth Callahan. And the other is Dr. Vance Tartar who for the past 15 years has been doing biomedical research into cells in his own private laboratory on the peninsula. It was Dr. Tartar who looked over our manuscript for this area and commented, "What's so good about plush accommodations? They just cost money and contribute nothing to the enjoyment of nature and the locale. I'm against this mindless escalation of expensive comforts."

You have to believe that the strength of Callahan's work and the senti-ments expressed by this scientist are at least influenced by the environment in which they have chosen to live. And what a place this is — backed up against the biggest bay in the state on one side and the world's largest ocean and put together by the interplay between that ocean and the most powerful river in the world.

In writing about the Columbia, author Stewart H. Holbrook noted that there is about 750 million horsepower in all of the rivers of the world combined . . . a fifth of this energy is in the United States and a third of that is in the Columbia. Twelve hundred miles long, it drops 2,650 feet. It doesn't just come out of the mountains, it beat them to a pulp and came through. And at the point where it forced its way past the barrier of the Cascades, it was found to be 300 feet deep — 215 feet below the surface of the sea.

This wall of water comes charging at the ocean . . .

And meets an equal and opposing force that brings it to a standstill . . . creating a visible and scary "hump" of water unlike any other in the world.

Together, they spew out Long Beach.

No wonder it's an attractive place to a couple of men like these and others with the same individualistic outlook on life.

Nobody but shipwrecked sailors arrive at Long Beach by accident — it's a place you have to go to on purpose — and one of the peninsula's most interesting long-time residents arrived there by the "accident" route. And a dramatic trip it was.

The incident occurred at 5:15 a.m. on November 3, 1891 when the British ship "Strathblane" was wrecked on the peninsula 9 miles north of the Columbia River. The vessel was 20 days out of Honolulu in a dense fog which prohibited the master from taking his bearings, and a defective chronometer ruined his dead reckoning. The Captain and 6 others died. His last words to one of those saved were, "I suppose this will be put down as another case of reckless navigation, but God knows I did the best I could."

The vessel was being pounded to pieces in a gale which followed the fog, when rescuers from the Ilwaco Beach Life-Saving Station attempted in vain to shoot a lifeline on board, and the sailors were obliged to jump into the surf. Surfmen joined hands with other local citizens to form a human chain that rescued most of the 24 saved. Dr. T. H. Parks, who had trained his horse to enter the surf, was a part of the rescue team.

Writing about the episode in the Winter, 1966, issue of *The Sou'wester*, quarterly publication of the Pacific County Historical Society, Eleanor Barrows Bower related the story as it came to her from the standpoint of Charles Angus "Jack" Payne, who was a 16-year-old cabin boy on the ship at the time. Payne subsequently became owner-editor of the *Chinook Observer*.

"As I was frantically trying to swim through the surf," Payne related, "I saw this huge gray stallion swimming toward me. I gave one look and turned back toward the sea, thinking I would rather drown than be kicked to death by a horse.

"But the people on shore were hollering, 'Grab his tail! He'll bring you in . . .'

"I did and he did."

Experiencing the peninsula is like being in attendance at the beginning and the end of the world. Nowadays some promoter would figure out a way of selling tickets to either event . . . and you can bet there'd be quite a crowd on hand.

And if it's crowds, not the beginning and the end of the world, you want to see, then August is the time to go to the peninsula . . . either August or a clam tide.

A lady writer named Marge Cocker wrote in the *Seattle P.-I.* that going there "only in the summertime is like eating oysters without lemon. You get the taste but only half the flavor."

The average car-cushion traveler probably can't see and feel the richness of life texture that has caused artist, Kenneth Callahan, to make this peninsula his permanent home, but our eardrums will convey to us the pounding of the surf on one side of the peninsula and our eyes can take in the mudflats on the bay side and contemplate the possibility that in the earth's biological beginnings some kind of creatures crawled out of that stuff and eventually gave birth to the human race.

You can get both sides of the picture at the same time by attending the *Wild Life Refuge* at Leadbetter Point. It's so wild up there that there isn't even a traffic light or stop sign . . . it's a fair walk, though, from the end of the road.

Seaview — (Pop. Nom. Elev. Sea level.) — You are introduced to the Long Beach Peninsula at Seaview where there is an information center and they give you a good map showing "see and do" things of the peninsula, and where you should buy a copy of the locally produced booklet, *A Guide to the Long Beach Peninsula and Nearby*. The "nearby" refers to Chinook, etc., Honcho'd by research biologist Dr. Vance Tartar and illustrated by local artists, it sells for $1.50 and takes you from place to place with artwork and explanation of each site as you go along. Most towns are one to two miles apart. The only longer stretch between is a 7 mile drive.

Uncommon shopping – *Wellington's Sea Cove* for shells, bottles, antiques . . . *Sea Chest* for Charles Mulvey's watercolors, driftwood, glass balls, etc. . . . *Hazel's Green Lantern* for bottles and "junque." There also are horse rentals about.

A word about beer – *Depot Tavern* is in — an old depot, of course!

A word about eating and sleeping — The historical old *Shelburne Hotel* which got a big play at the turn of the century has been restored by a fugitive engineer from the Boeing Company; antiques, etched glass in the doors, iron bedsteads; dinner, breadfast, brown bag lunches to go, family style dining room . . . *Lamplighter Inn* is new with pleasant accommodations.

Long Beach — (Pop. 968. Elev. Sea level.) — This is the metropolis and amusement center of the peninsula . . . and as good a time as any to mention that at low tide the peninsula is about 300 feet wide and 28 miles long. The folks say it is the longest driving beach in the world.

Prowling Long Beach

On the top of the visiting list as far as gardeners are concerned is *Clarke's Rhododendron Nursery*, on Willapa Bay side of Long Beach, the largest such nursery in the world and editorial office of the American Rhododendron Society. There are two huge greenhouses, each capable of propagating 20,000 plants from cuttings. The nursery offers 350 species . . . ships about 20,000 plants around the world. Blooming season extends through

June and visitors are welcome. *Marsh's Free Museum* has this perfectly hideous dried Alligator Man, also seahorses . . . shells . . . glass floats. Their new building is the first to follow the "early seashore" motif suggested by the Chamber of Commerce.

Uncommon shopping – *Milton York Candy*, making candy in Long Beach since 1894, great chocolates and saltwater taffy . . . *Ernie's Cottage Bakery*, stools for coffee with the pastry (present Ernie is grandson of original) . . . *Big Z* has 30 flavors of homemade ice cream . . . *California Street Gallery*, where you can watch David Campiche throw pots, and you can buy stoneware, as well as his wife's charming handmade clothes for children . . . *Bookvender*, a dandy bookstore . . . *Smiles Shop* for teenagers . . . *Cornell's Seafood Grocery*, with crab cooker in front . . . *Potpourri*, craft gift shop with weekend demonstrations . . . *Driftwood Boutique* . . . *Long Beach Cannery and Smokery*, 3 miles north of city center . . .

A word about eating – *Marylou's Tavern* is full of "locals" at lunchtime. Good clam chowder.

A word about sleeping — The Washington State Department of Commerce and Economic Development Tourist Promotion Division put the situation in a nutshell when it reported that accommodations on the peninsula are not what you would call plush, but all are clean and comfortable. Well over half of the hotel-motel accommodations on the peninsula are in and around Long Beach. In passing — *Shaman's* is popular locally . . . *Chatauqua* is a new condominium . . . *Ocean Lodge* has cottages with fireplaces . . . *Breakers* is on the ocean.

Annual affairs – *Fourth of July Fireworks and Arts and Crafts Sale* by Peninsula Arts Association . . . *Art Show* by the same Association late August . . . Annual *Lutefisk and Meatball Dinner* by the Grange first week in December.

Ocean Park — Just for fun, look for a house made of doors painted pink, and the *Wreckage*, made up of stuff that floated in to the beach; both houses south of the school. There also are horse rentals here, and visitors are welcome at the *Coastal Washington Research and Extension Unit*, Washington State University, where research is conducted into cranberry production — on the Pioneer Road to Nahcotta.

Uncommon shopping – *Sea Spray Gallery*, great photographic interpretations of the peninsula by photographer Larry Maxim. *Seattle Times* Columnist Don Duncan says: "Maxim is a rare combination of free spirit and perfectionist. While painting a business sign at his Sea Spray Inn recently, he was so pleased with the orangish paint that he sprayed it on his shoes.

"My happy shoes, he said, doing a dance."

A word about eating – *Roadhouse Restaurant*, style of early 1900's decorated with photos of that time on the peninsula. Seafood, breakfast in view of the fireplace.

◄►

One of the showplaces on the peninsula is *Cranguyma Farms* on Willapa Bay . . . and visitors are welcome. You can enjoy rhododendrons, azaleas, holly, bamboo and evergreens, and in August and September "U" can pick blueberries. And about October 1, "U" can watch them harvesting cranberries which they do in a tearing hurry and by flooding the bogs.

They have about 130 acres in cranberries, making it the biggest cranberry farm west of the Mississippi. It's that big because financier Guy C. Myers, who bought the property in 1941 opined he had "no use for anybody else's weeds," and in the cranberry business weeds are an item that can spread from an uncared-for farm to a cared-for one, creating nothing but problems.

The name Guy C. Myers should mean something to people who were around the Pacific Northwest in the 1930's . . . because Guy Myers was the guy who figured out the philosophy of revenue financing for bonds issued by Public Utility Districts, and how private power companies could get out of some of their more rural holdings by something a lot more profitable than via the condemnation route. He also handled financing of Rocky Reach Dam, which was the biggest sale of hydro-electric bonds in history.

Born in Wisconsin where they raise more than a couple of bushels of cranberries, Myers was aware that properly conducted cranberry farming — in spite of all of the grief involved — can be a very profitable enterprise indeed. (A good farm will bring in upwards of $2,000 an acre.) The farm subsequently was bought by Mr. and Mrs. Frank O. Glenn, Jr., a natural sequence since Mrs. Glenn is the late Myers' daughter.

If you stumble a little over the pronunciation of Cranguyma, the name came about like this: The "Cran" is for cranberries . . . the "Guy" for Guy Myers. The "ma" part gets a little more complicated.

First you take the "Y" off the Guy; you add it to the "ma" and then spell that part backwards. You get Amy, right?

That was Mr. Myers' wife's first name.

Nahcotta — (Pop. Nom. Elev. Sea level.) — If you time your visit here for weekdays either before or after lunch — until 4:30, you'll have a chance to see the operational headquarters of the fight to prevent the third great wipeout of oysters in this bay. It's the State Department of Fisheries' Willapa Shellfish Laboratory. Clyde Sayce, resident biologist, is the local "general" in the oyster preservation battle.

The individualistic oystermen on the east coast opine that "no biologist ever made a dime for me," but the biologists are big here as they try to figure out what gives with this fickle bay and how can they keep the commercial crop coming.

It took Charlie Russell, the Bruce Boys, and their successors about half a century to wipe out the original oyster supply in the bay. At the time, federal biologists warned them they should leave enough oysters on the beds to permit propagation, but when you're making a bundle, it's hard to believe a biologist. The oystermen then asked federal biologists for advice on how to propagate eastern oysters here and were told it couldn't be done. So they did the logical thing, they fired the federal guys and hired a local biologist, who told them the same thing. So they fired him and dumped millions of eastern oysters in the bay . . . and they didn't propagate.

By the 1920's, nobody had any oysters at all, not the original "natives" and not the "easterns."

Oyster lands that once had sold for as much as $3,000 an acre were going on the tax auction block for 50c. And that's when Gerard T. Mogan arrived on the scene at Nahcotta. That's the same Mr. Mogan we mentioned in Region I, who later became the "accidental father" of the Quilcene and Dabob Bay oyster industry. He established his headquarters in the Moby Dick Hotel here. Mr. Mogan was not so much in the oyster business as he was in the oyster "land" business. The old-timers on the bay still like Mogan and figure he made a contribution to the area. Longtime bay resident Stan Gillies notes than when Mogan initiated his real estate operations here he always asked the individual owner if he intended to bid for his own property at the tax sale. If the man said yes, Mogan would not bid against him. Otherwise, Mogan bought anything anybody would sell — which was about half the bay & at that four-bit figure.

Then he turned around and sold it to suckers from Seattle for $500 an acre.

Mogan was a high-flying man. Some of his literature read like this: "There is SIMPLICITY AND EASE IN OYSTER FARMING!" (The truth of that one, right there, is one you might consult an oyster grower about.) Mogan's published stuff also went along in this vein, "The oyster beds in Willapa Bay have a 75-year-record of raising oysters of high quality and in great quantity . . . . The oysters grow into enormous crops ranging from 1,000 to 3,000 bushels per acre without feeding or fertilizing . . . . "

Mogan established a model oyster farm in the bay with paths through it and advertised that people could come here and "walk on this bed or more around as easily as they would in their garden or orchard . . . . " And he surely sold oyster land.

Of course, he had a gimmick. A couple of American Japanese had figured out a way of bringing Japanese oyster seeds into the Pacific Northwest where they grew magnificently . . . especially in Willapa Bay where they established some kind of a record with shucked meat weighing three pounds from a single oyster . . . which is just a little large for the average oyster cocktail.

Mogan's sense of timing in selling oyster lands — during the stock market boom of the 1920's — couldn't have been better. And his timing in unloading limitless quantities of huge oysters in the channels of trade — 30 days before the 1929 stock market crash — couldn't have been worse. Thanks to the crash and subsequent hard times, during the thirties, they had oyster surpluses in the bay like you wouldn't believe. Then World War II came along and all those oysters that had been piling up got eaten. And waters of the bay cooperated with our war effort. Although the supply of seed from Japan was cut off, the bay came up with a couple of great natural sets of seed.

By 1946, 10,000,000 pounds of oysters were being harvested annually.

Today there are about 3,500,000 pounds being harvested.

While even this is about 7 times as many oysters as were harvested during the peak years of the native oysters at the turn of the century, there is plenty of cause for alarm. This year there's been a dramatic drop in seed production in Japan, and the biologists have got to figure out how to keep those baby oysters coming. Willapa is one of the last great oyster estuaries on earth. Some 96% of all oysters grown on the Pacific Coast of the United States are grown in Washington . . . and well over half of them are grown right here. If our grandchildren are to taste the flavor of real oysters, this is where the battle must be won.

Prowling Nahcotta

Seventy-year-old Ray Stone, the honorary chief executive of this miniscule mote on the population charts of the state, had this to say about Nahcotta:

"I'm the mythical mayor of a non-existent town, but I point with pride to the increase of pigeons from 4 to 800 under my administration. They keep the folks looking up and we don't have to paint City Hall. Our chief industry used to be windmills, but we made so many there wasn't enough wind to push all of them and we had to close down. We didn't have enough money to build a freeway, so we just built an interchange. You go up and around it and come back to where you started. Proves we don't spend our money foolishly . . ."

A retired biologist from the Shellfish Lab here, Stone keeps his hand in by conducting tours thru *Northwest Oyster Farm's experimental, shucking and processing plant* at the Nahcotta dock where it markets seafoods under the Jolly Roger label. It's one of the few oyster farms in the Pacific Northwest which really caters to visitors and the tour hours are posted on the door.

If you're an amateur oyster-eater, the chances are you'll want them well-done, which is in the same category as a well-done tenderloin steak — you don't get the "sizzle."

As Ray Stone puts it, "They're about the same price as a hot dog . . . and you don't get indigestion eating them."

A word about eating – *The Ark*, on the south side of the pier from the oyster plant, for thumb-sized oysters in cocktails or nicely panfried, not deep fried. With its peaceful view of Willapa Bay, the Ark is a welcome spot when you want to turn off the continuous sound of the ocean surf.

Oysterville — A dozen houses, a charming little post office, an old church and a store are all that remain of what for nearly 40 years was the county seat before the resolute South Bend folks took it away. But it's weatherbeaten and charming, especially the occupied dwellings, some delightfully restored, with colorful flowers surrounding them.

You can drive north to Leadbetter Park, but from then on it's shank's mares into the Migratory Bird Refuge. The *Leadbetter Point area* is a completely undeveloped Wildlife Refuge area, which is alleged to include bears among its inhabitants. There are no houses, you just drive through woods to sand. If you get out of your car to walk to the literal point, you'll find out it kind of hooks onto an island which it would be unadvisable to be caught on at high tide. Underfoot, strawberries and flowers grow in the sand, and birdwatchers can have a splendid time looking for the 200 varieties of birds to be found in this area.

Returning south on the bay side of the peninsula, you reach Highway 101 at Seaview and head east.

Willapa Migratory Bird Refuge — This is a few miles out of Seaview. the ranger here will supply you with information about birds you will hardly believe. He also can tell you about Long Island, to the north of here, which is not a destination for car-cushion travelers, because there are no ferries to Long

Island. However, this is well worth the stop because in addition to being there for birds, the ranger has a lot of information about the land and water the birds use in their flyway patterns, and a visit here will enhance your appreciation of the whole area and what's going on here to preserve this important estuary, labeled in a Congressional study as "one of the last remaining relatively unspoiled estuaries."

From here, head north on 101 to return to Aberdeen.

◄━━

Aberdeen-Hoquiam Tour 5 — Montesano, Elma, McCleary (Map IV)

Chances are you'll be taking this route either to or from the Puget Sound country, and you'll find yourself on one of the most parklike sections of freeway in the State. With appropriate weather, you'll get dazzling views of Mt. Rainier. Between Montesano and Elma, the Chehalis River veers south and provides another delightful way — the valley route, south to Centralia and Chehalis. There also is a woodsy "back road" through McCleary to Shelton. You'll notice some rise in elevation going out of Montesano and Elma, as the road leaves the river and cuts through the north edge of the Black Hills. McCleary is at an altitude about four times that of the other two towns. Your journey takes you from a wide river valley into dense second growth forests.

Montesano — (Pop. 2,847. Elev. 65.) — A residential town about half way between Olympia and the ocean beaches, Montesano is the Grays Harbor County seat. It's at the confluence of the Chehalis and Wynooche Rivers and was once at the head of navigation, although that was something of a dubious honor in the old days before they cleaned out the snags. In one of the early day trips, a freight canoe got hung up 20 times between Grays Harbor and the head of navigation.

The folks coming in from Olympia were mightly glad to see Montesano because it meant they could be upright men again. The trip to the Capitol was confined mostly to bear trails — and the bears usually were only four feet high, meaning that the men who had to follow them did so on hands and knees.

George Waunch was the kind of a guy who appealed to the popular imagination in those days. He could place 50 pounds on the palms of each hand and walk around with his arms outstretched their full length. Twice a week he carried 90 pounds of mail to Olympia on his back, a one-day trip each way. At log-rolling contests, he could sink the bit of the axe to the depth of the handle at each stroke.

And in case you're making the drive over the freeway from Olympia to Montesano, the first stage trip between the two towns made big headlines by covering the distance in eleven hours!

The first settler was a man from Maine, who came around the Horn instead of over the Rockies on his journey west. His exposure to mountains was derived largely from stops in San Francisco, Astoria and Aberdeen. His wife was a deeply religious woman and liked the idea of Mt. Zion as a name for their town. They liked the ring of Montesano, which amounts to the same thing, and thus named the town, as well as the mountain which rises behind the town. Today it's called the "Boy Scout Knob."

The folks here are pretty proud of the fact that their newspaper, the *Montesano Vidette*, is the oldest continuous business in the County . . . and even prouder that one of the two original owners retired after ten months with nearly $10,000 in his pocket. Profits on the paper in the early days came from the government requirement that people filing timber claims had to advertise notice of application and final proof. The originators of the newspaper charged $11 apiece for the notices. The profits that accrued to the newspaperman indicate how many timber claims were filed in the 1880's, particularly along the Wynooche River.

Stands of timber were so thick in some of the areas here they had to start at the edge and work in because it could only fall in one direction. This area has been called, with justification, the "Mother Lode of the Douglas fir."

Montesano's greatest day came on June 12, 1941, when, before an overflow crowd at the Montesano Theater, Governor Arthur B. Langlie gave the principal address in the dedication of the *Clemons Tree Farm* . . . and today you can't miss a large sign in town reading "Montesano Welcomes You. Birthplace of America's Tree Farms." The spot should be entered on the National Register of Historic Sites, and the sign really ought to read, "The Buck Stopped Here," because this is where the privately owned commercial forests of the United States touched bottom and started up again . . . .

With this farm the Weyerhaeuser Company proved to an astonished lumber industry that you could make a buck growing trees as a crop. You can obtain a map of the farm from one of the Weyerhaeuser offices some place, but you don't really need one to get the picture if you're driving from here to Raymond or from Raymond to Oakville via the back road through Brooklyn. You'll be in it.

It also sprawls up the Satsop River . . . comprising altogether some 200,000 acres. It was the first of 30,000 certified tree farms in the U.S., today covering over 68 million acres of privately owned timberlands. It's named for an old-time logger, Charlie Clemons, whose property formed the nucleus of this modern forest management enterprise.

When the folks first showed up in this country, the forests were the enemy of everybody. It was here the Indians and/or wild beasts lurked, people got lost, strayed or stolen and fables like Little Red Riding Hood helped to keep the kids out of the woods. Farm-thwarting stumps originated here. A lot of people are amazed to learn that farmers and fires decimated more forests east of the Missouri than all of the lumberjacks put together . . . and you have to take the U.S. lumber story with this kind of attitude in mind.

As late as 1890, a federal government employee, by the name of Major Powell, told Secretary of Interior, John W. Noble, that the best way of coping with the nation's forests was to burn them.

Powell went on to explain with relish how he, personally, had started a fire that had burned 1,000 square miles of forests in the Rocky Mountains . . . as a frame of reference, that's 64,000 acres — almost the size of the State of Rhode Island.

Powell was one of the two men who headed the United States Geological Survey and as such had spent the previous decade as an agent of Congress making a scientific analysis of the nation's lands.

His report was the shocker that brought about the Midnight rider.

This rider, creating the National Forest Reserves, was attached to a forestry bill at midnight on March 3, 1891. It stayed only because President Benjamin Harrison told congressional leaders he'd veto the whole bill if it didn't. They wanted the main bill and didn't have enough of a majority to over-ride his veto. That was the rider which ultimately made the Olympic National Park, Mt. Rainier National Park, the North Cascades National Park, and all the rest of our National Forests realities.

Outside of details like these, it wasn't at all far-reaching.

A decade later, a loosely knit group of individualistic capitalists from around the country strained every financial resource they could lay their hands on and coughed up $6,000,000 to buy a million acres of the Northern Pacific's land grant in the State of Washington. The group traveled under the name of Weyerhaeuser because one of their members, Frederick Weyerhaeuser, was the only one who ever could get them all pointed in one direction — even for brief periods. A contemporary, Matthew G. Norton, recalled that "Mr. Weyerhaeuser was not inclined to give up an undertaking which seemed to him to have great merit . . . ."

Off and on for the next twelve years, Mr. Weyerhaeuser got the men together from time to time long enough to blow $12,500,000 buying land in, to them, a somewhat improbable place called the Pacific Northwest . . . without getting a dime back in dividends. In 1912, the board rebelled and unanimously voted itself some income from all of these expenditures. Five years later, the newly formed Internal Revenue Service would opine the land was worth about $90,000,000. The nation's chief forester, Gifford Pinchot, who was prejudiced, would set the value at more like $900,000,000.

Pinchot was for nationalizing the forests.

And he had a point there, as you shall see.

Geographer, J. Russell Smith, estimated that when the folks first showed up in this country, primeval forests covered 821 million acres. In 1922 the Senate Select Committee on Reforestation held 24 hearings in the forested areas of the nation, and concluded there were only 138 million acres — or just over 16% — left . . .

And we were using our trees up 3 times faster than we were growing them.

Meanwhile, the lumber industry had acquired a bad reputation for a lot of things — among them the theft of fertile forest lands. The principal vehicle for their thievery was the Forest Lieu Land Act of 1897, under which, owners of land that had been included in a Reserve could select an equal amount outside the Reserve in exchange. The trick was to lay your hands on title to some lousy land within the Reserve and swap it for lush timberland outside the Reserve which you then sold at exorbitant prices.

Pieces of real estate, to the tune of 400,000 acres, changed hands in this way.

There were some 1,000 indictments and 126 convictions, the most spectacular of which were the indictments of Oregon's Attorney General, two of that State's Congressmen and the Mayor of Albany, Oregon. The sensation that rocked the whole country was the indictment of Oregon's United States Senator.

In the light of today's scandals, it is ironic that his name was John Mitchell.

Mitchell was 70 years old at the time and had been in the Senate off and on for over 30 years. On January 17, 1905, Mitchell brought ringing applause from the floor and galleries of the Senate with his impassioned denial of the charges . . .

But that didn't prevent the court from convicting him and sentencing him to jail later in the year . . . a sentence that was not carried out because of his death on December 8, 1905.

Meanwhile, the highly competitive and individualistic lumbermen of the nation defied the efforts of conservationists by moving into a region, removing the choicest trees (there was a time when they wouldn't take a tree that was smaller than 18 inches at the top and without a blemish) and moving out again, leaving a tangled mess on the bare earth behind them. Often devastating fires followed in their wake.

To be sure, they had help starting fires from the campers, fishermen and hunters, but in the 25 years prior to 1941, in the State of Washington alone, forest fires consumed an acreage larger than that of all the New England states — annually.

Most lumbermen gave lip service to conservation, but that was all.

Pinchot, behaving a lot more like a Democrat than a Republican, tried to work with them, gave up in disgust and ended up in the nationalistic corner . . . and the unregenerate Republican radicals polarized themselves in the laissez faire philosophy.

The problem was that private, state and national land was so intermingled, nobody could have separated them out. At about this point, the country spewed up a head forester by the name of William B. Greeley who thought that someplace in this mess, there ought to be a middle course.

The catalyst was the Pacific Ocean.

Norton Clapp, currently chairman of Weyerhaeuser's board, put it this way,"When we got to Grays Harbor there was no place else to go."

Greeley wrote, "The conviction became strong in my mind that industry itself was the great latent force for reforestation if the government could . . . shake off some of its shackles."

The chief shackle was taxation both on the land and on the product of the land, and a lot of lumbermen — including many within the confines of Weyerhaeuser — were of the opinion the company was out of its mind for retaining ownership of land twice the size of Rhode Island, in the State of Washington alone . . . enough so that a subsidiary called the Logged-Off Land Sales Company was formed to get rid of some of it. Among other things, this company tried to show farmers how to dispose of stumps and to try and farm land that was really only good for trees.

In the 1930's some of the big companies like Weyerhaeuser went on a "tax strike" to make their point about double taxation. On the other hand, the regulatory forces in the federal government started stiffening their stand on conserving the resource. George Frederick "Fritz" Jewett, a Weyerhaeuser board member, was moved to write "I feel stongly that unless the industry has a definite workable plan or course of action, we are going to be told what to do whether we like it or not."

Jewett's sentiment prevailed within the company; Greeley's worked out within the government. Weyerhaeuser committed 130,000 acres to the tree farm concept, while other owners, state, county and private, added 65,000 acres intermingled with or adjacent to the company land . . . and the Clemons Tree Farm came into existence something over 30 years ago. Since then, this concept has proliferated throughout all of the major timber holdings in the nation.

Greeley was right in his supposition that intensive forest management fell in the province of private enterprise and Clapp noted why: "Money from timber sales on National Forest lands goes into the National Treasury, but policy for the National Forest Service is made in Congress and there's no relationship between the operation and the sales. We've got to grow bigger and better trees faster and make more use of them in order to stay in business."

Forests in the Clemons Tree Farm are among the most prolific and intensively managed lands in the world. The company has the biggest privately-operated research team in the world . . . is the biggest owner of forest lands in the world. George Staebler, chief of the company's research group in Centralia, notes that since the advent of the tree farm at Montesano, utilization of the forests has been upped by 50%, and adds, "I have hopes that it will be increased by 300% before I die."

One of the cardinal reasons, of course, is the research which has made it possible to divert former waste products into chips for pulp mills. And it is typical that within the framework of our free enterprise system some mad genius has come up with a new labor-saving device.

It's a piece of machinery devised to split, among other things, the butt ends of logs called, delightfully, "lily pads" because that's what they look like floating in the water. If you've ever attempted to split the butt end of a log, you'll know what we mean when we say they are at the very least cantankerous. Until recently, there was nothing to do with them but throw them away.

But now Bill Zink of Bellevue peddles a Piqua Engineering Company device which divides log butts into pieces small enough to be fed into a pulp chipper. . . .

It's called — what else? — a "Lickity Splitter."

To get a further idea about tree-farming, be sure to note what the State is doing if you're in the Queets Rain Forest area above the Quinault Indian Reservation (See Region I map). There is a good highway up the Clearwater River through State Sustained Yield Forest Number 1. The blacktopped road has signs along it noting when the trees were planted and what's happening. The road comes out again at the Hoh River.

Prowling Montesano

The Grays Harbor Courthouse, a sandstone structure with a copper dome, is easily the most outstanding edifice in Montesano, and compares handsomely with any other similar capital in the country. Built at a time when timber tax returns were enormous, money was lavished on it.

Among other things in the Courthouse are murals by a Milwaukee, Wisconsin artist who clearly was unacquainted with the soggy weather in which our Indians dwelled . . . the kind of weather that would raise particular havoc with the headdresses of the Plains Indians. Nevertheless, in the mural depicting Governor Stevens' Treaty with the Indians, February 25, 1855, the Indians are wearing feather headdresses. In the actual signing of the treaty, there were no headdresses. The artist just thought they made a nice touch.

Did this little inaccuracy upset anybody? Heck, no! Our Indians liked them and started wearing headdresses.

Also in the Courthouse is the McKenzie-Elmer Plaque memorializing county deputy sheriffs Collin McKenzie and A. V. Elmer who were slain by John Turnow, known variously as the Wild Man of the Olympics, the Beast Man and the Human Gorilla.

In 1909, Turnow escaped from a mental hospital in Oregon. A year later, he killed a couple of young hunters, and for the next three years he was the subject of one of the wildest manhunts in history. A reward of $5,000 was posted for him and at times a thousand men were tramping through the forest seeking him. In March, 1912, the two deputies went after him and were found slain 13 days later. A year later three men surprised him in his hideout. Turnow killed two of the men before a bullet from the rifle of the third man ended his life.

Among the places to relax in town is the *Fleet Park*, given by Reuben Fleet, one of the town's more noteworthy citizens. It's named in honor of Fleet, a World War I flyer who entered the real estate and insurance business in town after the war and subsequently created Consolidated Aircraft of San Diego. Fleet, who also flew the first airmail from New York to Washington, never has forgotten his home town, returns here annually to give a dinner for his friends.

(Another famous resident has a mountain on the moon named for him. Dr. Howard P. Robertson studied with Albert Einstein after growing up in Montesano. When he returned and gave a talk on relativity to the Chamber of Commerce, it's reported nobody understood him.)

There also is a Parkway entering town, best viewed in the spring with blooming rhododendrons, tulips, daffodils, and *Lake Sylvia State Park,* at the site of the first sawmill in the county. The *Wynooche Dam* is a short distance away (36 miles) and is being developed into a handsome recreational facility.

The *W. H. Abel Memorial Library*, given to the city by the daughter of one of the town's most able attorneys, has one of the finest collection of books in the Timberland Library System.

Uncommon shopping — *"Finn" potatoes.* In 1950, Mr. and Mrs. Carl

Riipinen were back in Finland visiting the Old Country when they were served some potatoes that tasted so good they had Carl doing backward handsprings. He brought some seed potatoes back to his farm about 4 miles south of Montesano where they flourished and a whole bunch of other people shared his opinion of their flavor. Actually they are a yellowish Swedish potato with kind of a buttery flavor. They command a price of several cents a pound above the normal Irish potato in markets. In 1973 they were selling for 27 cents a pound in town and if you took the trek to the farm you could buy them out of a "dark bin" (light damages the flavor, the Riipinens say) for 19 cents a pound. They raise something like 150 tons in their 25-acre farm. People from around and about try and purloin seed potatoes so they can plant their own, but the family sprays them so the seeds won't sprout. If you'd like to try them on for size, cross the Chehalis River south on the Raymond Highway 107. Turn left past the welding shop to the end of the road (3 miles). Catch 'em in the fall while they last.

There's a good bakery in the *Thriftway Market* . . . and *Village Church Antiques* has an interesting collection in, of course, an old Village Church. The owner says "antique people look for the steeple."

A word about eating — *Beehive Restaurant* is preferred locally for its homemade pie and reasonable prices.

Annual affairs — *Farm Festival* in late June, events in the shopping center and arts and crafts exhibits in Fleet Park.

For further information — Write the *Montesano Vidette*, 115 W. Marcy, or call 249-3311.

Elma — (Pop. 2,227. Elev. 69.) — This is the crossroads town where you can take a cutoff highway up the Chehalis River Valley to Centralia and Chehalis, by-passing Olympia, go over the "summit" into Olympia, or take a couple of back roads into Shelton. It's a bedroom community for Aberdeen, Olympia, Shelton . . . with a high proportion of retired folk.

There are other variations of how the town got its name, but the one we like is that the settlers submitted the name "Elmer" in honor of Elmer E. Ellsworth, the first Union soldier killed in the Civil War. Postal authorities didn't think that was so hot, took off the "er" and added the "a."

Uncommon shopping — The *Satsop Bulb Farm*, featuring daffodils (they provided 50,000 of these flowers for the Puyallup Daffodil Festival in 1972) . . . *Heather Acres*, does a nationwide business with this plant . . . *Grey Gull Studio* where Ken Adamson does functional pottery . . . *Farmer's Market* antiques . . . take the Chehalis cutoff south to Oakville and the *Curfman Farm* which has a roadside stand selling the fresh produce of the 80 acres or so under cultivation, including in-season corn, beans, cauliflower and in the fall about 150 tons of pumpkins.

A word about eating – *Oaksridge Restaurant* on Hunter's Prairie, is locals' choice. At the golf course of the same name.

Annual affairs – *Grays Harbor County Fair* in mid-August.

For further information — Write the *Elma Chronicle*, 112 North Third or call 482-2422.

McCleary — (Pop. 1,324. Elev. 287.) — A neat little town on a grassy flat, a mile or so off the freeway, McCleary was founded by lumber baron

Henry McCleary who ran it on the basis that "a good kingdom was better than a bum democracy." He owned it and ran it as a company town for something over a quarter of a century.

When the Simpson Timber Company bought out Henry McCleary in 1942, it also acquired the town — water, light and street system — lock, stock and barrel.

Then Simpson turned around and offered the town for sale to its residents at bargain rates — 15 cents on the dollar. "For sale, one $40,000 town. Good as new. Only $6,000!"

They threw in another little enticement to help with the grocery bills — 450 primary jobs in the Sash and Door Factory. And on January 1, 1947, when Simpson went into the 100-year sustained Working Circle business with the federal government, McCleary became a very stable lumber town indeed. (Region V, Shelton, et al, tells the story of Working Circle.)

There remained but one further detail to be ironed out. As the forests grew, so did the black bear. In some areas they chewed the bark from as much as 80% of the young second growth trees. Working in conjunction with the Washington State Game Department and the U.S. Fish and Wildlife Service, a program has been evolved to control the bear population . . . which is entirely handy for the Bear Stew business.

It took a little doing for us to pry the bear stew recipe out of the secretary of the McCleary Chamber of Commerce, but we persisted and here it is: you "take a dozen-and-a-half to two dozen medium sized young black bears, and bone, trim and dice in one-inch cubes. . . ."

That's the start of the recipe for the gourmet climax of the *Annual McCleary Bear Festival* one weekend in mid-July. It's their famous bear stew which is fed to a multitude of maybe 5,000 . . . maybe 6,000 people. The meal is free as long as you have bought one of their festival buttons.

To the cubed bear, which should add up to about 500 pounds of meat, you add an additional 500 pounds of potatoes . . . 150 pounds each of carrots and onions . . . 50 pounds of cabbage . . . 35 pounds of celery . . . and 10 pounds of garlic. At this point, any of us could follow the recipe and get into the stewed bear business in competition with McCleary. But nothing has been said about the "spice pot." And nothing will be said about it. Because that's the secret ingredient that makes a McCleary bear stew better than any of the other bear stews you've encountered in your travels.

The folks in McCleary clearly do not intend for anyone else to get willy-nilly into a bear stew banquet. The difference between any old bear stew and a McCleary bear stew is this bouquet garni. And don't be misled by the counterspy propaganda that the "garni" consists of several pair of sweaty logger socks.

Beyond that, the cooking of the stew begins on Friday night and a night shift of cooks tends the stew which simmers away in about 15 huge thirty to forty gallon kettles in the kitchen at the city park. And just in case there may be someone prejudiced against this delectable dish, they provide about 300 pounds of baked beans . . . 3,000 homemade corn bread muffins and a truckload of watermelon.

For further information — Write the McCleary Chamber of Commerce, 130 Summit Road or call 495-3401.

REGION THREE

WHATCOM, SKAGIT, ISLAND AND SAN JUAN COUNTIES

A Word About Region III

Mankind meets himself coming and going at this end of the nation. In describing the situation, you find yourself somewhere between the lofty sentiments of the great naturalist, John Muir, and the practical approach of Lord Benjamin Disraeli.

Muir urged us to "climb the mountains and get their good tidings. Nature's peace will flow into you as the sunshine flows into the trees. The winds will blow their own freshness into you and the storms their energy, while cares will drop off like autumn leaves." And Disraeli commented dryly, "I don't know what the Kingdom of Heaven is run on, but the earth is run on oil."

You have both of these philosophic concepts along with a bunch of agricultural and oceanic "Oh, by gollys!" working for you in this northwest corner of the United States.

Driving along the bottom lands occupied by Interstate 5, it isn't hard to put yourself in the place of a modern Moses leading his people across the bed of the sea with the receded waters revealing the tops of otherwise submerged peaks to the west, the smaller hills around you dried by the parting waters but only for the moment . . . and the huge mountain masses to the east that still will be above the floods when they return.

The finest ferry system in the world is a drawbridge to the mental castles of contentment among the San Juan Islands, and the network of excellent highways penetrating the mountains are a lure to elevated islands of isolation for the soul.

But in between, you got trouble.

There's the petro-chemical industry tooling up to accept that black gold from the north slope in Alaska — with the Lummi Indians around the next point of land trying to make the best of both their world and ours, raising gourmet fish. The rich delta land of the Nooksack, Samish and Skagit rivers is poised between crunches of machinery and groceries. We need to run the world, all right. But the world's a little low on food these days, and here's one of the greatest spots on earth to grow milk and vegetables. We've got to have electricity, too. And man is faced with a choice of putting a whole bunch of dams on the mighty Skagit River or locating a thermo-nuclear plant there to turn on the lights in the metropolitan areas south of here.

There have been some stresses and strains over the location of the aluminum industry in the area and several, historically, in keeping the longest peaceful boundary in the world peaceful.

At the moment, mankind in this region resembles a dog chasing his tail.

And it's hard to figure out which end is winning.

Bellingham Tour 1 — In and Around the City, Lake Whatcom (Map V)

Located nearly two-thirds of the way from Seattle to Vancouver, B.C., Bellingham occupies a fine setting on an intimate bay of the same name. It also spreads inland over the valleys of 3 wandering creeks: the Squalicum, Whatcom, and Padden, although it's one of the few major towns on the Wet Side not located on a river. Sehome Hill rises to the south near the heart of town. From a high summit park are far-reaching views of Bellingham, the bay, the San Juan Islands behind Lummi Island, the Olympics, and sometimes Vancouver Island. On the waterfront, industry and shipping dominate the scene with warehouses, piers, railroad cars, and waterborne commerce. The harbor frequently is filled with a vari-colored fleet of pleasure and fishing boats. Bellingham residents live in neat neighborhoods, ranging from modern high density tracts, to fine older homes on the hillside near Western Washington State College. Highlights include the 1892 Whatcom County Museum of History and Art, and the Fairhaven restoration area. A few miles east of city center is Lake Whatcom. With its northern tip in the city limits, the lake stretches long and narrow to the southeast about 12 miles. Heading south out of town is the famed Chuckanut Drive, a real cliff-hanger with fine views.

Bellingham — (Pop. 39,700. Elev. Sea level to 640.) — The fifth largest city on the Wet Side of the Mountains, it clearly is the dominant urban area in the northwest corner of the United States. It's the seat of Whatcom County and contains 40% of the county's population. It's the major gateway to Canada and Mt. Baker as well as a center for oil refining, fish processing, aluminum and pulp production, boat manufacturing and agricultural products and the location of one of the state's oldest and most popular institutions of higher education.

With this diversified economic background and its location on an invitingly beautiful bay, it is entirely logical that it supports the biggest collection of sleeping and eating facilities in Region 3 . . . making it a good base of operations for your prowling.

For the first 50 years, thanks to coal, gold rushes and railroads, the fortunes of Bellingham jounced like a yo-yo on a wayward string. Concomitant with the violent economics of the period, there was the arduous effort of coalescing a whole bunch of different communities into one. Altogether, there was Pattle's Point née Unionville . . . Sehome . . . Whatcom . . . and New Whatcom-Old Bellingham and Fairhaven . . . .

Finally in 1900 the compromise that nobody really liked but couldn't object to *that* much — "Bellingham" from the bay on which all of them were located.

◆

As pleasant an illustration as there is of the community rivalries which existed is the one demonstrated by the arrival of that first vastly important Canadian Pacific train on June 22, 1891. You wouldn't believe the boom and bust conditions that had ebbed and flowed through Bellingham Bay for the twenty years previous to the arrival of this train. There were population ranges like up to 15,000 and back down to 20 poor souls rattling around a ghost town.

In one year!

Anyway, on June 22 — the day after the longest day of the year — the differences had temporarily been resolved and the train was coming in from Canada with the dignitaries on board.

The city of Whatcom had been appropriately decorated with colorful bunting. An Arch of Welcome had been erected over the track at Holly Street and Railroad Avenue (two streets that have survived consolidation) with the British flag on the east pillar and the stars and stripes on the west. Company F of the Sons of Veterans was on hand in full regalia along with Warren Burgess and his Coronet Band and, of course, the renowned Carpenters Union Band.

Six thousand joyful spectators were there to welcome the guests.

The maraschino cherry that topped the whipping cream on the ice cream sundae was to be the demonstration of the town's water pressure. Towns in those days were burning down all over the place and the folks here had so much water pressure, they insisted on installing iron water mains instead of the wooden ones generally in use at the time.

A fire hose in Bellingham could fire a 3-inch jet of water clear over the 3-story Victor block on West Holly. The welcoming committee decided that in addition to the static, wooden, welcoming arch, there should be an arch of "living water" over the track — much like the jets of water with which Seattle fireboats greet important incoming ships in Seattle's harbor today.

So the Whatcom and Sehome volunteer fire departments were called upon to do their thing . . . one arching from one side of the track and the other from the other.

Well, Whatcom got its fire hose fired up first and as the train was slowly approaching, the fellas playfully doused their counterparts on the other side of the track.

But, two could play that game as well as one; the Sehome guys fired right back. Well, if that's the way they were going to play it . . . .

The engineer of the train hadn't been instructed what to do in the event of a waterfight at the celebration so he kept on rolling ahead, but the men in the respective volunteer fire companies had forgotten about the 6,000 people . . . the visiting dignitaries . . . the celebration and the importance of the occasion.

With deadly accuracy, they were mowing down the opposition on the other side of the railroad track.

The arrival of the train failed to halt the hostilities.

Jets of water busted the windows of the coaches knocking off top hats, dousing Prince Albert coats, parasols and high-necked dresses.

It was an exciting welcome.

There are people to this day who swear it was that demonstration of

American exuberance which prevented Bellingham from being the American Terminus of the Canadian Pacific Railway.

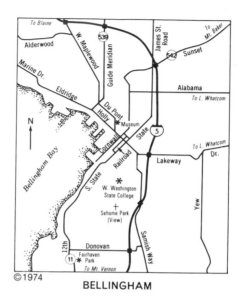

© 1974

BELLINGHAM

Bellingham's emergence as a town of metropolitan stature was initiated by the construction of a new town hall in 1892. This edifice was erected in spite of the fact that for years, the town's leading and only newspaper, *The Reveille*, had waged a consistent campaign aimed at holding the line on the city's budget at $400 a year.

The new building was to cost $50,000, which seemed like a little much for a structure in which to conduct $400 worth of public business, but there were those who contemplated the possibility that the town might grow, and they prevailed.

Historian Lottie Roeder Roth noted that "The beautiful City Hall was completed early in May, and was the pride of the city, with its sightly location, its handsome finish of native woods, and its architectural grace."

For years, *The Reveille* had another bee in its bonnet beside budget. This one was cows. How could the town attain any meritorious degree of urbanity when cows were permitted to roam the streets at will, especially at night when you couldn't tell the dung from the dirt? And furthermore the animals "disturbed the slumber of the citizens."

While the paper may have failed to hold the line on the annual budget it was triumphant on its 6-year campaign against loose cows, and on May 8, 1893, an ordinance was passed "restricting the liberty of cows to walk on the streets of the city between the hours of 7:30 p.m. and 6 a.m."

It was the first legislative act passed in the brand new, $50,000 City Hall.

But trouble loomed.

Mayor W. Miller vetoed the ordinance.

Attitudes about cows were polarized after that long editorial campaign, and the City Council was in *The Reveille's* pocket. Backed by the thrust of bellicose headlines the Council stiffened its resolve and passed the ordinance over the Mayor's veto.

But that was by no means the end of the problem.

The newspaper reported that the Mayor's cow was running loose. The City Council order the cow impounded, and the cops hauled her in.

No whit daunted, the Mayor broke into the pound and took his cow home. The Council responded to that one by having the Mayor arrested and charging him with "illegally releasing a cow from the city pound."

When Mayor Miller was summoned before the police judge, he demanded a jury trial.

An enraged City Attorney charged that a jury trial was ridiculous, but the Mayor's lawyers retorted that trial by jury was written into the U.S. Constitution as one of the guarantees of free men in our great nation.

The Mayor told the jury, "I was just passing by and she broke through the fence and follered me home."

The jury agreed. It held it was only natural that the cow, "seeing her old friend on the outside, had broken through of her own accord . . ." and they released the city's chief executive from the clutches of the Law.

The building in which all this early excitement occurred has been restored to its original glory and today houses the Whatcom County Museum of History and Art, listed on the National Register of Historic Places.

And even before it was finished last year, it was visited by an equivalent of nearly twice the population of the city annually.

It became partially government-supported in 1945 when Ordinance Number 6313 made it a Municipal Museum. A lot of ordinances had gone over the dam or under the bridge, as the case may be, since Ordinance Number 1, controlling cows, was passed in the same building, but none that finally tapped such constructive community support.

Passage of the ordinance, however, did not mean that Culture had come overnight to Whatcom County. For the next quarter of a century, there was massive passive resistance to the notion that this building could possibly be more important than a parking lot in the same location. The fact that for a long time it housed the John M. Edson collection of Whatcom County birds lent flight to the fancy, on the part of some, that the place was strictly "for the birds." But the Bellingham Public Museum Society, which had obtained use of the building in 1940, hung in there in spite of the odds that made the Perils of Pauline pale by comparison.

They thought they'd had it in 1962 when fire took out the tower and the clamor of the parking lot people rose to a crescendo.

Finis also was marked for the project with the failure of the $160,000 bond issue in 1964 and of a professional fund-raising campaign the next year. But help was on the way in the form of George R. Bartholick, an architect who prescribed restoration in 6 easy stages. (He subsequently redesigned the tower in sections that were lifted into place with huge cranes and fit so well it looks like it has been there from the time of original construction.)

There also was a lady by the name of Patricia Fleeson who took it into her head that the city which forgets its past has no future, and turned her hand to the difficult business of raising the money to pay for the dream. That's $665,000 ago. The sum includes federal, county and city money . . . and private contributions ranging from the $50,000 donated by Prentice Bloedel to an equally important $1.27 raised by a bunch of kids in a local neighborhood who collected and sold bottles for their share of the venture.

It became a joint City-County government project in 1968 with the City coughing up $44,000 and the County $11,000 annually, making this one of only two places in the United States with such effective governmental support.

As rich an addition as any to the Museum is Susan Hill Luhrs Barrow, who has a record as long as your arm in this kind of work and provides the spark that gives sparkle to all of the exhibits and to the activities of the 700-member organization, of which 45 are the docents who man the facility along with a paid staff of 6.

One of the things to look at in the museum is the handsome original woodwork, which was rubbed down with varnish, steel wool and elbow grease by a bevy of Lummi Indian girls under financing from a National Youth Corps program.

If Dirty Dan Harris were to be reincarnated 83 years later, he'd take one look at *Fairhaven Village*, another restoration project, and say, "Ef you would of asked me, I would of tole you this was the future of Fairhaven!" And if he were alive today, he'd have a piece of the action.

Dirty Dan legends are as close as they get to their own local Paul Bunyan in these parts, and he certainly was their most colorful historical character. He got his name on account of his unkempt appearance, eating and drinking habits, and living quarters. When Dan wanted to look distinguished, he wore a plug hat on his shaggy mane — and a white vest and frocked coat, neither of which concealed his red long-johns. Dan arrived on the Bay in 1853, and fell in with another man. Together they initiated the process by which Fairhaven finally came into existence and that enabled Dan to retire a comparatively wealthy man. He lived in style in Los Angeles for a while but managed to blow his wad before he died in 1890.

Dan's earliest enterprise was smuggling, which he did by rowing an enormous rowboat between Fairhaven and Vancouver . . . usually carrying that most easily assimilable of all goods. The Indians boarded him once and relieved him of a barrel of whiskey, and the next time they hijacked his load it was full of ipecac. They never asked for a repeat performance.

One of the legends of Dan concerns a couple of his pigs who did very well rooting clams for themselves on the tideflats. When the folks complained that Dan stole the results of the rooting, he said "I dunno. I only keep every other clam." And he was right collecting 50% interest on the other guy's labor was not unusual in those days. He served as a packer during the Cariboo gold rush and at one time bought a flock of 700 sheep which he drove from Salt Lake City to California and then brought by boat to Bellingham. One of his most prodigious efforts was that of clearing, grubbing and grading 12 miles of road in one summer, from the waterfront to Lake Whatcom, to enable the owners to bring in the machinery to start a coal mine.

Dan was an unregenerate Democrat right after the Civil War when few of them poked their heads above the trenches. And when Grover Cleveland won the Presidency, he had an American flag — big enough to cover a 5-story building — made in San Francisco, to fly for the inauguration. The flagpole had to be correspondingly high, but the problem arose when he gathered his fellow Democrats and they were higher than the pole and couldn't get it off the ground. Some sailors loading lumber at a nearby mill came to his rescue . . . raised the pole and hoisted the flag . . . and presumably joined in the consumption of the booze.

◄►

Ken Imus, a local boy who made good in the automobile business in California and way-places, doesn't wear a plugged hat, frocked coat, white vest or red long-johns. But in other respects, he's as much of a shaker and mover as Dirty Dan . . . and what he's done is breathe new vitality into old Fairhaven buildings with a restoration program rivaling in color and quality those in Seattle's Pioneer Square and Vancouver's Gastown — no mean accomplishment in a town with less than 1/10th the population of either of the other two big metropolitan areas.

Fairhaven still retains a separate identity, divided from downtown Bellingham by high Sehome Hill and spread in a bowl sloping down to a small cove and wharves containing a marina, ship yard, and Marine Park.

The new project involved 8 square blocks and a dozen brick buildings and is called Fairhaven Village. Projected costs of restoration may come to about $6,000,000 — including the restoration of an area left intact when the streets were raised, which is similar to Seattle's world-famous Underground. The heart of the reconstruction is a building called the "Marketplace," halfway up the hill, an outside-inside building housing dozens of shops around a 4-story central well and grand stairway.

The restorers have had 3 times as many applications for space as they could accept and they are being choosey about getting the best.

Dirty Dan would be proud of them.

Among the other enterprising efforts in the general area is an enormous development 5 miles southeast of Bellingham on Lake Whatcom called *Sudden Valley*. It's an 1,800-acre affair where a real effort has been made to preserve the environment. (They call it a "nondevelopment.") You may drive through it if you just stop at the realty office and ask for a pass.

Prowling Bellingham

Streets are sheer murder in the center of town because of the union of 5 original villages that never really got together on their streets. The 5 distinctly different patterns are easily recognizable on a detailed map — and only one (the smallest) 3-block square is a true north-south plan. To compound the problem, most streets are one-way in the downtown grid. Also frustrating is the fact that the bay makes a clean-cut right angle turn just below the Museum — about Central Avenue and Holly.

Easily the town's number one visitor attraction is the *Whatcom County Museum of History and Art*. Continuing exhibits include the art of the North Coast Indians . . . memorabilia of the early pioneers of the county . . . history of logging in the area . . . Whatcom seascapes . . . and landscapes.

You'll probably want to investigate the State's 3rd largest institution of higher learning, *Western Washington State College*, now in its 76th year and considered one of the country's more attractive campuses. Its location high on Sehome Hill in an evergreen forest looking out to the Bay has inspired Northwest architects to do some of their best work, and both residence halls and academic buildings have won national recognition for design. "Old Main" is a beautiful old building. W.W.S.C. includes 3 cluster colleges on its campus: Fairhaven College, which features independent study; Huxley College, part of the N.W. Environmental Studies; and Ethnic Studies, concentrating on minority cultures and histories. The student influence and color is obvious around downtown Bellingham and Fairhaven Village. If you'd like to participate in a touch of college life, drop in one of the coffee shops — at Miller Hall on the Square with the big fountain, or the one in Viking Union Building, operated by the Associated Students.

For a spectacular view, try *Sehome Park*, which backs up to the W.W.S.C. campus.

Two old homes listed on the National Register of Historic Places are the *George E. Pickett House* (the Pickett of "Pig War and Pickett's Charge" fame), 910 Bancroft, which is the oldest residence in the area and is presently owned by the Washington State Historical Society, and the *Gamwell House*, 101 16th St. You might like to see the *Roeder Home*, 2600 Sunset, where County Parks system presently holds craft classes; also the little downtown building, which is the first of brick in the territory.

You might not understand the tall, slim piece of *kinetic sculpture* on the City Hall lawn, so we'll note for you that it's called "Two Lines Oblique," and you're invited to watch the smooth constant counterpoint as its two arms seek their ever-changing equilibrium. Sculptor George Rickey comments that "All environment is moving, at some pace or other, under laws which are equally a manifestation of nature and subject to art."

On the performing arts front, the *Bellingham Theater Guild* on H St. has productions regularly. Call for current schedule.

There are a number of industrial tours you can investigate and you should call ahead for all of these or check with the Chamber of Commerce: *Bornstein Sea Foods*, I and J Waterway, fresh and frozen seafood; *Georgia Pacific Corp.*, tissue products division or bleached sulfite pulp products; *Port of Bellingham*, foot of Cornwall, to tour Port or perhaps visit a foreign ship; *Uniflite*, 9th and Harris, for a look at pleasure and commercial fiberglass boatbuilding; *Bellingham Cold Storage*, Squalicum Waterway, lots of cold fish and an interesting tour; *Whatcom County Dairymen's Association*, Ellis St. plant, processes ice cream, milk, cottage cheese — appropriate since Whatcom is the biggest dairy county in the 5 Northwest states.

Long narrow, *Lake Whatcom,* with its northern tip within the city limits and its southern end about 12 miles away provides a scenic trip via Lakeway Drive to Lake Whatcom Boulevard. This trip passes *Bloedel-Donovan Park, Whatcom Falls Park, Whatcom Creek* and *Bayview Cemetery.*

At *Park* at the southeast end of the Lake is the terminus of the *Lake Whatcom Railway,* where you can go for a delightful excursion on an old-fashioned train. There's a locomotive, 2 coaches and a business car, and if you like old trains, this is your bag. Project of a couple of young Bellevue men, Frank and Robert Culp, you can ride the train to Wickersham, some 5 miles away, between 11 a.m. and 3 p.m. on weekends and holidays during the summer. The round trip takes a couple of hours — with a stopover at Wickersham where the General Store does a land-office business when the train's in.

Uncommon shopping — *Fairhaven Village,* 11th St. near Harris, interesting in general, and look into the Marketplace building particularly — for shops like *Fairhaven Kite Co., European Delicatessen, Bead Patch, Artifacts Gallery, Creperie, Country Store, Wine Cellar, Yarns.*

"*Old Town,*" Holly near C St., is a block of second-hand and antique stores . . . *Hyde Leather & Crafts,* N. State . . . *Whatcom Museum Gift Shop,* Prospect St., crafts, pottery, jewelry from all over the world; cast metal folk art of 73 year-old Whatcom County craftsman Fred Bulmer. (He's provided city fathers with 600 "keys to the city of Bellingham" for visiting celebrities) . . . *Friday Night Auction,* Marine Dr., 7 p.m. every Friday . . . *Swap Meets,* Samish Drive-in Theatre, daytime on summer weekends, a kind of sell-swap bazaar.

A word about eating – The Leopold Hotel's *Chandelier Room* for fancy dining, Cornwall Ave . . . or the same hotel's *Good Time Charlie's,* jolly and contemporary, with entertainment . . . *High Country,* the Bellingham Hotel rooftop spot for prime ribs, rack of lamb, and panorama . . . *Cliff House,* N. State St. (no sign), small, smart steak place with great view, hatch-cover tables, captain's chairs . . . *Fisherman's Market & Shrimp Shack,* Holly at Central, plain and honest food . . . *Black Angus,* N. Samish Way by I-5, another in the series with good N.W. reputation for moderately priced steaks in nice decor . . . *Harbor House,* Squalicum Mall, fresh seafare such as salmon, steamed clams, Rockpoint oysters; breadfast, also . . . *Kovac's,* Bellingham Mall, for old country food like stuffed cabbage rolls . . . *Cap Hansen's* Tavern, E. Chestnut, fun and homey with good Reuben and other sandwiches . . . .

At Fairhaven: *Sofie's 1304,* charming atmosphere and variety like quiche, vegetable sauté, blackberry crepes, or chef's whim of the day . . . *Dos Padres,* casual with Mexican food, unusual dishes . . . *Fairhaven Village Pub,* cook-your-own-steak in cheerful early 1900 decor with old back bar, fireplace . . . *Fairhaven Fish House* (summer), lox and fresh fish, outside driftwood tables and benches.

At Sudden Valley: *Country Club Restaurant* on southside Lake Whatcom. Serves a gourmet-type menu with a flourish.

A word about sleeping – *Leopold Inn,* Cornwall Ave. "The Hotel" of Bellingham life. Motel units also . . . on N. Samish Way near Bellingham Mall is the motel cluster: *Aloha, Key Motel* and *Royal Motor Inn* are very good . . . halfway down the south side of Lake Whatcom is *Sudden Valley* and luxury clubhouse condominiums in beautiful setting, indigenous buildings.

Annual affairs – *Blossomtime Festival*, May, a county celebration with parades, a pageant and carnival . . . the *Highland Games*, June, Scottish dancing and sport events . . . *Lutefisk dinner*, 1st Saturday in December, at Norway Hall. The feast is open to the public, who annually consume some 1200 pounds of lutefisk, 1500 lefse and uncounted Norwegian meatballs and Christmas breads.

For further information — Bellingham Chamber of Commerce, 204 W. Holly, 734-1330.

◆

Bellingham Tour 2 — Lummi Indian Reservation, Ferndale, Blaine, Lynden, Edison, Chuckanut Drive (Map V)

Highlights of this tour include a visit to the Lummi Indian Reservation, Ferndale's Hovander Homestead Park, the industrial complex at Cherry Point, a sampling of Lynden's Dutch heritage, and a view-studded trip along Chuckanut Drive.

Scenically, the route heads north through the rich flood plains of the Nooksack, skirts saltwater harbors at Birch Bay and Blaine, then aims east through some of the lushest farm country in the State. It takes you along the South Fork of the Nooksack, which is separated by mountains from Bellingham, and then goes west through a low mountain pass by the southern end of Lake Whatcom, south again to Alger where it begins to emerge on a flood plain, and continues west to Samish Bay. Then to the highly scenic Chuckanut Drive which follows the precipitous coastline of Chuckanut Mountain to Bellingham.

We suggest you take local roads between the smaller delta communities. You'll see more of the countryside. The Whatcom County map from the County Engineers office, available for a small fee, is excellent.

To drive to the Lummi Indian Reservation, follow the signs to Marietta on local roads. You cross flat farmlands and bridge the Nooksack River . . . turn left and follow the shoreline road to Gooseberry Point. The Lummi Island ferry — which gives you access to a view ride around the island — docks here and there's a cluster of buildings which we'll tell about in a moment. Nearby is the Lummi Aquaculture Fish Farm. Looking westward to the island, you can see the Lummi Longhouse.

Lummi Indian Reservation — Don't anticipate being overwhelmed by Red Carpet treatment on the part of the Indians, many of whom are quite conscious of the fact the white shoved them off in a corner some place to get them out of the way of progress. The federal government has atoned some by dropping several million dollars into an Aquaculture Program that may or may not put other commercial fisheries out of business. One of the main thoroughfares of the Reservation still is the Garbage Dump Road.

The Indians are closer to doing their own thing here in the context of our modern industrial society than they would be working in the nearby aluminum plant. The Aquaculture Program employs a third to a half the total work force, raising Coho salmon and oysters for the gourmet market. You can see the 3 mile dike across the bay enclosing the rearing ponds and oyster beds.

There also is the Lummi Indian School of Aquaculture in which members of the tribe are teaching the basics of aquaculture to Indians from 20 other tribes that have water resources.

From time to time, they also are gainfully employed at woodcarving. Joseph Placid started the totem pole on the Bellingham Courthouse lawn and the late Joseph Hillaire finished it. Something seems to have been lost in the translation of its placement, however, because the canoe you see is going in one direction and the totem pole faces in another.

Joe Hillaire, a handsome, genial and articulate man, probably is the best-known member of the Lummi Tribe. Before he passed away, he became kind of a Professional Indian, available at a price for many kinds of functions. When we were managing the Boat Show in Seattle, we thought it would be appropriate to have an Indian carving a canoe at the show . . . and hired Joe to do it. Our first astonishment came when he insisted on a male cedar on the grounds they're easier to work with. Anyway, Joe had a good spiel and wore a headdress and made quite a hit, so we asked him back the next year. But we had a problem, "It's too much work to carve those canoes," Joe said firmly. "However, I'll carve you a totem pole for the same price." It didn't seem as appropriate as a canoe, but Joe was a popular attraction and we went along with the gag . . . except that each year the totem poles got smaller.

Joe went on to bigger and better things than the Boat Show. One of the high points of his extensive career in show "biz" was a job in Japan for a big show there.

There was a time when the local Indians would appear in a parade for the joy of the occasion, but they learned a thing or two about economics from the white man and these days, Indians in this kind of an affair go for $250 a bunch — $500 with headdresses. They've got it and if you want it, you pay for it . . . sounds like actors' equity.

They're not lacking a sense of humor, however, as is evidenced by the episode involving Alvin Casimir. Casimir and his wife have 7 children, and he was employed as a carpenter's helper in the construction of the oyster hatchery on Lummi Island. At the time the hatchery was completed, Dr. Wallace Heath, a biologist with a fervent belief in the productivity of Puget Sound and the Aquaculture Program, had been brought in to make the program work. A dike was built across the mouth of Lummi Bay, creating a 750-acre pond ideal for raising oysters and other fish. The federal government had applied $4,000,000 to the project.

But the whole thing hinged on getting the oysters in the hatchery to spawn. They tried everything known to the biological sciences, but nothing happened. Alvin became intrigued by their efforts and said, "Maybe I could help." The scientists humored the carpenter-helper with a "you gotta be kidding!" attitude. But what could they lose? Nothing they'd tried had worked, so they let Alvin try his hand at it.

The second he put his hands in the water, the female oysters emitted the milky fluid that bestirred the male oysters to action and several million baby oysters were underway. At first they thought it was a freak circumstance. But since that time, he's made more millions of oysters spawn . . . and clams, too. He's graduated from the bib overalls of the carpenter trade to the white coat of the laboratory business and now is the manager of the oyster hatchery.

Between the productivity of his wife and the oysters, Alvin is considered by everybody on the premises to be a man with a magic touch. And when one of the ladies in our group was introduced to him and extended her arm, half-a-dozen people hollered, "Don't shake hands! Don't shake hands!"

Uncommon shopping — Stop at *Isabelle Warbus' Crafts Shop* on Haxton Way (a mile on the left heading north, beyond the Aquaculture project) for Indian-made handicrafts and jewelry. Contemporary bead and bone necklaces and earrings, rawhide Puget Sound Indian drums, and leather medicine pouches. (When sold as purses, the bags didn't move; but as medicine pouches, they're a hot item.) Also on hand are books and pamphlets on Indian lore and arts.

A word about eating – *Fisherman's Cove* at Gooseberry Point, seafood, homemade pies and cakes, and pleasant surroundings looking across Hale Passage to high-rising Lummi Island.

Annual affair –*Lummi Indian Stommish*, 2nd weekend in June. Indian canoe races, salmon barbecue, dancing. Similar to the potlatches, it is one of the few Indian celebrations open to the public.

For further information — Write the Lummi Tribal Office at P.O. Box 309, Marietta, 98268; or call 734-8180.

Country roads past wooded patches and fertile farms lead to . . .

Ferndale — (Pop. 2,500. Elev. 26.) — A largely residential town along the banks of the Nooksack. Tree-lined streets are bordered by lawns, gardens and homes, most within view of Puget Sound and Mt. Baker.

Just across the river from downtown is *Pioneer Park* with its museum crammed full of relics and artifacts from early settler days. Especially fascinating are some old photos of the Nooksack in full flood.

Between Ferndale and the freeway is *Hovander Homestead Park;* follow signs and look for a putty-colored Victorian farmhouse, complete with white gingerbread trim, and handsome huge red barn. Both buildings have been restored and contain the original possessions of the Swedish immigrant family who settled here in 1903. Visitors are welcome daily during the summer, weekends during the winter months. Picnicking permitted on grounds bordered by a rustic fence, and fishing on the Nooksack which flows behind the homestead. An old water tower has been restored as a lookout — climb to the top for fine views of patchwork farmlands, the river, Ferndale and the mountains.

Uncommon shopping – *Snoop Coop*, W. Axton Road, antiques in the country . . . *Ferndale Bakery*, good bread, some German old-country types.

A word about eating – *Johnson's Fine Food*, W. Axton Road off I-5. Attractive white country-inn look, view of farmlands and Mt. Baker while dining.

A word about sleeping — *Scottish Lodge,* visible from I-5, half-timbered English type, two-story building surrounded by a golf course; pleasant outlook, and good accommodations.

To see the much-talked-about *Cherry Point* area, go out Mt. View Road from Ferndale. The road goes up a rise through farmlands, and suddenly there appears a forest of electrical towers at *Italco Aluminum Corp.* plant which is the largest producer of primary aluminum in the world. There's a totem pole, low olive-beige buildings and few people because it's all so automated. Doesn't cost much to shut her down, but the bill for starting her up again comes to $8,000,000; they have to rebrick the pots. The company employs 1,300 people and everybody around here has a deep interest in energy. North of Italco is the *Atlantic Richfield Corp. Refinery* and its many cracking towers, at this writing, the most modern in the world. South of Italco is the *Ferndale Mobil Refinery.* Each of the 3 has its own deepwater wharf for ships. Should be busy when the North Slope gets cracking.

From Ferndale north to *Birch Bay* you can take the main road direct or find your way to Pt. Whitehorn and a marine drive past *Birch Bay State Park.* The roads run through second growth woodlands and many birches from whence the name, and past small farms with frequent views of inland green foothills. At Birch Bay, the road hugs the shoreline of the circular cove and vacation cottages line the landward side. With the warmest salt water swimming around, Birch Bay has all the trappings of a popular summer resort: golf, roller rink, riding stables, a host of resorts, trailer parks and any number of eateries.

A unique enterprise is the *Birch Bay Fairyland Feather Shop.* Probably more chicken feathers in Whatcom County than anywhere in the State and the feminine accessories they make with them are not just for the birds.

For further information — Birch Bay Resort Owner's Association, Route 1, Blaine, 98230.

From Birch Bay, try the Birch Point Road and Semiahmoo Drive (one of our favorite Indian names) for a following-the-shoreline way into Blaine.

Blaine — (Pop. 2,000. Elev. 41.) — Biggest excitement here in recent years was the closing of the border in the late 1960's by students protesting the detonation of an underground nuclear device by the United States on Amchitka Island in the Aleutian chain. The students figured among other things that the detonation might trigger earthquakes. And the whole episode might have been even more exciting except for a technical problem that caused the U.S. to delay the detonation by 24 hours.

During the delay, the San Andreas fault slipped causing a lot of damage in California. If the bomb had gone off on schedule, the detonation most certainly would have been blamed by the students for the earthquake.

Three-quarters of a century earlier there was real excitement in town, when on St. Valentine's Day in 1891, railroads from Canada met those of the United States. A couple of polished railroad spikes were driven by solid silver hammers and the population of Blaine increased rapidly from 30 to 8,000.

One poor but proud violin-playing, wine-drinking homesteader named

Thomas Bunbary had eked out a precarious living for years on what turned out to be the most desirable property in town. Bunbary, who thought he would become a millionaire as the town boomed, turned down an offer for $160,000 for his land. When the boom went bust, he turned it over to the town in exchange for a promise of strings for his violin, a bottle of wine a day during his lifetime and after he died, a fine funeral conducted by a Roman Catholic priest. Today his land is the Blaine City Park.

Blaine lies along Drayton Harbor. The town's main street is just that. Best views are to be had from *Peace Arch Park* just north of town. The park itself includes landscaped lawns, color-packed flower gardens, picnic and play areas, not to mention the imposing white concrete Peace Arch monument. From the park, the view is westward over Drayton Harbor where gillnetters, purse seiners and crab boats ride at anchor alongside large and small pleasure boats.

A word about sleeping – *Dana Motor Inn*, on a waterfront street, is considered very good.

If you'd like to be able to say you've been to one of the oddest appendages of the U.S., cross the border at Blaine and drive 27 miles through Canada to cross back into the U.S. at *Point Roberts*. At low tide it's quite a spectacular drive around Boundary Bay and its exposed miles of sand. Populated mostly by Canadians, Pt. Roberts has occasional problems like shortages of water, or should it be a part of a National Preserve, or how far it is from the rest of its county. (Kaiser Wilhelm of Germany decided Pt. Roberts should belong to the U.S.) *Monument Park* has only original boundary marker on border between here and Montana. *Lighthouse Marine Park* has black rocks on beach.

From Blaine, roads lead east to Lynden through great agricultural land with one mountain range or another always in view.

Our secret black market geologist opines that the Nooksack Valley really ought to be considered a part of the Fraser River flood plain and if you include the area north and south of the border here, you have a massive conglomerate of deep, alluvial soil. But even on its own and despite the constant encroachments of urbanization, Whatcom County is no agricultural slouch. It's the leading dairy county of 5 northwest states . . . the number 1 producer of fresh eggs . . . number 1 in strawberries . . . number 1 in seed potatoes and timothy clover acreage . . . and number 1 in Western Washington, of farms with crop sales totaling $20,000 or more a year. With the current news that 1 out of every 7 persons on earth is literally starving to death, this rich soil could continue to compete with the industries and developers who like flat land for other purposes.

Lynden — (Pop. 2,850. Elev. 95.) — a town of neat stucco and frame houses, immaculate yards, and lots of churches — 17, to be exact. A look at the mailboxes reveals the Dutch ancestry of the town's residents, most of whom are retired farmers or merchants. Actually, 50% of the town is Dutch, and most business men still go home for lunch every day.

Many of the stores lining Front Street have been remodeled along a Dutch motif (not the ideal of the 50% of town that is Dutch). Don't look for any action on Sunday for in this town *everything* closes on the Sabbath.

Prowling Lynden

Most everyone in Lynden will want to tell you about *Berthusen's Park*, located 5 miles northwest of town on Berthusen Road. Willed to Lynden by Hans Berthusen, this 250-acre park bordering on Bertrand Creek has picnic tables and camp kitchens set in groves of virgin western red cedar and fir. A large red barn within the park is currently undergoing restoration, thanks to a successful "save the barn" campaign by townsfolk. We like the marker bearing Berthusen's words: "All that a man has when he comes to die is what he has given away."

Octogenarian *Fred Polinder*, a retired farmer, has a dandy collection of buggies, carriages, freight and milk wagons he has restored himself. He enjoys showing off his wheeled treasures at his home on 1040 Polinder Road, one mile southeast of town. Please call him first (354-2523), and let him know you'd like to visit.

You can visit *Consolidated Dairy Products* (Darigold), 3rd Ave., which processes butter, cheese, powdered milk. Largest cheese factory in world under one roof. Call ahead or check Chamber of Commerce.

Uncommon shopping – *Star Mercantile* on Front St. is an old-time grocery store where the brown sugar is still stored in bins and wrapped for customers in paper and string. Other bins hold what Hollanders call "church mints" — candy wafers to keep the small fry quiet in church. The store has stools for customers to rest on while their order is being filled from groaning shelves . . . *Leonard's Meat Market* near Main St., makes Dutch sausage and sells Dutch imported foods.

A word about eating — *Dutch Treat*, a small neat coffee shop with picnic makings "to go" . . . *Three Swans*, especially on Tuesday nights when authentic Dutch recipes are featured, also notable for having the first and only cocktail lounge in Lynden . . . *Snapper's Bakery*, outsized gingerbread cookies cut in shapes of Dutch boys and girls, deep-fried pastry called Olie Bollen, or banketstaaf, a delectably flakey almost pastry. Also for sale; a goodly selection of blue Delft Ware, chocolates, other Dutch goodies.

Annual affairs — Home of the heavy draft horses, Lynden is host for the *International Plowing Match*, in April, when teams of Clydesdales, Percherons and other draft breeds compete in the only contest of its kind held west of the Mississippi . . . *Farmer's Day Parade*, June . . . *Threshing Bee*, late August. Old-fashioned methods of curing and threshing grain, sacking up oats, old tractors displayed . . . *Northwest Washington Fair*, also late August. Attracts largest showing of dairy cattle and horses in State.

For further information — Lynden Chamber of Commerce, 525 Front Street, 98264; phone 354-4474.

Leaving Lynden, unless you're headed for Sumas and a less-used border crossing to Canada, head southeast in the broad Nooksack Valley through a pass created by the south fork of the Nooksack, into Deming. At the town of Nooksack, and at Deming, there are *graveyards of early settlers*. Deming lies in the mountain-surrounded "Y" of the north and south forks of the Nooksack River. (If you want to follow the north fork to Mt. Baker skip to the next tour, Bellingham Tour 3.) In this tour you head south on Highway 9, noting a *picnic ground* where your road crosses the north fork and an *Indian graveyard* a little beyond Van Zandt. Just north of Wickersham cut west through the mountains, past the southern tip of Lake Whatcom and turn south to Alger. Nearby is a good German restaurant, *Schnitzel Inn,* open for breakfast, lunch and dinner and featuring authentic German dishes. *Donovan State Park,* on Friday Creek is a likely place to picnic.

The Bow Hill Road will take you west across the freeway to Bow and Edison, on the fertile Samish River flats.

Somebody ought to start a movement about changing the name of Edison (for Thoma Alva) to "Dean," after a couple of her favorite sons who got into the sawmill business with more ingenuity and less cash than anybody.

The Dean brothers, William and George, were born in Scotland and George, at least, was apprenticed to the shipwright's trade. They arrived at Samish Landing about the time of the depression of 1873 with notions of building ships to haul lumber. And the cheapest way of getting the lumber consisted of chopping down trees and making it themselves.

They built a sawmill powered by a windmill, by topping two enormous trees, using one of them for a windmill blade and the other for bracing and to hold the handmade pulleys. They tanned their own leather for the belts and invented a cone-clutch and self-feeding arrangement that enabled them to turn out as much as 3,000 board feet a day . . . if the wind was blowing.

With this device, they were able to turn out finished lumber, even turned lumber, with homemade lathes built in their own blacksmith shop which was operated with homemade bellows. They ran the post office and store and built a small schooner with their own lumber which they used to ship that lumber to market.

In 1888, they built the sternwheeler "Mary F. Perley." She was 104 feet long, had a 20-foot beam and a hold 5 feet 5 inches deep, and served as part of the Mosquito Fleet.

Outright cash expended to get the whole plant going?

Fifty dollars.

A scenic side trip from here is the short distance out to Samish Island surrounded by cottages large and small, and no longer an island. Views are great and you can buy oysters in season at *Blau's Oyster Farm* and you'll find filberts for sale in their season, which is fall. (See *Footloose,* p. 47 for hike.)

Now go north from Edison and through Blanchard for a dramatic windup to your tour.

Chuckanut Drive — The Indians had a word for anything that was important to them and their word for a small bay lying adjacent to a large bay with a steep mountain rising from its shores was "Chuckanut." The people in the area and the highway department have called it a lot of other, and some-times less complimentary, things in view of the difficulties with which it has been maintained over the half-century since it was completed . . . and you will get a feel for the maintenance engineers when you drive it. It's steep and it's crooked, and the slide problems are horrendous when things get soggy.

Nevertheless, it was the first scenic drive built in the State of Washington and is famous in that respect, but mainly because it is so scenic. The views of Samish Bay and the San Juan Islands are spectacular along this concrete ribbon clinging to the rocky, forested cliffs of Chuckanut mountain, especially from Inspiration Point at 1,120 feet. In addition, it should be preserved as a museum piece . . . in a society which is bent on producing an eight-lane freeway that runs from the Canadian to the Mexican borders without a stoplight . . . even though periodically Chuckanut Drive gets a big hole in it.

The road curves something awful, but the views are tremendous, especially if you take the single land road in *Larrabee State Park* to the viewpoint at the top of Chuckanut Mountain.

You have to take a little mental reorientation course to appreciate its historical background, because when it started out, it was Bellingham's link with eastern Washington. Three-quarters of a century ago when this appendix to the State highway system was originated, the folks in the area were confident that Bellingham Bay would be the hub of shipping in the Pacific Northwest. This seemed like the most feasible route for a hookup with what then was known as Skagit Pass.

At that time the idea that it would connect with Seattle was only incidental.

A lot of people claim credit for the creation of Chuckanut Drive, but the guy who really put it together was a Bellingham engineer, J. J. Donovan. As you will learn later, Donovan was chiefly responsible for dumping the proposed highway across the Cascades north of Mt. Baker. But that didn't mean he was opposed to *any* highway emanating from Bellingham and crossing the mountains. He was, after all, an engineer and roads were in his blood. Nobody knew that Bellingham was not going to be the major metropolis in the 1890's, and everybody in the State *knew* there were rich mineral deposits for the taking once roads penetrated the vastness of the northern Cascades. So Donovan was able to apply a lot of clout at the legislature in Olympia, and appease hometown folks for quashing the more northerly route by obtaining State money for Chuckanut Drive.

In 1895, Donovan arranged for a meeting of the State Roads Commission with key leaders from Whatcom and Skagit Counties. There he sold everybody a bill of goods on what today is the North Cascades Highway which takes off as Highway 20 from Interstate 5 at Burlington.

(But, as Cicero said in 51 B.C., "There's many a slip 'twixt the cup and the lip . . .")

A year later the State Commissioners enthusiastically reported that the "Ruby Creek Trail" over the Cascades was practically a reality. In a letter to Governor John H. McGraw, the Commissioners noted that the whole project from Bellingham via Marblemount and "Twitsp" to the Columbia River could be completed for the $30,000 appropriated by the legislature.

They cited as proof of their estimates the fact a wagon road between 10 and 12 feet wide had been completed by Whatcom County from Fairhaven south to the Skagit County line. "Owing to the rocky and precipitous nature of the road," the Whatcom County engineer originally had estimated the cost at

$18,549. The construction men "effected some savings" and brought the 12-mile project in for a total of $11,000. (As a bit of added intelligence, the commission noted that the top wage paid on the project was $1.75 a day — from which $4.50 a week was deducted for meals.)

The Commissioner's $30,000 was a fairly steep sum, but then, of course, it included purchase of the right-of-way, too.

In its breakdown of the $30,000, the Commission figured it would cost $4,000 to continue the road from the Skagit County line to Blanchard where it would connect with an existing county road, and $20,000 from Marblemount to the confluence of the Methow and Twisp Rivers with $6,000 from there east to the Columbia at Marcus.

But speaking of breakdowns, the first one of considerable importance occurred shortly after the Commission had filed its report with Governor McGraw. Mount Vernon merchants saw no particular reason for giving their customers a better road to the bigger stores on Bellingham Bay. The Skagit County Commissioners had succumbed to Donovan's blandishments and purchased a right-of-way to meet with Chuckanut Drive at the Whatcom County line . . . but then they got a better offer . . . and sold the right-of-way to the Great Northern Railroad. This really frosted Whatcom County, which promptly sued Skagit County for breach of promise. That one ended in the State Supreme Court which found in favor of Skagit County. So Chuckanut Drive was a stub road that ended at the Skagit County line for the next quarter of a century. It would be 75 years before the dream of the Cascade crossing came to fruition — at considerably more cost than originally estimated.

Asked how far the $11,000 which built the original Chuckanut Drive would carry normal highway across the same terrain today, a State Highway Department engineer promptly replied, "Oh, about 100 feet."

Uncommon shopping — If the gate across a narrow gravel road off the Drive is open at the *Rock Point Oyster Co.* (near the Oyster Creek Inn) head down to the waterfront building to buy oysters shucked or in the shell. (Closed from April to October for seeding operations.)

A word about eating – *Chuckanut Manor*, south end of Drive, a roomy white frame restaurant for lunch or dinner with emphasis on oysters and other seafood, plus Friday night smorgasboard and weekend entertainment . . . *McFarland's Oyster Creek Inn*, looks modest but is extremely popular locally; oysters, seafood, wine and beer . . . *Oyster Bar*, 2 miles further south, also serves oysters, fantastic view.

Chuckanut Drive takes you right into Bellingham proper.

Bellingham Tour 3 — Deming, Glacier, Heather Meadows (Map V)

We're not all that committed to consultation with the weather-man before poking our noses outdoors, because most of the time, we get "hatless" rain. In addition, the basic theme of this book is that "there is no rain in hell . . . and if you don't like it here, we have a suggestion." But this is one trip you really should key to clear skies. Your destination — this enormous, glacier-covered peak — hangs there against the blue horizon like a gargantuan pile of sugar . . . and your whole distance from sea level to ski level is only about 50 miles.

For most of the trip, you're on the flat, rich delta land of the Nooksack River, but at Deming, you tuck in behind Sumas Mountain, following the Nooksack around the north side of the mountain. You enter Mt. Baker National Park at Glacier where Glacier Creek comes down off the mountain to join the river . . . and as you pass the various valleys, you can get sneak previews of the peak at close quarters. You buy your first lifetime memory with a view of glacial Mt. Shuksan, which is sort of the butler to the big mountain, although at first you may mistake him for the master of the household. But there won't be any doubt in your mind if you keep looking right as you reach the recreation area.

Take Highway 542 through lush farmlands, picking up the Nooksack on your way to Deming.

Deming — (Pop. nom. Elev. 203.) — Deming's business section — most of it, at least — is off the main highway but there's *Loggers' Landing*, under a sign reading "Cafe." (Their telephone number and parking lot both are labeled "Loggers' Landing.") Good local spot for breakfast or "coffee and . . ."

Annual affairs – *Logging Show*, second weekend in June. Local loggers compete with world champs at log rolling, climbing and axe throwing, with proceeds going to families of loggers injured or killed in accidents.

Mt. Baker — It isn't often that you get the kind of a quote from a government document like the one that follows, but then the U.S. National Park Service fellows are inspired by their subject matter and rhapsodize with words like these:

"The North Cascades near the Canadian border comprise a vast land of silent glaciers, tortured peaks, high eternal snows, deep-set forested valleys, and a variety of complex, delicate ecosystems. These features combine to form a unique area of breathtaking scenic grandeur and diverse recreational poten-tial . . . ."

The quote is from a Master Plan for the North Cascades approved in November 1970, and while it concerns itself principally with the area east and south of Mt. Baker, there is no way of keeping that mountain from being the star of the show. It's the geologic feature that anchors the northwest corner of the United States. The report goes on to note that "the North Cascades were probably lifted higher than the other sections of the Cascades and were more highly eroded, thus exposing harder central core rocks of great resistance (such as granites, schists, and gneisses). The end result is a series of rugged horns, peaks, and spires similar to those of the Alps in Europe . . . ."

There are three basic emotional experiences awaiting you as you leave Bellingham for the mountain. In the first, the eyes are assaulted with the magnitude of the high, vaulting peaks, which foster an impression of depth, scale and perspective; which prepares you in turn for the high, wide and magnificent vistas that will be yours when you arrive at your destination. Meanwhile, you are immersed in what represents the essence of the area's appeal: "waterfalls cascading from melting glaciers, patches of snow in mid-summer, blue ice above, alpine meadows in flower, and the other sensory stimuli related to these places; the sounds of thrushes and moving water, the cool, moist, fragrant air, the intense colors and various textures of rock, bark, prickly needles, succulent leaves, and wet snow; the taste of pure icy water, and the wild huckleberries; the feeling of swirling, wraithlike vapor on the face . . . ."

Particularly in a book called *The Wet Side of the Mountains*, it is significant to note that heavy precipitation resulting from the mountains' interception of some of the continent's wettest prevailing winds has produced a region containing over 300 glaciers — the largest and finest in the conterminous United States. There are 283 peaks over 7,000 feet high, 16 of them over 9,000 feet . . . and the 97 square miles of glaciers north of Snoqualmie Pass are three times that of all of the rest of the country combined, excluding Alaska.

Glaciers are big these days, with almost a million people visiting Mt. Baker annually to experience them, which is somewhat a far cry from the day more than 80 years ago when the previously mentioned J. J. Donovan ventured along this route up the Nooksack. You'll be making a right turn on the main highway hugging the northeast base of the mountains at Silver Fir Campground and heading for Heather Meadows. If you're lucky, pinnacled Mt. Shuksan will be appearing at about that time, and the following story won't be uppermost in your mind.

But it should take the secondary road straight ahead toward Hannegan Campground, you'll be in the general terrain followed by Donovan. Hannegan is named after Whatcom County Commissioner Tom Hannegan, who dreamed longer and more futilely about a cross-state wagon road in this area than anybody else.

◆

For half a century, Bellingham City Fathers were convinced that the main road across the Cascades would run north of "their" mountain. This seems a little incredible today, but those same people believed that Bellingham would be the major metropolis of the Pacific Northwest — on the grounds it would be easier for sailing ships to reach Bellingham Bay than to take that long tack trip up Sound someplace.

In 1893, the residents of Bellingham hit it lucky in the Legislature where the fellas were thinking for the very first time that maybe the state ought to get into the highway business. By teaming up with the legislators from Stevens and Okanogan Counties, the Whatcom County representatives got an appropriation of $20,000 for State Road District Number One. This was a major breakthrough. Instead of footing the entire bill for roads as they had in the past, the three counties would only have to cough up $7,000 . . . Stevens and Okanogan at $1,000 each and $5,000 from Whatcom.

A guy named Banning Austin, together with a couple other Sumas surveyors and engineers took on the job of surveying the route for $600, and in

May, 1893 reported he'd found a feasible pass from the north fork of the Nooksack River to the headwaters of Beaver Creek.

The Whatcom County Commissioners tendered the surveyors a vote of thanks and everybody set about blowing the $20,000 which was to take care of a road 200 miles long from Bellingham Bay to the town of Marcus on the Columbia River on the Dry Side of the Mountains.

Well, they got going great guns and by the end of the summer had spent $12,000 in construction heading from both the east and the west to the "Pass."

About that time, the contractor's bondsman cast a shadow of doubt on the project and a scandal ensued on the general grounds that "too many engineers spoil the broth." One of the leading lights of the State Road Commission resigned his post and Whatcom Lumberman Donovan, who was considered to be a man with a level head on his shoulders, was endorsed by the New Whatcom Board of Trade and the Whatcom County Commissioners for his replacement.

Donovan, who left town convinced that the project could be completed for the $7,000 that remained in the kitty at that time, explored the route with one John J. Cryderman, another state commissioner, in May of 1894. When they filed their report in August, it said no way could a road be built at that location.

The report pointed out that the proposed route never would be feasible because of high altitudes and impassable grades . . . and the fact that it ran smack into one of those 300 glaciers.

Outside of that it was fine.

With only $600, or $2-a-mile budgeted for the survey costs of the entire route, they had anticipated that Surveyor Austin might have to cut costs here and there, but this hardly seemed the logical spot. So they descended upon him with a greater, rather than a lesser degree of irritation, asking him what, in God's name, prompted his belief that there was a passable pass in the vicinity:

He responded that he was positive about the pass because he had seen a flock of wild geese fly through it . . .

And, of course, making this our first publicly financed, legally authorized, and totally authenticated Wild Goose Chase.

◄►

The Indians found the White man's frenetic activity distracting and had come to an abiding mistrust— which is one of the milder methods of expressing their feelings — about the American "Bostons" who had double-crossed them in a exquisitely infinite variety of ways.

Nevertheless, the following story, told by Eldridge Morse, editor, author and reporter, is one you'll appreciate if you pause at one of the outlook spots along either the Mt. Baker or the North Cascade Highway and contemplate the wilderness involved.

In August of 1881, Morse and another man thought it would be an interesting idea to cross the summit of the Cascades between the Skagit and Nooksack Valleys. It was only 10 miles over the divide . . . just a nice jaunt. So with minimal equipment, like one blanket and a frying pan, they started out on the Skagit side.

Now, the ordinary black bear, who runs unless there's no other alternative, leaves a footprint about 4 inches wide and 9 inches long. About the time they reached the banks of the Nooksack the two guys heard an eminently louder than normal crashing in the underbrush, found a bear track at least twice that size and concluded they had crossed the path of a very large cinnamon bear. They also concluded that it might produce a highly explosive encounter. While they were pondering methods of departing the premises with the utmost haste, they saw two elderly Indians coming down the river in a canoe.

Knowing the Indians held "Bostons" in less than high regard, the two men determined upon a course of pretending they were among supernatural creatures who inhabited the mysterious recesses of Mt. Baker. Their objective was to get a fast ride down river to the nearest hamlet. They pointed out to the Indians that their name was "S'Be-ow" and that their home was "everywhere . . . ." They didn't need to add that one of the powers of "S'Be-ow" was that it was a supernatural race that could assume the form of anyone. Nor did they need to add that members of this race could take Indians apart and put them together again.

Sometimes the "S'Be-ow" got a little careless on the putting-together part, which accounted for the number of crippled Indians in existence. This made Indians nervous.

The Indians were a little skeptical because these guys looked like the hated "Bostons" until Morse "took himself apart" by taking out a double set of false teeth. He clacked them at the canoers who promptly paddled them down river to civilization.

Glacier — (Pop. Nom. Elev. 881.) — Entrance to Mt. Baker National Forest and last outpost of civilization. A ranger station at the gate has all the information you'll want on things to do in the forest and Mt. Baker Recreation area.

A word about eating – *Graham's*, mix of general store, antiques, crafts, and restaurant with long wooden bar. Gary Graham, a Boeing "alum," is the genial proprietor of this long-owned Graham family business. Clark Gable wall photos, "Gableburger" ("over 104 sold right here in Glacier"), ice cream cones with jelly beans on top. Currently trying out a gourmet menu . . . *Mount Baker Inn* with food, beer, gas and ceramics . . . at the log-built *Chandelier Lodge*, the wooden bar is just made for carving initials, ceiling is hung with bear skins, and on a handy wall is what every skier needs: an "Excuse Board" for making up YOUR reason for not going skiing. The restaurant serves the only hard liquor around as well as good hamburgers and other items. Owner Bob Pederson is a walking compendium of knowledge of Mt. Baker and surrounding area.

A word about sleeping – *Snowline Inn,* Tudor style condominiums can be rented for luxury in the backwoods — pub, dancing, swimming pool, children's play area.

Out of Glacier, your road climbs through moss-hung Douglas fir with roadside viewpoints along the way. Even in summer there are patches of snow on the higher areas.

There are a couple of side trips you'll find worthwhile. *Glacier Creek Road,* one mile east of Glacier, provides the best roadside views of Mt. Baker.

You switchback along a timbered road with views along the way and then emerge in one steep swoosh to a high viewpoint. Mt. Baker and its multi-colored glaciers stare you in the face and Glacier Creek Valley spreads north-ward below you.

Seven miles east from Glacier you can hear *Nooksack Falls* as the glacial waters thunder into a narrow gorge. Turn off the main highway and drive half a mile. You can view the Falls from either side by walking across a bridge, through the trees and then right out almost to the cascade. Those enormous wire-banded hollow logs you see date from the turn of the century when they were used as a gravity feed water line for logging.

And now we come to the big event, *Heather Meadows*, the recreation area on this side of Mt. Baker . . . the 50 miles you've come from sea to ski in the Bellingham publicity brochures . . . .

But halt . . . first we must make a right turn instead of going straight ahead to Hannegan Campground — as we earlier suggested. Where you're headed now is over Austin Pass. Somewhat incredibly, this pass bears the name of the previously mentioned Banning Austin, the guy who goofed on the first wild goose chase.

Reacting from the trifling setback of the glacier-ridden survey route, the dauntless Mr. Austin proceeded with his characteristic vigor to find another pass through the Cascades to eastern Washington . . . and this time, he came up with what they finally named in his honor.

The only problem was that Austin Pass leads directly into Baker Creek, which leads into Baker Lake, which leads into the Skagit River, which leads to Puget Sound.

Somewhere his instruments must have erred . . . because they directed him south along the Wet Side of the Mountains instead of east over the moun-tains. Oh well, it's Austin Pass.

Now, before getting into the Heather Meadows playground, we think it only wise to fortify you with a quote from a brochure published by the Forest Service on the weather. It notes that the road to Artist's Point — the best viewpoint to see the top of the mountain — is not open until Labor Day and usually closes by October 15, like a little over a month in which car-cushion travelers can drive to the scene of magnificent Mt. Baker. The report then goes on with this cheering news: The longest rain-free period experienced on Mt. Baker rarely exceeds two weeks. This period is usually much shorter at the higher elevations (like the 4,742 elevation of Artist's Point). Further, several extremely misty, foggy days normally follow rainy periods, extending the disagreeableness. Snow may fall any month of the year above 5,000 feet . . . .

"Rain clothes and warm clothing should be available in the Mt. Baker National Forest at any season. Devils club, nettles and insects such as mos-quitos, black flies and no-see-ums (a small gnat) generally will be encountered . . . ."

The brochure concludes with: "We hope your visit will be an enjoy-able one."

While that summary doesn't cause the Bellingham Chamber of Com-merce to beam with pride, it does come under the heading of practical advice

... something that's worth following in view of the fact that you are in the presence of the American Alps. . . .

Austin Pass Ski Area — (Elev. 4,000.) — Lots of snow-oriented activity in the winter and, unlike some ski areas, beautiful during the summer months. Narrow footpaths run like patchwork through open meadows dotted with little lakes. At the parking area, trails lead past a display of native plantings. Surprisingly, the spectacular peak that most everyone photographs is nearby Mt. Shuksan.

To see Mt. Baker, you'll probably have to hike a couple of miles beyond the lodge area. But the walking's easy and the view along the route is tremendous.

A word about eating — Two day lodges serve cafeteria style. There also are areas for sack lunchers.

Annual affairs – *The Slush Cup*, held annually on July 4th weekend, officially closes the area's ski season. And it's a wild one involving skiing and icy ponds. The competitors get doused and soused.

For further information — Write the Forest Supervisor, Mt. Baker National Forest, Federal Office Building, Bellingham, 98225; phone, 676-8080, or call Ranger Station at Glacier, 599-8233.

Return via Highway 542 . . . unless you hanker for a wild goose chase.

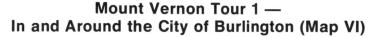

Mount Vernon Tour 1 —
In and Around the City of Burlington (Map VI)

M ount Vernon and Burlington and the flat land between them look a lot like Holland . . . except for a detail, the Cascade Mountains looming in behind them. Dairy and beef cattle graze right up to the edge of town . . . the rising flower bulb industry provides radiant color when the tulips, daffodils and hyacinths are blooming in the spring . . . summer brings lush green fields of peas (which provide nearly half of the nation's frozen product) and vegetables grown mostly for seed. Mount Vernon's streets are squeezed in between the freeway and the Skagit River. Burlington, a few miles north, got its start as a rail crossroads and is some distance from the River. Both hum with activity when the crops are moving, but are pretty peaceful the rest of the time. At any time, Mount Vernon is the dominant town.

Mount Vernon — (Pop. 8,804. Elev. 24.) — It kind of staggers the imagination, but this is the seat of the county where decisions are being made that may well affect the eating habits of the whole nation. The folks here are wrestling with the problem of the energy crisis for the entire Puget Sound Basin. And here is the governing body most intimately concerned with the development and/or "nondevelopment" of the most important river within the Wet Side of the Mountains. Skagit County is setting out to become the number one agricultural county west of the Cascades. And with urbanization and industrialization encroaching on Pierce, King, Snohomish and Whatcom counties, it is moving up in the ranks as our major "industrial-agricultural" complex. (Fewer big farms produce vastly greater quantities of seed and food than many smaller farms.)

Mount Vernon straddles a big curve of the Skagit River surrounded by flat farmlands on three sides and backed against the mountains on the east. Once this was the location of two enormous log jams on the river, and the one to the south was a mile long and centuries old. When these jams were finally blasted loose, riverboats could reach here and Mount Vernon began to grow.

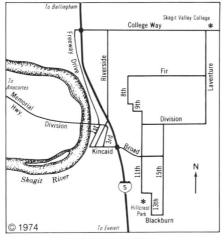

MOUNT VERNON

Burlington — (Pop. 3,337. Elev. 36.) — Maintains a separate entity, but it is essentially a partner with Mount Vernon as a center for the agricultural industry in the delta of the Skagit River.

The two towns are in the heart of a 150,000-acre flood plain containing some of the richest agricultural land on earth. The agricultural-industrial complex which makes up the backbone of the economy is valued at about $100,000,000 and they hope to keep it that way. Interstate 5, which came galloping through the valley, eating up land this nation may need for food, is the last of that kind of thing the county intends to put up with. A second Boeing, planting asphalt instead of peas, is discouraged by the fact that this will remain a flood plain ... and by zoning laws that are among the most advanced of their kind in the State. A requirement that there be 30 acres of land around each house in the rural zones, has proved totally frustrating to developers of multiple housing tracts.

On the other hand, garden and dairy products are record-breaking.

The Skagit-Samish lowland region has a network of sloughs and creeks which meander through the river deltas, maintaining the moisture content required for some of the most valuable crops in the State. There is a heavy concentration of both dairy and beef animals, and hay occupies almost half of the acreage. At the moment, it is second only to Whatcom County in strawberry production, and for vegetable seed it is without parallel. Mount Vernon and Burlington are the primary centers for processing milk, poultry, eggs, berries and vegetables . . . with peas the runaway leader of the latter.

Today, a mere 8% of the number of dairy farmers who were here half a century ago produce half-again as many pounds of milk. It's the number 3 milk-producing county in the State behind Whatcom and Snohomish. A few years ago, it was 4th, behind King County . . . but its production is moving up in the State's ranks.

Approximately 40% of the frozen peas in the United States come out of this delta country . . . 85 million pounds on land that is twice as productive as the national average. The mobile viners harvesting the crop in July and August is a significant sight.

Other astronomical vegetable figures include 14,000,000 pounds of cauliflower grown on 700 acres and 260,000 pounds of seeds for mustard greens (not the hot stuff, just the greens) which come at 15,000 seeds to the ounce. You're talking in trillions when you put it this way.

When the folks first started farming, they raised hay, barley and oats and other grains. The seed crops began with a spectacular crop of cabbage seed in 1918. The farmers got $1 a pound for it; since then there's been a saying around the valley: "The two best crops are 1918 — and *next* year!"

The County Agricultural Agent's statistical information on cabbage seed reads well — like 80% of the nation's production of this seed. It rates high on the financial ledger, too . . . $2.50 a pound. The area produces 90% of the nation's spinach seed — but they only get 20c a pound for it. Other national impressive seed crops are sweet beets . . . collard . . . Swiss chard . . . rutabaga and kale — all 80% of the national production; and turnips at 40%.

But the big news is the bulb business. Washington is the leading American flower bulb-producing state. And as late as 1969, the State Department of Agriculture was making the following statement: "Virtually all flower bulbs are grown on the flood plains of the lower White and Puyallup Rivers — the highest concentration in a four-mile radius around Sumner and Puyallup. Iris, narcissus and tulip bulbs . . . are the most important bulb crops, in that order . . . ."

When we came innocently down the pike asking about flower bulb production, we ran into a wall of silence exceeded only by the scientists involved in the construction of an atomic bomb. Nobody would venture an opinion whether or not the Skagit-Nooksack deltas had supplanted the Puyallup Valley as the leading flower bulb-producing area. (Puyallup is a little touchy about the subject.)

Finally, we asked Richard Nowadnick, Secretary of the Washington State Bulb Commission, to put the number of bulb sales for 1971 in writing so there would be no chance that we goofed. And here's the box score:

	Iris	Narcissus	Tulip
South (Woodland)	9,264,195	1,258,133	257,448
Central (Puyallup)	15,518,400	2,697.020	1,365,146
North (Skagit)	31,617,575	4,068,325	8,686,373

Their best bulb story is the one about a wealthy Seattle woman who sent to Holland for a batch of their finest tulip bulbs — money was no object. She got an apologetic letter back noting that her shipment was delayed because their supplier in Mount Vernon, Washington, was a little late in his delivery of them.

Prowling Mount Vernon

From March to mid-summer, the fields west of town are bursting with color. *Roadside flower stands* sell vegetables, cut tulips, daffodils, hyacinths. Some stands operate on the honor system of "Help yourself and make change," and some say "Cut your own." Berries and vegetables occupy the stands later in the season, as does honey.

The crest of *Lincoln Hill* is a residential area of some of the older and larger homes with views out toward the sunset . . . try 9th, 10th and 11th Sts. *Little Mountain City Park,* 910 feet higher than the city, views the landscape from Everett to Bellingham from its observation tower. (See *Footloose,* pages 65, 66). Beautiful rural drive is the *Clear, Beaver and Barney Lakes and Nookachamps Creek area,* northeast of Mount Vernon behind the hills. In the winter you are likely to see *trumpeter swans,* the largest of all North American waterfowl, also sightings of *whistler swans,* which are smaller and with a higher voice. Drive a short ways west of *Bayview State Park* on Padilla Bay, a warm, saltwater beach and vista. (See *Footloose,* p. 48.)

The 20-acre campus of *Skagit Valley Community College* on the north side of town, adds a higher education touch to the community. *"World's Largest Tulip Tree"* is on Cleveland St. (For the uninformed, a tulip tree doesn't bear tulips, only leaves shaped like them.)

Plants in the area you can visit include: *Stokely-Van Camp, Inc.,* S. 1st St., (visit late spring to Oct.) prepares fresh vegetables for freezing, call district manager; *National Fruit Canning Company,* Washington St.; *Burlington and Cascade Foods, Inc.,* Greenleaf St., processing strawberries and peas. *Dairy Farms* that may be visited: Matthew Paul, Riverbend Rd., Arthur Gadbois, Babcock Rd., Danny Miller Dairy, Gardner Rd., *Washington State Research and Extension Unit,* Memorial Hwy., "pea patch" of experiments to control pea wilt. For all above, call ahead or check with the Chamber of Commerce.

Uncommon shopping — Cheerfully advertised "Come and see us." *City Bakery,* 1st St., with Dutch motif, sells tasty cookies, coffeecakes, strudel, and irresistible breads like cardamon and roggerbrood, a Dutch rye that is heavy, dark pumpernickel. Tables for "coffee and" . . . *Wells Nursery,* E. Section St. and *Chenoweth Nursery and Garden Center,* 2nd St., both with good stock . . . *Sakuma Bros. Farm,* Burlington, strawberry and raspberry plants . . . *Gallery 22,* 1st St., gift shop with unusual, well-selected items . . . *Valborg's Gifts,* 1st St., and also at Skagit Valley Mall, some outstanding gift selections.

A word about eating — *Max Dale's Restaurant,* Riverside Dr., long-time local favorite, good meat, and blackberry cobbler . . . *Breadboard, Skagit Valley Mall,* spectacular 4-inch-high cinnamon rolls . . . *Mexico Cafe,* Memorial Hwy., small authentic and Mexican favorite of migrant workers . . . *Skagit Valley Community College Coffee Shop* for whatever, and college atmosphere . . . *Broaster,* Memorial Hwy., for breakfast near the farmlands, open 24 hours. In Burlington: *Axelson's* for talked-about clam chowder . . . *Canton,* good menu and pleasant Chinese family operation.

A word about taverns — *Duffy's Tavern,* Riverside Dr., hangout for local pundits: newspaper publisher, newsmen, radio staff; beamed ceilings, sunken dance floor, young and popular; good French dip sandwiches, pizza . . . *Tree Fort Tavern Pay Station*, Riverside Dr., huge photo murals of logging scenes and accent on lumbermen's era. Soup and sandwiches. Also young and popular.

 A word about sleeping – *Nor'Wester*, and *West Wind Motels*, both on Riverside Dr. and good.

 Annual affairs — *George Washington's Birthday Celebration*, in February. Gets front page stories across the country, what with "George" crossing the Skagit, parade, and raising of 13-star Betsy Ross flag at the Court-house . . . *Dairy Berry Days*, Burlington, late June, carnival, exhibits, and strawberry shortcake . . . *NW Square Dance Festival*, 3rd weekend in July . . . *Skagit County Fair*, 2nd weekend in August . . . *Skagit County Rodeo*, early September.

 For further information — Chamber of Commerce, 310 Pine St., Mount Vernon; phone, 336-2522. (Which also has a good folder of 1-day trips.) Chamber of Commerce, 701 Fairhaven St., Burlington; phone, 755-4331.

◄——

Mount Vernon Tour 2 — Sedro Woolley, Rockport, Newhalem, Washington Pass, Darrington (Map VI)

 The Skagit River is the most important single scenic entity on this tour. The trip takes you through the urban areas of Skagit County as far as Sedro Woolley where it shifts through rural regions in the lower valley with small towns and farms, then into semiwilderness and finally what probably is the biggest and most complete wilderness still in existence within continental United States — an area that you must get out of your car to really experience. Much of the time you are alongside of the river although huge dams lift it way above you when you get into the more mountainous terrain. Newhalem is your last outpost of man-made structures. And while the trip over Washington Pass into eastern Washington is one of the world's most spectacular this tour is confined to Western Washington, and we suggest that you do your turnaround at Newhalem back to Rockport and return to Mount Vernon via the Sauk River, Darrington and Lake Cavanaugh. On your trip, you will find our National Bird, the bald eagle, along the river, and huge hydro-electric dams serving the Puget Sound region. You will be passing within a short distance of the proposed new thermo-nuclear electric plant and find majestic scenery at almost any turn. But the big main event is the Skagit River . . . powerful, frightening at times, and always dramatic.

 The Skagit River — Region 3 has a lot of things going for it like the San Juan Islands and Mt. Baker, but the most under-written and over-ignored facet of this piece of geography near the Canadian border is the fantastic Skagit.

 To begin with it's the largest river between the Fraser and the Colum-bia. With 1.75 million acres, its basin and runoff are the most extensive in the

Puget Sound area. It's the only river with runs of all five species of salmon — Chinook, Coho, Pink, Chum and Sockeye — and is the single most productive river in the State for Steelhead trout. Its delta, which goes by the name of Skagit Flats, is the most important waterfowl wintering site on the west coast of the United States. The Skagit River is joined by the Cascade, Sauk, Suiattle and Baker, and to some extent the Samish, to form the previously mentioned delta.

The upper river valleys and mountains embrace forest lands capable of producing nearly a quarter of the saw timber in the Puget Sound area. It provides boating for a distance equal to the length of Puget Sound. It supports 8 hydroelectric facilities producing more than 58% of the power in the Puget Sound area. It is the gateway to the great new North Cascade Highway, the North Cascades Park, and Wilderness Area.

Outside of that, it doesn't amount to much.

A U.S. Forest Service Study of the Skagit River and its Cascade, Sauk and Suiattle tributaries published in March, 1973, has this cogent comment about the Skagit:

"This river is an experience. The compelling vertical scale of the mountain enclosure dominates all visual variety. From the broad sweep of the flat, level, grand expanse of the lower flood plain to the deep V-trenched bottom of the high country, the vertical enclosure is dramatically present. Whether from the river or the highway, the glimpses out 'looking around' are always controlled by the vertical backdrop — either nearby (foreground), or far away (background). The visual frame of reference is always seemingly upward from the base plane, the valley floor. Emotionally we experience a sense of awe, respect for the majesty of the wild lands on the skyline."

For about 10 miles to Sedro Woolley, you're in an urban environment dominated by man-made structures. For the next 30 miles, you pass through a rural atmosphere with fields of crops and forage, fences, barns, sheds, farmhouses, railroads, roadside stands and some residential developments. The next environmental change is to pastoral, about 6 miles west of Concrete, where there is an emotional sensation of being apart from the rest of the world in an area where man still is present, but agriculture no longer dominates and is replaced by the dominance of uncleared land intermingled with occasional farmhouses. You also become aware of the increasing proximity of steep mountain walls closing in on the valley floor, making the appearance of the river more frequent and apparent. The highway 5 miles north of Marblemount provides some of the most exciting scenic vistas on the entire Skagit River, including spectacular views of the glacier-clad North Cascades, Sauk Mountain and Eldorado Peak.

Up the tributary rivers, you get into primitive and then wild areas which are beyond the scope of car-cushion travelers, but nonetheless seem to be closing in on you as you get deeper into the mountains.

On our tour segment from Rockport to Darrington, you are behind mountains that separate you from the coast. You are in and among some of the finest coniferous forests in the world. In the Skagit-Samish basins, nearly 1 million acres are being harvested commercially on a sustained yield basis.

As you return down the Stillaguamish River and back to civilization, a metamorphosis occurs and your psyche reasserts its own importance — you're back in the scheme of things.

Sedro Woolley — (Pop. 4,620. Elev. 50.) — This is the last outpost of urban civilization, before you head into that 30-acre-per-house country and ultimately wind up in a big wilderness area set aside by the federal government in the vastnesses of the North Cascades. This town logically thinks of itself as the gateway to this enormous federally financed "nondevelopment". The idea is to preserve the area in the upper Skagit and over the Pass in varying degrees of recreational and natural states.

Among these is the inclusion of a huge chunk of the Skagit River, east of here, in the Wild and Scenic Rivers Act. In its preliminary report the Forest Service came up with a number of suggestions, including a recommendation that land for paths and toilet facilities along the river be acquired by outright purchase or easements at a cost of about $5,000,000: Of this sum nearly half would be spent for easements for footpaths that might later become bicycle paths (but never motor vehicle rights-of-way). The latter would be like having your cake and eating it for present landowners. The government estimated purchase of land outright at $1,000 an acre — for land that sold half a century ago for $5 an acre. The whole idea is that of protecting the environment against the onslaught of people expected to use the Park.

Beginning right away, that's expected to be a number 30 times the population of Skagit County . . . and increasing by at least 100% every decade for at least the next 30 years.

After that it is expected to really go up.

Some 42 governmental agencies are trying to persuade a bunch of Tarheels that this is a good thing. But they were the mavericks when they came here from North Carolina nearly a hundred years ago, and they haven't changed much. They brought a complete set of backwoods notions when they arrived in the first place, and added a few new wrinkles after they arrived. They want things to remain as they are — no more people.

Their idea is to sell the old family farm to some private operation for $100,000 and then have the Planning Commission prevent the new owners from building on it.

It's all in the great American tradition of free enterprise and they have some vivid recollections of historic financial transactions like the story of Charles Von Pressentin, who became the first settler in the town of Birdsview in May, 1877. Mr. von Pressentin sold a comfortable 10,000,000 board feet of timber for about $40,000 before he got down to the real use of his property — farming.

That they were individualists back in those days as well as now was evidenced in a case heard by Circuit Judge J. R. Lewis, who settled the hash of George Connor in 1878.

Mr. Connor was charged with "exhibiting a pistol in a rude, angry and threatening manner in a crowd of two persons. . . ."

In a precedent-shattering decision, peppery Judge Lewis held it did not take 3 to make a crowd.

He fined Connor 10 bucks and gave him 6 months in the nearest county jail — which was over at Port Townsend.

In spirit, things haven't changed much in the intervening years as you'll read when you come to the Rockport portion of this tour.

But back to the "last outpost of civilization."

The "Woolley" part of the town's name came rather legitimately from its founder, P. A. Woolley, but the Sedro section was the result of negotiations exceeded only by the diplomatic skill of Henry Kissinger.

The *Illustrated History of Skagit and Snohomish Counties* — the one written by a committee — gives us a look-in at Mortimer Cook, founder of Sedro with: "Mr. Cook's ambition was to bestow upon the new town a name such as no other town in America should have, and if such could be found he cared little whether or not it was euphonious or elegant.

"He eventually concluded to name the place 'Bug'."

Accordingly he posted a sign with that name at the riverboat landing. This annoyed the ladies of the communtiy, who promptly had a sign reading "Charlotte" posted above it. Mr. Cook threatened to tear the second sign down. The ladies threatened to print "Hum" in front of Bug or "House" after it.

One of the ladies happened to have an old Spanish dictionary kicking around the house and with a delegation of other women in the town called upon Mrs. Cook to enter negotiations with her husband on the matter of using the Spanish word "Cedro" on the grounds there were a lot of cedar trees about. Mr. Cook opined that was about as unique as the word "Smith." Mrs. Cook countered with a suggestion that an "S" be substituted for "C." He capitulated and "Sedro" was born . . . to be joined with "Woolley" as one town in 1890.

Prowling Sedro Woolley

A 23-mile excursion railroad runs from Sedro Woolley to Concrete, Memorial Day to Labor Day, on Seattle City Light's old *Skagit River Railroad.* Two round trips daily are pulled by *Old No. 6,* a steam locomotive recently brought out of retirement as a **State Registered Historic Site** in a park at Newhalem, to whistle and puff up the Skagit Valley again.

You can visit *Skagit Steel Works,* manufacturers of logging and home machine equipment. Call in advance or check the Chamber of Commerce.

Uncommon shopping – *Bob and Aggie's Second Hand Store* for antiques and collectibles.

A word about eating – *The Gateway,* located in a remodeled hotel, expensive but good seafood and steaks . . . the *Liberty Cafe,* with more modest surroundings and prices, great Friday night buffets . . . the *Sedro Woolley Bakery and Soda Fountain* for delicious pastries, especially the kringle, filled with almond paste and sugar-sprinkled.

Annual affairs — *Loggerodeo,* July 4 for 5 days. Logging contests and parade.

For further information – The Chamber of Commerce, Sedro Woolley, 98284, or call 855-6241.

From Sedro Woolley, the road follows the Skagit by neat farms and quaint barns, climbing gradually past the small settlements of Lyman and Hamilton, both at the elevation of 95 feet. Five miles further you will double your elevation to 192 feet at Birdsview.

From Lyman east, the road stays very close to the river as it loops and curves, widens for islands and narrows for channels. Up river it has been swelled by the Sauk and Cascade Rivers and in spring and early summer the river can have a frightening look — swift, deep, and so full that it is concave from bank to bank. You get a distinct feeling this is fishing country and plenty active in winter when the many fishing cabins and camps are full with pursuers of the Washington State official fish, the Steelhead trout. There are very few motels or restaurants, but lots of fishing supplies in stores and fishermen come and go year-round, not really being part of the permanent population.

Concrete — (Pop. 573. Elev. 216.) — The town started out as Baker in 1890 because it was at the confluence of the Baker and Skagit Rivers. The name changed to "Cement" when manufacture of that product began at the turn of the century and subsequently it got its present name. Concrete manufactured cement for 61 years until that became uneconomic. And although there is an estimated 20 million tons of limestone adjacent to the town and about 1 billion tons available in the valley, it is unlikely that the production of cement will be renewed if the Skagit is named as a wild river.

Concrete, largest of the upper valley towns, is built partially on a hillside, where the valley is at its narrowest point — just one mile wide. Two large maps in town point the way north to the area's many lakes, streams, and trails. Follow the one-lane bridge across the Baker River to see the *trapping pens* where salmon swimming upstream to spawn are caught below the dams (Puget Power's 2 dams), and trucked to rearing pens above the lakes. The action takes place during the fall salmon run.

Sidetrip north to Lower Baker Dam forming *Lake Shannon*, and Upper Baker Dam and its *Baker Lake;* and you'll find hot mineral springs, Rainbow Falls, a fish hatchery, resorts, and spectacular views of Mt. Baker and Mt. Shuksan less than 10 miles away.

This brings us to the spiral staircase of history.

Back in the late 1880's when the average man's ignorance of energy was even more abysmal than it is today, there was an argument between two traction companies in Seattle over which had the most powerful streetcars. To solve it, they hooked a car from each company together facing in opposite directions on the same track with the same trolley wire to stage a tug-of-war. After blowing some fuses, they concluded this was not the best method of proof.

But the real capper came on the day the first printing press was to be hooked up with electricity in Pioneer Square. The police cordoned off the area to keep the crowd back. One electrician, and only one, was permitted to enter the building and make the hookup. There were tears in the eyes of several onlookers when he disappeared from sight. They never expected to see him or any part of him again. Most of the crowd figured the building would blow.

That was the kind of battle against fear that used to be waged by the firms which make up the Puget Sound Power and Light Company. Today it is fighting its old enemy, fear, on a 1,500-acre site off the Skagit wilderness about 5 miles northeast of Sedro Woolley . . . the spot selected from among 100 possible locations for the state's first thermo-nuclear power development. It's one of those deals which public utilities have attempted with disastrous blow-backs from the voters . . . and now has devolved on this private company, which is a little less exposed to the political processes. At this writing the plant has been approved by the Planning Commission and the County Commissioners, but, like in the case of the electrician's connection to the printing press, some folks figure she'll blow and they'll all be killed.

But, Puget Power's public relations are pretty good, as evidenced by the incredibly comic election held in Seattle in 1950. For at least half a century, the company had been engaged in the process of consolidating the 128 entities which make up its present complex, and providing people with better electric power at lower rates. (One of the great examples comes to us from the apprecia-tive owner of an ice company in Granite Falls. Prior to Puget Power, he had to shut off his ice machine at night when it came time to open up the "picture show." The former power supply couldn't encompass both ice and moving pictures at the same time.)

The election stemmed from the fact that in 1902 one of the progenitors of Puget Power got a 50-year franchise to service the city of Seattle. This subse-quently put the company in competition with Seattle City Light, resulting in an awesome collection of duplicated poles and wires which the City Council decided to end when the franchise expired. The best way of ending meant voter approval of a $25,800,000 bond issue to purchase Puget's facilities in the city. Former Mayor William F. Devin, who was in office at the time, said, "I have never seen any political issue of any kind in which there was such unanimity of favorable public opinion. Both newspapers were for it. The Republicans and the Democrats were for it . . . the labor unions and the Chamber of Commerce . . . the P.T.A. . . . ."

The company, which had spent half a century "selling" itself to the public, set about the incredible business of getting itself "sold" to the public — for 25 million bucks.

Then, on November 7, 1950, news headlines blazoned the fact that the voters had rejected the purchase. They liked Puget Power and didn't think it was fair to put it out of business.

In a turnout of 123,700 the "no" votes totaled 952 more than the "yes" votes in the unofficial returns. It went to the absentee ballots and still lost by 189 votes. Then in the official recount announced on January 25, 1951, it turned out that the real count favored the purchase by a majority of 724. And City Light finally took over Puget's facilities.

Today, that faith in Puget Power is more important than ever before for those who would like to meet the current power crisis and at the same time save the river. The Federal Power Commission has identified 13 potential hydro-electric dam sites in the Skagit River basin . . . in addition to the 5 there now.

All of them together would produce less than the amount of electricity which the one thermo-nuclear plant could come up with. . . .

And one of the sights you'd see in this valley would be a river eternally dammed.

◄—

The valley is still listed as pastoral through Concrete to Marblemount, but it's getting farther away from the urban areas and more untouched forests are intermingled with fewer fields and farmhouses. Mountain walls are closing in, making almost right angles to the fields. In summer the wild flowers are riotous everywhere.

From mid-December to mid-March you have a chance to see an unusual sight. As many as 400 *bald eagles* winter in the area between Concrete and Marblemount. They congregate to feed on carcasses of spawned salmon and sometimes number up to 60 in one tree. Greatest concentration is along the Skagit near the confluence with the Sauk at Rockport. January, when a rainy day holds them near the river, is best sighting. The "Eagles of the Skagit Foundation" is trying to establish a 4,000 acre sanctuary here for our National Bird.

Rockport — (Pop. Nom. Elev. 225). — A few pages back we mentioned a negative attitude on the part of the planners toward motorcycles on pedestrian bicycle paths along the river. And there was nothing about an episode which occurred in the little town of Rockport on May 6, 1973 that dimmed the bright flame of public resentment against operators of these staccato mechanical devices.

Boasting a grand total of 70 post office boxes, which doesn't exactly qualify it as a major metropolis, Rockport enjoys a kind of peaceful coexistence with nature. But the quiet of the little town was shattered on Saturday, May 5, by the arrival of about 150 motorcyclists on a pleasure trip. They got into a beef with the locals that night at the Fish Inn Tavern.

Apparently unacquainted with the fact that a large proportion of the population of this area hails from the Smokies in the Appalachian Highlands of Tennessee and North Carolina, somebody in the bikers' group aroused the ire of one of the locals. And one of the creeds that comes from the Smokies is a tendency to clannishness that causes the group to respond as one when a crisis confronts an individual belonging to the clan.

As an upshot of the brawl at the tavern, Tim Roetman got his huge cement truck and ran it over a big batch of parked motorcycles.

This failed to endear these resolute mountain men to the lowlanders from out of state who proceeded to knock Tim Roetman, Jr. unconscious . . . which brought out the worst in the rest of the mountaineers . . . which brought out, eventually, some 40 law enforcement officers (Sheriffs, State Police) who attempted to restore the peace, a process which occupied their attention for the next 15 hours. Deputy Sheriff Albert Fagen had to have 4 stiches taken in his scalp after being clubbed. Three other people required medical attention.

Finally, late Sunday in the afternoon several trucks appeared to collect the remains of the mangled motorcycles.

Skagit County Sheriff John Boynton said, "They were scraping 'em up with shovels."

The two Roetmans were arrested for destruction of property. And on January 11, 1974, Superior Judge Harry Follman sentenced the senior Roetman to 6 weeks in the county jail and his son to 2 weeks in the same spot; and, of course the costs . . . which came to a grand total of $36 each.

The judge also put both men on probation for 2 years.

It cost them a little more than Judge Lewis fined the previously mentioned Connor — probably inflation — but the Roetmans didn't have to spend 6 months in the clink . . . .

And the folks are thinking of erecting a monument to them in the town square.

◆

A word about eating – *Totem Trail Cafe*, really great homemade pie — a good place to stop before heading farther into the mountains.

Keep a sharp eye on the road east from Rockport for a white *Episcopal Church* half-hidden by a house, that is the old depot from which the Seattle City Light train once departed for Newhalem.

The Sauk River, flowing from the south, joins the Skagit here, and a mountain loop highway branches south along the Sauk to Darrington. This tour continues east here to Newhalem. and Seattle City Light Dams (and Washington Pass, if you wish), but returns to Rockport for the loop trip.

Marblemount — (Pop. Nom. Elev. 313.) — This is the last of the "free enterprise" towns and the last open area before mountains hem in on all sides. Visit the rustic post office in town dating back to the early days, or load up on picnic supplies and film at either of the two well-stocked grocery stores.

A worthwhile side trip is the drive up Cascade River Road into part of the area designated as primitive and wild, to visit the *State salmon hatchery*. Then continue along the road for views of the Cascade River far below while 8,875-ft. Eldorado Peak looms to the right. At road's end, huge *glaciers* grind down mountain slopes, occasionally breaking off to thunder down hundreds of feet to rocks below.

If you are contemplating going beyond Newhalem along the new Cascade Highway, this is your spot for consulting with a ranger. As usual, they are totally informed and informative about everything from the dangers involved in canoeing on the Skagit or hiking in the wilderness to changing the baby's diapers. (This also includes where to stay or eat.)

The panoramas are fantastic and if you can lay your hands on a booklet entitled *North Cascades Highway*, do so if you're making this trip. If you can't, there are overlooks at Gorge Dam . . . Diablo Lake . . . Ross Dam and then one 34 miles up the hill from Ross Dam at Washington Pass.

Among other things, the booklet will advise you to take nothing but pictures and leave nothing behind you — especially your litter — and . . .

Fill your gas tank!

They are not kidding when they say this is wilderness.

A word about eating – *The Log House Inn*, built in 1885 with hand-hewn siding and 1890's atmosphere has the best food around.

A word about sleeping — Motel accommodations along this route are few and far between. Check locally as to what is available and adequate.

The road to Newhalem winds in and around heavy rock walls. Ferns poke out of mossy tree trunks, and the river runs dark green through a narrow gorge over moss-covered boulders dating back to early rock slides. Just before

Newhalem is *Goodell Creek Campground,* a good place to picnic among giant trees and sandy beach.

Newhalem — (Pop. Nom. Elev. 500) — It's a model City Light town and take-off point for *Seattle City Light's Skagit Project tours.* The highly popular tour includes first-hand looks at giant dam powerhouses and reservoirs, a trip up a near vertical mountainside via incline railroad, a boat trip on Diablo Lake, a colorful walk through the rock garden to astounding Ladder Creek Falls, and a family-style dinner. Advance reservations must be made through City Light's Seattle office. However, if you're just in Newhalem to look around, or take a self-guided mini-tour to *Ladder Creek Falls,* there might be an empty place at the dinner table . . . and the dinner is fantastic.

Newhalem is very tidy, well kept, and attractively laid out in a beautiful gorge of the river. Worth driving and walking around — especially the park area along the river and across the bridge.

For further information — Call Seattle City Light at 623-7600.

From Newhalem, the road climbs to Diablo Dam which derived its name from the fact that in the old days when the fellows thought they could find rubies and gold in the mountains, they had the devil's own time passing a turn in the river here. So they called it "Devil's Corner."

But then the area was taken over by Seattle City Light . . . and if you've ever worked for a municipality or any other governmental unit, you'll know that the customers always write. So there they were, stabbed with a terrible public relations problem. If they called it Devil's Dam, they surely would hear from the hinterlands.

So they called it "Diablo" Dam.

The folks who can speak Spanish are worldly enough to care less . . . and the others don't know . . . so no squawks.

The *North Cascades Highway* taps the North Cascades Pass and its two associated recreational areas, Ross Lake and Lake Chelan. As early as 1937 a federal study reported this area would outrank in its scenic, recreational and wildlife values, any existing National Park and any other possibility for such a park within the United States.

The Park Service is bracing itself for an onslaught of about 10,000 visitors a day and hopes it will be skillful enough to keep us from tramping the place to death — a realization that was not reached with Yellowstone Park until a century too late.

Stop at the *Ross Lake Overlook* to see the 24-mile-long reservoir stretching all the way to Canada through the North Cascades National Park and Pasayten Wilderness area. A striking topographic feature of the North Cascades is the approximate uniform elevation of the main ridgetops. Towering above are 2 dormant volcanoes, Mt. Baker and Glacier Peak, and several granitic peaks of exceptional height. This portion of the Cascades contains more active glaciers than any other area within the conterminous United States.

Continuing east on the North Cascades Highway, rushing Ruby Creek is the road's companion all the way to *Rainy Pass,* elev. 4,860, and then to *Washington Pass*, elev. 5,477, where it is time to take one last admiring view of the spectacular scenery before heading back. (No facilities for 75 miles between Marblemount and Mazama.)

Return to Rockport, and then drop down to Darrington along the Sauk River which cascades between converging valley walls. The Suiattle River comes down from its glacier on the east side of Glacier Peak to join the Sauk halfway to Darrington. Ancient barns dot the landscape, and frequent markers point the way to fishing and camping sites.

Darrington — (Pop. 1,120. Elev. 527.) — Darrington's most famous "forestry" product — and it is famous for forests — is Dr. Barney Dowdle of the College of Forest Resources at the University of Washington. It is a clue to his character that it's still "Barney," not "Bernard," and another clue is that he gives most environmentalists and the U.S. Forest Service fits.

Not only that, but he does it well, backs his statements with facts and is invited to speak at a whole slew of meetings all over the country dealing with the subject of forestry.

His general theme is that the Forest Service does a lousy job of handling the nation's forests and that economically our forests would be in a lot better shape today if they'd been left in the hands of the so-called robber barons. He also contends that Gifford Pinchot, the father of the Forest Service, had the wrong basic philosophy for most American forests.

Pinchot, for example, was trained in Europe where they used to practice selective logging exclusively . . . in Pinchot's day a forester went through the woods marking ripe trees. These were then cut down — very carefully — allowing the younger trees to grow to maturity. And it sounds like a great idea until you compare forests to agricultural crops. According to Dowdle, Pinchot's theory is in the same category as walking through a field of ripening wheat and selecting only the individual heads of grain instead of mowing 'em all down at once.

Dowdle makes the point that big companies like Weyerhaeuser cut forests, regrow them fast and recut them again because they have an economic motive. But there is no relationship between the amount of money the Forest Service produces and the amount of money it gets. The Service is beholden to Congress for its funds and Congress is influenced by a whole bunch of things besides forest management. So the Service loses $170 million a year managing forest lands that would show a profit and grow bigger and faster if they were operated by private owners.

This is due at least in part to the fact that the Service is in the position of managing this resource with a "bag limit" like you are forced to do with wild crops like deer or fish. Every time you think you've got it made on the conservation front with this philosophy some poacher nips in and nabs a bunch illegally — and you haven't got it made at all. It generates a philosophy of "Why should I refrain from taking this deer — so somebody else can get him?"

On the other hand, Dowdle points out, if your forests were privately owned, like a herd of cattle, the owners would not be forced to sell the product when the market is down — as often is the case under working circle forestry — or unable to sell more when the market is up. Private foresters could follow economic trends. They are motivated to keep forests healthy to take advantage of them . . . and make a buck at the same time.

On the question of clearcutting, which sets so many people's teeth on edge, you might take a look at the trees around Darrington — because, they're growing on land that once was clearcut. Dowdle makes the point that in privately owned forests, the owner would adopt the best practices to preserve the trees on his land. In this area, clearcutting is the best practice. It looks like the devil for a while, but it returns faster if it has been "mowed."

Dowdle likes to illustrate his point on selective logging versus clearcutting with a story about his grandfather and the apples grown on the old family farm which is still intact near Darrington. "When we were eating the apples he had stored for the winter," Dowdle says, "he always instructed us to pick out the rotten ones first. By the end of the year we discovered we'd spent the whole year eating rotten apples."

Darrington sits on the banks of the Sauk River in the shadow of snow-capped White Chuck and the Whitehorse Mountains, and backed against smaller Gold Mountain.

Well-marked scenic drives to forests, mountains, and streams radiate from the center of town. If you're feeling less adventurous, visit the *Stroll Gardens* right in town. (See *Footloose*, pages 72, 74.)

Uncommon shopping – *Darrington Hardware & Supply* will fill all of your shopping needs from intricate fishing gear to Scotch Tape. Highly recommended by local folks, and they're who count.

A word about eating — Homemade soup and homemade gossip at *Mr. Ed's* where a sign reads: "The customer is always right. Perhaps misinformed, inexact, bullheaded, fickle, ignorant, even abnormally stupid. But never wrong."

Annual affairs – *Timberbowl Rodeo*, last weekend in June. Logging contests, milking races and horse events . . . *Grange Fair* in August. Together with Arlington and Stanwood, *Stillaguamish Valley Frontier Days*, continuous through August. Fishing derby, boat races and fiddling contest.

From Darrington, our route 530 heads west through the picturesque Stillaguamish Valley, shadowed by mountains and crossing the "Stilly," as the river is known, or its creek tributaries along the way. (See *Footloose* p. 72-74). *Squire Creek County Park* along the way is a good place to picnic.

At Oso, turn off Highway 530 north to a gravel and dirt road that switchbacks up to *Lake Cavanaugh*, an undeveloped getaway spot, with spectacular valley views through tall timber along the way. This route continues on to Pilchuck Creek and Big Lake and on back to Mount Vernon. Should the road to Lake Cavanaugh not be passable, continue to Arlington and pick up Highway 9 north which leads past farms to Big Lake and back to Mount Vernon.

Mount Vernon Tour 3 —
Anacortes, San Juan Islands (Map VI)

Although there are some 172 of them — depending upon the height of the tide at the time — the highlights of this tour are 3 of the San Juan Islands: Lopez, Orcas and San Juan. These are serviced by Washington State Ferries, the most modern, comfortable and colorful mass transportation system on earth. (Shaw Island has ferry service but is largely residential and not covered in this tour.)

You head west from Mount Vernon across the flat, diked land of two river deltas, over a bridge to Fidalgo Island, and past a whole bunch of big oil tanks surrounded by green grass to Anacortes. The town slopes to a point on Guemes Channel and faces Guemes Island, which is largely privately owned and operated. Anacortes provides services for the San Juans and the nearby oil people and as a consequence, is one of the more cosmopolitan towns in Skagit County. which makes it pleasant for prowling.

The beauty of the ferry trip is the proximity of the islands it travels through . . . with sudden and surprising turns that open up new vistas and perspectives. Even the most hardened commuters get a kick out of criticizing the landings, and newcomers to the scene flip over the dexterity of the ferry crews in maneuvering the bulky boats into position at the docks.

Lopez is the most pastoral and least-populated of the trio you'll visit. Orcas has a fantastic, 360-degree view from the top of Mount Constitution. San Juan is the county seat and site of two historic National Parks.

You're traveling through water that's rich in marine life . . . among peaks of submerged mountains with precipitous, rocky shores that have occasional sandy beaches. A lot of the land is in the rain shadow of the Olympics and so arid that cactus grows naturally.

And the people? You've heard about the celebrated independence of a hog on ice . . .

Well, he learned it from them.

Anacortes — (Pop. 7,760. Elev. Sea level.) — You get into some of the background stories of a city like this, and you can't figure out whether to label them historical or hysterical. The railroad boom in the 1890's is a case in point.

What happened was this.

As you will learn in more detail later, Governor Isaac I. Stevens was charged by Congress with finding a railroad route from the Mississippi River and over the Cascade Mountains to Puget Sound.

Now, it is quite possible that Governor Stevens said something about Fidalgo Island (on which Anacortes is located) to his son, Hazard, because the latter bought a chunk of land here. What he may have said is not on the record, but what the real estate promoters said he said is very much a part of Skagit County history. *The Illustrated History of Skagit and Snohomish Counties*, an impressive turn-of-the-century tome that sells for about 150 bucks if you can find one, puts it like this: "In the interest of this great enterprise he examined all of the great harbors of the Sound with zeal and thoroughness . . . enthusiasm and pride in the performance of his great work . . . (that) have marked Stevens as the first hero of the territory.

"The result of this investigation was the choice by Stevens of Fidalgo Island as the proper terminus and Ward's Pass at the head of the south fork of the Skagit River, as the most desirable gateway to the Pacific . . ."

This kind of information excited the imagination of one Amos Bowman who bought the Steven's property from Hazard's sister in 1877 for $1,000 and set about promoting it as a railroad terminus. Bowman was something of a one-man band. He was a civil and mining engineer, a scow builder, pile driver, a notary public, the operator of the general store and a real estate developer. He named the town after his wife, "Anna Curtis" Bowman . . . and got really turned when somebody — probably the Northern Pacific Railroad, which was honeying around these parts at the time — offered him $10,000 for his townsite.

If somebody else was willing to pay him that much for the property, he figured that with the proper promotion he really could pick up a bundle. So he put together a publication called *"Northwest Enterprise"* and circulated it throughout the United states with the message that this was the terminus site selected by Governor Stevens. He said, obviously Stevens had bought it as an investment that would pay off when the railroad was built.

It took a little time, but by 1890, Anacortes was a boom town. There were 27 real estate offices on the island and they had agreed on a startling slogan for the place — "Magic Town" — not knowing or, perhaps not caring that there were "Magic Cities" sprouting like mushrooms all over the Pacific Northwest. In January, the population of Anacortes was 40. By February it was 500, by March 1, it was 2,000 and two weeks later, 3000. As the *Skagit Illustrated History* put it, "the boomer boomed, the promoter promoted, the gambler gambled, the grafter grafted and the sucker sucked . . . ."

The Northern Pacific had given serious consideration to this spot as the location of the terminus of a possible road out of Spokane along the northern tier of counties . . . but the N.P. was about half-railroad and half-real estate company. A boom for land it didn't own was the least thing it wanted. Bowman's propaganda campaign was the town's undoing. The Northern Pacific pulled out. Then, as the history book put it, "The great boom broke almost as suddenly as it had begun. In 1893, the hard times struck Anacortes with full force and many were the ruined fortunes and hopeless failures scattered along the shore of Fidalgo Bay."

But what were the magic words that Governor Stevens uttered that got Bowman going? They couldn't have been spoken to Amos because Stevens was killed in the Civil War before Bowman showed up on the scene with his proposed metropolis. And it certainly doesn't show on the record, for the record puts Stevens squarely and irrevocably in favor of what he called "Snoqualmoo" Pass in his 1,500-page report to Congress. He also referred to Duwamish (Elliott) Bay as the principal and most useful harbor in Puget Sound, adding, "Seattle is an admirable harbor for a great railroad, being landlocked, defensible, accessible and commodious . . . ."

In Steven's book, Fidalgo Island didn't even have a look-in as a railroad terminus. Stevens did admire Mt. Erie and mentioned that Fidalgo was "the first island on the north of Deception Pass . . . ."

What Stevens must have said to his son, if he commented on it at all, would have been, "Hazard, my son, this might be a nice place for a summer home."

One of the proposals that occasioned one of the more famous fights in Anacortes was referred to in Phil Bailey's scintillating weekly Seattle publication, *The Argus*, as the "Rape of Guemes Island," The Skagit County Commissioners are still smarting over the drubbing they took in 1966 at the hands of the guys of the "Save the San Juans" Committee which opposed locating an aluminum plant on that essentially residential piece of landscape. Bailey put it this way, "No company, be it an aluminum company, or Boeing, or a supermarket, should be allowed simply to purchase a piece of land because it is cheap or suits their purpose without considering the social and economic impact involved . . . ."

The attorney who headed up that fight against the aluminum people went on to bigger things on the national scene and probably will go down in history more because of his involvement on other fronts than in the "Rape of Guemes . . ."

His name: John Ehrlichman.

Anacortes these days is one of the more sophisticated towns in the county — what with the advent of refineries nearby, its forest products and seafood industries, the summer homes of wealthy Seattleites on adjacent Guemes Island and, of course, the folks from the San Juan Islands, who do a lot of shopping here.

Prowling Anacortes

Just to get your geographic bearings, drive up Mt. Erie, at 1,300 feet, the highest point on Fidalgo Island. From the summit you have a 360-degree view of three mountain ranges, the San Juan Islands, and a cluster of freshwater lakes at the mountain's base.

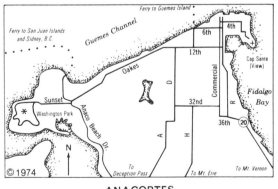

ANACORTES

Closer to town, *Washington Park's loop road* offers water views through Douglas fir — and usually a glimpse of a deer or two. At the *West Beach marker*, a trail leads to the shore and its rocky outcropping, teeming with sea life at low tide. Poke around, and you'll find sea urchins, tiny starfish and sea anemones in the many tide pools. (See *Footloose*, Pages 50-53.)

Cap Sante Park, on a headland jutting into waters between Guemes Channel and Fidalgo Bay, has a marvelous view spot overlooking the oil refineries, marina and general harbor activity. Picnic at *Causland Memorial Park*, 8th St., with its unusual stone wall, copied from an Austrian park. Or let the kids loose at the new *John Storvik Park*, until recently, a vacant lot, and now beautifully landscaped with playground sculpture, picnic tables and complete recreational facilities.

Best place to watch the harbor activity is the *Port dock* at the foot of Commercial Ave., where ships may be loading cargoes of canned salmon and lumber. Or catch the *Guemes ferry* for a short ride to that island where you can picnic and treasure hunt on beaches alongside the ferry dock. The return run provides fine city views as well as a close look at tankers coming in to the refineries.

Stop by the *Post Office* on Commercial to enjoy the contemporary Philip McCracken sculpture outside the building and the 1932 Kenneth Callahan painting inside. In an old Carnegie Library building on 8th St., check the *Anacortes Museum of History and Art*, displays — Indian artifacts, fascinating 19th century doctor's office upstairs, art downstairs.

In late spring, Anacortes fishermen practice another kind of art, mending their nets before heading north with their purse seiners. At *Bryant's Marina*, foot of 11th street, weathered fishermen repeat the age-old knots and ties on miles of outstretched nets with floats.

For a change of pace, visit the work of Italian *totem pole carver*, Paul Luvera, a retired grocer, who successfully sells them 'round the world. To see an outdoor display of his art, drive past his home at 2101 9th Street.

Browsers will enjoy the *Fisherman's World Market*, 7th and Commercial, a colorful collection of small shops and galleries in the handsomely renovated Keystone Hotel.

Plant tours are possible at: *Shell and Texaco Refineries*, March's Point, modern petroleum refineries; *Scott Paper Co.*, "R" Ave., manufacturing sulfite pulp from alder; *Publishers Forest Products*, 35th & "V" St., processing of logs to plywood and hardboard; *Whitney-Fidalgo Seafood*, 4th St., and *Fishermen's Packing Corp.*, 3rd St., for salmon and tuna canning in season. Call ahead on all, or check with the Chamber of Commerce.

Uncommon shopping – *The Thread Mill*, Commercial Ave., behind wild-colored windows. Kris Carlson stocks a tasteful mix of weaving supplies, jewelry, import yarns, and crafts . . . *Burton's*, Commerical Ave., has "art you can use" like Dansk, teakwood, porcelain, cast iron . . . *Marine Supply & Hardware*, Commercial Ave., owned by Mike Demopoulos, who collects items by the thousands, some of which date back to the '20's, perfect for male browsing . . . *Dorway's Antiques*, on Deception Road, especially for Victorian antique collectors . . . *Church Mouse House*, Second-hand shop run by Christ Episcopal Church — from pianos to antique stickpins.

A word about eating — for the view, the *Hatchcover Food and Grog*, "T" Ave., where you can watch ships from Japan take on lumber. Good for steaks and salad bar . . . *Perry's Skyline,* at Flounder Bay, with great views of the Yacht Basin.

A word about taverns – *Brown Lantern Tavern,* Commercial Ave., has a cozy log cabin interior and is quite fun — lots of local color.

A word about sleeping — Visiting oil refinery VIP's stay at the *San Juan Motel,* 6th & "O" Sts., in the middle of town . . . For island-goers, the *North Vue,* Ferry Terminal Rd., overlooking the ferry dock . . . *Holiday* and *Islands Motels* are on Commercial.

Annual affairs — Anacortes' sizable Croation population celebrates *Croation Spring Festival,* dinner in May before the fishermen head out to sea. Spring lamb and suckling pig on a spit, folk dancing, and native costumes . . . *Anacortes Arts & Crafts Festival,* first weekend in August; small, and quality, with a unifying theme; highly professional painting, crafts, poetry and dance . . . *Barbershop Quartet Show & Barbecue,* last weekend in July, features the An-O-Cords and big salmon bake . . .

For further information — Chamber of Commerce, 14th and Commercial Ave., Anacortes; phone, 293-3832.

Washington State Ferries — The road to "Ferry Land" is westbound, well-marked and well-patrolled. We don't know what the law's attitude on ferries is, but it surely believes in radar en route. Double-check to be sure you're in the right lane at the ferry landing or you may end up in Sidney, B.C., when all you wanted was Lopez. If you're island-hopping, make advance arrangements with the guy in the ticket booth.

Unless you're mid-day, mid-week and off-season, get there early or you may sit there until the next ferry and sometimes even the one after that. You will be loved, honored and obeyed if you're a foot passenger — and there's a parking lot for your abominable automobile at the landing.

It's about 45 minutes to Lopez . . . another 15 minutes to Shaw, almost entirely residential and not in the tour . . . 5 minutes more to Orcas . . . and an additional 35 minutes to San Juan. The "times" presume normal schedules. The island roads are good and the prowling productive.

You're boarding one of the vessels of the greatest ferry system on earth, as you will have an opportunity to personally observe.

The Washington State Ferry System, although confined for the most part to what has been called the "Mediterranean of the Pacific," annually carries 8,000,000 passengers a distance equivalent to 90 voyages circumnavigating the earth. It hauls more than a million tons of freight every 12 months. And it's the nation's largest ferry system.

The system's predecessor, the "Mosquito Fleet," a network of small boats darting around the nooks and crannies of Puget Sound like mosquitoes, performed its own singular service in the development of civilization on the Wet Side of the Mountains . . . and, our ferries shape as well as serve communities. They ply between the 3rd largest population center on the Pacific Coast on the east side of Puget Sound and one of the least crowded and most desirable land masses on the west side.

You may not have figured this out, but a whole slew of real estate people have, and real estate is the biggest booming business on the islands. The aroma of real estate people is strong in the land all the way from the Cascades to the Ocean. Sometimes it's sweet and sometimes not so sweet.

Commenting on our ferry system in the May-June 1971 issue of *City Magazine*, Urban Planner Talbot Wegg wrote, "You say you're a commuter? You say you live in a tastefully mortgaged rambler on a postage stamp lot in lovely Valhalla Village? And for this you endure a never-ending hour, twice a day, five days a week, 50 weeks a year, with the nightmare of American Transit?

"Which is your particular rack and pinion? The filthy train that can only freeze or fry but never runs on time? The lurching, roaring, stinking subway in which you once (you can even remember the date, April 1, 1954; April Fool's Day) found a seat? Or the diesel bus, which pollutes as it crawls, and transports you in a swaying gas chamber, from which you stagger forth, nauseated or asphyxiated, or both?

"If, as with 99.7 percent of the nation's transit riders, one of these is your sorry bag, you're not about to believe there is a mass transit system whose vehicles are clean, comfortable, and uncrowded; in which *everyone* sits down, can eat a leisurely breakfast, or even stretch out and catch those last few winks of sleep he missed at home. A mass transit system that runs on time comes rain or snow, hell or high water — except for one seasonal and unpredictable hazard, a need to slow down and dodge a pod of killer whales (running 25 feet in length and 100 in number) which frolic like elephantine porpoises in pursuit of salmon, but sure raise hell with the running gear . . . ."

Wegg neglected to mention a further thought-provoking consideration. The Washington State Ferry System has run for going on 25 years without a single passenger fatality.

And there is yet another cogent point. In addition to operating without fumes or fatalities, our ferry system has but infinitesimal use for asphalt, concrete or bridges . . . and for that matter could do very well indeed without automobiles. As Governor Dan Evans notes, "With more effective coordination of shoreside and seagoing transit systems, we should be able to reduce the number of commuters' cars on the ferries and hence in Seattle's streets and parking places.

"I look for the development of wholly new types of passenger ferries, perhaps like air-cushion vessels in use in the English Channel. (Ed. Note: Or like the new Boeing Hydrofoil that doesn't bust up when it hits a log.) Such technical improvements might well lead us back to smaller vessels operating in the manner of the old Mosquito Fleet . . . ."

Lopez Island — This the most pastoral of the three islands, and as the W.P.A. *Guide to Washington* published in 1941 noted, its temperature and climate are admirably suited to agricultural pursuits. (The south one-third of Lopez is in the driest zone on the Wet Side of the Mountains, as is the west and south side of San Juan. All the rest of the islands are "2nd driest.") The *Guide* also pointed to the fact that deer are not uncommon and it is not unusual to see them swimming the narrow passages between the various islands "in search of fresh pastures . . . ."

Well, the fresh pastures on Lopez are guarded by fiercely independent farmers who fail to welcome these graceful wild creatures of hill and dale grazing on their crops. The animals may find fresh pastures, but they also may find themselves on somebody's dinner table. There aren't many game wardens on Lopez and there are lots of guns. And the two butcher shops on the Island sell less meat per capita than any other two butcher shops in the State.

It's a closely knit Island too, and the presence of a newcomer is detected fast. We liked the story of the New York lady who called the Volunteer Fire Department on the Island. The lady's problem was that her son had not written her since moving to Lopez. The Volunteer Fire Department has a multiple ring that caused all 12 of the volunteers to pick up their phones at home. The New York lady explained her dilemma to the 12 good men and true, they descended on said son, and in a couple of days his mother had a letter.

One of the nice customs on the Island is waving, so just wave back if you're waved at as you drive by. An islander summed up his attitude toward strangers by saying, "During the summer most of the population is from Bellevue and California and in the winter, you are regarded with tolerance until you trespass and then the chances are you'll be shot."

Prowling Lopez Island

You take a long road through magnificent trees due south from Upright Head, which is where your ferry made contact with the island, past *Odlin County Park*. It's a place you will want to visit during your stay on the Island because it's got one of the best sandy beaches in the San Juans. You emerge from the trees and from then on you'll be encountering fields and woodlots . . . and roads that go mostly straight ahead, left, and right, rather than curving around things. As you head into town, make a note of *Betty's Place*, because that's where you get the most interesting food on the Island, but you must make a reservation.

Lopez — (Pop. Nom. Elev. 25.) — "Town" is to your right at the Chevron Station and consists primarily of a neat little general store. The Bay Restaurant is closed because "she" went to work at the *Islander-Lopez Resort* . . . and that just about has to be your destination if you're staying overnight.

The Islander-Lopez is on Fisherman's Bay, a deep inlet on the west side of the Island with gradually sloping shores which the Islander has taken the most advantage of. It really is a beautiful location . . . and there's great "driftwooding" on the spit that creates the bay.

A little farther along is *The Galley – Tavern, Restaurant, Cocktail Lounge* . . . with the tavern being the hangout for the "Locals." Just taken over by new owners who have remodeled and are providing some of the best dining out in the Islands. Away down to the south overlooking Mackaye Harbor is *Richardson's* "on the rocks," a dandy country store with everything from popsickles to Coleman lanterns.

Nearby is one we wish you could see but can't because it's privately owned; the home of the only man we know who has to mow his roof. (It's made of sod.) The other spot that you can visit to beachcomb and watch the ferries go by is *Spencer Spit State Park* on the northeast side of the Island. Other than that it's fun to drive around and look at the graveyard and the old square houses.

Lopez has not as yet been overwhelmed with population.

A word about eating – *Betty's Place* for home-cooked meals with vegetables from their own garden, served family style to a maximum of about 20 people. Advance reservations . . . *Islander-Lopez Restaurant*, great view of bay, open for dinner, also a coffee shop . . . *Fisherman's Bay Cafe*, features good pie and soup . . . the aforementioned triple-threat *Galley*.

A word about sleeping – *Islander-Lopez Resort* has an attractive 2-story motel building overlooking the bay and steady traffic from the boating crowd, and spectacular sunsets, Jacuzzi and regular pools . . . *Betty's Place* has a couple of rooms and cabins.

Orcas Island — This is the "resorty" Island, and has curved roads. The literature lays claim to 25 resorts tucked in here and there and about. They sort of go in and out of business without that much advance notice. The big deal here is real estate. The number of real estate offices here has jumped from 4 to 17 in the past several years and there seem to be a lot more going "in" than "out" of this business.

P-I reporter, Walter Wright, must have had a particular reference to Orcas when he wrote that San Juan County is "exceptionally Republican and incredibly white." One of the stories they tell on themselves concerns "The Presidential Election in which the Island voted solid Republican. Thinking of Nixon in 1972, the casual listener is inclined to mutter "What's so unusual about that?" And they pounce on him with, "For Landon in '36?"

Our favorite illustrative anecdote about the folks on Orcas may be apocryphal, but it is illustrative just the same. The story is that a gentleman farmer, fresh from Seattle and with limited knowledge of ranching, found himself rich enough to indulge in a lifetime dream of raising cattle. He bought some animals that had a reputation of surviving on twigs and branches. They weren't doing well and the "Vet" suggested that what they really needed was hay.

Hay was a new commodity to the "rancher" in question and he did what any other wealthy, upper-middle-class American from Seattle would do when he had a problem. He called Frederick & Nelson's about it. And pretty soon a "Frederick's" truck with a load of hay showed up at his ranch on Orcas Island.

Not everybody on Orcas is a retired millionaire, although there are quite a few of them in the "Gold Coast" area near Deer Harbor. There are some retired school teachers and a representative number of artists and craftsmen, who do very good things. But the pace for the Island was set in 1903, when the doctors told 47-year-old Seattle shipbuilder, Robert Moran, he'd damned well better get away from it all or he wasn't going to survive. He bought up 20 percent of the Island in order to do his thing (subsequently turned it over to the public in the form of *Moran State Park*) . . . and then went on to live to the ripe old age of 86.

This is a great "retirement" mecca for people from over half the states in this country and a few foreign countries, and population statistics show an enormous number of older people. But there's an adage about retirement that holds true here if ever it held true any place: You just can't retire from something; you have to retire to something. People who are running away from themselves don't get along here . . . and leave.

Outside of the real estate and resort people, the folks living on the Island want to "sink the ferry behind them" once they get on the Island, and just keep it like it is. (The ferry people will tell you a different story, although it may be that the people they hear from own real estate offices.)

There are 45 active organizations, but the one that charms us the most is the one involving the Seattle Symphony Orchestra. The orchestra, which has been doing neighborhood concerts around and about for some time, has a wise policy of not visiting any place under the auspices of a single organization. They want total community involvement. And here they get a county-wide involvement. The concerts are held on Orcas, but people come from all the islands in a ferry chartered for the event. Ladies of Orcas Island provide the transportation — once the ferry has docked.

And sometimes, because of limited seating facilities, it's a "bring your own chair" affair.

Prowling Orcas Island

You head north from the ferry landing on the west slope of a small mountain range until you reach the primary farmlands of the Island, which, prior to the advent of irrigation in eastern Washington, was the leading apple-producing county in the State and was the place where the Gravenstein apple was originated. Then you curve into . . .

Eastsound — (Pop. Nom. Elev. 30.) — The metropolis from which all roads fan out to the two wings that make up the Island. One drive takes you along the valley to West Sound with shoreline most of the way to Deer Harbor, a protected bay with lots of marine activity, boaters and a view of the massive cliffs on the opposite side from the high scenic road.

The whole Island is some 56 square miles, and all of it you can drive and is either scenic or quaint or both.

You haven't been to Orcas if you haven't driven to the top of *Mount Constitution*, the highest spot in the archipelago — and in Moran's park. It's an easy drive through a lot of northwest flora, and once in a while some fauna, to a castle-like stone turret. You climb its stairs to look out on a tremendous 360-degree view of Canadian and American islands and mainlands. The experts suggested replacing the picturesque tower turret with something more efficient, but before the islanders got through with them, they retired from the field dripping — with blood. The park is about 5,000 acres, has a lot of trails, lakes and camping grounds.

Also on this drive, is a drop down to the water to *Rosario*. Originally Moran's home, it's one of the three finest resorts on the Wet Side of the Mountains. If you have the necessary bucks and a reservation, this is probably the place you'll be staying. If not, it's worth dropping by for a drink or a meal.

The *Historical Museum*, at Eastsound, is made up of several home-steader log cabins which have been taken apart and reassembled and contains a lot of interesting Indian artifacts and pioneer memorabilia.

Scenically situated, *Deer Harbor* attracts many pleasure-boaters to its marina and it is developing accommodations and services for them, with buildings and boardwalk that retain the simple, turn-of-the-century look of its earlier days. There's a tavern-grocery store combo with pool tables and early-type beer license which enables you to serve yourself.

It's worthwhile to dip off into the side roads — some are pleasant remembrances of the Island's highly agricultural past, others take you to little water's-edge villages or resorts that are capitalizing on the best views and bays.

Uncommon shopping — At Eastsound: *Bungalow Cafe*, newly enlarged dining room overlooking bay at Eastsound, very reasonable ... adjacent, fascinating *Darvill's Books and Gifts*, advertises it has the greatest collection of old prints in America ... *Orcas Island Pottery*, in a cabin in the deep woods, with very good stuff and an interesting lady ... *Harbor Lights Antiques*, with marine view ... *Cottage Gift Shop* ... *Le Petite Bookends* ... *Dotty's A-1 Bakery*, good baked goods, like bread, cookies, pastry ... *The Joyeux Dolphin*, artist Pat Hegre's shop of local arts and crafts, antiques, decor accessories; also Eastsound's nautical headquarters, charts for boaters ... near Eastsound, *Crow Valley Road Pottery*, in a pioneer log cabin ... *Stonewall Antiques*, new in 1973, featuring nautical glass ... *Whaletooth Farm*, with old household utensils, postcards, memorabilia.

A word about eating — Look to *Rosario* for the best. The *Orcas Room* of the mansion overlooks the water, serves three meals daily; also *Discovery House*, on the water, for dinners, entertainment. Cocktails in both ... *Island Vista Coffee Shop*, overlooking ferry landing, noted for good hamburgers ... nearby *Cundy's Orcas Hotel*, dinners 7 days a week in large old frame building ... *Deer Harbor Inn*, for family-style cooking in a farmhouse atmosphere ... *Outlook Inn*, for homemade soups, pies, cakes, and a homey old building ... *Bartel's Resort*, pleasant view dining overlooking the strait ... *Chambered Nautilus*, rustic and attractive on Doe Bay, organic foods, sweet and sour ling cod, eggplant Parmigiana, cauliflower soup.

A word about sleeping – *Rosario* has everything ... *Deer Harbor Marina* motel, with harbortown atmosphere ... *Bartel's Resort*, year-round with view and dinner ... *North Beach Inn*, with housekeeping cottages spaced for privacy, breakfast and dinner ... *Beach Haven Resort*, log cabins with fireplaces ... *Obstruction Pass Resort*, with sandy beaches ... *Cundy's Orcas Hotel*, longtimer overlooking ferry landing ... *Outlook Inn*, which can sleep three families.

Annual affairs – *Family Festival*, in mid-May, has slalom bulldozer race, pancake breakfast, barbecue; with Mardi Gras at Friday Harbor ... *Historical Society Parade*, 3rd Sat. in July ... *Episcopal Church White Elephant Sale and Tea*, last Sat. in July. A 25 year tradition and lots of fun ... *Library Board Fair*, second week in August. Arts and crafts sale ... *San Juan County Horseman's Association Show*, mid-July, alternated with San Juan Island.

For further information — Write Chamber of Commerce at Orcas Island (no phone or formal office), or call any of the resorts.

San Juan Island — Thanks to the topography here you can drive the coastal perimeter of this Island more easily than the others and get marine views from as divergent places as treeless prairie and high, lime-filled cliffs. The central part of the Island still offers farming interspersed with woods and a couple of lakes. You probably will see eagles and hawks soaring overhead, most of them preying on the prolific rabbit population which has given rise to a sport called "bunny-netting." You sit side-saddle on a jeep and blast off into the night with flashlights, nabbing hapless bunnies, providing you have permission from local landowners.

This Island has the lustiest history of the bunch. The Indians used to fight other Indians. Then they fought the whites. Then the whites fought the whites. And now the whites fight the Planning Commission.

Friday Harbor — (Pop. 803. Elev. Sea level) — What with being a port of entry into the United States . . . the county seat . . . location of the University of Washington Biological Laboratories and the only moving picture show in the county . . . you readily can understand why this is the only town in San Juan County officially listed as having an urban population. And sometimes that urban population gets upset over proposed innovations.

As you're entering the neat little harbor, you might try to imagine what a five-story condominium would look like on the waterfront . . . because that's the most recent issue at hand, as the citizens try to cope with the crowds of people who would like to live on this island. And you might wish to note the Imperial Gardens Motel, which is where the battle lines were drawn in what was referred to in June 22, 1972 issue of the *Friday Harbor Journal*, as "The Big Debate" between the attorney for the condominium people and the Friday Harbor postmaster.

The paper noted the attorney used a "high tension presentation" and the postmaster used a "fishing rod" to make their respective points. The attorney denounced his opponents as telling "lies, lies!" And the postmaster merely suggested the condominium plan was "an outrage!"

The paper said the discussion was "heated."

The State Department of Ecology and the Attorney General's Office sided with the Citizens for Responsible Development of the Port of Friday Harbor and the Save Our Port Association. And on July 11, 1973, the *Journal* announced that Superior Court Judge Richard Bryan of Thurston County, (where the case had been taken to preserve some semblance of equanimity, we presume) had vacated the permit granted by the Town Council for the condominium. The net result of the whole flap is that there will be no condominium.

Lawsuits still are pending however, and you may have to inquire about the latest news on this front when you arrive here.

But, on April 15, 1973, the San Juan County Commissioners hired Lou St. John as the County's first Planning Director.

Shortly thereafter, Mr. St. John was quoted in the *Orcas Island Booster* in the following manner: "Quite frankly, the first day I set foot in Friday Harbor to take over my new job it was just like coming home. I love this area and feel that it is a wonderful to raise my family . . . ."

Two months later, Mr. St. John no longer was County Planning Director.

In a subsequent issue of the same paper, Mr. St. John was quoted as saying, "I simply could not accept the hostility shown me by the local residents . . . I could not subject my family to such erratic pressures as I have encountered in Friday Harbor . . . . They (the County Commissioners) told me they were sorry to see me leave and they tried to explain that as soon as the summer season set in that people would be too busy to carp at the Planning Department and things would settle down. But I could visualize the same trigger-happy business happening year after year. During the winter months the people are more or less trapped on the islands with little to do but work people over when they disagree with them. If that's their kind of entertainment, fine, but I don't care to be the subject of such harassment . . ."

"To this minor, but vociferous group, planning smacks of a Communist plot . . ."

This episode evolved from a highly self-expressive public meeting in Friday Harbor on May 7. And there you have it, a wonderful example of the rugged individualism typical of the kinds of people who live on islands anywhere in Puget Sound . . . most especially San Juan.

And, of course, the meeting occurred at their Madd Theatre.

Prowling San Juan Island

The flag you see flying from the waterfront, as your ferry pulls in, rises from the focal point of the main street — Spring Street. Along with a couple of trees, a couple of seats and a war monument, it comprises a miniature town square . . . and something of a traffic hazard. When you drive off the ferry go around it on the water side, or you'll be going the Wrong Way. Not long ago, "progress' demanded that this traffic hazard be removed, but the Garden Club Ladies rallied their forces and the square remains.

Friday Harbor is a pleasant little town reminiscent of about 1906, with an increasing evidence that the folks figure their economic bread is now buttered by tourists instead of limekilns, commercial fishing boats and agriculture. There are a lot of charming, unfussy, restored houses of turn-of-the-century vintage, not to mention some stores which have done a tasty job of blending the old and the new. The town isn't all that big and you will find the prowling profitable if you park your car and sort of wander around. Four blocks up from the ferry dock, you'll find the two-story, 1890 frame building that houses the *San Juan Island Historical Museum*, (summer Sundays 2-4 p.m.) with memorabilia of the early days.

Also on hand, is the unpretentious *County Courthouse*, where the picture of Kaiser Wilhelm I (the man who arbitrated the San Juan Islands into U.S. hands in 1872) may or may not be hanging. They took him down during the hostilities of World Wars I and II, but the janitor may have hauled him out of the basement again, now that ex-Chancellor Willy Brandt has visited this country.

Walk through *Sunshine Alley* and you'll pass a colorful wall *"mural"* painted block by block on the side of a cement block building by San Juan children. It has an indigenous quality with its emphasis on Indians, boats, whales and some mixed-up versions of the American and British flags. The previously mentioned Madd Theatre has its enjoyable moments, too. The *Strait of Juan de Fuca Players* take to the boards in early summer with melodrama or musical comedies.

North of town, turn in for a visit at the *University of Washington Biological Laboratory* — that's if you're there between 2-4 p.m. on Wed. or

Sat. This handsome cluster of buildings had its origin in 1923 and is there because the San Juan Archipelago has exceptionally abundant and varied marine flora and fauna. U.S. and foreign students and researchers work with uncontaminated seawater and often with living specimens. The locals tend to refer to this as "The Bug House." While you're around Friday Harbor, keep an eye out for the river otters that often live in boathouses.

Driving the Island, turn off Spring Street at Argyle and start south along Griffin Bay. The little island in the bay is *Dinner Island,* named because Captain Vancouver anchored and dined there in order to avoid trouble with the Indians ashore. A short way beyond, turn right and you will find the white frame *1873 San Juan Valley Community Church,* now used only for special occasions such as weddings and funerals. Adjacent are pioneer graves dating back to 1873 — the Protestants buried next to the church and the Catholics segregated in consecrated ground across the road.

You're headed for *American Camp,* 5 miles away and *English Camp,* at the opposite end of the Island. Both are National Park sites. It will not require any monumental effort on your part to find out why the "American" and "English" camps are National Historic Park sites . . . there are markers, books and pamphlets to tell you all about it. It all goes back to 1859, when an American by the name of Lyman Cutler (or Cutlar—depending on your source) shot a pig that invaded his potato patch. The owner of the animal, an Englishman, demanded that Cutler be brought to trial in Victoria. Cutler defied the British authorities and the whole Island got embroiled in the argument. The Americans asked for protection by the U.S. Government, which obliged with troops from Fort Nisqually. The British responded by moving in 3 warships. While the matter went to arbitration by Kaiser Wilhelm I, troops from both sides occupied the respective camps on the Island. Anyway, they called the whole thing the Pig War. It was a comic opera scene with the troops on either side staging parties for each other and the English Commander sending to Victoria for a bigger house so he could entertain more graciously. It finally was settled 13 years later.

A couple of stories not so generally known have tickled our fancy. The Pig War stemmed from the fact that the United States and Great Britain were a little hazy about which of three passages between Vancouver Island and the mainland constituted the boundary line when they settled the Oregon Question in 1846. One of the passages in question was Haro Strait — called "Canal de Haro" in those days. The Washington State Legislature was a little less than accurately informed about the whole thing, too. And on July 31, 1859, with magnificent aplomb, that body sent an irate memorial to Congress demanding that the line be fixed along "Canal de Arrow."

The business about the Hudson's Bay Company . . . and the boundary . . . and the Pig War was a little more involved. While the United States and Great Britain took the case of the boundary to the Kaiser, the Bay Company took its lawyers to Washington, D.C. demanding reparations for having been dispossessed of valuable lands, buildings, sheep and cattle trading and navigational privileges in Western Washington.

Among the acreage involved was all the land from the Puyallup to the Nisqually Rivers and from Puget Sound to the summit of the Cascades . . . 251 square miles . . . 167,000 acres. Governor Stevens opined the company should be paid only for places where it had buildings and fences. He thought this was worth maybe $50,000. As long as he was around, the company got short shrift. But Stevens was killed in the Civil War.

In 1865, long after Stevens died, the company presented a bill to the United States for $4,970,036.67. Finally, in 1869, the United States paid the company $650,000.

Three years later, the Kaiser rendered his decision in favor of the United States, a decision that set the boundary where it is today, and gave us the San Juans. But we weren't through with the Bay Company yet.

We suddenly discovered on May 24, 1872, shortly before the Kaiser's decision, that the company had neglected to pay us some $50,000 in back taxes, which we never did collect.

The neatest twist of all involved the soldiers we had sent to wage the Pig War. They came from Fort Nisqually . . .

For 20 years, the United States had been paying the Hudson's Bay Company $50-a-month rent for that fort . . .

Which, as it turned out, the Hudson's Bay Company hadn't owned in the first place.

At *American Camp*, you'll feel a brisk breeze blowing over this treeless prairie which commands a sweeping view across the Strait toward Pt. Town-send — undoubtedly why Captain Pickett, of later Gettysburg fame, selected this somewhat forlorn site. No buildings remain but 6 mounds which formed the earthworks for the artillery and plaques, including one for Lieutenant Roberts of Roberts *Rules of Order* fame. The boulders lying about are glacial "tramps" dropped during the Ice Age. Also listen for the melodic sound of *skylarks* in the only place they are found in the U.S. — having migrated over from British Columbia where they were brought by the English. Peale's *Peregrine falcons* winter in this area, also, and at any time of the year watch for bald and golden eagles and various owls.

Little holes along the edge of the road are rabbit warrens and undoubtedly you'll see white-tailed bunnies popping in and out. Further down at *Cattle Point* (so named because cattle used to be loaded there to and from Victoria) there is an unmanned lighthouse and the prairie gives way to sandy dunes bristling in season with American and Canadian thistles and cactus. This part of the Island lies in the Olympic rain shadow receiving only 14 to 16 inches rain annually. Nearby is the *Fish Creek* area where commercial fishermen dock their boats. The road goes west to *False Bay,* a little, almost round bay which earns it's name by virtually disappearing at low tide, but provides the warmest saltwater arond the Island, also good picnicking.

West, past fertile valley land that once — in 1912 — held the world's record for production of dry-land wheat, you'll be passing near the cattle ranch belonging to *the* author (*The High and the Mighty*, et al), Ernie Gann.

High on the edge of cliffs overlooking Haro Strait you come toward *Limekiln Light* and a landscape that surprisingly resembles California's Monterey Peninsula. This is the other part of San Juan Island that is in the driest zone in Western Washington.

San Juan County Park is a huge park on a bluff overlooking a little bay that is a favorite with snorkel and scuba divers. The park property was a gift from an eastern couple who had so enjoyed this lovely spot with their son, that they could no longer bear to come back to it after he was killed in World War II.

A far cry from the bleak, windblown prairie of American Camp, *English Camp* is civilized with its green "lawn" edging sheltered Garrison Bay. Some buildings remain, including a replica of the neatly painted white blockhouse at the water's edge. Newest replica is the tall flagpole — placed there by the National Park Service in the fall of 1972. The replacement went up exactly 100 years to the day from when the original one came down. (The British cut down their flagpole when their occupation ended to prevent any possibility of the Americans flying their flag from it.) There is a huge *big leaf maple tree,* said to be the world's largest. You'll see it in the movie filmed for the Washington Pavilion at Expo '74. After searching the State for a tree that would represent one that a little girl might think "God lived in," the filmmakers gave the big maple the part. On Mt. Young, behind English Camp is a small *cemetery* where seven Royal Marines and a Hudson's Bay official lie buried.

Roche Harbor — As you come into town, note brick limekilns built into the bluff on the right side. Here's where the fires burned and you can see remnants of the chutes above, where the limestone rock was dropped and slid down into the fires. A step further are more primitive arrangements of limekilns built by British soldiers during their occupation, around 1859-72. The ramshackle old sheet metal building was where the "cooked" rocks were ground into lime flour.

Tiny Roche Harbor is a startler, particularly in summertime; brightly flowering gardens lead the way from the dock up to the little *Hotel de Haro* which stands with barbecue courts, and more flower gardens and trellises adjacent.

It is the legacy from the earlier days when the rich deposits of lime-stone made one John S. McMillin an exceedingly rich man. After his arrival in 1886, Roche Harbor became strictly a company town controlled by him, and he and his wife embellished the place and loved to show it off to boatloads of business acquaintances who came for lavish weekends of wining and dining.

At the north edge of town, a dirt road leads into a forest where you will find Mr. McMillin's extraordinary *mausoleum.* In a quiet clearing a large circular cement platform supports seven 30-ft. Tuscan columns. In the center a cement table is surrounded by cement chairs, most of them serving as crypts for the ashes of family members, with their identification on the backs of the chairs. Now a marina and boatel complex has made this town a mecca for visitors, especially boatsmen, from both the U.S. and Canada. (Roche Harbor is also U.S. Customs Port of Entry).

In honor of the close international relationship, a ritual occurs each night of the year on the pier, just as the sun goes down and the afterglow lights the harbor. By recording or live bugler, "Colonel Bogie March," "Oh Canada," "God Save the Queen" and "Retreat" are played as one by one the colors that fly every day are struck for the evening. On Memorial Day, 4th of

July, Fair Day and Labor Day, a formal colorguard of U.S. Marines from Whidbey Island, conducts the evening color ceremony.

The road leads back southeasterly to Friday Harbor.

Uncommon shopping — First 3 blocks of Spring St. — named for a spring that has been covered over but keeps various businesses from having basements. *Ship Shop*, rough-hewn boards, high ceilings, nautical things plus clothes, dishes, paintings . . . *Boardwalk Bookstore*, on a new boardwalk . . . *Treasury House*, gifts and apparel in old false-front drug store with new front porch supported by columns from old schoolhouse . . . *Betty de Staffany's Town House Shops*, antiques, organic foods, gourmet cookware in an 1876 house . . . *Boutique Dubois*, colorful shop of giftwares, yarn, needlework in a '90's building embellished with old figurehead . . . *Ravenhouse Art*, reflects owners interest in good American Indian crafts and owners' own notecards and pictures featuring Indian designs . . . *Island Gallery*, in the former Odd Fellows Building.

A word about eating — Friday Harbor: *Sweet Tooth Saloon*, delightful ice cream parlor, church pew seats, sewing machine tables, bullet-shattered mirrored bar and tax-included prices because the old cash register can't ring up pennies . . . *The Mariner*, a sweeping view from the waterfront . . . *Rip Tide Cafe*, favorite spot for swapping local gossip during coffee breaks or cocktail hour, 7 days . . . *Imperial Gardens*, in new motel, featuring Chinese buffet Wed. nights, regular buffet Sun. . . . under construction at this writing is the *Great San Juan Salmon, Codfish, Cheese & Sausage Co.* on the site of the Old Reliable Deli. Roche Harbor: *Roche Harbor Restaurant*, cocktails, dockside on the waterfront.

A word about sleeping — Friday Harbor: *Moore Motel*, comfortable 11-unit older place . . . *Imperial Gardens Motel*, a little way out on Second Avenue, new two-story building, Japanese tea garden effect, covered pool . . . *Tourist Hotel*, modest 1882 hotel with 12 units . . . *San Juan Hotel*, recently charmingly restored in 1884 tradition. Roche Harbor: *Hotel de Haro* (Teddy Roosevelt's 1906 signature in register book), and Lyman Cutler's "pig-shooting" shotgun (hanging from a rafter in the lobby) in original modest 1880's style . . . *Roche Harbor Resort*, housekeeping cottages. Either place, swimming, riding horses, salmon fishing, Olympic-size pool and bunny-netting.

Around the Island there are other friendly places scenically situated, mostly modest, several offer bunny-netting charters. *The Oaks*, cabins near beach, east side . . . *Mar Vista* and *Snug Harbor Resort*, cabins on west shoreline . . . *Lonesome Cove* (north), cabins, good snorkel and scuba diving.

Annual affairs — *Friday Harbor Yacht Club Marine Parade*, 1st Sunday in May . . . *Memorial Day Parade*, Friday Harbor, organized and costumed groups march down Spring St., playing of taps at the WWI monument in town square. *Memorial Day Ceremony* at English Camp cemetery conducted by Marines from Whidbey Island, complete with raising of the Union Jack and 21-gun salute. A similar ceremony with U.S. Flag takes place at American Camp . . . *Lion's Club Rendezvous*, early August at Fair Grounds, for salmon, beer and camaraderie . . . *San Juan County Fair* – 3rd week in August at Fairgrounds, emphasis on horses, 4H beef, hogs and sheep, flower show . . . *One-Day Fall Salmon Derby*, Friday Harbor, about October 1 . . . *Winter Salmon Derby*, Thanksgiving to mid-March; King's Market, Friday

Harbor, weighs fish, keeps a running scoreboard. (Women tend to win.) . . .
Christmas Ship — Victoria Jaycees cruise islands with goodies for children,
symbolic of Islands' rapport with Canadian friends.

For further information — In Friday Harbor, the National Parks
Office, Spring St.; phone, 378-2240. Also, Girl Friday Service, Spring St.;
phone, 378-4600.

◄——

Mount Vernon Tour 4 — Skagit Flats, La Conner, Whidbey Island (Map VI)

La Conner, Deception Pass and Whidbey Island are the main
objectives as our route heads southwest from Mount Vernon along country roads checker-boarding the flat, diked farmlands of the Skagit River
delta. Weathered barns and farmhouses stand out against the near horizon; in the distance, lumpy headlands. These river flats serve also as
wintering ground for many species of migratory fowl, including the
snow goose and great whistling swans. From La Conner the tour crosses
the Swinomish Channel to Fidalgo Island. At Deception Pass, the
highway soars above the gorge where high speed tides boil through a
narrow gap. Whidbey Island stretches south some 60 miles, bisected by
the main highway. Rolling hills, dotted with farms and woods, border
the highway and there are views of the Strait of Juan de Fuca. The road
passes near the huge Naval Air Station and enters Oak Harbor, the
Island's largest metropolis. Several miles to the south, quaint
Coupeville spreads along the south shore of Penn Cove with its residences and picturesque waterfront. After climbing slightly to Greenbank, the road follows the Island's central ridge and skirts Holmes Harbor. At Columbia Beach is the ferry landing for the short trip to Mukilteo
and Everett.

Skagit Flats — An enormously fertile flatland created by diking the
delta of the Skagit River. Seattleites always did get along "putty good" with the
Skagit Flats farmers, but not 1 person in 1,000 today knows the biggest divi-
dend the major city on the Wet Side of the Mountains got from the investment
of a lousy 800 bucks . . .

This anecdote got its foundation in about 1864 when Sam Calhoun, a
shipwright at Utsaladdy, persuaded an Indian by the name of Sam Gallon (who
earned his title by drinking a gallon of hard likker at one sitting) to paddle him
around the delta of the Skagit River. The rest of the Indians thought Calhoun
was out of his mind when he proposed to farm this soggy spot. They and other
members of the intelligentsia of the period pointed out that Sam would be
hoeing his crops under water most of the time, because that's what the delta was
like when the tide was in.

But then, unlike Sam, they didn't know about dikes . . .

The biggest lump on the flats is Pleasant Ridge about 5 miles east of La
Conner and you might take a second look because that's where Calhoun

planted the first crop ever grown on the flats. His vegetables were prize winners and prolific. Of course, Sam also realized he'd have to dike elsewhere to keep the salt water out, but he'd done diking before and, as it turned out, some 10 years later, a guy named Ben Welcher invented a machine that could do a diking job for a little over $700 a mile, which was one of the keys to the opening of the 150,000 acres of the delta farming . . . .

Even today, dikes are the difference between paddling a canoe and driving a car over most of the acreage in the lower delta when the tide's in.

Calhoun found a couple of other characters hiding among the bull-rushes. There was Michael J. Sullivan, sole proprietor of a modestly success-ful smuggling business, who found this a convenient address whilst dealing with the U.S. Revenue agents. The other was Lyman Cutler (nee Cutlar), the forthright gentleman who shot the pig and caused the "Pig War." Mr. Cutler's friends had advised him that the geometric theorem, "Out of Sight, Out of Mind" was a good one to practice after the ruckus between the two countries got underway.

Sullivan gave up smuggling after the captain in one of the boats of the famous Puget Sound Mosquito Fleet gave him $1,600 cash at riverside for his first crop of oats. And by 1876, Calhoun was prosperous enough to have a foreman who ran an affidavit in the *Bellingham Mail* that the Calhoun proper-ties were producing between 60 and 100 bushels of hay, oats, barley and corn to the acre — a phenomenal amount in those prefertilizer days. By that time, knowledgeable farmers from all over the nation had flocked to the Skagit River delta and were making themselves comfortably welloff.

At least during the harvest season, it took every boat of the Mosquito Fleet small enough to navigate the river to haul the bounty of the land off to market.

And that's where the $800 investment came in.

Until 1877 two enormous log jams blocked the lower part of the river. Now, you may have seen log jams in your day, but we guarantee you've never seen ones like these. The worst one was above Skagit City on the south fork of the river. And if you have a burning desire to locate either it or Skagit City, try *Footloose*, p 62. Other than that, figure it was a little over halfway between Conway and Mount Vernon.

This jam had trees *growing* on it that were a couple hundred feet high and 4 feet in diameter. The Skagit County history notes that "there were from five to eight tiers, which generally ranged from three to eight feet in diameter . . . representing a total cutting space (when they started clearing the jam out of the river) of 30 feet . . . Beneath and between the tangled mass of debris the river was obliged to force its passage and in place beneath the lower jam there were twenty-four feet of water at the lowest stage . . ." The lower jam was about half-a-mile long.

The upper jam was at the bend in the river west of Mount Vernon, but it was twice as long and growing at a rate of about 400 feet a year.

Skagit City, which now consists of an old schoolhouse, was at the head of navigation and below both jams. Consequently it was the major town. Mount Vernon was just an idea in the head of one of the guys who was working his head off — trying to get somebody else to clear the jams out of the river.

Nowadays, our prodigal federal government would rush funds to a project like this, which would be duck soup for the Corps of Engineers. But Orange Jacobs, the Territorial Delegate to Congress (and a friend of the Skagit farmers) succeeded only in getting an army general out here in 1873 to look the situation over and estimate that clearing the jam would cost somebody other than the federal government $100,000 . . .

A hundred thousand bucks!? No way. They'd do it themselves!

Well, a group of 7 guys got started with money from a friendly Seattle banker who wisely took a mortgage on a Seattle lot that one of them owned, as collateral. They figured there were millions of board feet of merchantable lumber in those big piles, and they could make a fortune selling all this stuff.

They were cheered from the sidelines by everybody in the delta. They passed the hat right there and collected a couple hundred dollars. This project was even more important to some of the fellas in Seattle who had timber holdings above the jam, that were pretty to contemplate while the jams were in the river . . . but useless for logging as long as the jams prevented them from dumping their logs in the river and sending them down to collecting booms at its mouth.

So the Seattle lumbermen put the arm on some of their suppliers and together they came up with a contribution of $800, which wasn't much — but was by all odds the biggest single contribution the jam-clearing team got from anybody. The $800 wound up being 20% of the gross income from the project. It was a gesture the people in the valley never forgot.

A small item to remember here is that a Swede by the name of Alfred Nobel still was trying to persuade a skeptical world to try out a new product called dynamite that he had come up with, to replace the nitroglycerin that had been blowing innocent people to bits all over the world.

As the Skagit history says, "Brain and brawn, patience and judgment, with scanty resources of money, with little financial gain then or since were the distinguishing features of this, the greatest undertaking of the kind in the history of the county . . ."

Nature wasn't always helpful. Sometimes, it jammed the jam in tighter, but on one occasion, in the spring of 1877, it washed 5 big acres of logs out to sea, clearing the jam below the town.

That one fell swoop washed out the profits . . .

The banker foreclosed on the mortgage and the guys ended up $1,000 in the hole for their 3 years of dangerous back-breaking work. But they ultimately cleared both jams.

Concurrently, a few miles south, Seattle and the Northern Pacific were not getting on at all well. Congress had given the railway a grant of 50,000,000 acres of land with the stipulation it had to build track between the Mississippi and Puget Sound. Some 5,000,000 acres of that land was north of Seattle . . . which would give the company ownership of about 50% of the land between the Olympics and the Cascades.

To all practical purposes the Northern Pacific would own the whole Puget Sound Basin, which today holds the bulk of the State's population.

Of course, they had to build track to get it.

And the railroad played games with possible routes. It would file pretty maps with the U.S. Land Office from time to time showing that the track might go here and then again it might go there. And every place it *might* go — like the Skagit Flats — was withheld from settlement pending construction, which burned individualists like Calhoun, Cutler and Sullivan to a crisp.

Depression hit the world in 1873 and the railway was lucky to get track as far as Tacoma. The railway men figured that as long as they were that far and owned the town, lock, stock and barrel, they might as well make it the major seaport on Puget Sound.

They were doing a pretty good job of it, too. At least half of the businessmen in Seattle figured the big town would be where the railway touched tidewater, and moved to Tacoma. But the ones left behind were not about to take all this lying down and got into a big enough beef with the railway that the latter decided to put a quietus on this upstart village of Seattle for all time. It provided the Federal Land Office with a brand new map in which it proposed to touch tidewater at Tacoma with track up from the Columbia River, and then go east of the Cascades, south of Mt. Rainier, over Naches Pass — cutting Seattle off at the pockets . . . .

Or so they thought.

In the winter of 1877, Seattle ganged up with the Skagit Flats farmers who were delighted to add petitions from their 700 residents to Seattle's 700 businessmen and a little more cash and send Seattle City Attorney, J. J. McGilvra, to Washington, D. C. to see what could be done about screwing things up for the Northern Pacific.

The Skagit farmers added real weight to Seattle's arguments by pointing out they were being very well served by the Mosquito Fleet and why should the railway be given the subsidy of a land grant? That was a manifestly unfair advantage . . .

And the Federal Government agreed.

The result was the removal by Congress, of 5,000,000 acres of land in the heart of Puget Sound from the land grant — a neat 10% of the total the railroad was getting for crossing the whole country.

And did this ever burn the railway company. The company executives decided there was more than one way to skin a cat and set about dominating the Mosquito Fleet . . . by making Tacoma its headquarters.

But they were the source of their own undoing.

In those days, it took horses and mules to build railroads. Horses and mules functioned best on hay and oats . . . and by that time, the farmers on the Skagit Flats were raising more hay and oats per acre than were being raised on any other comparable piece of real estate in the nation. So the Northern Pacific — as well as the rest of the railroads that were laying track around and about the Pacific Northwest — got their hay and oats from the Skagit Flats.

And those independent captains of the Mosquito Fleet ships made Seattle their headquarters — bringing the railway to its knees, forcing it to connect up with Seattle . . . making the latter the major city on the Sound.

Joshua Green, who at this writing is the most venerable of the Mosquito Fleet captains still living, explained why.

"I made $200 a trip hauling hay and oats from Skagit Flats," he said. "I could only make two trips a week if my headquarters were in Tacoma. But I could make *three* trips a week if my boats were based in Seattle . . .

"Two hundred dollars more per week!

"It wasn't that I loved Tacoma less . .. but that I loved the profits more."

Prowling Skagit Flats

The territory you're passing through west of Mount Vernon is where all that early day activity took place. The upper jam was above Mount Vernon and the lower jam below it. Prior to the removal of the jams, Skagit City was the head of navigation. Today, it's barely a wide spot on a back road.

There is a significant side trip, however, to the multi-channeled exit by which Skagit finally takes to the sea. Head generally south on unnumbered roads to Fir Island and Conway.

Some 24,000 snow geese from Siberia winter in the *Skagit Wildlife Recreation Area*, in the lower delta. Best sighting is high tide on Fir Island, Jan. 15 to April, when they are in close, feeding on grasses and reeds. The geese, referred to as Skagit Snows, rest in the bay at night and move inland by day. When they leave for their nesting grounds, the entire mass lifts off in a 24 hours period between April 17 and May 5 — never before or after these two dates. (See *Footloose*, p. 68.)

La Conner — (Pop. 640. Elev. 40.) — This may seem like kind of a quiet little town — which is the way the residents like it — but a plot which was hatched here 90 years ago has sparked the current effort to cut King County into two pieces . . . never has the power of the press been more admirably demonstrated.

And it was the town's present paper, the *Puget Sound Mail* which did the demonstrating.

Things got underway on July 5, 1873 when one J. W. Power established the first newspaper in the northwest corner of the United States and called it the *Bellingham Bay Mail*. Those were the days when Whatcom County was a lot bigger than it is today and the town of Whatcom was the county seat. Mr. Power's chief financial support was derived from the publication of county notices.

Three months later, the *Mail* had occasion to engage in its first major fight. Those upstart farmers in the Skagit River delta at La Conner were circulating a petition to secede from Whatcom County, start a county of their own and call it Skagit. With vastly superior publishing power (La Conner had no newspaper at the time), Power was easily able to bring out enough support to squash the rebellion.

However, at the same time Mr. Power noted rather thoughtfully, that they were growing an awful lot of hay, oats and barley in the delta . . . and getting pretty prosperous.

Four years later, when the towns around Bellingham Bay were in dire economic straits, the *Mail* took a more conciliatory attitude to new demands for secession by the citizens in La Conner . . . like, "Let's let them have the county court and we'll keep the county seat." But things got worse instead of better on Bellingham Bay and by August 30, 1897, Mr. Power found himself with but a single advertiser. Two weeks later he moved his publication to La Conner, where the legal notices were printed, and changed the name of his paper to the *Puget Sound Mail*.

Bellingham Bay was without a newspaper until July 15, 1883, when one T. G. Nicklin, initiated publication of the *Whatcom County Reveille* with the stirring notion that his bugle call would wake people up at least once a week. In October of that year, he had occasion to really sound an alarm. By that time publisher Power had gotten himself elected to the legislature and, having come full circle, introduced a bill designed to create Skagit County. The *Reveille*, enthusiastically entered a campaign to defeat this outlandish action on the part of the Skagit delta farmers. A petition carrying 900 signatures was carried to the legislature protesting the division of Whatcom County and the bill calling for a new county was defeated in the Assembly Senate by a vote of 8 to 4.

The grateful citizens of Whatcom delegated to Mr. Nicklin the job of staying in Olympia for the rest of the legislative session as a watchdog in case the La Conner fellows got any further ideas about dividing up Whatcom County.

With talent like Nicklin protecting their interests in the Territorial Capital, everybody on Bellingham Bay relaxed and went about his business. Then, on November 30, 1883, without a warning peep from the *Reveille's* bugle, the blow fell. Word finally reached Bellingham Bay. A new bill had been signed, sealed and delivered . . .

Skagit County had sucessfully seceded!

Well, you know how it is when two old newspapermen get together. Power and Nicklin had had a little conversation over a cup of coffee in Olympia where they compared notes and agreed that with just one county they had to split the county advertising . . . whereas if there were two counties, each paper would get 100% of the income from each county's legal notices.

◆

Pioneer Monument marks the entrance to La Conner, reclining along the Swinomish Channel in a pocket of trees. Except for one small hill, the colorful village is a continuation of the agricultural plain. Weathered frame buildings house local businesses along First Street, backing on the waterway which links Padilla Bay with Skagit Bay. Purse-seiners, gillnetters, and pleasure craft share dock space along La Conner's waterfront, and homes line the bluff above First Street, spreading along the hillside beyond . . . all attracting artists in residence and motivating the area's placement on the National Register of Historic Sites.

Prowling La Conner

The town's whimsical charms are best displayed on First Street where a stroll up one side of the avenue and back the other will give you a look at most of the town's shops, and you'll pass the venerable *Puget Sound Mail* office.

Best views of La Conner are from the *Rainbow Bridge. Pioneer Park,* just before the bridge, is a good place to picnic. For vistas of the surrounding countryside, drive up the hill in back of town to the *Skagit County Historical Museum.* The looking is good inside the Museum too, with its regional exhibits of pioneer days.

The Swinomish Channel usually gets prolific smelt runs along about January or February and fishing for *saltwater smelt* is virtually a household sport here. Everyone, from small boys to housewives in curlers, line up on the bank and have a good time catching supper. You can join them too, and see why experts prefer the saltwater smelt.

Uncommon shopping – *Tillinghast Seed Company,* dates from 1891, even older as a mail-order firm. Store walls lined with bins of every possible flower and vegetable seed packet. Third generation Tillinghast, Ruth Dalan, helps make choices easier . . . *The Bookery,* well-stocked for browsing . . . *Pioneer Shop,* in the old hotel, for furniture, china and glass, lamps, even farm implements . . . *Hillside House,* now moved "down on the flat" from up on the hill, offers owner's hand-painted nostalgic floral designs on china plates, cups, bric-a-brac . . . *Den of Antiquity,* faded chartreuse curtains hanging outside the windows, has almost anything that is old, including clothes . . . *Craig's Pottery Gallery,* has wheel-turned and hand-built items, his and others . . . *Tallman's,* tiny shop in a tiny building, exhibits his own pottery . . . *Linda's Botanical Garden,* embellishes an old building with interesting greenery and good antiques . . . *Diamond Jim & Nasty Jack's,* has an eclectic mixture of barber and dentist chairs, oak furniture, Indian artifacts, iron beds . . . *La Conner House,* Sam Calhoun's brother's house tastefully restored by descendant of the Southwest's famed Wyatt Earp. Shop of kitchen and household accessories . . . *Swinomish Tribal Cannery,* visible across the channel, sells fresh seafood from local fishermen's catch, as well as processed fish.

A word about eating – *Courtyard Delicatessen,* Ulla and Jacques DeLourne (she's Swedish; he's French), tempting array of restaurant and deli items to the tastes of sizeable Scandinavian population; cheesecake, sherry cake or pickled herring, New York State cheddar cheese, crunchy rolls imported from a Vancouver bakery . . . *The Nordic Inn,* noted for Norwegian open-face sandwiches; in good weather, the brick terrace provides an openplace for the open-face . . . *The Lighthouse Inn,* overlooking the channel, has local fresh seafood, like oysters from nearby Similk Beach or Dungeness crab from the channel mouth; owner, Tore Dybfest, buys direct from fishermen and you can see the boats come in to deliver.

A word about beer — La Conner action is all at the *1890 Inn,* especially Wednesday night when schooners sell for a dime, and the gang comes rolling in from miles around. Live music, too.

A word about sleeping – *The Nordic Inn,* dating from 1907 as Hotel Planter, offers single rooms with community baths; rooms overlook First Street and have simple but authentic old furnishings.

Annual affair – *Smelt Derby,* held annually first Saturday in February, attracts thousands of freezing visitors to chance their luck in the channel's chilly waters.

For further information — The *Puget Sound Mail;* phone 466,3175.

The road leaves La Conner via the colorful Rainbow Bridge. Surpris-

ingly, you're on an island — Fidalgo — and the Swinomish Indian Reservation where fishing nets dry on front porches. The Swinomish Tribal Cannery
is on the water to the right. To the left is an Indian cemetery, its children's
graves bedecked with colorful plastic toys.

There are two alternate routes through the Indian Reservation. The
westernmost has the virtue of taking you past one of our favorite road names
— Pull and Be Damned Road — and Snee-oosh, which could be an opportunity to go to *Hope Island Inn.* It's not on Hope Island, but perched at the
water's edge looking at the Island. A very pleasant country inn, all white
and landscaped and good food; buffet on Sunday. You also have another shot
at the previously mentioned Mt. Erie (with, of course, nearby Lake Erie).
There is a spectacular 360-degree view and car-cushion travelers can make it
on their car cushions. (See *Footloose*, p. 52.)

The Deception Pass Bridge, arching above a narrow gorge between
Fidalgo and Whidbey Islands, offers one of the more spectacular sights on this
tour. The pass was so named when Captain George Vancouver learned it was
not a harbor as he first had suspected. The bridge is 1,350 feet long and 22 feet
wide, plus sidewalks. It's 180 feet above Deception Pass — which dumps 2½
billion gallons of water an hour into Rosario Strait at speeds ranging from 5 to
8 knots.

The bridge was completed in 1935, and the placement of the center
span is something Paul Jarvis, the engineer in charge of this ticklish chore,
never forgot. The bridge was completed from each shore, awaiting placement
of that huge section. One hot afternoon the cranes picked it up and put it in . . .

And it didn't fit.

Jarvis, an old hand in the bridge business, got out a thermometer and
his slide rule and realized the steel was too hot to handle at the moment, but it
was nothing a drop of 30 degrees in temperature wouldn't correct. So they
waited until 4 o'clock the next morning, turned on the floodlights, dropped
the section into place and it fit like — well, the way you see it when you drive
across the bridge today.

Deception Pass State Park, on either side of the span is one of our three
most popular State Parks, with annual visitors hovering around the 1-million
mark. It encompasses 1,800 acres and some virgin timber. There are nice
drives, views and 347 campsites for which you should make an advance reservation if you're around in the summer.

Whidbey Island — To clue yourself to the size of the Island, just
pretend you're leaving Seattle when you're at the north end and planning to
drive to Olympia 60 miles away — that's the length of the Island. But it's so
long, skinny, and contoured that no point on this Island is more than 3 miles
from saltwater, which you see on one side or the other most of the way. If
you're heading for the Keystone Ferry to Port Townsend, figure the amount of
time it would have taken you on old Highway 99 between Seattle and Tacoma
— and then add an hour for waiting (about 2 in all). Whidbey is the second
largest Island in the country and together with Camano Island, it makes up
Island County. The northern half of the Island is in the lee of the Olympia
rain shadow, making it dry enough in some places that cactus can grow here
naturally. Rainfall up here is about the same as the annual precipitation in

Rapid City, South Dakota, (about 17 inches) while at the south end, it doubles to nearly match that of Seattle . . .

The route takes you past the Pacific Northwest's major *Naval Air Station.* Commissioned on September 21, 1942, the installation was planned as a temporary establishment, but in December, 1949, it became big and permanent thanks to its favorable climatic conditions. With 6,200 military personnel and 1,200 civilian employees, it's Whidbey Island's largest industry, with an annual payroll of $71 million and a capital value of $276 million. It actually is two bases, 5 miles apart . . . the air station, Ault Field, and the seaplane base on Crescent Harbor — bracketing the town of Oak Harbor, and making that town bigger than either Mount Vernon or Anacortes, which comes as a matter of astonishment to most people not familiar with the Island. Even with our incomparable Coast Guard facilities on the wet side, the air-search teams at Whidbey NAS are comforting to have around. Originally put together to haul downed pilots out of the water, last year they went on 119 sea, mountain and river search-and-rescue missions — all civilian! The Naval Station is visitable — with groups, and usually on Thursdays, For details call the Public Affairs office, 257-2287.

Oak Harbor — (Pop. 10,445. Elev. Sea level to 65.) — It's a significant indication of the climate that the Garry oaks from which the town got its name flourish around here and have for several centuries. There's a full stand of them in a block-square city park and the tree by the post office is estimated to be 2,000 years old. But the dryness which permits the oaks to flourish makes problems, like the necessity for drilling wells 150 feet deep through stratas of manganese and iron which get into the water. The city had eight of them, but encountered arguments with the State Health Department over the quality of the product that they were serving.

Wilson Bow, the State Health Department's engineer in charge of this area, opined that the water gets so hard in some places you'd have a tough time chewing it. Hardness was rated at 163, which compares unfavorably with Seattle's, which is 10 . . . but not bad with Montana, which is 250.

Happily, the town's good neighbor at the Base long since had made the choice between more water-softening equipment and piping water from the mainland. The Navy's pipeline came across the Deception Pass Bridge and 11 miles down the Island to the Base.

A larger line was installed later by the city and about the time the State Health people started frowning on the Oak Harbor well supply, the town was able to work out a deal between their line and the Navy's line and in August, 1973 began using Skagit River water.

But that wasn't the end of the problem.

The Navy told us they had caught people illegally hooking up to their main line as it made its way down the Island.

"You've got water rustlers!" we delightedly informed Wallie Funk, publisher of the two Island newspapers, the *Whidbey New Times* and the *Whidbey Record.*

"That's nothing," Funk replied. "We also have sewer rustlers."

Well, that was one for the book.

Under deft questioning, Funk revealed that there's a community sewerage system at Penn Cove and for a long time the sewer commissioners suspected that some of the folks were making illegal use of their sewer lines. What the commissioner did, according to Mr. Funk, was put smoke bombs in the line and then checked homes to discriminate between the legal and illegal users . . .

Resulting in a process covered by either of two famous quotes, "smoking 'em out" . . . or "blowing smoke up their posterior extremities."

There was an item in the *Whidbey Island Record* on November 2, 1972 reading, "Dear Editor, It has come to my attention that certain persons are spreading the rumor that Eddie and I were 'kicked out' of our house in Freeland and this is why we moved to Langley.

"That's a damn lie and if you had come to either of us and asked for the facts, which incidentally would be none of your business, we may have told you why.

"But now you'll never know and I hope it drives you to distraction. Ethel Lieseke."

The above may or may not be as typical as it is comical, but it does show a degree of candor not often existing in the larger mainland towns, and it does provide a clue to the kind of individualistic thinking that goes on in islands in general and Whidbey Island in particular. It's in the same category as the lady clerk, three-quarters of a century ago, who was too lazy to put the "e" in the name, causing the Island to be spelled Whidby for decades until somebody looked up the proper spelling.

Prowling Oak Harbor

Oak Harbor has more "hustle and bustle" than other places on Whidbey. The main part of the town sits at sea level looking south toward Camano Island and curves with the crescent-shaped waterfront. Oak Harbor's front door is the beach and they have wisely kept it available as *City Beach Park*, where an outstanding civic band plays in the gazebo in summer. The first main street up from the beach is Pioneer Way, the "downtown" area and most shops, restaurants and accommodations are centered in a few blocks along here . . .

Nearby is *Flintstone Freeway*, a street built of rock and gravel on tideflats to form a mini-harbor for boats. Someone threw some extra rock together to make a replica of Flintstone's TV Stone-Age car and *everyone* takes a picture of this funny-looking "vehicle" . . . *Holland Gardens City Park*, a little way from downtown is a small open area with picnic tables and garden that features Holland bulb flowers in the spring and other flowers later . . . and a charming blue and white windmill building. Two tall flag poles fly big Holland and U.S. Flags, and in the summer there are shorter flag poles with the 11 provincial flags of Holland . . . all indicative of a predominant Dutch population.

Uncommon shopping — (On or near mini-parked Pioneer Way) *Piccolo Mondo*, smart boutique of fashions aimed at the younger woman . . . *Potpourri*, gay-looking shop of giftwares, candles, aprons . . . *The Little Gallery*, intimate gallery for prints, oils, crafts . . . *Collector's Corner*, antique furniture, spinning wheel, dishes . . . *Monique*, on Route 20, offers heavy-looking, traditional designs in table lamps, candlesticks, statuary. (Oak Harbor also has a number of pawn shops, like any other Navy town.)

A word about eating – *Chris' Bakery*, on Main Street — bakery with a view toward the harbor for "coffee and —", a friendly meeting place for locals. Danish pastries, doughnuts, cakes — and try for the cherry almond coffee cake. (When a drive was on to raise money for the park windmill, Chris baked a different huge coffee cake every Wednesday. Townsfolk came in, cut off their own piece of cake, put money into the "pot" and Chris turned the Wednesday coffee cake money into the windmill drive.) . . . *Candy Stick*, ice cream shop with an old-fashioned ice cream counter . . . *Pancho's Villa*, excellent Mexican food favored by Navy people . . . *Alfredo's*, good pasta and pizza. Makes own lasagne and salad dressing . . . *Island Cafe*, small in size but long in menu of Chinese food.

A word about sleeping – *Queen Ann Motel*, on Pioneer Way, has some kitchen units and King's Table restaurant adjacent . . . newest motel is *Acorn Inn*, west end of town.

Annual affairs – *Holland Happening*, last weekend in April; popular costume parade (Dutch and other), freshly swept streets, and Mayor plays Burgermeister in tall hat and frock coat . . . *N.W. Tulip Show*, shares same weekend, food, art and craft show . . . *Old-Fashioned 4th*, Fourth of July celebration held at City Beach with carnival atmosphere, parade, fireworks . . . *North Whidbey* (Riding Club) *Stampede*, late July, at rodeo grounds . . . *Naval Air Show*, alternate years in September. Whidbey's biggest event.

For further information — North Whidbey Chamber of Commerce, 5506 Highway 20; phone 675-3535.

Leaving Oak Harbor, on the south, a colorful drive is to take *Scenic Heights Road* about a mile out of town. The drive travels along bluffs above Oak Harbor to where the road drops and becomes Penn Cove Road, follows the water, and picks up the Island highway at San de Fuca.

Coupeville — (Pop. 703. Elev. 86.) — County seat of Island County, Coupeville is a charming old (1853) seaport town fronting on Penn Cove and with views of water and mountains wherever you look. There are a number of Victorian homes, lived in and kept up with pride, and there is pleasant open space between the buildings here which reflects the quiet openess of the Ebey's Prairie area adjacent to it. The general area is one in which to rest, enjoy and unwind.

Prowling the Coupeville Area

The Coupeville area, approximately 26 square miles, from the north side of Penn Cove to the Keystone Ferry — has been named the *Central Whidbey Historic District* and is now officially on the National Register of Historic Places. Meanwhile, the developers are breathing down the necks of the folks trying to contain the historic designation, and causing some tenseness in this "un-tense-looking" area. A local folder gives you information on historic places around the area and how to find them.

Heart of "downtown Coupeville" is a couple of blocks of Front Street — right on the waterfront — where 1880's frame buildings have been quite sympathetically restored and repainted in pleasing colors.

In addition to the delightful old houses and the handsomely restored grey and white church, whose bell still rings every Sunday, one can see *Capt. Coupe's (1853) house* (inhabited) with walnut tree which he planted there. It's at the east end of Front Street, and a few steps from the west end in a grassy plot, you'll find a display of preserved history in the form of the *Coupeville Blockhouse* (1885), *Indian dugout canoes,* and the *cross* that the Indians gave to Father Blanchet.

Across the street is the modest *Island County Museum,* with interesting local artifacts from early families — such as Capt. Coupe and the Crocketts — and, for such a small museum, a high-quality collection of N.W. and Alaskan Indian baskets, thanks to a gentleman who collected them as he went about these areas at the turn of the century, opening post offices. Museum is open Wed.-Sun. from April to Sept. Otherwise, by appointment.

In nearby *City Park* is a big slab of Douglas fir and a sign claiming that this tree was a sapling before Columbus discovered America.

Uncommon shopping – *Trader's Wharf*, big, old weathered wharf building, housing old and new whatever-it-is, like a flea market . . . *Old Town Shop,* false-front building with tasteful selection of cards, maps, gifts . . . several *antique shops,* a *candle shop* and a *weaving shop* . . . *Prairie Center Mercantile,* adjacent to Coupeville in Prairie Center, like an old general store — you can find anything here.

A word about eating – *Six Persimmons,* oldest building on Front St. (1864), oriental food with no choice of menu — you eat what they cook that day; weekends only . . . *Seagull Restaurant,* newly remodeled; food is best, including noted clam chowder, when Helen Williams is cooking . . . *Toby's Tavern,* good sandwiches and beer in folksy, 1890 building; photos, artifacts and nice-looking bar that came around the Horn . . . *Wet Whisker,* for ice cream, and coffee blends . . . *Burgerhaus* for hamburgers, shakes . . . *Captain Whidbey Inn,* 3 miles north, a charming, woodsy place for lunch or dinner, with cocktails and best food on the Island.

A word about sleeping – *Captain Whidbey Inn,* delightful 1907 madrona log house, accommodates only 37 people, so make reservations. Small rooms, venerable floor, community bathroom and lots of nostalgic clutter, plus old-fashioned hospitality. Also a few up-to-date cottages with fireplaces. On quiet waterfront of Penn Cove.

Annual affair — 2nd weekend in August, *Coupeville Festival Days.* Arts and crafts, sometimes a tour of homes, exhibits, salmon bake.

Between the Inn and tiny San de Fuca is the old *County Courthouse,* (about 1855) said to be the second oldest courthouse in Washington still in use.

For an historic side drive, take Sherman Road to its dead-end and back . . . to see the *old Sunnyside cemetery* and adjacent *Davis Blockhouse.* At the entrance to Ebey Road, you pass a lovely grey and white Victorian frame house, the *1892 LeSourd House,* then the *John Gould House* (1896) and the *Ferry House* (1860). As you drive along the serene, open, natural prairie space on Ebey Road, up the hill on the right is *Jacob Ebey's saltbox house.* Two miles from Coupeville on Ebey Road is *Ebey's Landing,* where the road is at sea level and there is a narrow strip of sandy beach and a vast panoramic view from Canada to Mt. Rainier. Five hundred-foot sandy bluffs rise from the beach to the *Enchanted Hills*, where ancient Douglas fir trees have twisted into fantastic shapes — and it is dry enough here that there is some cactus growing on the bluffs. This is a "unique shoreline" for Puget Sound, and the National Parks people are studying it in hopes of preserving 2-3 miles of seashore. (See *Footloose*, p. 54.)

If you are a history buff, you'll also want to look for the *Crockett Blockhouse* on Ft. Casey Road.

Easily the most dramatic episode in the history of Whidbey Island was the murder of Colonel Isaac N. Ebey by some northern Indians, who then cut off his head and took it with them. Most of the Colonel's mortal remains are comfortably ensconced in *Sunnyside Cemetery*, and there's a marker above Ebey's Landing, noting the approximate spot where he fell. But the mystery of the missing head still remains.

Colonel Ebey was quite a man. He was the author of the bill that created Pierce, King, Jefferson and Island Counties out of what had been Thurston County, and was instrumental in the creation of U.S. Mail service on Puget Sound and of the Third District Court. He was prosecuting attorney in that district and a probate judge. He succeeded in getting the folks to change the name of the State Capital from Smithfield to Olympia. He tried but failed in his attempt to have the State named Columbia and Lake Washington named Geneva.

His chief claim to fame was his appointment by President Franklin Pierce as U.S. Collector of Customs, the appointment which probably caused his demise. Some American had killed an Indian chief some place else and the Haidah Indians, who operated on an eye-for-eye and tooth-for-tooth basis, arrived at Ebey's homestead on the night of August 11, 1857. When he inquired what they wanted, they told him they wanted his head, killed him and took it — a gruesome event even in those troubled days.

There then ensued a 2-year search for Ebey's head, which was found in a Kake Indian village in Alaska and duly presented to the bereaved family for burial along witht he rest of his remains. At least that's the way the majority of the history books have it. But Jimmie Jean Cook, the Island's most meticulous historian, holds that only the scalp, not the head was returned.

Documents of the Territorial Legislature fail to shed any further light on the subject although that group of men passed a resolution on January 20, 1860 thanking one Charles Dodd for returning the relic. The initial paragraphs of the resolution thank Dodd for getting the Colonel's head, but the concluding one thanks only for returning the scalp. And at the moment, nobody knows for sure whether one or both are buried there.

As recently as 1973, the Smithsonian Institute in Washington, D.C. got into the act. In a letter to Dorothy Neill, historian and one of the more colorful and delightful people living on the Island today, Anthropologist Susan Olsen noted that the Smithsonian had received a death mask purported to be that of Colonel Ebey. She wished to have the head or scalp for purposes of making photo-micrographic and spectrographic tests to determine the authenticity of the mask.

Miss Olsen wrote, "What I need most is *one* hair off the good Colonel's head." She said she realized that this was a rather unusual request but added, "since everything from the time of Colonel Ebey's death has been quite morbid, I don't want to add to the occasion. It is, however, the only way we can scientifically make positive identification . . . it is absolutely essential. The contribution made to the Arts and Sciences for future generations would far outweigh the additional dent on the poor man's crowning glory."

To date, and in spite of vigorous effort, Miss Olsen has failed to have the grave opened.

Although it is not generally known at this writing, there also was supreme drama in the death of Judge Lester Carlos Still, the man who did more for the Island than any other single individual, and one to whom all of us should be appreciative. Judge Still owned a great deal of property, part of which now is the Oak Harbor City Park. He provided the right-of-way which gives the public access to the beach at Port Nugent. He played the key role in preventing the sale of timber in what has become one of the State's most visited parks at Deception Pass and an important role in the construction of the Deception Pass Bridge. He personally, with his own hands, built what now is known as the *Captain Whidbey Inn,* by all odds the Island's most interesting resort. And he had the first automobile on the Island, now the centerpiece of the Island County Historical Museum in Coupeville.

State Health Department records show the cause of his death was "cardio-respiratory failure due to barbituate poisoning . . . self-administered sleeping tablets . . . on October 18, 1960 in Anacortes." And the Skagit County Probate Court records include the following words from his will, "I hereby direct that no funeral services be conducted . . . that my body be cremated and my ashes must repose on my land at such location as my executrix may select."

Judge Still's niece, Margaret Still Harris, of Anacortes, executrix of the Judge's will, provides us with the high drama of his final days. The Judge was suffering from a terminal illness. He lived alone because he would not inflict his problems on somebody else and would not move into a nursing home. The Judge once told her, "I have made my own personal decisions all my life and I shall make the final one. My race with life has been run . . ." When he had made that final decision, Judge Still fashioned an urn for his ashes out of a piece of concrete pipe and wrote his initials and the date of his death in the wet concrete. The he placed a hot water bottle at his feet and a pillow at his head and covered himself with a blanket . . .

Thirteen years after his death, the urn was moved from his land to the Sunnyside Cemetery where his ashes now reside . . . but the memory Mrs. Harris holds was included in the last lines of a poem he had left for her when he made that final decision: "To live in the hearts we leave behind is not to die . . ."

Fort Casey, a fascinating State Heritage Site, is one of the coast artillery posts established during the late 1890's. Its scenic 110 acres includes massive cement parapets, guns, an interpretive center in the 1895 lighthouse (oldest on Puget Sound), picnic area, a couple of miles of saltwater beach for clamming, or fishing. (See *Footloose,* p. 56) Seattle Pacific College conducts summer classes here in the old barracks.

The United Sates Army refrained from building Fort Casey for half a century after it first was suggested. The delay was stimulated at least in part when an investigating major observed a cistern on top of a lighthouse located here and suspected it would be hard to come by an adequate water supply . . . and partly because of politics.

Admiralty Head was an entirely logical spot for erecting one of the forts necessary to guard Puget Sound in the days before the long-range artillery and the airplane. But there were a whole lot of communities around Puget Sound with more political clout than the folks on Whidbey Island. They all had reasons why they were the best location for the fort. Everybody was a military strategist when various chambers of commerce around and about thought up reasons for getting the garrison's payroll in *their* town.

Then on February 15, 1898, while on a good-will tour in Havana Harbor, the battleship "Maine" was blown up, killing 264 men and two officers. A Spanish investigation held the cause of the explosion was external. Congress appropriated $50,000,000 for defense purposes.

And the chambers of commerce on Puget Sound concluded, "Good God, man, we *all* could be blown apart by those guys!" So the politicking stopped and the Army built the fort where they thought it belonged. They named it in honor of Brigadier General Thomas L. Casey, Chief of the Army Engineers and the man who had engineered the construction of such notable structures as the Potomac Acquaduct in Washington, D.C., the Library of Congress building and the Washington Monument.

One of the features of the 5 powerful 16-inch guns at the fort was the design which enables them to sink into the ground for reloading. The lead "flew" in 1938 when 16,000 pounds of this metal used in the counter-weights disappeared, and the official anger motivated the Federal Bureau of Investigation to arrest a couple of W.P.A. workers for stealing it.

When you pass *Crockett Lake* — right alongside the road, near the State Ferry to Port Townsend — you might like to know it's outstanding for its wildlife, and birdwatchers have reported over 100 species of birds here.

A couple of miles south on Route 525, where the Island is narrowing to its slimmest span, is a road to the west, which leads to Ledgewood Beach, noted for its concretions. Commonly called *mud babies* from an Indian legend, these are the odd-shaped, small clay formations found on some Sound beaches.

North of Greenbank is the *Pomerelle Loganberry Farm,* largest in the world. Visitors may stop in any time as caretakers are there even in winter. Best time is August, when the crop is harvested for shipping out. It's worthwhile to stop here if only for the natural beauty of the site. From the top of a narrow rise you can see Saratoga Passage, close in on the east, and Puget Sound, close in on the west, plus Cascade and Olympic Mountains — a terrific piece of real estate.

For a side trip, south past Greenbank, look for signs to *South Whidbey State Park,* which tends to be less crowded than many State Parks. It's 100 acres of forest and beaches on Admiralty Inlet, with clams and hiking. (See *Footloose,* p. 58.) A couple of miles south, at Bush Point is a glorious view and a return to the highway on Bush Point Road. (Useless Bay, incidentally, is so named because it is shallow, open to the winds and tough on ships.)

A few miles further, past Freeland (for Freeland waterfront and Holmes Harbor, See *Footloose*, p. 60.) signs for *Maxwelton Road* lead you to brief, scenic side-trip to Maxwelton Beach and picnic area, with lighthouse, and a beautiful view of Kitsap Peninsula and the Olympic Mountains.

North, on Maxwelton Road, the highway winds through a bit of pastoral scenery and comes into South Whidbey's only incorporated town.

Langley — (Pop. 503. Elev. 50.) — sits on the waterfront facing Camano Island, with attendant pleasure boat activity and sports fishing about. A block-or-so shopping area, overlooking the waterfront, is developing attractively here . . . an artist has revitalized a frame building to house his gallery, plus a shop for knitters, sewers and weavers, and a smoke and pipe shop which sends its special odors all over the country, and there's a delightful barbershop done in Victorian decor, an antique shop, a shell shop with a cross-country business, a breakfast and lunch restaurant, specializing in homemade pies and an ice cream shop, with a deck in the back overlooking the water. And a new mini-park where you can sit on benches or read the community bulletin board.

For further information — Write South Whidbey Chamber of Commerce, Langley, 98260.

At Columbia Beach, where you get the ferry to Mukilteo, note *Virina's Weathervane Restaurant*. If you call ahead (giving Virina time to get the fresh fish she insists on), the restaurant will do a Luau for your party or a full Japanese dinner . . . which you enjoy along with the view over the water. Mukilteo folks like to do this and they enjoy going out to dinner by ferryboat.

REGION FOUR

SNOHOMISH, KING, PIERCE AND KITSAP COUNTIES

A Word About Region IV

What we got in Region 4 is people.

And what the people in Region 4 are trying to do is get out of it.

Mostly, it's just to go fishing, but one spectacular group effort on this front is sponsored by some malcontents in Woodinville who want to secede from King County.

They hope to create their own county and build a reverse version of the Berlin Wall that would keep people out instead of keeping them in. The territory they're shooting for is in the foothills of the Cascades. They want to call it "Cascade," but the name "Weyerhaeuser" County would be more appropriate, because it's the taxes they could collect from that company and a few others like it with rich timberlands that would foot the bill for running the proposed new government unit.

The region got started in 1851 when David Denny, Seattle's original real estate promoter, wrote a letter to his brother, Arthur, who was laid low with the flu in Portland, saying, "Come on up and found a town. There's room for 1,000 families here." The real population crunch was initiated, however, when the Northern Pacific's rails breathed new economic life into the Puget Sound Country exactly 100 years ago. Never in his wildest dreams — and he had some pretty wild ones before he died — did David Denny anticipate the runaway population inflation that has hit this region in one short century . . . . It's almost as bad as what they've got in California. The best evidence of what is happening to us lies hidden in the statistical reports of the Washington State Department of Agriculture. The most comprehensive of these reports was published in 1969 . . . and things have gotten more so since.

As it is today, some 80% of all the people who live on the Wet Side of the Mountains live in Region 4.

Kitsap County kind of pulls the average down with only 44% listed as urban population, a figure that should rise with the new Naval operations at Bangor. It should begin to emulate Snohomish, which has had the greatest switch to urban living in the last decade of any county in the State. Pierce comes in at 82% urban population and King County tops every place with 92%.

The thousand families David Denny figured there was room for has grown to 3,000,000 people in this region.

Interestingly enough, in spite of all its expensive sewer projects, King County still runs well in many agricultural products. In 1969, it was number 4 of the 19 Wet Side counties in total market value of farm products, and held the same relative position in dairy cattle. It was number 3 in farms with sales of $20,000 or more. There are those who will not be astonished that King nudged Thurston out by a bristle as number 1 in "hogs and pigs." Region 4 was number 1 in snap beans . . . although snap judgments are rapidly coming up.

And it's number 1 in the nation in "rhubarbs" . . . field and hothouse, that is.

165

Everett Tour 1 — In and Around the City and Mukilteo (Map VII)

Everett started out as and continues to be a major industrial city. The original concept was that it would process the products of a hole in the ground, but when they failed to materialize, the main thrust of the manufacturing was turned to wood products. This was the location of the Weyerhaeuser Company's pilot mill in the Pacific Northwest, and a trip around the waterfront takes you past the world's largest door company and other mills as well as a silver-domed alumina storage facility. In places the harbor looks like it's paved with logs. The tour takes you through downtown streets decked with flower baskets in the summer, past rows of modest homes reminiscent of the reputation as a mill town, and to hilltop vistas from fine residential neighborhoods, of Hat Island, the Olympics and sometimes Mt. Baker. It also follows the contours of the shoreline to the residential area of Mukilteo, which was the location of the signing of one of the most important Indian Treaties in the hisory of the Pacific Northwest. To enhance your enjoyment and appreciation of Everett check with the Chamber of Commerce for one of their Evergreen Trail directional brochures for the city tour, which should include Ebeys Island on the east side of town.

Everett — (Pop. 54,000. Elev. 30.) — What you don't get viewing it from your car cushions at 50 or 70 miles per hour, depending on the state of the energy crisis, is that Everett is on a peninsula made by a legal U-turn on the part of the Snohomish River ... that it's one of the most concentrated industrial complexes on the Wet Side of the Mountains, which you can see on a U-shaped tour of the town.

It got spewed out in a titanic tussle (well, it was *fairly* titanic) between two giants of industry, John D. Rockefeller, oil monopolist, and James J. Hill, empire builder. That the city of Everett, now the seat of Snohomish County and the 4th largest city on the Wet Side, was born in the process, was largely incidental in the minds of these men alongside of the BIG question of who lost and who won the battle.

The irony today is that the man who literally kicked the town to death is kind of a hero around the place. The one who applied the mouth-to-mouth resuscitation is considered something of a bum.

And the fact that this town is a classic example of the Wet Side's most important economic asset is overlooked entirely.

Now, on with the fight.

Everett started out innocently enough as a late-blooming lumber town in the late 1880's. It was crucified, dead and buried by John D. Rockefeller within a decade. And while it hasn't exactly ascended into heaven, it has survived to play an important role in our neck of the woods.

The initial mystery is that this spot was overlooked as long as it was. you had considerable stirrings in Seattle and Bellingham in the 1850's. Olympia preceded both of them and Tacoma came in about 20 years later. But it was nearly 40 years after the birth of Seattle that anybody gave serious consideration to Everett as a site for a city.

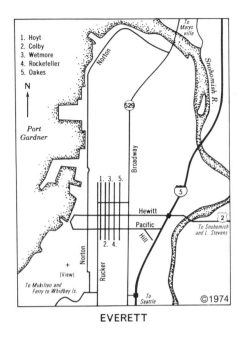

1. Hoyt
2. Colby
3. Wetmore
4. Rockefeller
5. Oakes

EVERETT

Actually, the process by which the town was created was initiated by two sets of men in Tacoma who figured that surely there must be a better spot than that. The key Tacoma figures were Wyatt J. Rucker, who has a street named after him in both towns, and Henry Hewitt, who found himself somewhat less than deified when he became known as the "father" of Everett. He missed getting a street named for him in the former town and nearly missed the same honor in the new town . . . although he also missed being strung up, which is something he didn't really miss at all.

Seattle was becoming the major railroad terminus in the late 1880's, in spite of the fact that the Northern Pacific Railroad owned Tacoma. The Northern Pacific was actually a transcontinental land development company with rails as a necessary adjunct to the sale of real estate. That Tacoma was a company-owned town caused many guys of spirit to kick over the traces and blow . . . and Hewitt was one of them.

He had come to the far west with $400,000 in his pocket from timber operations and was looking for some place more lively than Tacoma to enhance his fortune. Port Gardner Bay, where the Snohomish River completes its U-turn, looked like a neat, untapped resource for the manufacture of lumber. In the meantime, he was retained by the Northern Pacific to study the feasibility of running a line up to Bellingham. But, as he says in effect, in an "Inside story on the founding of Everett" which appeared in the *Everett Herald* on July 21, 1973, he couldn't get the Northern Pacific off its fat duff. (He didn't say it quite that way, but the feeling was there.)

But it was in connection with the Northern Pacific that Hewitt encountered the men after whom a couple more of Everett streets are named, Charles L. Colby and Colgate Hoyt. They had a New York investment banking firm and were members of the Executive Board of the Northern Pacific. Colby represented a couple more men memorialized in Everett streets, Charles W. Wetmore and Alexander McDougall, who had joined forces to produce some things called whaleback ships that looked like the forerunners of our present-day oil tankers but helped in the spelling of the word "disaster" for Everett — by the simple expedient of sinking. Among other things, Colby was looking for a new place to build whalebacks. And Everett seemed a likely spot.

Francis H. Brownell, an attorney for Colby and Hoyt, and another of the key figures in this entire operation, told about it in some reminiscences written in 1951: "The Northern Pacific Railroad, threatened by the rapidly approaching construction to Puget Sound of the Great Northern Railroad, decided in the late 1880's to build more directly west from Spokane in order to be the first to occupy the virgin zone of Central Washington and at the same time to construct a shorter route than the long detour from Pasco and up the Yakima River . . . . " It first contemplated crossing the Cascades via the Skagit Pass and following down the Skagit River to Puget Sound. This would make Fidalgo Island the Sound terminus. Copying the very profitable precedent of the Tacoma Land Company, a townsite company was formed and began buying land on Fidalgo Island. But the plan leaked. A boom started. Logged-off lands previously selling at $1 to $5 per acre shot up to $500, some even to $1,000 . . . .

What Colby's syndicate wanted was some sharp cookie who could produce a townsite for them without spilling the beans, getting everybody and his brother in the act and jacking up the prices before they owned the land. On a trip to Alaska with them, Hewitt pretty well convinced them he was the man to head the Everett Land Company.

The clincher for the deal came at the dinner table in Colby's home. The alert Mr. Hewitt saw Colby's son, Everett, reaching for a second helping of dessert. "That's it," he said, with a chuckle. "We should name our city Everett. This boy wants only the best, and so do we!"

So they gave Hewitt $800,000 to buy a townsite. They figured about 5,000 acres would do nicely.

Almost immediately, Hewitt encountered a revolting development. Rucker, the other ex-Tacoman, and his pals also had notions of building a city at this spot. But that wasn't the worst of it. Colby had just committed almost a million bucks for a town to be named after his favorite son, and the Rucker group was proposing to call it Port Gardner.

A sweating Henry Hewitt stopped that one dead in its tracks, even though he had to spend Christmas Day, 1890, doing it.

Rucker's combo owned 750 acres of land for which they paid logged-off-land prices. Hewitt offered them $27,000 for *half* of their holdings. He also signed a contract stating he would provide the town with a $35,000 dry dock . . . a sawmill capable of cutting 100,000 feet of lumber a day . . . one barge construction company valued at not less than $150,000 . . . a $400,000 paper mill — and a railroad line connecting Everett with the rest of the world.

It was a Merry Christmas for the Rucker people.

In the next 90 days Hewitt bought the 5,000 acres without letting any other land speculators in on the act. It was a prodigious feat.

An event that was going to shape Hewitt's new town had occurred the previous summer when a couple of prospectors spotted an outcropping of rich ore up the Stillaguamish River, about 40 miles east of Everett as the crow flies. One of them, a fan of Alexander Dumas, exclaimed, "This is richer than the Count of Monte Cristo!" A buddy of theirs took a look at it and added to the comment by saying, "Boys, the world is ours!"

Colby and Hoyt told about the country's newest hole, and that is when Rockefeller got in the act.

For years, J. J. Hill had sounded the same theme song wherever he went in our part of the country: "Timber is your greatest resource. Sell it off first and turn the land into farms. Then use the capital you have accumulated for the development of your mineral resources. Stop chasing gilded butterflies."

Rockefeller's attitude was: Big money doesn't grow on trees . . . it comes from holes in the ground. I ought to know!

Colby, Hoyt and Rockefeller were fellow Baptists attending the same church in New York. Rockefeller figured a good Baptist couldn't be all bad, so he bit the bait. And the Rockefeller name was magic. "Rockefeller never lost money on anything," they said.

A syndicate with Rockefeller as the heaviest investor decided to go the distance. And Attorney Brownell, who had a way with words, strung them together like this "In short, Everett would be the headquarters of a large and prosperous mining district. Visions of a possible Coeur d'Alene District of Idaho, of Leadville, Colorado, in its prime, and even Butte, 'the Richest Hill on Earth!' easily rose to mind. A successful Monte Cristo would do more to make Everett a thriving city than all the other proposed industries combined."

Hewitt opined philosophically that with enough iron and lead and gold and silver in the brand new smelter in Everett, Hill would have to come into line with a railroad line.

So they blew upwards of $8,000,000, and to hell with Hill. On April 27, 1893, Everett was incorporated as the Golconda of the Western World. It also was known as "Magic City."

But there was a problem. Whatever it was they wanted, Monte Cristo didn't have it.

With a trace of bitterness Brownell wrote, "The engineers who examined Monte Cristo erred in a most inexplicable manner . . . . It is difficult if not impossible, to explain the failure to thoroughly check the potential, if the engineers and others involved acted in good faith . . . . "

The death of Everett was a spectacle which Mr. Hill watched with energetic attention to the details as they emerged; and Rockefeller responded with the authentic vigor that had made him a millionaire in the first place. He fired Hewitt, Colby, Hoyt — Baptists or no Baptists. He instructed his confidential secretary, Frederick T. Gates, to enter Everett and clean up the mess.

It was a town Rockefeller never had visited.

With what Norman H. Clark described in *Mill Town*, his book about Everett, as "flawless efficiency," Gates extracted his money from the Everett Land Company . . . the nail factory . . . the paper mill . . . the shipyards . . . the hotel . . . the city lands . . . the street railway . . . the electric system and the water system. With the legal advice of Mr. Brownell, who also was attorney for the Land Company, he took his losses as they were necessary — and one of those necessary was the $2 million that had been spent on the railroad from Everett to the Monte Cristo mine.

It must have been a source of considerable inner satisfaction to Hill that Gates applied the money salvaged from the disappointing hole in the ground to timberlands, which ultimately netted Rockefeller a neat profit. And Rockefeller, who appreciated that sort of thing, may have found this something of a poultice. But he knew what Hill knew — and what Hill knew was that Rockefeller had dropped $8,000,000.

Loss of the $8,000,000 was bad; loss of face was worse. And Hill was preparing to grind it in.

As Everett sank slowly beneath the financial waves, Hill quietly bought up the bonds of the Everett Land Company for virtually nothing, so that on December 9, 1899, when the wreckage of the town of Everett was put on the auction block on the steps of the courthouse (which the Everett Land Company had built with its own funds), Hill's representative was there to make his grandstand play. His name was Wyatt J. Rucker. "Rocky" had blown $8,000,000 on the town.

Hill bought it for $1,500.

He also had thoughtfully, behind the scenes and in combination with J. P. Morgan, acquired effective control of the Northern Pacific Railroad.

Then Hill went into his magic act.

With a flourish, he pulled Frederick K. Weyerhaeuser — and the Weyerhaeuser Timber Company — out of a hat. Hill's Northern Pacific sold Weyerhaeuser and his associates 900,000 acres of timberland for $5,400,000. It was the greatest timber sale in history . . . and one of the results of the sale was the construction of the first Weyerhaeuser sawmill in the far west. It was on the site of the defunct barge works in Everett.

With the creation of a new Everett Improvement Company, Hill began breathing life into the prostrate town. To Hill, it was a matter of cosmic humor that timber from the lands of the Northern Pacific, which he described as a "real-estate railroad," should be shipped at a profit over the Great Northern, which was a *real* railroad.

Today, when you take Norton Avenue (Norton is a big name in Weyerhaeuser history) around Everett's perimeter, you will see the mills that give this city life. They are processing the product of our most important economic asset, the growing power of the land.

In your passing, you may note the broad thoroughfares marked Hewitt . . . Rucker . . . Colby . . . Hoyt . . . Wetmore — and Rockefeller.

If you look sharp, you may even see "Hill Avenue . . ."

It's a little three-block stretch down by the railroad tracks. And it may be more descriptive than commemorative. On the other hand, there's another street in Everett that we trust is more commemorative than descriptive. It's called "Dull Place."

Prowling Everett

The Chamber of Commerce has a nice green folder of *Evergreen Scenic Tours* that's very good. Number 1 is the whole shebang (2 and 3 are walking tours of downtown and riverside). Evergreen tree markers (green and mostly on poles) guide the way, more or less.

With or without a Scenic Tour, if you're like us, you might want to see the whole area from on high and then see it in particular. *Rucker Hill* from 35th and Kromer is a great shot looking north and getting the layout of the city, which is on a peninsula formed by a bay on the west and the Snohomish River on the north and east. It's plain to see why areas are commonly referred to as Bayside or Riverside. You can't miss the Rucker home nearby, a large brick mansion on estate-type landscaped grounds.

The waterfront is terrific: One long street, Norton, with great mills, plants, warehouses, is the lifeblood of the city. For another viewpoint try the *14th Street Pier* which you can drive out on and take a sort of loop road. The schooner, *"Equator,"* which is on the National Register of Historic Places, is tied up here. Stop for a look at the small boat moorage by Yacht Club (a handsome building) and visit an amazing tiny park of grass and small pyramid-type mounds, one of which has steps up about 25 feet where you can look around at neighboring piers. You could picnic here. It's called *Charles Jordan Memorial Park*. The Coast Guard and Fire Stations also are here. Other visit-able places are *Legion Park*, adjoining the Arboretum . . . the *Snohomish County Historical Museum*, which is full of memorabilia and some dandy costumes . . . a funny cedar stump house . . . *Grand Avenue Park*, a tiny strip park at north end of Grand that looks right down at entire waterfront. You see miles of logs, many look very weathered . . . bay almost looks paved with them. Turn around and you see Senator Scoop Jackson's handsome home. (You don't have to ask which house. It's obvious.) *Everett Community College* is oldest in State and has a lady president. You're welcome in the cafeteria in Student Union Building for snacks and atmosphere, which usually includes displays of what's going on in school. *Howarth City Park* south of city on bay has great beach with view and picnicking. It's below *Forest Park*, a beautiful old park with trees, mossy walls, full-grown shrubs and a small zoo.

A small park at municipal *Walter Call Golf Course* on Casino Road has unusual play equipment for little ones.

Mukilteo — (Pop. 1,360. Elev. Sea level.) — Take *Mukilteo Blvd.* through Forest Park to Mukilteo. The road loops up hill to a beautiful residen-tial area, which is a bedroom for Everett, and the terminal for the ferry to Whidbey. Nice viewpoint here as well as a lighthouse to visit.

Most history books refer to the treaty signed here by Governor Stevens and a number of Indian chiefs on January 25, 1855 as the Point Elliott Treaty. And it was here that the Indians gave away the site of the city of Seattle, because the treaty covers the ground from Point Pully — known more popularly today as Three Tree Point — to Canada.

The point of these points in the Indian Treaty business was significant and the wording used in Stevens' orders required that he "extinguish" the Indian's title to these lands. And that's what's coming back to haunt us now, as far as the Indians and their fishing rights were concerned. They were a foreign nation. We were taking land away from them literally by force of arms, and Stevens had to get that hunk of paper signed by whatever means he had at hand, or it would be impossible under international law to legally create an entity called the State of Washington.

A munificent congress gave Stevens $10,000 to estinguish the Indian rights to 100,000 square miles . . . *or a neat 10 cents a square mile!* So that was the original price paid for Seattle. A century later, the price for Seattle was upped to 40 cents an acre.

It is interesting to note that oysters were not included with salmon in the treaties. The white man already was making a killing in the sale of our native oysters to San Francisco. Salmon, on the other hand, was a drug on the market. They glutted and stank up the streams because the treaties were signed a decade before anybody figured out how to preserve this delicacy in cans.

Stevens had to offer the Indians something more than that dime a square mile. For reasons beyond the comprehension of the white man, the Indians considered the salmon important. And as far as Stevens was concerned, he was giving them nothing when he agreed to let them fish at their "usual and accustomed places . . ." which turn out to be such places as a river in the middle of the town of Tacoma.

And don't think he wasn't under some pressure.

A chief like Seattle, who had sold out to the whites, bellowed out sentiments that probably were written for him by a ghost writer, and was a major Fifth Columnist in the Indian War. But a smart cookie like Chief Leschi said, "If you are sincere about wanting us to be farmers like you say, then why don't you give us some of that rich bottomland the whites are grabbing hand-over-fist instead of the scraggly chunks you are foisting off on us?"

The white man honors Chief Seattle . . .

But he hung Chief Leschi.

To reach *Ebey's Island,* drive through rich bottomland of the Snohomish River and back. Take Hewitt Ave., east out of town, and the first turn-off from the viaduct to Home Acres Road . . . then follow the Swan Slough Road and River View Road past the GAR cemetery, auction barn and cross the river at Snohomish and follow south edge of river back to the Lowell-Woodinville Road and Everett. En route you pass the Jacknife Bridge, which is on the National Register of Historic Places.

Call ahead for tours of *Boeing Company*, Paine Field, 747 production and their largest facility which includes the largest building in the world; *Scott Paper Company*, Norton St. on waterfront; and *Weyerhaeuser Company*, on waterfront — sulfite, kraft, and lumber mills.

Uncommon shopping – *Tom Johnson,* Wetmore Ave., for tasteful decor accessories, antique things, ship dials, handmade stuff . . . *The Greenery*, Rockefeller Ave., for green-thumbers, and indoor plant decorators; young and trend-y . . . *The Red House,* Broadway, for primitives, wicker and antique furniture . . . *Everett Fish Company,* waterfront, for the adventuresome and particular; go early in the morning, May to September, to buy fresh fish (no more than two hours out of the Sound) from the fishermen . . .*Smoke Shop,* Colby Ave., leather clothing, custom work, for young, cool types.

A word about eating – *The Commitment,* Hewitt St., has to be number 1 in Everett. Coffee and lunch restaurant, handsomely appointed, and run by 2 local matrons who are superb cooks; and serve dishes like manicotti, quiche, shrimp-stuffed tomato, homemade pea soup, frittata or outrageously delicious cheesecake . . . *The Deli,* Colby Ave., hanging green plants and skylight atmosphere for luncheon and tasty sandwiches with beer or wine . . . *Moon Dragon,* Evergreen Way, ask Mr. Fook Yeung, the owner-chef (and a Kung Fu expert) to decide what he would like you to eat. It will be special and delicious . . . *Chalet Luise,* Hewitt St., good German food with all soups and sauces carefully and authentically made . . . *Jack's,* Hewitt St., a local 'Friday afternoon" place for color; super sandwiches at lunch . . . *Crickett's,* Oakes St., a hole-in-the-wall tucked between a funeral home and the Goodwill. Character-like liver'n onions, labor leaders, politicians and Mrs. Crickett. Sign on the side: "Keep the damn door shut" . . .

In Mukilteo: *Seahorse,* by ferry dock, lavish buffet on weekends, well-prepared seafood anytime; marine decor plus, of course, sea horses . . . *Taylor's Landing,* Pier 1, fresh seafood in a restaurant built almost over the water viewing the ferries and Whidbey Island . . . a local treat — park the car and board the ferry on foot to eat at *Virina's* on the dock at Whidbey; Polynesian, Japanese, and Philippine food. (See Whidbey Island, Region 3.)

A word about sleeping – *Holiday Inn,* on I-5 south of city, and *Imperial 400 Motel* and *Rodeway Inn* on Broadway.

Annual affairs – *"Ever on Sunday,"* in April, Greek food and dancing at annual dinner festival by Greek Community Club . . . *Salty Sea Days,* 1st week in June, on waterfront: parade, log rolling, concerts, dancing, salmon barbecue . . . *Paine Field Air Show,* 3rd weekend in July, two-day Washington State International Air Fair at Paine Field . . . *Waterfront Art Show,* 1st week in September, held in fishermen's net sheds on 14th St. Pier and sponsored by Creative Arts Association.

For further information — Chamber of Commerce, at 1532 Wetmore Ave., or phone 252-5106 . . . Weekends, any fire station with "HOST" sign.

Everett Tour 2 — Tulalip, Stanwood, Camano Island, Marysville (Map VII)

Our route goes north, crosses to Tulalip, the name of a large Indian reservation, a small bay and an even smaller town. Marine Drive winds down under the reservation entrance arch, formed by two totem poles topped by a canoe, to Mission Beach on the south point of the bay. A side trip goes around Lake Goodwin to visit wooded Wenberg State Park and its unusually nice beach. The main route heads north past Kayak Point, Warm Beach, with many small summer homes overlooking the Stillaguamish River delta, and miles of sand flats especially at low tide. Inland delta roads lead to Stanwood, and its once independent neighbor, East Stanwood. Then you go west to Camano Island, over three bridges with views of the river delta. The road is park-like, and stretches south 27 miles and back to the mainland, and then to Silvana through the Stillaguamish River Valley. Along the way there are big farmhouses and many handsome barns, with silos, turrets, or, in one instance, a pseudo-Russian cupola. Across the "Island" in the valley, the route goes south on Highway 9 and heads back to Everett over the Snohomish waterways.

The Stillaguamish Valley — Of the four rich river valleys north of Seattle, the Stillaguamish was the only one unencumbered by wheeler-dealers who were going to make it the western terminus of the transcontinental railroad. And while the delta of what the locals call the "Stilly" is smaller than those of the Skagit and Nooksack to the north, the agricultural impact of this one comes down to us with unadulterated clarity.

Eldridge Morse, the wandering newspaper reporter of the 1870's and 80's, put the whole thing in perspective in a government bulletin in 1883 when he wrote that the "Stillaguamish delta comprises all lands between the main river and Hatt's Slough . . . . The diking of the tide-marsh prairie shuts off all salt water and leaves nothing but river overflow to contend with . . . . It does not occur while crops are growing . . . . "

The other side of that coin comes from a brief incident in the life of a gentleman with the wonderful name of Bengt Johnson, the great dike builder of the area, who brought 128½ acres from the canny groceryman, Jack Irvine, for $600. Irvine thought he was taking in a sucker, but Johnson diked it and sold it to Sam Gilpatrick and Ed Dinsmore for $5,000. (You still drive over a hump made by a Bengt Johnson dike at Milltown, on the Skagit Delta.

The delta people, in turn, grew the kind of barley, oats and hay that established records in the agricultural journals and State fairs for the delta regions north of Seattle.

Like the Skagit, these crops were the "gasoline" that powered the oxen and the mules and the horses of the logging camps and railroads.

It is doubtful that the people who wrested the saltwater marshes from the sea and the rich, fertile fields of today from the underbrush were aware they were meeting the pre-steam-engine energy crisis.

They were too busy wresting.

Another "wrester" was Gardner Goodrich who took up squatter's rights near what today is the town of Stanwood. It was in the early 1860's and Goodrich had married an Indian girl so the Indians didn't immediately dispossess him. But they were more than a little irritated when Goodrich's agricultural ambitions clashed head-on with a traditional Indian burial ground.

Rather than have their dead float around through eternity, it was the Indian policy to bury people in canoes placed in the trees above the high-water mark. To the whites, this was a pretty grisly method of handling the problem and after due warning, Goodrich emptied the graveyard by burning the bodies that were dry enough and consigning the others to the efficacious removal system provided by the Stillaguamish River.

A group of 90 braves in three war canoes descended on Goodrich, demanding payment for ravaging the city of their dead . . . and while the squatter returned to his cabin for gun and knife to make that payment in Indian blood, Goodrich's wife warned the other Indians in their tongue that he was a "bad Boston man" and would do them all in. When he came out of the cabin bearing an arsenal, the Indians were disappearing around the bend.

It was this kind of determination that built the agricultural beachhead along the Stillaguamish.

Olanus Olson arrived in 1877 and between then and 1891 had by main strength and awkwardness cleared and diked 40 acres of land. The flood of 1891 took out 30 of the 40 acres. Willard Sly slashed himself with an ax while he was building a fence and died of the injury on April 4, 1867. LeRoy Fry reached his homestead land in a canoe and had to stand in the canoe in the river hacking at the under brush until he could clear a place to land and pitch his tent. Stryker Erickson's boat overturned while he was en route to Ut-saladdy and he was in the water all night before Indians rescued him — and was crippled for the rest of his life. One man was clawed to death by a bear which also died from the knife wounds the man had inflicted on the animal. Sam Brazleton nearly starved to death before a mail carrier discovered him in a trap that Sam had set to catch a bear. One man walked miles through forests so thick they required lantern light at 3 o'clock in the afternoon in the winter, carrying a two-year-old child in a gunnysack on his back and an infant in his arms; a forest fire had driven them off the trail and they found themselves lost in the forest. B. C. W. Schloman improvised a platform built on two canoes to bring in his first cows, at a time when a journey of 2 or 3 days up river from Stanwood to a new homestead was nothing out of the ordinary. Sam Ehrdahl had to pack hay on his back for two miles to feed his cow and it was 8 years before he could get a wagon trail into his place — not that it mattered much, because it was more than 8 years before he could afford to buy a wagon.

They lost their lives when canoes hit snags in the river . . . when steamboats blew up . . . when logging cables snapped and floods came and forest fires burned . . . and most of all they lost their lives to diptheria which ravaged them regularly.

In 1886, James McCullough wrote a letter to the *Seattle Post-Intelligencer* in which he extolled the Stillaguamish Valley as a home-hunter's paradise but suggested that no "picnic settlers" were wanted. The following year, just that kind of settler tried it out. According to historian William Whitfield, "The women were gowned in silk and were beribboned and be-feathered. The men wore silk hats, Prince Albert coats and kid gloves. They camped on the Emerson place, built half of a house, and one day they hailed a fleet of Siwash canoes and floated down to tidewater, with mildewed hopes and fallen feathers . . . " until 1885, the north fork was called "Starve Out Valley."

On the other hand, Michael Sill of Silvana split 200 rails on his 70th birthday.

There were other problems too . . . like in 1882 during extreme high water and with enormous effort, the tiny steamer "Gleaner" made it above the fork in the river at present day Arlington — once. But that got the north fork listed by the Army Engineers as a "navigable" river requiring a drawbridge which they couldn't afford to build. So they had to get a bill through Congress "un-navigating" it.

Stanwood — (Pop. 1,352. Elev. 5.) — Stanwood is on a tortuous bend of the river where two passes give access to the Sound. It no longer has any navigation activity except for occasional visits of the "W. T. Preston," a stern-wheeler snagboat on the National Register of Historic Places.

During the incorporation of Stanwood on September 29, 1903, Fred Pearson was elected City Clerk before they found out this was an appointive, not an elective office . . .

So they appointed Carl Ryan to the job.

In his first message to the City Council a year later, Mayor D. O. Pearson had to announce that the city already was in financial trouble. While the income to the city treasury was $421, they had spent $423.

Pearson was the "father" of Stanwood, and was much beloved by his fellow man.

Perhaps one of the explanations for this comes in the following from historian Whitfield, "Pearson had the reputation of being very lenient with the poor settlers, and while he made many friends and did more than any one other man to help the pioneers of the Stillaguamish, his kindheartedness was often taken advantage of, and it was common talk that the settlers went to Pearson when they needed credit and to Irvine when they had cash. The result was that Irvine was able to retire as a comparatively wealthy man in 1895, while Pearson barely weathered the panic of that period."

Prowling Stanwood

A scenic drive is north out of Stanwood to Conway across the delta and sloughs of the Stillaguamish and the adjoining delta and sloughs of the Skagit, with dikes and farms, all at sea level.

The area around Stanwood seems to reflect strong influence of the early Norwegian settlers. On the hillsides around the east are extremely orderly, well-cared-for tall, white houses on farmlands. In town, it's more midwest in tone, where the houses are smaller, squarer and set in green lawns on narrow paved streets. The remnant of an old brick highway goes through town. Curiously though, there is an effort to have an Old West look for several blocks on the main street. Buildings are painted burnt orange, mustard, rust and named Buckboard Tavern, Stanwood Hotel and Tavern Barber Shop, Central Tavern.

Call ahead for tours of *Twin City Foods,* on the channel, world's largest producer of frozen cut corn and green peas, and *Stokely-Van Camp,* processing peas.

Uncommon shopping – *Heritage House,* antique furniture, glass, and primitives; this was the home of D. O. Pearson, founder of Stanwood. It's a tall, weathered, faintly shrimp-colored house, now on the National Register of Historic Places ... *Viking Imports,* shop of Scandinavian wares ... *Gilbertsen Hardware Co.,* a small-town store with just the right mixture of old and new, and things you can't find anywhere else.

A word about eating – *Scandia Bakery,* one of the best reasons for going to Stanwood, has Scandinavian motifs, tables and chairs for coffee, tea, or fruit juice and their temptations, which include "real" lefse, cookies, pastries, and 25 different breads, one shaped like a mammoth mushroom, and hobo bread made of bits of dough from many varieties, so it slices in a marble effect; it could be mealtime anytime after 8 a.m. here ... *Buckboard Tavern* invites you to "Broil Your Own Steak" in their Old West surroundings ... *The Farmette,* pleasant dining room for quick meals; fresh shrimp in season, fresh eggs from the farm, fresh milk daily from the dairy ... *Jim Dandy Ice Cream Parlor,* old-fashioned sundaes and homemade toppings on 18 different flavors of ice cream.

Annual affairs — *Stanwood-Camano Community Fair,* 3rd weekend in August, unusually popular, with parade, carnival, barbecues, exhibits, art show ... *Lions' Lutefisk Dinner,* October, Swedish (or Norwegian) meatballs, lutefisk, homemade pie ... *Annual Lutefisk Dinner,* late October or early November, by Sons of Norway in nearby Silvana Peace Lutheran Church; famous event attended by people from far and wide.

For further information — *Stanwood News,* 530 Main St., Stanwood, 98292, or call 629-2155.

Prowling Camano Island

This Island is staunchly independent, holds itself as completely residential, and aloof from Stanwood and Snohomish County. Part of Island County, with a watery separation from the rest of its county, it is serviced by a satellite Island County courthouse in Stanwood, and the Island County Health Officer travels by private outboard to and from Whidbey. For car-cushion travelers, it's beautiful to drive around and look at the homes ... some residents commute from Camano daily to Seattle. *Camano State Park* has expansive views, from bluff and lengthy beach, trails, picnic and kitchen areas (see *Footloose,* p. 71). The western bulge of Camano, dividing the Island north and south, is in the Olympic rainshadow, making it part of the driest region on the Wet Side.

Uncommon shopping – *Ye Country Peddlers,* on West Camano Drive, lure trade with a sign about paintings, pottery and crafts by local artists.

A word about eating – *Hide-A-Way Cafe,* English wife of owner sets the flavor. Waitresses in long dresses and caps serve tea in "real" tea cups, other English food like Bubble and Squeak, Yorkshire pudding, English muffins. And they make their own pie.

A word about sleeping – *Cama Beach Resort,* run by the same family for years. Homey cabins on west "banana-belt" side with long sandy beach.

The drive on Highway 530 is one of the most pastoral, peaceful, and attractive on the Wet Side. It follows the Stillaguamish river most of the way at sea level in a middling-wide valley and all the houses look big, square, always cared for, and always lived in by the same family. Silvana, in the center of the valley, has a white steepled Lutheran church, a Viking Hall, a general merchandise store; besides a post office-grocery-bank cluster. And across a bridge, as though an intentional division, sits the local tavern. Even a sort of new community group which has popped up around the I-5 crossing doesn't intrude on the tranquility. This part of the valley, is called "The Island" which it almost is — by virtue of the fact that the Stillaguamish River and one of its tributaries almost surrounds it. The new community includes the *Turkey House,* a charming blue and white colonial restaurant with an excellent reputation for food — it suggests "Be ye warmed and filled . . . where every day is Thanksgiving Day." And nearby is the *Stillaguamish Tribal House* and the 2000-year-old *cedar stump* that was moved 5 times before it has come to rest in a highway rest area — all 20 ft. of its diameter. (The local *Cedar Stump Tavern* advertises, "Rest your rump at the Cedar Stump.")

Marysville — (Pop. 4,300. Elev. 15.) — Driving south on valley roads to Marysville, you go through farmlands with stands and U-pick signs selling strawberries, raspberries, blueberries in season, and later, corn.

The site where the first logging locomotive in the Pacific Northwest was built in 1883 — to run on maplewood tracks — Marysville was a longtime distribution point for farmers utilizing the diked flatlands of the Snohomish River. Today, it's the home of Reinell Boats, well-known in the Puget Sound region, and a bedroom community for the industries in and around Everett.

It's chief claim to fame in the minds of most people is a piece of pie — i.e., the kind you've been able to buy at the Village Cafe since 1937.

Uncommon shopping — On Highway 9 out of Marysville, *Covered Wagon Antiques,* for old furniture and antiques . . . at Frontier Village, *Antique Warehouse,* is well-thought-of locally; owner makes yearly trips to Europe for antiques.

A word about eating – *The Village Cafe,* in a new colonial building just off I-5, has more fame than Marysville to many of us natives. Its reputation for mouth-watering pies was such, that when they opened a second spot in Seattle's Food Circus, it was simply named The Pie Place. The simple but honest menu befits a meal before pie . . . nearby is *Caboose Cafe,* a jolly hamburger-type place in a red caboose . . . *The Coffee Shop,* attractive red and white exterior, for lunch. Sandwiches like crab salad, homemade rolls, and cheesecake . . . *Marysville Home Bakery,* for pastries, is noted for good Swedish rye bread. Tables for coffee and what you pick to go with it . . . a fun local tavern is *Bonnie and Clyde's.*

Everett Tour 3 — Granite Falls, Mt. Pilchuck, Monte Cristo,Darrington, Arlington (Map VII)

This circle tour which penetrates rugged mountain ranges is one of the State's most popular and is known as one of the Mountain Loop highways. Take Highway 92 to Granite Falls. There's a spectacular view, especially with the morning sun behind you, of the Olympics and Puget Sound, Everett, Seattle and Tacoma from a side trip up Mount Pilchuck. (This is the one you see with lights on during the winter from Interstate 5, because of night skiing.) There also is a side trip to nostalgic Monte Cristo. The main road takes you through the Mt. Baker National Forest, and up the south fork of the Stillaguamish, over Barlow Pass to the Sauk which merges with the north fork of the "Stilly" at Darrington and flows on down to Arlington where you can return to Everett via Interstate 5 on a more leisurely route via State Highway 9. This wild and vastly unpopulated country with periodic scenic spectaculars like the view of Big Four Mountain as you head toward Monte Cristo and an unbelievably beautiful shot at Glacier Peak where the White Chuck River joins the Sauk. The mountain loop road is not open year around.

Granite Falls — (Pop. 793. Elev. 396.) — Brick and frame buildings line the streets and include fine, fold, well-kept homes set on spacious lawns . . . and on the outskirts lumber mills being fed by rumbling logging trucks. There also are a couple of shake mills.

Uncommon shopping – *Otto Brenner's Granite Falls Rainbow Trout Farm,* where you can catch a trout without all the effort and risk of coming home empty-handed from one of the rivers . . . *Mary J.'s Custom Curing and Smoking Market* which has home-smoked meats like they once did it "down on the farm." Specialties are head cheese, ham, bacon, casing sausage and beef jerky. (Mary J. herself, is there and willing to talk with you.) . . . *Roberts Gallery* for pottery . . . *Forest Garden Nursery* for native plants and shrubs . . . *Mercantile Antique Store,* open weekends, and by chance and by reservation.

A word about eating and drinking – *Timberline Cafe,* "The" place in town to eat and gossip . . . *Friendly Tavern,* restored building, slightly alpine-style, local gathering spot.

Heading east you cross a good-looking bridge over the Stillaguamish, with a fishway along one side . . . and a short side lane to the cascading waters which give the town its name. The local chief of police notes that mountain cabins are multiplying in the valleys as city-dwellers seek refuge from crowds and find themselves bumper-to-bumper with other cars on pleasant weekends.

We have mentioned elsewhere and reiterate here that some of the most profitable stopping is at any ranger station anywhere for any kind of information about anything in the locality, and the Verlot Ranger Station is no exception. You will be entering the Mt. Baker National Forest here and leaving it shortly before reaching Darrington. Don't be too surprised if you see logging going on in the forest. That's a part of the multiple use program.

There's a rewarding side trip here. You drive through *Mt. Pilchuck State Park* to breathtaking views of the Cascade Range, the Olympics, and the

Puget Sound metropolitan areas. Part of the State Park is a ski complex including a lodge.

East from Pilchuck, the country becomes increasingly rough. The river flows below the road between basalt walls, while trees cling to steep slopes.

In the old mining town of Silverton, right alongside the highway, you may spot a few remains of the glory days. Just off the road are summer cabins. At nearby camping areas, picnic under the trees along the Stilly's banks. Snowy peaks, including spectacular Big Four, tower above.

The highway continues to climb, cresting at Barlow Pass, then descending to veer north along the Sauk. If the river seems to run backwards, in the opposite direction from the Stilly, don't let it bother you. Both streams eventually empty into Puget Sound, but drain from opposite slopes of a mountain ridge.

Side trip south from Barlow Pass to visit the historic mining center of *Monte Cristo*, that had so much to do with the birth of Everett.

John D. Rockefeller and James J. Hill may have given up on Monte Cristo nearly a century ago, but the ghosts of the prospectors who discovered the valuable metal will not be stilled. And a young couple of history buffs have heeded their call.

Still in their twenties, Don White and his wife have taken over the project of restoring the mining town to as much of its glory as they can. At the moment, there's room for plenty of camping or picnicking (for a small fee). They're making a lodge and museum out of a mining company's 2-story cookhouse and collecting all of the memorabilia they can find relating to the town's boom days. They provide groceries and simple meals. And they're in the process of putting markers on the streets.

The Whites have reactivated the direct-current electrical system, operated by their own waterwheel, but what is even more important is the resurgence of belief that the precious metals still are there in the hills and maybe one of these days there still will be a Golconda.

Keep an eye open for signs of the Monte Cristo railway. For a walk along the old railroad bed see *Footloose*, p. 77.

The northward leg of our mountain loop follows the Sauk as it cascades through alder and fir between valley walls. Look east up the White Chuck River for Glacier Peak, 4th highest in the Cascades (Mt. Baker wins 3rd highest by a measly 200 feet). Frequent markers point the way to fishing and camping sites. Now and then, a barn appears in a clearing.

Darrington lies on the flat along the Sauk's west bank (See Region 3, Mt. Vernon Tour 2), rimmed by peaks: Whitehorse, White Chuck, Prairie. Timber is the town's main resource, evidenced by the lumber mill and logging operations.

From Darrington, the road descends slowly to the valley of the north fork of the Stillaguamish. The river and its feeder creeks are crossed and recrossed as the road enters pasture lands. *Squire Creek Park* along the way is a good picnic stop.

At Oso, note attractive, *historic white schoolhouse*, and *Bradley's Antiques*.

Arlington — (Pop. 2,261. Elev. 103.) — Local business fronts on one long main street and beyond are small homes with colorful flower beds. New homes are near the river and overlooking the dairy farms. The town is just south of the confluence of the north and south forks of the Stillaguamish.

Prowling Arlington

There's a 1,200-acre industrial park which is near the Arlington Airport, a huge facility that formerly was a navy training base. Among the plants that can be visited with advance notice are *Glacier Cold Storage,* which packages vegetables with seasonings, *Portage Creek, Bradley Shake, Northwest Hardware,* and *Summit Timber Products,* all mills and wood processing plants; *Bayliner Boats* (fiberglass) and *Tanzer Yachts* (sailboats), and *Cascade Culvert,* culverts for highways.

Pioneer Park, one of the few privately-owned parks in the State, was a gift to the Stillaguamish Pioneer Association by an affluent pioneer . . . home away from home for senior citizens who find many activities in the clubhouse.

Uncommon shopping *– Ellis Photo and Postcard Company* for the biggest collection of State scenic postcards in the State . . . *Vienna Bakery,* third generation Austrian baking.

For further information— Arlington Chamber of Commerce, 300 N. Olympic; phone, 435-5514.

From Arlington, our route on Highway 9 aims straight and high south across farmlands with substantial barns and pastel farmhouses. Highway 9 was developed as an alternate road during World War II, in case Route 99 should be bombed out of use. It runs from Woodinville to the Canadian Border. Crossing the Snohomish delta sloughs back to Everett, cattle graze within the shadow of pulp and paper mills.

Everett Tour 4 — Snohomish, Monroe, Sultan, Skykomish, Stevens Pass (Map VII)

After you cross Ebey's Slough, you enter one of the prime agricultural areas of Region 4 through the town of Snohomish, a town which has mellowed gracefully with age. Next is Monroe, a major crossroads and State Fair town. Your route takes you through some of the richest dairy and berry land in the State to Goldbar, where you enter into the mountains and head for Stevens Pass, one of the State's most spectacular passes, especially in the fall when the leaves are turning or when the deep snow is on the hill.

Highlights of the tour are the visit to Snohomish, which is beginning to turn its collective face back to the river and thoroughly enjoying its rich historical heritage . . . the ruggedly rejuvenated town of Skykomish, a seemingly misplaced piece of King County, and the view-studded side trip to the Wellington site of the worst railroad disaster in the State's history.

Snohomish — (Pop. 4,753. Elev. 90.) — By pioneer forefather standards, Snohomish is a town that never made it . . . and the folks who live there today mutter "Thank God!" They're not bowing to the east when they say it, either. They're looking to the west to that industrial complex called Everett, that won the battle to be that industrial complex . . . and with the victory also won the terrible scars like the Everett Massacre with its 47 wounded and 7 dead . . . a lot of smokestacks and the smell of pulp mills.

Snohomish is one of the more charming towns on the Wet Side of the Mountains. It was the county seat for 30 years before Everett was born and by 1910, had accumulated 9 prosperous sawmills and an excellent hinterland of agriculture, a combination that produced a town with fine homes and tree-lined streets. On a promontory at the confluence of the Pilchuck and Snohomish Rivers, it affords a magnificent rural perspective of the river delta with Mt. rainier as the towering backdrop and the rising Cascades on the left.

The town owes its birth to the contretemps between the United States and Great Britain that erupted into the Pig War on San Juan Island. Even after the signing of the Oregon Treaty in 1846, peace between the nations was dubious insofar as the Puget Sound country was concerned. For years the military hollered there was no way it could keep in touch with Fort Bellingham if the British decided to move gunboats into our waters and, in 1853, Congress appropriated some money for a military road that would be inland from Steilacoom to Bellingham and out of reach of British guns in case hostilities in the area broke into the open. And Snohomish was going to be a river-ferry crossing for that road.

One of the great historic anecdotes comes from the construction of that road — or lack thereof. Private contractors were handed a contract for chopping a trail through the dense woods, and the easiest way to check on whether or not they were doing their thing was via a canoe trip up the Snohomish River. The army officer in charge of such inspections took that trip, and when he saw a wagon at the south bank of the river, he authorized payment for the work of building the trail that had enabled the wagon to get there. What he didn't know was that the contractors had not driven the wagon over a trail. They had just hauled it up the river to this spot in pieces. Then they assembled it so it "looked" like they had driven it there. This was the spot E. C. Ferguson selected for his "city."

In 1860, Ferguson, who would become the King of Snohomish County for the next 30 years, framed a house in Steilacoom and sent it up river by boat to be assembled at what today is Snohomish. The following year, Ferguson journeyed to Olympia to see if he couldn't get Snohomish County carved out of Island County. To his intense surprise, he found when he got there that the legislators already were at work with the carving job because they needed more counties on the west side of the Cascades in order to out-vote the eastern Washington delegations. They happily named him as the first commissioner of the new county, but he was a little late to have his town, Snohomish City, listed as the first county seat. The legislators already had handed that plum to the thriving community of Mukilteo.

The county was organized on January 14, 1861. The first meeting of the County Commissioners took place in Mukilteo three months later and it was easy to see that the 27-year-old Ferguson was the leading light in the political field. Not only was he a County Commissioner, but County Clerk, Auditor, Justice of the Peace, and Postmaster of the town where he had located his business, the Blue Eagle Saloon. He ran into something of a disappointment on the name of the town when the post office department dropped the "City" from Snohomish, but the department's attitude reflected an oft-repeated story of James J. Hill later on, that he'd only found four stumps in the whole territory that didn't have the name "City" tacked on them.

Ferguson's political maneuvering was evidenced early in the game when in July of that year there was an election (of which there is no legal record) held to move the county seat from Mukilteo to Snohomish. Young Ferguson wrote to the folks back home in Westchester County, N.Y., that he'd won a bitterly contested battle against the biggest town in the territory in the fight for the county seat.

It must have been bitterly contested all right because Snohomish only won by one vote . . .

The vote was 11 to 10.

On November 2, 1863, Ferguson's hotel and saloon was selected as the first County Courthouse . . . and from then on for the next 33 years, Ferguson ran Snohomish County. He was a simple man who believed in the direct approach, as is evidenced by the street system in the town of Snohomish today, It goes "A," "B," "C," and "1," "2," "3," and if you're going to the corner of 3rd and C you're not going to have a multiplicity of problems finding your way there.

But Ferguson was not a man with the kind of killer and acquisitive instincts that create captains of industry and builders of cities. He was able to raise a couple thousand dollars to explore a pass through the mountains at the head of the valley and seek a route to the gold fields, but he went over what turned out to be Cady Pass instead of Stevens . . . missing the major pass and, of course, failed to find gold. He figured Snohomish had to become a major crossroads because of the military road and got the franchise for the ferry across the river, but the United States and Great Britain settled their differences and Puget Sound was a much better highway. The Blue Eagle was the first, last and only stopping place in Snohomish for many years and as William

Whitfield says in his history of the county, "This was a good-sized, one-story building located near the river front at what now is the foot of Cedar Street. It was of course unpainted and was built of hewn timbers, home-made lumber and hand-drawn shingles. Here could be found E. C. Ferguson in all his glory, ready to serve drink or food, in his capacity of bartender and host, to hand out mail, as postmaster, to dispense justice, as magistrate, to transact business for the county as auditor or commissioner, whichever happened to be his title at the time, or to discuss the affairs of the territory as a legislator . . ."

Ferguson was president of the Atheneum Society and Telegraph Company, neither of which coined money for him, and promoter of the first newspaper in the county, *The Northern Star*, which failed to produce any measurable income. He filed the first plat in the county, which enabled him to do a fair business in foreclosures, and was vice president of a bank formed in the county by Jacob Furth, the prominent Seattle banker, but it was more of an honorary title than anything.

On the other hand, he opposed the advent of the railroad at a time when its supremacy over the riverboats was foreordained. Then he reversed himself and attempted a railroad in competition with James J. Hill, which is yet another way of putting your head in a buzz saw. Henry Hewitt tells of buying a piece of land from Ferguson for $4,000. In a couple of days he sold it to his brother-in-law, who quickly sold it for $128,000 to Hewitt's Everett Land Company, which turned it again in a few months to the general public for $500,000.

All of that, of course, was just money.

But the fight over the county seat involved Ferguson's heart and blood. He was the father of the county and the creator of the county seat in Snohomish. For the better part of his lifetime he had run the political affairs of "his" county. And in the 1890's, those city slickers from someplace else began their moves to take Ferguson's pride away from him, by moving the county seat to Everett.

It was a long, rough fight with no holds barred and all the money stacked on one side of the table. Ferguson had ridden roughshod over a lot of people for a long time, which didn't help him much. And fellows like Attorney Brownell, noted in our earlier tour about Everett, had participated in this kind of rough-and-tumble in the past.

In one of the oldest moves in the book, the Everett people took advantage of the fact that for years Stillaguamish farmers had been forced to go all the way to Seattle and back up the Snohomish River to get to the county seat — because that was the only way the steamers made connections. So what the Everett people did was make it appear that the impetus for moving the county seat came from some place other than Everett . . . They arranged to have the demand for moving the county seat come from the Stillaguamish Valley.

The next maneuver was a little complicated, and called for a few bucks. They would have a courthouse ready, willing and able to function as the Seat of Government once the folks voted to move it from Snohomish to Everett.

Now, there are laws in this country against this sort of thing. Cities simply can't go into the county-seat business, willy nilly, and in competition with the existing county seat.

On the other hand, they figured if they built a better mouse trap they had a better chance of catching a better mouse.

So, the way they worked it was this. The city legally could spend money on "parks." If the Everett folks would vote $30,000 to buy a "park" from the Land Company, the company in turn would use that money to build a courthouse in that park. Then, when the county moved its seat there'd be this brand new place to sit.

The city voters thought that was a splendid idea and voted 615 to 22 in favor of the park bonds . . .

And the Land Company ultimately built this neat new courthouse.

The next step was a petition filed on September 2, 1894 to move the county seat. The petition contained 1,884 signatures — making it mandatory for the county commissioners to submit the question to a vote of the people. They were riding high in Everett that day . . . not knowing that the efficient Mr. Gates was due in town to begin the process of the economic blood-letting.

In the ensuing months, a lot of hanky-panky was dedicated to the county seat campaign by both sides. The question went in and out of the swinging doors of the courts and the county commissioners like a dog chasing a cat. It finally devolved down to some mighty suspicious-looking poll books in South Snohomish.

Let's face it, the Everett people knew that most of the voters listed in those poll books were longtime permanent residents of the local cemetery. The question was, "How to prove it?"

And F. H. Brownell was equal to the occasion.

He had the residents of the graveyard subpoenaed to appear in person in court. It would have made quite a crowd too, because there were 200 of them. And, had they showed up, it would have been sensational news throughout the world . . . a story that would have dwarfed the county seat fight.

Mr. Whitfield sums it up with remarkable restraint with: "It was adroit, however, as it placed the South Snohomish officials in an awkward position . . ."

Finally, in December, 1896, the most famous of innumerable county seat fights in the State was settled in Everett's favor — after two years of legal maneuvering Everett got the county seat.

And it was on the steps of the courthouse constructed by the Land Company that James J. Hill later bought the town for $1,500.

◆

Prowling Snohomish

This tree-lined town bounded on two sides by rivers, in one of the loveliest on the Wet Side of the Mountains. It slopes to the south, with excellent views of the Olympics and Mt. Rainier from 10th and Pine . . . and there's a spectacular view of the Cascades from 5th and Ave. B. *Blackman's Lake*, partially in town, is at the top of the hill and the Blackman residence, now owned by the Snohomish County Historical Society and located on Avenue B, has been restored and turned into a *museum* which is open Sunday afternoons. Driving the tree-lined streets, Avenues A to D on 2nd to 5th Streets, you can see well-preserved and well-kept-up homes of the 1890 era . . .

Except for the one owned by John Patric, the local iconoclast, who lists himself as a "whale wrapper," and sort of lets things grow the way they will around his house. He advocates nonpayment of taxes and periodically runs for political office . . . publishes a small newspaper which does articles like, "The repairman will gyp you if you don't watch out." It refers to Senator Henry Jackson as "Scoop-shovel Jackson," and to the town as "Sodomish." He's not necessarily cheered in all quarters in town. His home is at 3rd and Ave. D, but you won't have any trouble spotting it. It's the one with the long grass.

Walk Avenues A to D on *Front Street* for a close-up of restored buildings, including a bank, theater, market and services . . . view between the buildings across the river to the *Seattle Snohomish Lumber Mill,* which will permit tours if you call in advance. *Silverbow Honey Company,* which processes the efforts of bees, welcomes visitors.

Eighty-five-year-old *St. John's Episcopal Church* is one of the most attractive buildings in town.

There's a *"bicycle tree,"* so named because you can ride a bicycle through it.

Pieces of incidental intelligence: Across the Pilchuck River, Short Street, of course, is next to Long Street . . . Snohomish has the only water-powered elevator for miles around (in the Snohomish Hardware Company on Ave. C). In 1974, parts of the residential and business areas were placed on the State Register of Historic Districts.

Uncommon shopping — There are 12 antique stores, among which these are especially good: *Baker's Antiques and Vintages, Another Antique Shop*, and *Bank Antiques* (in a restored bank building), as well as *Snohomish Exchange,* for frankly second-hand goods . . . *Pinkham's Interiors,* in restored Pioneer Market Building.

A word about eating – *Silver King Restaurant,* with back to the street and face to the river, with view of the mill and Mt. Rainier, sophisticated . . . *Snohomish Bakery* (everybody gathers here for bran muffins) is half bakery and half snack counter . . . *Fox and Hound,* looks east across Pilchuck with view of Cascades . . . *Barnacle Bill's,* near the City Hall is operated by Mayor and his wife; pool tables, ice cream and lots of company, both young and old (reminiscent of old E. C. Ferguson and the Blue Eagle) . . . for kicks, *The General Store, A Tavern,* early western memorabilia, fun and also food.

Annual affairs – *Tour of Historical Houses,* September, Historical Society members conduct the tours in period costumes (also worn by some of the customers). Everybody strolls and ends up at the museum.

For further information — Write Snohomish Chamber of Commerce, Snohomish, 98290; or City Hall, 1st St., Snohomish; phone, 568-3115.

Heading up the rich alluvial valley, you can understand why Snohomish County is number 1 in egg production, dairy cows and sweet corn in Region 4. It comes in second in red raspberries and peas. It is significant that dairying is by far and away the most important agricultural use of the land, bringing in more money than all other uses combined. Approximately 70% of the land you see is used to raise forage for cows.

Monroe — (Pop. 2,700. Elev. 68.) — Crossroads of Highways 2, 522 and 203 and in the middle of the rich dairy country. It's the home of the *Evergreen State Fair,* in late August and early September, the second largest fair in the State. For fresh dairy products try *Sno-King Dairy Barn. High Rock,* south of Monroe, is a favorite local Sunday hike with great views. (See *Footloose,* p. 78.) Nice approach into town from the south and an interesting route east is via the *Ben Howard Road* on the south side of the Skykomish River to Sultan. A side trip off this road is to a mini rain forest up *Cedar Ponds Road* to Youngs Creek.

Sultan — (Pop. 1,150. Elev. 114.) — Sultan River enters the Skykomish River here. Big logging and raspberry center. Visit the *Sultan Bakery* on Main Street, open sunrise to sunset, with coffee, peanut butter cookies, raisin bread with 499 raisins to the loaf, and during the summer they make homemade ice cream. Front window reads, "Old Fashioned Goodness." One suggestion for excitement: park on a county road at night and listen to the coyotes howl. For further information try Department of Natural Resources' office in Sultan.

Startup — (Pop. Nom. Elev. 158.) — Not where you "start up" into the pass, but named for George Startup, manager of the Wallace Lumber Company. Wallace River comes in here and they were afraid if they named the town Wallace, their mail would go to Wallace, Idaho. A 2 tavern, 2 church, 1 grocery store town. *Salmon Hatchery* on east edge of town, visitors welcome.

Gold Bar — (Pop. 504. Elev. 206.) — It's a 2 grocery (1 sells organic food), 1 company store and 1 tavern town. On east edge are roadside stands, one for honey and one for cider and wood.

Index — (Pop. 169. Elev. 532.) — Now you're starting to go up hill. The town is a quarter-mile off the highway . . . on the north fork of the Skykomish River about at the confluence of the north and south forks. One of the most impressively located towns you have ever seen; it's in a river gorge and the mountains rise steeply on the north and south. There are 3 valleys converging here, and *Bridal Veil Falls* is on one rocky face. Mt. Index provides a spectacularly beautiful alpine setting. Here's where a lot of people flee the crowds of the big cities and they really can get away from it all to their mountain cabins. Most important building in town — and you can't miss it — is the *Red Men's Wigwam, 1903.* It's on the National Register of Historic Places. Also present are *Index Tavern, General Store* and the *Post Office.* What more do you need . . . (See *Edelweiss Restaurant* at turn-off to town for . . . like hamburgers.) You see *Sunset Falls, Canyon Falls,* and *Eagle Falls* traveling north from here.

Skykomish — (Pop. 383. Elev. 930.) — From the highway, cross a bridge over the river to the town. Burlington Northern tracks are on the south side of town and sometimes there's a train every half hour, because this is a division point on the railroad. From here on, the trains have a real climb to Scenic, ten miles away and 1,100 feet higher. About 80% of the business in town comes from skiers. This is a dramatic spot with the river raging through and jagged mountains to the north and south and the trains growling and thundering.

The streets on one side are like this: 1, 2, 3, 4, Thelma and Helen.

Skykomish really is kind of a lonely part of King County. You've been in Snohomish County until you get here. It therefore did not surprise anybody much when a move was initiated to have the town secede from King County. However, it developed at the big mass meeting on the subject that the reason for the move was that the guy who initiated the secession movement wanted to start a laundromat and the zoning laws were easier on him in Snohomish than King County. So, they all decided to stay dirty and stick with King County.

A number of years ago, some ladies of easy (but profitable) virtue plied their trade in the top floor of the *Skykomish Hotel*. Molly Gibson, 80-year-old former manageress of this establishment, still lives in town, but no longer is connected with the hotel, which has become a really jumping party place. There's a night spot joyously attended by skiers and named after *Molly* . . . and the *Whistling Post Tavern*. There's a porch three stories high across the front of the building. The rooms are small, comfortable, and restored . . . and the weekend occupancy rate during the skiing season is 100%. We were delighted to learn it is owned and operated by a corporation named "Sweet Pea." There also is the *Chalet Restaurant* across the river. The decor of the town is a cross between the Gay Nineties, early 1900 railroading and 1974 skiers.

Annual affair – *Tunnel or Skykonish Days*, first week in August, bathtub race, band, races, arts and crafts.

For further information — Check the Post Office; phone, 677-2241.

From here, your normal route takes you to Scenic, but they also have thought up another historic site which you might want to visit because (1) the road's pretty good (2) the scenery is fantastic and (3) it was the scene of the third worst railroad disaster in the history of the United States. Came close to being the second worst, but a wreck in a New York tunnel beat us out by one death 8 years later.

When they built the present Stevens Pass Highway some years ago, they detoured the folks over the old route used by the railroad when the Great Northern came crashing through the mountains in a tearing hurry, to lend a major assist in bankrupting the Northern Pacific. And in so doing, it was necessary to build in some horrendous switchbacks before reaching the now-abandoned tunnel. It is considerably higher in the Pass than the present one, which, incidentally, at 7 miles is the longest tunnel in the western hemisphere.

The old road is 7 miles long, takes off from Scenic, to the west side of the pass and is surfaced with crushed rock taken from that original tunnel. It's only open in the summer, and if you drive it, you'll know why. You also will get a view of the present highway over the Pass and pause for a little respectful attention to the State Highway Department for the fantastic job it did in building the new road in the first place . . . and for keeping it open all winter in the second place.

The Highway Department crews are intimately acquainted with the snow pack. You can bet your life on it — and that's what you're doing when you drive over the Pass in the wintertime — especially if it's raining on top of a heavy load of new snow. In an article in the *Wenatchee World* in 1964, Stevens Pass Maintenance Foreman, Phillip Hanford, gave the reporter some clues. "A man has got to select his own men." Hanford said. "They've got to know where the chutes are and what areas are subject to slides (a chute is a steep slope down which the snow comes thundering whenever slide conditions are right).

"No matter how dangerous it is to be out, we go after them (people) stranded in a slide area," Hanford said . . .

And dangerous it is, as two State Highway Patrolmen found during a slide that year, because a slide caught and buried their car. And Patrolman Bill Edison reported what it was like."You hear the wind first," Edison said. "Then a puff of snow ahead of it . . . then your car starts rocking like a boat . . . and you feel it slide across the road." The two patrolmen had been searching for a school bus that happily (as it turned out) had passed through a raging blizzard earlier. The patrol car had stopped to allow a sno-go (plow) go ahead of them to take on a slide ahead when the snow hit. It buried their car but they were able to get out.

Ninety-six people on a west-bound Great Northern train that had been stalled west of the old tunnel at Wellington for several days were not so lucky when an avalanche hit on March 1, 1910. No trains were crossing the Cascades during that storm. (Farther south 200 people were trapped on a Northern Pacific train near Stampede Pass.)

It had been impossible to put the trainload of people in the tunnel because of a lack of ventilation. If they didn't maintain heat, they would have frozen to death and if they did, the fumes from the engine would have suffocated them. So they were on a siding just west of the old tunnel which was on the west side of the pass on the road you'll be traveling.

In her book *Northwest Disaster*, Ruby El Hult tells the story of a trainman who witnessed the disaster: "Just as he reached the bunkhouse, a new sound sprang into being behind him. He wheeled and in another vivid lightening flash saw White Death moving down the mountainside above the train. Relentlessly it advanced, exploding, roaring, rumbling, grinding, snapping — a crescendo of sound that might have been the crashing of ten thousand freight trains . . . Onward it rolled in a majestic wave, crumbling the whole canyon wall before it. It descended to the ledge where the side tracks lay, picking up cars and equipment as though they were so many snow-draped toys, and swallowing them up, disappeared like a white, broad monster into the ravine below . . ."

The man was describing the disappearance of 15 cars and 6 locomotives and plows . . . and the deaths of 96 people who had been asleep in warm coaches and pullmans in the middle of the night. The site of the Wellington Disaster is now registered as a State Historic Place.

The supreme ironic touch was added to the tragic incident by a King County Deputy Coroner. Representatives of Everett and Seattle funeral homes were on hand to do their thing. But the wreck occurred in King County, and he was the highest possible authority at the time a rescue train bearing the bodies paused at Everett. The relatives of the deceased victims who had lived in Everett were on hand to assume their share of the sad load. But he insisted that all bodies, whatever their place of origin, be taken to funeral homes in Seattle and then dispensed to various geographic locations like Everett . . .

Until an even higher authority asserted itself.

It was a large fist on the end of the arm of a tough trainman. It appeared perilously close to the deputy coroner's nose and was backed up with a booming voice that sounded a lot like God speaking to the deputy coroner. It said, "Release these bodies, or you get pitched off this train, yourself!" So he did.

A lot of half-asked historians have a little trouble figuring out the identity of the man who discovered Stevens Pass, and as residents of the Wet Side of the Mountains, you may wish to have this one on straight.

Governor Isaac I. Stevens, who was charged with finding a railroad route from the Mississippi to Puget Sound, sometimes gets the nod as the discoverer, but the credit belongs to John Frank Stevens, who was surveying the route for the Great Northern Railroad.

As a young fellow, the latter Stevens got some practical experience surveying the route for the Canadian Pacific Railroad. His first great national recognition came from his discovery of Marias Pass over the Rockies on a mighty cold night of December 11, 1889. Alone in the pass with the temperature about 40 degrees below zero, and unable to start a fire, he tramped in a circle all night to keep from freezing to death. It's the route now followed by Interstate 90 over the Rockies, and there's a statue of Stevens at the divide.

In 1890, he was assigned the chore of finding a route over the Cascades that was as near as possible to Wenatchee. In the spring of 1891, he had marked the route for the rails and by October, 1893, the last spike was driven connecting St. Paul with Seattle and making the latter the biggest town in the Pacific Northwest. Stevens designed the railroad tunnel that goes under Seattle. He also did the feasibility studies that resulted in the original Great Northern tunnel and the present 7-mile horse-shoe tunnel used by the Burlington Northern.

And, although, Major General George W. Geothals was the fellow who completed it and got the big credit at first, Stevens now is recognized as the Grand Architect of the Panama Canal.

Adjacent to the present tunnel route is Stevens Pass at 4061 feet elevation. There's an excellent ski area and basic amenities.

A Word About Seattle

Writing a book about Western Washington that refrains from emphasizing Seattle is a lot like ignoring a large lump on the end of your nose. It's the biggest and the best and the most of everything on the Wet Side of the Mountains.

On the other hand, this book is written of, by, at, with, for, from and to natives of this region, which automatically means that about 75% of all the people who qualify as our readers already live in and around the major metropolis of the State. So it is unlikely they need detailed directions for finding their way to Fourth and Pike. The fact is the *Wet Side of the Mountains was* compiled by Seattleites who used our town as a base from which to prowl the rest of the region west of the Cascades, and when you get into the reading of same you'll find the innate power of the major city intruding itself on the rest of the communities in many ways. All roads lead to as well as from Seattle, in spite of the fact that at one time or another practically every community on the Wet Side thought that it would become the major city.

But Seattle had the best port, nearest to the lowest pass over the mountains and attracted the most aggressive citizens, as you will see when you become involved with the pages that follow. She has the most rich men, poor men, beggarmen and thieves, doctors, lawyers and merchant chiefs. But all of this is something that all of us natives already know. And if we don't, the Seattle Chamber of Commerce and the Seattle-King County Convention and Visitors Bureau are ready at the rathole to tell us in case we try to scramble out.

On the other hand, this book may — in spite of our scrupulous care — fall into the hand of somebody who doesn't know the location of Fourth and Pike . . . who hasn't read *You Can't Eat Mt. Rainier!* or *Be My Guest in the Pacific Northwest* or *Sons of the Profits* — our previous books about Seattle. And that contingency also is handsomely cared for in our weekly full-color visitor publication, the *Seattle Guide*. Available in major hotels, motels, restaurants and tourist crossroads in the city and beyond, it provides on a current basis the kind of profitable prowling found in this book for the other communities on the Wet Side of the Mountains. If that doesn't do it for you, look for the Friday editions of the *Seattle Times* and *Post-Intelligencer*, which have complete informational sections headed "Tempo" and "206" respectively.

In addition, the map on the pages which follow will prove convenient on the matter of getting either in or out of town.

So join us in exploring the mushrooming old and new environs surrounding Seattle, that most of us can't keep up with.

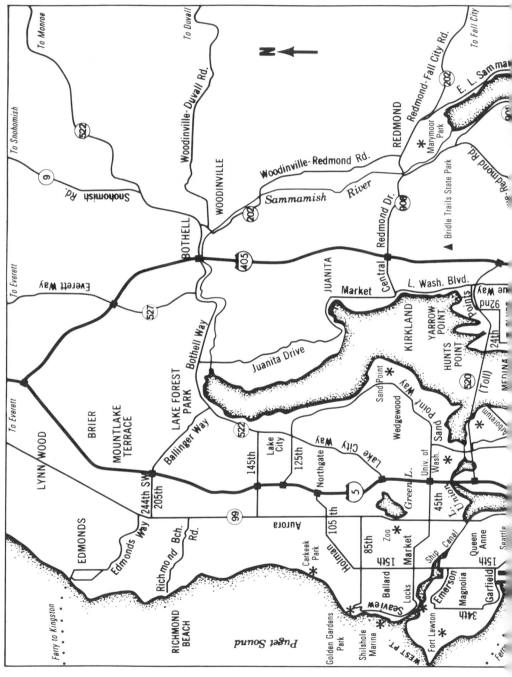

SEATTLE AND VICINITY

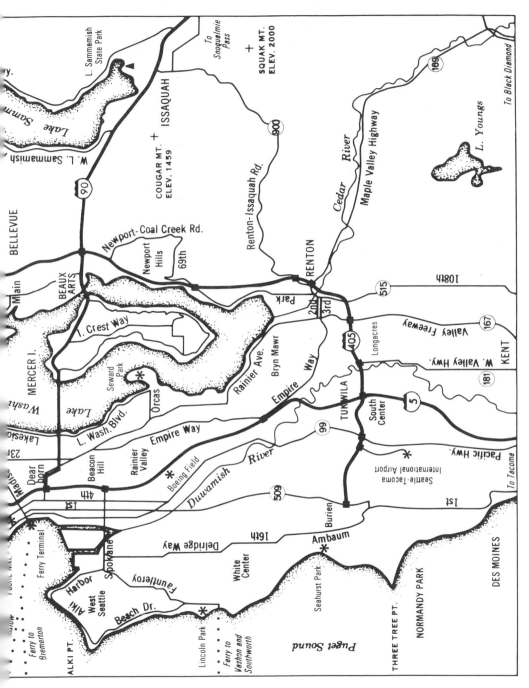

Seattle Tour 1 — Duvall, Carnation, Snoqualmie, Redmond, Bothell (Map VIII)

The main thrust of this tour is up the bucolic east side of the lower Snoqualmie River Valley, back the west side for a short distance and across over to the Sammamish Valley to Redmond, Woodinville and Bothell. Within spitting distance on the south side as 522 crosses the Snohomish River is the confluence where the Snoqualmie River joins with the Skykomish to become the Snohomish River. Highlights of the trip are a pause at pastoral Duvall, the fascinating activities at the Carnation Company's Experimental Farm and, of course, Snoqualmie Falls. You also will witness the urbanization of Redmond which incredibly was only slightly larger than Duvall 30 years ago . . . and see Bothell struggling to maintain its identity in the all-encompassing region now known as North Shore.

There was an item in the April 15, 1876 issue of the *Northern Star*, published in Snohomish, concerning the construction of the "Nellie," a little sternwheeler, in Hammond's Shipyard in Seattle to serve the farmers living in the Snoqualmie Valley.

"Farmers may now plant and sow, confident that they will have transportation, at reduced rates, to markets not only in this place but in Sound ports and San Francisco. None need hesitate. Put your hands to the plow; do something besides raise hay and vegetables, in short everything that will mature in this climate. We have been sapped and drained by the importation of breadstuff, feed and meats long enough . . . Remember, nothing can be put in the ground that has a value anywhere but can be shipped, when we have a boat that can run up the Snoqualmie River. We have waited long and impatiently, but relief is at hand. Up and be doing and make our valley blossom like a rose."

A few years later, the newspaper predicted that Snoqualmie Valley would be settled from its mouth to the Falls and from foothill to foothill. And the fact is that the 72-foot sidewheeler "Alki" was able to make the trip to Fall City, the head of navigation, at low water in July 1883 . . . although at times, the passengers had to get out and help her over Ben Stretch's riffle. She drew 4 feet, 3 inches. In those days all travel from Seattle to Snoqualmie Pass first went north to the Snohomish River and then south up the Snoqualmie.

Under normal conditions the flow of traffic from the east would have been down the river into what now is Everett, but Everett had not as yet been invented and Seattle, always the firstest with the mostest, had become the major port for the Mosquito Fleet, of which the "Nellie" and the "Alki" were two of the mosquitoes. Then she got the railroads coming her way and finally punched some groovey gaps in the hills and got the highway traffic.

This leaves the lower Snoqualmie Valley about as intensely bucolic as anything in the nearby geographic premises, giving us car-cushion travelers an easy way to get away from the telephone and the fumes of gasoline promulgated by other peoples' cars. Simplest way of getting there is by following Highway 203 out of Monroe heading for Duvall, Carnation and Fall City, to name a few of the little round dots on the map.

Just out of Monroe, the road goes right by *High Rock*, (see Monroe,

Everett Tour 4). There are opportunities to turn left into the foothills on roads that will return to 203 and if you have time, there are creeks and lakes and scenery, but our program should keep you fairly well occupied.

Duvall — (Pop. 575. Elev. 50.) — According to a recent issue of the *Sammamish Valley News*, a tall, nattily dressed Stranger breezed into Duvall's *Lake House Restaurant* and volunteered, "Boy! This town is a natural gold mine."

To him, Duvall's main street was an example of an old-fashioned rural community setting often seen in the movies. All the folks had to do was hire a hot-shot publicity man, blow a few bucks in advertising and promotion and soon great crowds would come and spend their money there. Having assayed this information, the effusive stranger sauntered out "slipped into his long sleek Cadillac, and sped southward . . ." (Presumably, we suppose, to Los Angeles.)

Duvall is located in lovely Cherry Valley, which we would like to think was named after cherry blossoms, but probably came by its appellation from an early settler by the name of Thomas J. Cherry. There's a nice *park* here, especially the part in Salmon Creek Canyon, where the band used to play on an enormous boulder called "Big Rock." Some Forward Thrust funds have been applied here . . . but, the results are charmingly rural in design.

Uncommon shopping – *Stillwater Trading Post*, which has good junk-funk and possibly a find in antiques . . . *Duvall Antique Shop*.

A word about eating — Is that the *Lake House* (and Puddle Room) has a nice view of the Valley — no lake, however — it's owned by some people named Lake . . . the *Silver Spoon* is in a restored building with farming memorabilia and good food.

It won't be novel if you sail through *Novelty* . . . former town named by a guy from Missouri who named it after his own home town which, in turn, thought it would be a "novel" name for a town.

Next is one of the most important establishments on the Wet Side of the Mountains.

Carnation Milk Experimental Farms — Visiting this establishment is a unique and rewarding experience which about 25,000 people share annually, in the shade of giant Douglas firs and beds of begonias in a wild variety of colors. You can wander on self-guided tours through gardens at the top of the hill and follow paths through a bit of the tangled old woods left standing as a reminder of old times . . . sit on a stone bench and look out and down on the valley below, dotted with black and white Holsteins and red and white Herefords. At the foot of the hill is a statue of Carnation's most famous cow, Segis Pietertje Prospect. She looks placidly over the green pastures and whitewashed fences of the farm she helped make internationally famous. In addition to superior strains of purebred cattle, there's a cattery and kennels in which 4 breeds of dogs are raised, Labrador Retrievers, Scottish Terriers, Beagles, and Brittany Spaniels. In 1974, the farms were undergoing a $1 million expansion. It should be noted Carnation is one of the 3 big dairy companies of the world. This farm is a small but vital part of its total operation. Milking at 1:30 p.m. daily; closed Sunday. For information call Seattle, 623-0510.

Here's a company that has put a river valley to its highest and best use.

A lot of our problem traces back to the alleged infallibility of James J. Hill, the Empire Builder. He was right so much of the time that his contemporaries gave him an Aristotelian omnipotence. If Hill said it, then, by God, it was right!

One of the points that Hill made repeatedly as he brought economically sound railroad transportation into the Pacific Northwest was, "Sell your timber and get enough money to finance other uses of your land." And one of the major uses he saw for our land was farming. If it was rich enough to grow trees, it was rich enough to grow grain, potatoes, and tomatoes.

So you could buy logged-off land for four-bits an acre . . .

Then you spent $175 an acre clearing it, or as most poverty-striken farmers did, you broke your back clearing it yourself. Then you found that most of it was only good for what was there in the first place — trees. So we came to the term "stump ranch" to connote a poor, run-down operation that looked like it was raising stumps. And our landscape still is dotted with them.

We leave these edifices to our ignorance alone, and spend millions in flood control to keep water off the industrial parks that ought to be on the hills in the first place . . . and irreversibly rob our valleys of their potential for producing food, which we may be short of one of these days.

But Carnation Farms is a beautiful example of what canny business judgment and man's ingenuity can come up with when it's applied productively to our rich bottomlands.

—◆—

Elbridge A. Stuart, founder of the Carnation Company, showed up on the scene in 1899 with a few bucks in his pocket and a new technological advance under which you evaporated the water from 3 pounds of whole milk and came up with 1 pound of condensed milk. You put it in a can. It would last indefinitely and you could ship it anywhere.

It was a revolution in the milk business.

With this kind of a money-making proposition going for him, Stuart bought a poor, run-down stump ranch near Tolt (they changed the name to Carnation in 1917 to honor the company) and started clearing the land. He tried contracting the clearing of the land for $35 an acre, which seemed a reasonable enough price to him, and the clearer went belly up. So, for the next contract, he upped the ante to $75 an acre — an astronomical amount to Stuart who was the son of a midwest farmer. But that man went down the tube, too, and Stuart took on the chore himself with his own farmlands . . .

And learned what a bitch-kitty clearing stumps was.

Happily, Stuart was not a person who folded easy and come the hell of clearing or the high water of floods, he persisted because he knew he had an end product in bottomland that was worth working for — the kind of soil that great cows are raised on — and by 1912 he had concluded he needed some great cows to raise on it. If he could get the right blood lines going in the right cows, he could get more canned milk to the cow than he could with a punk animal . . . which made nothing but good business sense to him. And in 1916, when he bought the herd of George V. Leighton of Boise, Idaho, he got his first huge break.

"After closing the deal with Leighton," Stuart wrote later, "He said he had a bull on the lot he'd give me if I'd haul him away."

Well, this bull was a mean, cantankerous critter that nobody liked. One keeper got so sore at the animal once, he let loose a shotgun blast that gave the keeper a lot of satisfaction and the bull the nickname "Old Buckshot."

But being an American Businessman, Stuart was not inclined to turn down a free offer — however unlikely the prospects of instant prosperity were from the deal.

And a fellow offered to corral the animal for 5 bucks, which seemed like a reasonable amount for high-risk capital and Stuart told him to go ahead.

That was King Segis 10th . . . the real start of the Carnation purebred Holstein-Friesian herd.

Stuart was a man who could and would put his money where his mouth was and he did exactly that at the National Holstein Sale in Milwaukee, Wisconsin on the morning of June 8, 1918 when a 6-months-old "milking bull" calf came on the auction block. The young bull's dam had produced 1,000 pounds of milk in one week — almost as much as grade cows gave in a year. The calf was the result of careful, scientific breeding. Before the bidding started, it was estimated the animal might bring as much as $5,000.

Stuart paid $106,000 for it.

The editor of *Better Farming* — a national farm publication — thought it was a phoney deal and demanded to see the canceled check. Then he thought Stuart had lost his marbles. Stuart gave him the economics of purebred life that showed that if the progeny of this animal only upped the production of milk 2 pounds a week it would make bulls sired by it worth $1,000 each and heifers worth $500.

As it was, the animal died when it was only 3 years old, from an infection caused by a nail. But the calves he'd sired in that time had sold for $86,000 . . . and the insurance came through at $50,000, so Stuart had made $30,000 on the deal.

Meanwhile, King Segis 10th had sired Segis Pietertje Prospect, known locally as "Possum Sweetheart . . ." the cow whose statue overlooks the green valley land of Carnation Milk Farms today.

She was the first of the "Iron Grandmas."

To get the proper perspective it is necessary to know that when Stuart got into the milk business at the turn of the century, the average American cow gave about 3,500 pounds of milk a year.

On December 19, 1920, "Old Possum" was officially clocked at 37,381 pounds in one year . . . 10 times what the average once had been.

And a whale of a lot of canned milk from one cow.

Carnation wasn't the only company that could come up with this kind of figuring, but it surely was in the right place at the right time with the right techniques. The fact that Stuart was running 20 condenseries made the payment of $106,000 for one bull calf possible . . . but the spinoff is astronomical, primarily because milking bulls or their frozen sperm are shipped all over the world.

Today the average cow in the United States produces 7,500 pounds of milk a year instead of 3,500 . . . and the average cow on the Wet Side of the Mountains being closer to the source of the new Carnation blood line and on comparable land produces 12,500 pounds. It's small wonder that 75% of the milk in our State is produced in Whatcom, Skagit, Snohomish, King, Pierce, Thurston, Grays Harbor, Pacific and Lewis counties . . . a matter of 4 billion pounds . . .

The fact that "every body needs milk" is the thumb in the dike as we scramble to make it unprofitable to put industry and housing developments in our rich valleys — before they're paved and housed over.

Carnation cows stay in the limelight for reasons that you will see when you visit the farms. One of them was the breeding of the first cow that produced 20 tons of milk in one year . . . 20 times her own weight in milk . . . the equivalent of nearly 2 tons of cheese . . . about 14,000 one-pound cans of Carnation Evaporated Milk.

And now we know where that old gag about canned milk came from. The company likes people to understand that its milk comes from "contented cows." (They even play music for them in the barns.)

But it was the little man who served as chief engineer of the "shit train" in the barns for 30 years who came up with the great quote when he saw his first red and white can of Carnation Evaporated Milk. Here was a character who could appreciate the condensation of it all and say: "My God! No tits to wring, no dung to fling. You just poke a hole in the doggone thing!"

—◄►—

Carnation — (Pop. 572. Elev. 90.) — The *Valley Memorial Park* here is a nice picnic spot with playgrounds and rest rooms. And not far away is a charming gray stone *Congregational Church* with beautiful stained glass windows. *The Gap* has good junk and antiques . . . and the *Tolt Cafe* has homemade pie. From here there are a couple of interesting side trips along the *Langlois Lake Road* to a county park, and the *Tolt River Road* into a wilderness.

In passing, as you're headed south, you might want to note a *pioneer cabin* in a large clearing on the right hand side of the road.

Fall City — (Pop. Nom. Elev. 389.) — We frequently have occasion to write about the "right man at the right time in the right place," but here you can insert the name George W. Gove ahead of the quotation marks and the word "wrong" three times in the place of the word "right."

If the history books are right, Captain Gove, who was born in Maine in 1838, went to sea when he was 9 years old. He became a master in the China Trade out of San Francisco where he made enough money to become master and owner of a batch of boats in the Mosquito Fleet on Puget Sound, beginning in 1874. His fleet consisted of the "Cascades," "May Queen," "Gleaner" and "Glide," and functioned on the Puyallup, White, Snohomish, Snoqualmie and Skagit Rivers. He was good at his trade and made a bundle.

A story that illustrates his finesse in this field concerns a farmer who asked him to wait for his chickens to lay 3 more eggs. That way he could fill a case. "Time, tide and the steamer Glide wait for no man," Captain Gove said sententiously, "But, chickens — that's different!" And he tied up his boat 45 minutes until the hens produced the eggs.

Gove, who was a robust man with chin whiskers, hauled hundreds of tons of hops out of the Kent and Puyallup Valleys between 1874 and 1882, watching the erstwhile poverty-stricken farmers grow fat on the proceeds from their crops. Finally, in the latter year, when the price on the market reached 10 times what it cost to grow them, Gove couldn't stand it any longer.

Dipping into the seafaring funds he'd been saving for the past 30 years, he embarked on a new career.

On December 11, 1882, he joined forces with Richard Jeffs and D. K. Baxter to incorporate the Hop Growers' Association which was capitalized at $120,000 and set out to create the biggest agricultural enterprise in the history of King County and the largest hop ranch in the world. Jerry Borst, the original settler in the upper Snoqualmie Valley was happy to sell the new corporation the nucleus of its farm. Borst was a man who knew land and when to sell and when to buy. He reluctantly parted with the "old homestead" — now a part of the town of Snoqualmie — for a price. With more alacrity than reluctance, other farmers in the area parted with their parcels — also at "the right price" — until the farm encompassed 1,500 acres above the Falls.

One of the old-timers of the White River Valley told historian Clarence Bagley that "the farmers more or less exploited the Association. The Association paid for every rail that it got from a farmer." Ranch-hands got about double the going rate for their work, and the transportation costs were sheer murder. This was the pre-railroad period and Gove had to use riverboats which, of course, couldn't ascend the Falls, which meant the head of navigation was at Fall City or at Moore's Landing even lower on the river.

Although in those days the wagon road was on the south side of the river, you can get your own impression of the problems Gove encountered when he attempted to take his supplies up the hill from the town to the ranch which covered the valley floor all the way from Snoqualmie to North Bend. It took a full day for a round trip, as many as 8 horses to haul a wagon up the hill . . . and a dozen trips to unload a scow at the landing. For years, it was necessary to haul about 500 tons of merchandise to the ranch up that hill and an equal amount in farm produce down the hill to the steamers during the harvest.

It was billed as the largest hop ranch in the world — which is highly questionable — but that just meant the venture could go farther into a deeper hole, for 7 years, with a San Francisco financier by the name of H. Dutard — generally known as the "bean and wheat king" — gradually inching his way toward ownership.

Finally, in 1889, Gove took the big plunge. He sold his entire fleet of ships and took over the active management of the ranch, which was indeed a big affair. In addition to what at times reached 900 acres of hops, it produced 5,000 bushels of apples and tons of potatoes . . . carrots . . . onions . . . turnips . . . rutabagas . . . pears . . . plums . . . berries and hay. During the harvest, it employed 1,200 people.

Fall City boomed.

Then Gove got the most brilliant idea in his entire career as a hop rancher. He would personally escort his hops to England and eliminate the

profit of the British middleman . . . those guys made all the money off his
crops and took none of the risk.

He triumphantly steamed full speed ahead — and went broke.

The middlemen were not without influence, and nobody would buy
from him. Storage charges ate him up. And the final forced sale ended his
career in the hop business.

Mr. Dutard foreclosed. Captain Gove turned to a small shingle mill,
and stuffing shavings into mattresses which he sold to logging companies for
two bucks apiece . . . and dreams of what might have been.

He died in comparative obscurity in 1924 at the age of 86 years.

Prowling Fall City

The biggest visitor attraction in Fall City is the *Snoqualmie Falls
Forest Theater and Family Park,* on a 100-acre tract at the foot of the Falls on
the south side of the river. You take the David Powell Road for 3 miles to get
there or ask anybody in town. The theater, itself, is in an amphitheater with
the Falls in the background. It's an active operation, supported by some 210
families, that provides a wide variety of events during the summer season
beginning with a Passion Play around Easter and staging plays, musical
events and barbecues through September. There usually are tours of the park
on summer Sundays but for further information try George Pratt, the director,
at 14240 Southeast Allen Road, Bellevue, 98006 or call 747-8989.

You can also see one of the *drying sheds* from the days of the great hop
crops.

Uncommon shopping — The *B-Frank Gift Shop* came by its name
more or less honestly when Barbara and Frank Stubbs were trying to think
what to call their store. She suggested that they might as well "be frank."
Specialize in plates and other objects made from slag glass, most of which has
come out of old churches.

A word about eating and sleeping – The *Sportsmen Cafe* features
hearty breakfasts and homemade pies . . . the *Colonial Inn* has homemade
cakes and muffins and a refreshment room called the Coachman Lounge . . .
and 7 rooms for rent overnight upstairs . . . and the *Kaschulmist,* a beautiful
Bavarian ice cream parlor in the restored 58-year old Fall City Hotel.

You come across a name like "Kaschulmist" and it kinda gets your
curiosity up. So we checked with RuthAnn Townsend who conspired with her
husband, Gordon, in renaming the place when they restored the 58-year-old
Fall City Hotel . . .

And, of course, it was absurdly simple.

"We wanted a Bavarian name," Mrs. Townsend, who is of Swedish
descent, said. "And we wanted to name it after our daughters, Karrie, Suzie,
and Mistie. So we came up with 'Ka-Shul-Mist'."

The "Ka" for Karrie wasn't hard to digest, and the "Mist" for Mistie.
But "Schul" as an abbreviation for Suzie didn't do much for us.

"Schul?," we inquired.

"Well," Mrs. Townsend explained patiently, "if we put "Suz" in the middle, it would sound Japanese, which doesn't go very well with Bavarian ice cream. So, with her permission, we changed Suzie's name to 'Schul'.''

So there you have it: *Kaschulmist.*

You gotta admit that "Karsuzmist" sounds like some kind of an oriental sneezing fit.

For further information — Call Kaschulmist, 222-5520.

Your route now takes you on the old road past the *State Game Department Hatchery* and on up to the *Snoqualmie Falls Lodge.*

A word about eating — If you've lived in the Pacific Northwest without eating at *Snoqualmie Falls Lodge* then you haven't *lived* in the Pacific Northwest. It's been hanging over the State's most famous waterfall (270 feet high) since 1916 when the chuck-holed road up there was referred to as an axle-buster — and we've busted our share of axles on it. You can go for other things, but the pan-fried chicken is the one to order. Takes about half an hour but in the meantime you can have a drink with the relish tray and potted soup which come with every order. The trademark of the place is the honey dropped from a spoon held about 3 feet in the air above the table.

The waitresses, mostly local girls, pratice this one in the kitchen sink until they get the hang of it and go "on stage." One diner reached for a piece of bread as the honey descended and came out of it with a sticky wristwatch, but that kind of thing is rare.

The Sunday Brunch has been a family affair for well over half a century and the restaurant presently is in the capable hands of Orville Graves and his son, Boyd, veterans in this business in this part of the country. Again, a hint that the "shoulder season" is less crowded, but reservations are advised.

Heading east about a mile along the upper Snoqualmie River we pass the *Puget Sound Railway Historical Museum* which houses the largest collection of railroad equipment west of St. Louis, the largest collection of logging railroad locomotives in the world and an operating steam locomotive. You can take a ride on a real steam-powered train, go on a guided tour of the museum and enjoy a picnic lunch. The elliptical station is registered as an Historic Site and the nonprofit association which operates this attraction hopes that one day it will have a train ride 11 miles long . . . at the moment it goes about a mile.

Snoqualmie — (Pop. 1,260. Elev. 434.) — The major visitor attraction is *Weyerhaeuser's Snoqualmie Mill* where you can take self-guided tours. The first all-electric of the company's mills, it began operation in 1917. You park at the visitor's Guest House and follow a white line through the mill. Periodic informational signs tell you what's going on. In town is a huge *15-foot wheel* which once was part of a saw needed for forest giants seldom found these days.

From here you go to I-90 for a trip back to Preston and a return to Fall City along colorful Raging River. (The trip to North Bend is covered in Seattle Tour 3.) From Fall City, this tour takes you on 202 through rural communities to burgeoning Redmond.

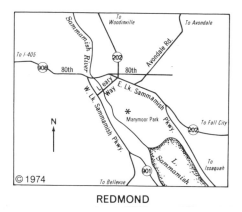

REDMOND

Redmond — (Pop. 11,634. Elev. 53.) — Maybe there's a message for all of us in the kind of thing they've been raising on a piece of property known as York Farm on York Road overlooking the Sammamish Slough and the lovely valley through which it more or less meanders. We say "more or less meanders" because it's been meandering a lot less than more since Man cut its length from about 12 to 6 miles after he lowered Lake Washington with the Lake Washington Ship Canal.

About a century ago, the slough was being used to ship coal from Issaquah to Seattle. It was lowered with the lowering of the big lake into which it flows . . .

An that's the last thing that ever got lowered in Redmond.

In 1918, the county got a brainstorm about reducing alcoholism by rehabilitating drunks in the healthy atmosphere of the Willows Farm at this location. The prisoners responded by raising cain with the whole countryside. They found it a wonderful location for the production of moonshine, which was a popular pastime in rural King County during prohibition. The place became sort of a country home for drunks, at least one of whom asked for a 90-day extension to his sentence, because somebody else would inherit the profits from a big batch of booze he had cooking.

The county gave up its abortive effort at controlling alcoholism here in 1932 and 10 years later, R. C. James, Jr., a Seattle businessman, bought the farm to raise Holstein cows, which he did with the aid of the Nelson brothers, Ray and Archie.

Their purebred herd produced almost twice as much milk as the State average and garnered enough blue ribbons that in 1958 the 69th Annual Convention of the Washington State Dairymen's Association named the Nelsons "Family of the Year," which produced a lot of nice publicity for the farm.

The farm gained even greater fame a couple months later when one of their employees, 17-year-old James Gubser, accidentally dumped a truckload of apple mash in the tunnel leading to the Lake Washington Floating Bridge and creating the greatest traffic jam ever experienced on that bridge.. . .

Scared the hell out of the military, too.

If a 17-year-old boy could do that much with a load of applesauce, what could an experienced saboteur do with one well-placed bomb?

What has happened to the York Farm is a striking example of the national trend that has converted 22,000,000 of the nation's 1 billion prime agricultural acres to nonagricultural use in the past decade. And here's the background.

An agricultural land use study published in December, 1973 by the Puget Sound Governmental Conference, which is seeking to solve some of the problems of Region 4, has cogent comments on the matter.

"Prior to World War II, the highest value placed on a parcel of land was, more often than not, a direct indicator of that land's agricultural productivity. After World War II, however, the concept of 'highest and best use' evolved and land became valued by what type of urbanization it could best support . . . the average per acre value of farmland in the Central Puget Sound Region rose from $247 in 1945 to $1,233 in 1969. The average per acre value in King County went from $290 to $2,068 in the same period . . .

"Specific tracts of farmland in close proximity to the major urban centers are currently being taxed on assessed valuation in excess of $10,000 per acre!"

In effect, the farmer is paying more for the right to farm his land than he can make by farming it. Inheritance taxes also are based on the "highest and best use of the land" and in many cases these are higher than the agricultural value of the land. In the old days, when a farmer retired, he sold his farm to another farmer to get a nest egg. Today, he sells it out of agriculture and into urbanization.

The study adds, "In short, the net result of land value is to push agriculture off of the land. Spatially, this effect is most noticeable immediately around existing urban centers and is keyed to zoning patterns contained in local jurisdiction comprehensive plans. As local jurisdictions seek to increase their tax base by expanding industrial and commercial zones, land values in these zones escalate even before the zoning goes into effect, no matter what the use happens to be . . ."

Labor costs more . . . quality standards are higher . . . prices are not rising to compensate for the increased costs and it becomes almost impossible for a farmer to attract investors.

The study concludes with, "from an agriculturist's point of view, it would appear the region would be better off without him . . . ."

If the trend were to continue unabated, the agricultural industry in this region probably would cease to exist by the year 2010.

The great white hope for agriculture seems to be in the kind of evolving policy evidenced in Skagit County — that if land within an agricultural zone is accepted as undevelopable, speculation purchase of that land would cease and the market evaluation is tied to its agricultural productivity. (Another theory is that public funds will have to be used to preserve our agricultural lands.)

Now back to the specifics illustrated by York Farm. In line with the trend to urbanization, the City of Redmond levied a sewer assessment of $66,000 against the James property . . . for a facility which the farm needed like James needed a hole in his head.

At about the same time, the Rocket Research Corporation, which was located elsewhere, raised the roof off one of its experimental cells and became unpopular with the rest of the folks in the neighborhood . . . especially when they realized the company was producing a nonnuclear explosive 3 times more powerful than nitroglycerin.

With taxes being raised the way they were, James deducted 15 acres of his land along the slough which he gave to the county for park purposes. He sold the rest to Rocket Research for a bundle and got out of the milk business.

The population of Redmond has increased from 530 to 11,536 in the past 30 years.

Prowling Redmond

The key showplace in the area is *Marymoor Park*, a 600-acre tract along the bend in the Sammamish Slough. There's room for picnicking, baseball, model airplane flying, a kiddies' play area. There also is a *Prehistoric Indian Campsite and Dig* which is on the National Register of Historic Sites. But the star of the show is the Marymoor Museum which is located in the north half of the mansion erected by J. W. Clise, a Seattle mortgage banker, at the turn of the century. It was a hunting lodge and then a model dairy farm.

The *Marymoor Historical Museum* has rooms dedicated to pioneer scenes and is operated by volunteer members of the King County Historical Association whose president is one Mary Hanson, who notes with pride that her volunteer chore is cleaning the bathrooms. Everything done in the museum is done with volunteer help. This includes opening the place to the public twice a week (winter hours, Tues. 10-2, Sun. 1-4; and summer, Sat., Sun. 1-4.) Operating on the premise that living history is important, there are demonstrations of pioneer skills the first Tuesday of the month . . . with classes in subjects like baking, spinning, and soap-making during the winter. These are highly successful and you can sign up. The museum is on the National Register of Historic Sites along with an old *Dutch Windmill*.

For a walk on *"The Yellowstone Road,"* which isn't really yellow but once was part of a much longer brick road, see *Footloose*, p. 102. It's a red brick road about a mile long built about 1910, once part of the only road to Yellowstone National Park. From Redmond drive east on Redmond-Fall City Road to 196th Street. This is Old Brick Road and runs north to Union Hill Road.

Uncommon shopping – The *Homestead Nursery* has some of the finest rhododendrons in the Pacific Northwest. Also there are bike rentals.

A word about eating — The highly successful *O-Brien's Turkey House* attracts a clientele from miles around. Another locally recommended is *O'Banion's* — named after Dion O'Banion, a Chicago gangster, 1920's decor, features one-price steaks and pizza.

Annual affairs – *Marymoor Museum Open House* in late April where there are live demonstrations of pioneer skills . . . some 1,500 kids on bikes attend the 3 day *Redmond Bicycle Derby* in August.

For further information — Greater Redmond Chamber of Commerce, 16210 N.E. 80th; phone, 885-4014.

You better have a good map with you up around the north end of Lake Washington these days — especially if you're an oldtimer — because they've got new roads until your eyeballs pop right out on the dashboard. Good Ol' Woodinville and Good Ol' Bothell and fairly Good Ol' Kenmore (although not so ol' as Woodinville and Bothell) are working themselves into a new entity called north shore (without capitals). What with big interchanges and huge population growths in a couple of new entities called Lynnwood and Mountlake Terrace, and an almost total disregard for county lines, things are pretty confusing. The school district was sort of stuck with being called by an anonymous number or hitting on a name. They hit on North Shore. (They, unlike the "north shore directory" people, capitalize their North Shore.)

And the old Sammamish Slough is now officially called the Sammamish *River*.

Things are being upgraded to go along with the fact that this is an important bedroom community for Seattle and Everett.

Woodinville — (Pop. Nom. Elev. 50.) — They've got a lot of horse sense in Woodinville for the simple reason that they've got more horses per capita here than anywhere else in the United States and they angle their attitude toward horses . . . all of which must reflect approval from Above on the part of the town's founder, Ira Woodin. He left Pioneer Square in Seattle, where he started the town's first tannery, because in 1872, with a population of 1,100 the place had become too crowded for comfort.

In those days, the route here was by rowboat or coal barge, and usually involved a certain amount of hiking through trails in the forest.

It also is possible to ride (on horses, not motorbikes) on a dandy road maintained along the *Tolt River Pipeline* by the Seattle Water Department. Check the Water Department for map.

Bothell — (Pop. 5,386. Elev. 54) — About half a century ago, there was a row of signs along the highway between Woodinville and Bothell reading consecutively over a distance of a couple of hundred yards, "if the highway department . . . does not fix . . . this crooked road . . . of floating bricks . . . we'll vote them out . . . of politics!"

And you can't help wondering if now the folks who put up those signs are satisfied. The closest counterpart is hitting a jackpot in a slot machine in Las Vegas. You'd never be able to read those little signs on the highways that have proliferated in the area today.

Bothell notes that it has 175 services and businesses to take care of your every need, which is what they must do to handle the influx of surrounding population, but we're a little wistful about the old days and remember the historic incident when the late eminent Jurist J. T. Ronald and his friend George Bothell had their little political encounter.

Unlike most residents of rural King County back in 1895, Ronald was a

Democrat. He was running for prosecuting attorney of King County. Bothell and everybody else in the town he and his father had founded was a Republican. Ronald had to nominate himself as chairman of the meeting (a motion which Ronald seconded) and then introduce himself as the speaker . . . and then give his speech — to an audience that was 100% Republican.

When the results of the election were announced, he was the only Democrat in the precinct to get any votes — and he got all 30 of them.

There also were the good old days when Joe Ryan was mayor of Bothell and had all the fire hydrants painted white so the dogs could see them more easily . . . and walked in the Fourth of July Parade scooping up the equine "accidents" which he dumped on the doorstep of the drugstore that night.

Prowling Bothell

About as good an historical reminder as you can get in King County is the *Bothell Historical Museum* on Main street. Here are memorabilia of three-quarters of a century ago. Located downtown at the site are the log cabin in which the first white child in town was born, the community's first school-house, and an early pioneer residence.

We were totally charmed to note that Mrs. Marshall Paris, a member of the Bothell Historical Society, prepared the information on the 3 buildings for their nomination as State and National Historic Sites . . .

Because a decade ago, Mrs. Paris wrote the following note to the *Seattle Times* Troubleshooter:

We have read several times about the early-day Seattle store fronts and sidewalks which are still intact underground in the First Avenue and Yesler Way vicinity. Are tours of this area available to the public?

The Troubleshooter suggested that Mrs. Paris and any others interested in underground tours write William C. Speidel. That was on August 3, 1964. Two days later, some 300 persons or organizations had written letters . . .

And Seattle's now internationally famous Underground tours were launched.

Another reminder of the good old days is *Norm's Resort* at Cottage Lake where you can swim and play just like you could swim and play a half a century ago.

There also is a neat place called "*Rhody Ridge*" located at 17427 Clover Road in Snohomish County, which borders the north city limits of Bothell. It's operated by Merline and Founta Butler who bought the land in 1958 and donated it to the county in 1970. It's an arboretum with about 100 varieties of flowers and trees and about 1,000 rhododendrons, azaleas and other shrubs. Open on an irregular schedule and you can find out when by calling the Snohomish County Park Department at 259-9317.

A word about eating — If you haven't already figured out a reason for visiting the north shore, then the *Schnitzelbank Restaurant* is a sufficient one all by itself for the trip. It's just north of Kenmore on the west side of the Bothell Highway where you not only get beautifully prepared, authentic Bavarian cooking, but fixtures carved by one of the most talented men imported to the Pacific Northwest from Germany . . . and on weekends some jolly, genuine "oompah" music.

Annual affairs – *Speedboat Races* on the river in April . . . *Fourth of July Parade and Fireworks* . . . *Raft Races* from Hollywood to Bothell in July . . . and most spectacular is the lighting of the world's highest living *Christmas Tree* (it was born in 1898) on the first Friday in December.

For further information — Bothell Chamber of Commerce, 486-1245.

Seattle Tour 2 — Juanita, Kirkland, Medina, Bellevue, Renton (Map IX)

This tour takes you through the dreams of yesterday and the realities of today around the perimeter of Lake Washington, which was pretty much of a wilderness a lot less than 50 years ago. As a trip through nostalgia for some of the old-timers, it will be an astonishing experience. Leisurely old Lake Washington Boulevard, the mecca for a Sunday Drive in the old touring car, is all but lost from sight . . . busted up by bustling suburban communities. If you can find Kenmore, you can find the right turn past Inglewood Golf Course and over the hill to Juanita Beach, which has got a bunch of gourmet restaurants in place of the old hot dog stand. And Kirkland is a welcome sight as a town that has seized control of its waterfront and its history and is making the most of both. The Points — Yarrow, Hunts and Evergreen — have done a masterful job of retaining their residential "rurality." And Medina is the same unthriving metropolis it was when the ferry landed there. Bellevue, you will never recognize. It's a modern, automobile-oriented metropolis with residents who are looking some place else for a "second home" away from the big city. Mercer Island still is a place with wonderful "drives," but the residents are a lot closer together on those drives. Renton is still Renton, although you'll be a little hard put to find it among the huge industries that have found their homes here.

You'll have a tough time finding remnants of the old Bothell highway, reputed to be the first all-automobile highway built in the United States, but you should be able to ring some kind of a bell if you reach . . .

Lake Forest Park — (Pop. 2,545. Elv. 30.) — When former Seattle Mayor Ole Hanson selected this site for a residential development in 1912, he figured it to be an oasis in the wilderness. He planned the area as a park of large individual plats of an acre or more together with winding roads, parkways and an impressive entrance facing the lake, because, of course, that's how the folks were going to get there — via the flotilla of little steamboats that plied Lake Washington. That gave him the idea for the name of a splendid residential community — on the lake but in a forest — Lake Forest.

It's still an oasis of residences in a parklike atmosphere — but part of a wilderness of heterogeneous housing developments. And without the traffic light at the entrance, you'd risk life and limb getting to the lake which the original developers thought would be the town's perpetual connection with the big city.

A mile or so beyond the park look for the old Inglewood cut-off which is known today as 68th Avenue Northeast in an area generally known, but not incorporated, as Kenmore. In the conglomerate of cross-roads business, it's hard to find, but that's the one you need to follow this tour.

Juanita — Is a very popular swimming beach because the water's warm — and clear, since the advent of Metro.

A word about eating – *Juanita Inn*, has good pizzas . . . *Frosty's Village*, has good view of lake . . . *Spud Fish & Chips*, has some of the finest, freshest fish and chips in all of Region 4 . . . *Domani's*, for good Italian food.

Kirkland — (Pop. 15,275. Elev. 17.) — This city had the most colorful Founding Father of any town on the Wet Side of the Mountains, and at the moment isn't even aware of his existence. Nonetheless, he walked with presidents and kings and wrought great events on this earth in addition to the creation of Kirkland.

He even told Jacob Furth, the boss of Seattle at the time, where to get off at. Furth didn't like it, but he did get off.

The founding father's given names were Smith Jones, which admittedly isn't an admirable start for naming a town . . . like you'd have a little problem with wild laughter elsewhere from people receiving letterheads reading "Smith Jones, Washington." The fact is the name was inflicted upon him by his father at a time when there was very little he could do about it, and he spent a lifetime overcompensating for it.

He did his best though. Upon reaching his majority he caused the name "Leigh" to be placed in front of the "Smith Jones" . . . and subsequently used only the initials of his two middle names. So he was known informally to his friends as "Leigh" and to newspapers as "L. S. J." Hunt. The name is more familiar to people today from the fact that he also was the "father of Hunt's Point . . . which, in its own perverse way, is as good a method of introducing him to the present generation as any.

Hunt never lived on Hunt's Point. His 14-room mansion was on Yarrow Point. But the trees at the end of Hunt's Point interfered with his view of the Olympics, and he bought the Point so he could cut down the offending trees.

Mr. Hunt interjected himself on the Pacific Northwest scene in 1886 by informing the owners of the *Seattle Post-Intelligencer* that if they didn't sell out to him, he would put out a competing publication and drive them out of business. The owners were a bunch of Seattle businessmen who had never owned a newspaper before and hastily sold; not knowing *he'd* never published a newspaper before, either.

Now about Jacob Furth being Boss. Not only was he the leading banker, he also was the political boss. Pioneer Henry Broderick put it this way, "You didn't have to ask Mr. Furth first if you wanted to run for public office. On the other hand, if you wanted to *win* . . ."

With two such positive people as Hunt and Furth in the same town, it was inevitable that they should clash . . . and equally logical that the clash should come over money. In this instance, it was a little matter of $10,818.

Hunt had an incredible capacity for conversation and a burning belief that whatever he did was "right, mete and good." And in 1887 when Peter Kirk was contemplating the construction of a steel mill in Tacoma, Hunt jumped into the act. Kirk was operating on the not unintelligent theory that Tacoma's location as a seaport and its proximity to the Wilkeson-Carbonado-Fairfax coal fields made it a logical spot for a steel mill . . . a condition no righteous Seattlelite would stand for. Hunt had only been in Seattle for a year, but he had brought his righteousness with him. Even a site on a lake unconnected with a port (there was no canal then) near Seattle was better than the oceangoing facilities available in Tacoma.

Hunt was nothing if he was not a shrewd judge of men, and it undoubtedly was at this point that he suggested the name Kirkland to Mr. Kirk. But he had additional pieces of bait. The townsite bore a strong resemblance to Kirk's home, Workington, England, and there was a possibility that a steel mill might fail, but a land company selling townsite real estate around a proposed steel mill certainly would not.

The whole idea made sense to Kirk and in July, 1888 he joined with Hunt and others in the incorporation of the Kirkland Land and Improvement Company which immediately acquired 5,000 acres of land in the area now comprising Kirkland.

The mill, which was to be located up on Rose Hill, near Highway 405, was incorporated on August 18, 1888 as the Moss Bay Iron and Steel Company of America . . . and even Furth, normally the shrewdest of bankers, got sucked into the act and became a member of the board of the mill. But a year later it was out of money, and the fellas dropped it into the nearest garbage can in favor of forming a new corporation called the Great Western Iron and Steel Corporation.

And this is where Hunt's conversational capabilities came into play. He persuaded John D. Rockefeller to invest along with a former U.S. Secretary of War, the Governor of Michigan, Boston's richest millionaire banker and, in addition to others, Senator Jacob Sloan Fassett of Elmira, New York, who felt that Hunt could do no wrong.

These men put $750,000 in cash into the new corporation.

But the steel mill promoters had guessed wrong on a lot of fronts. They figured on more of a market for steel than there was, which held back investment capital. They relied on somebody else to give them a rail line to the mine, which didn't materialize. And they hadn't fully explored the potential supply before they got started. Hunt had talked Furth into investing $10,000 of the bank's money in the enterprise and during the panic of 1893, the bank got a judgment against Hunt for the money.

Furth, who felt Hunt was the golden-tongued orator who had done all of them in despite their better judgment, tied a can to Hunt's tail and ran him out of town, an action for which Hunt never forgave Furth.

Everybody thought he was gone for good, but Hunt, who was only 39 years old at the time, fooled them all, and his adventures would fill a book. For instance, he became the "father of Egyptian long cotton." He was one of the instigators of the Russo-Japanese War and out of that became President Theodore Roosevelt's chief advisor on Oriental affairs. At a White House dinner one night, he told the President about the big game hunting in Africa, which resulted in the President's famed expedition to that country.

But Hunt's crowning achievement as far as we are concerned came from the deal with the King of Korea. Wandering throught that country, he noticed that natives were crushing rich gold ore deposits by hand.

Backed by $100,000 from Senator Fassett, who had not lost faith in him in spite of the fiasco at Kirkland, Hunt talked the king into a concession for a hastily formed corporation called the Oriental Consolidated Gold Mines, which extracted the precious metal with modern machinery.

Fassett did not lose on that one. His share of the $15,000,000 they made was $7,500,000. He figured $7,500,000 was a fair return on a $100,000.

Hunt, of course, got the other $7,500,000.

Although the statute of limitations long since had expired, Hunt came back to Seattle after that one — for two days — and gave the most expensive dinner ever provided in the city's history. It cost $200,000 — plus the food. The people who attended found checks under their plates totaling that amount.

He had invited all of his creditors to that dinner and paid everybody in full . . .

Except Jacob Furth.

And there you have it, a ready made plot for a Kirkland Creative Arts League musical comedy called "The King and I."

It could be staged at their center which is in one of the original town buildings, now on the National Register of Historic Places.

Prowling Kirkland

A Chamber of Commerce brochure on the subject notes that Kirkland is "nestled around Moss Bay on beautiful Lake Washington . . ." but Arline Stokes, who handles the publicity for the town's annual summer festival, couldn't help adding that there is no bay and there is not moss. Outside of that, the Chamber's brochure is fairly descriptive.

There was a bay until the Lake Washington Ship Canal was completed in 1916 and the lake was lowered 9 feet. And there was moss until Metro showed up on the scene. However, the bay really got its name from a bay near Peter Kirk's home in England.

The Chamber has an angle there when it cites Kirkland as a "City of Parks." Park Director David Brink made the point in 1972 that the town has the most public waterfront for each citizen — of any city in the State. When the town merged with nearby Houghton in 1968, the combo came up with 3,500 feet of publicly owned waterfront. Brink pointed out that this desirable objective was brought about by a number of factors, including court decisions restricting over-the-water construction of apartments, which lowered the costs of acquiring such land for public purposes . . . together with

State and Federal grants which enabled the combined towns to create a waterfront park out of street ends and former gasoline storage tank property. Brink also pointed out the town's marina has become the "poor man's yacht club" for boaters from around the Seattle area . . . and forms the only public access for boaters to go ashore from a pier on Lake Washington, and with "free parking" for 48 hours. The Park also has a children's play area with unique driftwood playground equipment and a pavilion. Newest addition to the scene is the restored codfish schooner "Wawona," designated a National Historic Ship, a permanent, waterfront attraction donated by Northwest Seaport, a nonprofit historic ship organization.

Another feature of the Park is the free-form *Kirkland Centennial Fountain* by the late James Fitzgerald . . . made possible by a combination of public subscription and county and State matching funds.

It is of considerable significance that this town, which like many other towns on the Wet Side of the Mountains, turned its back on the water, now has returned to the water . . . and you not only will find civic activities related to the lake, but the stores have learned that store fronts on the park are better than those facing the street.

Octogenarian Louis March, who has lived on the lake in Kirkland since 1905 was so taken by this activity that he gave the town some 300 feet of waterfront, which the municipality was able to parley into at least double that amount with matching funds based on the property March had donated.

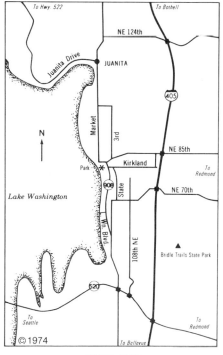

KIRKLAND

Three-quarters of a century ago, Kirkland thought it was doomed to oblivion because it failed to become a smoke-laden repeat of Pittsburgh, Pennsylvania . . . and today's residents thank God that it did.

The *Peter Kirk Building* on Market Street, is landmarked by its cupola, and candle-snuffer roof. In 1962, a group of citizens pooled $5,500 of their own money to create the Creative Arts League and partially restore the building as an arts and cultural center. Today, the restoration goes on and it's a place where people can develop their talents and interests in painting, sculpture, pottery, literature, dance and, of course, drama.

There's fine riding through the 480-acre *Bridal Trail Park,* east of the Kirkland business district, between Kirkland and Bellevue. It's a densely wooded State Park, serving as a mecca for horse people on the east side, with several stables around the park. Central Park Stables is the only public one and you can rent horses here and trail ride with a guide. Hours are 9-5 Tue., Thur., Sun. The park looks formidable when you're driving around, rather impenetrable, and is surrounded on three sides by homes that are horse-oriented, with many developments having a name related to horses, and there are horses in every paddock and back yard. The park superintendent would like to encourage more hikers.

Uncommon shopping — The fact there are 10 antique shops ought to prick up the ears of some of our readers. Among them are *Busek Vintage Days,* 124th N.E., *Good Old Days,* Commercial St., *Marcella Ashton, Potpourri,* Kirkland Way, *Red Barn, Tumbleweed,* Central Way, *Utility Room,* 100th N.E., and *Woodshed Antiques,* Lk. Wash. Blvd. — together they vend a wide variety from primitives to early American . . . *Fiber to Fabric,* 4th St., has supplies and instructions for weaving, spinning, needlepoint, knitting, stitching and macrame . . . A number of shops face on the park, one of the more interesting ones being the *Saints Alive Thrift Shop,* Central Way, sponsored by the Episcopal Church and supported by many local groups, merchandise both by donation and on consignment. Proceeds benefit the whole community, not just the church . . . One of the best for good buys is the *Kirkland Custom Cannery,* 8th Ave., built by the W.P.A. in the thirties to can vegetables grown locally, it now cans fish exclusively, from May through October. Retail shop open through Christmas, features canned "Thunderbird Smoked Salmon" in gift packs . . . *The Thumb,* Peter Kirk Building on Market St., *Creative Arts League gallery and shop* . . . *Cellar Gallery,* Kirkland Ave., featuring work of local artists and craftsmen.

A word about eating – *Flame Restaurant,* Central Way, probably the best known, for steaks . . . *Dona Maria,* Market St., posh Mexican, and *Le Provencal,* Central Way, posh French, both dinners only, and reservations advisable, *Happy Day Taco and Grub Company,* Central Way, informal, hole-in-the-wall Mexican food with good tortillas, enchiladas . . . *Happy Clam,* on Marina Dock, for snacks . . . *Fog Horn,* next to new Houghton Park with fireplace in the center of the room and lake view.

Annual affairs – *Lake Washington Saddle Club Horse Show,* in July, one of the big ones . . . *Kirkland Summer Celebration,* mid-July . . . *Kirkland Creative Arts League's Annual Pot and Craft Show,* in November, glass blowing, whittling, painted tile, sand casting, weaving, collage kits, batik, stoneware, hanging lamps . . . In December, the same organization presents one of the outstanding Christmas features in Region 4, the *Enchanted Castle,* in

MAP I REGIONAL MAP — THE WET SIDE OF THE MOUNTAINS

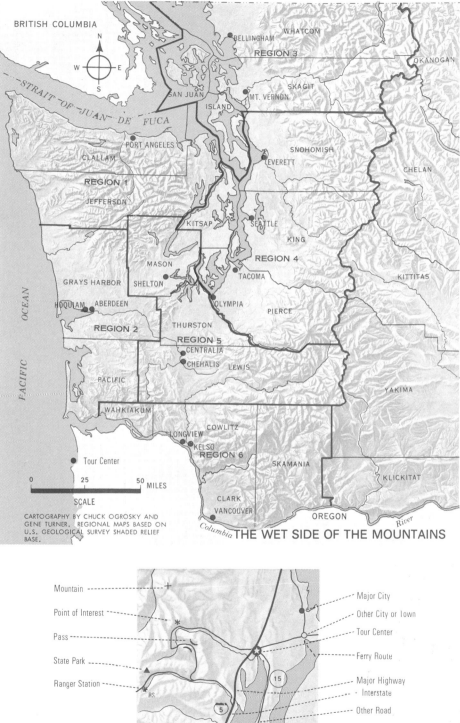

BRITISH COLUMBIA

N
W   E
S

STRAIT OF JUAN DE FUCA

WHATCOM

BELLINGHAM

REGION 3

OKANOGAN

SAN JUAN

SKAGIT

MT. VERNON

ISLAND

PORT ANGELES

CLALLAM

SNOHOMISH

EVERETT

CHELAN

REGION 1

JEFFERSON

KITSAP

SEATTLE

KING

REGION 4

MASON

TACOMA

KITTITAS

GRAYS HARBOR   SHELTON

HOQUIAM   ABERDEEN

OLYMPIA

PIERCE

REGION 2

THURSTON

REGION 5

CENTRALIA

CHEHALIS

LEWIS

PACIFIC

YAKIMA

WAHKIAKUM

COWLITZ

LONGVIEW

KELSO

REGION 6

SKAMANIA

KLICKITAT

CLARK

VANCOUVER

OREGON

Columbia   River

THE WET SIDE OF THE MOUNTAINS

PACIFIC OCEAN

• Tour Center

0   25   50 MILES

SCALE

CARTOGRAPHY BY CHUCK OGROSKY AND
GENE TURNER. REGIONAL MAPS BASED ON
U.S. GEOLOGICAL SURVEY SHADED RELIEF
BASE.

Mountain   - - - - - - - +
Point of Interest - - - - - - *
Pass - - - - - -
State Park - - - - - - ▲
Ranger Station - - - - - ★
RS

Major City
Other City or Town
Tour Center
Ferry Route
Major Highway
Interstate
Other Road

15

5

MAP II REGION I — PORT ANGELES TOURS (EAST)

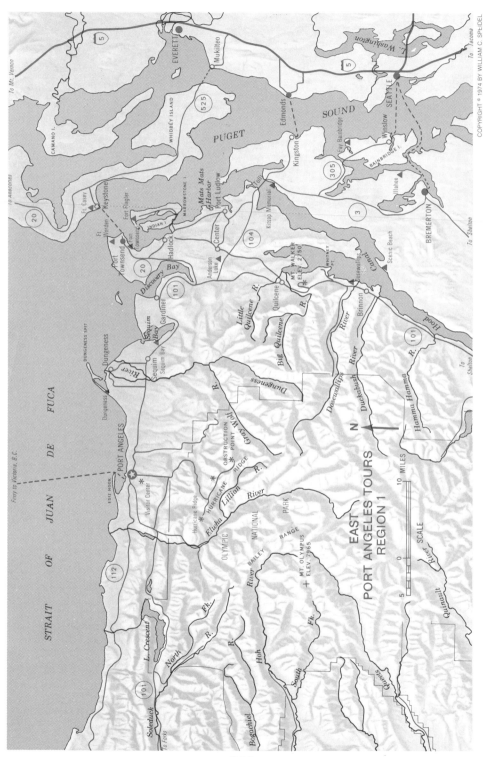

MAP III REGION I — PORT ANGELES TOURS (WEST)

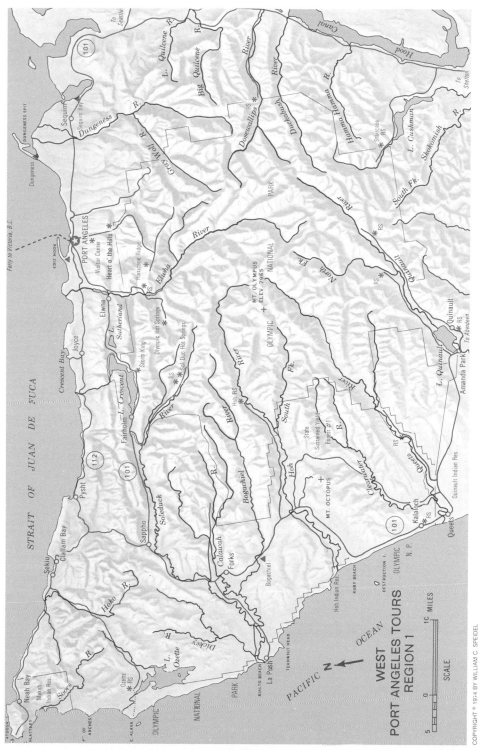

WEST
PORT ANGELES TOURS
REGION 1

MAP IV REGION II — ABERDEEN-HOQUIAM TOURS

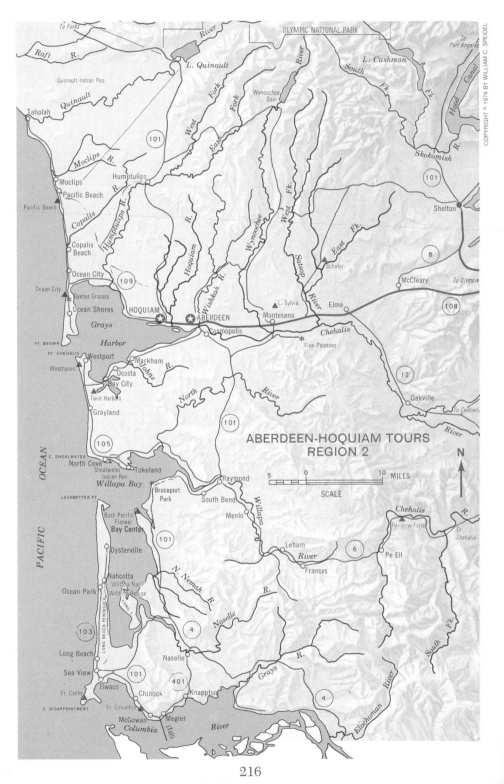

MAP V REGION III — BELLINGHAM TOURS

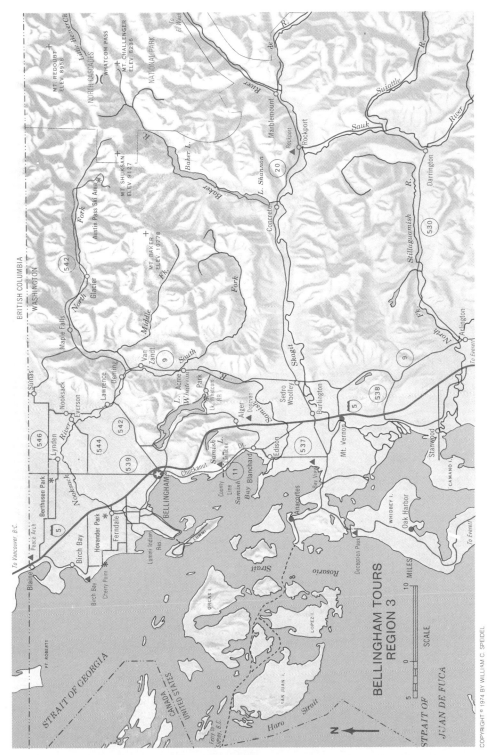

BELLINGHAM TOURS
REGION 3

N

MILES
10

5

0

SCALE

MAP VI REGION III — MOUNT VERNON TOURS

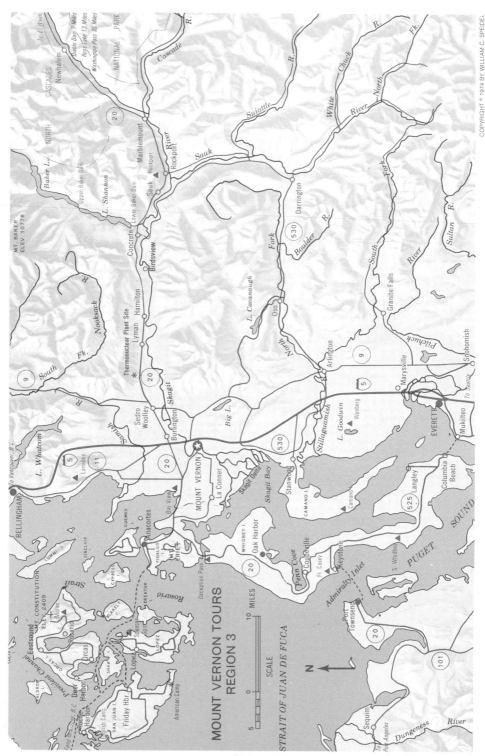

MOUNT VERNON TOURS
REGION 3

SCALE
MILES

STRAIT OF JUAN DE FUCA

PUGET SOUND

N

MAP VII REGION III — EVERETT TOURS

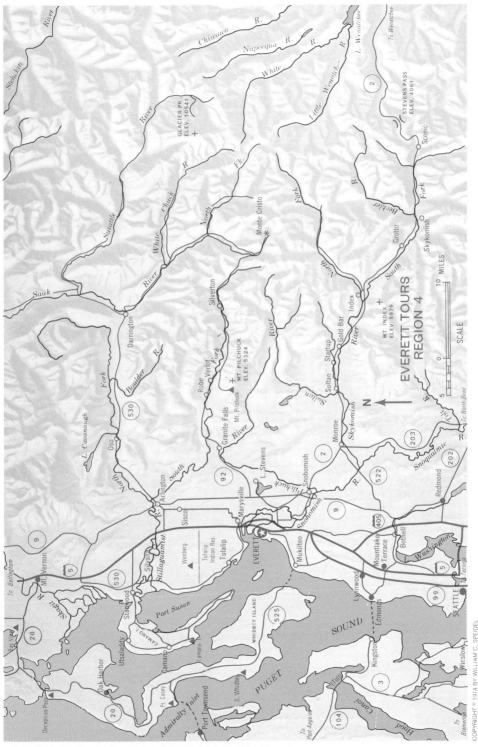

EVERETT TOURS
REGION 4

MAP VIII REGION IV — SEATTLE TOURS

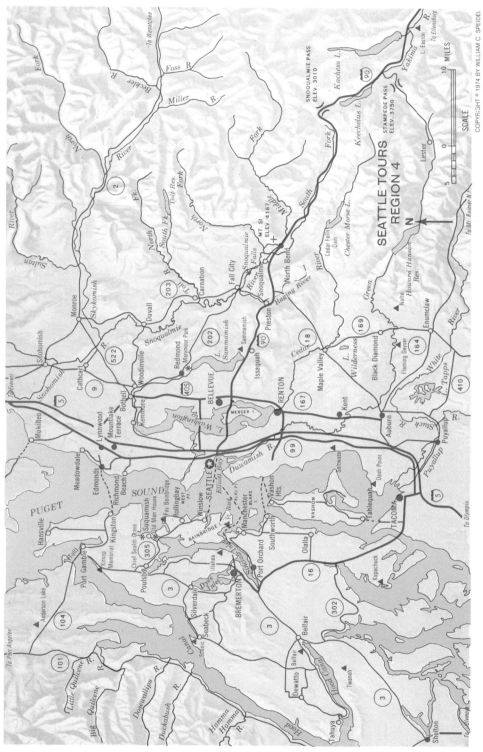

SEATTLE TOURS
REGION 4

COPYRIGHT © 1974 BY WILLIAM C. SPEIDEL

MAP IX REGION IV — SEATTLE TOURS

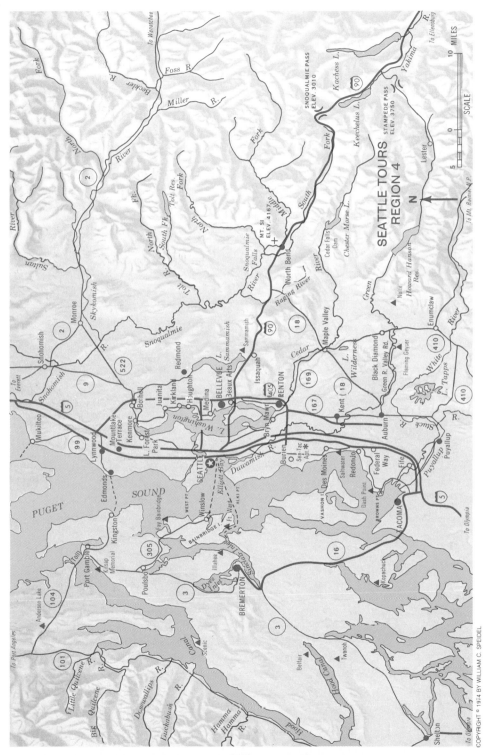

SEATTLE TOURS
REGION 4

MAP X REGION IV — TACOMA TOURS

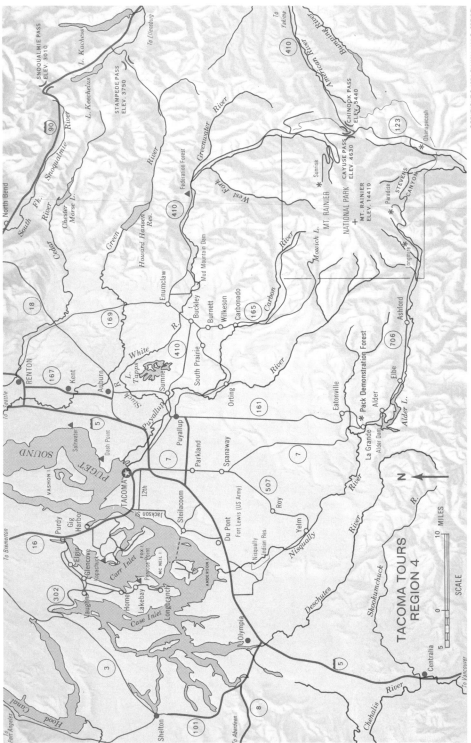

TACOMA TOURS
REGION 4

MAP XI REGION V — OLYMPIA TOURS

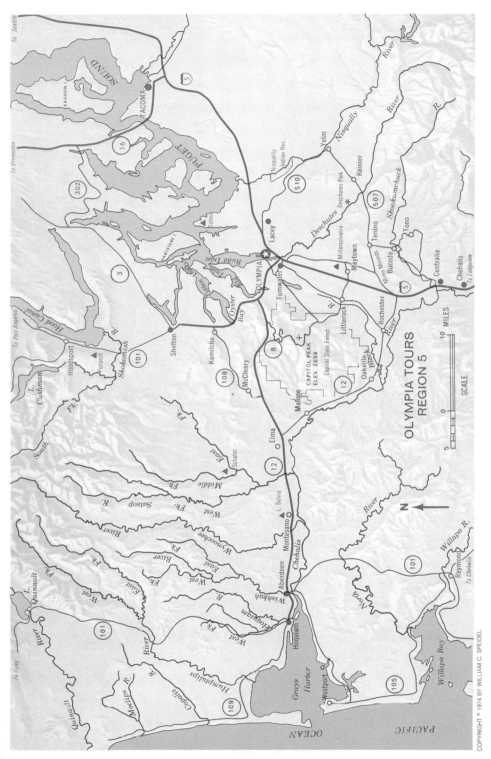

MAP XII REGION V — SHELTON TOURS

SHELTON TOURS
REGION 5

COPYRIGHT © 1974 BY WILLIAM C. SPEIDEL

SCALE

MILES

224

MAP XIII REGION V — CENTRALIA-CHEHALIS TOURS (WEST)

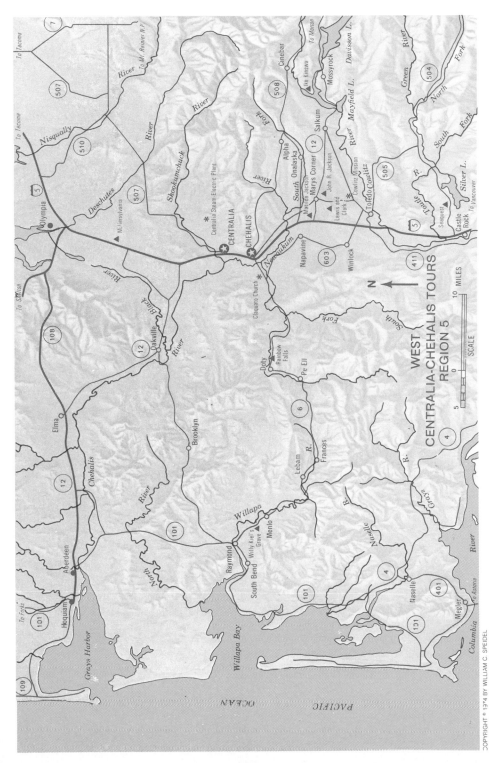

CENTRALIA-CHEHALIS TOURS
WEST
REGION 5

SCALE

MILES

COPYRIGHT © 1974 BY WILLIAM C. SPEIDEL

MAP XIV REGION V — CENTRALIA-CHEHALIS TOURS (EAST)

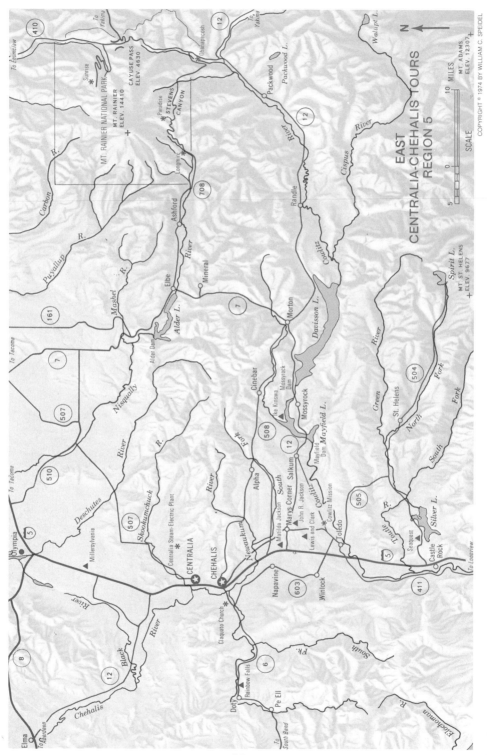

EAST
CENTRALIA-CHEHALIS TOURS
REGION 5

COPYRIGHT © 1974 BY WILLIAM C. SPEIDEL

SCALE

MILES

MAP XV REGION VI — LONGVIEW-KELSO TOURS

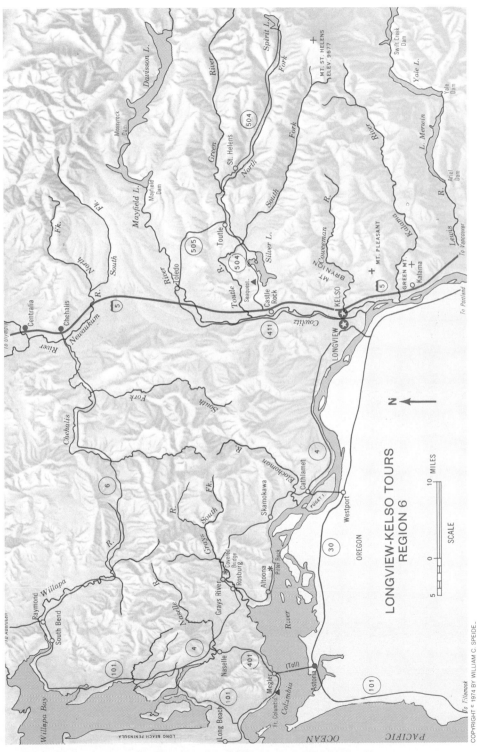

LONGVIEW-KELSO TOURS
REGION 6

N

SCALE

5   0   5   10 MILES

PACIFIC
OCEAN

227

MAP XVI REGION VI — VANCOUVER TOURS

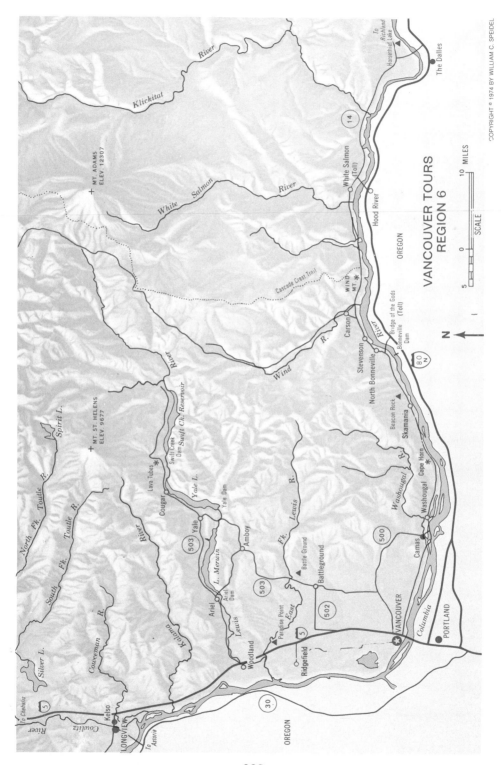

Peter Kirk Building with three floors of storybook land together with little half-hour playlets.

For further information – Kirkland Chamber of Commerce, 113 Lake S., Kirkland; phone, 822-7066.

From here follow the shoreline as much as possible past the attractive residential areas of Yarrow and Hunt's Point to Evergreen Point and . . .

Medina — (Pop. 3,455. Elev. 20.) — This is the "Gold Coast" of the east side of the lake and once was a ferry landing (the ferry landing is now the Town Hall). You get a thumbnail sketch of the town today in a few well-chosen words from a brochure introduced by City Clerk Bernice Snowden with, " . . . Medina is and probably always will be a residential community in the strictest sense . . . the residents of Medina historically have shared a protective attitude toward their heritage of tall trees and quiet waters . . . This often unspoken yet abiding determination has given Medina the unique distinction of having three times as many parks as gas stations — and twice as many schools as grocery stores . . . within the city limits are three parks . . . two public docks, and two elementary schools. There is only one grocery store and one gas station . . . "

By last count there were 1,000 dogs in town, approximately one dog for every three people.

Uncommon shopping – *Medina Grocery*, an old 1910 country grocery, with oiled floors, yellow wooden walls and ceilings, even has delivery service; many call orders in, and some customers have never been in the store; merchandise includes gourmet foods . . . *Wells Medina Nursery* — contemporary nursery with arcade to keep customers dry on rainy days, plants cool on hot days; natural setting wooded area, drinking fountain, aggregate walks.

Annual affair – *Medina Day*, last Saturday in August, events for kids.

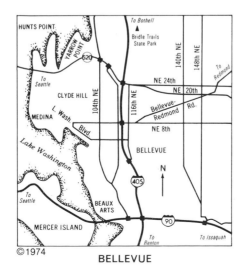

© 1974

BELLEVUE

Bellevue — (Pop. 62,900. Elev. 200.) — Thirty years ago, when the unincorporated village of Bellevue held its annual Strawberry Festival in June, a crowd of 3,000 arrived to eat hundreds of pounds of shortcake and tripled the population of the place. Today, a crowd of about 125,000 arrives for the Annual Bellevue Arts and Crafts Fair — and barely doubles it.

Twenty years ago, Kirkland was twice as big as Bellevue . . . Renton was 4 times as big . . . Everett was 30 times as big. Now Bellevue's the biggest of the bunch.

Wha hoppen?

To the casual observer, it was the first Lake Washington Floating Bridge, but the fact is the fellas came up with two things — Prestige and Free Parking. The former we'll deal with at length later, but the latter is summarized by John F. Herman, who was the long-range planner in 1953 when the town was incorporated and for the next 18 years: "Bellevue pioneered the philosophy in the United States that the public streets were dedicated to the movement of traffic . . . and that parking was the responsibility of the property owners adjacent to the thoroughfare, whether it was a business or a private home. The idea was revolutionary at the time."

And it was Bellevue Square, the first regional suburban shopping center in the Pacific Northwest, that added the Prestige.

In addition to providing 2 square feet of free parking for every square foot of shopping space, it left a big madrona tree standing in the middle of a parking lot and shook the free enterprise system to the base of its foundation. A tree in a parking lot? That took up valuable parking space!

The Square capped the climax by decorating that tree every year with Christmas lights and thereby symbolized not only the fact you could park free and shop in this suburban atmosphere where there were so many trees they could afford to leave one in a parking lot, but that you could live in and among those trees like a country squire . . . and the chances are that if the tree had only been coniferous instead of a madrona, Bellevue would be bigger than Seattle today . . . maybe still could.

◆

The Bellevue Chamber of Commerce has done nothing to tarnish this thought.

In the most elegant brochure of any chamber on the North American continent, it makes the point that Seattle may be a nice place to visit but a Bellevueite would hate to have to live there. While grabbing your attention with a deft picture showing that their town is the major crossroads of freeways heading out to every point of the compass, the chamber notes that Bellevue has been able to plan ahead without distressing decisions about leveling existing buildings to meet the challenge of increased population. After casually noting it was named an All-American City by the National Municipal League, the brochure talks about developing new shopping centers and industrial parks in the lush countryside, while "new residential areas mushroom artistically in the natural splendor of Bellevue's forested and water-rich terrain . . ."

Some of the headings in the all-encompassing brochure read: "THE CITY OF PLANNED OPPORTUNITY . . . COME GROW WITH US . . . THE GOOD LIFE . . . A

LAND CLOSE TO GOD." This is pretty good, too — "Think of this: broad sweeps of lawn, stone fireplaces, boathouses, seaplane ramps, bridle trails and trees everywhere. Hidden park-like home areas . . . For the discriminating there are $200,000 homes with yacht anchorages . . . $31,000 to $80,000 homes designed by talented architects . . . and scattered country acres from $15,000 to $31,000 where your own dream home may some day nestle among tall firs, overlooking the grandeur of the Cascade Mountains and vistas of sparkling waters . . ."

The headline we liked best reads: "A LAND CLOSE TO GOD."

Further statistics are pretty fancy. Seattle expanded its boundaries by 34 annexations in about a century. Bellevue's had 44 annexations in about one-fifth that time. The school population doubled during the 1940's . . . increased 5-fold in the 50's and has doubled again since. Some 80% of the kids who graduate from that system enter college, and of those 50% complete a 4-year course. The brochure says the per capita income is $10,000 — twice that of the State and nation as a whole . . . the average home costs $27,500 and appreciates 5% in value annually . . . some 80% of the city's population is under 45 years . . . and 46% under 18.

Paradise on earth? Heaven brought to the "uncommon" man? Well, there *is* one fly in the ointment.

It's known locally as "454."

It used to be called "Glencourt 4" before the telephone company switched its phones entirely to digits. "Glencourt 4" (now 454) generally encompassed the "Points" — Evergreen, Hunts and Yarrow (to the Kirkland city limits) — and south through Beaux Arts Village to the Sunset Highway (now I-90). It became the diamond-studded, gold-medal, all-purpose, socially-accepted *sign of success* for young executives on the make in the big corporations around and about the Puget Sound Trough. So, Ma Bell had to put in some "455's."

And that's when the circuit breakers broke in the real estate offices.

"Love the house," the people over $10,000 and under 45 say. "Love the location. Love the view. Love the $27,500 price. Er . . . what's the phone number? 455? Sorry."

Now there may be individualists who couldn't care less about the 454, but they belong in Ballard.

Of course, some people have made it without 454. Look at Norton Clapp. He's 455 . . .

He also is Chairman of the Board of Weyerhaeuser.

◄►

Prowling Bellevue

There's *Chism Beach Park*, a lakeside park with amphitheatre setting in a large undeveloped area, which offers swimming beach, picnic tables, charcoal grills, trails and a quacking mallard population. *Bellefield Nature Park* is a plant and wildlife preserve with plank catwalks over waterways and walking paths. (See *Footloose*, p. 94.) *Kelsey Creek Community Park* was created from two former farms whose buildings remain and also includes *Yao*

Park (named after Bellevue's sister city in Japan), an oriental garden with a stone lantern sent from Yao.

For a magnificent view of Lake Washington, Seattle and the Olympic Mountains, drive to *Somerset*. You might want to look in on *Bellevue Community College* on its new campus, a 95-acre maple-wooded site on a hill. *Beaux Arts Community* has winding roads, charming homes and luscious (nearly tropical) flora . . . Chamber of Commerce has a do-it-yourself tour map for the asking. A word to the wise. Get one!

Safeway Distribution Center, 124th N.E., gives morning tours. Call ahead or check Chamber of Commerce. The *Bellevue Lake Driving Range* for golf practice made easy. The balls collect in the bottom of a lake and roll back to you . . . not stoop, no squat, no squint. You might combine your tour with a performance at Bellevue's *Playbarn Theatre*. It has a good reputation in amateur theatre circles and performs mostly weekends at Crossroads Center.

Uncommon shopping – *Cracker Barrel*, N.E. 10th, used clothes (average 2½ months old) sold on consignment, some treasures . . . *The Gazebo*, N.E. 8th, plants and antiques . . . *Sonnett's Sweet Shoppe*, Main St., mix of Victorian and contemporary decor; homemade candies, party mints, bells, hearts, any flower or color, hard candy dishes (you can eat the dishes) . . . *Crockery Shed*, 102nd N.E., in an older brick home, stoneware in graceful shapes, fine workmanship and glazes . . . adjoining *Gail Chase Gallery* . . . and still adjoining *Bell, Book and Candle*, a great bookstore — Mary Ann Robertson gives her store its character . . . and still, still adjoining *Apogee*, women's wear in appealing old brick and split cedar building . . . *The Weed Lady and Crazy Quilt Gallery*, located in old storage shed behind Apogee, with a rain barrel on the roof for water supply for plants. Much charm and warm feelings, "discovery" shop. Homemade soup, breads and cider Wed. noon.

Main Street in "old" Bellevue, false-front small buildings, is an interesting street to browse for antiques, like at *Black Jack Antiques*, and other specialty shopping. Can pick up a map of all shops in any one.

The Brenner Brothers Bakery (and fine restaurant and delicatessen), Bellevue-Redmond Road. A family place (Mama's making cabbage rolls in kitchen) varied pastries and meats. "Pastrami & corned beef Yesler Way," cheese buns, fruit pie tarts, cherry butter-nut cookies, apple or cheese strudel, and the bagels of which they bake many dozens daily. Get their homemade dill pickles before supply runs out . . . *Bud's Select Meats*, 106th Pl. N.E., unusual meat market, prime cuts of meat, stuffed pork chops, stuffed beef flank, marinated steak on stick, squab, pheasant, ducks, capons, geese, deli meats, salads, cheese . . . *Johnston's Seafood*, 106th Pl. N.E., with vintage wine cellar as well as good selection of fresh fish . . . *Bottega*, Bellevue Square, tasty gift shop, home accessories . . . *Panaca Gallery*, Bellevue Square, of Pacific Northwest Arts and Crafts Assn., features only NW artists and craftsmen . . . *Arthur's Bakery*, 107th N.E., has fancy cake decorating, can reproduce anything; also known for lemon queen cake, cheese cake, French pastries . . . *Yabuki Nursery*, one of the oldest nurseries selling vegetable plants, flower stock — whole family involved.

A word about eating – *Crabapple*, Bellevue Square, excellent menu. Relaxed and sophisticated cut-stone decor beneath huge tree, not a crabapple . . . *Jonah and the Whale*, Holiday Inn, elegant food (rack of lamb, etc.) and internationally recognized chef . . . *Casa del Rey*, Northrup Lane, small and very personable dining in a converted home; must have reservations . . . *Brenner Brothers*, Bellevue-Redmond Road, great for lunch, midday snacks, supper . . . *Victorian Inn*, Main St., quaint English atmosphere and unusual menu, like paella on Sat. . . . *The Pie House*, homemade . . . *Cook's Nutrition*, Main St., downstairs below natural food store, all natural foods served in restaurant . . . *Frederick & Nelson Rhododendron Room*, Bellevue Square, lunches, hot fudge sundaes, typical F & N excellence . . . *Harry's of San Francisco*, 105th N.E., hofbrau type food and super sandwiches . . . *Benjamin's*, N.E. 4th, with great view of Bellevue and Seattle, contemporary decor, huge servings, open 24 hours including Breakfast of Champions 4 a.m.-11 a.m. . . . *Black Angus*, 105th N.E., stainless steel dance floor, reasonably priced, modular seating . . . the irrepressible gay-Nineties *Farrell's* ice cream parlor with a Mt. Rainier Sundae disproving our book, "You Can't Eat Mt. Rainier!" See photo of us eating one . . . *Mad Anthony's*, 112th N.E., early American decor-colonial food: game pie, steak and kidney pie, peanut soup . . . *Sir Loin Inn*, 116th N.E., choice beef and lavish salad bar . . . *Apple Pan Dowdy*, Bellevue Way N.E., old-fashioned American dishes in old-fashioned oak atmosphere . . . at Crossroads, *The Fox*, has a good chef and intimate dining . . . *Yangtze*, with Northern Chinese food.

A word about sleeping – Bellevue *Holiday Inn* and *Thunderbird Motel*, both excellent and have everything, Bellevue-style . . . *Bellevue TraveLodge*, also follows suit . . . *Fortnighter*, 100 N.E., for a week's stay or more, twice-weekly maid service.

Annual affairs – *Rhododendron Show*, mid-May . . . *Miss Bellevue Pageant*, early June . . . *Bellevue Village Mall Festival*, late July . . . *Pacific Northwest Arts & Crafts Fair*, Bellevue Square, last weekend in July, attendance over 120,000 making it the largest outdoor art show in the U.S., plus the No. 1 for quality of the Wet Side.

For further information – Chamber of Commerce, 550 160th N.E., Bellevue; phone, 454-2464. (Note that "454" prefix.)

En route from Bellevue to Renton, you can route yourself for a tour of *Mercer Island*, which is a pretty fancy suburb of Seattle that once was called "East Seattle," but has incorporated itself to control its own destiny. I-90 bisects it, but if you take to the perimeter road around the Island, you get some excellent views of the lake and the surrounding mountains ranging from the Cascades to the Olympics. There are a lot of nice homes tucked among trees.

South of I-90, it's a fair chore to stick to what was the old Lake Washington Boulevard, but if you keep edging to the water whenever you have a chance, you'll catch sight of it now and then. Once in awhile there's a lake view and you also will see some stretches of the old highway. Most people prefer 405.

Renton covers the flats formed by Cedar River and the former Black River at the southern tip of Lake Washington. The Cedar is the principal river now feeding the lake. Until the Lake Washington Ship Canal was built, the Black River, a few hundred yards west of the Cedar, drained the lake (except at times of flood when overflow from the Green River Valley flowed into the lake). The Black now is a mere ditch west of town. The Cedar, which once meandered through town, has been channelized and directed expeditiously to the lake. The town is extremely flat and you have little indication it is even near water, unless you drive up Renton Hill where there is a fine perspective of the whole area.

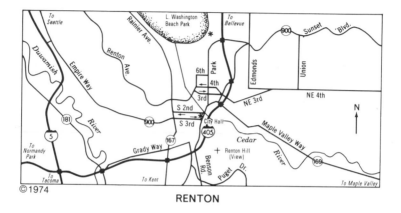

RENTON

Renton — (Pop. 26,386. Elev. 40.) — You sort of hesitate to suggest that Renton is always the bridesmaid and never the bride, but the fact is she's been used and re-used by some of the so-called stars of the show for the past century or more.

For instance, Seattle was in deep trouble when the Northern Pacific selected Tacoma as its transcontinental terminus on Puget Sound in 1873. Half of its business community deserted to set up shop in the new terminal town. Real estate prices in Tacoma soared while those in Seattle dropped to rock bottom. Tacoma's population skyrocketed past Seattle's and the latter was on the skids right down to the bottom of its skidroad. In a frantic effort to save itself from total psychological destruction, Seattle had a big Mayday Picnic — famed in chapter and verse in her history — and started to build its own transcontinental railroad. Renton was to be the first stop.

That was a nice gesture, but it takes more than a picnic to build a railroad.

Then, James M. Colman, one of those tough cookies who built Seattle into the Pacific Northwest's major city, made a deal to build a railroad out of Seattle provided he could make whatever bucks there were to be made on the project. Everybody else thought, "Hot Dog!" and handed him the problem. They thought he was projecting a line to Walla Walla and transcontinental connections. But he had a simpler solution that was a lot more relevant to his own economic future. There was coal in them thar hills at Renton, and a fortune to the guy who could figure out a cheap way of getting it to tidewater. Colman not only was the man who figured out how to do it, but he also figured out to file a claim for one coal mine faster than the man who had discovered it. And it was the Colman Coal Road to Renton that brought the Northern Pacific to its knees and bailed Seattle out.

What did the town of Renton get out of it?

Blue collar jobs in the coal mines.

By 1877, Renton was a rough and ready mining town and on Sunday, February 11 of that year, the way was paved for adding a star of dubious distinction to the town crown. A guy named John Thompson was having an argument with another guy and an innocent bystander by the name of Solomon Baxter intervened on the other guy's behalf. Whereupon Thompson shoved a knife through Baxter, who died on Monday. On Tuesday, the case was presented to Judge J. R. Lewis, the jolly judicator from Seattle, who had a jury impaneled by Thursday. The jury convicted Thompson on Friday and on Saturday, Judge Lewis sentenced him to be hanged.

And Renton got the credit for the first and fastest legal conviction of a white man in the Territory.

Approximately 20 years later, when Seattle was decimating its population with typhoid fever, somebody got the bright notion the folks in the city would have to stop drinking the water out of Lake Washington. The easiest way of getting clean water was by gravity flow out of Cedar River . . . through Renton.

So it was Renton's streets that got excavated to provide three pipelines carrying Seattle's water.

One of the big efforts at the moment is the restoration of the Duwamish Valley as Seattle's prime industrial property, a project that would be a lot simpler if the Lake Washington Ship Canal was there instead of where it is today. It also would have followed the course of the Lake's original outlet through Renton's Black River. But Seattle had made so much money as the shipping center for Renton coal it was able to maneuver the route about as far away from Renton as you can get. Seattle then sold Renton on the more northerly canal route on the grounds that all of Lake Washington would become industrialized and Renton would be the major industrial town on the lake. But the new canal lowered the lake 9 feet and moved Renton's waterfront two miles north of town.

Finally, in 1909, the Chicago, Milwaukee and St. Paul Railroad made use of Snoqualmie Pass, with a route that took it through Renton to Tacoma. Five years after that a biennial report described the Sunset Highway as "A highway starting from the Pacific Highway at Renton, Washington; thence over the most feasible route by way of Snoqualmie Pass; thence by way of Wenatchee, over the most feasible route, through Waterville and Spokane, to the State Boundary . . . " (And thence to New York City.)

Renton had it made. The Pacific Highway came south out of Seattle and went to San Francisco and the Sunset Highway went east all the way across the northern tier of the United States. These two major highways intersected at Renton.

Then somebody invented a thing called the Lake Washington Floating Bridge.

And there Renton sat holding the empty bag, two miles from the water and no place as a major crossroads.

Next, the United States Navy said, "We will utilize that flatland between you and the Lake because it makes an ideal location for the construction of a flying boat."

But there was a problem. The flying boat would "boat" just fine . . . but it wouldn't fly.

Then Pacific Car and Foundry, the largest foundry in western United States, started providing a big payroll . . . and Boeing moved in to produce 1,100 B-29's for the World War II effort. Renton's population tripled in 3 years . . . and Life Magazine did a story on "Renton's Juvenile Wolf Packs," a condition the town finally licked by giving the kids productive things to do.

Pacific Car and Boeing do a lot for the economy of Renton, but they're not an unmixed blessing. There are times when the population of workers in these two places is double that of the entire town. The automobiles of all those people have to be moved to and from work . . . and the resulting traffic congestion periodically causes an upheaval in the city administration on the grounds of "Why doesn't somebody do something!"

And once again, Renton is at the wrong end of the psychological stick. The blue collar workers live in and around the town, giving it the sobriquet of "lunch-box city," but the guys in the supervisory and upper management positions have moved to Bellevue, which has replaced Seattle in the minds of the folks here as Renton's number one nemesis.

Welsh coal miners and Italians built Renton in the original instance. It is made up mostly of working class families who live in neat, well-cared-for homes. Only 3 mayors in the town's history have been college graduates. Bond issues have a tough time here; when they acquire a park or a fire engine, they pay cash for it. It took three shots to build the new library-city hall complex, and those where the first new municipal buildings in 52 years. Baseball games get a big public play, but cultural events must scratch for existence. The voters are mostly Democrats — but conservative Democrats. It's a town of people who try to mind their own business.

And that's why it's such a shock when Sex periodically rears its ugly head.

◆

There was the much publicized episode in 1930, for example, when Police Chief Oliver Martin announced that he was "gunning" for restauranteur Tom Rubattino. Rubattino, it seems, had exposed Martin to public embarrassment and the police chief was going to "get" him.

What Rubattino had done was round up some members of the City Council, and together, they had burst into a beauty parlor where Police Chief Martin was making love to one of the beauties.

The beauty, as it turned out, was Rubattino's wife.

The city council fired the Chief, and a lenient judge told the Chief to go and sin no more.

In an article provided by the Renton Chamber of Commerce for a publication called the *Cities of America*, one of the major points made went like this: "The thing that gives this town its spark is the school system. We all get a thrill out of it . . . "

The biggest spark ignited the biggest thrill in 1966, when somebody discovered that a course in the high school which had been taught for the previous 20 years under the heading, Family Living, was nothing more nor less than *Sex Eduation!*

"My God," somebody said, "they're promulgating promiscuity among the puberty of the people's public schools!"

And the "fit hit the shan."

In the resulting uproar, the distraught school authorities announced they would open the Family Living course to adults on Wednesday nights as long as the latter evidenced enough interest to show up.

Before they were through, the entire adult population of Renton had taken this "refresher course," — 1,000-strong for 12 straight weeks.

This, however, was a summer zephyr alongside the operations of Dr. Frans A. Koome.

His operations were abortions.

Now, abortions are not new to the medical profession. And Renton had no corner on the market. For instance, this region's most famous abortionist for several decades lived in the socially acceptable Bellevue area. But Dr. Koome had a new twist — he made no bones about the fact that he performed abortions. To make things even more inconceivable, he lived next door to the Chief of Police and his modern, tastefully appointed clinic was within a stone's throw of the city's new municipal buildings.

But the authorities had a problem.

Dr. Koome is a very good man. He does excellent work. And they couldn't find one single patient who would testify against him in court. This caught the imagination of the entire State and the voters went to the polls and legalized what Dr. Koome was doing.

That relieved the tensions some between the good doctor and the boys in blue, but the final breakthrough came when he helped them catch a desperate criminal on the afternoon of July 6, 1971.

What happened was this. A fellow walked into the Economy Department Store in downtown Renton and shoplifted an overcoat. When owner Ike Benveniste questioned him about it, he socked Ike on the chin and escaped with the merchandise. Now, Ike's pretty popular with the police. The police are proud of their record against crime. And downtown Renton isn't all that big. Within minutes, a police cordon had been thrown around the entire business district. Not even a rat could get through.

But the criminal had evaporated into thin air — until Dr. Koome called police headquaters . . . and we can hypothesize the conversation:

Dr. Koome: "I say, I've got a somewhat unusual case to report . . . "

Police Sergeant: "Sorry, Doc. This isn't the Mayo Clinic. This is Police Headquarters."

But Dr. Koome wasn't reporting an anatomical anachronism. And what he did report *was* police business. A 55-year-old man, wearing a new over-coat, had ducked into Dr. Koome's waiting room, picked up a magazine and was pretending to be a patient.

His next waiting room was in the city jail.

One of the more sensitive sides of Renton's psyche is that people living someplace else reap the benefits while Rentonites do the productive blue-collar work . . . and like the fact that a whole slug of men in the middle-executive positions in Pacific Car and Boeing get their paychecks in Renton and spend them on those prestigious 454 phone numbers and "average" $27,500 homes in Bellevue.

But Don Custer, native son, former mayor of Renton and articulate spokesman on behalf of his favorite city, gets the last word on that one when he notes, "On the other hand, our homes are paid for."

Prowling Renton

The most spectacular building in town is the *Renton Public Library*, a low, modern building which bridges the Cedar River in *Riverside Park*. A provocative time to visit it is during September and October when the brilliant red, sockeye salmon are ascending the stream to spawn. (The story of how this salmon run came into existence is told in the introduction to Seattle Tour 4.) There is parking around the new municipal complex of which the library is a part, and the park along the river to wander through.

Although you will need our map to get around because of the enormous impact on the city of Boeing and Pacific Car, Rentonites are rightfully proud of the new face-lifting of the central business district which has cost nearly $3,000,000 and includes an area 30 blocks square. A railroad track has been removed from one of the main streets. Power and telephone lines have been undergrounded. Old light standards have been replaced with new, decorative ones. There are new curbs and gutters along with decorative sidewalks and streets, including trees and planters. It's the first renovation of the town in half a century and represents an all-out attempt to restore the vitality of the heart of the city. Involved were the Washington State Department of Highways, Forward Thrust, the property owners, power and telephone companies, Federal Highway Administration and Urban Arterial Board as well as the city and the Burlington Northern Railway.

A major attraction is the *Carco Theater* in Cedar River Park, which was built with a $100,000 grant from the Piggott Foundation. It is used for dance recitals, church revival meetings, and little theater performances. It's a handsomely designed building in a landscaped, rolling terrain along the river.

Pleasant *Lake Washington Beach Park*, just north of the Boeing Company, is especially popular during the salmon runs on the lake. *Longacres Race Track*, located a few miles away is particularly beautiful because the fertile land on which it is located permits magnificent plantings to go with an equally spectacular view of Mt. Rainier. The race track is the heart of the thoroughbred horse breeding industry in the State . . . one which is undergoing tremendous expansion. The *Barbee Mill*, last remaining sawmill on Lake Washington, owes its existence to the fact that some kids had a fish fry on the property in 1958. Their cooking fire expanded into a holocaust that wiped out the mill, but the insurance made it possible to rebuild a $2,000,000 mill modern enough to compete and remain in existence. Visits by appointment.

The Boeing Company, from which the Greater Renton Chamber coined the phrase describing the town as "Jet City," occupies the third largest building in the world — and is tied with the Pentagon for cubic volume. Doesn't look that big but compare it to one of the automobiles parked there and you'll get a better perspective. Visitors usually at 1 p.m. Tues., Wed., and Thurs., but better check ahead. Slide presentation and mock-up of the lounge of the 747. Boeing airport and buildings occupy most of the land between the city center and Lake Washington.

Uncommon shopping – *Old Country Shop*, S. 2nd, European-style delicatessen that takes pains to please . . . *St. Charles Place*, Wells St., antique shop in old restored building, and hobby of doctor who travels to England for his stock . . . *Bud Austin's Drug Store*, a real old-fashioned one with a soda fountain in the middle of it and sundaes, "Green River," sandwiches like it used to be.

A word about eating – *Kingen's*, Airport Way, a family restaurant with good, honest food plus smorgasbord on Tuesday nights . . . *Rubattino's*, S. 3rd., has been here for over 50 years, and is the oldest restaurant in the State still in the original family; open 24 hours and here's where the local characters are, starting with breakfast . . . *Beef and Brew*, Sheraton Renton Inn. "Best damned salad bar in town," and serves brunch on Sunday . . . *Black Angus*, Airport Way, Intimate surroundings and reasonably priced steaks; some from their own beef raised on the dry side of the mountain.

A word about sleeping – The multi-storied *Sheraton Renton Inn* is one of the finest on the Wet Side, with 24-hour coffee shop and posh dining room.

Annual affair – *Renton Aviation Festival*, July 4.

For further information – Call Greater Renton Chamber of Commerce, 300 Rainier Avenue S.; phone, 226-4560.

Return to Seattle along 167, which again provides you with some nice lake views.

Seattle Tour 3 — Issaquah, North Bend, Snoqualmie Pass, Stampede Pass (Map VIII)

This route takes you across the Lake Washington Floating Bridge, the engineering marvel that changed traffic and population patterns in the metropolitan Seattle area . . . across the northern tip of Mercer Island and past Lake Sammamish. You shouldn't miss Issaquah, nestled in a valley between Squak and Tiger Mountains with a fantastic view of Mt. Rainier . . . then over High Point which is more historic than high because it was through here that the energetic residents of Seattle and King County diverted traffic that normally could have followed the Snoqualmie Valley into what today is Everett. North Bend, lying at the base of Mount Si (most "climbed" mountain in the State) is remodeling itself in the pattern of an alpine village. Next is Snoqualmie Pass, the lowest and most important in the Cascades. Here also is the most popular ski area in the State. A delightful summer side trip takes you over the pass to the south end of Lake Keechelus and back into King County over Stampede Pass. It's rugged, often single lane and spectacular into the county's most isolated small town, Lester.

Issaquah — (Pop. 4,435. Elev. 97.) — A historic mining town that has made it gracefully into the 20th century and attracted a wealth of creative people as residents. It lies in the valley between Squak and Tiger Mountains and has a clean, clear stream running through the middle of town. The main east-west artery of the State pulses only half a mile away, but leaves Issaquah relatively untouched to serve as a crossroads community mostly for people who have fled the confines of Seattle and the Renton industrial complex.

On a clear day, the view of Mt. Rainier framed in the "V" between Squak and Tiger Mountains, provide a unique new perspective of the great peak. And Issaquah Creek supplies and is also supplied with salmon by a hatchery in the middle of town. A nice amenity with salmon rapidly becoming one of the most precious commodities in the entire world.

And now we think it would be nice to tell the folks in Issaquah about Daniel H. Gilman, who was the "father" of their town.

Gerrie Armbruster, one of the young matrons who operates *The Boarding House*, a nifty little restaurant that serves homemade food, opined that Gilman was at one time one of our Territorial Governors. And while this is the most outlandish example of misinformation in Issaquah about the man who created the town, it is not a radical departure from the general level of information on this subject within the city limits. And it's not without reason. Mr. Gilman was a pretty scarce commodity around the premises even during the brief time when it bore his name. Most generally, he is confused with his brother, L. C. Gilman, who made most of the biographical history books where Daniel H. did not. Other evidences of Daniel's sojourn in the Pacific Northwest come from Gilman Avenue and Gilman Park in Seattle and the proposed Burke-Gilman Trail, which is much in the news at the moment.

"Our" Mr. Gilman, following his graduation from the Columbia Law School practiced law in New York from 1877 until 1883, when he came to Seattle and concocted the notion of building a railroad in competition with the Northern Pacific which still was actively trying to put Seattle out of business.

The road would start from what today is Alaskan Way and Columbia Street and run north along the Seattle waterfront, on what became Railroad Avenue to accommodate his railroad . . . to Ballard and along what today is the north side of Lake Washington Ship Canal (which was not there at the time) . . . around the north end of Lake Washington (which *was* there at the time) . . . and past Kirkland (which was not) . . . along the east side of Lake Sammamish to tap some coal mining property at what today is Issaquah . . . and then over Snoqualmie Pass.

The ultimate terminus of the road was to be Deadwood, South Dakota.

Gilman fell in with Thomas Burke, another comparative newcomer to Seattle, and after about 18 months the two of them dug up $500 from some big-time spenders in Seattle to send Gilman back to New York to get the rest of the money for the proposed railroad . . . which would come to, in round numbers, $10,000,000. Much to the astonishment of everyone concerned, Mr. Gilman came back from New York with pledges of $450,000 in cash from people who could actually produce real money. But there was a catch. Seattle businessmen had to up their original investment from $500 to $50,000 which would bring the cash total to a well-rounded $500,000. This in turn, would build the first leg of the road as far as present-day Issaquah, tapping rich coal resources the folks had known about for the previous 20 years but been unable to adequately develop.

That struck a responsive chord in the hearts of Seattle's businessmen, who always look on a deal in which the other guy invests $9 to your $1 as a 50-50 proposition.

Besides, it could scare the hell out of the Northern Pacific.

On April 15, 1885, the Seattle, Lake Shore & Eastern Railroad was incorporated by a bunch of Seattle men with Mr. Gilman, who always was long on promoting and short on cash, as the manager. Three years later, practically to the day, the road started servicing the coal mines. For the next 16 years the mines in the area averaged 100,000 tons of high-quality coal a year — which amounted to about 10% of the coal that came out of the county during that period — and made that leg of the S.L.S. & E. a very profitable operation indeed. It did scare the Northern Pacific. The N.P. secretly acquired control of it to keep James J. Hill from getting it — and then found out that Hill didn't want it.

The trustees of the railroad wanted to do something nice for the man who had put the whole thing together. And, inasmuch as it was against their principles to part with cash, they thought the nicest thing they could do was name the town in his honor. Gilman appreciated the honor, but the bank refused it as collateral for some of his other promotions . . . which created a condition in which his interest in the town of Gilman was negligible.

And, inasmuch as there already was another town called "Gilman" in the Territory, the U.S. postal authorities proved less than appreciative of the honor . . . to the extent that they called it Olney . . . which was a name drawn out of a hat some place. So if you wanted to address a letter to Gilman, Washington Territory, you addressed it to Gilman, but if you wanted to address a letter to "Gilman," you addressed it to Olney. Well, this created a certain amount of confusion as well as discouragement among the local citizenry who endured these conditions for 11 years . . . and they were determined to come up with a name related to the area. They kept asking the Indians "What is this place?" As best they could tell everything in the area was called "Squak." Lake Sammamish was "Squak Lake." It was in "Squak Valley" near "Squak Mountain." So the Indians would say something that resembled, "Is a Squak!" Which nobody liked. Then somebody suggested that they were trying to say, "Is a Squaw!" The male chauvinists involved at the time didn't want to rename the town after a woman, so they cut out the "S," added an "H," and came up with Issaquah, which seemed cool to all concerned, including the post office fellas. And on March 6, 1899, the new name appeared in a city ordinance.

Did Mr. Gilman care?

Heck, no. He'd left the Pacific Northwest 11 years before.

Prowling Issaquah

From Front Street, there's the previously mentioned perspective of Mt. Rainier up the valley formed by the Tiger and Squak Mountains. These together with Cougar and Rattlesnake are the closest mountains to Seattle. (See *Footloose*, pp. 97, 99.) There are *view roads* up Cougar and Tiger Mountains. A *drive north* to Pine lake goes past Laughing Jacob's Lake and a thickly forested park and picnicking areas as well as a number of fine country homes. A *drive south* to the Sycamore residential hillside provides a look at a planned community and houses that blend with Northwest landscape.

Out of Issaquah from I-90, you can head for *Lake Sammamish State Park*, the second most popular from the standpoint of attendance in the State. In July of 1973, for an example, an average of 9,500 people were clocked through the gates — per day! (Number 1 State Park from the standpoint of attendance is Saltwater . . . and number 3 is Deception Pass.)

Sammamish has a bathing beach which boasts some of the warmest natural swimming water on the Wet Side of the Mountains. It is loaded with picnic facilities, has a lot of woods and wide open spaces and is a bird sanctuary . . . to attract the kind of people who are for the birds.

Issaquah Historical Society and Museum, located in the old town hall and jail, is open weekends and there are summer tours of historic sites. Inquire ahead about visiting *Darigold Ice Cream* plant . . . plus, of course, the *State Fish Hatchery* in the middle of town.

Uncommon shopping – *Georgie Porgie's Goodie Factory*, for Squak Mountain bread and apple fritters . . . *Browse & Barter*, second hand, some antiques and books . . . *Fonky Hand-Me-Downs*, oak furniture, iceboxes, beds . . . *The Golden Era*, American antiques, weapons . . . in Gilman Village are *The Victorian*, for distinctive antiques, *The Calico Cat* for women's clothing, handmades and custom sewing and the *Country Mouse*, for good local handcrafts . . . *The Wooden Spoon*, art gallery and crafts . . . *Wessex Books*, owned by an English couple, in an old brick building . . . *Cackleberry*, for antique glass and mirrors . . . *Boehm's Candy Kitchen*, for fine, handmade Swiss candies . . . *The Mercantile*, in the former Grange Building has a number of small stores and workshops . . . *Perry's Stained Glass Studio*, owned by a young couple who refer to themselves as craftsmen in stained glass and whose work has a lot of acceptance in the Pacific Northwest.

A word about eating – The previously mentioned *Boarding House* in Gilman Village. Homemade soups, breads, salads and desserts for lunch; and about twice a month they are open for dinner if enough people inquire about it . . . *Pick's Restaurant*, operated by a descendant of pioneer Governor William Pickering . . . *Fasano's*, popular place for fish and chips . . . *H & H Tavern*, for local color in the middle of town.

Annual affair – *Salmon Days Festival*, in the fall, parade and salmon barbecue and watch the sockeye salmon run coming up through the middle of town. Good viewing from the bridges.

For further information – Write Chamber of Commerce, Issaquah, 98027; or ask at City Hall, Sunset Way by the tall flagpole; phone 392-6477.

In view of the elevations to be found in the rest of the Cascade Range, the name "High Point," for a little hump 502 feet high between Issaquah and North Bend doesn't seem like it has very much to do with the price of fish. But from the standpoint of Seattle, it commemorates the spot where the psychological war was won.

In the old days when they were talking about the Snoqualmie Pass Highway, they had in mind taking a canoe from Seattle up the coastline and then up the Snohomish River to the Snoqualmie River as far as the Falls and then hiking over the mountains. Then Seattle got its railroad track into Renton and into Issaquah, pulling traffic in those directions instead of north by the traditional river route that normally would become the route of the highway. Finally, in 1908, Highway Commissioner Joseph M. Snow submitted a map of the State of Washington showing "State Roads Located and Proposed." And that's where they departed from the script about traffic, like water, flowing downhill; and built the road over High Point that ultimately became I-90.

Elevations of various places in the area will give you a clue. North Bend comes in at 456 feet. Fall City is 389. A few miles down the river you're at Carnation with a mere 90, which in turn drops to 50 feet at Duvall and sea level at Everett. High Point, on the other hand, meant routing the highway over a hill to move traffic around the south rather than the north end of Lake Washington. That 1908 map was published at a time when Everett still was uncertain about its status as a city, while the Seattle leaders were in there with both feet, politicking the highway in their direction.

And the proposed route on the Highway Department map showed the highway coming down out of the mountains and making a left turn between North Bend and Issaquah instead of making a right turn down the Snoqualmie River. At that time, a Stevens Pass Highway wasn't even on the drawing boards. And the only way you could get to Everett or any other town on the Sound north to the Canadian border, was around the south end of Lake Washington through Seattle.

A further flourish was added to the concept in the 18th Biennial Report of the Highway Department for the period 1938-1940 and reads like this: "In choosing the site for the Lake Washington Bridge utmost care was taken that it be on the most direct route possible from the city center of Seattle east over the Snoqualmie Pass Route . . . "

But the real battle had been won 30 years before.

If you happen to be in the market for a *carousel horse*, you might pay particular attention to the 356th Street exit, which is about 2 miles west of the Snoqualmie Falls exit. That's how you get to the home of Ernie Jenner, a carousel carver for places like the Smithsonian Institute. Start looking for his mailbox about a mile north of Interstate 90 on 356th. You're welcome to browse if he's there, and if you're in the market, he'll do you one of the inside horses for $450. An outside horse may run as high as $7,000. . . but you could get a whole carousel for a mere $200,000.

North Bend — (Pop. 1,631. Elev. 456.) — They had a little trouble getting this one named and it's been known variously as Snoqualmie, Mountain View and South Fork. All of them had a point, like the first one notes it's in the Snoqualmie Valley. The second suggests they have a view of nearby Mount Si, their favorite mountain. South Fork was pretty good because it's on the south fork of the Snoqualmie River . . . but North Bend pinpoints it better as the "North" bend of the south fork.

Right now the town has the dubious distinction of being the only town which Interstate 90 goes right through the center of. The folks there say the only way to get across the highway now is to be born on the other side. Plans are to bypass it. The local "Built It Now!" organization doesn't much care where the bypass goes — if only they'll build it now.

This is your last real sign of civilization and it is wise to check if your gas tanks and tummies are full and bladders — especially if you have children — are empty before you ascend the Pass.

Prowling North Bend

Snoqualmie Valley Historical Museum, beyond the library, has a lot of antique farming and logging equipment. A walk along the dike of the south fork, Snoqualmie River is in *Footloose*, p. 120.

Uncommon shopping – *George's Buttercrust Bakery*, for Greek delicacies, and Mount Si' crushed wheat, cinnamon, cheese and onion breads. Pastries like eclairs, cream puffs; have coffee at the coffee counter — everyone in North Bend does . . . *Orange Door*, a shop that sells handcrafted wares like quilts, knitted items and other products of heretofore undiscovered hidden talent.

A word about eating – *Mar T Cafe*, homestyle food prepared "from scratch" in a simple homey restaurant. Variety, tasty and local patronage . . . *Mount Si Golf Course Restaurant*, for lunch with a great view of "the" mountain and rolling greens. Buffet dinner weekly and night view of reflections in golf course pools . . . *Hangchow Restaurant*, good food in a Chinese restaurant in an alpine building that was once a bank.

Annual affair – *Alpine Festival*, August, firemen water fights, flea market, raft races, horse-riding events.

For further information – North Bend Town Hall; phone, 888-1211.

Snoqualmie Pass — (Elev. 3,010.) — No Cascade pass is a Sunday school picnic when the wind's up and the snow's down, but if you want to cross the mountains, Snoqualmie's your best bet. It's the westernmost. It's the lowest. It's the one with the easiest approaches and the smallest "hump" at the top. The Indians had used it for centuries before the white man showed up. To the early trappers and Hudson's Bay men, it was the regular route. Physically, historically and economically it was a natural trade route. They grew the steaks at one end and sold them at the other . . . the wheat on one side, and the bread baskets on the other.

The other way of traveling between the two places involved going down the coast from the major population centers and then up the Columbia — a distance of perhaps 500 miles plus the lethal Columbia River Bar — versus 100 miles directly across.

As one early settler wrote the *P.-I.* in 1868, it was an easy route except for one small "gordge."

In the spring of 1853, Isaac I. Stevens resigned an Army position as Executive Director of the Coast Survey office (predecessor to the U.S. Coast and Geodetic Survey) to accept the appointment as the first Governor of Washington Territory and to head up an expedition to determine the most practicable route for a railroad to connect the Mississippi River with Puget Sound.

Functioning under the overall direction of Secretary of War, Jefferson Davis, it was the largest, best-equipped and most detailed of 4 railroad surveys being conducted at the time. These surveys were the greatest effort ever mounted by the United States government to explore the vast and virtually unknown American West. Initiated half a century after the Lewis and Clark Expedition, this was second only to that in importance, although Davis himself was extremely partial to the southernmost of the 4 routes, which made it tough on this one.

Created and paid for by Congress, it consisted of astronomers . . . zoologists . . . geologists . . . meteorologists . . . botanists . . . ethnologists . . . interpreters . . . hunters . . . guides . . . herders . . . teamsters . . . topographers . . . artists . . . cartographers . . . doctors . . . soldiers . . . photographers . . . packmasters . . . wagonmasters . . . quartermasters . . . sappers and civil engineers, of which Stevens was one. It was charged with surveying a swath of land 250 miles wide and 2,000 miles long from St. Paul to Seattle. It was exploration on a grand scale.

It specifically was charged with finding a railroad pass through the Cascade Mountains to Puget Sound.

Stevens fell all over himself to give his great and good buddy of the Mexican War the opportunity of producing that plum and acquiring fame and advancement in the Army as a result of it.

His Great and Good Buddy was Brevet Captain George Brinton McClellan.

There is a piece of landscape called *McClellan's Butte* (which really should have the "e" deleted) on the south side of the Snoqualmie Pass Highway about halfway between North Bend and the pass. And you have our permission to lean out the window and give it the razzberry when you drive by . . . because McClellan retarded the development of Snoqualmie Pass by more than half a century.

The thing that scares you is that the Democratic Party nominated this nut for the presidency of the United States 12 years later . . . and he came within 400,000 votes of Lincoln when the latter ran for his second term. Lincoln must have had McClellan in mind when he said, "You can fool all of the people some of the time, and some of the people all of the time. But you can't fool all of the people all of the time.

Lincoln had learned by then that McClellan, unlike Grant, was constitutionally incapable of "taking Richmond." At the start of the Civil War, McClellan was known as "Young Napoleon" in the drawing rooms of Washington, D.C. — which was where he did his best military work rather than on the field of battle. By the end of the war, he was referred to as *"Little Mac,"* a term that ranked and rankled him for the rest of his life.

But in the spring of 1853, Stevens was one of the people that McClellan had fooled. And by pulling every string at his command, he had McClellan relieved of an obscure job in the wilds of southwest Texas and bundled off to Fort Vancouver and the limelight of the Cascade Pass. McClellan was to be second in command of the expedition, yet he had an easy assignment. Stevens would direct the explorations over the 1,800 miles between St. Paul and the "north" bend of the Columbia River. McClellan's job was the other 180 miles from the coast over the Cascades.

At the onset, Stevens explained to his right-hand man that while the route down the Columbia was fairly well-known, the objective was Puget Sound. Seattle, with its magnificent harbor was believed to be the best western terminus. Following the Columbia meant a swing of 150 miles southward and another 200 miles to the north again, which would add greatly to the cost of the railroads. Congress probably would approve the cheapest route. Thus a feasible pass through the Cascades north of the Columbia became the bottleneck through which the railroad *must* run.

In view of his vast lack of accomplishment, it is noteworthy to point out that in the medical report submitted by the team surgeon, Dr. J. G. Cooper, not one man was injured or sick during the entire time of McClellan's summer excursion in Washington Territory — during which he wrote enthusiastically and in detail about the pleasures of catching trout and the possibilities of panning for gold.

To begin with, it took him 3 weeks to find the exit from Fort Vancouver.

On July 18, 1853, he finally ventured forth.

In the ensuing 180 days, he was directed to, but failed to find, Cispus . . . White . . . Cowlitz . . . Carlton . . . Chinook . . . Stampede . . . Deception . . . Stevens . . . Cascade and Harts Passes. But most of all, he failed to find the pass that Stevens and all of the white hunters, trappers and settlers had urged upon him. And that was Snoqualmie Pass. What he said was he ran into an Indian at Lake Keechelus who told him the snow was 20 to 25 feet deep in Snoqualmie Pass during the winter and there was no way of getting through.

When Stevens and McClellan met at Fort Colville on October 18, 1853, the former, who had an army of men three times the size of the latter, had coverd 10 times as much mileage in equally tough terrain as the latter. The two guys were jovial buddies that night. They stayed up all night belting a few and talking about old times. But 10 days later, McClellan was *ordered* to go to Puget Sound via Snoqualmie Pass . . . or possibly Naches. Then he discovered that he had neither the proper pack animals nor needed scientific instruments and couldn't make the trip. With relief, McClellan wrote in his journal, "I therefore succeeded in having the project crossing the mountains abandoned . . . " Later, he added, "The old proposition (that I thought long since dead) of going over the Cascades . . . with an odometer was renewed. I objected so strongly to such a performance that I think it is now abandoned — forever, I hope."

But he hoped in vain.

Stevens' diary adds to the light of what followed: "Had I possessed at Camp Washington the information which I gained six days afterwards at Fort Walla Walla, I should have pushed the party over the Cascades . . . but McClellan was entitled to weight in his judgment of the route, it being upon the special field of his examination . . . " (McClellan meanwhile had headed down the Columbia and up to Olympia.)

So, Stevens again *ordered* him to explore Snoqualmie Pass . . . this time from the west side of the mountains. That order wiped out Snoqualmie as a railroad pass for the next half century. McClellan couldn't have found it if he'd had a helicopter. McClellan wrote, "I have done my last service (when I have finished this expedition by going to the Snoqualmie Pass from the Sound) under civilians & politicians. The great consolation is that I was detailed on this service without either my knowledge or consent — and I do not regret the service I have seen, the duty I have performed nor the lesson I have learned. Certainly, I will not consent to serve any longer under Governor Stevens unless he promises in no way to interfere — namely to give me general orders, and never say one word as to the means, manner or time of executing them — even under those circumstances I should hesitate." With that attitude, there was no way McClellan would cross Snoqualmie Pass. After the usual 3 weeks of pawing the ground for traction, he presumably went as far as McClellan's Butte where, on January 7, 1854, 4 inches of snow stopped him dead . . . Four inches of snow and a real knowledgeable Indian who told him that no way could anybody cross over until April.

And it was the same damned Indian who had talked him out of it before!

Ten days later, A. L. Tinkham, who had been Stevens' assistant when the latter engineered and constructed Fort Knox, came breezing through Snoqualmie Pass with a report that snow conditions would be much easier to cope with than those through the Alleghenies. Tinkham, a civil engineer, had showed up at Walla Walla after 42 tough days on his trek through the Rockies . . . and went right on to make Snoqualmie without difficulty.

After that one, Stevens required McClellan to reduce his reasons for not crossing the pass to writing and then refused the latter's request to delete the example of incredible incompetence from the report that went to Congress. Stevens not only made himself an enemy for life, but an enemy for Snoqualmie Pass, and in the amazing processes of Washington, D.C., this was critical. Jefferson Davis wanted a railroad along the northern route about as much as he wanted to preserve the Union a few years later. He buried the information sent from Stevens and Tinkham. And in his report to Congress on February 27, 1855, wrote: "The examination of the approaches and passes of the Cascade Mountains, made by Captain McClellan, of the Corps of Engineers, presents a reconaissance of great value, and though performed under adverse circumstances, exhibits all the information necessary to determine the practicability of this portion of the route, and reflects the highest credit on the capacity and resources of that officer."

In other words, a railroad over the Cascades was impossible.

The Civil War interfered with everybody's railroad plans. By the time they came up again, Stevens was dead. McClellan, back in the drawing rooms of the east coast, had become president of two successive railroads — both of which bounced him when they got to know him. But he was sitting there as the big expert when the Northern Pacific and Great Northern were contemplating their passage over the Cascades and neither of these lines opted for Snoqualmie Pass.

It remained for yet another man and a new era to popularize Snoqualmie Pass and built it into the artery that provides the lifeblood between the Wet and Dry Sides of the Mountains. And he would not even be born until 10 years after McClellan made his grim decision to sabotage any pass in the Cascades . . . and that pass above all others.

His name was Ford . . . Henry Ford.

Born on July 30, 1863 in Greenfield, Michigan, he was an apprentice machinist by the time he was 16 years old and became obsessed with the notion that motors attached to wheels could replace horses and provide people with propulsion without effort.

By 1903, he divested himself of his overalls long enough to form a company named in his own honor to manufacture a thing called a motorcar. Six years later he was a ripe plum for a promotional idea submitted to him by the backers of the Alaska-Yukon-Pacific Exposition in a town a long way from Detroit called Seattle.

At 3 p.m. on June 1, 1909, President William Howard Taft pressed a Golden Key in Washington, D.C., that opened this exposition in Seattle and at the same time rang a bell in New York City. The Mayor of New York, poised for the sound of that bell, fired a golden pistol into the air, and the first motorcar transcontinental race ever attempted was underway as 6 wheezy "gas-breathed" vehicles sputtered down the street.

Five of them were Fords.

Three weeks later, Ford was waiting anxiously in Seattle for the outcome of the race when he heard that Snoqualmie Pass, still covered with snow, was hell on wheels. He donned his overalls and trekked up there to help dig Ford Entry Number 2 out of the mud and if necessary carry the thing over the pass on his back. The car left the pass at 3 p.m. on June 22 and arrived in North Bend by 10 o'clock the next morning. It was 1 hour and 45 minutes more to Renton from there and another 45 minutes into Seattle where Fire Chief Harry Bringhurst, met her at the city limits to escort her through the cheering crowds. With fire bells ringing, Chief Bringhurst headed for the Exposition Grounds followed by Robert M. Guggenheim, who had offered a trophy worth $2,500 and $2,000 cash for the driver winning the race. Next was the driver of the Model T, Harry B. Scott, followed by Henry and 150 cars who had joined the procession en route down from the pass. At 12:56 p.m., June 23, 1909, the winner of the transcontinental race entered the main gate of the

AYP. The car was 22 days and 56 minutes out of New York City. A crowd of nearly 15,000 people cheered.

Interviewed by the press, a jubilant Henry Ford suggested there was a Ford in our future.

He said, "The happenings of the past three weeks will awaken the conscience of the American people that this country can become the most mobile and prosperous nation in the world. And I am confident they will build a road system that will bring it about."

The Chicago, Milwaukee and St. Paul railroad also ran through the pass that year.

And speaking of Snoqualmie Pass, neither Ford nor his driver made any bones about the fact that it was the toughest part of the whole trip, putting the deserts and the Rockies to shame. The Washington Good Roads Association rallied around that one and promoted a good Snoqualmie Pass highway as its first order of business.

And on July 4, 1915, Governor Ernest Lister made it to the pass from Seattle at the head of a motorcade in the incredible time of "just over 7 hours!" He had cut the record made by the Ford in half. Speaking at the opening of Highway 10 (now Interstate 90) to automobile traffic, Governor Lister told dignitaries from both sides of the mountains, "This motorcar highway is more important to the area than the transcontinental railroad."

To get some feel of what the folks went through in crossing on the old *Snoqualmie Pass Wagon Road* a century ago, stop off the highway at the Denny Creek Campground exit where you can take a historic walk on a mile-long section of the road built in 1868. You'll find remnants of the puncheon, the decaying remains of some of the trees so big that it took two men 3 days to cut one in half and another 3 days for oxen to haul away. There's lots of other stuff and the trail is marked. The road is on the State Register of Historic Places, and application has been made to put it on the National Register. (Also, see *Footloose*, p. 124.)

Prowling Snoqualmie Pass Area

Some 250,000 skiers annually take on the slopes at the *Snoqualmie Ski area*, which makes it one of the most heavily populated ski areas in the world, and during the season, it operates 7 days a week. On Saturdays, some 250 school buses bring kids here for their shot at it . . . and thanks to the new short skis, this sport is available to people in age brackets ranging from 3 to 80 years. It's just a step off the highway for car-cushion travelers, and if you'd like to get the flavor of one of the most popular ski areas in the world you can stop off here. Accommodations range from the posh *Restaurant Continental*, which is open year-around, to cafeteria service and include the *Slide Inn Tavern*, which has huge windows overlooking the slope. This was one of the first big-time ski areas in the country . . . and the first to have interdenominational church services on Sunday — in, of course, *St. Bernard*, a small chapel adjacent to the main buildings.

At the south end of *Lake Keechelus*, you will encounter a right turn to *Stampede Pass* and come west to the town of *Lester*, which is back on the Wet Side of the Mountains in King County. Mostly a logging road, it has not been tailored to perfection like so many of our highways, but you get a real taste of the wilderness and a couple of interesting places to picnic en route. There is only one road — because there wouldn't be room enough in the narrow valley for another. Access in winter to Lester has to be by train or by the courtesy of the Tacoma Water Department to leave the gate open through their water shed.

Seattle Tour 4 — Maple Valley, Black Diamond, Auburn, Kent (Map IX)

This tour sticks to the foothills and valleys on the Wet Side. It starts our rather unpropitiously with a lot of bulldozer dirt-moving at the mouth of Maple Valley but soon starts following the meandering Cedar River through a green valley that sparkles with fall colors from the changing leaves to the bright and spawning salmon in the stream in September and October. At Landsburg you cross flat tableland where enormous coal-mining activity spawned Black Diamond three-quarters of a century ago. Coal is gone but the town remembers its glory days and basks in one of the finest perspectives there is of Mt. Rainier. You descend through the gorge of Green River to the jam-packed, industrialized Auburn through sprawling Kent, a bedroom community en route from agricultural to urbanization and industrializaton, and back through flat, river bottomland to Seattle. Generally, it's an area where man has monkeyed around with rivers and come up with amazing, amusing and spectacular results that give environmentalists fits and bring joy to the hearts of the bankers.

Maple Valley — Don't be discouraged by the entrance to the valley which currently is undergoing a lot of earthmoving. It gentles off into the small valley of the Cedar River shaded by trees that once were predominantly maple but now are alder. Mushrooming residential developments proliferate the green valley floor around the meandering course of the river which is crossed and recrossed by automobile, railroad and foot bridges. Once a major route across the mountains for fur traders and prospectors (via Meadow or Dandy Pass to Lake Keechelus), it is a rapidly developing bedroom community. Evergreen forests cover the hills with second growth and there still is much pastureland . . . on which are grazing more horses than were there before the advent of the automobile.

The main tourist facility in the lower valley is the *Aqua Barn Ranch*, occupying one of the oldest homes in the valley. It was built in 1895 by Samuel Denny, a cousin of Seattle's founder, Arthur. As was a Denny custom, he also married a Boren . . . Carson Boren's youngest daughter, Mary Louise. Today, it's quite a recreation center — especially for young people. There's a motel restaurant, swimming pool (where 10,000 people have learned to swim), horses, riding arena and trails.

But the unique feature of Maple Valley, penetrating the burgeoning evidences of civilization, is the man-made salmon run which qualifies as amazing, amusing *and* spectacular. Best time to see it is in late September and October.

What successful nimrods used to say in the old days — and may say today for all we know — is that "you've gotta be smarter than the fish!" A crack like that was usually good for brief laughs before the conversation went on. But Dr. Lauren R. Donaldson, the big salmon and trout expert from the University of Washington School of Fisheries, easily tops that old gag by adding, "And that's something the human race will never be!"

This is particularly true of salmon . . . and more especially true of Pacific than Atlantic salmon or steelhead. The former are born in a particular stream somewhere in the northeast Pacific Ocean. Some of them have to have a lake attached to that stream. And they come back to that exact same spot where they were born . . .

And they only have one shot at it, because they die.

Avalanches and giant trees blocked off the previous courses of streams while these animals were at sea. When they came back, what they did was adapt to the new situation — whatever it was. And a man like Donaldson, who has performed miracles with fish that are second only to the demonstration of Our Lord is like an infant crying in the night as far as total knowledge is concerned.

The aboriginal Indians worshipped the salmon. Donaldson is one of the pioneers in understanding the mysterious and infinite force which they represent.

The salmon swimming up Cedar River are the result of one of the damnedest sets of coincidental circumstances you will ever see.

This story begins back in the late 1880's when the residents of Seattle were absolutely convinced, as you will recall, that Lake Washington would be industrialized and that Kirkland would be the Pittsburg of the west, and needed a canal to the Sound.

We got the canal 20 years after the main reason for wanting it had ceased to exist.

But we did get it, and that's the point here.

Then, in 1926, while The Lord looked down on us sadly shaking His head and saying, "They know not what they do!" the Puget Sound Power and Light Company proudly presented us with a brand new dam on the Baker River. Now, we're not faulting Puget Power for this. And The Lord only shook His head instead of firing a big bolt of lightning at us and striking the population dead . . . because God knew we needed electricity. Except that in the light of today's knowledge, the State Department of Ecology would never okay a dam at that site . . .

Because that was the only river in the whole United States with a sockeye salmon run.

For whatever reason, sockeye have got to have a river-lake combo in connection with their life-style. In British Columbia, for instance, the folks are risking brownouts (at the moment) rather than permitting damming of the

Fraser River and endangering the sockeye runs. Among other things, sockeye, which has that economically priceless red color in the cans, is the money fish up there. They rate it above the king, which has the top value down here.

Well, the State and Federal Fisheries guys went crazy trying to find some place else — *any place* else — in the United States where they could redirect the force represented by these fish. They milked eggs from the females blockaded by the dam and planted the resulting fry any place where there was a river-lake combination that seemed even remotely suitable.

There were 5 — only 5 appropriate places.

By 1937, about the time when they were figuring out a few more things about our salmon, there was a big run of sockeye to the Birdsview Hatchery on the Skagit River which ended up with a surplus of 4,000,000 eggs. State Fisheries fellows figured that May Creek, Lake Isobel and the Snohomish River was a combo that would prove particularly enticing to sockeye salmon. So they planted half a million eggs there. It was one of those deals on which you couldn't lose.

Not one single adult salmon returned.

They dumped another half a million in the Samish River . . . and when only 400 had returned by 1940, they forgot about the Samish River. They put another half a million in Bear Creek, which is an outlet for Cottage Lake and flows into Lake Washington . . .

And got 2 back.

They tried Cedar River on for size with 600,000, but when only 400 came back, they forgot about that one, too.

But Issaquah Creek . . . there was a bonanza! That looked like a real good one from the very beginning. They planted 1,357,000 fry and got back a whopping 9,099, which looked pretty big alongside of 400 and 2 and none at all. For a while there they thought they were smarter than the fish, but the Issaquah Creek run faded into gradual oblivion and the fisheries guys went on to bigger and better — well, at least "other" — things.

Meanwhile, in spite of the fact that it had failed miserably in the "industrial test," Lake Washington proved to be a wonderful receptacle for the effluent of sewage treatment plants catering to a basic necessity of a proliferating population. The lake got so nutrient rich with algae that you couldn't see your feet when you stood in the water . . .

A pretty punk place for people . . . but the hottest spot on the Wet Side of the Mountains for sockeye salmon . . . which meant the whole of the United States.

In the fall of 1950, one of the Department of Fisheries patrolmen got a call from some folks living along Cedar River about some terrible-looking red fish with hooked snouts messing up the water and wouldn't he *do* something about it?

Now an interesting point to be made here is that in the old days when the lake drained out through Black River and into Puget Sound, there never had been a sockeye run. And, as far as anyone knew, the fish planted in the creeks around here long since had died off. Nevertheless, the fish described on the telephone with that first call sounded suspiciously like sockeye.

Well, the Fisheries Department men did something about the funny-looking red fish, all right. They said "Holy jumping Jehosophat!" and they weren't far from summing the whole thing up.

They estimated that about 25,000 fish spawned in Cedar River that first year. And while there's many a slip between the cup and the biological lip, the Department of Fisheries experienced little difficulty in reviving its interest on this front.

"Interest" was the only thing they had at first, because it takes a run of about 100,000 fish to undertake a management program. But by 1964, they had counted 70,000 fish, which was pretty exciting. In 1967, there were 200,000 and the run was increasing exponentially.

Four years later it hit 600,000!

This, of course, called for a big uproar among fishermen over who got to catch what fish . . . and they had to monkey with the State laws and the rules and regulations and a bunch of economically injured feelings to let purse seiners in Lake Washington so a lot of the fish could be caught and they wouldn't die and stink up all the expensive residential property the sewer systems were supposed to take care of.

There probably won't be a run to match the one in 1971 until 1975, but here's a neat instance where mankind is doing something right — on purpose. By controlling the flow of Cedar River, which the Seattle Water Department can do, they can get 3 times as much spawning as they could get under natural circumstances. They start out with a flow of 90 cubic feet per second until the salmon have hatched along both sides of the river. Then they up the flow to about 200 cubic feet per second, which gives the next wave of animals a whole new shoreline to hatch in. Finally, they up it a 3rd time to 600 for the final hatching process and hold it there until the spring when the fry go downstream to live in the lake for awhile.

Meanwhile, however, something else has happened that may or may not upset the balance again . . .

Metro has cleaned up the lake.

Will Lake Washington continue to be the biggest sockeye salmon rearing pond in the United States?

Maybe we'll find out in 1975.

But back to the original question. Have we been smarter than the fish? Well, we spent several million dollars 20 years after the fact to industrialize Lake Washington with the Hiram Chittenden Locks and the Lake Washington Ship Canal.

And we were bright enough to build fish ladders alongside the locks so the poor fish could climb into Lake Washington if that's where they were determined for some abstruse reason to go.

But do the salmon use those fancy fish ladders?

Heck, no . . .

They ride up in the locks.

Maple Valley — (Pop. Nom. Elev. 343.) — Is a crossroad with stores, a highly visible old railroad station, and a fine new *County Library*. For a side trip, turn left up hill to 216th St. and go to Black Diamond via Landsburg where Seattle City Light has a *dam* and their slick little *Park*. You can see the sockeye milling around at the base of the dam in season. An annual affair, the *Cedar River Boat Race* starts from here in June. Continue on through Maple Valley and take right turn to Lake Wilderness. *Lake Wilderness County Park* has swimmers, boats and golf balls. People connected with the University of Washington think deep thoughts in the fancy facility here and then talk about them. You can drive around the *King County arboretum* and look at the nice private residences and gardens on the lake if you want to.

Black Diamond — (Pop. 1,164. Elev. 610.) — As you come up the hill to the town limits, Mt. Rainier comes down the road to meet you if you have thoughtfully selected a day when the Mighty Mountain is showing itself to mere mortals. Old King Coal built this place and when he was deposed, it went down the tube so far they thought it was gone out the other end like a lot of other ghost towns around here, but the good roads and uncommon shopping like the *Black Diamond Bakery* saved it. That Bakery is one of the most famous institutions on the Wet Side of the Mountains. And all they do is bake bread the way people used to *have* to bake it — in brick ovens with wood fires. Chances are if you're on a Gray Line Bus en route to Mt. Rainier, you'll stop here . . . and if you aren't you'd better call ahead for a reservation for the kind of bread you want (but don't try it on Mon.). Suggestions for profitable prowling here are sourdough rye . . . flakey meal . . . Crystal Mountain and Mt. Rainier breads. They also sell pies and Black Diamond candy. It looks and feels like coal and is licorice-flavored. They don't make a dime on this and you don't pay tax — it all goes to help support the Volunteer Fire Department.

Black Diamond's most colorful character has to be Ben Bieri, a graduate architect from Kansas who has a ball living in the "exclusive Morganville Section of Black Diamond" building and selling beautiful clay objects at *The Pottery*. For years he has been trying to move from this Tar Paper Shack to the exclusive Barn up the road and may have made it by the time you show up. He notes in the flyer announcing his annual *Valentine Day Bowl Sale* that "If you received this, you were on the Tar Paper list which has been placed in a time capsule to be opened in 23 B.C." For the lushes, he adds . . . "What's 'er name is south of the border; however before she was deported, she brewed a VAT of her notorious O*T*H (over the hill) and DRANK it . . . but there will be something . . . "

Uncommon shopping – *Frank Zumek's* Kolbase, in the IGA meat market at the north side of town is sausage made like they used to do it in the old country. If pressed, he'll show you the smokehouse which bears a strong resemblance to a Chick Sales edifice. He sells about 2,400 pounds prior to Christmas and Easter.

A word about taverns – Social life of the town centers around the *Boots Taverns* "where everybody goes," and the *Morganville Tavern* which has a solid silver dollar bar and a sign directing you to the restrooms which reads, "Sitty Hall."

For further information – Black Diamond City Clerk, TU 6-2560.

On the road out of Black Diamond take a side trip to *Green River Gorge* and park near the 200-foot-high bridge for gasping view which includes a small island on the north and a waterfall on the south. You can take the pretty trail down to the river through moss, ferns, pools, salal. (See *Footloose*, p. 155.) There's also a lodge resort with cabins, restaurant, snack bar and picnic grounds with fire pits.

Continuing the tour, go west off the main highway about half a mile south of Black Diamond on *Green Valley Road* to Kummer . . . Green River . . . *Flaming Geyser State Park* and Auburn. There's a picnic area at the Park and you can see the Green River's gorgeous gorge. (See *Footloose*, p. 150.) It's a pleasant drive on primary county highway with picnic spots, and a beautiful green valley winding down through farmlands to civilization.

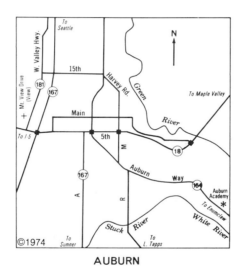

AUBURN

Auburn — (Pop. 21,870. Elev. 90.) — Right off and at the onset, not to mention the beginning, we want you to know that we are *White River Valley* people . . . not Kent Valley . . . or Green River Valley . . . or Duwamish Valley.

And the fact that there is no *White* River in the White River Valley is quite beside the point.

And we are happy to note that the White River Valley Historical Society and the White River Feed Company and the White River Buddhist and the White River United Presbyterian Churches — not to mention White River, itself — all are on our side.

Actually, from time immemorial, the White River originated in a couple of glaciers on the northeast side of Mount Rainier. It tumbled down between Enumclaw and Buckley, then through Auburn, where it was joined by the Green. With 75% more water added to it by its new helper, it flowed on through the Valley which was named in its honor and dumped into Elliott Bay between Seattle "Forefather" Charlie Terry's onion farm and what now is the

Spokane Street Viaduct. Once it passed Renton, where it was joined by the erstwhile Black River, it really was the "White-Green-Black River." And with a mess like that on their hands, the folks decided to call all 3 of them the Duwamish River, which is about as good a name as any, although it basically was the White that was the main show.

The only problem is that the White River no longer is there.

The confusion crept in the peace table following the Twenty-Years War between King and Pierce Counties, when a whole bunch of Chamber of Commerce people from Seattle, Orillia, Kent, Auburn, Sumner, Puyallup and Tacoma met in Auburn on December 24, 1906 and agreed to submit the problem to Hiram Chittenden of the Army Corps of Engineers. Chittenden brought in a broad spectrum of engineering talent when he went to work.

The Twenty-Years War had started in 1887 when a bunch of White River farmers north of Auburn got some dynamite and blew a hole in the west side of the river, diverting it down the Stuck River and into the Puyallup River in Pierce County so farmers in the latter valley would get the benefit of the water from the fall floods. The following year, the Puyallup farmers blew a hole on the other side of the river, thus giving the benefit of the fall floods to the White River Valley farmers.

The Chittenden report puts it this way, "From 1887 to 1892 there was a good deal of interference by citizens of both counties with natural conditions near the point of separation of the two streams. Due mainly to artificial causes, the channel shifted back and forth several times in the next six years . . . "

In 1898, the White River guys let go a charge that caused a high bluff to slide into the river filling the north channel completely and funneling the entire river down the Stuck . . .

And as far as the King County farmers were concerned, the Pierce County farmers were "stuck," period.

Then came the famous blast of July 4, 1899.

By that time, the King County Commissioners had an armed guard posted on their side of the river to prevent any monkey business. But somebody gave the guard some money and he took an official leave of absence to go bet it on the Independence Day horse races at Enumclaw.

At the crack of dawn, and accompanied by a newspaperman who reported the whole incident, a band of twenty men "armed to the teeth" sneaked across the river from the Pierce County side. The P.-I. reported it in part like this, "The perpetrators of the deed — the farmers of the White River call it a dastardly outrage — were farmers whose lands are annually threatened by the Stuck River floods, aided by adventurous spirits from Tacoma, some of whom looked upon the affair as a unique Fourth of July Celebration. Looked at in that light, the event was a brilliant success . . . "

By 10 o'clock in the morning, 2,000 pounds of dynamite, costing 13¢ a pound, had been planted along a 250 foot stretch of the river just west of what today is the Auburn Academy, about 1½ miles south of Auburn on Highway 164. Then everybody slipped back across the river to open a keg (not dynamite) and start celebrating the founding of America.

Shortly before noon, one man in a canoe slipped across the river, lit a fuse and hastily paddled back. The news story adds that "eight mighty charges of dynamite costing approximately $40 apiece were detonated. The explosions shook the earth for miles around and tons of mud, water and shattered timber were hurled higher than the surrounding tree tops . . . Farmers who live near the scene say in sober earnestness that they saw huge logs shoot into the air higher than the sixty-foot bluff overlooking the slide . . . the shots were heard and plainly counted in Auburn . . . The leaves on the trees were torn off as if by a hail storm . . . and acres of mud are covered with splinters and mud from the log jam . . . Hours after the dynamiters had hurried stealthily from the spot, the poisonous gases of the explosion hung low over the scene and filled the lonely valley as with autumn mists and both rivers ran black with debris . . . "

King County retaliated in 1899 by starting construction of a high embankment across its side of the river on the grounds that the Stuck River might overflow its banks and flood out King County farmers . . . which meant it would have to flow uphill, backwards and against the current of the White River.

What they really were after was insurance that Pierce County farms would enjoy the benefits of White River floods in perpetuity.

The Chittenden report notes that this action "culminated in 1900 in an injunction suit brought by Pierce County to restrain King County in an alleged attempt to divert the White River permanently into the Puyallup Valley. Each county produced a formidable array of evidence from old settlers, engineers and others to prove that the natural route of the White River to the sea had always been through the territory of the other county; and that any work which it or its citizens might have done near the point of separation of the two streams had been solely for the purpose of preventing the other county from interfering with natural conditions . . . "

Well, Pierce County won that round. And then on November 15, 1906, both counties lost when a flood arrived that inundated both valleys, wiped out railroad bridges and killed people. And in 1907, they sat down around the peace table and handed the chore to the engineers for action.

The Chittenden Report stated that geologically, the main channel of the White River was north to Elliott Bay, in spite of the fact that there were occasional overflows at flood times into the Puyallup Valley. On the other hand, the report noted that the river trip to Seattle was 40 miles while the river could reach the sea at Commencement Bay, Tacoma, in 20 miles. So the engineers recommended that a man-made left turn at Auburn be constructed and that 3½ miles be cut from the meandering Puyallup River and that it be enlarged and channelized to cope with the new course of the White.

The engineers also recommended that inasmuch as King County would be the principal beneficiary it should pay the lion's share of the bill. And that's when the legal profession got into the act. It was tough enough to persuade the King County Commissioners to go along with the notion of doing something, *anything*, to help Pierce County. After that, they had to figure out whether it was legal for one county to spend money in another county.

That one took 7 years.

Finally, in 1914, they initiated an Inter-County River Improvement on the White-Stuck and Puyallup Rivers. They finished the project in 1919, but not before the White River had one final shot at returning to its traditional channel.

In a report filed in 1920, W. J. Roberts, chief engineer of the project, wrote that only prompt action on the part of the engineer during the floods of January, 1919, saved the diversion dam which routes the river to Commencement Bay. Roberts wrote, "Prompt action on the part of the engineer was successful in filling the eroded section of the undercut before any serious damage resulted (but) I have no hesitation in saying that had the dam not been there at the time of the . . . flood at least a portion of the White River would have cut its way again into the Auburn district . . . "

The White River's been around for a long time and it knows where it wants to go . . . and it's just lurking there, waiting for its chance to get back to the White River Valley where it belongs.

When somebody said, "Don't raise the bridge, lower the river," he thought he was being funny, but the folks in Auburn went him one better. The first homestead in the site of the city was located on the banks of the White River . . . and they removed the whole river.

A lot of other areas might have considered moving the town, but the people in Auburn have their own way of doing things.

Halfway between Seattle and Tacoma, it has been a major intersection from the time of the railroads, and it got an enormous boost on April 10, 1913 when the town became the western freight terminus of the Northern-Pacific Railway with 50 miles of trackage and a payroll of 750 people. Transcontinental trains were broken up here and dispersed around the Pacific Northwest. Ten years later it trembled to the shudder of 67 trains a day routed through the tracks here by four transcontinental railroads . . . together with 57 daily interurban trains. And in 1926 a change in railroad policy knocked off 90% of the railroad repair and dispatching personnel. It was an economic body blow that staggered the little town, but in World War II, the United States Army reactivated the dispatching yard, bounced the population to around 6,000 and paved the way for a population boom the city fathers still are having a terrible time coping with.

In 1961, the General Services Administration moved into some of the 604,000 feet of covered warehousing space left by the Army after the war and provided some 800 jobs. But the really big boom began with the arrival of the Boeing Company in January, 1966 with an investment of $120,000,000 in an assembly plant that presently employs — in nice round numbers — 8,000 people.

Auburn traffic has been all choked up over that one ever since.

Service stations outnumber churches for the first time in the town's history. The city's operating budget has soared five times and even with the aid of huge federal matching funds, they're having a trying time just coping with the number of human beings involved in all of this.

It would be illegal, immoral and probably fattening not to mention that the town originally was named to honor Lieutenant W. A. Slaughter who was killed nearby during the Indian War. And if you scratch the surface even slightly, someone will tell you with a small chuckle why they changed the name: When the railroad came in, runners from the hotels attended the arrivals of trains and urged passengers to the hotels they represented. The town's leading hotel was honorably named after Lieutenant Slaughter.

But somehow it didn't have the right ring to it when the runner shouted "This way to Slaughter House!"

But the same token, the most elite organization in town takes its name, "Daughters of Slaughter," from the fact that the members have descended from people who were here when the town bore the Lieutenant's name. And if you meet a Daughter of Slaughter it does not necessarily indicate you are in immediate danger of mayhem.

Prowling Auburn

The *White River Valley Historical Museum*, on H St. S.E. is open afternoons on Thursday and Sunday, and filled with lovingly collected memorabilia. It is on the edge of *Les Gove Park*, which has picnic tables, should you feel like combining history and food. Up on the hill to the east of Auburn, *Green River Community College* is housed in good-looking buildings on a beautiful campus, has a lively college atmosphere; try the coffee shop. There's a *Bicycle Path* along the bank of the Green River from Auburn to Renton that's just as scenic for walking, as it winds through farms, pastures and towns. A *State Game Farm* is located on R St. S.E. and you may visit to see deer, pheasants and other birds; also visit the State's *Green River Hatchery* on Route 1. Or, by calling ahead, you can arrange a tour of the *Federal Aviation Administration* traffic control center, *Boeing Co.* fabrication plant, or *Burlington Northern* roundhouse.

Uncommon shopping – *Cugini Florists*, Auburn Way S. Attractively arranged store of gifts, china, as well as flowers . . . *Forest Villa Bakery*, Auburn Way S., popular locally for bread et al . . . *Frank Natsuhara Store*, W. Main, Oriental food and gifts, started as a supplier of berry crates . . . *Auburn Pottery Co.*, Auburn Way N., clay flower pots and saucers, and may have that size you've been looking for. One of only two such plants in the west, the company has been here 50 years run by the same family.

A word about eating – *O'Farrell's Char-Broiler*, Cross St., locals like their hamburgers . . . *Concord Inn*, Kent Municipal Airport, offers an unusual view for lunch — at the end of the runway . . . *Other Side of the Tracks*, W. Main, literally and figuratively, in restored old building with sofas from Seattle's Pantages Theatre and chairs from Seattle's Rainier Club; soups and salads . . . *Rainbow Cafe*, E. Main, features "Tom Matson, steak," named after father of local 2nd-hand car dealer . . . *Clover Leaf Cafe*, Auburn Way S., homemade bread and pies . . . Taverns with food: *Flapper Alley Tavern*, Auburn Way S., tasty sandwiches and chicken . . . *Jack's Tavern*, Auburn Way N., mighty good homemade Italian pizza.

Annual affairs – *Old Fashioned Spring Festival*, late April. Sidewalk display of arts and crafts, sale of produce, all on Main St. . . . *White River*

Buddhist Church Festival in fall; dances, booths for sale of produce, delectable Japanese food . . . *Veterans' Day Parade*, November 11. The one-hour march is considered one of state's biggest.

For further information – Chamber of Commerce, 24 B N.E.; phone, TE 3-0700.

Kent — (Pop. 16,805. Elev. 42.) — A booklet about Kent by Richard S. Beyer, the sculptor whose work in the Kent City Hall is a "must" for car-cushion traveler, has the following food for thought:

> A man has an idea
> He would cage it
> But it breaks out
> It would kill him
> He hides
> He cannot sleep
> There is no peace in the day
> And the tide comes in on his castle
> Disordering his life like a man in the constellations
> There are those who have answered to ideas and
> gone to jail
> The cost is like the cost of a wife.

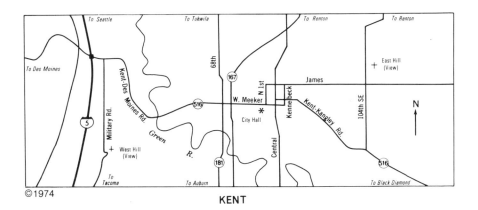

©1974

KENT

Now, this kind of thing has proved pretty puzzling to a lot of the residents of Kent — mostly among those who think the creation of the present city hall has to be among the nuttiest notions ever inflicted upon mankind by a majority vote of the people . . . a vote which allowed the city fathers to blow nearly 2 million bucks on this outlandish enterprise.

But we shall see what we shall see.

The town of Kent was ushered into existence on July 3, 1888 by the ubiquitous Ezra Meeker, who at the time was enamoured with all the money he was making from selling hops in England. He thought it would be good public relations to name the town for the English County of some of his ritzy friends and one of the great hop-growing areas of that country. The English couldn't grow enough hops to satisfy the demands of the brewers in the business of providing English pubs with the British national beverage. And in 1888, close to a million pounds of hops were grown around here for overseas shipment.

It annoyed the hell out of Meeker a few years later, when a Methodist Conference publicly thanked God for the destruction of the hop crop. This remarkable action on the part of the Methodists resulted in a news story in the *P.-I.* reading, "A Curse on the Hop Crop." Preacher Hanson of Puyallup reported to the conference that he had some good news from the great hop country . . . the crop had been cursed by God. "Whereupon Bishop Bowman said, 'Good' and from all over the room voices could be heard giving utterance to the fervent ejaculation, 'Thank God.' "

Meeker blew his cork in a letter to the editor on June 6, 1895, saying that the church in which the Rev. Mr. Hanson had been preaching for "a year past was built in great part by money contributed from gains of this business 'cursed by God.' For myself I can inform him that, as a citizen of Puyallup, I contributed $400, to buy the ground upon which that church edifice is built, every cent of which came from this same hop business 'cursed by God.' I would 'thank God' if they would return the money and thus ease their guilty consciences . . ."

This caused something of a furor in the White-Green-Black-Snoqualmie-Duwamish-Puyallup River valleys where overnight the main money crop had died. For an equivalent today, ask some eastern Washington farmer what the impact would be from the sudden demise of the entire wheat crop . . . or if Boeing suddenly went out of business in these same valleys.

The Methodists strategically removed Mr. Hanson from his post in Puyallup and assigned him to a distant parish that was less susceptible to the vagaries of a lynch mob.

Ah, those were the simple days with the easy answers . . .

Ezra was one of the world's most colorful characters and we divide him up between Kent and Puyallup, although the latter really has the main claim to fame on his front. Nevertheless, the principal annual celebration in Kent is called "Ezra Meeker Days," and the main east-west street in town was named by this worthy gentleman in honor of himself — a step which he devoutly wished he had taken in his younger days when he gave Puyallup the name it had today instead of calling it Meeker.

And they have a pretty good reason for honoring him. Because it was through him that the White River Valley was changed from an economic disaster to one of the most prosperous river valleys in America. Some historians say it was *the* most prosperous valley.

To understand the transformation, we take you back to the two decades before Meeker introduced the hop crop.

Things were tough all over in hinterlands of Seattle in the two decades following the 1851 settlement of that city as evidenced in an unpublished manuscript of Charles H. Ballard of the White River Valley who wrote, "About the only thing that could be raised to sell was potatoes . . . The potatoes were hauled to the Alvord landing, then they would be taken to

Seattle by a couple of hired Indians in a canoe. They brought in Seattle from 30 to 50 cents a bushel . . . the latter price being considered a regular bonanza. Father would go to Seattle on horseback, sell the potatoes and take goods in payment, and load them in a canoe and come back up the river, the Indians taking about four days for the trip . . . Father tried raising wheat to make flour. The country had such early rains and so much moisture that it always grew so rank that it would fall down before it was ripe enough to be cut . . .

"We were desperately poor at first . . . "

Roads posed no particular problem in much of Thurston and Pierce Counties, but from King north they were a muddy impossibility most of the year. Ballard noted that in the fall when they were trying to haul their harvest to the landing, the wagons frequently would sink to their axles in the stuff and sometimes become buried in it. "When the road got so it was almost or quite impossible to haul over," Ballard wrote, "those interested would get out together and cut another route around, which in a short time would be about as bad or worse than the first. In some places there were several openings through the woods that one could take his choice of . . . "

Sometimes a man would take the long walk from Kent to Seattle — just to sell a bucket of eggs.

To begin with, the folks didn't have enough capital to invest in dairy herds that could produce quantities of butter that in those days sold at the fabulous price of 50c a pound — easily the equivalent of $2.50 today. The population of Seattle was well under 1,000 and even though it was the trading center for the logging camps around and about, there was only so much of a market for produce. The roads were nonexistent and there wasn't enough money in transportation on the river to warrant the steamboat travel that was so prevalent, for instance, on the Columbia River.

What the farmers needed was a crop that could be sold for a bundle of money in the world markets.

And that's when the hop crop popped.

It started out innocently enough when Isaac Wood, owner of the first brewery in Olympia, imported a few hop roots from England to plant in the garden around his house. On March 15, 1865, he sent three pecks of roots to Jacob V. Meeker, who had a claim near Sumner in the Puyallup Valley, via one of Meeker's sons, John. John packed them on his back the 20 miles, pausing for a bit at the home of his brother, Ezra, who relieved him of enough of the roots to plant 6 hills of hops at what now is Pioneer Park in Puyallup.

With the rest of the roots, Jacob Meeker planted four rows of about 100 feet each, and that September sold the hops to Brewer Wood for $150 . . .

It was the most money paid for any crop any place in any of the valleys in the region that year . . .

And the farmers went hop happy.

The elder Meeker died in 1869 and Ezra went on to be the hop king of all the nearby valleys tributary to Puget Sound, which included all of those colored rivers mentioned earlier. Ezra, who was not behind the door when they were dispensing the brains, put it with his usually direct simplicity,

"Any crop you can sell for ten times more than it costs to raise, is a good crop." It wasn't always that good. On the other hand, sometimes it was better. Meeker was lucky, too. In the early 1880's when the going got good in King and Pierce Counties, the Germans were getting tricky about the hops they sent to England. They would label inferior hops as top quality, which infuriated the English brewers who could do little about it because Germany was the biggest hop-growing nation in the world . . .

And that's when little old Ezra in his homespun clothes and philosophy of producing an honest product for an honest price wandered into the winner's circle in London, England.

Before the Germans got the message and mended their ways, Ezra had sold one crop of his hops for one year in England for a cool $500,000.

Pretty good for a country kid from Puyallup!

In 1883, a decade before the hop crop died forever, Meeker wrote a book on how to raise hops in which he said "The hop crop in this whole region has never failed or become attacked with disease, as in older hop districts of the world, hence the growers of Washington Territory have enjoyed the singular good fortune to have full crops when prices were high . . . During fifteen years' experience no enemies of the hop have appeared or disease attacked; it is the hope and belief of hop growers in Washington Territory that the peculiarity of their climate will always protect them from the ravages of disease so destructive elsewhere." He predicted the crop would continue 300 years.

Meeker reported later that for 22 years in the hop business there was not a single year in which he lost money. Others fared almost as well, if not on so grand a scale. On an average during the so-called "hop-craze" of over 20 years, this plant brought in the equivalent of Washington's strawberries, which is the most important berry crop in the State today. The steamboat business on the rivers was built on hops. The old mansions you see dotting the landscape were built on hops. And the dairy herds in the valleys got their start with hop money.

Then one evening in the fall of 1895 Meeker saw what he later referred to as the "barometer of poverty." He wrote, "I stepped out of my office, and cast my eyes toward one group of our hop houses. I thought I could see that the hop foliage of a field nearby was off color — did not look natural . . . I walked down to the yards a quarter of a mile distant, and there saw the first hop-louse. The yard was literally alive with lice. . . ."

Meeker said he went to bed that night a rich man and woke up to bankruptcy — along with every other hop grower in Western Washington and Oregon. Even a small, isolated hop ranch, the only one in Skagit County, was decimated.

Half a century later, the big annual affair in the valley was Kent's Annual Lettuce Days when a bevy of beautiful maidens in bathing costumes and carrying pitchforks stood in a huge bowl of lettuce, mixing it with mayonnaise onto the world's biggest lettuce salad.

Today, most of Kent's lettuce comes from the Salinas Valley in California. Four times the total population of the town during its "salad days" have jobs with the Boeing Company alone, and they're manufacturing equipment like the Moon Buggy that hauled the astronauts around that planet.

The rich valley soil has a carpet of asphalt and concrete.

It was the Eagle Gorge Dam which made the difference.

There are a lot of people who cling to the thought that this is the great tragedy of the White River Valley, but the Seattle Chamber of Commerce obviously is not one of them . . .

And the structure that made a "dammed bit of difference" is named in honor of Howard A. Hanson who, as chairman of a rivers and harbors subcommittee of the Seattle Chamber in the late 1920's, expanded his campaign for Eagle Gorge to other communities in King County. As literature about the dam published by the U.S. Army Engineers in the Seattle District states, "The flood control of the Green River and its tributaries was discussed by the Associated Improvement Clubs of South King County on May 9, 1928 . . ." and the dam "is a monument to the faithful and persevering efforts of that large group of organized citizens as well as Colonel Hanson and many who helped."

The primary purpose of the dam is cited as "prevention of flood damage in the Green River Valley . . . Assurance that cropland will not now be flooded is expected to result in a higher type of agricultural development in the valley. Hay and field cropland and will be farmed more intensively, and greater value of production will be realized. This type of benefit termed 'farm-land enhancement,' can be expected to provide approximate annual benefits of $290,000 on a long-term average basis . . ."

By the same token, it was estimated that the flood-control reservoir would enhance industry to the tune of $570,000 annually.

The idea was that the valley could have its cake and eat it, too. Agriculture would be enhanced by flood control. At the same time the land could support industry that would expand the prosperity by a value of about 2 to 1 over agriculture. The two could peacefully coexist, and we'd have $3 where we used to only have $1.

But that's not the way she turned out. Seattle's running out of industrial land within the city limits and moving up into the valley. For agricultural purposes, the land was worth about $1,000 — perhaps $2,000 an acre. For industrial purposes, it may be worth as much as $42,000.

The lettuce these industries are producing isn't the kind you put in salads. It's the kind you fold up and put in your wallet.

But a further complication now is setting in. We're a nation that at the moment is concerned about whether or not we can raise enough food to feed ourselves. Holding valley lands for agricultural purposes may end up costing the taxpayers the $42,000 an acre . . .

The cost is like the cost of a wife.

Prowling Kent

You can get a quick look at what's happening to this valley from Interstate 5, but for the best overview, take off on Military Road and go out to the end of one of the dead-end streets. You'll see the whole valley . . . what man is doing to and with it, and Mt. Rainier magnificently in the background.

The most significant pausing place inside Kent is the new — and controversial *City Hall — Library* complex. The sculptures were carved in the raw brick before it was fired at Newcastle and a lot of them are really worth writing home about . . . one of which is the history in brick of the rise and fall of the strawberry crop. These berries are depicted along with the bulldozer tracks that crushed them for the industrialization of the valley.

One neat touch is a hand reaching out through a wall to pluck one of the berries.

It's the actual wall of the city jail.

And speaking of jails, if you have to be incarcerated in one, this is the place to be. It's as comfortable and convenient as a modern hotel . . . and a work-release program enables the inmates to check in and out on about as normal a basis as you can get under the circumstances.

The time to visit the City Hall is Thursday afternoon when there are conducted tours of the building, which is bricked inside and out, and the meaning of the sculptures is explained . . . along with the concept that the City Hall is a place that should be visited for other purposes than registering beefs, paying taxes or being tossed in the clink. (In case you can't make it on Thursday, there's an attractive booklet about the sculptures — although they're a little hard to match up with the booklet if you aren't being guided.)

Plants which can be visited if you make advance arrangements are *Boeing*, for the people-moving equipment and *Warn Industries*, the ones who developed the 4-wheel drive for jeeps.

Uncommon shopping – By far and away the most uncommon in the area is that at the *Fantastic Cake Box*, Kent-Kangley Rd., for pastries which have a lot of fame. Also coffee, and open 7 days a week . . . *Green River Cheese and Dairy Products*, Peasley Canyon Rd. for cheese and dairy products . . . *Gingham Square Delicatessen*, Benson Rd., small, nicely done, with antiques and lox, bagels in happy mix . . . *Jerry's Agate Shop*, W. Valley Rd., 250 tons of polishable rocks along with the equipment to do the polishing.

A word about eating – A "sleeper," patronized heavily by the locals and truckdrivers for lunch is *Our Cafe*, E. Valley Rd., plain food, good soup, modest prices . . . *The Coachman*, Smith St., tasty pies, rolls, bread, made on the spot . . . *Meeker's Landing*, W. Meeker, popular clam chowder and buffet, dinner, dancing, Old West atmosphere . . . *Moonlite Inn*, N. 2nd, best-known night spot and bar — likely place for "overheards" . . . Kent covers a lot of territory, clear over to I-5 in places — and includes such famous family dining as *The Farm Inn*, and *Rose's Inn* on Pacific Highway South.

A word about sleeping – *The Dunes Motel*, W. Meeker. It's not Las Vegas, but that's good.

Annual affairs – *Ezra Meeker Days*, in July, has parade . . . *Fun Feast Festival*, Memorial Day, with parade and barbecued chicken.

For futher information – Chamber of Commerce, 604 W. Meeker, 854-1770. City Hall (24 hrs.) 220 S. 4th, 852-2412.

Seattle Tour 5 — Bainbridge Island, Poulsbo, Port Gamble, Kingston, Edmonds (Map VIII)

Seattle puts her best foot forward to the ocean from which she sprang and if you haven't seen her from the water side there's no way you can have an in-depth appreciation of her beauty. And a ferry ride to Winslow on Bainbridge Island provides an unparalleled marine perspective of the Queen City.

You also visit Bainbridge Island which most people feel is populated entirely by millionaires, and you'll have a chance to tour the rural backroads and judge for yourself. Shortly after leaving the island there's a side trip to Chief Seattle's grave, which is a lot more venerated by the whites than by his fellow Indians ... then on to Poulsbo, a colorful Scandinavian town plopped in our midst ... and along Highway 3 to Port Gamble which is en route to recognition as a National Historic Place. It was a tidy New England village created out of whole cloth in the dense forests of the Pacific Northwest. It presently is undergoing authentic restoration. The tour takes you to Foulweather Bluff where the water from the incoming tide splits left into Hood Canal and right into Puget Sound and back via Point No Point and one of the hottest salmon fishing spots on the Sound. You return via the Kingston-Edmonds ferry and see what the mainland looks like to a sea captain, landing in Edmonds, a pocket of civilized living amongst the urban sprawl.

Seattle-Winslow Ferry Trip — The human relationship between the operators of the Washington State Ferry System and its regular patrons is unlike any other on the face of the globe ... and reminds us more than anything else of the old woman who lived in a shoe taking care of all those obnoxious kids, or perhaps a mother hen with a bunch of chicks: She doesn't want anything harmful to occur, but sometimes they drive her right out of her mind.

That's why we refer to this splendid fleet of vessels as our "folksy ferry system." Babies are born on board. Packages and messages are delivered to worried wives at one end of the run from anxious husbands at the other end. Captains get retirement parties. Citizens sleeping in their cars are banged awake. Docks are whammed and whistles blow and people wait in lines. But so far, the ferry system hasn't lost a paying customer yet.

The entire operation is geared to the poorest-paying customers of the bunch — the guy we call the Professional Ferry Patron. He's the one who rides on the commuter ticket. You may not realize this, but he "owns" the ferry that he rides on. And while the State may run it for him and pay all the bills, it's his private yacht. And perodically, the State must be jacked up and "put down," a feat that requires unending dexterity on the part of the Professional Ferry Patron. However, he has plenty of time, energy and enthusiasm for this pursuit ... which allows him to vent his spleen without getting fired from his regular job.

Professional Ferry Patrons have one common denominator: An abiding conviction that the Washington State Ferry System always is wrong.

Now, if somebody else tries to get into the act, that's something else again. When Julia Butler Hansen tried to get a bridge put across the sound, the Professional Patrons marched on Olympia with banners flying and the band playing, "The Old Gray Mare, She Ain't What She Used to Be!" The PFP's even raised *money* to fight the bridge.

We often have tried to characterize the Professional and the closest we can come to the epitome of this person involves the last billboard on Bainbridge Island. The folks there simply don't want billboards on their island, but there was one persistent entrepreneur who insisted on erecting one. Our ideal PFP went up there one night with his chain saw and cut the billboard into small rectangular squares.

The PFP has no admiration for the Amateur Ferry Rider like you. You don't have the right change. You don't know which is the right lane. You don't know where you're going when you get off the ferry. And you don't know how to drive aggressively when you're on it. You are the reason why the speed limit on board a Washington State Ferry is only 5 miles-an-hour . . . ever since some dumb amateur drove on one end and off the other — before the ferry left the dock. (Luckily, he was bailed out before he drowned.)

The PFP's established control of the situation immediately after the State took over the privately-owned system in 1951. Historically, the Black Ball people had given one long and two short toots when its ferries approached a landing, and the State had the temerity to change it to two even toots.

The howl that went up was heard around the world . . .

Well, at least around the Sound.

Want to know how that one came out? Listen for the "tooot toot-toot" of the tooter when your ferry toots for her landing at Winslow.

The coffee, of course, is a continuing "criminality" pumped from the bilges and parceled out in plastic cups. And the howl that went up with the increase of price from 15 cents to 20 cents a cup was backed by angry PFPs who brought their own coffee from home and drank it with determined deliberation in the cafeteria.

The ferry system is enormously proud of its new super ferries, but the PFPs refer to them as the "soopers," the "sooper doopers" and the "sooper *pooper* doopers." When the time between Seattle and Bainbridge was cut from 45 to 35 minutes, the ferry managers blushed with pride but the PFP's informed them crisply this left no time to finish the newspaper on the morning run. The splendid decor of the new sooper pooper doopers was described in letters to the editor of the *Bainbridge Review* in disparaging terms. The warm orange colors were garish, and the ornate mirrors in the ladies' room over-done. Dave Averill, publisher of the *Review*, had to run an extra section in his paper to encompass all the comments, which referred to the carpeting as "silly" and the new low-backed seats as a hazard to health, welfare and safety. If you leaned back in those new low-backed seats you could crack the head of the guy behind you, and both of you would end up with skull fractures.

The ferry system raised the seat backs, but it was in more of a quandary when it came to the "no smoking" areas and the piped music. Letters were equally divided that the areas were (1) too big and (2) too small. The music was too loud and too soft. One of the great historic incidents on the music front came during an early morning commuter run when a couple of Amateur Ferry Patrons put some rock music on the juke box and awakened a sleeping PFP. He took out his knife and cut the cord supplying electricity to the juke box. Burned off the blade of his knife, but it stopped the music — permanently — on juke boxes on the early morning runs.

The ferry system thought it would oblige pedestrian passengers at Winslow by enclosing the long walkway to the terminal. But it made the mistake of enclosing it in white plastic instead of clear glass and it now is known as the "longest john in the world."

Early in the morning, The PFP's grope their way aboard and to the men's or women's facilities as the case may be, or to the coffee shop or to the table where their bridge group's deck of cards is stuffed behind the seat cushions, or to *their* seat to continue sleeping.

Now the ferries may appear to be as identical as peas in a pod to the amateur rider, but each has its own idiosyncrasy. The women's john is at one location and the men's at another. The coffee shop is here on one and there on another. But generally they are constant because the way you see your ferry pointed today is the same as it was yesterday and the day before and so on for the past 20 years. They start out from the ferry barn going in that direction and return to the barn that night ready to repeat the performance the next day.

It's one of the constants in the life of a PFP.

Then somebody in the system had a diabolical idea. On April Fool's Day, 1974, they would strike back in kind at their tormenters by turning the ferries around when they left the dock that morning. Things would be wrong end to. Men would push their way into the women's can. The deck of cards would be under the wrong seat cushion. The coffee shop would be at the wrong end and general confusion would prevail among the professionals —

A silent gesture of retaliation.

Besides, it would make a neat twist to end this story in this book. And so for a year all of us plotted with glee at the anticipated confusion that lay ahead.

And then a couple of days before the big event, somebody in top management had a worrisome thought: Suppose somebody in the engineering crew below decks also was as much of a creature of habit and pulled the wrong lever at the right time, smashing the boat to into the dock?

So as we went to press with the story of the ferrymen's revenge we got a reluctant call from Ralph White of the Ferry System, telling us we'd have to change the copy. They wouldn't be able to turn the ferries around on April Fool's Day.

To use a British nautical term, the ferry management had been frigged again.

Winslow — (Pop. 1,604. Elev. 20.) — This town occupies an infinitesimal proportion of the total landmass and yields a clue to the fact that the land on Bainbridge is almost entirely privately owned. Its big fear is what one town official called Bellevue-ization. And from the standpoint of car-cushion travelers it yields little in the way of profitable prowling. A former City Councilman who, happily, operates one of the shopping exceptions, voiced a prevailing opinion on the island when he said what most residents feel: "I'm here — everybody else keep off!" If he were really trying to be "with it" on the island, he probably should have called his business establishment "The James Junquetique," but he just calls it *Jim's Junk Shop*.

Prowling Bainbridge

Most cars zip across the island on the limited access highway, but there's a nice walking tour of *Fort Ward*, which slopes to Rich Passage (see *Footloose*, pp. 128-29) and the beach at *Fay Bainbridge State Park* has an excellent view back to the mainland.

Uncommon shopping – *Bainbridge Arts and Crafts*, outlet for local artists and craftsmen. Nonprofits and very good . . . *Gifts of Bainbridge*, in balconied green shake building. Baskets, flowers, candles, pewter, other fine wares displayed on owner's antique furniture . . . *Berry Patch*, decor and kitchen accessories, like casseroles, pottery, in warm atmosphere with fresh flowers around . . . *Genii Boutique*, women's clothing and go-withs of the well-bred country look . . . *Country Mouse*, peppermint stick-ish children's shop for ages 0 to 12 . . . *Town and Country Florist and Nursery*, handsome displays and large collection of indoor plants, hanging and standing.

A word about eating – *The Martinique*, the "sophisticated" restaurant with a French Provincial look . . . A new one, *Island House*, operated successfully by son of the local banker in a restored house, is appealing; baked chicken is very tasty . . . *Lemon Tree Restaurant*, coffee shop for good sandwiches at lunch; lots of local trade.

Annual affairs – *Bainbridge Island Grand Old Fourth of July Celebration* . . . and a spontaneous "non festival" *Scotch Broom Festival*, in May. Informal parade of *anything*, decorated generously with scotch broom.

For further information – Chamber of Commerce, 264 Winslow Way E., 842-3700.

After you cross the Agate Pass Bridge, pausing to look at a handsome totem pole at the far end, you are on the Kitsap Peninsula. Immediately turn north for a side trip of particular interest to Indians, Seattleites, and historians.

Suquamish — (Pop. Nominal. Elev. Sea level.) — On a hill at the west end of the main street is an Indian burial ground containing *Chief Seattle's grave*. A stone monument marks the final resting place of the Indian chief for whom the city was named. A granite shaft reads: "Seattle, chief of the Suquamish and Allied Tribes, died June 7, 1866, the firm friend of the Whites and for him the city of Seattle was named by its Founders."

About as good a comment as you'll find on the name comes from an article by Mary R. Daheim in the December, 1973 issue of *Pacific Search*: "Seattle has a peculiar northwest ring. It sounds like a bubbling spring, the tide coming in, a river flowing among the trees. Seattle sounds like water."

The mellifluous qualities of the name are disregarded in the Indian legends handed down from father to son, where the chief comes off as the Benedict Arnold of the Wet Side of the Mountains. The chief was remarkably adept with his footwork — like beating a murder rap that was lodged against him by the Hudson's Bay Company before the Americans showed up on the scene. Seattleites bought and paid for him.

And he was worth it. Smart chiefs like Kitsap and Leschi were for wiping out the white population before it engulfed them. But Chief Seattle figured he couldn't beat 'em and was the first person put on the city's payroll. As such, he talked a couple thousand Indians into staying here when the rest of them undertook the annihilation of the town's population as a signal for a general uprising around the Sound. As near as we can determine, he got about 600 times in cash as much as the $24 those east coast Indians got for Manhattan Island. They said it was just for the use of his name but it really was to keep his fellow Indians in line.

The Chief's grave was a pretty crummy affair for a long time because he was sort of betwixt and between the two races, but about 15 years ago, the American Legion in the area undertook the chore of an annual celebration in his honor. The legionnaires gave the Suquamish Indian Tribe a percentage of income. They called the annual affair in August "Chief Seattle Days" and provided such things as Indian dancing, canoe races and the like.

In 1973, the Tribe took on the program itself and George Gibbon, spokesman for the tribe, put it this way in a *P.-I.* article on August 17, "(they were) charging for everything and offering the Indians a 10% cut of the take."

The Indians put an admission charge of 50 cents for the 3-day event, which included free camping on the reservation. They offered the Legion "10% of the take," but the Legion indignantly turned them down.

Well, they may not like him, but Chief Seattle showed 'em the way.

◀▬

Poulsbo — (Pop. 1,962. Elev. Sea level.) — It isn't prominently displayed among the world's most widely dispersed facts, but Poulsbo not only is the metropolis of the north half of Kitsap County, it's the Gooeyduck Capital of the World. (Normally spelled Geoduck.)

The former may not send you into roseate dreams of high expectations, but you should also visit Poulsbo if you'd like to get the feel of Norway without spending all that money with SAS to have it cart your body to that country. And instead of being more than 8,000 miles, this one is a lot less than 80 from downtown Seattle. It has the look of a Norwegian fishing village and some of the commercial buildings are painted with the peasant designs —called rose-maling. In order to get more of the feel, we suggest you try it on for size on the weekend closest to May 17, which is Norway's Independence Day, a time when Poulsbo folks assiduously cultivate things Norwegian ... which pleasures the people there because about 90% of the people in town and the approximately 20,000 in the town's service area are Norwegian.

And now about the Gooeyducks.

Ever since somebody said it 2 or 4 hundred years ago, the world has trotted obediently along repeating the line about a "rose by any other name is just as sweet ... "

And it simply isn't!

You take the Spider Crab for an instance . . . As long as they called it that, nobody would touch it with anything shorter than a 10-foot pole. Even then, they sort of dropped the pole and ran. It's a monstrous-looking creature and anybody eating it today with relish (or mayonnaise or baked) would think twice before the next bite if one of them came crawling across the table. And for a long time, that was its only protection against the human race.

Then, about 30 years ago, somebody got the bright idea of calling it "King" Crab. By 1966, Alaskans harvested 159,000,000 of them. Meanwhile, the Russians and the Japanese got into the act. And now all three countries are fighting over who gets what part of a harvest totaling about a third of the '66 figure. All of that's not so bad.

But now it's happening to the Gooeyduck.

And Puget Sound *is the* Gooeyduck country. It's possible to find them as far south as California and as far north as the Queen Charlotte Islands, just like it's possible to find Kelvinators on the North Slope of Alaska, and corn some place besides Kansas. But this is the heartland of the Gooeyduck right here inside the Strait of Juan de Fuca.

For several thousand years, the Indians were the only ones who'd venture the consumption of this terrible-looking animal that more than anything else resembles a man's penis — and a mighty big man at that. And they would just as lief have kept the gastronomic qualities of this animal to themselves. But in the early days of the white settlements around Puget Sound when there wasn't much else to eat but clams and the pioneers' stomachs rose and fell with the tide, some of the folks who were either (1) more venturesome or (2) hungrier, tried them. Wow. What flavor!

So they "clammed" up, and Gooeyducks became the best-kept flavor secret on the Wet Side of the Mountains. It was handed down from generation to generation by the "sons of beaches" who lived on the shores of Puget Sound. Go back in the hinterlands — maybe as far as Tukwila — and they never heard of a Gooeyduck.

Nobody in his right mind would put a Gooeyduck up for sale in a fish market. Mothers would cover their daughters' eyes when they walked past the stalls.

The Indians used to say that the Gooeyduck could be found only 2 days a year — at the time of the "mad moon," which wasn't a bad way of keeping nosey people out of the act.

What with their names, size, shape, tides, beachheads, and secrecy, the Gooeyduck was a fairly well protected animal — enjoyed only by people willing to lie down in the wet mud and reach into a hole up to their armpits to participate in this gastronomic delight.

Then somebody invented scuba diving, and the State Department of Fisheries discovered there were 200,000,000 of these animals living and dying in vast populations on the bottom of the Sound beyond the reach of human beings operating with shovels and stovepipes at mad-moon tides. Department scuba divers did a census and found they covered about 20,000 acres . . . and their minds went click . . . click . . . click to the commercial value of the fishery . . .

Because those guys also had eaten Gooeyducks.

Now there may be some confusion in your mind about the spelling of the name of this animal, which is perfectly all right with us, because confused people are liable to leave more Gooeyducks for us. But out of pride in our post as purveyors of information, we'll give it to you as Don Page, Marine Editor of the *P.-I.*, put it in his column on December 6, 1969:

"What's in a name? Our most magnificent clam has to be a hardshell creature indeed, just to live with his name. 'Geoduck, goeduck, gweduck' . . . take your choice. Even the dictionaries and encyclopedias can't agree.

"State Fisheries' official name for the big mollusk right now is 'geoduck,' That sounds like a Greek word meaning 'earth duck.' Which is ridiculous. Big G.D. isn't a Greek. His name is derived from the Indian . . .

"Webster's dictionary back in 1948 called G.D. 'gweduc.' Said it came from the Nisqually meaning 'dig deep.' By 1964, though, Webster was giving 'geoduck' as preferred spelling, from Chinook jargon, with alternate spellings of 'geoduck,' 'gooey-duck' or 'gweduck or geoduck.' The latest World Book called him 'goeduck'."

We might sail for "gweduc", which is probably as close as the white man — who wasn't even calling it anything until about 100 years ago — ever will get to the name it went by with the natives for the previous 5,000 years. And we're doing that on purpose, because who on earth would want to buy a Gooeyduck — except us?

One of the original descriptions of this animal was provided in 1881 by one John A. Ryder, who said, "When first dug and laid upon its back, it resembles a fat, plump duck." Ryder also observed, "Its flesh is, I think, the most delicious of any bivalve I have ever eaten, *not* excepting the oyster . . . " (Italics ours.) Cedric Lindsay, the State Department of Fisheries man in charge of the fate of the Gooeyduck, added that this animal has no taste of iodine, the like of which you find in most of our Puget Sound clams . . . and opined that its meat is sweeter than that of the famed abalone.

Lindsay says, "In many fisheries, there was no research until the supply was depleted. We're in a lot better shape (on gooeyducks). We had a good handle on how big the population was before we started leasing." He was referring to the fact that for about 5 years before a commercial harvest was permitted by the State Legislature, the department went over the potential fishing grounds and leased them under strict supervision on a basis of about a 100 to 1 ratio of protection for the resource. Lindsay said it was the objective of the department to harvest these animals as though they were a stand of timber being harvested on a basis of clearcutting. "You plan your operation," Lindsay said, "so that by the time you harvest your final stand, you've grown a new crop to be harvested."

Gooeyducks thrive in Puget Sound because it is one of, if not *the*, richest nutrient-bearing bodies of water in the world. At the moment, the State is leasing about 1,000 acres of the 20,000. A Gooeyduck reaches merchantable size in about 10 years . . . giving a leeway of 10 years for reproduction. However, only about 500,000 of the 200,000,000 animals are being harvested annually. At that rate we wouldn't get all the way around the barn for 400 years. This could be the neatest trick of the bio-economic week if it could continue that way, what with Olympia oysters down 96% . . . Dungeness crab — at least in the San Francisco area — down 90% . . . abalone down 65% . . .

If these animals would only continue to be known as "Gooeyducks."

But the guys marketing them were not behind the door when they passed out the brains and they're being sold by the *Washington King Clam Company* as King Clams. Headquarters for the company is here in Poulsbo. And if you want the marine gourmet treat of your life, drop by and pick up a pound or two. They come as steaks — which is the way to buy them, because they're too tasty to become chowder — or chopped, like for chowder.

In our book, they may be spelled K-i-n-g C-l-a-m . . .

But they're pronounced, "Gooeyduck."

Prowling Poulsbo

Poulsbo started out as, and still retains the flavor of, a small cod fishing village in Norway, although the cod fishing both locally and in Alaska presently has gone by the boards. Made up of substantial wooden and brick buildings, it sits on the picturesque shore of Liberty Bay, surrounded by green hills.

At Christmas time, two local artists paint shop windows in gay if somewhat corny and slightly Norwegian Christmas motifs . . . a Viking ship outlined in lights is stretched across Anderson Parkway along the waterfront. It can be seen from the other side of Liberty Bay . . . and you might even hear strains from Grieg if you keep your ears open.

All of this, of course, represents what we mean when we suggest that the readers of this book are able to attend this sort of thing "off-season" . . . off-hours and mid-week — well, at least off-tourist season.

One that you can and should enjoy doing mid-week off-season is visit the *Marine Environmental Center* from 9 to 3 Monday through Friday down next door to Joe Engman's place, the *Key Point Oyster Company* . . . and adjacent to the *Washington King Clam Company.*

Anyway, at the Environmental Center, which is one of two in the country (the other's on the east coast) elementary, high school and junior college students are doing things with, for and about our marine environment that the most advanced PhD's didn't even have an inkling of 25 years ago.

Engman has a plug coming because he gave the North Kitsap County School District — along with a whole bunch of other districts in the area — a renewable 20-year lease on the building they're using to teach Kitsap County students more about the marine environment that surrounds them than any of their age in the history of the world. The lab maintains running seawater 24-hours a day where the kids check the water quality in Liberty Bay . . . do aquaculture experiments and have a sound-picture unit that tells you what they're doing. Visitors are welcome.

And in the course of events, of course, they find out a bit about what Joe Engman's doing, which is raising oysters, employing, among other things the use of cultch on strings originally employed in Japan. (See story in Region 1, Tour 3.)

Uncommon shopping – The most uncommon, of course is the *Washington King Clam Market* . . . *Bauer's Bake Shop*, for Viking doughnuts (and coffee), shortbread jelly cookies, 30 kinds of bread . . . *Carson's Rexall Drugstore* for town's largest supply of Scandinavian imports . . . *Yarn Barn*, bonafide, roomy old red barn sitting alone in the countryside, decorated with rose-maling and jammed to the rafters with yarns, craft items and sewing supplies, very popular . . . *Vickie's Antiques & Collectables* for bottles, insulators, oak furniture . . . *Lemolo Meat* for smoked salmon, but best of all, Peter Keim's homemade sausages. He has 95 varieties plus pre-shrunk bacon. Peter notes his prices are a little higher, but you aren't buying the water that usually adds to the weight of these products. Very interesting man and, as he says, "a little bit out of the way on beautiful Lemolo Bay" . . . *Ole's Place* for junque . . . *Little Norway Seafoods*, for gooeyduck steaks, imported cheese, fruit soups, Swedish candies . . . *Viking Oyster Company* for tours and retail sales.

A word about eating and drinking – The *Viking House* with big windows overlooking Liberty Bay . . . *Iskrem Hus & Sandwich Shop* for ice cream, homemade pies and soups . . . *The Pulsbo Inn*, medieval English decor . . . *Pete's Tavern*, with wooden cigar store Indian out front and livery stable decor.

Annual affairs – *Annual Codfish Derby and Dance* of the Yacht Club, February, with "Biggest Jerk of the Year Award" . . . *Viking Festival* (Norwegian Independence Day) in May has art show, Nordic dancers, Saturday luncheon which includes homemade open-face sandwiches, pea soup, waffles with strawberries, coffee, bread, and lefse; Sunday smorgasbord starting at 11:30 features baked salmon, halibut, meatballs, turkey, ham plus rullepolse, sylte, potato sausage, boiled tongue, pickled herring, Nordic cookies and like that.

For further information – Poulsbo City Library, 779-2915 or Chamber of Commerce, 779-4740.

Port Gamble — (Pop. Nominal. Elev. Sea level.) — This is the home of the oldest continually operating sawmill in America. Colonel Ebey was the first one to lose his head over Port Gamble and the chances are that you won't be the last. To all outward appearances, it's a tiny New England town transferred, elm trees, pitched roofs and all, from East Machias, Maine.

Why it was never called "West" Machias is one of the world's little-known or worried-about wonders.

The fact is that unlike Arthur Denny, who came west to found a town and built Seattle, Andrew Jackson Pope and William Chaloner Talbot came to Puget Sound to found a lumber empire. Denny was deeply involved in the naming of his city and the two empire builders couldn't have cared less about what their location was called if there was plenty of timber and the price was right.

Nonetheless, East Machias, which even today is not listed among the American cities with a population of 2,500 or more, has everything to do with the fact that Port Gamble is being restored as a National Historic place . . . because the founders of the town hailed from a long line of people who lived in that neck of the Maine woods, and nobody ever forgot it.

There's the story of a man who fell off the dock at Port Gamble in the old days. He was floundering, spluttering and in danger of drowning, but nobody paid any attention until someone looked at him more closely. "Blow the whistle and call out the mill crew," the observer shouted, "He's from East Machias!"

Little old Port Gamble, with not enough population today to rate a listing by the Association of Washington Cities, had as much to do with the development of Puget Sound as Seattle. And a modicum of knowledge of the historic background helps us figure it all out.

Pope and Talbot showed up in San Francisco at a time when lumber was selling for between $100 and $500 a thousand . . . and the freight for getting it there around the Horn was four times the cost of the lumber in the first place. There was lots of timber in Humboldt Bay, California and around Portland, but the crossing of the bar in those two locations was a wonderful way of losing your ship and its cargo. What the fellas wanted was a sheltered harbor with a good anchorage and access to lots of tall timber.

They'd heard a lot about Puget Sound from Captain Lafayette Balch who was supplying San Francisco with piling and timber from that place and decided they would build a mill there — sight unseen. Their story also supplies us with the reason northern Puget Sound developed faster than the Olympia area which was settled six years earlier.

The answer is wind . . .

Not the kind you find in City Halls, but the kind that propels sailboats. It took a lot less wind to push a lumber schooner from Port Gamble or Seattle to the open ocean than from Olympia. That took time, and time was money every day and every hour of the day — except Sunday — to Pope and Talbot. So you can imagine how impressed Captain Talbot was when he noted a geographic location described by him in *Time, Tide and Timber*, a history of the company:

"About five miles from the entrance of Hood Canal, a small peninsula jutted out to form a little sheltered bay. It was about two miles long and half a mile wide, with a contracted entrance. On the west side, there was a level sandy spit for the mill plant. Magnificent timber grew so close to the water's edge that entire trees were mirrored in the blue of the bay . . ."

Before they were through, Port Gamble would be as cosmopolitan a place as there was west of East Machias and north of San Francisco. Telephone lines connected them with Seattle and other points on the Sound and the telegraph linked them directly with San Francisco. At their social functions, a well-stocked larder provided them with many-course dinners, each served with its appropriate wine and the men ended the meal with brandy and cigars. They were wearing well-tailored broadcloth suits while they were doing it. And the ladies in the other room were clad in satin and velvet made in the latest styles of the day.

But nobody ever forgot East Machias . . .

Not even when somebody went to all the trouble of contacting the Rand McNally map company for a special map of Maine to be presented as a gift to the bosses of Port Gamble.

As a gag, they'd had Rand McNally omit East Machias from the map.

Prowling Port Gamble

Today you'll see the results of 6 years of an on-going restoration program. The New England-style homes are being spruced up and there is talk of duplicating the original townsite plot. The *1853 Port Gamble General Store* will have a historical museum in the basement and Pope & Talbot is bringing all their company papers here to develop a company library. *St. Paul's Episcopal Church*, built in 1870, still is used each Sunday. The *pioneer cemetery* also includes the grave of the first U.S. Navy man to die in action in the Pacific in World War II and it is a National Historic Site. An interesting sidelight at the General Store is the free museum on the second floor of Tom Rice's *seashell collection.*

Although most car-cushion travelers probably will be racing for the Kingston ferry from here or taking the toll bridge to the big Peninsula, it is possible to wind your way from the head of the bay on which Port Gamble is located and up through the Port Gamble Indian Reservation to scenic Foulweather Bluff, which is the place where Puget Sound officially begins. Your return to the south takes you through Hansville, which is flat, isolated and bears a strong resemblance to the end of the world for everybody but salmon fishermen — to whom it is the beginning. This is a great spot to start out fishing from . . . and they have the necessary facilities.

From here, it's an absolutely straight shot 9 miles to the intersection that gives you a left turn to the ferry landing at Kingston, and on to Edmonds. You "freeway" it most of the time on the east side of the Sound.

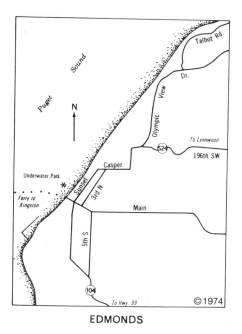

EDMONDS

Edmonds — (Pop. 24,000. Elev. 9.) — Now here's a place that could use the advice, counsel and consent of its Founding Father, one George Brackett, a man with a profound instinct for doing the right thing at the right time in the right place.

At the moment, the City Fathers are attempting to provide the kind of small-town, homespun atmosphere that goes with a place that once was called Brackett's Landing — in an area where people are popping up like pox in the Black Plague and automobiles are producing super duper shopping centers in big blobs all over the terrain.

It also is a little difficult to do in a town that has grown from 2,400 to 24,000 in a couple of decades. While you're trying to get down to the bottom of the town through the skein of crossroads which tangle up the approaches, you'd swear they'd never make it. The fact that some 500,000 people, one way or another, wish to pass through Edmonds annually, either coming or going from Kingston on the ferry, does nothing to materially lighten the load of traffic . . . nor is a marina designed to hold 800 craft in the city's front yard doing much to alleviate the general aura of congestion.

But the "fathers" are doing what they can. In a calendar printed and distributed by the municipality a couple of years ago, it was pointed out that "we see continued growth as an undesirable thing and a threat to our way of life. We see that more people means more houses, more streets and fewer trees . . . more furnaces, more fireplaces and more trash burning . . . more automobiles which pollute the air, cause traffic congestion and create parking problems . . .

"Our goal is to remain a small, low-density, rural-type community.

"In accordance, we are determined to resist all pressures to increase the population density and industrial development."

A lot already has been done to preserve the quality of the residential area where the folks have been willing to pay the price of higher assessments for nicer yards and better homes. Areas once zoned for multiple dwellings now are restricted to single family units. Streets once adapted to the streamlined, one-way concept have reverted to the old two-way system.

They've removed the parking meters and provided off-street parking — a little matter in which the Washington State Ferries came up with a big assist by providing off-street parking for the 160 vehicles that make up a full load of a super-ferry.

Recognizing they're bucking the trend of big shopping centers, and in order to attract small, individual and specialized shops that *en toto* make up what a shopping center offers, they've removed the business-and-occupation tax that has proved so onerous to so many small business people in other cities. In the past year, barrels of paint have been applied to the stub part of the main stem which leads down to the ferry dock. Building colors on the main street are carefully coordinated and they're shooting for a concept of personal contact between shop-owner and customer in stores that have a turn-of-the-century flavor. In addition to the waterfront park named after Brackett, there's an underwater park set aside for scuba divers . . .

And the Edmonds City Council has unilaterally declared a three-mile limit off its shores against drilling for oil.

All of this takes a little doing under the democratic system, and Brackett could see the whole population problem thing coming even as he named the town after Vermont Senator George Franklin Edmunds, who had fathered the Act bearing his name that extirpated the population-producing process of polygamy in Utah. The Post Office read the "u" as an "o" in "Edmunds" hand-written name, but Brackett figured the spirit of the thing was there . . . and what was spelling to a young logger in those days anyway?

Brackett, who owned the town bag and baggage and was its first mayor, was a forthright man. He met the first Chinese who attempted to move in and told him to "beat it," which the gentleman did. Brackett bought the place for $650 and sold it for $36,000. That was in 1890.

Then, three years later, when he didn't like the way the new fellas were running things, he repossessed it . . . and then sold it again in 1900 for $139,000 to some men who would take care of it right.

Maybe before they're through, today's fathers'll need some of the direct approach practiced by old George Brackett.

Meanwhile, you might like to see how they're doing . . . and by following our usual advice about midweek and off-season try the following prowling.

Prowling Edmonds

For a once-over-lightly, try the scenic drive to *Woodway Park*, an exclusive residential section southwest of town, or *Sunset Avenue* which runs along the waterfront. Of course, you also will get a good look at the town, either coming or going, on the ferry. One of the features is an *underwater park*, and there are 3 *city parks* which have fire pits on the beach in which you can build fires without a permit. It also is one of the few sandy beaches on the Sound. You might want to take a look at the old brick *Carnegie Library* which is slated to become the local historical museum. It's on the National Register of Historic Places.

Uncommon shopping – *Balinka Jrs.*, boutique and clothing for younger people . . . the *Edmonds Bakery*, goodies and coffee . . . *Busy Bell Antiques* . . . *English Curiositea Shoppe*, collection of English antiques and tea-room featuring lunches, tea and cakes served in the English manner . . . *Peggy Harris Gifts* . . . *Party Harbor*, everything for a party; decorated in a Puget Sound harbor theme with gulls, pilings, etc. . . . *Patty's Place*, hand-arts crafted by over 80 artists . . . *The Reminder Shop*, collection of dolls and collector's items in a Doll House setting . . . *Underhill's Shoe Store*, what it says, plus a gallery of arts and antiques . . . *Wooden Spoon* for kitchen ware . . . *Llubs Art Gallery* for imports from Norway . . . *Decorative Arts* for picture framing . . . *Gallery North*, gallery and art school.

A word about eating and drinking – Best known is *Henri De Navarre*, one of the few excellent French restaurants in the Pacific Northwest . . . *Fog Cutter West*, intimate, sophisticated, with entertainment . . . *Los Amigo's*, Mexican food . . . *Aust's Steak and Oyster House* . . . *Angelo's Bella Casa* . . . *Peking* . . . *Parlour Car Tavern*, features cooking your own steak.

Annual affairs – *Edmonds Art Festival*, second in size only to Bellevue's, 3rd weekend in June . . . *Fourth of July Celebration.*

For further information – Chamber of Commerce, P.O. Box 246; phone, 776-6711.

◆

Seattle Tour 6 — Vashon Island, Port Orchard, Bremerton, Silverdale, Seabeck (Map VIII)

This tour takes you to Vashon Island, the highest of the up-Sound islands and one with a main highway, replete with views, along the top.

We mentioned at the start of Region 4 that what the people want is "out" . . . and you'll see where they're headed to "get away from it all" in large tracts of wilderness on the Kitsap Peninsula, as well as down the west side of Colvos Passage to Olalla. A once-thriving Port Orchard, which wrested the county seat from all other contenders, is awakening to its rich historic background and reaching for restoration and is good prowling. Bremerton, the biggest city in Kitsap County, is "Navy" to the core, with the battleship "U.S.S. Missouri" at the Puget Sound Naval Station, as its most famous historic site. Green and Gold Mountains west of Bremerton offer fine views for the more adventuresome car-cushion travelers along with the side trips to Belfair, Tahuya and Dewatto, past the ghosts of the early-day loggers and the endless acres of second growth timber. Return to Bremerton and the ferry to Seattle which provides you with the most dramatic approach to the city in existence.

◆

This story is about a little old lady schoolteacher . . . and a Lieutenant Governor . . . and how they saved Puget Sound from a fate worse than death.

If you're an oceanographer you will know that Puget Sound is a fjord. But unlike most fjords, Puget Sound lives and breathes. Twice a day a gallonage of water equal to twice that contained in Lake Washington goes whooshing out the Strait of Juan de Fuca exhaling the Sound's bad bodily fluids; and then sucks in good clean ocean water. Three or four times a year, the Sound "exhales" clear down to the bottom of its lungs and cleans up places like Hood Canal.

Right now, it's pretty much pollution-free, but uncontrolled growth could kill it even today when the State is looking over everybody's shoulder about maintaining environmental standards. And a bridge 15 years ago would have let the population growth get out of hand long before we could cope with it, so the following was critical to the future of our favorite body of water.

Which brings us to the little old lady and the little old Lieutenant Governor . . . and a little old bridge.

Senate Bill 154 of the 1959 Legislature proposed a modest 20-million-dollar bridge from Bainbridge Island to a nearby piece of mainland. When the bill was returned to the Senate from the House of Representatives, it had been amended to provide a big hunk of concrete that would bisect Puget Sound at Vashon Island at a cost of $500,000,000!

To use one of the buzz words of the trade, it had been "scalped." The hair on its head had been removed and replaced with a new wig. This provided a bridge from Fauntleroy to Vashon Island and then from Vashon Island to the mainland on the west side — instead of the short Bainbridge bridge.

Senate Bill 154 was returned to the floor of the Senate from the House on March 12, 1959. It was the 60th and last day of the session.

Senator Riley moved that the Senate consider Senate Bill 154 as amended by the House. Senators Greive, McCutcheon and Hess demanded a Call of the Senate. A Call of the Senate was ordered. The Sergeant-at-Arms locked the doors of the Senate Chamber. The Secretary called the roll. All the members were present. And the fight was on.

Greive then read the bill as amended by the House. It was as in depth as an accurate report of the Second Coming of Christ.

Riley moved that it be referred to the Committee on Highways, which meant "Goodbye Bridge Bill." Nat Washington, chairman of the committee, favored the bill but a majority of his committee did not. Once it landed in the hands of that committee, it never would be returned to the floor for a vote of the whole Senate. And that's where the battle lines were drawn.

Greive leaped into the fray by noting that when there was disagreement between the two Houses of the Legislature the rules required that a conference committee composed of 3 people from each place be called to iron out the differences. He noted that this *must* be done "in every case!"

Old-timer Victor Zednick, who enjoyed pointing out the facts of life to the young fellas, pointed out there was no difference of opinion yet because the Senate had not acted on the amended bill. And Riley added, "We will not know until the Committee on Highways has taken this bill under consideration as to whether or not there is a difference . . ."

Riley provided the folks with a decided "dig" here. He said, "I would like to direct the attention of the Senate to another point. I think the record will show that action on Senate Bill 154, as amended by the House, was taken *last* week, but in the ordinary process, for some mysterious reason, the message did not come to the Senate . . ."

Interruptions came thick and fast and finally Senator Washington got the floor to state that the House amendments had not "changed the scope of the bill."

Zednick commented on that one by observing that the amendments added $150 million to the cost of the project and added, "If that doesn't enlarge the scope, then I don't know what does!"

Senator Washington retorted that the amount of money didn't have anything to do with the "scope" of the bill as it merely called for "a" bridge.

Senator Dale Nordquist brought things into focus with, "I will take it from your remarks that you are seeking not only to sidetrack your own committee, but the Rules Committee?"

Senator Washington: "I am trying to do that. I have confidence in the body of the Senate in making up its mind whether we win or lose and I want it decided on the floor of the Senate . . ."

Senator Greive then got back into the act by suggesting that the bill be passed and that then the courts could decide whether or not the amendments had changed the scope. And old Vic Zednick commented, "The speech made by Senator Greive is a speech he might make before the Supreme Court, and what they would decide is another matter. We are determining now a matter which should be decided by the President of the Senate."

Senator Riley: "The scope and object of the bill was a short little bridge with a six-mile stretch of road, for a $20 million expenditure. The scope and object of the amendment to Senate Bill No. 154 is a $200 million project. (Ed. note: Estimated ultimate cost totaled $500 million.)

"If this matter were before us on the second day of the session instead of the sixtieth, I am sure the chairman of the Committee on Highways would say, 'Yes, I would like to have this bill in my committee . . .' My point of order is in your hands, and I leave it to your determination as to whether this amendment changes the scope and object of the bill."

Greive came in on another tack to get the matter to a vote. He moved that the Senate resolve itself into a Committee of the Whole to consider the matter. Zednick said, "Mr. President, Senator Riley's original motion is still before the Senate."

Greive then tried for a vote on whether the matter should be referred to the Committee on Highways.

And that's when the whole thing assumed the aspects of a Perry Mason Murder Trial. Senator McCutcheon moved that the Senate recess for lunch.

Greive objected, but Cherberg ruled in favor of lunch. The way he put it was, "The Senate will be at ease, subject to the Call of the President."

And they all trooped out to lunch.

At 2:30 p.m., the roll was called by the Secretary who reported to the President that everybody was present and Cherberg said . . . "The President believes that he can resolve this situation to everyone's satisfaction by merely stating that under the provisions of Rule 62, the President has ruled that the amendment as presented by the House to Senate Bill No. 154 changes the object and scope of the bill. Therefore the Senate rules require the President to refer Senate Bill No. 154 and the House amendments thereto to the appropriate committee and that it *shall* take the course of an original bill.

"If the President's memory serves him right, he was taught by his English teacher, Miss (Florence) Carlson, of Queen Anne High School, that 'shall' means 'mandatory'.

"One thing remaining to be said is that the President knows in his heart that he is right on this one . . ."

Thanks to Lieutenant Governor Johnny Cherberg — with an assist from a little old lady schoolteacher at Queen Anne High School — Puget Sound was saved from the inroads of the Phillistines . . .

And there's still a fjord in your future.

Vashon — (Pop. Nom. Elev. 220.) — Deep in the heart of every real estate man and most of the members of the Chamber of Commerce, there lurks a desire for a bridge from Vashon Island to the mainland in Seattle. But like the folks on Bainbridge who shudder at "Bellevue-ization," the average Vashonites dread the prospect of being "Mercerized" like the populous island by that name in Lake Washington.

And when aroused, they're capable of direct action.

There was something of a "to do" in official circles in 1911-12, for instance, when Vashon attempted to secede from King County. State Senator Ira H. Case, a resident of the Island, got a secession bill passed by the Senate before the astonished County Commissioners knew what happened. They had to drop all other lobbying for a while to blunt the secession movement in the House.

And thanks to agitation which began a year before, the Motor Ferry "Vashon Island" was launched on June 28, 1916 and began Des Moines-Portage service five months later.

It was the first motor ferry on Puget Sound.

In 1951, the resolute residents of the Island lobbied a bill through the legislature creating "Washington State Ferry District Number One" which permitted them to operate their own ferry in opposition to the gigantic, privately owned Black Ball Line. To protect his franchise, the energetic Captain Charles E. Peabody, head man of Black Ball, ordered his captain to land at the ferry dock.

The captain was met by a determined group of islanders wielding various farm implements — like axes — and baseball equipment — like bats — and beat a strategic retreat by reversing his engines and refraining from making contact with the irate citizenry.

It was one of the things that tumbled Black Ball Ferries into the publicly owned transportation system that exists today.

A year ago the county started charging admission to the garbage dump . . .

And somebody burned down the ticket office.

Then there was the little problem of the Justice "Courthouse" on the Island. Someone thought the word "In" should have been inserted in front of the word "Justice," and during the July Festival Days in 1970, he put a bomb through the window. It blew the interior of the building to pieces, devastating nearby automobiles and smashing out windows across the street.

The insurance on the fireproof structure was $10,000 . . . the damage, $35,000.

The Judge said, "We simply don't approve of this kind of thing." The confessed bomber was admonished not to blow up any more Justice Courts and released.

◆

Most of the time, the folks on Vashon are peaceable enough. It's only when their ire is aroused . . .

But it does tend to remind officialdom that while bridges across Lake Washington are a military and economic link via Snoqualmie Pass with the

Dry Side of the mountains, the same compelling motivation does not exist when it comes to hooking Seattle to the Olympic Peninsula via a ribbon of concrete touching on that potentially explosive Island.

The average visitor, however, is welcome.

In the winter of 1972, a 17-year-old Swiss girl by the name of Maya Hofer wrote her ski instructor asking him which were the best skis in the world and he reluctantly informed her they were not made in Switzerland. "The best in the world are K-2 Skis," he said. "They're made in a place you never heard of, called 'Vashon Island, U.S.A.'."

But indeed she had heard of Vashon. She had won a scholarship to attend school in the United States and was living on Vashon Island at that very moment. Shortly thereafter she broke one of a pair of borrowed skis on the slopes at Snoqualmie Pass. Bill Kirschner, President of K-2, upon hearing this story, presented her with a pair — which as any skier knows — represents no small investment.

It's a pity you can't visit the K-2 Factory, but the ski business is fiercely competitive and the K-2 people would just as soon not have their competitors learn about the newest wrinkle any sooner than necessary. New wrinkles consist of things like figuring out how to incorporate K-2's red, white and blue colors in the tops of their skis, a feature that immediately was copied . . . but K-2 was a jump ahead by then and had innovated the same colors on the *bottoms*, which, of course, are highly visible from below on skiers riding chair lifts.

The current effort involves ski boots. The sole leaves a K-2 imprint in the snow.

K-2 provides jobs for 500 people . . . the equivalent of about 10% of the 5,000-6,000 permanent residents of the Island.

Prowling Vashon Island

The center of the Island is higher than most islands in the Sound and provides sweeps of scenery that encompass both the Olympics and the Cascades. On a good day, Mt. Baker and Glacier Peak loom up in the distance, and there is no more spectacular perspective of Mt. Rainier than the one from *Inspiration Point*, high above Quartermaster Harbor. There are some delightful walks at *Dolphin, Robinson,* and *Jensen Points.* (See *Footloose,* pp. 142-147.)

Uncommon shopping – The most uncommon shopping on the Island is at the *currant farm* near the center of town. During the season, "U" can pick — and this is the only place in the entire State of Washington where a commercial crop of currants is grown . . . *Wax Orchards*, which produces 200 tons of pie cherries annually, is the only orchard of its kind on the Wet Side of the Mountains. You can buy them frozen in 10-pound plastic containers mixed with sugar (and pie recipes are available). You also can buy cherry juice and apple juice and a new beverage which is a mixture of cherry juice and honey. In December, combine this one with a trip to *Mitchell's,* which is nearby and sells "farmed" Christmas trees. The trees are "planted" in among towering evergreens. A big bonfire warms the hands of the red-cheeked and rubber-booted sales people and the whole thing makes for an unusual adventure that has become an Island tradition. In addition to the above, there's *Minglement Emporium*, for handmade items, crafts, natural foods, mostly local . . . *Little House*, decor accessories, clothing, kitchen items, toys, in remodeled cottage . . . *Red Caboose*, gifts and antiques in railroad car . . . 4 country-flavored "general merchandise" stores: *Country Store*, antiques, clothes, garden stuff, furniture . . . *Portage Store*, on Maury Island beach . . . *Harbor Mercantile*, in Burton . . . and *Tahlequah Store*, south ferry dock, for mainly food items . . . *Books By the Way*, new and used books by a potbellied stove, in historic old feed building. In summer, look for occasional signs along roads selling berries, corn, milk, or vegetables for fresh-from-the-farm goodies. Also sometimes local pottery is for sale on sawhorse-supported display tables in some casual grassy plot.

A word about eating – Try the really fresh french fries at the *Northgate Lunch*, north ferry dock. Popular spot for Sunday omelet breakfast . . . *Lloyd's Bakery*, chocolate chip cookies, raisin, pumpernickel, and "Speidel Onion" breads.

Annual affairs – *Home Tours*, in May, so popular they put on extra ferries to handle the crowds . . . *The Festival*, in July, parade and booths.

For further information – Any real estate office; they also have maps.

You can continue on to Tacoma from the south end of the Island but this tour returns you to the north end and the ferry to the Kitsap Peninsula at Southworth.

The wave of the future also is headed down this road — which is another way of getting to Gig Harbor — because the folks from the cities are getting away from it all with second homes here . . . and for that matter throughout Kitsap County, which is the least populated in the "big four" of the Puget Sound Governmental Conference: Snohomish, King, Pierce and Kitsap.

Olalla — They really ought to designate Olalla as an historic site, because it's a pure example of the kind of community the Mosquito Fleet once served — a summer colony of buildings around a dock. The old Mosquito Fleet sign reading "Olalla" still is there at the dock along with a post office, garden center, general store and gas station. Father commuted to Seattle or Tacoma while the family spent the summer at the beach. This is especially attractive in that it centers around a long lagoon . . . and Kitsap County has thoughtfully provided matching decor on the bridge for the picket fences around and about. If you are now or have been addicted to alcohol, Olalla is a famed place because there's a physical, mental and spiritual drying-out facility there that has helped a lot of people off the booze.

For viewing from the outside but not visiting is the 1912 *Charles B. Nelson House*, which is on the National Register of Historic Places. It is turreted and painted a classic white with black, and commands a complete view of Colvos Passage.

Uncommon shopping – *Country House Antiques*, on the way down the hill to the water at Olalla. It's barn-red and white . . . open "by chance and by reservation," and features primitive and country furniture.

You get another taste of the same thing you'll find at Olalla if you take a left at the sign pointing to Fragaria (botanical name for strawberry). The flavor of it all is reflected en route from signs like "March's Funny Farm," or "Ken Bradbury and Relatives."

Southworth-Port Orchard — If you have not opted for the Olalla run, we suggest you continue north at Colby instead of following Highway 160, the main road. This takes you along the coast route through Manchester and Retsil and prepares you for the fact that "Port Orchard is Port Orchard is Port Orchard." There are views of the Olympics on your right and neat homes on your left. The ferry does some twisting and turning through Sinclair Inlet along here to get to Bremerton. One time a big Navy craft was attempting to do the same thing and the nice homes on the left had some astonished people who woke up one Sunday morning to find a battleship in the front yard. (It floated off at the next tide.) The route takes you past the *Retsil Veteran's Home*. It's name is taken from that of Governor Ernest Lister (spelled backwards).

Port Orchard — (Pop. 3,900. Elev. Sea level.) — Kitsap County's second largest town and the county seat, it underwent a face-lifting in 1971 and today two blocks of Bay Street, the town's main thoroughfare, are covered with a cedar marquee. Colonial type lanterns and wooden store front sign embellish the covered walkway.

For the last 75 years or so, there's been a bit of a problem about the difference between "Port Orchard" and "Port Orchard." *The Guide to Washington* normally is the most accurate historical record in existence, but it leads the parade in getting things all fouled up this time.

So, with the aid of the local historical group and Miss Chloe Sutton, an 86-year-old "walking encyclopedia" of information about things concerning Port Orchard, we thought we'd sort of neaten things up, pat History on the head and send it on its way.

For about 100 years after Captain Vancouver named Port Orchard Bay after a young fellow on his ship — not for a bunch of fruit trees he found growing there — the problem of Port Orchard was pretty simple. It was the whole body of water on the backside of Bainbridge Island.

Then in 1854, when Captain William Renton got tired of having his sawmill beaten to bits by the waves at Alki Point and moved the machinery to Port Orchard Bay, he neglected to add a specific location to his address. Letters were written in longhand in those days and that was an extra word you didn't have to put in. Besides everybody knew what he meant.

Port Orchard was Enetai.

Well, that was simple enough. Everybody knew that if you wanted to go to Port Orchard, you went to Enetai.

But then in 1871, Renton's mill burned down and shortly thereafter a twenty-year effort was initiated here and in Congress to locate a Puget Sound Naval Yard at Port Orchard. But that Port Orchard wasn't Enetai at all. It was a place on Sinclair Inlet, an arm of Port Orchard Bay. And everybody, including the Congress — which kept not voting for the Navy Yard — knew where that Port Orchard was, too. It was on the *north* side of Sinclair Inlet.

Then in 1886, a fella by the name of Sidney Stevens platted a town on the *south* side of Sinclair Inlet. He had enough pride in his own first name to call his town "Sidney." And everybody knew where Sidney was . . . and the little steamers of the Mosquito Fleet stopped at Sidney, where they were promoting a Navy dry dock.

Meanwhile, some guys got going on a place we now know of as Annapolis — and called it Port Orchard. So we had Port Orchard Passage, and Port Orchard and Port Orchard and Sidney all in a cozy little group there at Sinclair Inlet.

Then during the Gay Nineties, things started to hum.

The Port Orchard people on the north side of the inlet got their town incorporated. And some other people in the same location platted a town called Charleston right next door. The two towns got in a big bust over which one would be the post office address and Charleston won.

And the guys building Port Orchard at Annapolis had a beef, and half the town — two people — left in a huff to take up residence in Sidney, a few blocks up the inlet. With a swollen population like this, Sidney went after and got the county seat away from Port Madison. Breathing triumph in every pore, Sidney decided that it, not Port Orchard, should be Port Orchard.

But the State legislature said, "Look, we already got one town called Port Orchard," and turned down their plea.

The real Port Orchard on the north side of the Bay decided they'd better cinch things down and change their postal address from Charleston to Port Orchard. But when they got there, the cupboard was bare. Sidney had sneaked in ahead of them with the endorsement of the State's entire Congressional delegation and got themselves named Port Orchard as far as the post office was concerned.

So then the mail for Port Orchard went to Sidney.

Ten years later, W. L. Thomson, one of the publishers of the *Port Orchard Independent*, which was located in Sidney, got himself elected to the legislature. In 1903, without a by-your-leave from anybody, Thomson sneaked a bill through the legislature and got it signed by the Governor officially changing Sidney into Port Orchard.

And that's where Port Orchard is today.

If you don't believe it, just check with the *Sidney Museum of History and Arts* . . .

Which is located in Port Orchard.

Prowling Port Orchard

The liveliest organization in town is the Sidney Museum group. They are the shakers and movers who are making the town into a cohesive unit that hopefully is turning its face back to the sea where the town got started. One of their prime objectives is the restoration of the old *Sidney Hotel*, which you can arrange to visit by calling its owner, Mrs. Lora Mahon. The hotel, which looms large on the landscape, has been an apartment house and a poorhouse as well as a hotel and the Museum Association was formed for the specific purpose of saving the structure. It now is on the State and National Historic Registers.

The Association also has opened the *Sidney Gallery* in the Pioneer Masonic Temple. They've done a sprightly job of restoring the interior with barn siding and that sort of thing, and have classes, shows and artists in action on the premises. They have acquired a log cabin further up the hill. Its restoration also is a part of their ambitions.

Some of the town rests on pilings and the rest climbs the hill to the Courthouse which has a splendid view of the Bremerton Navy Yard and the Olympics from the south side of Sinclair Inlet. A neat way of seeing the Bremerton Navy Yard from the water is by taking a 10 minute trip on the Horluck Transportation Company's boats which haul commuters from Port Orchard to their jobs in Bremerton.

Uncommon shopping – *Elder Crafts Shop*, you have to be 55 to enter your stuff for purchase here, and they have dolls, quilts, knitted items ... *Thrifty Nickel Shop*, run by the Episcopal Church ... and of course the *Sidney Gallery*, which really has quality arts and crafts.

A word about eating – *Myhre's Restaurant*, with a downstairs coffee shop and terrace restaurant upstairs which opens after 5, is main eating place in town ... *Smith's Coffee Shop*, is a gathering place for locals.

Annual affairs – *Art and Historical Celebration*, the last weekend in May and *Fathoms of Fun*, on July 4th weekend.

For further information – South Kitsap Chamber of Commerce, 742 Bay; phone, TR 6-3505.

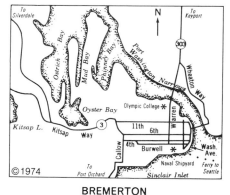

BREMERTON

Bremerton — (Pop. 39,400. Elev. 12.) — This town is the result of the most brilliant, single real estate coup ever perpetrated on the Wet Side of the Mountains. It was brought off by a young German immigrant still in his 20's and it very well may turn the Olympic Community College into the Stanford University of the Pacific Northwest.

William Bremer was born on June 12, 1863, in Seesen, Germany where for a time he served as an apprentice in his father's banking business. He got further training in the financial field in Hamburg. In 1888, two years after his arrival in this country, he showed up in the real estate business in Port Orchard (only it was known as Sidney in those days) across Sinclair Inlet from a piece of property the United States Navy had been buzzing about for almost 20 years.

In an article written in 1943, Rear Admiral C. S. Freeman, U.S.N., who was Commandant of the Puget Sound Navy Yard in Bremerton at the time, described what the original buzzing was all about. After pointing out that in the 1890's there wasn't a single shipyard on the Pacific Coast that would accommodate a major warship, Freeman wrote:

"It fronted on a natural bay, of such depth and extent as to be able to accommodate the entire fleet at anchor. The depth of the water was right up to the shoreline, and the nature of the bottom was such as to make periodic dredging unnecessary. Further, the site was practically impregnable from attack by sea. Although it was connected to the Pacific by an excellent channel, this channel could be easily defended along its shores, and its waters quickly mined in case of threatened attack." (Those who rode the ferries to Bremerton during World War II will recall they had to wait while the Coast Guard did what it did to let the ferry through . . . and there was a lot of concern whether some bright Japanese submarine captain might try to follow a ferry.)

Anyway, a young Navy Lieutenant by the name of A. B. Wyckoff had been trying fruitlessly for a decade to interest his superiors and Congress in a Naval Station, preferably with dry dock facilities, in this location. A group of energetic eastern Senators who figured the west coast was expendable, blocked all attempts to nail down the facility until 1890 when the Congress finally let an amendment slide into the Navy Appropriations bill that enabled the expenditure of $9,600 for that hunk of real estate the Navy was so excited about.

In those days, a lot of loggers worked at their trade as a regular thing and proved up during the off season on homesteads. And one Andrew Williams was no exception. He had homesteaded a place called Point Turner in 1872 and got his patent on a key 168 acres on October 15, 1875. You could figure the value of that land at the time at, and let's be liberal about it, maybe clear up to $320. Even 13 years later, you could get yourself a pretty good piece of view property in the area for in the neighborhood of a couple hundred bucks . . . but not one the Navy was interested in buying.

In 1888, when the news got around about the potential Navy Yard at Point Turner, Mr. Williams suddenly put a value on it of something well above the $320 . . .

The price went to $32,000.

The Navy only had $9,600. It not only had a financial capacity limited to $9,600 by those lawmakers on the east coast, but it had a need for more than the 168 acres owned by Williams. Wyckoff was having a hell of a time even getting that much of an appropriation. And it looked like a decade of effort on his part was headed down the old torpedo tube again . . .

But 1888, also was the year that young Bremer added himself to the scenery on the Wet Side of the Mountains . . .

He was so excited when he got the news about the Navy and Mr. Williams that he neglected to wait for more conventional methods of transportation. He leaped into a rowboat and rowed across Sinclair Inlet to meet with Mr. Williams.

Bremer was 25 years old at the time . . . and he had the $32,000 in his pocket.

Williams, who gulped when he named the price, must have gulped again when he got it.

Bremer added some more acreage to the Williams property and offered Wyckoff and the United States Navy 190¼ acres for a neat $9,587.

There was a whole thirteen bucks left over from the $9,600.

You gotta admit that it's only in the American tradition that in addition to the 190¼ acres which he sold the Navy, Mr. Bremer thoughtfully acquired some property around the outskirts of the Navy Yard. And it's not entirely astonishing that he called it "Bremer's Town."

After all, he owned it.

Mr. Bremer lived in Seattle and did the things that wealthy owners of towns did in those days, like join the Arctic, Rainier and Seattle Golf Clubs. In 1891, he was married to Miss Sophia Stensel of Wisconsin. He died in 1910 at the age of 47 years. The Bremers had three children, Matilda, John and Edward.

And none of them had children.

So there were headlines in the *Bremerton Sun* when the will of John, who followed Matilda to the grave, was probated and revealed that he had left his share of the estate in trust with his younger brother Edward for the Olympic Community College located in that city.

When we asked Edward Bremer, who is 73 years old at this date, if the proceeds from the estate of the biggest landowners in the fifth largest city west of the Cascades would go to the kids in the college, he replied, "Yes, I guess they will."

Prowling Bremerton

The star attraction of course is the venerable battleship *"Mighty Mo."* Some 300,000 people a year visit this National Historic Site in the *Bremerton Navy Yard*, where you can stand on the deck where the Japanese surrendered. Visiting is from noon to 4 p.m. on weekdays and from 10 to 4 on weekends and holidays. *Naval Museum* on the ferry dock . . . *Kitsap County Historical Museum*, in the old post office in the center of town . . . nearby *Great Northwest Building*, Pacific Ave., has the highest view.

For a feel of the area, drive the *Rocky Point Road* or *Marine Drive* northwest of town. They go out on two peninsulas pointed north . . . or else cross the Manette or Warren Ave. Bridges over the *Port Washington Narrows* and look back from the hillside to the town and the Olympics.

Uncommon shopping – *Navy Supply Center*, at the Puget Sound Naval Shipyard, near the "Missouri," is open to the public Saturday mornings. As *Sunset Magazine* put it, "Shop at the Department of Defense;" everything from tools to railroad ties, depending upon what happens to be surplus at the moment . . . *Three Gables Home Craft Shop*, Charleston Beach Rd., for macrame, oil paintings, candlemaking supplies, handwoven rugs, copper enameling, etc. in Amy and Ralph Jacobson's home . . . *Harriett's Antiques*,

Highway 3, for table settings, decorator items . . . *McGavin's Bakery*, Callow Ave., Dutch, Indian and Swedish breads, egg rolls, tortes; all delicious . . . *Little Norway Seafood Shop*, Charleston Beach Rd., for fresh oysters, red snapper, Swedish farm cheese and other Scandinavian cheeses.

A word about eating – *The Hearthstone*, Kitsap Way, quite posh and has a great overlook of Oyster Bay . . . *Crazy Eric's*, one of a chain of regional drive-ins relating to the Scandinavian population and providing shakes and hamburgers . . . *Sammy's Triangle Cafe*, 1st St., steel yourself to the crummy look, this is a "character place;" bacon and eggs breakfast is "out of sight" . . . *Carriage Inn*, Bremer's Dept. Store, Burwell St., pleasant atmosphere for breakfast or lunch . . . *International House*, 4th St., small German deli with daily "sandwich specials" . . . *Skipper's Tavern*, on 1st St. dock, for a taste of local Navy and Shipyard color.

A word about sleeping – *The Hearthstone Inn*, has water views and balconies and is considered best, although the *Chieftain*, with mountain view, and *Westgate Motels* are very good. All three are on Kitsap Way.

Annual affairs – There are three big ones in May; *Armed Forces Day Parade, Annual Jazz Festival*, at Olympic Community College, and the *Rhododendron Forest Theater Productions*, put on by the Mountaineers (follow the Seabeck road to the Mountaineers Forest Theater. It's a forest setting where you sit in a natural amphitheater and look down on the players below).

Side Trip to Belfair, Dewatto and Tahuya — We always thought that last name came from a bunch of independent Indians saying "What's it to ya?" at their first encounter with early map makers.

Belfair is at the end of Hood Canal at its eastern loop and they have very good homemade chocolate pie at the *Belfair Cafe*. Heading west on Highway 300, on the north side of the Canal, you come to *Belfair State Park*, comparatively new and has picnic facilities; and on to Tahuya, where visiting the *Tahuya Grocery* is worth at least the price of a package of cigarettes or a coke. It's barn-red and white and looks as though somebody chewing on a straw ought to be rocking on the big front porch.

The road to Dewatto, from Musqueti Point along the Canal's edge, is for the adventuresome and summertime. To Dewatto across the top of this peninsula, it's across newly logged and newly tree-farmed land to the long, sheltered bay and 3 buildings of a ghost town. For a handsome view of the Olympics from the unusual angle of the east side of Hood Canal, turn on the Lake Aldrich Road to *Paul Sharp Scenic Park*. There's a decaying old log chute, picnic spot and spectacular outlook. Lots of room for present-day pioneers who want to get away from it all.

One route heads east over the Manette Bridge to *Illahee State Park*, which has good nature trails and a sandy beach and is less crowded than many parks; on the mainland side of the part of Port Orchard Bay that goes up past Bainbridge Island's backside. This route takes you past the *Keyport Torpedo Station*, where there's a sign reading "Our tasks are trimmed and pointed to the sea," and a small shopping center . . . or you can cut west at a number of places that go more directly to Silverdale.

Silverdale — It is really a two-part town — the one you usually see when you're headed north on Highway 3 for the Hood Canal Bridge and wouldn't dream of stopping at — and the neat little town to the east. All of a sudden, you're on short little streets that dead-end in the bay in two directions. It's quiet and sort of 1900-ish with some old pilings where the Mosquito Fleet once came by.

Uncommon shopping – *The Art Cellar Gallery*, representative of the better Northwest artists and open half days Wed., Thurs., Sun. . . . *Halfway House*, a delightful "find" in a 2-story log house. You enter through what once was the entryway of someone's home, go past interior design offices into the 2-story main room, with a big fireplace at one end and all sorts of interior decor items for sale like furniture, rugs, antiques. The local folks think that Ann Schlick who runs it is "fey . . ."

A word about eating – The best place for miles around is *The Poplars*, named for a row of poplars and open from 7 a.m. to 2 a.m. Bright, clean, cheery coffee shop, and a restaurant with a medieval red and black decor and dim lighting in the evening. Good Shrimp Louie with lots of shrimp is a feature . . . *Bauer's Bakery*, by the same people mentioned so favorably in Poulsbo; with equally impressive baked goods here; also tables for snacks.

A word about sleeping – Rather two words, *The Poplars*. What's a nice place like this doing in a place like this? We suspect they're part of the tooling-up process by which the county looks to taking on 6,000 more workers for the Trident Submarine program scheduled to be initiated at the nearby Bangor Naval Station.

Next you skirt the submarine base and head south along the east side of the Canal through farmlands, past lots of "Northwest Scandinavian" farmhouses (sort of tall, white, spare and tidy) and, if you're lucky, unsurpassed views of the Olympics.

The town of *Seabeck* is quite a startler. You come around a bend and here's a pleasantly preserved New England village. It is mostly a location for interdenominational church conferences, but the buildings are handsome, the grounds lovely and there's a snack bar and a grocery, where you can rent a rowboat in the little town on the big bay. It's the kind of thing that can, but rarely does, happen to a former logging operation. There's an old *Indian cemetery* on a path behind the nearby school.

You can go on to *Scenic Beach State Park* and *Holly* (through a rhododendron and evergreen terrain for the adventuresome) and then back along the north side of Green Mountain, which in addition to a sensational view, has a picnic area on its peak; and Gold Mountain, the only "high rises" on the Great Peninsula. Both mountains have roads to the top. For a walk here . . . (See *Footloose*, p. 127.)

Then back to Bremerton and back to Seattle on one of the reasons we believe in ferries.

Tacoma Tour 1 — In and Around Tacoma (Map X)

Highlights of this tour are the enormous old railroad station as you enter town from the freeway . . . the new Pedestrian Plaza in the heart of town . . . a trip to the Port of Tacoma across the 11th Avenue Bridge . . . the Old City Hall and the Tacoma Art Museum and Allied Arts Center across the street from one another . . . the State Historical Society Musem and, of course, Point Defiance Park — one of the most talented parks in the entire Pacific Northwest.

It is a part of wisdom while you are in Tacoma not to dwell on the name of the Mighty Mountain some 70 miles to the southeast. Tacoma Chamber of Commerce literature mentions that "Geographically, Mt. Rainier belongs to Pierce County . . . that its original name was "Ta-y-ma," "Ta-co-ma," or "Tak-ho-ma," or "mountain that is God," but that Captain George Vancouver named it after a less majestic personage — a rather unpopular admiral of the British Navy. Tacomans suspect Seattleites of lobbying Congress to retain the name "Rainier." And there is a poem written by Ralph Chaplin in 1961 — 36 years after the official adoption of the name "Rainier" for the mountain — called *Only the Drums Remember:*

> *High in the heavens where all clean things are*
> *Still stands the Mountain underneath a star,*
> *Timeless and patient, waiting to reclaim*
> *Its ancient title to the Indian name*
> *It bore with pride before the white man came*

All of which proves that Tacoma is still in there pitching.

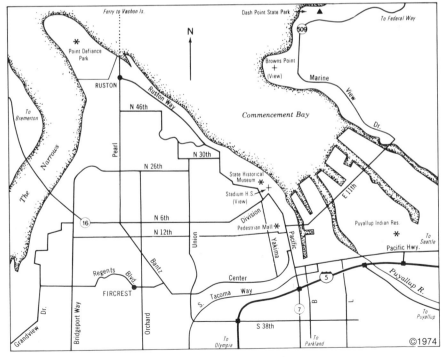

TACOMA

Tacoma — (Pop. 155,000. Elev. 21.) — As the runner-up in the population race between the two cities, Tacoma takes an awful beating by comparison with Seattle, which is three times as big. But that doesn't mean the founders in Tacoma were dumber than those in Seattle or that they didn't try as hard or that their topographic assets were any different.

You take a look at a map of Puget Sound and you'll find that Commencement and Elliott Bays are as much alike as twin dents in a car fender . . . and the hinterlands backing them up belong to the same club. Seattle took advantage of the fact that she's located midway on the Sound while Tacoma is sort of tucked down at one end. Seattle has the further edge of proximity to Snoqualmie Pass, the lowest pass in the Cascade. And when the chips were down between two more or less equally matched antagonists, these were lethal advantages.

But if you look at it another way, outside of Seattle, Tacoma is twice as big as the next largest city on the Wet Side of the Mountains, and three times the size of the third largest. And Tacoma's got a lot of fascinating things going for her that make profitable prowling profitable.

The one that currently fractures us is the historical background of Tacoma Plaza, the pedestrian mall they're working on in the heart of the central business district right this moment. This was an area that was supposed to roll over and play dead when the Tacoma Mall was built some distance from downtown several years ago. The mall's a great place, but it hasn't got the plaza location's kind of history going for it.

On March 2, 1892, the cops found one Salvatore Conchilla, a Sicilian fruit peddler, with 34 stiletto thrusts in his body and his head bashed in to sort of "top" things off. The corpse was the result of Tacoma's first really admirable vendetta.

And 7,000 people formed a line clear around the block to view the remains at the undertakers . . .

The first day!

It would be correct to state that the murder created quite a stir even outside of Tacoma and was a matter of intense satisfaction to the Pierce County Sheriff J. W. Price. You see, he happened to have on hand a piece of brand new, unused hangman's rope he'd bought at a special, 4 years previously. But the convicted killer he bought it for had the audacity to escape before it could be used.

Well, the county got around to convicting another poor Sicilian for the new vendetta murder. It was an election year, Sheriff Price was a good political campaigner and made the most of the situation . . .

He sent out engraved invitations to the hanging!

They were engraved on purple cards with the picture of the convicted murderer in the upper lefthand corner. The invitations read as follows: "You are respectfully invited to attend, and this card will admit you to the execution of SALVADOR PICANI to occur on Friday, July 1, 1892 in the Pierce County jail yard at Tacoma, Wash., J. W. Price, Sheriff."

You must admit that at this point, things did not look favorable for Mr. Picani, who could have used Perry Mason as his attorney in the worst way. But Perry hadn't even been invented yet.

Instead, a Roman Catholic priest, who was entirely unsympathetic to Sheriff Price's problem either with the unused rope or the election campaign, made a big speech about Picani at a luncheon meeting at the Tacoma Commercial Club. A couple of legislators were at the meeting and they asked what they could do. And the priest said maybe they could get a law passed requiring the State Supreme Court to review the case.

So they did.

But Governor John H. McGraw was unsympathetic to this new case. A former sheriff from King County, he'd been through a couple of tough election campaigns himself. He believed in supporting the local police, so he vetoed the bill.

But he'd goofed on his dates and didn't affix his veto to the bill until the day *after* he had to do it, if his veto was to count . . . and it became law without his signature.

At this point there was quite a hoo-hah going in Tacoma on this matter. And much to Sheriff Price's disgust, the Pierce County Prosecuting Attorney folded on the case and moved for dismissal . . . which was granted.

Price not only had to account for his unused hangman's rope and the engraved purple invitations, but old Jim Frace presented him with a bill for the construction of the scaffolding in the jail yard. And F. E. Johnson was hanging around with his bill, too. Johnson had provided a brand new and expensive electrical mechanism for springing the trap. There was nothing for it but to dismantle the whole contraption and remove it from the jail yard, cancel the invitations and call the whole party off.

Even the honored guest had canceled out.

It turned out later that Mr. Picani hadn't done the job at all. Another friend of the deceased had inflicted the stab wounds and departed for parts unknown.

The party may have been ruined at the time, but part of the new Tacoma Plaza occupies that former county jail yard. What a wonderful gesture to bring that rope and the scaffolding and the electrical trap out of retirement for resurrection in the new mall. It could be dedicated to the nonhanging of an innocent man in Tacoma . . . and what a tourist attraction!

There are some other items of history that a lot of people are bent on saving in downtown Tacoma. Tacoma Allied Arts already has established itself in the former city jail. When you come into town along Pacific Avenue there's a grand old *Union Station* on the right that's an outstanding example of the heyday of railroading when the fellows would blow $750,000 on an edifice of this kind.

The railroad station is a little big for the average backyard, but the architects have singled it out as one of the Northwest's best in design and somebody ought to be able to figure out something to do with it . . . along with the old 1893 *City Hall* with a clock tower that could tell time to the north, east, south and west to the accompaniment of chimes if they were working.

The Washington State Historical Society Museum nearby, formed in 1890, is just north of Stadium High School, a structure rich in Tacoma history.

In the 1880's when high-flying railroader Henry Villard was flying high with the Northern Pacific, he set out to blow $750,000 jointly with the Tacoma Land Company, a subsidiary of the N.P., on a big resort hotel. It was to have, among other things an enormous view of the harbor and Mt. Rainier, and an automatic electric potato peeler. The railroad hit hard times and by 1891, the Land Company found itself with half a million dollars worth of partially constructed seven-story hotel which it boarded up.

At 7:15 p.m. on October 11, 1898, the structure was hit by a mysterious fire which Tacoma historian Herbert Hunt suggested could have been set by somebody. Hunt noted that there was some black smoke coming out of some oil cans and, "It was the third costly fire that had visited Tacoma within three weeks . . . all were in the hands of Henry Longstreth, who had been appointed receiver of the Tacoma Land Company the June before."

The ruins sat for six years and when the railroad reluctantly began to tear it down, some of the folks thought it would be a splendid location for a high school and others thought it was terrible, but the "yeas" prevailed. Then somebody got the notion that the gulch next door would make an excellent stadium and an equal number disagreed. The architect for the job, prowling around in the gulch, found a dead man hanging in a tree and rather than having it known from then on as "deadman's gulch," they got going on the stadium. There were some squatters in shacks in the gulch who didn't want to leave. One woman stuck around and got a little hysterical when water, stones and mud for the fill came through her back door. Convinced that the stadium people meant business, she departed by the front before her house was buried.

The first step of the school building, completed in 1906, is a lulu. Twenty-feet long, 6-feet wide and 16-inches thick, it was cut from a boulder deposited nearby by a friendly glacier several thousand years ago. It took 26 horses to bring this big rock into town where it was cut up. The second step is from the same rock but lacks the same generous dimensions as the first.

◆

A little farther along, at Ruston, is the *American Smelting and Refining Company* smelter which reduces about 10% of the copper ore in the United States to the kind of metal that brings electricity into your house. You can visit this industrial plant; it's rich in the kind of history that created a real estate boom in Tacoma in the 1890's.

One William R. Rust arrived in Tacoma in 1887 with a mere $30,000 in his pocket, which he had acquired in some Colorado mines, and proceeded to build a smelter. At 7 a.m. on September 15, 1890, they fired her up and a short time later a representative of the Guggenheims suggested his people might go as high as $1,000,000 for the smelter, which would be a nice return on Rust's $30,000 investment of 3 years before.

"I might consider $4,000,000," Rust replied complacently.

"You gotta be kidding!" the Guggenheim man gasped.

"Not only not kidding," Rust said, "but $4,000,000's only my price today. Next week it's going to be $5,000,000."

And sure enough, the next year when the Guggenheims bought the place, it was for $5,000,000 . . . well, that is $5,000,000 plus $500,000 in the incidental expenses Rust had been put to while they were making up their minds. They couldn't afford to let a man like that go, so as part of the agreement, Rust remained on to run the show.

The folks in the neighborhood liked Rust so well they named a town, Ruston, after him. Tacoma now surrounds it, but Ruston's a town today with a bonafide population of 688 people. And has its own cops.

And that takes us to *Point Defiance Park*, the outlet of Tacoma's most effective, satisfying and delightful energies . . . the place for the most profitable possible prowling in the second largest city on the Wet Side of the Mountains.

There's some difference of opinion over who named the Park, but our story is of the men who were surveying the 638 acres in 1854. When they got to the Point, one of the surveyors said, "A fort here and a fort there (pointing to Vashon Island), could defy the world. We'll call this Point Defiance."

The land originally was set aside for military purposes. However, when it kept on not being used by the military, Tacomans started putting pressure on in Washington, D.C. to make it a park. It finally was pushed through in the nation's capital by a real estate developer and the operators of a streetcar line because a park in that spot would be mighty good for business, and in 1888 President Grover Cleveland signed the necessary papers and it became a city park.

Lobbying was a little cheaper in those days; the promoters had to part with only 500 bucks to get the job done.

The Army, however, kept one little string attached — which turned out to be quite beneficial in the hands of a couple of capable Junior Leaguers about three-quarters of a century later. The string stated that the Park could be used for military maneuvers at any time it seemed advisable.

It is difficult to assert which of two jewels in the crown of the present-day "Tacoma Spirit" at Point Defiance is the more illustrious, the sea otters in the *Aquarium* or the *Lidgerwood Skidder* at *Camp Six*. But both are priceless prowling for the car-cushion traveler.

The otters were brought here from Amchitka, one of the islands on the Aleutian chain. And in addition to being among the few in captivity, their antics charm children ranging in age to maybe 90 years old.

And then there's *Camp Six*.

Camp Six is unique in that it is the only outdoor museum of its kind, and is listed on the National Register of Historic Places. It was designed by a veteran logging engineer, Marc Titlow, to demonstrate a "two-sided" logging operation on a 20-acre site in the forest at Point Defiance. All of the equipment is the authentic, best of a kind . . . and in most cases, the last of the type. All were brought from the woods, patched up and repaired and are displayed as they were used during the era of steam logging.

On weekends in summer you can ride a logging train operated by the PDQ & K Railroad (Port Defiance, Quinault, and Klickitat), if you're an adult with four-bits or a kid under 12 with two-bits.

Camp Six — typical of logging camp location designations — was the sixth and best possible site offered for such an operation in the Park's 638

acres. In it, are such logging equipment as a caboose . . . skeleton flatcar . . .
Willamette yarder . . . Washington duplex loader . . . high lead . . . flatcars . . .
Dolbeer donkey . . . Kapowsin bunkhouses . . . Quinault camp cars . . . the
venerable locomotive, Shay No. 7 . . .

And, of course, the Lidgerwood Skidder.

For years, various timbermen had talked about lobbing together a
museum of the logging equipment which had built the Wet Side of the
Mountains in the first place, but it wasn't until the Tacoma Junior League did
a feasibility study in 1958 and some very forthright younger women — many
of them daughters and granddaughters of those freewheeling timber barons
— took a hand in the game that the whole thing got put together.

Mavis Kallsen, who presently is nearing the mid-century mark herself,
went into some of the details. (She had quite a hand in the League's activities.
She wrote about it for the Goeduck Publishing Company in 1969.)

There was all of this steam equipment scattered from the Quinault to
the Klickitat forests and no neutral central place to exhibit it. So the problem
was getting the equipment, finding a place for it and then moving it into
that place.

In 1964, the League put up the initial $20,000 and its members began
to talk with influential people like their relatives, the Tacoma Park Board and
the State Parks and Recreation Commission.

When the gals got going, so did the camp.

There was a little problem of obtaining the no-longer-used steam
equipment, but that was solved in one meeting of Tacoma timbermen with
enough clout to keep a sustained yield program going in our forests for the
next 1,000 years. They also would come up with a hand in moving that
equipment out of the forests, along the highways and into position in the Park.

Then there was the problem of preparing the place to receive it and
that's where a lawyer friend uncovered the clause about military "maneuvers"
at Point Defiance. Pretty soon an Army general in a helicopter was flying overhead and 125 guys from the Army Engineers moved into bivouac operation
in the dense forest of the Park.

The railroad "crew" laying the donated ties and track was made up of
volunteers from the drunk tank of the Tacoma City Jail — with a major assist
from a friendly union leader who was on the board of people who put Camp
Six together. And the crew had never eaten so well as they did from the
homemade cookery of the Leaguers who served them hot lunches from the
tailgates of their station wagons. A couple of the guys went out and got drunk
again after their sentences expired, so they could be back on the job again and
eat those lunches the next day.

And things went swimmingly until they came to the Lidgerwood
Skidder, the most powerful steam force ever applied to logging. A monster
weighing 300 tons, it was rail-mounted and could be moved to a logging site
where it could log an area 3 miles in diameter. The skilled men who operated
it were the elite corps and highest-paid loggers in the woods. They also held
the most dangerous jobs. Its record day's work was 72 cars of logs. The one at

Point Defiance was the last of 100 and had been in operation for a quarter of a century in Weyerhauser's Mt. St. Helens area.

But 300 tons . . .

How would they get it to Point Defiance?

Even when they took her apart, the base weighed 150 tons. It took four days to move her up Interstate 5 from Longview because every time they went around a curve they had to jack up the leaning edge or she'd blow the tires on that side of the 18-tire flatbed trailer.

That would be $9,000 worth of tires.

And that's what she did at a peak traffic period in a bottle-necking underpass at Tumwater. There was a lot of irate drivers who waited several hours for those tires to be replaced . . .

And the resulting traffic ticket came to 600 bucks.

But those were the only casualties in the creation of Camp Six as it is today. And the Lidgerwood Skidder is up for inclusion in the National Register of Historic Places.

Prowling Tacoma

Your best bet is to go to the Chamber of Commerce in the Winthrop Hotel building for instructions and map of the Drive-Yourself Scenic "Kla How Ya" Trail starting at 9th and A Streets. At the very least, it should be a fascinating full day, what with stops and all. (See *Footloose*, p. 188.)

We call your particular attention to the log-loading at *Blair Waterway* on the Port Dock, where thousands of millions of feet were shipped to the Orient in 1972 . . . and to the channel off *St. Regis Paper* where on the morning of January 14, 1899 the four-masted, full-rigged 2,579-ton British ship *Andelana* sank in 180 feet of water carrying 17 to watery graves. Because of legal problems concerning salvage, King County's boundary subsequently was moved 12 miles north beyond Brown's and Dash Points.

For tours of the harbor, *Riggs Charter Service* will cover the waterfront for you, and on summer Sundays they go to Blake Island in connection with the Indian salmon bake dinners at Tillicum Village. There is a new *Tacoma Art Museum* at 12th and Pacific, in the vicinity of a number of galleries. And to see homes of 1890-1910 period considered to be among the most well-kept houses and architecturally interesting on the Wet Side of the Mountains, loop back and forth between 4th and 9th Streets from Yakima Avenue to L St. *Point Defiance Park* should be rementioned for its restoration of *Fort Nisqually*, the 1833 Hudson's Bay fort, as well as the *Fort Nisqually Granary*, nationally registered as an Historic Place. The city of Tacoma puts on a salmon barbecue at the beach in the Park every Wednesday evening in July. (See *Footloose*, p. 190.) By calling ahead or checking with the Chamber of Commerce, visitors may see *Nalley's*, S. 35th, Northwest's largest processor of salad dressings, pickles, potato chips; *St. Regis Paper Co.*, Canal St., kraft pulp and paper; *Lindal Cedar Homes* S. 19th, factory of pre-cut homes; *U.S.S. Cabezon*, Hylebos Waterway, "thick-skinned" deep-diving submarine, or by checking the Port of Tacoma office, you might be able to visit a foreign ship in port.

One of the not-to-be-missed spots is the previously mentioned *Museum of the Washington State Historical Society* on N. Stadium Way. This is where writers like us mine pure historical gold, but it also has exhibits that make history come alive to the average visitor. And if you're at all curious about Ezra Meeker, the covered wagon he trekked across the county with is on display here.

Uncommon shopping – *The Tacoma Mall* is the biggest one of the bunch with some 85 enclosed stores ranging from the large to the small and exclusive; we don't have to tell you to go there because you will anyway . . . *Allied Arts Gallery*, in the old city jail on Pacific, will give you a list of a whole batch of galleries within walking distance . . . *Washington Plaza Building*, on Pacific, is new and has a great fountain and all that good stuff you've come to expect in such a contemporary complex of shops . . . *Stadium Toys and Crafts*, on Tacoma Avenue . . . *Windjammer Marine*, Ruston Way . . . *Ocean Fish Company*, Ruston Way, has lots of good fresh fish; for a taste that may be new to you if you're not Swedish, try the pickled salmon . . . *The Basket Shop*, So. K St., has thousands of baskets . . . *Larson Nursery*, Bridgeport Way, has some of the finest rhododendrons in the northwest, but the doctor won't let Mr. Larson work between 12 and 1 . . . There also is a place to rent *bicycles* on Pearl St. . . . *Gunderson's Jewelry*, Broadway, is venerable and fine, with distinctive designs . . . *Connoisseur Shop*, Tacoma Ave. N., beguiling bibelots for collectors . . . unusual number of delicatessens thrive here — among the noteworthy; *Hess' German Delicatessen and Bakery*, Bridgeport Way, homemade breads; *International Kitchen*, N. Pearl; and *Jim's Delicatessen*, Regents Blvd. . . . *Lakewood*, a colonial shopping square by the poshy lake area, is abounding with a considerable number of good antique shops.

A word about eating – *Clinkerdagger, Bickerstaff & Pett's* Ruston Way, shingled, and with leaded windows, restaurant is built on pilings over the water, has intriguing atmosphere of an old English pub, costumed waitresses, heavy beams, high-backed booths, good food, and reservations "a must," any time . . . *Lakewood Terrace*, Lakewood Center, a pleasant spot for continental dining; excellent food and varied menu . . . *Bavarian Restaurant* — and nearby *Bavarian Delicatessen*, N. K St., a German restaurant that features wild boar and venison . . . *Black Angus*, 11th & A St., good for steaks and lounge entertainment . . . *Honan's*, St. Helens St., longtime popular downtown facility with relaxing atmosphere; hangout for newspaper people . . . *Ceccanti's*, Pacific Ave., excellent Italian food in a well-designed brick building . . . *Johnny's Dock*, at the Port and Tacoma Mall, does as brisk a business as anybody — especially with deserts — and probably makes a killing in Johnny's Seasoning Salts . . . *Cliff House*, Brown's Point, is very good on steaks and chops, unsurpassed view if the moon or mountain are out . . . *Steve's Gay Nineties*, South Tacoma, a whole bunch of restaurants rolled into one theme and very popular with the family trade.

A word about sleeping – *Lakewood Motor Inn*, at Lakewood, is a quieter suburban motel in a handsome Williamsburg-style building and *Rodeway Inn* is near the Tacoma Mall; both are superior accommodations . . . *Doric Tacoma Motor Hotel*, St. Helens St., is handily downtown . . . *Sherwood Inn*, 84th and I-5, is complete resort . . . *Holiday Inn*, Pacific Highway E. is east of the Port Dock . . . *Rose Motel*, S. Tacoma Way, is smaller . . . all three of the latter considered very good.

Annual affairs – *Daffodil Festival*, March through May, attracts 2,000,000 visitors with events including Grand Floral Parade, Floral Marine Parade, Junior Daffodil Parade; valley and fields of daffodils are spectacular ... *McNeil Island Prison Art Show and Sale*, October, Rhodes Store, Broadway; sponsored by Amer. Business Women's Assoc. and includes oil paintings, pastels, watercolors, copperwork.

For further information – Tacoma Chamber of Commerce, 752 Broadway, 627-2175.

Several important military installations are located within easy distance of Tacoma, two of which contribute significantly to both the population and prosperity of this region.

McChord Air Force Base — (Pop. c. 5,000 military; 1,200 civilian)

— A one-hanger, dirt strip in the early 1930's, "Tacoma Field" was deeded to the government and became "McChord Field" on May 5, 1938. From that meager start it became our country's largest bomber-training base in World War II, even training some of the aircrews that flew the B-25s in the renowned Doolittle Tokyo Raid. An $81 million-dollar-a-year industry in Region IV, it is the home of 18 major Air Force units. The headquarters of the formidable North American Defense Command's 25th NORAD Region and of the Aerospace Defense Command's 318th fighter-interceptor squadron, it is probably best remembered for the 62nd Military Aircraft Wing — which played the major role in returning our POWs from North Vietnam. The base is semi-visitable, by prior arrangement.

For further information – call Chief of Information, 984-5637.

Fort Lewis — Named after Captain Meriwether Lewis, of *that*

expedition, "The Fort" claims to be the 10th largest city in the State . . . and it well might be just that. It maintains a ten-year average population of 41,000 (25,000 military); has more than 3,000 sets of quarters; more than 700 miles of roads; 30 miles of railroad and 57,600 acres of timber on its 86,000 acres of real estate which grows to *340,000 acres* when sub-installations are included. One of the largest and most modern military complexes in the world, Fort Lewis has been on the scene since ten thousand laborers and carpenters took less than 60 days to build 1,757 heated and lighted buildings and 422 other structures capable of housing 60,000 troops for deployment to the "war-to-end-wars" in 1917. These same workmen donated labor and material to erect the historic Fort Lewis Gate, one of the few structures surviving from the original "Camp Lewis" cantonment. Originally the home of "Washington's Own" 91st Division, it is presently the home of the 9th Infantry Division acclaimed by some as "The Northwest's Own." For military history buffs it should be noted that Fort Lewis has at various times also headquartered such famed divisions as the 2nd, 3rd, 4th, 32d, 33d, 40th, 41st, 44th, 71st and 96th. With an annual military and civilian payroll in excess of $172 million, its impact on the region becomes even more visible when you consider its total annual expenditure of nearly $350 million.

—◆—

Our favorite story about Fort Lewis has no conclusion, simply because it is more fun to speculate. In proper U.S. Army tradition, the home of the Commanding General of the Fort is located at the head of the parade grounds. In this case the site of that home is such as to command (also) one of the most spectacular views of Mt. Rainier that can be had. Well, on Memorial Day of

1930 the 91st Division Monument was dedicated on the parade grounds. An emotionally understandable but physically gross piece of work, it was installed directly and closely in front of the general's house — backside to him. So, for the past 44 years any commanding general who wishes to enjoy his superb view of *the* mountain must take glass in hand and lead his guests out on his lawn. About what do we speculate? Who was the general — or general's lady — that approved such an installation, and what were their feelings toward their immediate successors?

Visitors are welcome at Fort Lewis and there are many interesting things to see and do, including the Military Museum in the old Fort Lewis Inn. There is an information booth at the Main Gate entrance just inside the Fort from the north cloverleaf on Interstate 5. Phone 968-5210.

For further information – call Public Information Office, 968-2511.

Tacoma Tour 2 — Puyallup, Sumner Enumclaw, Cayuse Pass, Mt. Rainier, Paradise, Eatonville (Map X)

The highlights of this trip are Ezra Meeker, cow manure, raspberries and rhubarb in the lower Puyallup Valley and the Osceola Mud Flow, pickles and Mt. Rainier when you get to the higher reaches.

The trip takes you through Puyallup, heart of one of the richest raspberry-producing areas in the United States and the site of the mansion built by Ezra Meeker, the Wet Side's most prominent pioneer. Timing your trip for either the Daffodil Festival in the spring or the Western Washington Fair in the fall, would be appropriate. The Western Washington Experiment Station in Puyallup is working on a very deep problem caused by cow manure. The tour then goes through Sumner, which is the pie rhubarb capital of the world and the timing there should be January or February if you want to get some fresh hothouse rhubarb. You ascend to the upper White River Valley — an area created by the Osceola Mud Flow — and can visit the Farman's Pickle factory, manufacturers of the best dill pickles in the world. From there you take an awe-inspring trip around Mt. Rainier and back to Tacoma.

Highway 410 from Tacoma to Puyallup parallels the Puyallup River, though the river seems more like a canal here. Concrete revetments were built by the United States Engineers and Flood Control Agencies, hence the canal look. (See *Footloose*, p. 172, for a walk along the North Levee Road.) This also is the route of the Daffodil Parade from Puyallup to Tacoma. Beautifully cared-for berry fields and a cucumber farm with a sign "Cukes for Sale."

Puyallup — (Pop. 15,000. Elev. 49.) — You won't get far in Puyallup without hearing the name of Ezra Meeker, and you should listen because one of these days the name may be even more famous than it is today.

Born in 1830, Meeker crossed the plains on the Oregon Trail in a covered wagon in 1852 . . . recrossed the country with oxen and another covered wagon in 1906, later on by automobile and in 1924 by plane.

Ambrose Bierce once said that "A statesman, unlike a politician, has the virtue of being dead," a pronouncement that applies to pioneers as well as statesmen. And the growing tendency to venerate Ezra, the most publicized pioneer we've got on the Wet Side of the Mountains, is a case in point. It would make him very uncomfortable indeed if he were here. In his day he was the Arnold Palmer of "professional pioneering."

Meeker was the kind of a guy who got things done . . . and while he was doing them, the Marquis of Queensbury Rules were only incidental to the operation. If they didn't happen to suit the occasion they were moved to a seat behind a post in the top tier of the highest gallery of the theatre, William Allen White, the Pulitzer Prize-winning publisher of the Emporia, Kansas, *Gazette*, looked on him as a phony, which was wrong. He was just a "pro."

When Meeker first emerged on the Pacific Northwest scene and needed a few bucks, he landed at Kalama where he notes in his autobiography, *The Busy Life of Eighty-Five Years*, that a lot of people were helping themselves to the timber on government lands. And he was no exception when he made up a log raft of "merchantable timber" to be sold for $6 a thousand at nearby Oak Point Mill on the Washington side of the Columbia. But Ezra had reckoned without the power of the river current and found himself and his log raft swept past the mill in the general direction of disaster on the Columbia River Bar.

In the 40-mile trip that ensued, Ezra managed to beach his logs at Astoria — where he sold them at $8 a thousand, turning apparent disaster into an extra 2 bucks a thousand. He had an instinct for turning a profit.

Meeker, as a member of a jury, was one of two men who held out against the other juriors and public opinion in general, by voting for the acquittal of the later-to-be-martyred Chief Leschi. He turned down Seattle as a scene of his operations on the grounds he could smell the stink of it 5 miles out in the bay. He frankly confessed that he couldn't have cared less about the splendor of Mt. Rainier at the head of the Puyallup Valley when he was fighting his way up the river to create the town of Puyallup. "It was land we wanted," he wrote, "whereby we might stake a claim, not scenery to tickle our fancy . . ."

As a banker, Meeker was something else again . . .

The Puyallup Bank of which he was the president had a lot of cash lying around at the time of the panic of 1893. He could see the institution headed for bankruptcy. He also knew that the bigger banks in Tacoma would want their money out before his bank folded. The story is that he sent out armed men at night with the bank's total supply of cash and forced his Puyallup depositors to take their money whether they wanted it or not. He disclaims the gunpoint part, saying he had not armed the men to force money on depositors but as protection against possible robbery while they were returning the depositors' money.

The big banks failed to appreciate this maneuver and some bank officers tried to physically restrain him in one of their offices while they summoned the sheriff. Meeker was small but tough and one of the bankers got a punch in the nose for his pains.

Meeker made a less than dignified but wholly effective departure before the Law showed up. In his autobiography, he airily dismissed the episode with, "The attempted hold-up in Tacoma resulted in nothing more than a serious scuffle, the loss of a collar button or two, with plenty of threats but no action . . . " Meeker frankly didn't take money all that seriously. When the hop louse hit the crop, years later, he knew he was headed for financial ruin. He had loaned a total of $100,000 to other ranchers in the various valleys, but instead of foreclosing, he forgot the money.

But the most hysterical story in the book of autobiographical sketches concerns his encounter with the New York Police Department at the time he was trying to persuade Congress that it should commemorate the Oregon Trail. That was in 1906 and Meeker was 76 years old when he started out on the adventure. It proved to be a 2½-year trip in a covered wagon drawn by a pair of oxen . . . just like those that had brought 300,000 pioneers across the continent in the conquering of the West.

The difference was that he was eastbound.

His ultimate objective was a conversation with President Theodore Roosevelt in Washington "city," but he saw no disadvantage in taking a wave of publicity along with him into the nation's capitol.

You get the picture pretty well in the following: "After leaving the Trail behind me to head for the nation's capitol, I somehow had a foreboding that I might be mistaken for a fakir . . . My beard has grown long on the trip across; my boots were some the worse for wear and my old-fashioned suit (understood well enough by pioneers along the Trail) that showed dilapidation, all combined, made me not the most presentable in every sort of company . . . The press, with but one exception (Ed. Note: William Allen White), had been exceedingly kind and understood the work . . . "

When he got to the Erie Canal, he decided to go along the towpath instead of being forced to drive over a hill. He noted that while this was illegal, a lot of people did it and he saw no reason why he should be an exception. The drivers of the mules who towed the canal boats, however, did take exception when their mules encountered Meeker's oxen and ordered Meeker's assistant to "take that outfit off the towpath!" What ensued resulted in the towmen "swearing at the top of their voices and the women swearing in chorus, one of them fairly shrieking."

Meeker added that "my old and trusted muzzle-loading rifle that we had carried across the plains more than fifty-five years ago," handily restored "order to the situation" and calmed things down. One of the towmen threw up his hands, "bawling at the top of his lungs, 'don't shoot, don't shoot . . . ' "

"But," Meeker continued, "it took New York City to cap the climax — to bring me all sorts of experiences, sometimes with the police, sometimes with gaping crowds, and sometimes at the city hall . . . "

The problem lay in a city ordinance that prohibited the driving of cattle on the city streets. The first encounter with the cops came at Amsterdam Avenue and 161st Street on his first day in town.

He writes, "A policeman interfered and ordered my driver to take the team to the police station, which he very properly refused to do . . . I saw the young policeman attempt to move the team, but as he didn't know how, they wouldn't budge a leg, whereupon he arrested my driver and took him away.

Just then another policeman tried to coax me to drive the team down to the police station; I said, 'No, sir, I will not' . . . The crowd had become large and began jeering the policeman. The situation was, he couldn't drive the team to the station, and I wouldn't, and there we were . . . "

Meeker called in the reporters of the *New York Tribune* and the *New York Herald* and made his position clear. He had come to New York all the way from a town called Puyallup in the State of Washington in order to drive his covered wagon down Broadway and he was not going to leave the city until he had done so.

The police were mad.

The Board of Aldermen was confused.

And the press was delighted!

And there they were for the next 30 days . . . stalemated.

First the aldermen passed an ordinance granting him the right-of-way down Broadway. The city attorney opined the aldermen had exceeded their authority. So they passed an ordinance saying he couldn't drive down Broadway. But the acting mayor vetoed it. And while they were waiting for a court decision on the question, Meeker drove his oxen down Broadway . . . illegal but effective.

On November 29, 1907, twenty-two months after he had left Puyallup, Meeker found himself in conversation with the President of the United States, who had popped out of the White House bare-headed to witness this phenomenon at close range.

" 'Well, well, well, WELL,' was the exclamation that fell from his lips as he came near enough to the outfit to examine it critically . . . Roosevelt had bounded out of his office without bothering to put on his hat," Meeker wrote. He recorded the President's reaction: "Addressing Senator Piles (Sam, of Washington), the President said with emphasis, 'I am in favor of this work to mark this Trail and if you will bring before Congress a measure to accomplish it, I am with you, and will give it my support to do it thoroughly . . . ' "

On the question of his hometown, Meeker writes: "Puyallup . . . is of Indian origin — as old as the memory of the white man runs. But such a name! I consider it no honor to be the man who named the town (now city) of Puyallup. I accept the odium attached to inflicting that name on suffering succeeding generations by first platting a few blocks of land into village lots and recording them under the name Puyallup. I have been ashamed of the act ever since . . . "

His biggest problem was the people who emphasized the "Pew" and not the "allup."

It was especially discomfitting to him in London in the 1880's when his wife, Elizabeth Jane, was presented to Queen Victoria — which really was a fair-sized social item back in Puyallup. Those two homespun pioneers must have made their own kind of impression on London society and he recalls one singularly unhappy occasion when one of the London swells was trying to recall the name of the place that Meeker came from. The man said, "I say, Meeker, I cawn't remember that blasted name — what is it?" Then the whole drawing room crowd roared with laughter at the "Pew" in front of the "allup."

Meeker also comments on the shots that vaudeville comedians took at the town . . . like "Pew-lupe," "Pull-all-up," "Pewl-a-loop," and "Pay-all-up." He wrote, "Then my cup of sorrow was full and I was ready to put on sackcloth and ashes . . . Puyallup has been my home for forty years, and it is but natural that I love the place, even if I cannot revere the name . . . "

Actually, the correct pronounciation, according to Meeker, is "Peuw-Al-Lup."

This kind of information was in the back of our mind when we called the Western Washington Research and Extension Center in Puyallup, an organization which has a greater impact on our lives than most of us realize . . . and it certainly is the most advanced professional and intellectual research institution in all of Puyallup.

"What," we asked, "is the most important research project on deck at the Research Center today."

"Shit," was the candid response.

Dr. David Allemedinger, director of the Center, was somewhat disconcerted when he learned that one of his colleagues had used this non technical term to an outsider. And it may turn out as something of a shock to the powers that be at Washington State University, of which the Center is a branch organization. On the other hand, it would have been less of a shock back in the days when the University was the Washington State Agricultural College and more confined to barnyard terms. The word, itself, of course, antedates both the University and its Research Center.

It's just that used in juxtaposition with the name of the Indian Tribe for which the town was named, it assumes an added connotation that must have been the crowning indignity for the ghost of Ezra Meeker.

Actually, the Center is one of the main bastions in the battle against paving the Wet Side of the Mountains from the ocean to the summit of the Cascades.

These men and others like them are the difference between profit and loss to the agricultural industry on the Wet Side. For instance, berries are big, especially strawberries; and for years, a variety called the Northwestern, was the biggest of the bunch, economically. But when those cold east winds swept down off of Mt. Baker, they wiped it out along with a whole bunch of berry farmers in Whatcom County. In addition to that, reusing the same fields brought on a fungus called "root rot," not nice, but descriptive. What with cold winds, and root rot and the importation of 120,000,000 tons of these delicacies from Mexico, the strawberry business on the Wet Side was headed straight for perdition.

However, 12 years of experimentation at the Center came up in the nick of time with a berry that would measure up to the Northwestern in quality, productivity and firmness — and withstand those cold northeast winds. It took the Federal Government to limit Mexican imports to 80,000,000 tons of strawberries with Dr. Allmendinger, who takes this sort of thing personally, said, "we can live with."

The Center deals with a lot of other agricultural problems too. There's the matter of machine-picking. About 90% of all the raspberries grown commercially in the United States are grown in Oregon and Washington. And 54% of these are grown in Whatcom and Pierce Counties. Whatcom is having it tougher than Pierce on the all-important matter of picking the berries. Unlike Pierce, Whatcom is not adjacent to a couple of big cities and a fairly decent supply of pickers. Now, raspberries are about the only berry that really has been holding its own against the onslaught of urbanization; and if you can't get them picked, there's no point in growing them. So, like with the tomatoes in the Sacramento Valley, it became essential they come up with a berry that could be picked by machinery. Not only that, but they needed a berry, like the new strain of whole tomatoes you find in your cans today, that could be picked when it was ripe without getting squashed in the process.

So the Center scientists produced one with even higher quality than the previous berry. It was more productive, could be machine-picked even when ripe and, above all, resisted root rot.

Anyway, they called the new berry the "Meeker" in honor of Ezra.

There are continuing problems, like the yellow corn that kept coming up with black kernels, until the Center advised farmers to pick fertilizer with less sulphur in it . . . and, from time to time, the question of blonde peas crops up. Now what do you do with an albino pea in a nation in which the green of the green pea is the criterion for the state of "greenness?" You might try dyeing it, but you'd have the Food and Drug people on your neck.

That's one they haven't solved yet . . . along with a current crash program concerning a fungus that appeared in the 1972 cabbage seed crop in the Skagit Valley. As you will recall, this area is the biggest producer of cabbage seed in the world . . . and in 1973, fungus spread by those seeds cost millions of dollars in crop damage clear across the country.

But the ongoing, year-in-and-year-out problem is the previously cited product referred to in American drawing rooms but not on American farms as "cow manure."

Dr. Russell Murdock, who was in charge of this work at the Center, removed it yet a further step from the colloquialism of the barnyard when he did a paper on the subject entitled, "The Land as a Receiver of Animal Waste."

The problem is this: Even before Olympic Swimmer, Mark Spitz, got on the telly with his previously mentioned pitch about every *body* needing milk, we were a great nation of milk drinkers. And it is something we should be especially cognizant of on the Wet Side because some of the best milk in the world is produced here. But the problem is that for every 50 pounds of milk a good cow like a Holstein gives, it also produces some 90 pounds of Animal Waste. When you multiply this by the average amount of milk per capita drunk by Americans and the waste that is produced along with it, our figures show the enormity of the problem. It comes to 97,664,251,290 pounds. (our multiplication.)

The trouble is that it stinks.

If it didn't stink the home gardeners of America would rush to Animal Waste Centers all over the country to buy it because it's the greatest natural fertilizer The Lord ever produced. As it is, we have an over-supply. And what do you do with it?

In California, there's an enormous pile of this stuff which they refer to as "Mt. Shitney." At the moment — the unit cost of chemical fertilizer is less than that of animal waste. But scientists predict that future generations will mine that mountain like it was pure "gold." It would render the "rush" of the Forty-Niners in that state pale by comparison.

The problem on the Wet Side of the Mountains is wetness. It never gets dry enough to build a mountain like the one in California . . . and even if we did, the organic chemicals working within the pile could explode . . . resulting in an eruption that would be remembered a lot longer than a similar cataclysm on the part of Mt. Rainier.

So what they're doing is going to the opposite extreme and trying to figure out a way to liquify the stuff. And the way they do that is through the creation of a lagoon . . . depending on the wet weather to help conditions that will make this stuff self-propelling to the impoundment basin. On commercial farms, they shoot the liquid over the land from gigantic squirt guns adapted from military flame-throwers. The manure guns at the Center can send a stream out 250 feet.

In the course of their efforts along this line, ingenious Americans have come up with some kind of a gigantic honeybucket that sells for $4,500 and is equipped with used tires taken from Boeing 707's. Scientists at the Center opine it is unlikely — even when it rocks along at full speed — that this machine will exceed the safety restriction cast into the rubber on the sides of those tires reading, "This tire not to be driven at speeds in excess of 180 miles an hour."

Now, it's one thing to broadcast this stuff wholesale on a farm where it can be pumped out of a pond and spread over the land. There's another problem, however, when it comes to containing this material in a bottle. It has a tendency to work, a lot like home brew. And when it works, it has a tendency to blow the bottle apart which would be admittedly disconcerting to the average, plump, middle-aged American gardener.

Nevertheless, in view of its past successes with things like strawberries, raspberries and black corn, we have confidence in the ability of the Center to come up with an odorless but effective product.

What better poultice could there be for the ghostly psyche of the town founder than to have this developed in a town pronounced "Pew Allup?"

Perhaps they even could invent a non explosive bottle . . .

And name it the "Ezra Meeker Beaker."

◆

Prowling Puyallup

The 17-room *Meeker Mansion*, E. Pioneer Ave., was built in 1890, and soon became the pivotal point around which most of the civic and cultural activities of the valley revolved. Literature on the subject reads, "The effect upon those who visited the home was immense. The uniqueness of the six exquisitely decorated fireplaces, the brilliance of the ballroom socials; the delicately carved woodwork and the stained glass windows; the magnificence of the landscaping — entranced those who were to visit it." The mansion is now on the National Register of Historic Places, and is owned and operated by the Ezra Meeker Historical Society.

At *Pioneer Park* there's a life-size statue of Meeker done by Victor Alonzo Lewis.

The *Frontier Museum*, on 23rd St., has lots of historical relics. The *Paul Karshner Museum*, in a building at Stewart Elementary School, is the only one in the State owned by a school district. Artifacts from Indian tribes, rocks, minerals, fossils, and preserved animals, birds, and insects; and open to the public during school hours, Tuesday through Friday.

You can visit the *Research Center*, on Pioneer, from 8 to 5, weekdays, although the chances are you would be better of watching for one of their "Field Days."

For the best overall view of the town, try to drive up *South Hill*, a residential area so attractive that some 16,000 people — a population greater than that of the town, itself — have built homes there in the last couple of years.

There's no way anyone in the Pacific Northwest can be uninformed about the *Puyallup Daffodil Festival*, and if you've missed seeing those flat fields of brilliant blossoms against the backdrop of Mt. Rainier in the spring, you can't really qualify as someone "living" in the Pacific Northwest.

The same is true of the *Western Washington Fair* in the fall. It is all of the fairs of the world rolled up in one gigantic evidence of the productivity of the Wet Side of the Mountains. It comes a time when the maple is brilliant in the woods and the Puyallup River is quiet in its deep embankment in the valley and you should take the kids out of school in the middle of the week to go there unless, of course, the whole class is going anyway . . . in which case you will be deprived of one of the warmest and most exciting experiences of your life.

Note: Because Puyallup and Sumner are virtually twin cities and the Chamber of Commerce for both is between the two towns, we include "Shopping, Eating, Sleeping" and "Annual affairs" at the end of the Sumner section.

Highway 410 is an easy approach to Sumner from Puyallup because it continues to follow the Puyallup River and crosses it just after the White River joins the Puyallup from the north. If you are continuing to Buckley, be prepared to turn right on 410 *immediately* after crossing the bridge or you'll miss it.

Sumner — (Pop. 4,325. Elev. 75.) — This is the "pie rhubarb" capital of the United States . . . and as far as the pie is concerned, the statement probably could be expanded to include the world. People have long been acquainted with this edible plant in China, but it's dried and used there for medicinal purposes. In 1973, some 11,000,000 pounds of this vegetable, often referred to as the "pie plant," was processed through an organization variously known as the Puget Sound Vegetable Growers Association, The Sumner Rhubarb Growers Association or Washington Rhubarb Growers Association.

It comes out of the hothouses beginning in January when the flavor is more delicate and "pie" eyed gourmets gather 'round with glee. From about April through September, you also can get "field" rhubarb. The hothouses are heated, windowless buildings which give the plant a "good color" . . . delicate pink. The stems are thinner and less likely to be stringy. If the stem is exposed to sunlight, it comes off green, which is not exactly our idea of a color for rhubarb pie. The big leaves, of course, protect the stalks and keep them red even in the field. Hothouse rhubarb is grown in the field for 3 years and then transplanted indoors.

All of the rhubarb grown commercially in the State comes from King and Pierce counties ... with about twice as much grown in the latter as the former. There are about 50 growers and the largest farms are 75 acres ... the total crop sells for about $1,600,000 annually, which isn't a bad "pie" to cut among some 50 growers.

Of the 54,000,000 daffodil bulbs produced in the State annually, approximately half of them are grown on the 500 acres in this area devoted to this culture and sold throughout the world via the Puget Sound Bulb Exchange with headquarters in Sumner. It also is a major center for strawberries, raspberries and blueberries, which become ripe in that order during the season.

Prowling Sumner

Underneath a spreading butternut tree is the 1870 vintage home of Mrs. Lucy V. Ryan which houses the *Sumner Public Library* which has artifacts of a bygone era along with the books.

Up on the ridge above and to the north of Sumner is the Puget Power White River Project, *Lake Tapps Dam and Reservoir*, "Multiple Use Power Project Developing Public and Private Recreational Resources." Unbelievable lake with a contoured shoreline — like a mud splat on a wall — and lots of stumps. Nice homes, lake-type and permanent; islands are named "A" and "B." *Bonney Lake* community borders the south end of the lake and has a Swiss Park and Hall. The dairy business is the attraction for quite a colony of Swiss and in many of the towns nearby you see signs like Swiss Chalet in nearby Orting and Anton's in Puyallup.

Uncommon shopping – Throughout the valley there are roadside stands which sell rhubarb, strawberries, raspberries and blueberries — vegetables, in season. There are U-pick berry privileges at discount rates. Some of the world's best daffodil and tulip bulbs may be purchased at various farms. *The Coach House*, Puyallup, for primitives, antiques, collectables ... *Colony House*, Sumner, antiques, also furniture and clock repair ... *Main Street Antiques*, Sumner, specializes in fine 18th Century furnishings. *Pioneer Bakery*, Puyallup, for doughnut holes, cinnamon buns, German chocolate cake, sourdough bread on Friday and special "grab bags" daily ... *The Danish Bakery*, Sumner, is one of a kind with sidewalk cafe and publicity gimmicks galore that cause the locals to call him the "Dick Balch of the Bakery Business;" nonetheless, the coffee and Danish served here is one of the Wet Side's real treats. (Owner's name is Ole Nielsen and some of his gimmicks include a dog day, in which kids bring their dogs in to be weighed and he sells the kids a cake for a penny-a-pound — with the dogs usually ending up eating it. He has a measuring stick outside his bakery and kids sometimes can buy a cake for 1¢-an-inch in their height. More recently he decorated a whole 1974 Mustang like a wedding cake.)

A word about eating – All in Puyallup: *Anton's*, the *Black Kettle* and *Blue Boy* all are sophisticated places ... *Forbidden City*, good Chinese food ... *Nettie's*, local gathering spot.

A word about sleeping – The *Tamarak Motel* in Puyallup and the *Sumner House*, in Sumner, good accommodations.

Annual affairs – The tremendously worthwhile *Daffodil Festival* which goes on and on in the spring . . . and, of course the venerable *Western Washington Fair*, where Fisher Flouring Mills serve their famous scones and jam and the ladies of various nonprofit organizations fill the air with the delectable odor of onions being fried to serve on their hamburgers.

For further information – Puyallup Valley Chamber of Commerce, 2823 E. Main (Highway 410 going east); phone, 845-6755.

From Sumner, you can go up the Puyallup River Valley to the sleepy valley town of Orting, with side trips to Wilkeson and Carbonado. The town of Wilkeson is where in 1883 they started cutting into a big hunk of rock for St. Luke's Episcopal Church in Tacoma (which is still standing) and probably will be cutting for some time to come. Wilkeson sandstone was put there about 50 million years ago and is 10,000 feet deep. Beyond Wilkeson is the isolated town of Carbonado (named for the coal). Here also is the Carbon River entrance to Lake Mowich in Mt. Rainier National Park.

Otherwise you go from Sumner to Buckley on Highway 410 up the side hill of the valley and into Buckley like somebody aimed you at the town with a musket and then pulled the trigger.

Unless you've time to dawdle, we suggest the 410 shot to Enumclaw, where you have the definite feeling of rising up the plateau created by the Osceola Mud Slide, which divides the area generally into the upper and lower valleys, a condition which gave rise to one of the more hysterical-historical Wet Side stories.

By way of background, the White River has come out of the mountains at this point and has slowed down to a walk. It's called "White" because of the glacial mud it's carrying to the bottom of the hill.

You should take an opportunity to become intimately observant of the White River. It honeys around Buckley and you'll cross it en route to Enumclaw. You'll be paralleling a railroad line and have an opportunity to judge for yourself whether you would like to drive a horse and buggy across a trestle or try crossing the river in a rowboat. This is one of the old fords of the White River you'll read about shortly.

Enumclaw — (Pop. 4,900. Elev. 742.) — The community is on this mud flow plateau between the White and Green Rivers. If you have the feeling you're on the launch pad for the final assault on Chinook Pass when you reach this delightfully level town on the verge of Mt. Rainier, it's because you are. You've climbed 670 feet in the 15 miles from Sumner. And the Mountain, of course, towers nearly, 3 miles above your head.

The antics of politics are not always admirable, but neither are they new, in spite of the fact that the nation is holding up its collective skirt in horror currently at the sight of a muddy mess called Watergate. So astute a politician as Nikita Krushchev noted that politicians are the same all over, adding, "They'll promise to build a bridge, even when there is no river . . ."

But there was a river and no bridge between Enumclaw and the rest of civilization back in the 1890's when the only road money available was that which citizens in an area could clobber from their county. State and Federal highways were a thing for the future, and when the White River was raging, you crossed it at your own risk . . . an action that proved repeatedly fatal to either the unskilled or the unwary.

The town got going in 1885 with the advent of the Northern Pacific Railway, which at least gave the upper valley contact with Tacoma while the railroad company braced itself for the final assault of Stampede Pass. The company was in a tearing hurry to get rails across the Cascades before James J. Hill could beat them to the punch further north at Stevens Pass. And if you don't think they were risking the lives and limbs of their men in doing it, you are mistaken. The Pass got its name from a survey crew that rebelled against a tough foreman. He woke up alone in camp one morning to find a message notifying him that everybody else had "Stampeded."

You may feel you have come up some hill from the valley on your trip at this point, but you've seen nothing yet. You've risen an average of 26 feet a mile, while the rest of the trip over Chinook Pass will average out at about 4 times that much.

The railroad knew from the start it would have to tunnel, but in the meantime, it pushed over the top of Stampede Pass with a series of hair-raising switchbacks. The motive power for the trains weighed 148,000 pounds and the locomotives were the most powerful built in the United States to that date. It was only a brand new device called the telephone that made the trips over the top possible. With it they could let the engineers know in advance whether the track was still there under conditions that called for the invention of another new mechanical wonder called the rotary snowplow. The trains were "blocked" across. At each switch, the switchman got a receipt for the train that was coming through. Speed was kept at a minimum. A brakeman was required for each two cars and it was his responsibility to make sure the brakes on his cars were in working order and used. As it was, they lost two trains to the chasms below, but because everybody was acutely attuned to the danger involved they managed to leave the trains before the latter left the tracks.

In driving the tunnel through later, the Tacoma contractor, Nelson Bennett, made a net profit of $10,000 a month for the 25 months his crews were at work. And the newspapers heralded the enormous safety factor in the construction.

Nevertheless, every other month a man was killed on the tunnel construction alone.

The total number of men who lost their lives in the whole construction project which put that first railroad over the Cascades probably isn't recorded, but it was not inconsiderable.

In the meantime, the pioneers' choice of getting to Enumclaw by any route other than the railroad involved a certain amount of risk. They could, of course, bump a buggy along the railroad track, but the horses really didn't care for crossing the trestles and showed a tendency to bolt at inconvenient times and places, like over a river. One of the systems of holding the local roads together involved the use of stumps. Trees in the middle of the road were cut only low enough so the axle of the wagon could pass over them. That way the roots held the edges of the road together. But in the wetness of the climate, ruts would develop at the edges. Axles would hit the stumps, drivers got pitched off, and broken legs became a regular hazard of teamsters' trade.

The real insoluble problem, however, was hops as far as the upper valley folk were concerned.

This plant introduced an average income to the lower valleys of $1,000,000 a year for a period of 20 years, which was phenomenal . . . and, of course, that brought people. Riverboats, which provided the transportation of the hops to the market had a nasty habit of hitting snags and sandbars and dumping their loads unprofitably into the water. With money and people, came political power . . . which enabled the lower valleys to elect their own men as county commissioners. And these men steered county funds into roads that serviced the hop fields in the lower valleys.

And this is where Nelson Bennett's construction crews provided a service to the town of Enumclaw that was way beyond and above the creation of the railroad. In the late 1880's some 2,000 men were living in the now defunct town of Stampede, a few miles up the Green River from Enumclaw, but still part of King County.

We're indebted to Arthur E. Griffin, founder of the first general store in Enumclaw, for the story of how the manpower used in constructing the Stampede Tunnel was applied to the political field to provide a road from the lower to the upper valley. Griffin, who became a lawyer and then was elected to the King County Superior Court bench, tells about it in a newspaper article in the clipping file of the Enumclaw Public Library. The article, published in 1939, credits Johannes Mahler, another one of Enumclaw's pioneers, with the idea for using the railroad manpower . . . which may be one of the reasons why the folks in the area have named their newest and finest recreational facility Mahler Park.

The problem they had was getting enough votes to the Republican caucus. In those days if you were the Republican nominee in King County, you were assured of winning the election. On the other hand, not all of the men who participated in the construction of the tunnel had that kind of political leanings. As a matter of fact, not an inconsiderable number of them were members of the Populist Party, and many later would become activists in that radical group called the Industrial Workers of the World.

Judge Griffin summed the situation up in these words: "Mr. John (Johannes) Mahler . . . is entitled to much credit for assistance in getting permanent roads located and opened through the whole Enumclaw district. The election of Mr. Frank Nickerson and Hon. Lou Smith as County Commissioners in the south district put Enumclaw on the map by improving the roads in the locality . . .

"The Republican caucus at which Mr. Nickerson was selected, held in Seattle on the night before he was nominated, was a fight between the upper precincts against the older districts in the Duwamish Valley. In building the Cascade Stampede Tunnel many workmen were employed and the Tunnel Precinct was entitled to a large number of delegates. When Sam Lafromboise went to the locality, the precinct had but one, the section foreman, eligible for a delegate. This deficiency was overcome at the caucus by John Kelley, Democrat, appearing on behalf of the Tunnel delegation . . ."

So there you have it, a Democrat at a Republican caucus casting by proxy the votes of Populists and I.W.W.'s.

They, of course, couldn't have cared less; because their names had been taken from the headstones of men who long since had been buried at the West End Tunnel Cemetery . . .

The judge adds this final note of homely philosophy with, "Names . . . of the unfortunate hardrock workers, whose lives had been sacrificed that others might ride through the tunnel in ease, by proxy in the hands of Mr. Kelley, aided materially in putting a good man in office . . ."

Prowling Enumclaw

In spite of the risk that it might mean to our own personal supply, we will flatly state that the *Farman Brothers Pickle Company* manufactures the best dill pickles in the world. This company produces around 5,000 tons of pickles annually and is one of the major Enumclaw employers. In August their cucumbers come fresh daily from Skagit County, the state's number 1 cucumber pickle producer, to be held for processing during the balance of the year. The state of Washington produces 14,000 tons annually, with Farman's creating nearly 50% of the state pickle supply.

It's only a drop in the bucket to American consumption of 4.4 million pounds of pickles daily — but, oh what a tasty drop!

Make arrangements ahead of time to visit them while you're here. Other visitable spots are the huge Weyerhaeuser *White River Mill* and *Garrett Industries*, a local concern that leads the way in the manufacture of logging equipment.

One of the things they do in Enumclaw is climb Mt. Pete née Pinnacle or Peak or Mt. Peak, an 1,800 foot pinnacle that's easy enough to climb, gives you views as far away as the Olympics and has a strange formation of columnar basaltic rock near the top. (See *Footloose*, p. 160.)

The King County Park, adjacent to the County Fair Grounds, has a huge swimming pool, and *Mahler Park* is nice for picnics.

Shortly after you leave Enumclaw you come to a side trip of about 5 miles to the *Mud Mountain Dam*, one of the highest earthen dams in the world. There's a vista point and a picnic place.

Uncommon shopping – On the Crystal Mountain road just outside of town, you'll find Julian Joubert, referred to in an article in *Puget Soundings* by authoress Pat Lucas, as the "King of the Bees." Mr. Joubert, who cannot walk, nevertheless owns and tends 300 colonies of honey bees — the honey of which he sells from a picturesque moss-covered stand. And he can tell you more about bees and the different flavors of honey than you ever dreamed existed . . . *Wetzel's Auction Sales Pavilion*, auctions cattle as well as household goods or what-have-you every Sat., and horses one Fri. a month; very good lunch counter, local color . . . *Osceola Pottery*, good studio which sells pottery as well as offering classes . . . *Rainier Bakery*, (Home of Good Living), natural foods and store-owned and operated by 7th Day Adventists; popular for their sunflower seed bread . . . *Slaughter House Antiques*, local

word has it that this shop is very reasonably priced and big on brass beds . . .
Christopher House, in home of Eleanor Uhlman, daughter of 1st doctor in
Enumclaw; gallery and shop reflects many exotic things from owner's former
residence in Persia.

A word about eating – *4 Seasons*, Chinese in decor and food, quite
sophisticated; owned half by Victor Graham, president of the Chamber of
Commerce, and half by a Chinese partner.

Annual affairs – *King County Fair*, 3rd week in August, deliberately
small and old-fashioned in scope, sells corn on the cob, dripping with
butter . . . a very tidy fair . . . *Folk Dance Festival*, August, held at county park.

For further information – Enumclaw Chamber of Commerce, 1612
Cole; phone, 825-2519.

Mt. Rainier — (Elev. 14,410.) — What makes Mt. Rainier so
frightfully lethal is about a billion gallons of water bubbling at the bottom of
the crater. Otherwise, it would just be one of your run-of-the-mill "dangerous
objects," like Fujiyama in Japan, Popocatepetl in Mexico, or Vesuvius in Italy.

In 1971, a couple of geophysicists from Scripps Institute of
Oceanography at LaJolla and the Nuclear Science Laboratory at Los Alamos,
New Mexico, spoke on the subject at the annual fall meeting of the American
Geophysical Union. They noted that Mt. Rainier has the potential explosive
power of a hundred nuclear bombs like the one at Hiroshima. In the course of
their talks, they cited Rainier as the most dangerous of the "most dangerous
objects on earth." The potential danger, they said, came from the fact that our
mountain has molten rock with steam sealed in it by frozen rock above. "If it
exploded like the volcano that made Crater Lake," they said, "It could destroy
Seattle." What they wanted to do was tap the base with pipe and use the steam
for geothermal power.

The United States Geological Survey men most acquainted with our
Mountain, Dwight R. Crandell and Donal R. Mullineaux, aren't quite such
alarmists — although they do suggest that if the Mountain melted it would be
a hell of a mess.

The beauty and character of our Mountain stems from its solitary
height and tentacles of the glaciers that embrace it in about 34 square miles of
thick ice. It's the greatest single peak glacier system in the lower 48 States.
The fact that Rainier sticks up there 7,000 feet above the rest of the Cascade
Mountains and covers a total area of 100 square miles, makes it an enormous
interceptor of those wet winds from the southwest. In 1955-56, for instance,
with 83 feet of the white stuff, it enjoyed the greatest snow pack of any place
in the United States — including Alaska. Almost any year, it packs snow in a
lot faster than it melts, and that's what makes a good glacier. For a century
after experts started thinking about that sort of thing in 1840, the glaciers were
receding about 70 feet a year. But, beginning in 1950, they started advancing
again at approximately the same rate.

So, in one state or another — ice, rain, snow, fog — there's a lot of water
in and around that Mountain. Lovely to look at when it's white. But it
could melt.

And that's where the USGS fellas figure the real danger lies.

Contrary to previously held geological opinion, Mt. Rainier did not blow its tip several centuries ago. It simply got cooking with gas which transformed hard rock into hot, wet clay that oozed off into the White River Valley, lowering the former peak of the cone by upwards of 1,000 feet.

They discuss the subject with admirable restraint in Geological Survey Bulletin 1238, in which even the title is printed without capital letters and reads: "volcanic hazards at mount rainier washington." The bulletin notes that a glob of wet clay, sand and rock with dimensions of about half a cubic mile, descended into the valley about 5,800 years ago in what was known as the Osceola Mud Flow.

We can't help noting that's equal to a cube in which one side is more than 5 times the height of the Space Needle in Seattle. And some Green River Community College kids are, if you will pardon the expression, bringing the matter even more down to earth. They're members of an anthropology class who currently are excavating the slide for the oldest dated human tools yet discovered in the Puget Sound area. The class has uncovered more than 200 stone projectile points, scrapers, a drill and other tools.

Gerald Hedlund, the class instructor, came up with a chilling thought when he said, "I can't see any alternative but that people were living here at the time of the mudflow." (There is no way of telling whether the people were trapped or had enough warning to flee.)

The trouble is that stuff moves along at a right good clip.

A rockflow toppled off a Little Tahoma Peak on December 14, 1963 and shot down the hill at speeds of from 100 to 300 miles an hour.

The big Osceola Job, a viscous mass like wet concrete, towered 500 feet high when it passed the present site of the White River Camp Ground . . . buried the sites of Enumclaw and Buckley under 70 feet of mud and stretched out almost to Auburn.

Nobody knows when there'll be another big event like this. It could be today . . . tomorrow . . . next week . . . next month . . . next year, or a thousand years from now.

The thing to do is look what's cookin' on Mt. Rainier.

The danger signals could be steam jets and clouds of water vapor, possibly accompanied by explosions and rockfalls . . . increase in fumarolic activity . . . abnormal glacier melting . . . increase of sulphur and chlorine in fumarolic gases . . . .

You can count on one thing . . . .

If Mt. Rainier starts smoking, it may be hazardous to *your* health.

◆

When you're visiting the Mountain, you'll see the devastation of the Kautz Mud Flow of December 1947, a rain-inspired natural event for which interesting comparative statistics have been compiled: Man's biggest concrete dam, Grand Coulee, required 12 million cubic yards of concrete. The Kautz debris conglomerate used 50 million cubic yards. The Osceola slide (the biggest of many) took care of 1,500,000,000 cubic yards — right off the top of the Mountain.

Prowling Mt. Rainier

If you're car-less or have friends visiting and can't take them yourselves, we suggest the *Gray Line Sightseeing Tour* of the Mountain. It's one of Gray Line's most popular packages and is operated seasonally from late May through October 30, weather permitting. Tours leave Seattle at 8:45 in the morning and return at 6 p.m. (Although you can make advance arrangements to stay overnight at Longmire or Paradise.) The drivers are thoroughly informed and tell colorful stories about the Mountain.

Also lots of books have been written about the Mighty Mountain, but one of the best for this kind of a trip is Ruth Kirk's, *Exploring Mount Rainier*. It describes in detail and with lots of color the specific areas you may wish to visit. In addition, you also can pick up more detailed information at the various centers you'll pass, so we'll just give it to you once over lightly.

Ten miles further along the main highway is the *Federation Forest State Park* made up of 612 acres of virgin forest. There also is an interpretive center and a couple of walking trails, each of them about 1 mile long. (See *Footloose*, p. 164.)

Sixteen miles further, you pass the entrance to the *Crystal Mountain Ski Area* — the fanciest ski area on the Wet Side of the Mountains and one you should plan to visit any time of the year. Attractive alpine lodging and restaurant facilities are available from November to May . . . and from July 4 through Labor Day, the chair lift operates for car-cushion travelers. If it's a nice day, a ride on the chair lift — which may cause some people to gulp a little although it is perfectly safe — affords you the most magnificent perspective of Mt. Rainier in existence. It's right there!

Five miles further is the entrance to *Sunrise Park*, which is open to automobiles from late June through early September and affords the highest viewpoint you can drive to in the park (6,400 feet). Here is the White River Campground — the spot almost reached by the most recent rockslide on the Mountain — together with a look at Emmons Glacier from which the slide slid at speeds of from 100 to 300 miles an hour. There's a visitor center at Sunrise in which the geologic history of the Mountain is displayed . . . and rangers conduct walks and talks in the summer. You may not see forever more on a clear day, but you do have a chance at views that include Mt. Baker, Glacier Peak in one direction and Mt. Adams, Mt. Hood and Mt. St. Helens in the other.

Five miles further along, our tour leaves Highway 410 and takes Highway 124 through *Cayuse Pass* to *Ohanapecosh*, which has a visitors' center and a grove of Sitka spruce 1,000 years old. You can continue on 123 here down to Morton, but our tour takes us along the *Stevens Canyon Road* (closed in the winter). There's a ranger here to explain a display depicting glacial erosion.

At *Box Canyon*, which is 115 feet deep and 13 feet wide, there's a ranger-naturalist to tell you more about glacial erosion.

Eleven miles further you come to *Paradise*, and you'll see that the fellow who named it wasn't kidding, if the Mountain is "out" at the time of your arrival. (It's open year-round although you must come in from the west side during the winter.) There's a visitor center, illustrated programs, walks and talks, cafeteria and some lodging along the simple lines required in National Parks.

You descend past *Narada Falls* and a viewpoint where it is worth stopping to take a look at *Nisqually Glacier*. Then in 5 miles you're at *Longmire*, which is the *Mt. Rainier National Park Headquarters* and has the same general amenities as those found at Paradise plus a relief model of the mountain.

Another 3 miles down the hill is a pausing place and an exhibit telling about the previously mentioned *Kautz Creek Mud Flow*. If you've wondered how active the landscape can be, here's an example of what we're talking about.

You leave the park and head through the tiny towns of Ashford, National, Elbe and Alder. In the latter is a viewpoint at Alder Dam, Tacoma's first publicly owned hydro-electric dam. Then on through LaGrande, which is perched 400 feet above the Nisqually River in a remarkable canyon.

One of the more significant and longtime Wet Side efforts is the *Pack Demonstration Forest* of the University of Washington's College of Forest Resources. Here ecological studies are made of who's doing what to whom in our forests. It's a 2,200-acre facility in which conditions are maintained that range from the untouched forest primeval to a logging camp, clearcutting and a model mill. At the entrance is a log section of a tree about 1,800 years old. The area is loaded with trails, some of them with handsome views of Mt. Rainier. (See *Footloose*, p. 178-183.)

Eatonville — (Pop. 860. Elev. 800.) — After wandering through all that wilderness, you really owe yourself a piece of blackberry pie, which is obtainable along with homemade soup at the *Mountain View Cafe*. This is not your run-of-the-mill, tame, blackberry pie with the big seeds. It has the added touch found only in the wild berries with the tiny seeds, a rare piece of pie found in few places in the world outside of the Wet Side of the Mountains.

Here also, almost anybody in town will happily point out *Indian Henry* to you. It's a rock formation on the Mountain which, viewed with imagination, shows the profile of an Indian, complete with headdress.

Indian Henry, was a guide around these parts, and well-liked by everybody. But the problem was his 5 wives. A judge came along and notified him polygamy wasn't allowed in this country and insisted that Henry divest himself of 4 of the 5. Polygamy didn't mean much to Henry, but he was scandalized just the same. The judge was proposing to destroy an economic empire of berry-picking, back-packing and farming. "Judge," he exclaimed. "One woman simply can't do all the work around the place!"

Just out of Eatonville is a chunk of land called *Northwest Trek*, which gradually is being developed into an enormous wild native animal farm. Eventually you will be able to walk all the way around it, outside a high wire fence, and view moose, deer, buffalo, elk, mountain sheep.

En route back to Tacoma you can take either Highway 161, which routes you back through Puyallup, or Highway 7, which goes straight into Tacoma. Allow a little time on either of these because you're reaching into heavy population densities as you get closer to town and with the local traffic, the going is slow.

Tacoma Tour 3 — Gig Harbor, Fox Island, Purdy, Vaughn, Longbranch (Map X)

This tour takes you over the only bridge that crosses the Sound. It's located where the Sound narrows before it exhausts itself in a series of bays and inlets created by the massive glacier which lost its gouging power reaching for Olympia. The tour concerns itself with the 2 major peninsulas just west of Highway 16. It takes us through tunnels of trees with an occasional breathtaking view of Mt. Rainier, a lot of pleasant beaches, and summer homes. Highlights include state parks, one of the State's more unusual fish hatcheries, a couple of good oyster estuaries, and diminutive Gig Harbor. The latter's one of the most exciting and only "all women" shopping districts on the Wet Side of the Mountains. We mentioned earlier that what the people in Region 4 wanted was out of Region 4 and here is another area where they are going. The farther you get away from the city, the more vast the open spaces between homes.

The Narrows Bridge is a spectacular sight all by itself and in addition to being the only bridge over the Sound, it's the only location where there also is a bridge *under* the Sound . . . because, of course, the original bridge at this location, lies on the bottom. Nobody believed it was going to go. Bridges simply didn't. We drove across it once or twice when the wind was blowing and it was quite an experience. You could see waves of steel running across ahead of you that would cause cars ahead to disappear in the troughs and then loom above you on the crests . . . and you knew your car was doing the same thing.

After it blew down in 1940, the engineers took the problem of the winds which blew it down to the wind tunnel at the University of Washington, where they built a scale model of the original bridge and then with smoke to provide visible identification of the wind currents, they duplicated the forces that had blown down "Galloping Gertie." After months of testing and figuring out what had to be done to resist a wind force that was brand new in bridge building, there came the dramatic day when they duplicated the original destructive force and brought the model of the old bridge to collapse.

Then they designed a scale model in the wind tunnel that would not collapse under those same wind forces . . . and it's the full-sized verion of that one which you drive across today.

Take an early left after you cross the bridge and head for Wollochet which meant "squirting clams" to the Indians and generally means "private" to the people living along the shores of the bays. One of the most interesting roads follows the shoreline of deeply indented Wollochet Bay and more or less culminates in a place called Bay View where you may be able to guess what you get a view of.

A little further along is Fox Island, which is so privately residential the principal reason for visiting it is the spectacular view afforded you of Mt. Rainier when you cross the bridge to the island. A right turn at the end of the bridge takes you around the north end in a circle tour of a residential area, then south through the small community on the Island, and back to the bridge.

The rest of the island is more of the same plus a whole bunch of dead-end roads. Fox Island's most famous homeowner is Dr. Dixie Lee Ray, Chairman of the Atomic Energy Commission.

A rewarding trip takes you along Horsehead Bay to *Kopachuck State Park*. It should be noted that Mt. Rainier is a major scenic attraction throughout the trip. It appears low and near at surprising turns and places along the route. A charming, narrow valley leads to the park past horses, cows, ducks, pastures and ponds. The park, comprised of 104 acres, is heavily wooded, has a flat, sandy beach. The walk to the beach is about 4 blocks and there are picnic tables tucked around in the woods near the parking lot, which may help you decide where you wish to picnic.

Gig Harbor — (Pop. 1,595. Elev. Sea level.) — The town has a bona fide fishing village look which may be at least in part due to the fact that it's been a fishing village for the past 93 years . . . and still is, with fishing boats heading for the rich salmon-laden waters from right outside the bay's entrance all the way to the Gulf of Alaska. The bay's a remarkable geologic formation built like an isosceles triangle with the narrowest point at the entrance. (It's about 100 feet wide.) The bay, itself, penetrates about a mile into the landmass. The northern side is steeper and heavily wooded while the town is on the more gentle, southern slope.

The dominant population group is a combination of Croatian, Slavic, Austrian. Either by accident and design, or by design and design, the neat collection of imaginative shops of this village are owned by women. The plan for smart and unique shops started about 4 years ago when the wives of some of the business and professional men who had fled here from the big cities decided they wanted to do more with their spare time than sit around in rocking chairs eating chocolate bonbons or dedicate their energies to some charity.

So now they've come up with the DAGHLM — pronounced "Dagh-Lm," as in E-lm tree — and standing for the Downtown Association, Gig Harbor Lady Merchants. Their idea was to establish a variety of nonduplicating shops so they wouldn't be competing with one another. And each gal strove to make hers better than the one which preceded it until the shopping world started beating a pathway to their door.

Neat restoration jobs have been done of only existing buildings and the number of shops and restaurants has expanded to include an area about a mile along the waterfront and spreading to the surrounding hills . . . with an amazing degree of acceptance by the downtown of the "up" town merchants. It is a real tribute to the persuasive powers of the women who got the whole thing going in the first place.

Now tragedy has struck. They have voted themselves a sewer district . . . the kind of thing that has been the precursor of disaster for so many fine communities on the Wet Side of the Mountains. As long as they were limited by the health department to a smaller number of buildings they had no real problems. But now a sewer system has opened Pandora's box, and it will be interesting to see if the women can do a better job of handling the onrush of civilization than the predominantly male power structure has been able to do elsewhere.

Under any circumstances, it's great now and it will be intriguing to see how they cope with the advent of this monster.

To get the most from this community walk the mile, in and out, up and down, among the 35-40 shops divided by the head of the bay and "new" town. Places to lunch, tea, or gather local "overheards" for a shopping break; circle to several worthwhile spots outlying (i.e., antique shops, nursery, lapidary shop).

Uncommon shopping – *White Whale Gallery*, one of the Northwest's finest . . . *Candles and Wine of Gig Harbor*, 10,000 gal. wine barrel brought in and dismantled to form the walls and atmosphere . . . *Beach Basket*, site of old sawmill, mill machinery used for props and display of baskets, etc. . . . *Galleries O'Broclain*, upstairs lobby of 1924 hotel, now collection of shops . . . *Mostly Books*, self-explanatory . . . *"Century 19" Millwork*, also self-explanatory . . . *The Bath Locker*, in a former courtroom . . . *The Wharf*, marine antiques . . . *Country Store*, 2nd hand shop of Orthopedic Guild in old cabin . . . *Scandia Gaard*, 105-year-old original home, later a barn, now Scandinavian gifts.

A word about eating – *Scandia Gaard*, Peacock Hill Road, unbelievable location atop high hill looking down on "fjord," lush meadows, most spectacular view of Rainier. A whole complex including a village, museum, town square for celebrations, gift shop and restaurant. Latter is in the "big house," 95 years old, and serves Scandinavian, open-faced sandwiches, desserts, genuine smorgasbord, Staircase Room, for cocktails, under stairs. Smorgasbord and prime rib dinners Thurs., Fri., Sat. . . . *Poggie Bait Ice Creamery*, hatch-cover tables, pennants, charts, oak chairs and homemade soup, sodas, parfaits, Banana Split Binnacle, salads . . . *Shorline*, at head of bay has contemporary decor, big windows for watching bay activity, float for boat-diners . . . *Lost Alaskan*, in Olympic Village, ham 'n eggs and man-type food. Local color in taverns: *Three Finger Jack's*, on pier, music and lively, boaters habituate . . . *Harbor Inn Tavern*, sort of German tavern, good hamburgers.

Annual affairs – *Harbor Holidays*, 1st of June, century-old blessing of the fleet, parade, food-arts-crafts, crowning of queen, dance.

For further information – Call Gig Harbor Town Hall, Pioneer Way, 858-2116, or any member of DAGHLM.

Purdy — (Pop. Nominal. Elev. Sea level.) — This is a crossroads town at the site of an old Indian campground and it's easy to see why they selected it. In addition to the level beach and generally easy approaches, it was loaded with Olympia oysters for feasting before the white man appeared.

Most people driving here mentally drool over the wonderful beach on the south side of the causeway and pay scant attention to the muddy lagoon on the north side. And the fact is you're not welcome on the north side, because it's a privately owned oyster farm which sells its product only to wholesalers. But it was over this piece of property that one of the most important legal decisions of the present century was rendered on June 22, 1967.

You're looking at Burley Lagoon, and in view of what happened we would call your particular attention to some long thin poles stuck in the mud and the probable presence of some scows, which, for your information are about 12 by 30 feet.

The pregnant history of this lagoon goes back to 1895 when the brand new State Legislature responded to a concern that civilization was too much with us and that our oysterlands were a priceless part of our heritage . . . and passed a law which provided that as long as these beds were used for raising oysters they could be privately owned. But if for any reason they ceased to function in this capacity, the land would revert to the State which, in turn, would find somebody else to operate them as oysterlands.

The land had functioned in this capacity for the previous several thousand years and proceeded to do so for the next 67 years, at which time the Pierce County Commissioners adopted a comprehensive plan for the orderly development of the county.

The comprehensive plan followed precedent by setting Burley Lagoon aside as oysterland.

Now, one of the problems which we have mentioned previously is the frightening decline of the world's oyster supply. You also may recall the paper by state biologist Ron Westley in which it is pointed out that by raising oysters on string hanging from rafts, the Japanese have managed to produce 10 times as many oysters on the same amount of land as can be raised by letting the oysters lie flat on the ground. And Jerry Yamashita, the proprietor of the Western Oyster Company, which owns these lands, decided he would try raft culture of oysters in this lagoon. The State Department of Fisheries, which views the State's declining oyster production with considerable consternation, cheered lustily from the sidelines. If Yamashita could make it work, the graphs on oysters might start going up instead of town.

There didn't seem to be a cloud on the horizon as far as this move was concerned, but it was necessary for Yamashita to file a notice of intent with the United States Army Corps of Engineers, which has charge of determining whether things people propose to do will be a menace to navigation. And all you have to do is take a quick look at the lagoon and we think you'll agree with us and with the Army Engineers that the materials in this lagoon are unlikely candidates as a major menace to navigation.

Nevertheless, it was incumbent upon the Engineers to post notices of Yamashita's intent to augment his bottomland oyster-growing with raft culture. Frankly, nobody at the time considered this move to be in the least bit controversial . . .

But they reckoned without the retirement of one William S. Johnston from the paint-contracing business in Tacoma.

Mr. Johnston was the owner of a piece of property on Burley Lagoon, and he and his wife planned to retire there . . . and Burley Lagoon was headed for the classic confrontation of land use that has clobbered thousands of acres of irreplaceable estuary land in the Pacific Northwest with the advent of high-density population demands. Nobody familiar with the background of the lagoon gave Mr. Johnston serious thought. However, when he went to the Pierce County Planning Commission to protest the creation of raft culture on the lagoon, the planners pointed out that the commission might consider rezoning the area to Suburban Agricultural, which would permit a slaughterhouse and a fish farm, but would put a stop to oyster growing. So, on December 17, 1965, Mr. Johnston petitioned the commission for a rezone to Suburban Agricultural.

And that's when things started getting a little out of focus.

Mr. and Mrs. Johnston circulated petitions which they got signed by people from far and wide and arrived at a Planning Commission meeting on February 8, 1966 with the petitions and the press. Incredibly, the Planning Commission turned against its own master plan and voted to rezone Burley Lagoon as Suburban Agricultural, which would have effectively put the lagoon off limits to oyster growing.

To further put the nails in the coffin, Mr. Johnston caused a libel action to be filed in the United States District Court in Tacoma which read, "In Admiralty, No. 2892 . . . William S. Johnston, on his own behalf as well as on behalf of the United States of America, libelant . . ." This point was that those oyster scows you see weren't carrying running lights on the night of February 20, 1966 . . . which was not unusual because there had been no running lights on scows in that lagoon for the previous century.

Now, there are some interesting sidelights to libel actions like this. There were 6 scows and each of them liable to penalty of up to $500, of which the libelant could collect half the penalty. So Mr. Johnston stood to make as much as $1,500 on the deal. That, however, was only one side of the coin. Johnston also would be required to pay for the salaries of 24-hours-a-day worth of watchmen on the scows, which would have gobbled up his whole profit in 20 days. So nothing much came of that outside of the newspaper publicity.

Mr. Johnston, who was devoting a lot of attention to this project at the time, next appeared in Pierce County Superior Court on April 14, charging that those bean poles were a menace to navigation. That one kind of went by the boards a month and a half later when the Army Engineers held that the scows were not a menace to navigation. And, as you can observe, they were considerably more substantial than the poles.

Then on June 13, the Pierce County Commissioners voted to put the Western Oyster Company out of business by upholding the rezone ruling of the Planning Commission.

So Yamashita took the County Commissioners to court on the grounds that they were being arbitrary and capricious . . . which brings us to the final and precedent-setting decision rendered by Superior Court Judge Bartlett Rummel on June 22, 1967.

To Yamashita's horror, the judge announced that the County Commissioners were not being arbitrary and capricious in upholding the zoning of the property as Suburban Agricultural. But then the judge went into a further explanation. He pointed out that fish farming was legal under the ordinance. In the actions taken by Johnston, the Planning Commission and the County Commissioners, the general presumption had been that oysters did not qualify as fish. But no previous court decision had been rendered on the matter.

The judge solved Yamashita's problem by simply ruling that an oyster was a fish. It's one of those unbelievable things, but the news story of that decision went via the wire services all over the world with most of the headlines reading: "JUDGE RULES THAT OYSTERS ARE FISH!"

Perhaps he had in mind the old saying, "An oyster is a fish built like a nut . . ."

Anyway, they're stilling growing oysters here.

—◆—

While you're in Purdy, you might like to know that *Pearl's Restaurant* makes a specialty of wild blackberry pie. Two worthwile side trips en route to Vaughn are the *Washington State Fish Hatchery* and the *Minterbrook Oyster Company* at different locations on Minter Creek. At the latter you'll find fresh oysters for sale either in the shell or in jars and at the former, you'll find them raising the All-American Salmon.

—◆—

In the Biology Business, you never know for damned sure exactly what's going to happen, although with an animal as intelligent and adaptable as a salmon, you can be pretty sure of positive results if you get a few human beings around who are as smart as the fish. Most of the time, however, the positive results come from dumb luck on our part.

In the case of the Minter Creek Hatchery, it was a little of both.

Out of it came the "All-American Salmon."

The big complaint from fishermen was that while we were successfully raising millions of salmon in our hatcheries, they departed from Puget Sound and went up to Canada to be caught. So, the Washington State Department of Fisheries was doing all the work and those foreigners across the border were catching all the fish.

The order went out from State Fisheries Director Thor Tollefson: Provide us with a fish that will bite "American." Not only that, but come up with a fish that will return to Puget Sound during the summer when the weather's good. This seemed to a lot of people like a pretty improbable request, but luck stepped in at the Minter Creek Hatchery.

The hatcheries are always conducting one kind of an experiment or another with these animals and at the time this particular order came out, Art Gallaghan and his redoubtable crew at Minter Creek already had initiated a feeding experiment which required them to hold the fish in the hatchery until they had finished eating a specified amount of food.

When salmon are ready to leave the hatchery, they do two things. They gather at the outlet of the facility, indicating their desire to go to sea. They also stop eating. In the past, when this happened, the hatchery crew released them to go their way.

This time, the experiment required they keep the fish in the ponds whether they ate or not. For a while, the animals pouted around the outlet to the pool and refused their food. But after a while, like kids when they get good and hungry, they started eating again, and behaving normally. And it wasn't until two months later they collected around the outlet to the pool again, the signal for departure.

This time, they let 'em go.

But somehow the fish knew it was too late in the season for the round trip to Canada. So they shortened their normal cycle and stayed in Puget Sound. And in addition to that, they bit on a ratio of 60 to 1 over salmon that previously had been released earlier and had gone to Canada.

So now we have American Salmon raised in American hatcheries which swim in American waters and bite on American hooks at the end of

American fishing lines wielded by American fishermen. Their pictures are taken with American cameras in American fishing boats. They're cooked by American housewives with American butter and salt and pepper and served on American dinner tables to American people.

Next year, they'll have American flags tattooed on their American bellies . . .

And every tenth fish that you open will contain a music box that plays, *"God Bless America!"*

◆

Vaughn — (Pop. 300, Elev. Sea level.) — Is a minimal town, but on a beautiful small bay encircled by homes and ending in an inviting spit. There's a great view from the nice old cemetery on a steep hill to the north — a good place for a peaceful picnic. Then seek out modest signs to *The Old Farm Antiques* run by Luke and Esther Marlatt. In their delightful restored barn showroom and workroom, they sell, repair, and refurbish mainly early American (1785-1875) antiques, and also do chair-caning. *Vaughn Community Church*, worth driving down to bay, east end, is the only church we've seen with beach propery and its interior is completely shingled, simulating Swiss churches. Check pastor in house behind for a look inside.

To go on to *Penrose Point State Park*, follow signs south through Home (former commune) and Lakebay, which also sports a Bay Lake adjoining it. Penrose has a mile of beach for clamming, swimming, picnicking, and trails set in "Nature's Arboretum" — a wide range of Northwest plants abound. (See *Footloose*, p. 212, which gives a 2-mile hike here on beach and bluff.)

Many side roads disappear through trees and small farms, and any real signs of life seem to be on the waterfront private home sites. The round trip to Longbranch, an almost landlocked harbor, (sailors delight) also is more of same. The return to Purdy and Highway 16 to Tacoma can be varied by more shoreline scenery going through Glen Cove and Elgin.

Tacoma Tour 4 — Steilacoom, Nisqually, Yelm, Roy (Map X)

This tour takes you on the back road to Steilacoom, past an enormous gravel deposit put down by the Vashon Glacier, and down the hill to the Sound, crossing Chambers Creek to Steilacoom, the oldest incorporated town in the State. It has a number of very old buildings and is virtually untouched by commercialization. You then take Interstate 5 to the Nisqually exit and the delta of the Nisqually River, the least-spoiled estuary in the United States. A recent purchase by the federal government plus land previously bought by the State Game Department probably means it will retain its present status as dairyland and a bird refuge. The route then follows Highway 510 up the Nisqually River to Yelm where there is the largest antique shop on the Wet Side of the Mountains. At Roy, Highway 507 cuts through the back side of the Fort Lewis military reservation and back to Tacoma via Parkland and Spanaway.

To take the colorful backroad to Steilacoom, turn left from Highway 16 onto Bridgeport Way and angle right at the Chambers Creek Road ... following Steilacoom directional signs. You go through a vast gravel pit where the Vashon Glacier died and dropped millions of tons of glacial till in a pile about 250 feet high that will keep a couple of sand and gravel companies busy for the next 20 years. In the fall you can see salmon "climbing" Chambers Creek. And you drive through the busy *Boise-Cascade Mill*; if you're there during regular working hours, you'll see logs being bandied about by big machines. You'll pass *Sunnyside Beach*, which is a good swimming spot and arrive in a town which may be several hundred feet below Lakewood Center, but still "looks down" on the higher spot.

Steilacoom — (Pop. 3,064, Elev. 50.) — Now here's a town that ought to be investigated by some kind of an Un-American Activities Committee. It's got both history and view property and they've deliberately voted against making a buck at either.

This incredible circumstance surfaced only last year with the election of Mayor Lyle Dunkin, a guy who had bulled through an ordinance creating an Historical Preservation Area. This, the members of the present local power structure opined, held back the tide of developers and speculators until a permanent preservation ordinance could be passed covering the older portions of town. Now they've got an Historic Review Board that must pass on the demolition of older buildings and the construction of new ones. And believe us when we tell you there were a lot of people in town who felt this was un-American.

The thing that pushed the ordinance through and elected Mayor Dunkin was the existence of Lakewood Center, 3 air miles uphill from downtown Steilacoom. They're so ritzy they "ride to the hounds" in residential Lakewood. But the folks in the town of Steilacoom take the attitude that regardless of what they call it in Lakewood, the place is "going to the dogs." Mrs. Emogene Waggoner, of Steilacoom laid it on the line like this for *P.-I.* Reporter Jack Mayne, "Lakewood used to be a pretty area, with trees and streams and open space. Now it's just cement and blacktop; a classic example of ugly urban sprawl."

A fellow named Lynn Scholes said they didn't want to make Steilacoom into either a Victorian or Wild West town. What they're trying to do is preserve it for themselves and their children. And if as a spinoff some people wanted to visit, they'd be welcome.

Attaining this plateau resulted in one of the hottest mayoral campaigns in the town's history, which begins earlier than any other town in the State . . . because it was the first town to be incorporated in the State of Washington. It has the first courthouse, the first church in the State, and a Methodist minister who preached the first sermon with a Bible in one hand and a gun in the other to maintain order in the pews. It has the oldest Roman Catholic church in the State and, until it was torn down a few years back, the first jail — now commemorated by a marker. It was the starting point of the first highway. It even has a couple of homes built more than a century ago listed on the National Historic Register.

On top of that, it has great view property . . . an oasis in a desert of urbanization begging for commercialization.

The next election campaign ought to be hotter than the last.

Prowling Steilacoom

You can drive through town in a few minutes and see some of the neat old buildings, some of which have been thoughtfully restored, and visit the *Steilacoom Historical Society Museum*, which is in the basement of the town hall and open Thursday and Sunday afternoons. There are some level, sandy, view beaches and a trip on a county ferry to Anderson Island, which is the big piece of land you see across the channel. The *Ferry Dock Lunch* not only is the most outstanding restaurant in town, it's the only restaurant in town . . . and the hamburgers are great. (For a town walk see *Footloose*, p. 192.)

Annual affairs – There's a *Salmon Bake* on Sunnyside Beach which attracts 1,000 people in early July and a *Cider Squeeze* in early October. Bring your own apples and for a small fee you can get them squeezed into cider in one of the old presses available for the occasion. This could become the most popular celebration on the Wet Side of the Mountains in time.

For further information – Call the Town Hall, 588-3490.

The tour now takes you along Interstate 5 a piece, to exit 116 and the road to *Old Nisqually* which is a crossroads in the heart of the area where the federal government blew $175 million worth of money collected from duck stamps to buy the 1,300-acre Brown Corporation Farm. Tacoma and Olympia had been nosing around the Nisqually Delta with the notion of making it a super-port. They broke their last pick about 4 years ago when the Thurston County Commissioners turned down a request to zone 1,100 acres for industrial use. The Brown Farm is north of Interstate 5 and some west of the little village of Nisqually.

Just south of Interstate 5 and the nearest neighbor to the Brown Farm is the land of Swiss dairy farmer Fred Schilter.

Schilter had a cogent comment on the federal purchase. "A big port would have driven me out," he said. "That wouldn't have been good for me, and it wouldn't have been good for the country.

"Someday we're going to need all the land we can get to feed the nation."

The Nisqually Delta has been described as the least-spoiled of all the major estuaries in the nation . . . and we might as well start accustoming ourselves to astronomical figures for the purchase of this kind of land. Few people associate the whole problem with the energy crisis. So it's worth remembering that it takes a whole big bundle of energy to make the chemical fertilizers necessary to turn poor land into productive farms. In light of this alone, it's worth saving these rich bottomlands — regardless of the cost.

The question really is, "How much would you be willing to pay for the last glass of milk on earth?"

The tour now takes you up the Nisqually River to . . .

Yelm — (Pop. 632. Elev. 350.) — You're getting out into prairie country here and there was a time when the folks thought it would be quite a garden belt.

The Hudson's Bay Company maintained a herdsman's station here along with a ferry for crossing the Nisqually on the trail to Fort Vancouver. Later, James Longmire, for whom Longmire on Mt. Rainier is named, become one of the early settlers. Shortly before World War II, they got an irrigation district going with the notion that this would be a major berry-growing center. And for a time, berries were an important crop. But the war took young people away. They didn't return and the folks finally voted to dissolve the irrigation district . . . which was done to the tune of a loss of maybe a quarter of a million dollars. That ended up as a lien against the property and gave the area a bad name in the banking business. The debt's been cleared up, but the bankers are still a little leery about loans here . . . and locals opine it has set development back 20 years.

The real reason for stopping at Yelm is Mrs. Rodney H. Coates. That Mrs. Coates is something else again . . . like, she's serving her second term as mayor and modestly admits to the ownership of the biggest and best antique store on the Wet Side of the Mountains. Mrs. Coates, who is 68 years old, once was asked if being a lady mayor didn't pose difficulties.

"Not if you follow those two titles in consecutive order," she replied.

She operates on the philosophy that the shortest distance between two points is the truth. If the object under discussion happens to be a spade, that's what she calls it . . . and what she calls the *Daily Olympian* is "double zero." (From time to time, Mrs. Coates and the *Olympian* have held differing points of view.) She made what the *Olympian* considered news when she fired a handsome young deputy policewoman for wearing an abbreviated costume to work. "There she was at our Prairie Days celebration in the city park with those brief britches and a regulation police pistol hanging from her hip." Mrs. Coates said,

"I told her I didn't think Yelm was ready for a policewoman in hot pants."

Now Mrs. Coates is preparing for a conversation with the Civil Liberties Union on the question of discrimination. "If a police *man* came to work wearing hot pants, I'd fire him," Mrs. Coates firmly declared. "I've got civil liberties, too." People who work for Mrs. Coates are aware of her philosophy that they must either "hit the ball or hit the road."

Mrs. Coates found herself left to her own resources when she was 14 years old, "facing the world head on with no more than an 8th grade education and a desire to really earn whatever salary I got." She never has taken charity from anybody and there were times during the depression when she and her son faced prolonged periods of actual hunger. "You were glad to get any kind of job in those days," she recalls. "Now you can't fire anybody short of getting an Act of Congress."

Nineteen years ago, Mrs. Coates trimmed all four sides of a 9 x 12 rug to make it small enough to fit on the floor of the covered front porch at her home . . . and went into the antique business. She decided to call her establishment *Garden Gates Antiques* . . . not because she planned to specialize in garden gates, but because she thought the name had a nice ring to it.

In the intervening years, the cash register also has had a nice ring to it, because that original store has grown into a building 30 feet wide and 300 feet long. She buys out whole estates . . . recently purchased an antique store that was going out of business and acquired 3,000 items in one purchase.

Her whole inventory? Somewhere between 75,000 and 100,000 items.

Is it the biggest?

Well, it's surely not the smallest.

Annual affair – Prairie Days is week-long in early August, featuring old-time costumes, bicycle races, carnival and parades.

Your route now takes you through *McKenna* and *Roy*. In the latter there are two *Annual affairs* — both rodeos that attracts crowds of between 2,000 and 3,000 the first weekend in June and over Labor Day.

The return to Tacoma then goes through the open prairie land of east Fort Lewis and via Spanaway and Parkland.

REGION FIVE

MASON, THURSTON AND LEWIS COUNTIES

A Word About Region V

What the planners did was attempt to divide the Wet Side of the Mountains into 6 easy pieces that could be coped with in the planning processes—instead of the 19 counties that had evolved in approximately the previous century.

And what they came up with was a big hole in the middle. The problem was they either had to divide it into a whole bunch of pieces, which would be self-defeating in the simplification they were seeking, or lump it all together in one big chunk. And the latter is what they did. They called it the South Puget Sound Region.

South Puget Sound Region (our Region V) starts about half way up the west side of the Sound. It ends up at the summit of the Cascades and includes such diverse elements as the oysters in Hood Canal and the vast recesses of the Gifford Pinchot National Forest, while also encompassing the grasslands of Lewis County, which is the largest county on the Wet Side. Included in the area are such disparate towns as Shelton, the only town in Western Washington with no economic worries about the future . . . Olympia, where the state of the State is decided . . . Centralia, which subscribes to the *Seattle Times* and *Post-Intelligencer,* and her sister city of Chehalis a couple of miles away, which subscribes to the *Portland Oregonian* . . . Winlock, which has the largest egg in the word, and Morton, which still considers itself to be part of the State of Kentucky. The latter was ameliorated some in the past half century as far as Mountain Dew and the revenooers are concerned, but the job of game warden in eastern Lewis County still is one of the least sought-after positions in State government.

The attractions for the car-cushion travelers also are widely diversified with some of the highlights being the last family-type logging camp out of Shelton . . . the interesting and often novel processes by which all of us are governed in Olympia . . . gargantuan coal mining facility out of Centralia and the largest and most modern salmon hatchery in the world out of Toledo. Natural wonders of the region are as far-ranging as the southern tip of the Olympic National Park, the eastern side of the Willapa Hills and the southern approach to Mount Rainier.

Beginning in the mid-1840's, this county was the principal travel route for the settlement of Washington Territory, as emigrants made their way from Vancouver up the Cowlitz River to the head of navigation, and then occupied themselves with the frequently muddy trek the short distance to Olympia where they could get back into something comfortable — like a boat — for dispersion throughout the Puget Sound region. And today, of course, the bulk of the county lies on the main line of railroad from Seattle to Portland, with Centralia being approximately at the mid-point of the trip.

The first wave of settlers was followed by the lumber barons who moved in like a lot of locusts with the cut-and-get-out techniques that set the conservationists teeth on edge, but everybody reckoned without the growing power of the land. And now that man has become convinced that he can make a buck in timber as a crop, you will be a witness to luxuriant second-growth forests. The cropland of the lowland prairies is devoted mainly to feed crops. Over 85% of the acreage is in hay, grass silage and small grains for local livestock feed. This also is one of Washington's most important areas for producing commercial certified clover. Red clover is the predominant seed crop. Grass seeds grown are mainly bentgrass and fescue. Milk produced in the lowlands regions is shipped to both Seattle and Portland . . . and one of the most consistent crops throughout the whole, sprawling region is that of Christmas trees which, if you will pardon the expression, "crop" up everywhere.

One of the ironies is that with all of this water around it, the fact that it's the biggest and the "mother" of our counties, Lewis County is not touched by any commercially navigable waters. It's the county with the most "inland" feel of all of the counties we visit.

For the rest of the ares, however, the Department of Commerce, etc. has noted that "Water is the dominant resource of the South Puget Sound Region. This region's system of inland waterways, freshwater lakes, streams, bays and inlets offers tourists a wide assortment of water-oriented activities . . . . "

Which isn't a bad unifying feature in a book called *The Wet Side of The Mountains.*

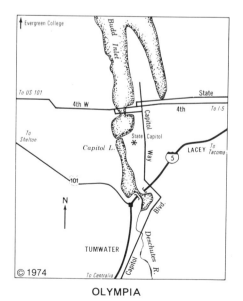

OLYMPIA

Olympia Tour 1 — In and Around the City, Tumwater and Lacey (Map XI)

Beer, government, education and history — in that order — are the chief attractions that bring visitors to the capital of the State of Washington. The town, itself, slopes to the central business district which is largely on filled land in Budd Inlet, the southernmost point of Puget Sound. This is the spot where the settlers toiling up from the Columbia River first touched Puget Sound. Nobody here ever quite forgets it and memorabilia of that struggle is to be seen in the State Capitol Museum, a handsome, restored mansion near the capitol campus. Education does come in for its share of attention, too. An archaeological museum at St. Martin's College at Lacey, east of Olympia, attracts a lot of people . . . and the brand new Evergreen College west of town on Eld Inlet nestled in a forest of evergreens is another major drawing card. The domed roof of the Legislative Building, on a knoll in about the middle of town, dominates the entire scene and is the spot where our laws have been ground out for the past 50 years. Visitors by the thousands flock to conducted tours here.

But by far and away the biggest attraction is beer. About 100,000 people a year visit the State Capitol . . . and over 300,000 take a conducted tour of the Olympia Brewery in Tumwater.

Olympia — (Pop. 23,600. Elev. 71.) — Clearly the most outstanding structure in the state capital is the Legislative Building. The official guide book notes that "with its massive white dome, its monumental design, and its placement in relation to the other buildings, it has the general effect of a broad base from which an adequate dome rises."

The 187-foot dome is the 4th highest in the world and 1 of 2 domes of sold-stone construction in the United States. It took stone masons 15 months to complete the masonry, the pieces of which ranged from a few pounds to 18 tons. The book continues with, "the two-tone bronze doors at the main entrance are ornamental with a series of bas-relief panels depicting pioneer life. The interior is marked by the use of several tints and kinds of imported marbles. Throughout the structure lavish detail has been used.

You're even more impressed and more likely to speak in hushed tones if you're inside the building when music from an organ on one of the balconies sonorously rolls and reverberates around the domed ceiling. You are awed by the majesty of this magnificent masterpiece. And well you might be . . .

They blew over $7 million on it.

The idea was to make it as inspirational as St. Peter's Basilica in Rome. For a while the architects designing it had in mind making it as big if not bigger than St. Peter's. But some skeptic brought over an Italian engineer familiar with the weight of that structure. After testing the ground on which our dome has been erected, he promised us that if we tried to duplicate St. Peter's, it would fall flat and kill a lot of innocent bystanders.

Enough important people with a vote on the question believed him and we scaled her down to the present size. Even so, as the day of the grand opening approached, it was a pretty impressive bunch of rocks . . . especially in view of the structures that had been used to house our legislative bodies in the 5 previous locations used for their deliberations. Early in the game, we rented a Masonic Hall. The first official legislative building was a frame structure 40 × 68 feet and 2 stories high. The total expenditure was limited to $5,000. Twenty years later, it was in such a desperate state of disrepair they had to spend $5,274.35 just bringing it up to code. for the next 26 years, the legislature functioned in the former Thurston County Courthouse, which the town of Olympia sold to the State.

A lot of governors got a lot of political mileage out of the building of the present legislative building ... but none who stuck in his thumb and pulled out a plum got one like that which Governor Roland H. Hartley extracted from this political pie without even half trying.

To Governor John H. McGraw goes the credit for the excavation of the basement of the new building. To Governor John R. Rogers, who succeeded McGraw, goes credit for the quote: "No capitol of this state ever will be constructed on a McGraw foundation." And that's where the capitol site sat for the next 26 years . . . .

It was a hole in the ground.

In the meantime, various guys got in their licks. Great architects designed the building. But governors gave it new directions. At one time or another that long flight of steps you may have climbed swung around like a weathervane in a high wind. They did a complete circuit of the compass, east . . . west . . . south . . . north.

Governor Ernest Lister wanted to junk the elaborate plans selected in a competition of 186 of the nation's top architects. His idea: Construct an office building on the west side of Capitol Way and run the State "like any other business."

The original plans called for a building that faced the east "as do all great capitols of the United States."

Governor Lister's proposal gave it 2 "easts" to just one "north," a "south" and a "west." For a while, it looked like the "easts" had it, but Governor Louis F. Hart got cornered by the "north" faction which was dominated by the Washington Chapter of the American Institute of Architects. That outfit had pitched hard for "north" in 1911 ... and in 1919, in one super power play, they swung her around to the north again and started construction before Governor Hartley took office.

Now, you've really got to know Hartley to love him. Amy Albright, who was his right-hand gal and loved him, told us about him from a sanitarium where she presently is spending her declining years. To her he was the most honest, effective and misunderstood governor the State ever had. However, this is a question on which there is a certain amount of disputation.

Hartley had but a few years of grammar school. At the age of 14 years he was on his own, at 15 a cook's helper and at 16 a teamster in a logging camp. When he was in his early twenties he did three important things. He studied penmanship and bookkeeping for a while at a private academy . . .

And he married Nina Clough, the boss' daughter.

By the time World War I came along, he did one more important thing:

He made a million dollars!

Some of the comments by contemporary writers about Hartley provide us with a fair character sketch: He was a flamboyant speaker . . . conservative industrialist . . . hated unions, social workers and reformers with a passion . . . proudly bore the title 'Colonel', although he never had been in battle and got the title from the governor of Minnesota who owed Hartley's father-in-law a political favor . . . he had no use for educators, especially Henry Suzzallo, president of the University of Washington, whom he fired . . . he was fastidious in appearance, had a mercurial temper . . . and if you attempted to change his mind about almost anything you had a very good chance of being disappointed."

At one time or another during his gubernatorial career there were movements to (1) recall and (2) impeach him. And the legislature got up enough votes to officially censure him for his abusive language and dictatorial manner. He was the last governor to leave office with a surplus in the State Treasury ($3,000,000). He believed the least government was the best government and considered the much-talked-about welfare programs of the 1920's as "so much altruistic twaddle." He served as mayor of Everett and as a legislator from that district.

He was elected Governor of the State of Washington in 1924.

Several years later a political writer who had covered the scene in Olympia for one of the newspapers that paid particular attention to state politics, had this summation of his impact on those around him: "His first four years in office were probably productive of more political melodrama than any other comparable period in the history of the state . . . he was in conflict, during the term, with the legislature, the land commissioner, state treasurer, state auditor, attorney general, secretary of state, superintendent of public instruction and countless semi and non-political organizations . . . he antagonized virtually every organized group in the state. A heated but unavailing effort was made to recall him . . . industries, labor, the farmers and organized groups in general were against him . . ."

With all that going for him, Hartley felt he had a mandate from the people to run for a second term.

His closest advisors promptly swooned.

And that's the way things stood when the naive proponents of a beautiful capitol building came innocently down the pike.

On September 30, 1927, when Hartley's stunned backers were attempting to adjust their thinking to a fruitless campaign, the contracts were let for the furnishings of the new building . . . and they were first class. Nothing was "store-boughten." Everything was custom made. Each individual part matched every other part to create a single, lavish entity that, as one woman reporter put it, "would surprise and delight the homemakers of the state . . ."

Those were the days when a high percentage of the people in the State thought "interior decorator" was a polite term for "bartender." You have to figure that every newspaper in the State was solidly opposed to Hartley. But a new device called the radio had come into play. Hartley had a resonant voice.

And the interior decorators provided that voice with a campaign song . . .

Called "The Solid Gold Cuspidors."

Whether or not they were solid gold didn't matter. They were cuspidors that had cost the State $100 apiece when even the best homes and most modern hotels in the country only had $30 cuspidors. The outfitting of the capitol had not been his responsibility and he could use the extravagance of others as an example.

Hartley got on the radio with his cuspidor campaign during the early months of 1928. From the response, he realized he might have a winner in this one. He invited the folks to Olympia to see what he called a "Temple to Mammon rather than a Monument to Representative Government!"

There was a lot of curiosity about cuspidors, but Hartley realized he had to do more than issue invitations. So in August he denuded the building of these newly blossomed additions . . . loaded them into the back of a truck and initiated what a delighted press happily labeled, "The Great Cuspidor Caravan!"

On August 28, 1928, there was one of a running series of articles in the *Seattle Star*, which had assigned a man to ride the caravan. It appeared on Page 1 under a headline reading "Crowds Flock to Cuspidor Caravan!" and reported that "farmers left their orchards, laborers their jobs, and merchants closed their shops to see the cuspidors." Some 1,500 people in Okanogan County came to stare at those objects d'art in one day.

Hartley didn't just come within spitting distance of winning, he won . . .

And became the first governor of the State ever elected to a 2nd term.

Prowling Olympia

This should, of course, include a visit to the *legislative building* where there are tours every half hour in the summer, Monday through Saturday. There's an organ recital in the rotunda at noon on weekdays and from 1 to 3 on Sundays, which is really inspirational . . . and we'll never forget the time when President Harry S. Truman sneaked away from his bodyguards in the middle of the night to try his hand at this organ. You can also visit the greenhouses on the capitol campus, and if it's summer, nearby there's a spectacularly colorful hedged garden of perennial flowers.

The *Washington State Library* is a low, flowing pavilion at the south end of the capitol campus with lots of glassed areas and an impressive Mark Tobey mosaic mural inside. On the lower level in the *Washington Room of Pacific Northwest history*, there's a Kenneth Callahan historical mural that runs completely around the walls above the bookshelves. This is "our" room; If you wonder where some of the hard-to-come-by information in this book came from, this is the place. Two knowledgeable librarians in this room, Hazel Mills, head of the department, and Nancy Pryor were the ones who dug up the information for many of our anecdotes, but we absolve them of all responsibility for the treatment we accorded their facts.

In addition to information, there are invitingly comfortable leather chairs, coffee, and no "no smoking" signs.

While not actually contiguous with the capitol campus, the C. J. Lord house a short distance away, is considered part of the campus and houses the *State Capital Museum,* which is the pride and joy of the town. Lord was a banker and prominent in the all-out fight at the turn of the century which retained Olympia as the site of the capitol. It is an active and attractive museum which retains many items of historical significance, and is used for style shows of antique costumes, meetings and musical concerts. There also is a *Victorian Pharmacy Museum* where you can find swamp root, Oregon Kidney Tea for backaches and Williams Pink Pills for Pale People. It's in the State Board of Pharmacy offices in the Washington Education Association Building. *McAbee's Tower House Mansion* at 11th and Central was built in 1887, slated for demolition to make room for a high-rise building and saved by its present owners who have restored it and brought in antiques from all over the world. Visiting 11 to 6 Sundays and holidays, or by appointment. (Small fee.)

The Evergreen State College — TESC as it's known on campus — opened in 1971. It is the first state-owned 4-year college opened in over 70 years. Five miles northwest of Olympia, it has a 1,000-acre campus of natural forests, rolling hills, grassy open spaces and over 3,300 feet of saltwater beach on Eld Inlet. There is a remarkably successful marriage between contemporary design in concrete buildings and the thick evergreen forests immediately around them. The open brick-and-cement courtyards and paths leading to a variety of housing in cul-de-sacs among the trees creates an integrated whole. The lighting comes from poles so high that you don't have the impression of individual lights at night, but rather an overall luminescence.

Educational goal of the college is the development of a learning community which reflects the "real" (as opposed to "ivory tower") world and provide a climate of problem-solving. The college places strong emphasis on the interrelationship of fields of knowledge rather than treating academic disciplines as separate entities. Instead of studying such subjects as sociology, economics, psychology, biology or art independently of one another, team members work to pull the disciplines into a clear and related focus.

This kind of thing has its own individual chuckles, too. A team was studying Hood Canal to submit an enormous 400-page report on all aspects of the past, present and future of this body of water.

One of the projects involved netting fish by sending a purse seine out from shore. The tide was right only at 1 o'clock in the morning, so that's when this particular class convened. And the report revealed that something in addition to pure science had evolved from the effort. It advised future generations to back the boat out and drop the net from the bow or the latter would get tangled in the propellor. It also noted that if dogfish are netted with other fish, you'd find the specimens you were after in the stomachs of the dogfish.

The best, however, concerned the study of an ancient Indian encampment along the shores of the Canal. The camp had apparently involved the presence of an untoward number of dogs. And the Indian name for the place translated into English as, "You can't step out of your tepee without getting dog excrement on your moccasins."

Capitol Lake Park, a former tidal basin, offers interesting walking or bicycling, and in the fall you can view the salmon runs from a viewing platform (see *Footloose,* p. 196). *Priest Point Park,* East Bay Drive is 253 acres of heavily forested terrain with picnicking, playgrounds, nature trails and beaches. (See *Footloose,* p. 200.) Plans are underway to build a replica of the mission that once was there and from which the park got its name. There are 21 lakes of all sizes in the Olympia, Tumwater, Lacey area.

You might try the *Port Dock*, where arrangements can be made for you to visit one of the foreign ships, frequently in port.

The best overall scenic view in the area is from the top of *Capitol Peak* west of Olympia in the Black Hills. It's about an hour's drive each way from Olympia on a road that's both narrow and steep, but spectacle is worth it, giving you a different view of the Olympics and Mt. Rainier than usual.

Tumwater — (Pop. 5,460. Elev. 89.) — The *Olympia Brewing Company* clearly is the number one visitor attraction of this outstanding location on the Deschutes River . . . attracting 59 times the population of the town annually for guided tours of its plant. It also employs about 13% of the population in the plant itself. For some 70 years, the company also has employed the use of a slogan, "It's the Water," to denote the fact that all Olympia beer is made with water from an artesian well selected by its founder, Leopold F. Schmidt, in 1896.

Recently, the words "and a whole lot more" have been added with an earned connotation that far exceeds the necessities of advertising. "First Citizen" is a more appropriate appellation, with the most recent contribution to the community being the $3 million *Tumwater Valley Recreation Area*, which includes a championship golf course in which mountains of earth were moved to raise the valley floor an average of about 5 feet . . . tennis courts . . . 2 swimming pools and winding pedestrian paths. The restaurant, *Tumwater Valley Inn*, is generally considered one of the finest in the area.

The Schmidt dynasty has been one of perfectionists who have produced the largest single brewing firm on the Pacific Coast and the 12th largest in annual sales in the nation. There's an anecdote about Leopold Schmidt which illustrates his meticulous attitude toward cleanliness and his detestation of waste. He found his executives were tromping past some rusty nails on the floor, and cleaned them up himself. When they replied they'd been too busy for this kind of work, he suggested sternly, "Well you know . . . it was by picking up rusty nails like this that I built this brewery . . . think it over." In 1957, both houses of the state legislature paid unanimous tribute to Peter G. Schmidt upon his death for his contribution to the industrial development of the state.

It's the Water . . . and the rusty nail attitude . . and a whole lot more.

(Incidental intelligence report: The Brewery and Victoria, B.C. attracted almost as many visitors coming to the Century 21 Exposition in 1962 as the Fair, itself.)

Alongside the Brewery is *Tumwater Falls Park* which follows the Deschutes River in its descent to Capitol Lake. There are play and picnic areas by the upper falls and small dam, and self-guided tours in wooded trails to the lower falls and its bridge (made famous by Olympia Beer labels) and back. It is especially choice in the spring when enormous plantings of rhododendrons are in bloom. And again in the fall when you can see the salmon coming up the fish ladders. (See *Footloose*, p. 198.)

Tumwater is noted for being the end of the Oregon Trail . . . and most of the maps seem to show it about on top of Bing Crosby's grandfather's home,

Crosby House. A tiny white house surrounded by freeways, it is the oldest in Tumwater (1860) and is open Thursdays, 2 to 4.

Lacey — (Pop. 9,880. Elev. 185.) — Nearly 20% of the population is represented in Panorama City, an attractive retirement community located on the pioneer Chambers estate, adjacent to Chambers Lake and Chambers Prairie.

There's an excellent collection of anthropological and archaeological artifacts including Indian arrowheads, woodcarving, leather, stoneware, pottery, etc., at *St. Martin's College.*

Also in Lacey on the beautifully wooded college campus is the headquarters of the *Washington State Department of Ecology* which isn't exactly a tourist attraction because they don't encourage visitors who just want to find out the meaning of the word "ecology." Nevertheless, this is the heartbeat of our concerted effort to make the environment in Western Washington worth living in.

The campus boasts the largest pavilion for sports and other activities in the area.

Uncommon shopping – *Olympia Artists' Guild,* picturesque outlet for local artists and craftsmen, in a remarkable old building which once was the office of Foss Tug Co. — and the "Peggy Foss" still ties up alongside . . . *Morningside Industries Gift Shop,* N. Capitol Way, an outlet for items made by the handicapped; you can visit the school which provides sheltered work training . . . *The Chamber Pot,* Custer St., people doing pottery for fun and for sale . . . *Marble Elegance Imports,* E. 4th, specimens of Taiwan marble, stone ground so sheer the light shines through translucent lamps . . . *Out of Sight,* French Rd., gifts accentuating the sea; hard to find among the tall evergreens, but worth it . . . *The World Shop,* Harrison St., gifts from all over . . . *Bigelow's Little Gallery,* S. Capitol Way, paintings and crafts by local artists . . . *Childhood's End,* S. Capitol Way, pottery, jewelry, candles, clothing . . . in November, December, *Sharp's Christmas House,* Craig Rd.; decorations, greens, dried materials, swags, wreaths in a family home . . . *Olympia Cheese Co.,* Lacey, has Swiss, smoked, caraway, cheddar, provolone cheeses . . . *Koehler's Bakery,* Capitol Way, tantalizing European pastries and breads; also a delicatessen and coffee shop, and open at 7 a.m. for a fragrant breakfast . . . 3 good bookstores: *Word of Mouth,* Overhulse St. S.W., *Pat's Bookery,* Capitol Way, and *The Bookmark,* Lacey . . . and a number of antique shops: *Antiquerie,* W. 4th, estates bought and sold . . . *Gingerbread Haus,* 4 miles west of Mud Bay, art glass, dolls, silver . . . *Olympia Coins,* Route 4, clocks, guns . . . *Lilly and Woodie's,* Martin Way, American oak furniture, depression glass, storm lamps . . . you can also buy *oysters and clams* where old Olympia Highway crosses Eld Inlet at Mud Bay.

A word about eating – *Tumwater Valley Golf Club Restaurant,* one of the newest and considered especially choice, is simple, comfortable with a qualified chef reflected in well-prepared meals; restful view over the golfing greens — good place for breakfast . . . *Jacaranda,* Port Dock, perched over the inlet with excellent look at Olympics; special Sunday buffet breakfast . . . *Falls Terrace,* S. Deschutes Way. Entrance on busy street belies an intimate restaurant with a dramatic view into Tumwater Falls Park and Deschutes River; after dark, area is lit and the Brewery looms like a medieval castle . . . *Golden Carriage,* S. Plum, generous portions, huge cinnamon rolls, and moderate prices . . . *Governor House,* hotel on S. Capitol Way, tasty meals and pleasant service, features champagne dinner for two . . . *Davis' Brown Derby,* S. Capitol Way, 4υ years of home-cooked food, and best pastries and pie in town . . . *Tyee Motor Inn,* S. Tumwater, terrace restaurant overlooking landscaped grounds; popular, and delicious food, like Oysters Rockefeller . . . *The Divot,* S. Tumwater, great, hot sandwiches called fringers of turkey, ham, sausage, clams, ad infinitum . . . *Panorama Dining Room,* Panorama City, Lacey, second floor view over homes, gardens of retirement community; good food, try it for breadfast, too . . . *Greenwood Inn,* Evergreen Park Dr., sophisticated restaurant overlooks Capitol and Capitol Lake . . . *Olympia Oyster House,* W. 4th, featuring our famous native oysters.

A word about sleeping — Because of State Capitol business, Olympia is like a convention town with a plethora of very good facilities: downtown, *Governor House* (Holiday Inn), S. Capitol Way, tall and new . . . *Carriage Inn,* S. Quince, excellent . . . *Brown Derby Motor Inn,* S. Capitol Way, newest . . . *Golden Gavel,* S. Capitol Way, smaller type . . . *Greenwood Inn,* Evergreen Park Dr. on beautiful grounds, Olympia view, even "suites with pools" . . . *Tyee Motor Inn,* S. Tumwater, cabana units, fireplaces . . . *Holly Motel,* Martin Way, smaller.

Annual affairs – *Silver Tea and Pound Party,* last Wed. in May, is only public affair at Governor's Mansion; sponsored by Thurston County Children's Orthopedic Hospital Guilds . . . *Olympia Homes of Interest Tour,* May, biennially, put on by YWCA . . . *Olympia-Maytown Flower Show,* June . . . biggest event of the year *Capital Lakefair,* second weekend July, sidewalk bazaars, dances, tournaments, queen's coronation, hydroplane races, skydiving, twilight parade, fireworks. Simultaneously, *Outdoor Art Festival* of Tumwater Allied Arts at Tumwater Falls Park . . . *Thurston County Fair,* August . . . *Kiwanis Pancake Feed,* October at Community Center . . . *St. John's Antique Show,* November. Sponsored by Episcopal Church.

For further information — Call Olympia area Chamber of Commerce, Legion and Washington, 357-3362.

Olympia Tour 2 — Rainier, Tenino, Littlerock, Rochester, Oakville (Map XI)

You're heading into Prairie Country on a big scale on this tour . . . penetrating or touching Weir, Smith, Ruth, Violet, Frost, Grand Mound and Mima Prairies. It is thought-provoking that only 125 years ago, this was the main route of the pioneers taking possession of a new land recently acquired from Great Britain . . . and a mere century ago the region was bustling with the activity of the first railroad punching north from the Columbia River to Puget Sound. This trip takes you up the Nisqually River Valley via Yelm to Rainier, across the Deschutes River into Tenino and Bucoda, and then a broad open prairie to Maytown, nearby Millersylvania State Park, and Littlerock. From here the route circles around the Black Hills and *their* Black River through Rochester to Oakville and the Chehalis River Valley north. You return back to Olympia via McCleary. Highlights are the world famous Mima Mounds and the huge seed-processing plant and tree nursery of Weyerhaeuser at Rochester.

You can reach Rainier by Highway 510 as noted on our map through Yelm or by taking an unnumbered Rainier Road across Weir Prairie out of East Olympia or out of Lacey on S.E. 46th.

Rainier — (Pop. 390. Elev. 430.) — This is the only town in the State named in honor of our most famous mountain. And in addition to being strategically located for a splendid perspective of "The" Mountain — which all of these prairie towns have — the town has something else in common with the mountain it was named after. Rainier, the mountain, is the highest landmass in the State. And Rainier, the town, is the highest point on the railroad line running from Portland to Seattle.

Annual affairs — *Rodeo* in May, which includes motorcycle racing, a very popular activity in this region . . . *Team Pull* on "Father's Day" in which workhorses demonstrate their strength.

En route to Tenino on 507, the *Deschutes River Park* makes a nice picnic stop.

Tenino — (Pop. 962. Elev. 200.) — Although it's a downhill pull for the railroad, which drops some 230 feet in the short distance from Rainier, Tenino clearly is enjoying a population boom, having a net gain of ten people since 1940. Tenino also is rich in history. In the first place, there's been a lively discussion for about three-quarters of a century over how the town got its name. Legend has it that it was named for either a railroad car or engine with the numbers 1090 on it when the Kalama-Tacoma spur of the Northern Pacific came through in the 1870's. It's a nice thought, but it probably came from the Indian word for "Junction" or "Fork" and dates back to an Indian legend. Coyote told some poor downtrodden California tribes he knew of a swell place to settle. They followed him and it was in this locale, originally called Tenalquot Prairie, where he showed them this well-watered, pleasantly wooded area rich in game and exclaimed, "Ten-alquelth!" (the best yet!)

◆

In 1890, the Northern Pacific pulled one of its usual tricks, moving the station a short distance out of town with the notion of disposing of real estate more profitably. As in Yakima, the owner of the hotel here put his edifice on rollers and rolled it to the new location. Some 500 people followed the hotel. But the city fathers of the original town screamed their eyes out . . . and, unlike Yakima, the hotel was put on rollers again and rolled back to its original site — followed by 500 people.

Tenino made worldwide news in 1932 by printing wooden money . . . together with a net profit of $11,000 from people who bought the money as a souvenir. It started something of a trend and the State printed its tax tokens on wood for a while during the depression. More recently, the folks here printed up another batch of wooden money — and sold it all. This probably will become an annual event.

The nice part of it all is, they call it lumber "jack."

Tenino sandstone was used in the old Seattle Public Library, the old Capitol building in Olympia, and the Science Hall at Washington State University. They had a big blast at the quarry on February 17, 1912 — two carloads of powder — and the 375,000 cubic yards of rock dislodged formed the first Grays Harbor jetty. Today, *the old quarry,* which is in the City Park, forms an enormous and inviting swimming pool with a mossy, fern-covered wall.

Tenino's population boom — some 30 new homes have been built in the past year — is due to the construction of the Centralia Steam-Electric Generating Plant 10 miles south, a project that will be more fully described in the Centralia section. Whatever else, the new feel to the old town resulted in passage of a $60,000 bond issue in 1972 that's being used to build a park with various play facilities like tennis courts, picnic tables, ball fields and nature trails and one day maybe overnight parking.

Best time is in the spring when prairie flowers like camas are in bloom and best view is from Blumauer Hill south of town . . . a small *Weyerhaeuser Park* is on the Deschutes River near McIntosh Lake.

You can visit the *Wheaton Farm* where eggs are raised in quantity, and the *Agnew T-9-0 Ranch* where thoroughbred horses are raised.

Annual affairs – Old Time Music Festival, in March, fiddling and folk-music . . . *Oregon Trail Celebration,* on Labor Day weekend with old-time costumes on the folks, muzzle-loading gun contests, parade, logging show.

Head south on Highway 507 for side trip to . . . .

Bucoda — (Pop. 425. Elev. 254.) — On the Skookumchuck (Indian: "swift river") River. The coal, which presently motivates the steam-electric plant, brought 3 settlers to the area, John M. Buckley, Samuel Coulter and John D. David who contributed the first 2 letters of their surnames to give the town its appellation. That was in 1890 and was a principal means of erasing a very bad taste that had become associated with the town's former Indian name, Seatco, which had designated it for the previous 35 years. It was the location of the first Territorial Prison. They used convict labor in the coal mine under a contract with private individuals. A scandal in the 1880's resulted in the creation of the State Penitentiary at Walla Walla.

Lying in the Skookumchuck River Valley, Bucoda is a cozy little spot that has proved attractive to retired people, trailers and mobile homes. The folks are very proud of their *Volunteer Park* (sponsored by the Volunteer Fire Department in 1958). It's on a bend in the river . . . has moss-covered maple trees, rest rooms, picnic tables and ball park where men working in the Mutual Lumber Company once played quite professional baseball.

Annual affairs – *Rebecca Annual Turkey Smorgasbord,* in April . . . *Annual Reunion* of people from Tenino, Bucoda, Tono and Mendota, the last weekend in July.

Tono — Barely qualifies as a widespot in the road. There was quite an agate deposit here although rockhounds have been digging for them for the past half century and you've got to move a lot of earth to find one these days. We tried it once. It was a great outing, but we drove a few miles into Centralia where they have a "rock" store with an enormous supply of rocks for polishing from all over the world. And they were a lot easier to "mine."

Maytown — Its principal claim to fame, other than being a somewhat wider spot in the road, is that it is en route to *Millersylvania State Park* on Deep Lake, which is a lovely spot and well-populated summer weekends.

See *Footloose,* p. 206 for trip to *Scatter Creek Wildlife Recreation Area* for wild flowers, picnics, birds . . . and p. 204 for Millersylvania State Park.

Littlerock — Is the place where you can get instructions for reaching the *Margaret McKenny Camp and Picnic Area* (named after the conversationist and naturalist best known for her book, *The Savory Mushroom*). This is a Department of Natural Resources Camp with picnic tables, foot, bike and bridle trails and parking for horse trailers. It also provides access to *Capitol Peak* (2,658 feet) which provides "capital" views of the surrounding area, including lower Puget Sound and Olympia. Nearby in an old lake bottom, the Weyerhaeuser Company has 60,000,000 seedlings planted, of which about half are transplanted elsewhere annually. *Capitol Forest* provides intriguing trails and a look at Mima Mounds.

Annual affair — South of Littlerock, *Harness Races* are run in August.

Mima Mounds — The word "mysterious" usually is put in front of the word mima in describing these mounds which originally occupied about 30,000 acres in and around the prairie of the same name. One of the best places for seeing them lies in the land between Gate and Littlerock. And so far, nobody has figured out how they came into existence. Nevertheless, they're a Registered National Landmark.

Earlier explorers dug into them, presuming this was a great Indian burial ground. Then they thought they might be ant hills or fish nests — following glaciation. Some of the earlier settlers opined they were buffalo wallows. What would appear to be the most logical is that they are of glacial origin. But Dr. Victor Scheffer, mammologist with the United State Fish and Wildlife Service in Seattle, has by far the most interesting and provocative theory.

He believes they were built by pocket gophers.

He backs up his theory with the following arguments: They are regularly spaced animal territories built by small gophers from southern Washington who invaded the area when the galciers receded. He refers to the area with the colorful title, "Pimpled plains," and notes the pocket gophers are extremely conscious of the territorial imperative. The mounds look pretty big for such a small animal, but somebody checked out the activity of one group of these animals and found the average gopher could move from 5 to 8 tons per acre annually. And all rocks in the mounds are small enough to be carried by a gopher.

The gophers feed on the roots of plants, and mounds like these only are evident in localities where either hardpan or a high water table limits their vertical activities . . . which forced the gophers to build mounds — much as pioneers in the Midwest prairies built sod houses.

Scheffer points out that even when the mounds are on sloping ground, they remain essentially circular, whereas had they been built by glacial action they would carry channeled patterns of rain, wind and frost, which they do not do . . .

Anyway, you may be looking at the structures built as a social structure of little animals. (See *Footloose*, p. 211.)

Rochester — (Pop. Nom. Elev. 149.) — Just about anybody can observe with equanimity the apparent devastation left behind by the harvesting of a corn crop in Kansas. The word has trickled through to the public that with superior seed, fertilizer, farming methods, and by our own experience, that there'll be another crop of corn on that spot next year. But we still get the jitters when we see a field of clearcut timber of the Wet Side of the Mountains.

Even so knowledgeable a man as Secretary of the Interior Rogers Morton told *P.I.* political writer Shelby Scates in 1973: "Every expert I talk with tells me otherwise, but every time I fly out over the Northwest, I have fear in my heart that we are overharvesting our timber."

Just like the rest of us, Morton can fly over clearcut cornfields without lathering up his pores because he knows that next spring, the field's going to be green again. But he's going to be dead before that timber crop is ripe. So the devastation looks like the end of the world to the Secretary . . . but only by standards of the life expectancy of Secretaries of Interior. Adding a couple of zeroes to the 1 year represented by the corn crop is tough for finite human beings to encompass . . . in spite of the length of time that Weyerhaueser has been telling us "timber is a crop."

Actually, The Lord has been treating timber as crop for several centuries longer than even Weyerhaeuser has been in existence. The Douglas fir crop of the Pacific Northwest has grown up, been devastated by fire and grown up several times. The difference is that God, unlike Weyerhaeuser, doesn't have to file an annual report with His stockholders. He doesn't have to modernize His equipment. And He doesn't have the State Department breathing down His back to do something about the balance of payments with Japan . . . or the devaluation of the dollar . . . or supplying jobs to people in the area.

All of us appreciate the profound statement by Joyce Kilmer that "only God can make a tree."

On the other hand, Weyerhaeuser and the other big timber companies in the Pacific Northwest can make it grow a hell of a lot faster, and straighter and taller. You should see what George H. Weyerhaeuser, president of the company, had to say on that subject in the 1971 Annual Report. The company had planted 73 million new trees in 104,000 acres that year. They had rehabilitated 6,800 acres of formerly nonproductive lands and seeded another 34,000 acres. Some 47,000 acres had been thinned. Another 123,000 acres were being fertilized.

"Seedling nurseries now are producing 61,000,000 new trees annually," the report said. "Seed orchards have been established to furnish superior seeds to those nurseries . . ."

Genetically superior seeds . . .

There's the key to the whole operation.

That's what they've got going here at Rochester and a few miles away at Mima. This is the place that Rogers Morton ought to visit for a psychological restorative after flying over the clearcuts — or you, looking at the clearcuts that show up in our satellite picture on the inside front cover. This is really where it's at and you will be impressed if you plan to pause in this area to get a look at the seed and nursery operation. Out of all the millions of acres available, this is the spot that Weyerhaeyser selected as the best location for the selection of genetically superior seed and nursing those seeds into little trees that can be planted in the forests and speed up the time schedule that God is so Almighty casual about.

What they have here in Rochester is referred to as the Seed Processing Plant. This is your guarantee that 60, 70 or 100 years from now there's going to be a crop of great big trees to harvest. It's the existence of this place, and others like it, that make it feasible for us to ship logs to Japan. And if you don't think that's important to you, consider this: For a decade — until last year — the United States operated at a trade deficit around the world. In other words, we were buying more stuff from them than they were buying from us. All sorts of nasty things happened, like the devaluation of the dollar.

So the State Department got on the backs of some of the big companies and told them, "shape up and ship out." Weyerhaeuser could handily use the spare change it got from shipping logs to Japan . . . a move that enabled the company to blow $200 to $300 million in modernization like at the huge complex in Longview.

The State Department's collective ulcer relaxed some when, in 1973, the balance of payments shifted to the plus side by about a billion dollars for the first time since 1960 . . . and logs shipped to Japan picked up about 25% of the total tab. Your income and ours had just a little bit more security . . .

All because of a process that relates back like a pyramid standing on one of its points to the Seed Processing Plant in Rochester, Washington . . .

And this is where we pause a moment to adjust our semantical skirts.

The dictionary doesn't make all that much of a big thing about the difference between seeds and nuts. Those diminutive objects that are seeds to the Weyerhaeuser Company are nuts to a squirrel.

From the viewpoint of a squirrel, for instance, the processing plant here has got to be the world's biggest Nut House. Now, to the uninitiate the attitude of a squirrel toward this processing plant probably couldn't matter less. But this isn't true of the residents of this valley who rely on the squirrel for a nice adjunct to their living. Every fall, these people go out in the woods and gather cones from coniferous trees which they sell to Weyerhaeuser's big Nut House. At the moment there are 133,000 pounds of seeds in cold storage here. They get about half-a-pound of seed from a bushel of cones. And the pickers are paid anywhere from $2 to $3.50 a bushel for cones . . . so that supply of seeds represents somewhere between $500,000 and $1,000,000 to the pickers, let along the processors.

Picking cones is a big deal here. Kiwanis Clubs organize picking expeditions to finance worthy projects. Families take along a picnic lunch and combine "togetherness" with cash to send Susie off to school.

There's no way a human being can climb to the top of a 200-foot-tall Douglas fir where the prime cones are growing. And that's where the squirrels come in. Operating on the theory that these seeds are in reality nuts, the squirrels set about laying in a choice supply against the coming winter. What they do is chew them loose from the tops of the trees and let them drop to the ground. Then they gather them and store them away in a hollow log some place. A good active squirrel will easily put in a double shift, 7 days a week from Labor Day to mid-December collecting nuts.

What the pickers do is cover the ground under the trees before the squirrel comes down to do his gathering and haul away the fallen cones. If a picker gets real lucky, he'll find a squirrel cache — which is the equivalent to a city slicker of walking down the street and finding a couple of $20 bills lying in the gutter.

Fortunately for everybody concerned, including these small animals, the squirrels gather about a 1,000-times more nuts than they'll ever use. They're nuts about nuts and go kind of crazy gathering them in. As long as there's a nut to gather, they'll gather.

So we get back to the original premise that timber is a crop. Rogers Morton can tell that to his ulcers so they'll simmer down. The State Department can point with pride to the balance of payment. Ford can note the dollar has been stabilized. The Weyerhaeuser Company can pour a quarter-of-a-billion dollars into plant improvements. And you and I can rest secure in our economic future.

There will be a time when man can harvest seed from genetically superior trees in his own orchards for all of this.

In the meantime, the whole world operation hinges on stealing nuts from nonunion squirrels.

In his book *The Mountains of California*, naturalist John Muir referred to the Douglas Squirrel (Sciurus Douglasii) . . . "Nature has made him master forester and committed most of her coniferous crops to his paws. Probably over 50% of all the cones ripened on the Sierra are cut off and handled by the Douglas alone, and those of the Big Trees perhaps 90% pass through his hands: The greater portions of course stored away for food to last during the winter and spring, but some of them are tucked separately into loosely covered holes, where some of the seeds germinate and become trees. But the Sierra is only one of the many provinces over which he holds sway, for his dominion extends . . . far northward to the majestic forests of Oregon, Washington and British Columbia. I make haste to mention these facts, to show upon how substantial a foundation the importance I ascribe to him rests. . . ."

Prowling Rochester

This is a quiet, open town on a flat prairie. It gives the impression of a coastal "Midwest" community.

Weyerhaeuser Seed Processing Plant is where you'll see how the seeds are extracted from the cones after being sorted by locality. They're dried, threshed and cleaned, and photographed with a polaroid X-ray to make sure the hulls contain seeds and not insects (sometimes they only get enough seed for the bugs). Good seeds then are packaged and frozen until they're needed.

The next logical visit is 5 miles north at Mima to the *Weyerhaeuser Tree Nursery* which is the second step in the key to high yield forests and is set up to show you how it all works. It's something to see the raised plats of trees on a bright cold day — with drops of water shining like diamonds on the perfect 8 inch firs — where once corn grew.

Both of these locations are attractively done . . . coordinated green stain on board and batten wood buildings, shake roofs — including the chief forester's home — and beautifully landscaped, of course.

Nearby, in an oak grove back of the forester's house, there is an *old pioneer cemetery*. Poking through the overgrown orchard which it occupies, you might find the *grave of William Packwood*, explorer and guide for whom the town of Packwood was named.

Uncommon shopping – *Bright's Ceramic Shop*, outlet for local potters.

Annual affair – *Strawberry Festival* in June, with all the roast turkey and strawberry shortcake you can eat for a nominal price.

Curving north around the bottom of the Black Hills on Highway 12, you follow the Chehalis River Valley downhill through farming communities to . . .

Oakville — (Pop. 443. Elev. 72.) — You can find a real "Main Street, U.S.A." here. It's nice and wide. There's a shake mill here and a lot of retired people. It's a faily major stopping point for people taking the cutoff on the west side of the Black Hills between the coast and Centralia-Chehalis.

Uncommon Shopping – *Oakville Treasures*, antiques in an old brick bank building . . . and across the street *Beaux Art Galleries* . . . and *The Only Tavern*, which makes it unique in "shopping" for beer.

Annual affairs – *Chehalis Indian Tribal Days*, in late May for rodeo, foot races, salmon or oyster bakes . . . *Fourth of July Celebration* in Oakville, for parade with floats and horses, queen and fireworks.

For further information — Call City Hall, 273-5710.

At Malone, a wide spot — well, a *fairly* wide spot — you can cut around the northwest side of the Black Hills back to the freeway and return to Olympia.

Shelton Tour 1 — In and Around Town, Camp Grisdale, Oyster Bay (Map XII)

A quarter of a century ago, the Simpson Timber Company bet its life that it could achieve a successful marriage with the U.S. Forest Service for the ensuing 100 years. A lot of skeptical people thought the marriage would never work out, but the comfortable, prosperous town of Shelton — the economic offspring of the marriage — is living proof that things are going well to date.

Your best bet for approaching the town is from Olympia via Highway 101 where there's a sign "Christmastown U.S.A.," and you can pause at the crest of a hill and look down on the only city in the State that doesn't have any economic worries for the next three-quarters of a century.

A visit to Simpson's mill here, its modern, dry, log-sorting yard, a few miles out of town, and Camp Grisdale, the last family-logging camp combination in the country, are prima facie evidence of successful modern forestry practices. Continuing past Camp Grisdale, you visit the recreational area created by Wynooche Dam, and return past Schafer State Park.

To the southwest of town is the Olympic Oyster Company, last remaining stronghold of the tiny native Olympia oyster. It can be visited . . . and it, too, is related to Simpson. A drive around Oakland Bay, which once died, reveals the restorative powers of which Puget Sound is capable. And all around the town are evidences of the people from Region 4 who are fleeing to second homes. Mason, a county with a population of 20,000, had real estate sales, mostly homesites, totaling $26,000,000 last year.

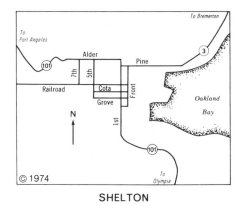

SHELTON

Shelton — (Pop. 6,600. Elev. 22.) — On February 25, 1944, Charles Linza McNary, Senator from Oregon, passed on to his great reward confident that the crowning achievement of his 27 years in the United States Senate soon would become public law. McNary, father of the Bonneville and McNary Dams on the Columbia River and one-time vice presidential candidate on the Republican ticket, was known to his colleagues as the "forestry" senator. He was instrumental in the passage of a law in 1924 which ultimately brought a virtual end to the fires that had devastated the nation's forests for centuries. In 1937, he brought about the Farm-Forestry Act, designed to preserve our forests through the education and cooperation of the nation's farmers.

During his entire career in the Senate, the star to which Senator McNary had hitched his wagon was that timber should be treated as a crop that needs 100 years — in western forests — to grow to its best size for harvesting. And that a watershed "Working Circle" should be planned on the basis of a century. In most important western forests, the government was the owner of the upper reaches of the watersheds. The lower portions were in private hands. From 1937 on until the end of his life, McNary dedicated his zeal to the creation of a law that would permit federal cooperative agreements with private owners of forest land within a sustained yield unit for coordinated management of the unit.

Finally, at the end of 1943 an exhausted 69-year-old McNary dropped Senate Bill 273 in the hopper. Under the terms of key section 2, the private cooperator, having pledged his entire facilities and lands to the success of the contract, was to be sold timber at appraised value without competitive bidding, harvesting timber on his own lands as well as on federal lands under federal rules and regulations. He was to provide for recreational, wildlife and water resources and reforestation for defense against fire under federal rules of forest practice.

Two months later, McNary was dead.

A month after his death, by standing acclamation, the United States Senate voted unanimously to make that bill into Public Law 273. Many of the senators had tears in their eyes. On March 29, 1944, President Franklin Delano Roosevelt solemnly affixed his signature. Everybody believed the new law would revolutionize forestry practices in the United States.

The Simpson Logging Company, incorporated in 1895, was the first applicant under the new law.

And on December 12, 1946, Simpson (now the Simpson Timber Company) and the United States Forest Service signed a 100-year contract to provide continuous tree crops under multiple use management as stability for the communities served by the Unit.

There was dancing in the streets of Shelton . . . (and in McCleary, Elma and Montesano).

Well there might be. The W.P.A. *Guide to Washington*, published a few years before, summed up the situation in the area covered by the new Working Circle. Logging operations, it noted, had eaten their way steadily inland, consuming in less than a generation forests that had taken hundreds of years to produce . . . employees "are buying little acreages, improvising small impermanent homes, and after clearing their land, attempting to supplement their wages . . . by gardening, berry growing, poultry raising, and dairying; thus they are helping transform a dismal logged-off region into an agricultural community. While the remaining stands of timber disappear from nearby forests . . . the development of farms will give the town a chance to survive . . . " (The latter was in particular reference to McCleary, not Shelton, although both are within the Working Circle.)

Mills at Bordeaux, Littell, Doty, PeEll, McCormick, Dryad, Walville, Frances, Globe and Lebam died. The communities withered into ghost towns to the point where the Northern Pacific branch railroad out of South Bend became known as the "ghost line."

As the Mason County seat, Shelton was somewhat better off. It also had a payroll from a pulp mill, but the latter was not an unmixed blessing. A screaming bunch of oyster growers in and around Oakland Bay, on which Shelton is located, had the mill in court with a charge that the effluent was killing off their oysters. And God knows the mill had tried to do something about it. Management pumped is effluent to the end of the Hammersley Inlet with the hope the stuff would go some place else, but the tide brought it back in. They tried burning it, but burning water leaves something to be desired in the way of economic efficiency. They pumped it to a gravelly flat several miles north of town, but the water in the nearby wells came up looking a lot like iodine, a depressing sight to the owners of the wells. And they did not neglect to inform the mill of their depression.

Finally, the mill shut down — a devastating economic blow to the town which then raised $166,00 by public subscription to get oyster growers off the pulp mill's back so it would get that payroll going again . . . which it did.

But there were periodic closures through the '40's as the realization grew that while it was the right process for greater utilization of our forest products, the mill was in the wrong location and it ultimately ceased functioning permanently.

So there was dancing in the streets when Simpson signed the contract.

And what a thing it has been for Shelton where the main mill is located . . . (and McCleary and Elma and Montesano).

And for God . . .

And for country . . .

But mostly for Shelton. The late Chapin Collins, publisher of the *Montesano Vidette*, put it like this: "In Shelton, company shops and railroads have been removed from the center of town, replaced by a parkway and shopping centers. McCleary has changed most in its homes. Color has replaced company-town gray. Gardens bloom. New stores, new bank building, new schools, new water and sewer systems, new city hall, new park — all attest that something happened here that never happened before . . .

Employment in the woods has gone from 1,400 in 1947 to 2,400 in 1973 . . . The payroll has been upped from $6.4 million to $29.4 million . . . Bank deposits have gone from $14 million to $102 million . . . bank loans from $1 to $41 million.

All of this against a population increase of 1.45 times.

In the meantime, in the first 25 years, Simpson had spent $20 million in plant improvements. It has paid the Forest Service nearly $50 million and the latter, in lieu of taxes, has paid 25% of that amount back to the counties involved. Simpson pays 25% of the Mason County taxes. And the folks there never heard of a school levy.

A trio of foresters commenting on the woodsy end of things in the *Journal of Forestry* for August, 1972 noted that the more than 1,300 miles of logging roads had cut yearly average fire losses to less than 10 acres . . . given access to good hunting, fishing and recreation to 120,000 people in 1971 (up to 150,000 last year).

The three gentlemen observed that, "The 1947 mills at Shelton and McCleary have been entirely replaced by modern plants, well adapted to converting logs from the unit into lumber, plywood, insulation board, doors, pulp chips and other products . . ."

The gentlemen also estimated that 775,000,000 board feet — three-quarters of a billion — *more* timber has been harvested under sustained yield from the lands in the Shelton Unit than would have been possible had the same National Forest and Simpson lands been managed independently for sustained yield . . . and it can keep on going this way for 1,000 years!

McNary's dream come true?

Not quite.

For this is the only cooperative sustained unit of its kind created under Public Law 273 which was supposed to be the great panacea for forestry ills.

Well, the problem was people.

Some other companies and communities thought this would be a neat idea, but in the 6 areas where they tried to put it in operation, none of the communities could agree on which one of them would be getting all this gravy. The Forest Service threw up its hands and said, "Forget it!"

Other people piled on the Simpson situation with charges of "monopoly!" and "favoritism!" making the Working Circle a hot political potato for the Forest Service, and for Congress which gives the Forest Service its annual budget. So, to make sure it wasn't open to criticism, the Forest Service started looking over Simpson's shoulder with a fine-toothed comb — and you can't hardly get a scrutiny finer than that!

No big bundle has been made. Much of the money for improvements in the Sustained Yield Unit has come from profits made by Simpson outside the unit. Other companies, observing the operation, failed to embrace the idea to their economic bosoms . . . and the Forest Service, with a keen eye on Congress and its future budgets, has done no recruiting. So Simpson's the only one fulfilling Senator McNary's dream . . . and William G. Reed, who was president of the company when it made the deal, has his own thoughts on that . . .

"We could have made more of a profit," Reed wryly opines, "if we'd put our money in a good savings account."

◄▬►

Mason County has the distinction of being a vacation home country with no building code. At one time there were 26 speculative developments in one year's time. The number of seasonal homes now surpasses that of year-round houses. The population multiplies 5 times in the summer and puts a real strain on Shelton, the only large and complete town in the county, for necessary services, like hospital facilities, etc. Ecological impact forces frequently lock horns with the development people. Mason County encompasses the contrast of one of the State's best developments — Weyerhaeuser's Hartstene Pointe — to some of the worst looking in the same county — rows of flags strung along roads and signs like those of used-car lots. Mason's miles of salt and fresh waterfront, views of mountains and sea, and its mid-position to a number of cities is a powerful lure for our more affluent (and effluent) society and second home sites.

Prowling Shelton

This is a comfortable town with a couple of creeks running through backyards and under streets, a parkway in the middle and a general knowledge that for at least the next three-quarters of a century its economic future is assured by the written contract between the Simpson Timber Company and the federal government. Shelton makes the brag that thanks to the ITT Rayonier research facility here it has more PhD's to the square inch than any other small town on the Wet Side of the Mountains. It also has the feel of a small town where you can walk anywhere, especially to the main shops which line both sides of the parkway in the center of town. The town also supports both a yacht and country club. Many of the comfortable homes of the pleasantly prosperous town are in the residential areas of the surrounding hills.

There was a time when the loggers wouldn't haul a log that was less than 11 inches in diameter out of the woods, but now, thanks to the $2.7 million Simpson blew in the renovation of Sawmill 3 in 1972, logs down to 5 inches in diameter are processed into quality lumber from commercial thinning of the second growth forest. The combined saw and chipper also produces chips for pulp and the generation of electricity for the mill. During the energy crisis, Simpson offered to supply the town with electricity if things got tough.

They really should erect a shrine of some kind in this town and call it "Saint Simpson."

Plant tours of Simpson Mill 3 are available twice a day during the summer work week. Check at the gate or the Chamber of Commerce.

The drive to *Camp Grisdale* is a neat one on a good road that goes through Egypt Valley, south of South Mountain, the south-most mountain of the Olympics, and across 13 rivers. About 7 miles out of Shelton you will pass the most modern log-sorting yard in the State. They don't toss logs around like they used to in the old days. Some 70 cars of logs a day come in from Camp Grisdale. The enormous jaws of a big crane clamp around a flat-car bundle of logs, and they are sorted by species and ultimate use. Then they're banded and taken to the bay where they are let carefully down into the water, instead of being dumped in as they once were.

At Matlock is the *Simpson Seed Nursery* which got its start from 15 superior, fast-growing wild trees. From Matlock, you loop south across the Satsop River to the Wynooche River Valley and north to Camp Grisdale, which is tucked into the Weatherwax Ridge just north of Reed Hill, named after Mark Reed, who succeeded Sol Simpson as the big man of the company. (Just to remain impartial, the folks also named another piece of the landscape, due east of here, Simpson Hill.)

Grisdale is the last remaining family-logging camp combination in the country. You can get a folder on this forest community when you get there, but here's what you see: family homes . . . bunkhouses . . . machinery shops . . . community hall . . . logging equipment and atmosphere.

A 3-mile drive north is new *Wynooche Dam* and its 6-mile-long reservoir stretching into the Olympic National Forest.

You return to Matlock and head south to *Schafer State Park* where you'll find large stands of fir and big-leaf maple . . . swimming . . . picnicking, etc. . . . then Cloquallam in Goose Prairie and back to Shelton.

Another scenic drive with a goal is on the south edge of town where a road goes east following Hammersley Inlet, Shelton's channel to the Sound. The forested road winds past suburban homes to a point where you can look east to Squaxin Island, reservation of the Indians by the same name, or south to tiny Steamboat Island and its shoulder-to-shoulder houses. Continue on around this peninsula along Skookum Inlet and south through Kamilche to Oyster Bay Road.

The Olympia Oyster Company — Although most people aren't aware of it, William G. Reed is the president of the Olympia Oyster Company on Totten Inlet, a short drive south of town where the last great stand is being made against the encroachment of civilization on our native Olympia oyster. And if you should encounter Dave McMillan, manager of the company, on your trip here, you will not get a favorable report on the influence of pulp mills on his favorite oysters.

Actually, it's the people population explosion that has done these delectable little oysters in. The pulp mills probably have their fair share coming, but then so do the rest of us who use so much more paper than we did at the turn of the century, you wouldn't believe it. (More on that subject will be brought out in the next region.)

Historically, overharvesting depleted the Olympias down on Shoalwater (née Willapa) Bay before the pulp mills made their appearance. But southern Puget Sound, where diking systems, like those that date back to the original oyster culture by the Romans in Naples nearly 2,000 years ago, made the natives an enormously profitable crop. Then the mother lode died in Oakland Bay and people brought in the Japanese oyster . . . which brought with it the oyster drill. This drill has a tough time penetrating the shell of the larger Pacific oyster, but the thin shell of the Olympia is duck soup for it.

Manager Dave McMillan lays awake nights these days trying to figure out how to beat the Japanese oyster drill, which has proliferated in Oyster Bay, and save his oysters from extinction. But this drill is not the only enemy of the Olympia oyster. Dave's battles to save them are legion.

When Dave isn't busy cussing the pulp mill people, he's busy cussing the bluebill ducks. The air gets bluer when he sounds off against pulp mills. But for your in and out, long term, every day bread and butter cussing, the bluebill get the blue ribbon, not just with Dave, but with any grower who has ever tried to raise Olympia oysters.

The problem is that a man can scare off the other ducks, but he barely annoys the bluebills (to birdwatchers, scaups) . . . and does the bluebill love Olympia oysters. They're only about as big as a silver dollar, shell and all, and what this duck does is swallow them whole. The bluebill dives for them in about 20 feet of water and gobbles them as fast as he can swallow them. They've shot bluebills and examined them to find as many as 35 Olympia oysters in one duck. They're layered like shingles all the way down his throat to his gizzard.

Before the white man appeared on the scene and Olympia oysters were scattered from here to California, even the bluebills had to work for their dinners. But when oyster growers began diking the lands three-quarters of a century ago, the oysters were concentrated behind the dikes. The dikes are placed in semicircles, squares and rectangles. And you can tell the shape of the particular dikes underwater when the tide's in, because the bluebillls are congregated on top of the water in semicircles, squares and rectangles depending on which dikes they're working.

The ducks, however, are protected animals, much to the frustration of the oyster growers. As early as 1914, the United States Biological Service sent a man out from Washington, D.C. in response to the angry demands of the oyster growers in the area. He noted that the ducks were eating something like 8,000 oysters a day, and added, "The protective measures consist in chasing the ducks or by shooting at them and scaring them by whistling the boat horn. The efficiency of these methods is very low however, if they are not accompanied with real danger to the birds, which after a short experience disregard the shooting with blank cartridges and pay no attention to any noise-making devices . . ."

The oystermen claimed the federal fellow was wrong . . . that the ducks were eating 35,000 oysters a day and the big boss of the Biological Service proceeded to make the biggest mistake of his life. He demanded proof. So the oystermen sent him 1,000 ducks . . .

Each with 35 oysters in his gullet.

You can readily understand that 1,000 ducks, each containing 35 oysters, made quite a pile on some bureaucrat's fumed oak desk. So, sort of a gentlemen's agreement was reached that the oystermen could shoot at the bluebills with intent to kill to the tune of maybe 150 ducks per year. The rest of the time they'd have to get rid of these birds by waving their arms and making-noises.

Working on a budget of 150 dead ducks annually, the oystermen have tried various devices. To begin with, they know these ducks will fly around exactly 6 feet out of shotgun range. And as soon as the shotgun is gone, they start feeding again. However, if the shotgun is loaded with blanks, the ducks don't even bother to get up off the water. They tried sending a patrol boat out from shore on a regular schedule. But after two days the ducks left the feeding grounds exactly three minutes *before* the boat was scheduled to leave.

They tried automatic exploders floating over the dikes. The first day, all the ducks flew away. The second day, the ducks sat on the floats holding the exploders and didn't budge. One ingenious oysterman floated a bag of gravel with a stick of dynamite in it. The first day it blew gravel all over the place, and he killed three ducks. The second day, they ducked underwater moments before the dynamite went off. (That was a coordinated "ducking" by about 500 ducks.)

Then somebody got a bright idea. They would put a whole bunch of rafts out over the dikes. All but one would have mannequins instead of men. Then they would shift the man around to different floats on different days so the ducks wouldn't know which float had the live man and ammunition on it.

You've gotta be kidding!

No matter how well they disguised the real hunter, no matter how many times they switched him around with the mannequins (and sometimes they would have him lie stiff and carried him like they would a mannequin), the ducks always knew which float had the live man. They did their feeding around all the other floats and stayed out of shotgun range of the real man with the real gun.

Then the oystermen decided they would get a duck to utter a distress call and broadcast it over the area. But no way could they get a cry of distress out of a bluebill duck.

So, what they do now is employ a full-time patrolman who goes out at irregular intervals in the patrolboat with the shotgun and live ammunition to keep the ducks uncomfortable and on the move and hold down on the number of oysters that are strictly for the birds. At today's prices, one day's oysters for a duck is $3.50. And there are some 10,000 ducks in the area from October to April.

McMillan says, with grudging admiration, "God dispensed so much wisdom in that bird, you wouldn't believe it!"

You can see the operation of the processing plant of the Olympia Oyster Company from 10 to 2 Monday through Friday and purchase shucked Olympia and Pacific oysters and marvelous clams in the shell. The Olympias are frightfully expensive, but if you have never eaten them you can't qualify as a bonafide resident of the Wet Side of the Mountains.

In addition to bringing in the hated Japanese oyster drill, the new oysters in the Pacific Northwest also "hosted" the arrival of the Manila clam, which is a delicious addition to our gourmet economy and can be purchased at the Olympia Oyster Company which farms them along with native rock clams in unbelievably prolific quantities. The farmed clams grow in quantities like a dozen to the square foot, available maybe a couple of inches below the surface.

So add clams to your purchase of oysters here and you'll go away with a couple of gourmet prizes that are well worth the trip.

(Once again, we point out that if you find oysters growing in profusion on some beach, they belong to somebody else. And if you take them, you are a thief . . . and in the same general bag in the eyes of oyster growers as were the cattle rustlers they used to hang from the nearest tree in the less formalized days of the west.)

Uncommon shopping – *The Shop* for local arts and crafts . . . *Blue Lantern Antiques*, Highway 101 at McCleary cutoff, furniture, primitives, glass and knowledgeable owners . . . *Gatehouse Gift Shop*, Sanderson Field Hwy. 101 N., cedar plant boxes, picnic tables, ceramics treated by Exceptional Foresters, retarded boys . . . *Barden's Antiques & Trading Post*, Olympic Highway S., huge old bottle collection . . . *Gems Etc.*, W. Railroad, for rockhounds.

A word about eating – *Heinie's Broiler*, W. Railroad, cheerful and friendly local gathering spot, menu in logging terms like Rigger Slinger, serves local oysters, mouth-watering sandwiches . . . *Harper's Broiler*, S. 1st, if you hanker for buffalo meat, pardner, they have buffalo burgers and buffalo dinners . . . *Mac's Corner Tavern*, Cota St. middle of the block, usual tavern atmosphere, but local secret is the food: veal scallopini, potatoes that taste like — *potatoes*, spring stew bowl topped with ladle of fresh green peas, $2 filet mignon breakfast . . . *Taylor Towne Restaurant*, Olympic Hwy. S. 6 miles, "oysters and Manila clams fresh daily" and must be — this close to Oyster Bay.

A word about sleeping – *Thunderbird Motel*, W. Railroad, two-story, good facilities, comes equipped with Timber Coffee Shop.

Annual affairs – The 4 day *Mason County Forest Festival*, in May, "green" theme, Paul Bunyan parade, "second growth" junior parade, loggers' show — one of the best on Wet Side.

For further information — By all means blow four bits for the Annual Edition of the *Shelton-Mason County Journal*. Or ask Forest Service Ranger, Olympic Highway N., or Chamber of Commerce, 3rd and Cota; phone, 426-2021.

◆

Shelton Tour 2 — Hoodsport, Lake Cushman, Union, Allyn, Hartstene Island (Map XII)

This one takes you over the hill to the Great Bend of Hood Canal where you'll have a chance to buy tough salmon and tender cigarettes from the Skokomish Indians who have a roadside stand adjacent to a fancier white man's stand which sells shrimp fresh from the canal.

Heading north along the Canal on Highway 101, you can buy shrimp from a stand at Hoodsport where there is a ranger station, fish hatchery and a restaurant that knows how to cook oysters. Here you take a left to Lake Cushman, owned and operated by Tacoma City Light . . . with a good resort and a lot of vacation cabins. You can drive from this road to the Hamma Hamma recreation area, and you have a shot at a road into the Olympic National Park to Staircase.

All along the canal there are oyster farms where you can buy or watch them shucking, or both. From Hoodsport, you return south to Union and Alderbrook Inn, the most famous and venerable on Puget Sound . . . and up toward the head of the Canal where you return on Highway 3 to Allyn, the big huckleberry, salal, sword fern and Christmas tree town, and a neat little church.

Continue south along a shoreline unmarked road to grapes of Grapeview, the stretch of Stretch Island and the heart of Hartstene Island where they have the kind of a second home development you could be proud of, and then back by whatever seems like a handy route to Shelton.

Lower Hood Canal — The Olympic Highway (101) goes arrow-straight to the Great Bend of Hood Canal where the glacier apparently was blunted and turned northeast. This elbow is the wettest area in the Puget Sound Trough and rainfall measures 83 inches annually. An adventuresome side trip may be had by turning up the Skokomish River Road here to Camp Govey, and seeing the highest bridge in Washington, a 380-foot steel arch railroad bridge. There's a ranger 8 miles in from the highway who can put you in the right direction — or check with the Forest Service in Shelton.

The highway splits here inside the Skokomish Indian Reservation, east to the dead end of the Canal, or north with this tour along the base of the Olympics. You pass the Skokomish Tribal Center, a Shaker church, and a backyard cedar shake mill on the way through the reservation.

Uncommon shopping – *Bonnie Bee's*, Potlatch, country-style food like raw honey, natural cider, barrel-cured kraut and homemade cheese . . . *The TePee*, Potlatch, owned by a Tepee Indian from Montana. Indian crafts from Alaska to Southwest — baskets, moccasins, purses, beadwork, dolls, drums, and — tepees . . . look for *stands at the "Y,"* where you can buy some of that Indian smoked salmon. Hard-cured and built to last, it takes a bit of gnawing, but it's one of the few places on earth you can buy it and the flavor is delicious. You also can buy cigarettes here depending on the attitude the courts currently are taking with regard to Indians and State taxes. We suggest the cigarettes are tender on the grounds this is a tender subject with the Washington State Tax Commission. If conditions are right, however, you can buy your favorite brand at substantial savings.

This west shore also is a great spot to buy *Hood Canal shrimp*, fresh from pots marked by colored flags bobbing right out there in the canal beyond you. The shrimp fishery here used to be enormous, but, of course, the white man came along and virtually wiped it out. Thanks, however, to the fertility of Hood Canal, they're coming back. At present there aren't enough for a big commercial fishery, but all the locals along the Canal have got their shrimp pots and obtain their own supply. You can buy them here if you're early enough in the day and driving by between April and October. The fresh ones are tiny and superb, and taste a lot like sweet nuts. But don't let anybody pawn off frozen ones on you . . . .

There are *oyster farms* all along the Canal where you can get these delicacies fresh, either in the jar or in the shell. There are some public beaches, but there won't be any oysters on them. And you do everybody a favor including yourself if you put out a buck or two and buy them instead of stealing them from the private beaches which is the only place where they're plentiful. You also can watch the shucking line, which is fascinating. But take a tip: Try to resist buying them in months without an "R" in them. Nothing wrong with oysters in the summer, except that they're a lot like sex . . . always good, but sometimes better.

West, up a service road at Potlatch State Park, there's a drive and a hike to the *Lost Canyon of the Skokomish River* (see *Footloose*, p. 216).

Hoodsport — (Pop. Nom. Elev. Sea level.) — A waterfront-business, hillside-residential town that is the middle one of the 3 metropolises on the Canal. (Other two are Quilcene to the north, Union to the south.) It provides services for Canal and Lake Cushman vacation homes, plus sporting a ranger station and a *State Fish Hatchery*, which you can visit. There's not a lot of verve to the name Hoodsport, but it's easier on post office than the original Indian name: "Slalatlatltulhu."

Uncommon shopping – *Spouting Whale*, for arts, crafts, books, antiques. Appealingly nautical Northwest . . . *Skipper John's Roadside Stand,* for fresh Hood Canal shrimp.

A word about eating – *Skipper John's* has a cheerful yellow and white colonial look, and an appropriate menu like steamed clams, oysters . . . *Old Mill* on the waterfront, is special for oysters . . . *Hoodsport Cafe,* where the rangers and other locals meet to eat. "Goeduck", shrimpburger, homemade chowder and oyster stew.

A 4 mile drive up a rise of 748 feet out of Hoodsport takes you to *Lake*

Cushman, formed by Tacoma City Light's two dams on the Skokomish River. The lake stretches 10 miles into the Olympics which rise steeply on the south and northwest. (See *Footloose*, p. 218, for road to the top of Dow Mountain.) The development of the lake is a tasteful combination of recreation area, vacation homesites, resort, services and *Lake Cushman State Park* — all on the north side looking across at mountains and wild country. A turnoff at the second dam goes to the Forest Service's 35-acre *Denny Abl Seed Orchard.* (Inquire at ranger station for self-guided interpretive trail.)

   A word about eating and sleeping – *Lake Cushman Resort* has casual dining (a genuine trapper's cabin is part of the knotty pine interior), together with a sophisticated menu and a great view over the lake. Dancing in the Liar's Den, breakfasts in the Village Store and Grill. The lodge operates from April through September. Tidy, stained cedar, housekeeping cottages, tucked in among the trees, are open all year and are popular, surprisingly, most winter weekends.

   At the far end of the lake, the road is sandwiched between a rock face and the water, and you come to a neat picnic spot, *Bear Gulch,* which is a babbling stream, big trees and bridged. Then you're at *Staircase,* one of the 12 entrances to the Olympic National Park (one of 2 on Hood Canal). Ranger station, parking. Cross bridge and walk in ½ mile past giant prehistoric trees and along the north fork of the Skokomish, tumbling down a literal staircase of boulders —- noise resounds endlessly.

   For the car-cushion traveler there are spectacular views in the *Hamma Hamma Recreation Area* accessible through the Lake Cushman road via Jorsted Creek or west out of Eldon. Check your local forest ranger.

   At this point our tour returns us to the Skokomish "Y" and east on 106 where we encounter . . .

   Union — (Pop. Nom. Elev. 10.) — This was Union City in 1890 — and had been for over 30 years, but they really began to believe their own propaganda when the Union Pacific dropped in with crews of men to start railroading. Acres were selling for 1,000 bucks apiece and they had the usual "terminal" disease of the day — which terminated with the panic of 1893. Finis to the "city" part was marked by the postal service in 1904. It's now a marina-grocery-gas station town, plus Hoodpoint Oyster Co., "fresh oysters daily."

   But they still have an abiding sense of humor. There are two memorial monuments in town . . . one of the ubiquitous Captain George Vancouver and the other to Frans Philip Johnson. And Johnson has all the better of it, because his is in the form of a drinking fountain. He's been honored because he was the handiest handyman for miles around.

   A word about eating and sleeping — One of the finest and oldest resorts in Western Washington is the *Alderbrook Golf and Yacht Club* at Union. Most generally it is known to us old folks as *Alderbrook Inn.* It was born in 1913 on 10 acres of the kind of beach and gently sloping property everybody wishes he owned on the Canal. It now occupies 435 acres and has year-around accommodations which include hotel and motel rooms and an excellent dining room . . . once was listed by Life Magazine as one of the few "Famous Roadside Inns of America For Fine Foods . . . " Gives you a dandy place to satisfy the inner man and put your head on a nice pillow in the midst of a lot of scenic attractions . . . great for meetings, retreats and conventions *Robin Hood Inn*, near Union, dining room and coffee shop in steep red-roofed lodge under the trees. Homemade pie, quality food and atmosphere.

Uncommon shopping — One of our favorites is the *Flagwood Gift Shop*. It has items in keeping with the high caliber of Alderbrook, and is within strolling distance, as is the Dalby Waterwheel nearby, a moss-covered, fern-shaded relic of a past era.

This is the popular, populated side of the east Great Bend (we doubt if the residents like it called the appendix or hook, both of which it resembles). Varied and attractive homes abound here, many are newer shingled and "articulated shed roof" styles. Past *Twanoh State Park* — great trails, swimming, flora, and very popular (see *Footloose*, p. 214), the road goes to another "Y" where this route swings south on Highway 3 to . . .

Allyn — (Pop. Nom. Elev. Sea level.) — Allyn got its start in a big way in about 1854 with a guy named Joe Sherwood who was known as the "Hercules of Allyn." He was 6 feet 7 inches tall, weighed 300 pounds and operated that most cantankerous of all production lines, a sawmill run by a waterwheel. Allyn's a center for the production of about 600,000 bushels of green huckleberry . . . 17,500 of red berry "huck," 300,000 of salal, and 99,400 of sword fern that you'll see on the ferries en route to the floral shops of the United States.

And this is about as good a time as any to bring in some statistics that mellow the hearts of the folks in Mason County, and give Shelton the sobriquet "Christmastown U.S.A."

The world's greatest Christmas tree growers live in Mason County, utilizing 80,000 acres for the promulgation of an annual crop of some 2,000,000 trees worth from a buck to a buck and a half apiece to the county's economy. Some 200 people are employed year-around and during the pre-Christmas rush an additional 1,000 get $20 a day for 6 weeks.

It takes 10 to 12 years to bring in a Christmas tree orchard and from then on there's a sustained yield of about 40 trees to the acre. The objective is "trees that are dense, uniform, dark green with fresh green foliage and a well-balanced crown with evenly spaced whorls that sweep gently upwards . . ."

There's a whorl of difference to Mason County trees, which brightens the eyes of kids as far south as Mexico City and west to the Philippines. About 80% of the crop is sold in California.

Worth seeing here in Allyn is the 1909 Congregational Church now rendering religious services to the tune of the Episcopalians as *St. Hugh's Episcopal Community Church.* And this church by any name is just as sweet, with a stone from Lincoln Cathedral in England embedded in the altar. (Saint Hugh is buried there.) An impressive attraction is a beautiful carved wooden lectern in the shape of an eagle and made in New York in 1840. It looks a lot like a toy church, but the average attendance annually is 54 a week.

You might inquire locally as to where you can see one of the most spectacular petroglyphs on Puget Sound. It's 3 to 4 feet high and 20 feet long, on the beach above the high tide mark at Case Inlet.

If you haven't tried oysters yet — or if you have — *Sargent's Oyster Company* here has some of the finest around.

From Allyn, take the waterfront road past the "exercise" islands, Reach and Stretch.

Grapeview — (Pop. Nom. Elev. Sea level.) — This is sort of the gateway to Stretch Island and consists mostly of a post office. On the Island is the old winery where the Island Belle grapes — better for juice than wine — were developed beginning in 1878. You can pick your own during the fall and the rest of the year there are some of the memorabilia of the winery, ships models and pictures of the old days in *The Olde Winery-Bottles, Antiques, Ship Museum.* Perhaps you also can see the 100-year-old grapevine, 12 to 18 inches thick with a 30-foot spread. There also is an 1890 house on the beach — not for visiting.

Back to the mainland and continuing along Pickering Passage, with its open, sloping farms and vineyards, you come to the *Werberger Winery,* the last remaining winery in the area. It imports its grapes for the wine it bottles, but you can pick for yourself in the fall and during the rest of the year picnic at a nice place provided for that purpose by the winery and see their operation.

Grapenut note: The 4-H Club here is called the "Grapenuts."

You go back to Highway 3 for a short distance to get the road to Hartstene.

Hartstene —*Hartstine . . . Hartstein . . .* take your pick. An enormous Island with a new bridge is next down the pike. The Quadrant Corporation, a subsidiary of Weyerhaeuser, has constructed four sample duplex residential units and a community building for your contemplation. This is one of the first-rate 2nd home developments that the folks from Region 4 are fleeing to. Heavily wooded Island with most of the houses along the beaches and out of sight. There's a wonderful *State Marine Park* on Jarrell's Cove in an orchard and one of the few places around where manzanita is prolific and huge. Park is a big item for mariners, but car-cushion travelers can use it too. It also has pleasant picnic areas and a viewpoint of the jade green cove.

Uncommon shopping — Four miles south of bridge on Maple Road, signs lead you to *Hartstene Island Gallery,* where potters John and P. J. Dunlap do "Designs in Clay." He's an ex-Boeing engineer, living as he wants to. She does clay wall hangings, living as *she* wants to. Their pottery is much in demand at regional arts and craft shows.

Across the bridge back to the mainland, turn left and swing along the north side of Hammersley Inlet, with another view across to Shelton, and back through Agate to Highway 3 and return to Shelton.

Centralia - Chehalis Tour 1 — In and Around the Cities (Map XIII)

With a combined population of some 16,000 the Centralia-Chehalis urban complex represents more than a third of the total population of the largest county on the Wet Side of the Mountains, with Chehalis being the seat of Lewis County. Some 80% of the county is occupied by forest lands that for the most part are part of modern forestry techniques that treat timber as a crop. And the rest of the land is in grass. Lewis is the most "midwesty" county we have on the Wet Side and is the only one that doesn't border on some piece of navigable water. The political tenor of the two towns is conservative and the rivalry between them is not. Centralia is twice the size of Chehalis, but the latter charges that the population of Centralia was counted when the passenger train was standing in the station. Centralia is the north-south midpoint of the Wet Side, but is more oriented to Seattle, while Chehalis gravitates more to Portland. The Southwest Washington Fair, which has permanent fairgrounds between the two towns, attracts some 125,000 people every fall and is by far and away the biggest fair south of Puyallup. The two towns are nestled against the foothills leading to Rainier, which is slightly northeast of them, but open on the south to some of the most impressive prairie country on the Wet Side of the Mountains. Just north of Centralia, a magnificent electric-generating plant is digging into the nation's most abundant supply of fossil fuel-coal. The two towns border on the Chehalis River less than 4 miles apart but two separate rivers run through each town to join the Chehalis: The Skookumchuck (Centralia) and the Newaukum (Chehalis).

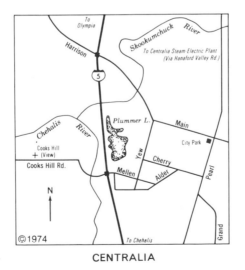

CENTRALIA

Centralia — (Pop. 10,207. Elev. 184.) — In the beginning, there was George Washington ... not the one who "fathered" our country, but a man of remarkable parts who platted the town in the original instance and then became independently wealthy with a dozen or more subsequent plats and may well have left a barrel of gold coins buried somewhere inside the city limits.

Mr. Washington also was black.

There's a marble bench in George Washington Park in the center of town commemorating Mr. Washington's contribution to the town. The park is on Washington Avenue. And Mr. Washington is buried somewhat obscurely in the George Washington Cemetery. But the color of his skin caused him a lot of trouble in his lifetime up to the point where someone tried to kill him by substituting a bottle of carbolic acid for the wine he kept on his nightstand. The attempt failed and he lived to the ripe age of 84 years.

In a fascinating pamphlet called *Centralia, The First Fifty Years*, the students of Centralia and English teacher Miss Herndon Smith, have compiled a remarkable tribute to this man born of a slave and a white English girl in Frederick County, Virginia on August 15, 1817. His father was sold to someone a distance away shortly after he was born and he was taken in by the family of James C. Cochran, which turned out to be the most important decision the Cochrans ever made because from the time of his maturity, he took care of them for the rest of their lives.

He could hit a tack in a piece of paper with a rifle bullet fired 40 yards away . . . cook . . . spin and weave and make all of his own clothing from shirts to suits. When schools in Missouri refused him entrance, he taught himself to read and write and do arithmetic. He was so skilled with an axe that he could lay a watertight floor that looked like it had been planed. He could tan his own hides to the point where they were soft as buckskin and knit himself a pair of long wool socks with double heels and toes in an hour-and-a-half.

He was of sufficient stature that the state of Missouri, by a special act of the legislature, granted him all of the prerogatives of a white man except that of holding public office, but another special act prohibited him from manufacturing whiskey which caused him to come west, bringing his foster parents with him. When Oregon territorial law prohibited the settlement of blacks, he transferred the title of this Centralia land to the Cochrans hours before a couple of white men tried to liberate him from it. The Cochrans subsequently deeded it back to him and he gave them $3,200 "so they might have ready money for any emergency . . . ."

When he was 52 years old, he married a woman with a son by a previous marriage . . . bought her the first sewing machine owned by anyone in the area. And she, in turn, helped him with the naming of the streets which still exist today as Diamond . . . Gold . . . Silver . . . Pearl . . . Iron . . . Rock . . . Oak . . . Cedar and Hemlock.

A neighbor from one of the southern states built an 8-ft. fence between them when he first arrived and then knocked a gate through it when he got to know "Uncle" George, who had a philosophy of life that "I want to do right by my fellow man, then I'll never lose anything by it."

A friend, Vernon Dunning, administered to him for 72 straight hours when an enemy had switched the bottle of carbolic acid for that of the wine and saved his life. Somebody else tipped him off that the banker was a crook. He took his money out in gold coins, becoming the only man ever to wheel a fortune in gold down the streets of Centralia in a wheelbarrow. And 3 weeks later the bank went belly up.

He was the only black man to found a town in this State.

And writing in the *Seattle Post-Intelligencer* for December 10, 1972, reporter Walter A. Evans noted, "but no blacks live in a town a black founded . . ."

The *brick railroad station* is listed as a National Historic Site.

The downtown still has many old brick buildings, brick streets . . . and has a "feel" of being old. It is updating and beautifying its central business district by adding landscaped parking — where a penny still buys you some time on the meter — and with pedestrian malls that cut through the middle of the block. And the most interesting of the old establishments is the *Olympic Club* which still has a cigar counter at the entrace so you won't be contaminated by exposure to booze if you just want to buy a cigarette, along with an iron fence that closes at night, swinging doors, leaded glass windows and a Tiffany lamp over the old mahogany bar. Customers shoot billiards near a coal-burning round oak stove.

Above the entrance in faded gold leaf lettering a sign of a bygone era reads: "Ladies' Patronage Not Solicited."

Not so faded is the memory of a dreadful Armistice Day of 1919 commemorated via the bronze statue of a World War I soldier in the city park. Centralia American Legionnaires started battering down the door of the IWW hall 3 doors north of Second Street on the west side of Tower Avenue. Angry members of the Industrial Workers of the World had anticipated the attack, opened fire from within the structure and from nearby promontories and buildings, killing three of the Legionnaires on the spot.

The fourth Legionnaire met his death from the revolver of a Wobbly he was pursuing near the river. (Wobblies reputedly got their name from a Chinese restaurant owner who catered to IWW clientele in Canada saying, "I likee Eye Wobbly Wobbly.")

The murderer died at the end of a rope attached to what for years was known locally as "Hangman's Bridge." (Now replaced.) The coroner's verdict was suicide and two days later, the *Portland Oregonian* noted on Page 1 that the man had broken out of jail . . . fled to the river . . . hanged himself . . . climbed up to the bridge again and changed ropes . . . jumped again . . . shot himself several times . . . cut the rope . . . and finally drowned in the river . . .

Some suicide!

The rest of the Wobblies were hunted by posses, one of which came across a man in the woods while combing the countryside. The posse shot him down before it learned that he was not a Wobbly, but a member of another posse. This was unofficially listed as an "unlawful error."

A number of the Wobblies were convicted and an appeal upheld on the grounds they were not protecting life and property when they opened fire from up and down and across the street, but the saddest epitaph was laid on by the son of the Legionnaire shot in the woods when he said to the men who killed his father, "I don't blame you fellows. Don't think that I do for a minute. It's tough to lose Dad — but you fellows did your duty."

◆

The most spectacular event in Centralia's recent history, however, is the advent of the $237,000,000 Centralia Steam-Electric Project which has made Lewis County the largest producer of electric power of any county in the State.

Of particular significance is the fact that more than 10% of the total project was incorporated in new features of operation like the ash condenser to protect our environment with the very latest technological advances in this field.

There's a total of at least 500 million tons of coal in the presently explored area with seams that vary in thickness from 8 to 50 feet. Earth and rock on top of the coal is removed with a gigantic, 56-yard dragline shovel and set aside. A mine shovel digs the coal and the company replaces its huge divots with the good soil that has been set aside. And this is where the grass and tim-ber-growing capacity of the land comes into important play. A Douglas fir forest needs open land for reforestation. And while the grass holds the earth in the beginning, nursery trees also are planted as the mining proceeds . . . so that when the coal supply has been exhausted a crop of valuable Douglas fir will replace it. The whole operation is a tribute to the ingenuity of man and his new technological knowledge of the natural processes here.

Everything about it is the biggest and best and most. Coal was disco-vered in the county well before 1900 and by the turn of the century, mines were turning out a whopping (for the time) 100 tons a day. (It takes some 20,000 tons a day to feed the maw of the present monster.) Coal production lasted until the 1930's when diesel took over the power for the railroad locomotives that passed through Centralia regularly and refueled . . . a change that proved to be an economic body blow to the town. They had a saying about the coal in the old days . . . that you put in a bucket of the stuff and got out two buckets of ashes. Under present-day technology it is cleaned and ground into a fine powder that burns about like gas. In order to get one ton of clean coal, 5 tons of earth and rock must be removed — and at this new plant they figure to move 6,000,000 tons of coal annually.

They do this with enormous equipment — like a machine with a boom the length of a football field. But the control room is one of the most remarkable pieces of gadgetry concocted by the mind of man. One individual in this room can run the entire plant except for the coal mining and preparation. Throughout the plant are 1,100 nerve ends for the computer in the control room. If anything goes wrong, lights flash and buzzers sound and the computer's printout machine ticks out a written record of what got busted or burned.

Television cameras are trained to monitor the furnaces and the gauge showing the water level. The operator is telemetrically in touch with the Skookumchuck Dam 10 miles away. He can control the amount of water released from the dam and then recover this water from a pumping station 12 miles downstream from the dam. He also can direct the activity feeding coal into the plant.

We were lucky enough to encounter Bob Beadnell of Pacific Power and Light, which is one of the prime movers of the project. A personable and persuasive man with a lot of knowledge about power needs, Beadnell gave us some food for thought about power prognosticators and the future of the plant.

In 1918 when horses and mules were our chief source of motive power and there were 25,000,000 of them (the highest in history), they were eating up one-fourth of the harvested crop acreage in this country. At that time, prognosticators were predicting that the product of all arable land in the country would be needed just to feed power animals within the next 50 years . . .

And we would be up to our you-know-what in horse manure.

The point of that is that while the supply of coal here may be limited to 5 or 10 years, it buys us time for new technological advances in solving our ever-increasing energy needs.

Prowling Centralia

The *Steam-Electric Plant* is about 12 miles north of Centralia in the Hanaford Valley. The road's good and there's a viewing platform from which visitors can take in the whole operation. A Centralia miss, landscape architect Jane Garrison, who did the landscaping for the central business district of Centralia, also is applying the same talent to the landscaping around the plant.

To see other scenic drives — especially in the spring — try *Cook's Hill Road*; Mellen Street west up the hill, for a great view; or the community of *Grand Mound*, northwest of town for colorful prairie flowers. The *Centralia Timberland Library* at the City Park is one of the few Carnegie Libraries still surviving in its original building . . . and for a look at some *fine old homes* try Mrs. Washington's Iron, Maple, Pearl, Silver or First Streets. The *Lewis County Game Farm*, Mt. Vista Road, produces 12,000 Chinese pheasants annually to make hunting attractive, and welcomes visitors interested in seeing how the birds are raised. *Fort Borst Park*, located on a small lake, has an original blockhouse from the days of the Indian Wars of 1856 along with picnic tables, cooking facilities and play areas for the kids. There also is older and more casual *Riverside Park* with similar facilities along the Skookumchuck.

Centralia Community College on Oak Street does about higher education for this combined prairie and mountain area. You can snack at the college cafeteria, if you've a mind to.

If you want to see "State Fair" come to life, be here in August for *Southwest Washington Fair* time. It's like nothing else on the Wet Side. The facilities of both towns are jam-packed for the 6 days and activities range back and forth between Centralia and Chehalis — with the fairgrounds in dead center. With lively *Morton's Logger Jubilee* (40 miles east) combining at the same time to draw the big crowds to this area, it doesn't seem possible anybody can be at home in the rest of southwest Washington at fair time.

The fair grounds get big use all year — by about 200,000 people . . . of these about 125,000 come for the main fair, which is third largest in Western Washington.

Magyar (Hungarian) Museum, old Highway 99, has a large collection of dolls, Indian and Eskimo exhibit, Australian collection.

Uncommon shopping — The *Look Nook Antiques*, 803 N. Washington, some antiques and collectibles in Mrs. Hayward's home.

A word about eating – *Hallmark Restaurant*, Harrison St., is new and efficient at largest motel in area . . . *Nor'wester*, Alder St., pleasant, with cheerful waitresses, and apple crisp in season . . . *Chef John's Steak House*, S. Gold St., family place for locals, who like the salad table . . . *King Solomon's*, Mellen St., attractive atmosphere . . . *C & B Cafe*, Harrison St., family-style with homemade soups and pies. You can eat breakfast at 6 a.m., lunch until 4 p.m.; dinner on Friday and Saturday . . . *The Country Cousin*, Harrison St., barn siding walls, hung with farm tools and equipment, but city-slicker type menu.

A word about sleeping – *Hallmark Inn*, Harrison St., resort-type facilities . . . *Lake Shore*, Lakeshore Dr., rooms open out to small lake . . . *The Park*, Belmont St. and *Motel Ambeau*, Alder St. also are good.

Annual affairs – *Lawn and Garden Show* in March . . . *Rabbit and Primrose shows* in April . . . *Appaloosa Horse Show* in June . . . all in July — *Buck and Kids Goat Show, Motorcycle Races*, a very good *Rose Show*, and *Arts and Crafts Fair*, sponsored by Orthopedic Guild, luncheon, artists and craftsmen at work . . . for Centralia and Chehalis, biggest is the *Southwest Washington Fair*, second week in August . . . *Washington and Oregon Horse Game Finals*, Labor Day weekend . . . most spectacular event, *Horseless Carriage Swap Meet*, in September . . . all in December — *Boy Scout Show, Indian Three-Feather Fair* and *Northwest Pigeon Show*.

For further information — Chamber of Commerce, 500 N. Pearl. or call 736-3161.

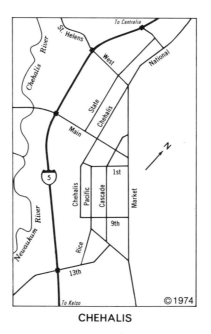

CHEHALIS

Chehalis — (Pop. 5,727. Elev. 185.) — It's sort of hard to believe that Chehalis is semiofficially listed as a foot higher than Centralia because it started out life as Saunders' Bottom, eminently qualifying it for a book called *The Wet Side of the Mountains* because a lot of people stopped here whether they wanted to or not. They couldn't go forwards or backwards, sideways or up.

They were bogged down in a donation claim taken by a guy by the name of S. S. Saunders.

It was a swampy spot at the foot of a promontory euphoniously referred to as Mud Mountain on the main-traveled trail from Fort Vancouver to Olympia. And as apt a description as any of the conditions there "even in September" comes from the one given by George B. Roberts who told a historian, "The road through this bottom in the wintertime was a terrible road to travel. It was almost impassable, being in many places little better than a lake, its soil being of a sticky, stiff, muddy character . . . even in September . . .

"One time I was wading through the bottom, myself and horse covered with mud, when I came upon old John Southerland, a man well-known to many old and new settlers in Pierce County, with an overturned wagon and four horses in the middle of one of the worst mud-holes. Legs, shoulders and sides of bacon were scattered all about, and poor John was in a deplorable condition."

An interesting observation to be made here is that old Southerland wasn't in the least bit worried about his condition.

He knew that John R. Jackson would come along and "save his bacon."

We like to think this is where that expression originated — right here in Chehalis.

And if anybody could save anybody's bacon in those days, it was John R. Jackson whose farm, The Highlands, was located at the high point between the Cowlitz and Chehalis Rivers and who, with the aid of his stepsons, built the first courthouse in the Territory. It's a sixteen-by-twenty-six-foot cabin that still is preserved off old Highway 99 twelve miles south of Chehalis.

Old one-eyed John (he lost his left eye in a thicket in Scotland during his youth) was a lusty, long-legged Yorkshireman, sharp and smart in a trade deal. He sold a $150 team of horses once for $300 and the guy who bought them wondered to his dying day why he had paid so much. And John was in a key location for making a buck. At the age of 48, John lucked out and married a widow by the name of Matilda Koontz who not only provided him with four lusty boys, but was the best cook anywhere for miles around. John's house became a favorite hostelry for people heading into Puget Sound, and boasted such eminent travelers as Ulysses S. Grant . . . Philip Sheridan, George B. McClellan and Isaac I. Stevens — something Matilda never forgot although she outlived her husband by 17 years.

Immigrants to the country who wanted to become naturalized citizens and land some of that donation land had to visit Jackson's courthouse. They found hospitality at Jackson's house (and "court" house). Among other things, for instance, Jackson was the first assessor of the first county (Lewis) of what has become the State of Washington. The folks in Clark County are inclined to dispute this, just as they dispute whether Clark or Lewis was the real head of the Lewis and Clark Expedition. But the dates give Lewis County the edge in this argument. On the other hand, the Lewis County people like to think that Jackson was the first American settler north of the Columbia when Thurston County's Mike Simmons should get the nod.

Anyway, the immigrants had to visit Jackson's courthouse where they found a shrewd, likable trader who was willing to do business.

Jackson's contemporaries opine that many a foreigner became a naturalized citizen of the Unites States without answering any of those tough questions immigrants get thrown at them today . . . without knowing that the country had a constitution . . . or even a president.

Either way, John prospered without breaking his back as a farmer and the route through Chehalis — Saunders' Bottom to the contrary and notwithstanding — became part of the main-traveled route to Puget Sound, which it still is.

And John lived long enough to help save some financial "bacon" for the United States in an argument over land value with the Hudson's Bay Compnay. As one of the landowners he testified on land values when the United States was arguing with the Hudson's Bay Company over how much money it had coming (See Pig War, Region 1.)

When the Northern Pacific first came through Saunders' Bottom in 1871, the company tried to make a deal for land with Eliza Barrett, Saunders' widow, but she wanted too much money, so the company platted a townsite on Newaukum Hill 3 miles south. But the only way of getting to the hill was along the railroad track and across a trestle, which annoyed the folks to no end, so a delegation called on General J. W. Sprague, superintendent of the line in Kalama.

That had to be one of the world's classic mistakes because Sprague was the guy who had bought the 40 acres on which the station and hopefully, from Sprague's standpoint, a new town called Newaukum would be built.

But during the visit, Sprague let an important cat out of the bag.

If a red flag was waved, the train had to stop.

So the folks at Saunders' Bottom got themselves some red bunting and flagged down the train every time it came through. Finally the railroad decided it was cheaper to use a warehouse the folks had thoughtfully provided at that location than to start a competing town on the hill.

In 1875, Saunders' Bottom (nee Saundersville) became the County Seat and in 1879, the legislature converted the name to Chehalis and folks are about evenly divided over whether that means in Indian "shining" or "shifting" sands. Anyway there's a lot of sand around and a lot of references to Chehalis. It's at the confluence of the Newaukum and Chehalis Rivers.

It's a pity the I. P. Callison Company doesn't have tours because it probably is the largest producer of mint extract in the world — like for Wrigley's Gum and MacLean's toothpaste — and grinds the bark of the cascara tree for commercial laxatives. This is the most fertile cascara country in the world and a lot of folks around and about make a buck gathering the bark for Callison.

Periodically, when the wind is right, you get a real whiff of mint in town and some years ago, we utilized that lovely odor with telling effect. We handled the publicity for the opening of Callison's new mint reduction plant and put a few drops of peppermint essence in the envelopes containing the news releases. When those envelopes were opened in city rooms throughout the northwest, every newspaper in the area knew a freshly "minted" news release had arrive.

There is a further phenomenon that makes Chehalis important.

It is called Mary McCrank.

Mary has a restaurant a few miles south of the city limits on the old Highway 99 where she has been serving home-cooking for approximately 40 years and when later historians cover this same territory, they'll rate her right along with Matilda Jackson as one of the finest cooks the region has ever known. Mary is outspoken with Irish wit and warmth, frequently critical and often annoys the local folks, but the world beats a gastronomic pathway to her door. No booze, and her chicken is like the kind that grandmothers who knew their way around a wood stove cooked. Mary's greatest pride is that actor Charles Laughton (of Henry VIII fame) once ate there. Better try her midweek and midwinter or you may have to wait in line.

About the Wet Side of the Mountains, Mary opined, "Why not? If California can sell its sunshine, we should be able to sell our rain."

Prowling Chehalis

There's an *International Rose Garden* in the park at City Hall on the upper side of Market Street, and try *Pennsylvania Avenue* and higher up the hill to see where wealthy Chehalins live. The red brick *railroad station* is worth a passing fancy and the *Lewis County Historical Museum* on Washington St. has regional pioneer items, Chehalis Indian art, children's toys and dolls; 1-4 Thursday and Sunday afternoons or call Mrs. Charles Deichman, 736-4319.

Try *Newaukum Hill* for view of 3 mountains, Rainier, St. Helens, and Adams. Take the *Coal Creek Road* (across from Wayne's Photos) to Logan Hill Road and back the north fork of the Newaukum — where you also might find some agates — and then back to Old 99 south of Mary McCrank's. For additional entertainment try driving to *Wallace's Wild Animal Farm and Glass Blower* (an interesting combo) a few miles south of town on Interstate 5. *Recreation Park* near the 13th Street entrance, has an outdoor swimming pool, kitchens, picnic tables, a locomotive and the *McKinley Stump*, Chehalis' pride and joy and mentioned in any mention of Chehalis.

McKinley, of course, never spoke from the McKinley stump although it was cut in Pe Ell for that purpose. Original tree was 300 feet high and produced 30,000 board feet of lumber which made the whole thing worthwhile even if the president was a "no show." *Matilda Jackson State Park* is 6 miles south, *Lewis and Clark State Park* 8 miles south, *John R. Jackson Courthouse* is between the two parks — all three are on old Highway 99.

Uncommon shopping – *Orange Door Gallery* where local artist Hallie Schuster has a shop behind her home, open from 9-5 Thanksgiving to Christmas Eve or by appointment . . . *La Plaunts Antiques,* with glassware, furniture, some American and some European . . . *Roscoe Doane,* Market St., has a skylight gallery of watercolors, like of the Claquato Church, and at 82 loves to talk with people . . . monthly antique auction managed by *Dowling's Antiques,* Chehalis Ave.

A word about eating — See copy above for *Mary McCrank's Dinner Inn* and make your plans accordingly. Homemade pies, corn relish, jam, in an old-fashioned, comfortable house . . . if you like peanut butter pie, try *Kit*

Carson's, Kelly Rd. . . . *Candlelight Cuisine*, Market St., serves country break-fasts, merchant lunches, and candlelight dinners . . . *Pine Gardens*, National Ave., is a Chinese-family-operation whose fried shrimp lures the locals.

A word about sleeping — *Cascade Motel*, Kelly Rd. at 13th St. has comfortable accommodations and peanut butter pie next door.

Annual affairs – Most affairs are at the fairgrounds (see Centralia).

For further information — Chamber of Commerce, 886 Market St., or phone 748-8885.

◆

Centralia-Chehalis Tour 2 — Pe Ell, Winlock, Toledo, Salkum, Mossyrock, Morton (Maps XIII & XIV)

This tour first takes you west along Highway 6, through prairie and farm to the summit of the Willapa Hills, an enormous tree-farming region (as a side trip). It then follows the main route south by which the settlers came from the Cowlitz River to settle Puget Sound, past Winlock which has the biggest fiberglass egg in the world, to Toledo, which once was the head of navigation of the Cowlitz, and into Salkum, which has the most modern fish hatchery in the world, and past the Mossyrock Dam, which is the highest in the state, through Morton, which still has a substantial population of people who migrated here from the Appalachian Mountains of Kentucky, West Virginia and Virginia. It then enters the southern portion of Mt Rainier National Park thru the northern part of Gifford Pinchot National Forest, which rivals the North Cascades area as an impressive piece of Washington Wilderness. The route returns through some of the Wet Side's most extensive prairie country with a side trip to Mary's Corner and the Jackson Courthouse, the first north of the Cowlitz . . . with the original building still standing.

Head west out of Chehalis on the Willapa Hills Road (Highway 6). It is unusual in that about half of it follows the Chehalis River to the summit of the hills, and if you were to continue to Raymond and South Bend, you would parallel the Willapa. This is beautiful river valley country with grassy pastures and lots of hay and corn fields. It's a gently curving road with prosperous-looking homes and big barns along with a lot of dairy cattle. One of the barns we like looks a little like a red and white pin-stripe suit. From time to time, you are reminded of the crop of trees dominating 80% of the country by the logging trains coming down out of the mountains. There are lots of railroad bridges across the Chehalis which follows a leisurely, winding course at this point. As you get into the foothills you find a lot of land dedicated to Christmas Tree crops — with U-Pick signs on them. The road is fast if you want it to be, but it is realtively untraveled and conducive to a leisurely pace. The hills look old and worn down, reminiscent of the Scottish Highlands, and close in after you as you take your turning route to the summit.

Rainbow Falls State Park — is on the Chehalis and has one foot on the prairie and another in the foothills. Picnic facilities are near 4 or 5 tumbling falls cutting through the rock on broad steps.

Pe Ell — (Pop. 540. Elev. 412.) — Pe Ell, which still is in the prairie, once was big in lumbering and may be again. But at the moment, it's a little like a ghost town in an open valley where the Chehalis River has just come down from its beginning over Huckleberry Ridge. There are proper little mill-type houses around the main street along with a clear evidence they still cater to the satisfaction of the inner man: The baker and the liquor store are one and the same enterprise.

Continuing west about 1½ miles you gain about 300 feet in altitude and come to the summit of the Willapa Hills at . . .

Pluvius — (Pop. Nom. Elev. 746.) — It was named Pluvius by an early homesteader who testily observed that it had rained cats and dogs for 362 consecutive days and recalled that it "was most damnably cloudy" the other three. But he stayed on and on, seeming to delight in cursing and reviling the place.

Though once listed in the U.S. Postal Guide, there appears to have been no official postmaster ever appointed, or any actual post office ever established. There was once, however, a station for the Northern Pacific Railroad. Local report is that: "This place was named by Mr. E. H. McHenry, former Chief Engineer of the Northern Pacific. The name is from Jupiter Pluvius, the Roman god of rain, and is due to the fact that it rained incessantly during the construction of the line of the Yakima & Pacific Coast Railroad. The station was established in 1892."

Oregon historian and author, the late Stewart Holbrook, once reported that he could find not one single sun dial in Pluvius. You cross a bridge, one end of which is the Chehalis River drainage basin and the other in the Willapa River basin.

Our route now calls for a return to the *Claquato Church* and State Highway 603, although from Pluvius the road continues to Willapa Bay. The church was resurrected from the dead about 10 years ago and has been restored with pride by the locals around here as the oldest Protestant Church in the State. It originally was built as part of one man's contribution to an effort to make this spot the county seat. The tower is an excellent example of mortise and tenon work. Erected in 1853, it stands on a small hill beside a cemetery overlooking the valley.

This route goes south through Napavine, which was a big logging community half a century ago, but has settled down to more of a trading center for people who like to live in a spot with a good view of Mt. Rainier. You're following the route the early settlers took going north from Cowlitz Landing to Puget Sound overland. Presumably it was a little less muddy than the trail closer to the river because the Federal Government made this the military road . . . and the grades must be okay, too, for you're closely paralleling the main line of the railroad to Portland and California along in here.

You'll be heading southeast when you come to . . .

Winlock — (Pop. 896. Elev. 308.) — We kind of hate to do this to you, but not enough so we won't, and we call upon a variation of the famous quote from so many murder mysteries: "Eggs marks the spot."

It all started in the 1920's when the completion of Highway 99 all the way from Seattle to Salem, Oregon, was just about the biggest event of the decade for the Pacific Northwest. To celebrate the occasion, the towns along the route were asked to enter floats in a caravan that would make its triumphant trip between the two cities.

Winlock wasn't exactly on Highway 99, but who cared . . . and the more the merrier. There were a lot of Finns in the area with 10-acre tracts and small flocks of chickens. And somebody got the bright idea of mounting a paper-mache egg on a truck as the key symbol of the community effort. Well it turned out to be a great idea and a smash hit. And it got the town of Winlock more attention than it ever had enjoyed.

When the folks who had joined the parade got back home, everybody was pretty enthusiastic about the attendant publicity, and they decided to improve and enlarge on the situation. So they erected a big concrete egg on top of a couple of 20-foot poles near the railroad tracks and announced that this was the "Egg and Poultry Capital" of the Pacific Northwest. This was a great idea and attracted a lot of attention.

The fact that it was not the Egg and Poultry Capital of the Northwest came under the heading of nonessential information. King County was number 1 at the time, followed by Whatcom and Pierce, but *they* had a lot of other things besides chickens to crow about. And Winlock, which was number 4 for about half a century, made up for its lack of production in a thing called enthusiasm. Who could fault a town for being enthusiastic about eggs? Not King, Whatcom and Pierce which were tossing the top three spots around among themselves until Whatcom took over the permanent number 1 spot a decade or so ago. It would be like putting down motherhood.

A couple of disasters struck the Winlock egg production. New methods of feeding made it uneconomic for the small farmer to compete in the marketplace, which drove the majority of the folks in the egg business in Winlock into some other kind of endeavor. Then in 1963, the heavy blow fell. Dry rot set into the posts holding up the big concrete egg. And, as Dick Sarvella, the Egg Day Chairman in 1973, said with practiced urbanity, "Like Humpty Dumpty, it had a great fall and broke into 1,000 pieces."

A large body of the constituency in town — aware that Winlock was losing ground fast in the egg-production statistics of the Pacific Northwest were pretty gol darned sure that if the King's men had been unable to put Humpty Dumpty together again, there was nobody in Winlock capable of that miracle.

But they reckoned without some of the old timers in the Lions Club . . . you know, men who remembered that the first egg producer in Winlock was a man named Gordon Egbert. So there was the usual division of opinion that comes to a town over whether or not the tradition should continue . . . and, by golly, the pro-egg people won out. The Lions Club raised the $1,500 necessary to get a new egg . . . and they put her on a pedestal. The Winlock Garden Club did the landscaping around it, and every year the Lions paint it up all fresh for the annual Winlock Egg Day in mid-June.

They took a couple of precautions this time, however. Sober heads pointed out that egg production in the county had slid so badly some of the stores were shipping eggs in from out of county. So, instead of noting that Winlock was the Egg and Poultry Capital of the Northwest, the new sign accompanying the new egg reports that this is the *"largest egg in the world!"*

The new egg is made of fiberglass and if it comes tumbling down, it may go rolling down the road, but it won't break.

Next time you're in the neighborhood in June, plan to drop in for Egg Day, which always falls on a Saturday. The VFW and the American Legion — and their Auxiliaries — cook 100 dozen eggs and make them into egg-salad sandwiches. You'll be safe. The men do the boiling and chopping. It's the women who do the sandwich-making.

A parade starts at the south end of Main Street and winds clear through town, across the railroad tracks and the highway and the bridge over Olequa Creek and right up to the Winlock Miller Elementary School. The whole two blocks of the parade route is lined with between 3,000 and 4,000 spectators.

Everybody's there except the women making the egg-salad sandwiches in the grade school cafeteria. And when the parade's over, everybody, including the women making the egg-salad sandwiches, has a great feed.

Winlock may not be number one in eggs . . .

But it sure is Number One in Egg-Salad Sandwiches!

Several thousand words have been written about the fear and wonderment which struck the hearts of man at the sight of the Yacolt Burn in 1902, but none of such direct simplicity as those penned by C. C. Wall, in the *Lewis County News* in Winlock, 70 years after the holocaust.

The Yacolt Burn is the name given some 100 forest fires that exploded simultaneously in some 700,000 acres ranging from Bellingham, Washington to Eugene, Oregon and from the summit of the Cascade Mountains to the sea. It took the lives of countless animals and 35 human beings and scared the hell out of everybody who witnessed it. Cinders covered all of Portland to a depth of half an inch and they had to turn the lights on in every town in the disaster area at noon on September 13.

The most dramatic deaths were those described by Stewart H. Holbrook in a book called *Burning An Empire*. Two families, comprising a party of 11 people, including a baby and 5 other children were heading up the north fork of the Lewis River for Trout Lake on a picnic. They were about 2 miles above the Yale post office when it happened, and Holbrook knew what he was writing about when he wrote, "Down a draw in the hills came a sheet of flame, roaring like a hurricane, exploding into balls of fire that went off like torpedoes. . . ." None of the party lived to tell the tale, but an experienced man like Holbrook and others acquainted with forest fires could read the telltale signs . . . the blackened iron hoops of the wagon were there . . . the bodies of the people who had only gotten 150 feet. The two horses had been unhitched. Humans and horses had headed for Speelyai Creek, less than 100 yards away. None had made it. This story was repeated with varying degrees of drama with the other 24 people who met fiery deaths.

At the time, each individual community thought that it alone was experiencing the holocaust, but afterwards, foresters pieced the whole conflagration together. The consensus was that fires of one kind or another had been smouldering since May. On September 9, an east wind as dry as tinder began to come down out of the Cascades. The sleeping fires began to awaken the next day. Each fire created its own local wind that sent it scurrying down the nearest draw. On September 11, the relative humidity dropped to the vanishing point.

Holbrook put it this way: "No one who has not seen the fury of a fire in the Douglas fir country can have any conception of how mighty it can grow in a brief time. A Douglas fir jungle has almost the same explosive properties as a pile of gunpowder, a great big pile. When a fire gets going in this jungle it is said to blow up. This is about the only term to describe it . . . . "

Most writers have attempted to encompass the fire in terms of human enterprise . . . like a farmer burning slash here . . . or sparks from a logging locomotive there. But the truth is that God created the conditions that caused the Yacolt Burn. Douglas fir forests can't regenerate themselves in the shade of other trees. And Nature was simply manifesting one stage in the forest management process that had been in existence for centuries. It just happened that mankind was a witness to this one. And while the foresters were able to reduce the conflagration to technical terms — after the fact — the human beings exposed to it *felt* the fury of the flames.

In the towns nearest to them, people were convinced that Mt. Rainier . . . Mt. St. Helens or Mt. Hood were erupting. In Woodland a religious revival meeting echoed a widespread feeling by shouting, "Glory to God! The last days have come!"

As man has assumed tighter control of the forests, the fires have lessened. But there have been nine major fires in and around Yacolt, in Clark County, since the terrible fire of 1902. Firelanes and a network of roads built by the timber companies and the Department of Natural Resources . . . lookouts, aerial fire fighting techniques and tight controls over logging practices have virtually eliminated another burn like the one called Yacolt (although, ironically, the town of Yacolt, itself, was spared). But the thought still should be yours when you contemplate throwing away that match. And, as we mentioned earlier, C. C. Wall laid it on the line the best.

The Lewis County News in Winlock reproduced the story on January 20, 1972 from a history of the area written by Wall. And it related to the Yacolt Burn.

"My grandfather, Bryson Wall," he wrote, "wanted to telegraph to New York to see if it was dark there. Someone asked him what he thought of it and he replied, 'Well, I think we've just been living too fast, and God Almighty is putting on the brakes.'

"About 11 a.m. the sun began to break through the screen. When it first broke through it had all the appearance in the world of a huge red ball of fire.

"At this time quite a few persons went on their knees and started praying. Then as the sun dissipated more of the smoke, the red fiery condition began spreading over the heavens. It was then that several women in town ran to the mill to be with their husbands when the end came . . . . "

And that's when Wall, who was a child at the time, had to make his determination about the safest place on earth.

He wrote: "It certainly did look like the end. The writer was at the store with his Daddy, until this red fiery situation came about, but Daddy wasn't comfort and protection enough then, so I hightailed it for home to be with my Mama when the end came."

This route continues southeast on 603 to the freeway and then a scant distance south to the Toledo or Highway 505 exit. You are driving into Grand and Cowlitz Prairies, part of a 300-square-mile open prairie stretch in the heart of the inland Wet Side. Noticeably this is grassy country with oak trees and wild flowers like the bright blue camas, an edible bulb used by the Indians as we use the potato.

Toledo — (Pop. 639. Elev. 142.) — What they've got going for them here is history and monkey business. The history stems in part form the fact this was the head of navigation for the Cowlitz River for a long time.

In "nostalgicating," if there is such a word, you can do a better job of getting into a proper mood if you're armed with the following facts: This was the main route, bar none, for the tide of immigrants from Portland-Vancouver to Puget Sound. Oceangoing steamships were few and far between and the trip up the coast was perilous to say the least. And it hung in there as the principal thoroughfare for 67 years — a lot longer than either Highway 99 or Interstate 5 have been in existence.

Beginning in 1851, there was the Cowlitz River Canoe and Bateau Line, but as wheat, barley, oats and produce began to be cultivated in the prairie, they needed stern-wheel riverboats to handle the trade. Fittingly enough, the first one was the *Cowlitz*, built in 1857 for this trade. It was 76 feet long, 17 feet wide and drew 3 feet 6 inches of draft. Five years later, the trade was so brisk it erupted in a price war among the little steamers, many of which were no more than a disreputable shack on a raft with a paddle wheel at the stern.

It took 24 hours to go from Toledo, the head of navigation, to Portland and cost a buck. They stopped anywhere there was anything to pick up from a can of milk to a ton of hay. Meals were 25c. During the price war, that's what the price of the passage dropped to.

In 1879, the *Toledo,* which was 109 feet long and drew 4 feet, entered the trade and it was from this craft that the town got its name.

The *Chester,* which entered the trade in 1897, and plied the river until 1918, was the bloody-end in shallow-draft riverboats. It set the pattern for boats in the Alaska Gold Rush trade in the following year and brought a new up-river penetration for the boats of the Mosquito Fleet. Wagons could just drive alongside the *Chester* and transfer passengers or freight. Brought in by the Kellogg family, famous in these parts, she was a hundred feet long.

She could navigate channels a foot deep . . .

And old-timers said she could travel the Cowlitz River in a "heavy dew."

To refresh your memory a little and counteract all that propaganda they pump out about the Monticello Convention in Longview, we will give you a few dates and places in Washington's history. For the first five years after we signed that agreement with Great Britain to settle the "54-40 or fight!" fight, the Oregon Territory extended from California to the Canadian border. The Capital of the Territory was way to hell and gone down in the Willamette Valley, which annoyed the guys in Puget Sound all to pieces. Not only was Puget Sound the tail of the dog, it never got wagged.

So, as part of the Fourth of July Celebration in Olympia in 1851, a fella named John Chapman give a big oration about dividing up the existing territory at the Columbia River and naming the area north thereof "Columbia." One thing led to another and on August 29, 1851 they had a convention at Cowlitz Landing — which to all practical purposes these days was Toledo. And they fired a memorial off to Congress which ended up with: "The committee most respectfully requests that Congress will pass an act organizing a separate territorial government north of the Columbia River; with the immunities and privileges of her most favoured territorie, and that the territory be known and designated as 'Columbia Territory.' "

Well, Congress had the notion that the folks might confuse the Territory of Columbia with the District of Columbia. And for about 18 months they debated the matter, unable to come up with a suitable name. Finally, to make sure they had eliminated all possibility of confusion, and with erudite precision, Congress met in Washington and decided to call the new Territory "Washington."

Meanwhile, the settlers out here got impatient and had another convention at a place called Monticello (née Longview) and re-asked the Congress to name their place "Columbia." But by the time the new memorial got back there, some congressman said, "didn't we already name that place Washington?" And somebody looked up the minutes of the previous meeting and sure enough they had. So they sent a letter off to the fellows out there telling them the new territory had been created before their letter arrived in the nation's capital . . .

Yet all our history books say the Monticello convention was the one that got us Territorial status.

You just can't trust a historian.

The fact is that Longview just has more muscle than Toledo and the latter town has had to take a backseat on the matter of organizing Washington Territory, but it's not about to take a back seat on the question of the Apes.

There are two ways of getting to Ape Canyon on the north side of Mt. St. Helens. You can go through Castle Rock or you can go through Toledo. But Toledo has nipped in ahead of Castle Rock by claiming to be the *shortcut* or "Via" route and "Gateway" to Ape Canyon. The irony is that Toledo is taking aim at Longview for stealing its glory on the formation of the State. But Longview has long sinced ducked and it's that poor innocent bystander, Castle Rock, which gets hit in the face with a dead fish.

Anyway, back in 1849, three brothers were prospecting in the Mt. St. Helens area. They encountered Indians who informed them of some terrible hairy creatures in the high mountains. The Indian arrows bounced off the creatures' chests and a lot of brave braves got killed in the rough and tumble that followed . . . so the Indians quit the premises.

The brothers dismissed this as so much superstition and found gold in such quantities as you would never believe. There were nuggets as big as a man's thumb. So one of the brothers stayed behind that winter to protect their claim while the other two went into town for supplies. Fortunately for historical accuracy, the brother who was left behind kept a diary and Ray Wallace, Toledo sportsman and author, takes over on the story at this point. "The last time he wrote in his diary was December 18, 1849 (when) he wrote that he saw large giant sized hairy animals coming towards his cabin, no one knows what took place, the story has been told many times by early day pioneers that they believe that he shot and wounded one of the giant sized hairy animals and those hairy type animals tore the door off of the log cabin, the cabin showed where there had been a terrific struggle, as the table and chairs were all broken to bits and the diary was found on the floor the next spring when the other two . . . brothers returned to the cabin . . ."

Mr. Wallace notes that the white man gave the animals "a name called the Mt. St. Helens Apes and they still are called that every time one is seen . . ."

Which is a new refinement in weasel-wording, because very few people have taken a sober look at the Mt. St. Helens Apes. Fred Beck, however, was one of them. Beck told Wallace the Apes were prehistoric animals which had been preserved in ice for millions of years. They stayed alive by eating the fish which also had been encased in the ice with them. Then in the 1800's the Apes used their big ivory claws to claw their way out of the ice and attacked Indians, carrying off squaws.

Mr. Wallace says that Fred Beck killed one of the apes in about 1920, but it toppled off into a deep canyon, now called Ape Canyon.

A U.S. Forest Service brochure on Mt. St. Helens and Spirit Lake, published by the Department of Agriculture, however, completely denies the ridiculous piece of Wallace fiction about the super Apes. You know how the Federal Government is about this kind of a tall tale.

It wasn't 1920. And it wasn't Fred Beck who killed that ape at all.

It was 1924 and it was a party of miners. They were in their cabin and "huge creatures being at least 7 feet tall and covered with long black hair showered them with large boulders. The next morning, they encountered the creatures and shot at them. One of the creatures was believed slain, but its body rolled over a cliff and into a deep ravine destined to be known as Ape Canyon.

"Searching parties were immediately mobilized from the Longview area to visit the mountain region to seek out the headquarters of the apemen. These parties, however, found no trace of the apemen but did find the cabin with huge boulders around it and the inside torn to shreds . . ."

If you would like to locate the scene of the crime, go to *Timberline Campground* and somebody will tell you where to get off at.

Prowling Toledo

This is a tranquil town on the north bank of the Cowlitz River. You can get a cup of coffee, a sandwich, a full meal and a beer at *The Landing*, which is about half a block from the river . . . and you can dance there if you've a mind to.

You also can make arrangements for a *ride on the Cowlitz River* by contacting Roy Ridenhour. Roy will take you on the float trip — which is not like shooting the rapids or anything like that — if the river's not too low and he's not busy on a construction job someplace. And even if he is, he knows a guy in Olympia he can get to do it. The trip can take a couple of hours or all day. Roy's been charging $15 a person, but what with the energy crisis and all, he probably will have upped his rate by the time you call him at 985-4045.

Heading east on an unnumbered road, you come to the *Cowlitz Mission*, started by Father Francois Blanchet in 1838.

French Canadian trappers for the Hudson's Bay Company came to this area. They became acquainted with the Indians, grew to know them, liked them, and even married some. They settled here and after about three years realized that they really needed a priest for religious guidance as they had been brought up in the Catholic Church.

They began trying to get one, and one man even walked overland to find one.

Finally, Father Blanchet came to take care of the people. He had just returned from 7 years at a New Brunswick pastorage. From there he was assigned to Montreal (which was the head office for the Hudson's Bay Company) and the Church assigned him to come to this little place.

He arrived November 24 or 28, 1838 and was joyously received. He administered to the people, baptized them, married them, etc. And he established the Cowlitz Mission. There are still some descendants of those trappers living here now.

On the site of the original church now stands *St. Francis Mission,* the 4th church to be built there. You can read a plaque here which tells the story of Father Blanchet and his mission.

Blanchet built several Catholic Churches in the Northwest. He lived to be about 89 and is buried at the St. Paul Cemetery in St. Paul, Oregon.

Salkum — (Pop. Nom. Elev. 551) — Kinda tough about old Don Wink. Thirty-eight years with the Department and all . . . and here he is stuck with those dammed left wingers. The thing that makes the canker sore is that Don's hatchery is only 10 miles as the crow flies from those young upstarts at the Salkum Hatchery. And there's always Harry Senn around to rub it in.

But, how in God's name do you figure out ahead of time what a salmon's going to do?

In order to appreciate the warmth of different opinion on this front, you probably will have to take two separate trips out of Toledo up two separate river valleys. But they may very well be trips you plan to take anyway . . . and this is a little fillip to enhance your enjoyment of the country. Don's hatchery is well below Coe's Dam on the north fork of the Toutle. You can reach it either out of Castle Rock or Toledo on the road to Spirit Lake. The Salkum facility is below Mayfield Dam on the Cowlitz.

It wouldn't be so bad if Don's hatchery hadn't made such a big "rep" by producing "Mother Toutle" fish for the Great Lakes fishery. Some years back the fisheries' biologists, egged on by Dr. Lauren Donaldson, shipped a bunch of Coho salmon eggs back to the Great Lakes. There were some from Oregon, but the ones from Washington came from the Toutle River Hatchery. Anyway, it was a big success and they restocked salmon in the Great Lakes. And it made a lot of history and the Toutle River Hatchery was pretty famous throughout the fish world.

Toutle River was everything.

Salkum was nothing.

And when we say nothing, we mean *nothing*! For an example of Salkum's nothingness we dip into a direct quote from the official *Guide to the State* published in 1941: "Salkum is a cluster of dilapidated, nondescript houses and two mills, the latter closed down as a result of the depletion of the timber supply in the vicinity. Today (1941) only a few people remain in what was a flourishing sawmill town a decade ago. The adjacent country is largely wasteland, where willows, alders and vine maple almost conceal the bleaching stumps, tombstones of forest that have passed away . . ." (That's what they thought of clearcutting in those days.)

Then that smart-assed Tacoma City Light built the Mayfield DAM.

Tacoma and the State Department of Fisheries went round and round and round like a brace and bit over that one. To put it succinctly, dams are damned by departments of fishery. At first Tacoma only offered them the State of Washington. Then they enlarged it to the 5 Pacific Northwest states . . . and the 11 western states . . . and the whole United States . . . and finally the world.

And that's when State Fisheries said, "Put a fence around it and it's a deal."

What Tacoma City Light said was, "We'll provide a hatchery that will produce as many if not more fish than there were in the river before we built the dam."

And State Fisheries said, "Yeah, what kind of fish?"

"What *kind* of fish? *Fish* fish!" (Those City Light guys are always telling us not to kill-a-watt, but deep in their hearts they couldn't care less about fish.)

"Well, we don't want scrap fish, for one thing," State Fisheries said, burnishing its fingernails on its coat lapel. "So, we'll need a fish sorter. Then we don't want you to think you can fill us up with Coho and call it a good thing. Chinooks use that river, too, you know. State Game is going to want you to take care of the Steelhead crop. Then we'll need hospital facilities . . . antibiotics . . . anaesthesiologists — that sort of thing . . ."

"*Hospital* facilities . . . *anaesthesiologists!*"

Well, Tacoma City Light, exhausted but triumphant, acceded to that one and sank back figuring they'd given State Fisheries the world. And that's when State Fisheries came up with the final stipulation about a fence.

"The fish must, of course, be right turners . . ."

The benumbed City Light guys looked up piteously from their prone position on the ground. They'd heard of a lot of things before but none of them included an right- and left-handed fish. So State Fisheries explained patiently but firmly that when the fish from this hatchery left the mouth of the Columbia they had to turn right and go up the coast of Washington.

"We got not one, but 2 'Salmon Fishing Capitals of the World!' to think about," State Fisheries added reasonably. "Ilwaco and Westport. And, of course these fish have got to take another right at the Strait of Juan de Fuca . . . and take another right again . . . and up as far as, let's say, Seattle."

Well, the upshot of it all was Tacoma City Light blew $26,000,000 on that fancy fish hatchery equipment on the Cowlitz, with that automatic fish sorter .. and the hospital facilities ... and the antibiotics and the anaes-thesiologists. They sort out the scrap fish and they meet specific quotas for specific salmon.

Ken Kral, fisheries biologist for Tacoma City Light, notes with evident satisfaction that, "We have met or exceeded our commitment for Steelhead, Coho and Fall Chinook and next year, we'll be doing the same with the Spring Chinook."

What does all this mean?

Well, State Fisheries figures it produces a catch of about 4 million salmon for the commercial and sports salmon fishery combined. And while a salmon caught in the commercial fishery is worth $4 to $12 apiece — depending on the kind of salmon it is — a good Chinook is worth as much as $60 to everybody concerned in the sport fishery. And it certainly does a lot for the economy of Ilwaco and Westport . . .

And Tacoma City Light hatcheries produce about 1,000,000 of those fish.

If you figure they're all caught by sport fishermen — and, of course, that's the way we're figuring because that's the biggest figure — then you're looking at a catch of $60,000,000 worth of salmon . . .

And our hat's off to Tacoma City Light . . .

But what about the famous Mother Toutle fish?

"Ask him where his fish go," Harry Senn, biologist with the Hatchery Division of State Fisheries in Olympia urged. "Ask him where they go."

So we asked Don Wink about his hatchery, which produces perhaps 100,000 salmon for the fishery, what he thought about the Salkum Hatchery and he said, "It's nothin' but a Fish Factory . . ."

Then we asked him were his fish went when they left the mouth of the Columbia. He pretended not to hear the question and noted that for four years now they'd been processing Cowlitz eggs . . . but the dreadful truth was finally extracted. Mother Toutle fish turn left when they reach the mouth of the Columbia . . .

Sixty-dollars apiece worth . . . to be caught in Oregon or California.

Those "left-wingers" go "south" with the loot!

Heading east on U.S. 12 out of Salkum, you're on the main White Pass Highway with Mayfield Lake on your left. It's kind of calm prairie country heading into the foothills. Then you cross *Cowlitz River Bridge* across the Cowlitz Canyon.

The State Highway Department is pretty proud of this bridge. Completed 7 years ago, it is the longest concrete arch bridge in North America. The length of the base of the arch is 520 feet. It's total length is 1,136 feet and it's 255 feet above the water. After crossing the bridge, you turn a corner and there, bang, is the shock of Tacoma City Light's enormous *Mossyrock Dam.* It's the Northwest's highest dam, rising more than 600 feet from bedrock and 365 feet from the riverbed. Davisson Lake behind it is 23½ miles long . . . has but 52 miles of shoreline, indicating what a narrow area it covers. It was named for Ira Davisson, Tacoma City Light Commissioner from 1918 to 1940. It covers the former towns of Riffe and Kosmos.

Mossyrock — (Pop. 409. Elev. 533.) — Got its name, not surprisingly from a nearby mossy rock, a promontory that sticks up about 200 feet and formerly was burned regularly by the Indians, presumably so blackberries would grow in the area. Nowdays, the land's too valuable for blackberries and it's planted in Douglas fir. The town's principal economic base these days is tourism.

As you leave Mossyrock, you're leaving the broad valley and heading into Kentucky Mountaineer country and to Morton, one of our most favorite towns on the Wet Side of the Mountains.

Everywhere on the Wet Side of the Mountains there is increasing evidence that Seattle wouldn't be the big city she is without her hinterlands. And we're not just talking about groceries and the milk supply the big town gets from the farmers in the valleys. We mean people who come forward in time of Seattle's need.

And Morton's Gracie Hansen is a case in point.

Morton — (1,231. Elev. 945.) — It's about as far out in the backwoods as you can get. It is completely surrounded by mountains. You have to take a couple of lefts and a right through a narrow valley to even get there. And Mount Rainier, looming up close behind Morton, provides periodic spectaculars to lift the souls of its people.

It's a rich pocket of land in the wilderness so like the pockets of land in Kentucky, West Virginia and Virginia about a century ago, it caused an exodus from that country. The Appalachian Mountains had been logged out at the time and for a people who depended on mountains and forests for survival, this was the promised land. In 1940, Dr. Woodrow Clevinger, who presently teaches at Seattle University, did his Master's Thesis on the subject of their migration.

One paragraph in the thesis gives you the idea: "The railroad journey to Western Washington is vivid in the memory of these pioneers. Tales of incidents and humorous experiences on the long trip enliven reminiscences in Lewis and Skagit counties. One family from Pike County, Kentucky, brought along several lean "black and tan" coon hounds and some of the men carried rifles. Another family brought its own food supply for the entire trip — a large box of corn bread, home-cured bacon, apples and home-canned beans. Some individuals displayed pistols, long knives,and jugs of whiskey in the railroad stations in Chicago and Cincinnati . . . The migration between 1890 and 1920 brought the culture and living standards of Appalachian America and modern America into close juxtaposition . . ."

The folks from the southern Appalachians were unaccustomed to regulated hunting, trapping, fishing and moonshine whiskey, which had a tendency to make things lively from time to time — especially during Prohibition. They tell the story locally about one guy who had a still in his barn near the main highway out of Centralia. He piped the product to a faucet behind a big billboard. And if you wanted some Kentucky Lightning, you just drove up to the billboard with your jug and he turned on a spigot to fill it.

The purity of the Appalachian attitude has dissipated some as the kids have grown up and gone to school, but the virulence of antagonism in these mountain valleys to the Game Warden (called Wildlife Agents by the State Game Department) remains undiminished. Jim Knodel, the agent for 3,600 square miles in Gifford Pinchot National Forest and a whole lot of other forest land in this area . . . and his wife . . . and his children in school, clearly feel the prevailing attitude of the folks in the valleys. Knodel estimates that the illegal take of deer, for example, far exceeds the legal take . . . and that well in excess of 70% of the people in the various valleys leading to Mt. Rainier have tasted and enjoyed poached deer — even if the actual cooking process called for roasting.

And Jim Marvin, publisher of the *Morton Journal*, makes a real effort to get his facts straight. "They don't write a letter to the editor," Marvin declared, "They pay him a personal visit — with a pitchfork clutched in their fists."

So Louisiana-born Gracie Barner, whose stepfather, George, was Mayor of Centralia, married a logger and arrived in Morton and for 6 years between 1953 and 1958 was the producer of the Morton PTA Follies. "At first it was wonderful," Gracie said. "Everybody wanted to be in the Follies. Each year, you had to ask the people who had performed the year before or their feelings would be hurt. So, toward the end there, we had a cast of well over 100 . . . and it was growing. Some of them were very good and some of them were not. But almost all of them felt that a shot of some kind of stimulant was a prior essential to an appearance in front of the footlights. I would spend the whole year writing the script, but once they got on stage, they'd start ad-libbing and after a while it got too rich for the Morton PTA."

After the 1958 Follies, Gracie was in tough mental, emotional and physical shape. The Follies, which were her lifeline to sanity, had gone down the tube. She was divorcing her husband and had undergone major surgery. "It was a case of quiet desperation," Gracie said.

That's when her friend Esther Lester (wife of Reg Lester, the Buick dealer in Morton) said, "Why don't you put on some kind of follies at the World's Fair in Seattle?"

Now the thing to remember is that in and among all of those mountains, you still don't get any reception on your car radio. If it wasn't for the cable, you wouldn't get any television either. Disappointed, sick and depressed, Gracie had not gotten the word. "What fair?" she asked.

Gracie's stepfather had slipped her a quarter to see the Sally Rand Show at the San Francisco Fair when she was a little girl — which turned out to be a big disappointment. And throughout her life, her notion of a big time deal was a ticket to one of the Hollywood musical spectaculars at the local movie house.

The upshot was an announcement by his secretary to one of the executives of the Century 21 Exposition that "there's a Mrs. Hansen, producer of the Morton PTA Follies, in the outer office and she wants to see you."

Gracie, who is short, plump, black-haired (and shrewder than you think) was ushered in and the bored official pretended to be charmed with a visit from one of the ladies of the Morton PTA. People from Morton might one day buy a ticket to the Exposition — if it ever got off the ground.

He got the shock of his life when the demure little lady answered his first question about what she proposed to do.

"I want to put on a tit show for the Fair," she said.

He never forgot her. For that matter, nobody who ever has met Gracie ever forgets her. She's gentle in her way, but her tongue can have a razor's edge, like when she says about her departure from the mountain people, "I shook the mud of Morton from my feet," At a meeting, with banker Frank Jerome present, she got a great laugh when she said, "No wonder bank employees embezzle money. The banks don't pay them enough to live on."

Gracie was a little depressed after her first contact with Fair people, and even more so when she set out to raise $25,000 to put on her show. What she did was get a job with investment banker, Robert Chinn. During her lunch hour, she was going around trying to tap people for the money. It looked like she might get somewhere until she found out it would take at least $125,000. Then she was even more depressed until Chinn suggested that she try getting smaller amounts from a number of people instead of all of it from one backer.

Well, Gracie was the owner of an idea whose time had come. "I had asked the men in Morton what they remembered about past World's Fairs," she said, and everyone of them said it was the girlie shows. "The Fair people had figured out things like the Science Pavilion and the Monorail and the Space Needle," but they didn't have the essential ingredients of a big fair . . . the sex and cotton candy . . .the fun and excitement."

What Gracie didn't know was the proximity of the Century 21 Exposition to bankruptcy in the summer and fall of 1961. At one point, 10 Seattle businessmen who dug in their jeans for $2,500 apiece meant the difference between continuing the struggle for 1 more day . . . or folding the Fair on the spot. And Art Cooperstein, who was comptroller for the Fair, opined at this writing, 12 years after the event, that "if she showed up with money any time before the big advance ticket sale in November of 1961, her contribution was extremely important."

Gracie walked into the Fair offices prior to November of 1961.

She had $90,000 in her figurative fist.

Ewen C. Dingwall, Vice President and General Manager of the Exposition is not without fond recollection of Gracie. "She was a personality from outside of Seattle who had a tremendous impact in certain fields of the Fair," he said. "I saw those Methodists and Baptists standing in line outside her show, waiting for a little taste of wickedness."

Gracie put herself in the hands of Bob Karolevitz and Guy Williams, a couple of public relations people with more than a modicum of native intelligence. And while it was out of character, they billed her bluntly as a "madam."

They put her in the hands of various kinds of couturiers who equipped her with costumes reminiscent of the Gay Nineties. Feathers had a lot to do with them. A golden cadillac and a red apple with a bite taken out of it also were a part of the ensemble. When a show girl burst out of a paper apple to initiate the publicity campaign, Gracie endeared herself to the press with her first candid announcement, "You know this is just a publicity stunt."

Gracie was just that forthright in all of her contacts with the press. PR man Williams put it this way, "Karolevitz and I got a lot of credit we didn't deserve for outpublicizing everything else at the Fair. But there's only so much the press could write about a Space Needle and a Science Pavilion and a Monorail. Once the newspapermen checked Gracie out and found she was for real and not another phony, they went to town with her. She's got a bright mind and a quick wit. She and her show made great copy."

It was the kind of copy Murray Morgan referred to in his book summing Century 21 when he wrote, "Have sex — spelled S-E-X — and plenty of it, the experts forewarned . . . "

Gracie Hansen's Paradise International was the hit of the midway. And bared bosoms were really *something* for Seattle. Even today when tops and bottoms and every other part of the human anatomy are matters of routine exposure in a lot of places, bosoms are not a part of the Seattle scene. And serving booze along with bosoms is a matter of great concern throughout the whole State. Even under the aegis of the Fair, the censors had their eyes peeled for propriety with a capital "P." Gracie's show was in excellent taste and it packed them in.

But there were a couple of supreme ironies attached. The extravaganza, which ended up costing not $25,000 or $125,000, but $260,000 ran into management problems and lost money. And while the breasts were the big lure, it was a little dog named "Louie" that stole the show.

Louie was a nondescript animal who had been carefully trained to do absolutely *nothing!* His trainer, Bob Williams, played the role of a doting father with a backward of offspring of no talent whatsoever. Nevertheless, Williams kept hoping out loud — and the audience kept hoping with him — that the dog would do something, anything, right. The act was good for a lot of belly-laughs, the biggest of which came at the very end when the dog just collapsed on the stage while the audience collapsed in the aisles.

"Look," Williams would say triumphantly, "He's *breathing!*"

◆

It's a general concensus that the Morton Loggers' Jubilee is about the liveliest one in the state. Informed local opinion holds that not all of the life is contributed by the spirits dispensed in the state liquor store. The notion prevails that the St. Regis, Weyerhaeuser, and U.S. Plywood operations which ship 17,000 carloads of material out of town annually by the Chicago, Milwaukee, St. Paul and Pacific Railroad are not the only profitable operations in the deep woods. There's that previously mentioned manufacture of White Lightning. As one of the locals opined, "Maybe that's why Morton is such a sleepy little town."

Anyway, the Loggers Jubilee is a joyous occasion attended by some 3,000 people and participated in by real live loggers who come down out of the mountains to compete. Esther Lester's son, Reg, Jr., comes up from California to be master of ceremonies and Donald Jastad is the local boy the folks root for the hardest. The rest of the year Don lives in Tacoma where he practices dentistry. He's the only contestant with the letters "Dr." in front of his name.

A word about eating — The *Wheel Cafe* in the center of town is pretty much it. Good coffee and gathering spot for locals, plain and simple fare. As one of the locals said, "Rosellini's it ain't!"

Annual affair — *Loggers' Jubilee*, in mid-August, parades and logging show; community and church dinners, loggers' breakfast.

For further information — *Morton Journal;* phone, 496-5405, or City Hall.

From Morton, you can take a trip up through an ever-narrowing corridor of privately owned land in the Cowlitz River Valley. It becomes increasingly engulfed by Gifford Pinchot National Forest until a few miles after leaving Packwood, you're entirely in the forest. And by the time you reach Ohanapecosh, you're in the Rainier National Park. We always wondered where a delightful name like Ohanapecosh came from and now somebody has told us and we're delighted.

Some Indian looked into a clear pool at this spot and uttered this exclamation, which in Indian language meant, "God, what beauty!" Nobody knew whether he was referring to his own reflection or that of Mt. Rainier.

Just beyond Ohanapecosh, you take a left to the Box Canyon road and Paradise — if you're traveling in the summer. It's closed in the winter.

You also can take Highway 7 north out of Morton to Mineral where there's a lake with an outstanding reflection of Mt. Rainier when the weather's right. And here you can join westbound Tour 2 out of Tacoma.

Our route, however, calls for returning on State Highway 508 via Cinebar and Onalaska. (The Alpha Road west of Cinebar will take you to the previously mentioned Jackson Courthouse.

REGION SIX

WAHKIAKUM, COWLITZ, CLARK AND SKAMANIA COUNTIES

A Word About Region VI

The most exciting thing they've got in Region 6 is the Columbia River. And for a connoisseur of excitement, it's got a lot going for it. Known historically as the "River of the West," it packs more power than any other river on the North American continent. Beginning in Columbia Lake in British Columbia at an altitude of 2,650 feet, it drops to 1.40 feet above mean sea level at the bridge between Vancouver and Portland. The overall length is 1,210 miles.

The region is rich in history thanks at least in part to the fact that the British thought it was a neat river which they would like to own *en toto* . . . and a bunch of radical American settlers thought this was a pretty punk idea. And it was because of the disputation over the future ownership of this magnificent body of water that the famous American slogan "54-40 or fight!" cropped up. Lewis and Clark made a name for themselves by taking an expedition down this stream and the Hudson's Bay Company subsequently assigned one of their toughest characters, Dr. John McLoughlin (known as the "despot of the Rockies") to the chore of posting "no trespassing" signs, as far as Americans were concerned, on the north side of the river. One of his principal successes consisted of enhancing a big real estate development called Portland, on the south side of the river. But a rag-tag bunch of resolute Americans finally succeeded in putting him down.

This was the last really major conflict between the United States and Great Britain — despite the subsequent "Pig War" on San Juan Island. In the city of Vancouver, they've lucked out in getting a huge piece of property in the center of town that played an enormous role first in the introduction of civilization to the Pacific Northwest and later as a U.S. Army post called Fort Vancouver. This was the place where the State of Washington really began, and it only recently has been turned over to civil authorities. Located on the banks of the river, it now is being developed as a major historical site and a means of providing amenities for this town that few American cities possess. The fort should be a must in your visit to this city.

Up river in Camas is the forerunner of the pulp mills that have proved to be one of the major stabilizing industries on the Wet Side of the Mountains. Further along is the Columbia River Gorge where east and west weather fronts collide head on, and beyond that the Bonneville dam, which began the process of harnessing the power of the river in 1936. It was a move which initiated the production of finished products instead of just raw materials in our part of the world . . . a matter which a number of conservationists fail to appreciate today, but one which loomed of vast importance at the time the dam was created.

Vancouver is one of the two major population centers of the region, with the Longview-Kelso complex comprising the second. One of the musts in Longview is a visit to the Weyerhaeuser facility here. It's the largest processing plant of forestry products in the world and Weyerhaeuser presently is spending in excess of $200,000,000 making it even more productive than it has been in the past. Kelso is the county seat and by far the older — but smaller — of the two cities.

We also feel it incumbent upon ourselves to inform you that this region's alluvial flood plains not only are number 2 in snap beans for the whole State but number 1 in filberts. Along the Columbia and on Puget Island is the most specialized cucumber acreage in the State and the flood plains also are big in cabbage, carrots, lettuce, potatoes, mint and flower bulbs.

Two of the towns that tickle our fancy are Stevenson, the seat of Skamania County, which once got kicked out of the State, and Cathlamet, where the smoked salmon frequently is "poached."

We're sure you will be intrigued by the solitary splendor of Mount St. Helens, which recently was voted one of the volcanoes most likely to erupt in the United States, and Spirit Lake, the body of water which the mountain created for itself, but we still stick to the fact that the mighty Columbia is the major attraction. One of the best places to get the feel of it is from the top of Beacon Rock, a State park that once was given to the State of Oregon.

We find it thought-provoking that while other rivers wind their way around the mountains, the Columbia had the power to plow right through a mountain range.

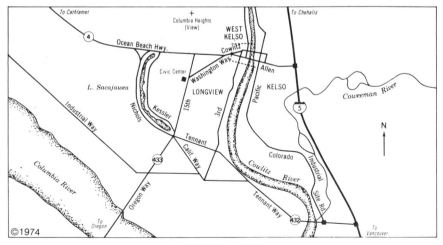

LONGVIEW-KELSO

Longview-Kelso Tour 1 — In and Around the Two Cities and Kalama (Map XV)

This is another set of twin cities where the rivalries have existed in varying degrees of virulence over the years . . . a condition inherent in the fact that Kelso was a recognized settlement for three-quarters of a century before Longview was organized; and now Longview's more than twice as big. Ladies from one town will go to social events staged in the other, so things can't be as bad as they once were. The Cowlitz River, flowing in from the north, divides Kelso into 2 parts and empties in the Columbia south of both of them. The Coweeman River comes into the area from the east . . . and at one time or another all three of these rivers have contributed to the rich delta land on which the two towns are located. The rivers also raise problems periodically at flood time. Kelso is the seat of Cowlitz County and Longview is the biggest planned city in the United States after Washington, D.C. The town was planned for a population of 50,000 — which is both good and bad. The streets are broad and the park system magnificent. But the anticipated population has not as yet materialized and there are pieces of vacant property where they thought there might be buildings. Regardless, it's interesting to see how they've coped with realities that didn't turn out to be quite the same as the planners had anticipated.

Longview — (Pop. 28,400, Elev. 13.) — Any time you get into the expenditure of $50,000,000 you're going to find some crossed tempers, broken backs and busted noses somewhere in the pile before the deal is completed. With private instead of public money, it's more so . . . and the privately constructed town of Longview was no exception.

◄►

It was the largest completely planned city in the country after Washington, D.C. and R.A. Long, the chairman of the board of the Long-Bell Lumber Company, was the man who did most of the planning. Long believed in the democratic form of government as long as everybody did things the way he wanted them to. If they didn't, it was "off with their heads!"

On December 6, 1922, there was a meeting of the 18-member board of directors of the Long-Bell Lumber Company, biggest of its kind in the United States, on the eighth floor of the R. A. Long Building in Kansas City, Mo. They were there to determine whether they should go ahead with Long's mad idea of building a model city in a land of swamps and brambles from scratch . . . especially in view of the fact it would take up all the "scratch" the 47-year-old company could lay its hands on.

Long, who was 72 years old at the time, carried into that meeting with him the abiding belief that the success of a business depended on the "choice of men to fill responsible positions . . . to build the organization from within instead of without . . ." Long also was a deeply religious man, and it was by custom that Frederick Bannister, who had served the company for a quarter of a century and recently had been named president, should open the meeting with a passage from the Bible. His selection on that occasion was the 67th Psalm, which begins with: "God be merciful unto us, and bless us; and cause His face to shine upon us . . ."

Events reveal that Bannister's heart just wasn't in it. He was asking The

Lord to change His whole basic policy with regard to this piece of landscape so Long-Bell could make a buck in a location where nobody else had been able to before.

This was the site of the historically significant Monticello Convention which had met on November 25, 1852. What the convention did was ask the Congress to pass a law creating Washington Territory. It was a great convention and has been much celebrated since.

The fact that Congress already had passed a law creating Washington Territory is quite incidental. Monticello was wrong in claiming credit for getting the Territory created. But it was right politically when it used this piece of misinformation with telling effect in persuading the State Legislature to make it the seat of Lewis County a couple of years later.

The Lord responded by visiting a flood upon the place in the winter of 1866-67 and destroying it. After that, the land here was considered pretty good for dairy cows, but pretty punk for people . . .

So you can imagine the intense enthusiasm with which the homesteaders and their descendants embraced the news that Long-Bell would pay anybody any price he had the courage to ask for his land.

Being stalwart pioneers, they had the courage to ask and get approximately ten times the going rate for land that could be visited anytime, en masse, and virtually unannounced, by the waters of the mighty Columbia, not to mention the equally devastating, if not so mighty, Cowlitz River. The bill for the land came to $2,600,000.

So, of course Long-Bell had to build a dike around the town. It was 14 miles long . . . 300 feet wide at the bottom and 100 feet wide at the top.

Going in, they estimated it would cost about $800,000.

The final bill came to $3,200,000.

These were the kinds of things that made Bannister nervous.

As it turned out, The Lord wasn't all that merciful to the men who got the town going, either. He didn't bless the minutes of the meeting or cause His face to shine on the people who attended. Long's ability to chose the right man for the right spot wasn't infallible, either. Mr. Bannister, who had called upon The Lord in the first place, finally worried his way around to the conclusion that old man Long finally had flipped his lid. So he resigned the position he'd dedicated his adult lifetime to getting and instituted a lawsuit designed to make the creation of a new town in the mudflats a legal as well as a practical impossibility.

And he had some arguments that proved interesting to the Missouri courts. There was all that stuff about the flood. The profits from the lumber company were being diverted to the construction of a town — which was a far cry from the lumber business that had made Long-Bell prosperous in the first place.

Mr. Bannister convinced the Missouri Attorney General that Long-Bell had sold millions of dollars of local improvement district bonds illegally to the citizens of that state for the purpose of engaging in a gigantic real estate venture on the mudflats of the Pacific Northwest. The venture included, the complaint charged, a "model town that would contain hundreds of thousands of inhabit-ants." The complaint also charged that Long-Bell had no business in the hotel business or the construction of sidewalks, streets and sewers. It further charged that vast sums of money had been illegally diverted from the legitimate busi-ness of the company for the construction of boulevards, parks, community buildings, a civic center and the establishment of a big lagoon.

In his book, *Longview, The Remarkable Beginnings of a Modern West-ern City*, John M. McClellan, Jr. summed it up like this: "In short an effort was made to take management of the company away from Mr. Long and the other officers, sell the properties in Longview for what they would bring, and confine the company's activities in the west entirely to the manufacture and sale of timber."

A lot of people thought Mr. Bannister had a point there.

All of this took months, ended up in the Missouri Supreme Court, which upheld the contentions of the Long-Bell attorneys that everything was really "legit" and the fellas could go ahead with their town. McClellan covers the impact of that decision on Bannister like this: "Not long after he died suddenly, whether by his own hand or not the public never knew for sure."

All in all, before they were through, the company spent some $50,000,000 — nearly a million dollars more than its own net worth.

A lot of thought, attention, and prayer also was given to the question of naming a town built by Mr. Long.

They thought of Tom, Dick and Harry, Jim and John. Then somebody had a *great* idea. Why not use the word "Long?"

All of this deep thinking culminated one day at a meeting of directors at Mr. Long's 1,600-acre farm, (built at a cost of $1,500,000) 20 miles south of Kansas City. The group had gathered there for the specific purpose of enlisting the aid of The Lord in deciding on a name. Mr. Long had caused the tele-phones to be disconnected so they wouldn't be disturbed by outside earthly agencies.

The name of the farm was *Longview*.

Well, they thought about names.

They thought of Long-Bell, but that was too commercial. Besides, the people in Kelso already hated the new town to pieces and wanted to call it West Kelso. They thought of Long Port, but the port wasn't all that long; and it wasn't really definitive of the spirit which caused the creation of the town in the first place.

Then, somebody suggested "Longview."

To this day, nobody remembers who made the suggestion.

S. M. Morris and Jesse Andrews, two of the board members, liked that name Longview a lot and argued for it. And as the battle of the name raged back and forth across the conference table, with the two Longview voters on one side and others on the other, Long leaned over behind Morris and said, *sotto voce*, "Stand your ground, man. Stand your ground!"

It was like a message from God, and accompanied by a bolt of lightning followed by a great clap of thunder. With their eyes blinking from the blinding light the board sank back exhausted and someone said in solemn tones, "Let's call it Longview!"

And that's what they did.

But you know how it is with The Lord. He's got an awful lot of work to do and sometimes the details slip past His watchful eye. This was not the case with one of the postal clerks in the Post Office Department in Washington, D.C., who informed the company in a distressingly routine form letter that they were out of luck on the name of their new town. There already was a town called Long View, in Benton County. The board had better come up with something new in the way of a name or the postal department would do it for them. The Post Office system of naming towns consisted of pulling a name out of the nearest hat.

Some of the fellas felt that this was the end of the line and they'd better check again with God. But Mr. Long was not one of them. Maybe there was a chance that the people in Benton County would relinquish the name of their town in favor of something else. Mr. Long had not come all this way and blown all this dough without a notion of leaving his footsteps on the sands of time. Maybe a few well-spent bucks . . . .

Mr. Long was quite aware that thanks to their deeply courageous attitude, the dauntless pioneers of Lewis County had charged Long-Bell $2,600,000 for about $260,000 worth of flood-plain property. There was little reason for him to expect that the owners of some desert property in Benton County would lack the same financial pluck.

But he had the bit in his teeth for fair by now. This was the high point of his life and from here on out, everything would be down hill. He would go for broke and hang the costs. Long-Bell employed the services of the Portland law firm of Dey, Hampson and Nelson to talk with the people in old Long View to see if anything could be worked out. The three gentlemen arrived at the original Long View with whatever pomp and circumstance they deemed appropriate and entered into negotiations with the town fathers. The arrival of Dey, Hampson and Nelson created quite a stir in the old town — because 3 men doubled the male population of the town, which consisted of 3 families.

R. M. Klinefelter, the postmaster, was a shrewd businessman who drove a hard bargain. He extracted from Long-Bell the price for the construction of brand new station facilities. These consisted of a platform for the mail sack that was dropped by the Seattle, Portland and Spokane train as it sped by this flagstop with a Long View of the Columbia River.

The total cost was $25.

◆

For a quarter of a century, the wiseacres of the county chuckled and chortled over the story of the flatland furriners from Kansas City, Mo. who thought they could build dikes around the town for a mere $817,359 and ended up blowing $3,250,000. Nobody around had spent that kind of money for dikes. Wesley Vandercook, the chief engineer for the Long-Bell Lumber Company, had even taken a trip to Holland to find out about building dikes.

Then on April 1, 1948 there was a government report that was no April Fool's joke. It noted that snow in the mountains which fed the Columbia Basin ranged from 20 to 42% deeper than ever before. A month later the Weather Bureau in Portland noted that the runoff of the Snake, the Columbia's largest tributary, was going to be late that year and might peak at the same time as the main stream. On May 19, there were cloudbursts in British Columbia. There were other ominous signs throughout the Columbia Basin. Clark Fork River suddenly rose 6 inches . . . some dikes broke outside of Bonners Ferry, Idaho, and a dam gave way in Lardner, B.C. . . . water covered an airfield at Vancouver . . . 5 sawmills closed down . . . piers for a new highway bridge tumbled into roaring water . . . 1,000 families were driven from a trailer city at Pasco.

And then there was Vanport . . . a war housing project on the south side of the River named for Vancouver and Portland.

Some 18,700 people lived there in temporary housing under the jurisdiction of the Portland Housing Authority. On Sunday, May 30, there were 800 cars parked in front of those homes in Vanport. Between the town and the river was a dike made up largely from a fill for a railroad construction along the river in 1907.

Writing for *The Nation*, in the issue of June 12, 148, Richard L. Neuberger, later to be a United States Senator from Oregon, had this to say:

"At 8 a.m. May 30, 1948, circulars were shoved under the doors by the Portland Housing Authority reading 'You will have time to leave. Don't get excited. The dikes are safe at present. 'You will be warned.' Eight hours later, a wall of water toppled onto Vanport. The people had warning — five or six minutes . . .'"

Thanks to the time of day, only 14 lost their lives. Had it been 12 hours earlier, the death toll easily could have exceeded that of the Johnston Flood in 1889 (2,200). President Harry S. Truman declared Vanport a disaster area. The town never was rebuilt.

The list of towns that were all or partially flooded in May and June of 1948 is impressive . . .

Missoula . . . St. Regina . . . Lardner . . . Bonners Ferry . . . Northport . . . Wenatchee . . . Ellensburg . . . Yakima . . . Pasco . . . Kennewick . . . Richland . . . The Dalles . . . Portland . . . Vancouver . . . St. Helens . . . Kalama . . . Washougal . . . Camas . . . the Puget Island dikes failed . . . the Johns Dike at Klatskenie . . . and Kelso.

Thirty-five people lost their lives.

Property damage was estimated at $100,000,000.

It took 10 days and nights of careful attention to additional sandbagging . . . but Vandercook's Dutch dikes held and Longview was spared.

The $3,250,000 worth of dikes was a bargain.

Prowling Longview

To get the best feel of what man has done to this formerly sodden piece of landscape, take Industrial Way and turn toward the Columbia River on Ditch or Dike Road. It is built on one of the most remarkable pieces of engineering outside of the Netherlands and is based on the principles used in that country. You get a view of the River on one side and everything ranging from the Yacht Club to the garbage dump on the other.

Without this dike, Longview dies as its predecessor, Monticello, did more than a century ago.

To get a good over-all view of the whole area, turn north on the Longview end of the Cowlitz River Bridge and go up *Columbia Heights Road* to the top of the hill. On the right is the Cowlitz River Valley and turning left to Cedar Gates, the Columbia River widens and winds out to the sea.

Sacajawea Park is *the* Longview park. Formerly a swampy area, it was made into a long, narrow lake, bordered by trees, lawns, walkways, and a pleasant residential area.

One can hike or bike around it or even ride a horse (bring your own) — boats and bikes for rent. The lake's for sailing, canoeing, rowboats, no motors; also there are 3 play parks, one of which can be closed and locked to keep kids in and safe.

A few years back, an over-abundant population of squirrels lived in the area around Sacajawea Park and the Monticello Hotel. The problem was, they were getting run over . . . then Amos Peter, a general contractor, devised and built a *Nutty Narrow Squirrel Bridge* to get the squirrels across the street. To see the bridge, look up from the locomotive in the park area near the Monticello Hotel . . . At Lexington, *Riverside Park* is on the west side of the Cowlitz River about 6 miles north of Longview. Picnicking is good with a community kitchen and a ball field . . . *Hollywood Gorge* also is a great spot.

Tours are available at the *Weyerhaeuser Company*, Industrial Way, the world's largest single integrated manufacturer of forest products. Their Longview branch is the largest of their operations and is comprised of three sawmills; a plywood plant; a pulp and paperboard mill for production of sulfite, kraft pulp, paperboard and container board; a chemical plant producing chlorine, chlorate and caustic; presto-log, bark products plant and research market development centers. Call ahead for tours and schedules. *Reynolds Metals Company*, Industrial Way, makers of pig aluminum and extrusion bullet sheeting has tours on Thursdays at 2 p.m.

Uncommon shopping – *Patchwork Gallery*, Commerce St., a small corridor-type shop featuring crafts like local Eden Valley Enterprises stoneware . . . *Gay Nineties Treasure House*, Vandercook Way, Mr. and Mrs. Ralph Gay have old junk and (perhaps) antiques heaped to the ceiling. (To shop here you need time.) Furniture, bikes, dishes, glassware, books, magazines, etc. etc. etc. . . . *Bonita Art Shoppe*, Commerce St., fine gifts, crystal, glass, china, sculpture, paintings, and a delightful little lady . . . *The Guest House*, 4119 Pacific Way, Abby Aanerud has choice array of collectibles and antiques, Wed. Thurs. 1-5 . . . *Art In Crystal*, 327-23rd, showroom in Albert Arnits' home, of hand-engraved, imported crystal. He is one of the few glass engravers west of the Mississippi . . . *Longhorn Western Store*, Ocean Beach Way, western wear, hats, boots.

A word about eating – (Amongst the 7 ice creameries and 9 drive-ins) *Hodge-Podge Ice Cream Parlour*, Washington Way, sundaes, sodas, shakes, sandwiches, also delicatessen . . . *King's Table*, 14th St., a good buffet, nice for children . . . *Henri's Restaurant*, Ocean Beach Hwy., "Continental cuisine in the grand manner." Crab and shrimp louies, cheese bread . . . *Bart's*, Washington Way, western decor and noted for steaks, lobster, cappucino coffee . . . *Pietro's Pizza Parlor*, Commercial St., Old West-style parlor . . . *Fran-Paul Pantry*, 15th St., gourmet hot dogs, sandwiches, varieties of ice cream, served casually, family place . . . If you like nostalgia, try the *Monticello Hotel Restaurant* (in old hotel), which rose, at first, all alone out of a farmer's field in 1923 a six-story, steel, brick, and white terra cotta structure with mahogany paneling in the lobby. It was the first tall building in town. A single, 18-car train delivered its furniture from Chicago. If you're old enough to remember Aimee Semple McPherson, the Los Angeles evangelist, then you're old enough to remember her mother, Ma Kennedy. And if you remember Ma, you surely remember, "What a man!" Hudson. He was the man Ma married in the autumn years of their lives, right there on the banks of Lake Sacajawea. After that, Ma's picture hit the American press riding her horse, Billy Sunday, into the lobby of the Monticello Hotel . . . *Masthead Tavern*, Ocean Beach Hwy., delightful tavern with marine feeling but carpeted floors, different levels, basket chairs hanging at the bar. Dark beer, spiced wine and Reuben sandwiches.

A word about sleeping – All centrally located and comfortable: *Monticello Motor Inn* . . . *Hudson Manor Motel*, Hudson St. . . . *Miramar Motor Inn*, Hemlock St. . . . *Town Chalet Motor Inn*, Washington Way.

Annual affairs – *Lower Columbia Arts and Crafts Festival*, mid-June. Sponsored by Longview Junior College and includes demonstrating, craftsmen and crafts for sale . . . *July 4th Fireworks*, Lake Sacajawea. Shot off from Lions Island . . . *Cowlitz County Fair*, last of July. Fairgrounds between two cities . . . *Labor Day festivities*, on Lake Sacajawea, tree climbing, concessions, band, kid's races . . . *Tour of Homes*, in December, put on by YMCA. Four outstanding homes each year.

For further information – Longview Chamber of Commerce, 1563 Olympia Way; phone, 423-8400.

Kelso — (Pop. 10,300. Elev. 22.) — For 50 years, Kelso, which started out as Freeport, and Kalama battled over which one was to be the seat of Cowlitz County. And then for all but about 10 of those years, Castle Rock joined the fray, making the regular elections a three-way free-for-all in which practically everybody in the county voted. Each of the 3 towns saw that all of their voters got out and voted at each election. Freeport, now West Kelso, became the County Seat in 1868. In 1872 Kalama won the honor. But everybody kept on trying and finally in November, 1922, Kelso won the County Seat back. It was the biggest single coup in Kelso's history. But the jubilation didn't last long. Six months later they started selling lots in a new town to be called Longview and rivalry in one form or another has existed between the two municipalities ever since.

On a hot night in August, at a mass meeting in the Kelso Auditorium, the citizens of that town swallowed their pride and on the grounds that one big city was better than two resolved that "the citizens of Kelso, to effect such ends, are willing that such city will be given such name as may be selected by Mr. R. A. Long . . ."

Long turned them down.

The Kelso paper ominously editorialized that Longview would feel the wrath of God in the form of a flood which "years ago destroyed the arrogantly proud settlement of Monticello that stood where Longview now stands, and washed it down into the sea."

The Chambers of Commerce of the two towns cooperate in joint promotions. And these days, unlike those, sees Kelso women inviting their counterparts in Longview to social functions. But it has taken half a century to effectuate the peace.

For a time, the Long-Bell Company added fuel to the flames by attempting to coerce its employees to live and shop in Longview. Letcher Lambuth, brought in to handle the real estate operations for Longview, failed to endear the folks in Kelso when he opined that one day Kelso could be incorporated with Longview as "East Longview."

At one point, the pro- and anti-Longview forces got themselves all tangled up in the First Christian Church of Kelso. The Rev. Mr. Charles L. Thornton, pastor of the church and an anti-Longview man, found himself padlocked out of his church by the pro-Longview people. With the aid of 50 of his loyal followers, he put a rope on the lock and pulled it off the church door. Then, singing "Onward Christian Soldiers!" the group marched in.

A seriously annoyed Board of Trustees of the church then fired him.

But the Port fight was the best.

As soon as the Long-Bell people had showed up on the scene, some farsighted Kelso men went through the legal procedures necessary to create a Port District and then sort of laid back in the weeds. And sure enough, in 1924 and 1925 there was agitation to create a public Port in the area.

But where would it be? The Longview people, being energetic, ambitious and all that sort of thing, wanted it at the foot of Oregon Way in Longview. And if the Longview people wanted it in their town, then the Kelso people wanted it some place else . . .

Any place but Longview.

The Port Commissioners, wary of getting in the middle of this kind of a fight, strategically decided to place it on a ballot where the entire county could voice an opinion, and on August 1, 1925, the vote was better than two-to-one in favor of Longview. So they assessed everybody for the necessary $111,000 it took to dredge the dock and build the 950-foot pier. But when dedication day rolled around on April 15, 1926, there was this huge sign painted across the front of the building.

It read: "Port of Kelso."

And, of course, that was legally correct. Nobody had thought to legally change the name of the Port District at the time they voted on the location. The Port of Longview remained the "Port of Kelso" until December 7, 1929 when the necessary legal change was made.

Prowling Kelso

One of the most charming assets of Kelso is the *Cowlitz County Museum* in the County Courthouse annex. It is loaded with Indian artifacts, a doll collection, a log cabin and reproductions of a county store, post office, barber shop, livery stable, kitchen and parlor of a stagecoach inn.

The road along the Cowlitz south of Kelso is also a good one to be on to view smelt dippers in January, February and March or to join in the fun yourself for there are several places along where there are pole rental signs . . . *Tomlinson Beach* is one of these. Kelso makes a big thing of the winter smelt-fishing . . . which is indeed a big thing. Thousands of people line the banks of the Cowlitz River dipping for smelt when they're running. Beautiful little fish that make wonderful gastronomic music on the dinner table.

Kelso has the dubious distinction of having more taverns per capita than anywhere around. On one street in West Kelso there are 5 in a row, next door to each other.

Visitors can tour *Tollycraft Boat Corp.*, weekdays, 1:30-4:30 p.m.

Uncommon shopping – *Fraser's Bakery*, Allen St., doughnuts, breakfast pastry, peasant and French breads . . . *The Designers*, N. 1st, (rock shop) opals a specialty . . . *Jule's Antiques*, Main W., mostly bottles, dishes, and glass, and some furniture. To reach owner call Aaby, 1st number in phone book . . . *Davies Jewelers*, S. Pacific, Mr. Davies is one of only 3 gemologists in the State. He's quite a character, too . . . *Kelso Sale Barn*, Sale Barn Road, auction every Friday, furniture.

A word about eating – *Peter's Gay 90's Restaurant*, S. Pacific St., for anyone who loves stained glass. The food is well prepared and the decor is something else, a huge and ornate stained glass window, "Yesler" from the Seattle Hotel in Pioneer Square, beautiful lamps, windows, pictures, art objects reminiscent of the 1890's.

A word about sleeping – *Holiday Inn* of Kelso-Longivew, Kelso Dr., considered the best for some distances around here. Dining room and coffee shop, adjoining.

Annual affairs – *Smelt Eating Contest*, 1st Sunday in March, at the Eagles . . . *Highlander Summer Festival* (this relates to sister city, Kelso, Scotland), July . . . *Cowlitz County Fair*, 1st week in August. Fairgrounds between the 2 cities . . . *Annual Lutefisk Dinner*, 1st Sunday in December, at Sons of Norway Hall. Lutefisk, meatballs, lefse, and Norwegian cookies . . . *Sons of Norway Bazaar*, Norwegian items: rose-maling (type of decorative painting on wood), wood carving, baked items, hardanger (Norwegian embroidery cutwork).

For further information – Kelso Chamber of Commerce, 1407 Allen; phone, 523-5922.

There is a three-mountain side trip out of Kelso for some spectacular views of the Cowlitz and Columbia Rivers. All 3 mountains are low enough to drive up easily . . . just right for car-cushion travelers. The first is taking Brynion Street going out of Kelso east right up *Mt. Brynion*. The second is to *Mt. Pleasant*, east of Carrolls, off I-5 about 5 miles south of Kelso. The Pleasant Hills Road meanders along the Cowlitz River and on this road you can view *Rutherford's Nursery & Azalea Gardens*, in a park-like setting beside the River. The prize-winner to us, however, is the view of the Columbia Valley and far-off Portland from *Green Mountain* out of Kalama about 5 miles farther. You go south up the hill from in town on Cloverdale Road. It takes a little prowling and poking because nobody has thought to promote it, and there's no viewing area as such. But once you find your way there, the sight is spectacular.

Kalama — (Pop. 1,120. Elev. 21.) — This town lies east, parallel and immediately adjacent to Interstate 5. The business area is below the freeway, and the residential area goes up the steep hill. On the west side of the freeway the Army Engineers have built a berm to protect the changing sandbank. Kalamans advertise they're where "Water, Rail and Highway meet."

The first cabin on the site of what presently is Kalama was built by the famous pioneer, Ezra Meeker, in February, 1853. One of his happiest recollections came from the time he lost a raft of logs that he was trying to take down the Columbia to Oak Point, about 30 miles from Kalama. (See Tacoma Tour 2.)

In 1871, the people of Kalama were pretty sure theirs was to be the new Portland. In keeping with customary practices in those days, the real estate department of the Northern Pacific had bought up as much land as it could lay its hands on here with the notion of making a buck by locating the terminus here, and killing off Portland. For a time, when the railroad shops were here, things boomed, but Portland, unlike some of the other towns along the line, wouldn't be budged. A year or so later, they moved the shops to Tacoma and Kalama failed to become a metropolis.

Prowling Kalama

There are 2 nearby *fish hatcheries*, 5 and 6 miles up the Kalama River respectively.

Uncommon shopping – The main street generally has turn-of-the-century-type buildings. *Country Store* has curios and antiques . . . *Kalama Trader*, freight-damaged goods and bottles . . . *Antique Clock Shop*, a house perched on top of the hill on the foundation of the old water tower, mostly mantle and wall clocks . . . *Holly House Antiques*, home and shop of Virginia and Earl Rae. Well-cared for home, with mansard roof, formerly was the old Northern Pacific Hospital. The shop is next door and has good antiques, not curios. If they're not open and you're a serious buyer, call about an appointment.

A word about eating – *Kalama Cafe*, recommended locally . . . *Phyllis Cafe*, at the bus stop, good food at reasonable prices.

A word about sleeping – *Columbia Inn*, rates as good. Restaurant attached.

Annual affairs – *Kalama Community Fair*, last week in July, parade, etc. . . . *Amalak* (Kalama spelled backwards), 1st week of November. Annual carnival of the Federation of Women's Clubs in the Community Building. And anybody who is anybody shows up.

For further information – City Hall; phone, 673-3801.

Longview-Kelso Tour 2 — Cathlamet, Puget Island, Skamokawa, Altoona, Naselle, Megler (Map XV)

You may get rained on a little on this tour because the average rainfall along the north side of the Columbia here is 90 inches a year. But it's a great experience in a colorful and vastly unpopulated part of the state. (They didn't even have a road into Cathlamet from the rest of the state until 1929. And even then, you knew you'd driven something by the time you reached your destination.) The tour takes you into Cathlamet, a small pocket of individualistic thinkers who think that restoration of history to a living present is the neatest thing since the invention of sturgeon fish balls. It's nestled above Puget Island, which is an interesting place to be even if the revenooers have removed all the stills. The tour takes you along to Skamokawa (with the end pronounced "way"), Grays River and its "not-quite-white-water run," and there are smorgasbords at Cathlamet and Naselle worth timing your trip for. You see Pillar Rock and cross the Megler Bridge for a return trip with view of Washington from Oregon and cross back over the famous Longview Bridge.

Cathlamet — (Pop. 652. Elev. 340) — We'll tell you how modest they are in Cathlamet: They only list their population at 650, in spite of the official record cited above. Of course, it's a real population boom if you go back 30 years when only 621 people lived there. Cathlamet is the county seat of the smallest county in the State, and politics always has been big here. At their first election in 1854, they named 13 office holders . . .

With only 8 voters.

In 1905 little old Wahkiakum County beat out the big counties to the north and east by having its State Legislator, Joe Megler, elected Speaker of the House. There were some pretty important soreheads in King County after that one. They tried to make trouble for Joe, but got more than they bargained for. And in his *History of Brookfield* (The Joe Megler Story), historian Carlton E. Appelo, tells about one of the times Joe held his own: "Feb. 21, 1905 . . . the Elks were having a celebration on Tuesday in Seattle and this was followed on Wednesday by Washington's Birthday so there was strong pressure put on by the House to vote a 2-day recess. Megler felt that his body should stay in Olympia and work. With the fastest gavel west of the Pecos and an ear which heard the ayes over the noes when the vote came up for adjournment merely overnight, Speaker Megler kept his House colleagues working in Olympia while the Senate celebrated in Seattle with the Elks . . ."

And whom do you think they've got from Cathlamet in Washington, D.C. today? Congresswoman Julia Butler Hansen. Bridge-building Julia's from an old, old family in Cathlamet. And while her 1857 home isn't open to public tours, it's restored and pointed at with pride by everybody in Wahkiakum County.

Cathlamet is one of the joyous "finds" you encounter when you really get prowling Western Washington. Perched on a steep bank above the Columbia River, it's a picturesque, orderly little town with a lot of historic buildings and a wonderful view of the rolling hills of Oregon across the broad expanse of the river. And early-day restoration is rampant.

The most exciting moment in the 20th century history of Cathlamet came at 1:15 p.m. on Saturday, August 26, 1939 when President Franklin D. Roosevelt pressed a golden key at the White House which cut a ribbon in Cathlamet officially opening the Puget Island Bridge. Julia was new in the Washington State Legislature at the time, but that bridge is proof positive that the fellows who made up the bulk of the legislature knew she was there.

But Julia's not the only effective woman in Cathlamet. Those ladies who keep pushing the Equal Rights movement could use a page or two from the Cathlamet book of *Women in Action*. During the *Summer Arts Festival*, the ladies turn to and wash all the windows along Front Street, which then becomes a gallery of business show windows displaying the arts and crafts of the region . . . with many artists and craftsmen actually at work.

And the *Wahkiakum PTA Smorgasbord* . . .

Man, is this a wealthy reminder of the origins of a lot of the women in this county! You can sample such delicacies as magnificent sturgeon fish balls . . . and the line which formed to the left a decade or so ago when this feast was initiated, was so long they had to do something about it. With an efficiency that marks the talents of any well-organized housewife, the ladies now give you a card which tells you when to show up for their feast. That frees you from any worry about "when do we eat?" and . . .

Enables you to browse and buy at the local shops.

Prowling Cathlamet

Wahkiakum County Historical Museum is located at the bend of River Street on a small bluff above the river. It contains tools, clothing, books, etc. from the bye-gone days. And for a buck, you can buy a map of Wahkiakum County and Cathlamet historical sites, and the charming Historic Northwest Calendar with sketches of Washington and Oregon landmarks (one of whose artists, Carolyn Feasey, also is a Cathlamet Woman in Action). Open most afternoons in the summer and Thursday-Saturday in the winter.

Wahkiakum County has over 55 miles of Columbia River shoreline and contains 65 miles of streams, sloughs and man-made waterways, and there are lots of ways for you to take advantage of them. *White's Island*, reachable by foot at low tide (you're 7 miles from the ocean here but you notice the tides), is owned by the State and has a network of sloughs for prowling by boat; and *Sand Island*, used for Japanese Prisoners of War during World War II contains artifacts left by the prisoners after their incarceration. *Abe Creek Park* offers a view of the Columbia through shade trees, and *Hayes Park* in the area of a Crown Zellerbach tree farm has a gravel bar where youngsters can go wading in the Elochoman River, together with picnic tables and fire pits . . . . The county Port District has developed a new, sheltered boat moorage with launch ramps, parking, picnic and play area.

You can call in advance and get a scheduled tour of Crown Z's *Cathlamet Managed Forest*, 2 to 3 hours of visiting all types of modern logging operations, or take your own self-conducted tour on hard-surfaced roads. Of prime interest is the Crown Z sorting yard at the west end of town with a viewing platform for visitors.

There are a couple of really unusual opportunities in and around Cathlamet. First, a golf course with a great view of the Columbia as you approach from the east. It only has 5 holes, but you can play it *twice* for a buck; and second, the sturgeon fishing at the *State Fishing Beach* on the Cowlitz-Wahkiakum county line. You are allowed to catch one sturgeon every 7 days, it must be over 3 feet and under 5 feet and anything else is illegal.

They call a lot of sturgeon you get in these here parts "smoked . . ."

A lot of it also is "poached."

Uncommon shopping – *Macrame Shop*, on Front Street.

A word about eating – *Marie's . . . Jim's . . . Paul's Canteen* (The Dock Tavern) for beer and snacks . . . and the *Hole in the Wall*, red and black, with checkered tablecloths and shake walls, run by high school kids and featuring "malts" when we were there.

Annual affairs – Now here's a county that flips for annual affairs — all in all, there are 6 of them in Cathlamet. *Cathlamet Little Theater*, April . . . *Wahkiakum PTA Smorgasbord*, 1st week in May, pickled herring, lefse, rhumkake, rosettis, fatigman, ham, roast beef, pies salads — all homemade . . . *Norway Independence Day*, May 17 . . . *Kid Parade* and *Invitational Softball Tournament*, June . . . *Summer Arts Festival*, 3rd week in July, Queen Fair Contest, loggers' breakfast, logging show, square dance, parade . . . *Annual Melodrama and Poster Art Exhibit*, 2nd week in August.

Speaking of annual affairs automatically bring us to the subject of Bob Goodfellow, a gentleman from Eatonville. Goodfellow opened a drugstore in Cathlamet in the late 1920's. But he had a problem. There were two doctors in town at the time, neither of whom would send their patients to druggist Goodfellow for their prescriptions. By formulating and mixing their own medicines, the doctors could pick up a buck or two on the side.

The ordinary druggist might have died there and then, but not Bob. He got ahold of a young fellow by the name Harold Fritz who was fresh out of medical school and starting a practice in Tacoma and persuaded Dr. Fritz to come to Cathlamet. As it turned out, one of the previous doctors who'd been practicing in Cathlamet had neglected to attend medical school before entering the practice of medicine, and left town in a fair hurry after Dr. Fritz appeared on the scene. The other one lasted 3 months and then relinquished the field to Dr. Fritz — who sent his patients to Goodfellow for their prescriptions.

Cathlamet was an isolated community in those days . . . one of the last in the State to get a road built in. Prior to that, medical care and everything else required water transportation.

A few years back, Goodfellow retired from the druggist business and went into "annual affairs" as a volunteer . . . which is why they have so many in this community. His "office" is in Jim's Cafe.

For further information – Call the *Wahkiakum County Eagle*, 795-3391.

While you're about Cathlamet, you can browse *Puget Island* — often referred to as the town's "Little Norway," where less than an hour's drive will cover this essentially residential area, with a small fishing fleet and a superior view of freighters plying the Columbia River from the 14 miles of dikes. Sixteen ferries a day leave the Island for Oregon between the hours of 7:15 a.m. and 11:30 p.m.

Continuing along the river there is some fine fun ahead — and that includes at least one great gastronomical adventure if you arrange to be around at the right time of the year.

First, you take off to Skamokawa (Ska-mock-away). It once was the number 3 town on the river, preceded only by Astoria as number one and Portland as two. Nowadays, if you drive too fast, you'll miss it. Start looking for it about 8 miles west of Cathlamet.

Skamokawa — (Pop. Nom. Elev. 1C.) — Once in an area referred to as "Little Venice," it's located along a slough at the mouth of three creeks — with the stores backed on the water. Left of the abandoned grade school is a sandy beach where you can picnic, if you can do so without the benefit of picnic tables. You also can get a closeup of big freighters, because that's where the channel goes. If you climb the hill behind the Redmen Hall, you can have a splendid view of the Columbia if it isn't foggy — although it's sometimes foggy, and some opine it was fog over the water, mistaken for smoke, which gave the town its Indian name, Smoke Over Water.

A Chicago businessman by the name of Pierre Pype is blowing a bundle on restoration of the *Redmen Hall*, and naturally, it's referred to locally as a "Pype Dream."

Listed as a partial ghost town, there are signs that Skamokawa may be restoring and turning back to its sternwheeler past on the River.

Uncommon shopping – *Hoby's General Store* is located on pilings over the slough. With your purchase, you also can be filled in on local lore by Hoby Thatcher and his wife, Clara . . . *Dodge's Antiques and Agates*, a mile east, has antique dishes and glass, with a collection of rocks for polishing or already polished . . . also coffee and cookies.

A word about eating – The level of local humor is indicated by the name of the leading, and only, restaurant which is called the *Duck Inn*. There's a bar and live and lively music when the folks come gather round on weekends. It's on the slough, but faces the highway. The water's always been there but the road is fairly new.

Annual affairs – *Skamokawa Firemen's Ball*, 3rd week in May . . . *Wahkiakum County Fair*, mid-August. Typical small county fair and delightful.

As long as you've gone this far, you might as well head up the gap and over the "pass" (760 feet) of KM (first initials of long-gone logging men) Mountain, where if you're lucky and energetic you might find some fossils.

Lewis & Clark, stopped along in this area, a fact of which you will periodically be reminded.

About a mile east of Grays River, there's an attractive sign explaining the *Grays River Covered Bridge* (built in 1905, 158 feet long and 14 feet wide with a 4-ton load limit), which is in the valley below. It's on the National Register of Historic Sites and you can drive it if you're of a mind to.

At Grays River is a Valley Tavern where the folks gather on weekends and there are hummingbird feeders in the windows, and a general store. This is pastoral, inland valley country and an area of picturesque barns — one of them is an unusual round style.

A word about eating – *Grays River Inn*, comes well recommended by people for at least 20 miles around. Fifty kinds of hamburgers, and homemade soup that you should get there early for or you won't get any.

Annual affairs – *"Not-Quite-White-Water Run,"* 2nd week in June, on Grays River.

At Rosburg, there is a worthwhile side trip on Highway 403 heading to the mouth of the Grays River. En route you can go up the Eden Valley Road to visit *Eden Valley Enterprises*, various art forms made by personable David (photographer) and Elaine (potter) Meyer. Name of the business may be changed to Black Silver-Mud Stone by the time you get there, but the phone is still 465-2577. Better inquire how to get there. It's complicated.

From Eden Valley the road hugs the Grays River Bay around a bluff to Altoona, once a fish cannery, and a vast Columbia River with dozens of sand and grass islands. To the east is *Pillar Rock* which rises 75 feet from the river bottom — usually about 25 feet showing.

Pillar Rock is big in local history, and in its way is a symbol of something or other. It caught the eye of Lieutenant William Broughton of Captain Vancouver's crew who named it on October 25, 1792. Seventeen years later Lewis and Clark climbed the hill above it and came up with the famous quote about seeing the "Ocian and oh the joy of it!" They camped here that night. At the time, an estimated 50,000 Indians were eating an estimated 18,000,000 pounds of salmon annually.

On August 20, 1841, the meticulous explorer of the Pacific Northwest, Captain Charles Wilkes, named and described Pillar Rock like this, "The rock is 25 feet high and only ten square feet at the top; it is composed of conglomerate or pudding stone, and is fast crumbling to pieces. I found great difficulty in ascending it . . ."

By 1832, the Hudson's Bay Company had a salmon saltery here and was shipping the fish to the Hawaiian Islands. About that time, the white man introduced something the Indians never had experienced before. And for lack of a better name, we'll call if influenza. The Indian system of treating this ailment consisted of getting up a good sweat in a hot box and plunging into icy water. The disease, complemented by the treatment, decimated 80% of the Indian population in the next 20 years . . . which meant that the salmon run in the Columbia went virtually unchecked until June 13, 1866 when one George W. Hume arrived at nearby Eagle Rock with the know-how and the equipment to put salmon from this river in cans. A lot of the cans blew up when bacteria got working inside, but those that didn't were shipped to all kinds of improbable places in cans painted with red lead . . . and the salmon boom was on.

On June 12, 1878, a salmon cannery was constructed here. And a dozen years later there were 1,000 fishing boats in and around the Columbia, some 39 canneries shipping an enormous pack around the world. The Columbia River catch of salmon ran to over 30,000,000 pounds. Pillar Rock was a key location on the north side of the river for canning this harvest. It was a busy place.

And historian Appelo describes it today, "It is ironical that now that (the community of) Pillar Rock can be reached by road, has a daily mail run by automobile and a school bus run, has electricity, has dial telephone service . . . (one) finds that the salmon industry which made it such an important factory . . .

now has declined to the point that it scarcely maintains the canning lines at nearby Astoria . . ."

The salmon catch of the Columbia is well below a third of what it was during the several thousand years that it served as the mainstay of Indian life here.

◆

Returning to Highway 4 you can go left to Naselle in Pacific County, or cross the Megler Bridge into Oregon for a return back to Longview via the Oregon side.

And here's a neat reason for going to Naselle: About a decade ago, this community was in need of an ambulance and they came up with an idea for raising the money with the *Firemen's Smorgasbord.* It's held in the school of this predominantly Finnish community in the middle of May, and the goodies bring maybe 1,300 people from all over. No price is asked for the dinner — just contributions to maintain the ambulance dropped into a fire pump can. It's an 8 course meal in the Finnish tradition with 60 to 70 hot dishes . . . 40 salads . . . smoked salmon . . . pickled dishes . . . Swedish potato sausage . . . homemade breads . . . fried chicken . . . baked ham . . . turkey . . . oyster casserole and sturgeon casserole. All done by the best cooks in the area . . . .

Ah, man, is it good! Remember the middle of May and be thankful. And call Buddy Nelson at the Post Office for details.

Then on to Megler and back to Longview via Puget Island or the Longview Bridge.

It's a good highway on the Oregon side and affords you great opportunities for looking across the Columbia at the State of Washington. It also provides you the best opportunity of getting an overall perspective of the Longview-Kelso combo, especially when you get up on that big bridge.

In 1921, when the Oregon State Highway Commission authorized a survey for a bridge west of Portland, the folks down there thought the whole thing was a grand idea. They didn't get around to building it, although Portland businessmen thought it was a wonderful method of providing the people of southwest Washington with easy access to the wide variety of shopping in Portland.

But a few years later, when the previously mentioned Wesley Vandercook proposed to build such a bridge, it occurred to everybody that the bridge went both ways and some of the Oregon people might want to do some shopping in the fabulous new town called Longview.

So all hell broke loose.

In 1926, bills were introduced into both Houses of Congress authorizing private parties to build the bridge.

All of a sudden, it became Longview versus Portland . . . the Lower Cowlitz Valley versus the Willamette Valley . . . the State of Washington versus Oregon.

And while R. A. Long had declined an opportunity to participate in the construction of the bridge (he had his hands full at the moment without adding a bridge to his troubles) the fact that Vandercook was associated with Long-Bell was enough incentive for the Portlanders to start slamming Long-Bell.

Portland Commerce, the official publication of that city's Chamber of Commerce, carried an item reading in part, "they have a big lumber corporation, boasting a townsite of *small proportions* the lots of which would be given higher value through building a bridge across the Columbia . . ."

They never should have written that part about "small proportions" in reference to Long's dream town.

He blew his cork and decided to show them whether or not he had any political clout after half a century of honorable operation in the South. Southern congressmen and senators got "turned on" via the 145 Long-Bell retail managers in their areas. And pretty soon the bridge issue was up to President Calvin Coolidge for signature or veto. The respected *Portland Oregonian* took the position that this was a tempest in a teapot and the *Oregon Journal* tore into its rival publication (they're both under the same ownership now) asking "Why didn't Longview, the Seattle publishers, *The Oregonian*, and the bridge profiteers advocate the building of a dam across the Columbia at Longview and make the job complete?"

The upshot of the whole thing was the Portlanders brought "Old Ironsides," that heroic frigate of the War of 1812 into the act. They demanded that if there had to be a bridge, then, by God, it would have to be high enough for the "U.S. Frigate Constitution" to pass beneath it under a full complement of sails. The "specs" on the bridge were thusly changed from a height of 159 feet to 195 feet and the span from 750 to 1,125 feet.

And that's the way she is today.

"Old Ironsides" doesn't sail under it very often these days, but you sure get a great view from the bridge.

Longview-Kelso Tour 3 — Castle Rock, Silver Lake, Spirit Lake, Mount St. Helens (Map XV)

From the standpoint of the car-cushion traveler, Mount St. Helens and Spirit Lake, which it manufactured for itself, are the stars of this show, along with an approach up the Toutle River valley below the Green Mountain Range. There are periodic spectacular views of the cone of the mountain, which is our version of Mount Fujiyama. However, this is also a fine opportunity to drive the east side of the Cowlitz to the cozy little town of Castle Rock before taking off past Silver Lake, the largest natural lake in the county, and into a vast mountain wilderness.

Castle Rock — (Pop. 1,680. Elev. 52.) — This attractive small community is divided by the seemingly peaceful Cowlitz River, southbound. The majority of businesses and residences are on the flat area east of the river. More homes clamber up the bank and have exceptional views across the valley. The town is named for a rocky upthrust, one acre square and 150 feet high, south along the river.

The adjacent river area is a favorite of smelt fishermen and in January and February the river looks like a carnival, with the banks lined with smelt dippers and watchers. There's a dandy *riverside park* for picnicking.

Castle Rock competes with Toledo as the gateway to Mount St. Helens these days, but half a century ago, its importance was based on the fact that it was the gateway to one of the finest stands of timber in the world, to the west of town. This stand was the key that opened the door to the creation of Longview as a planned city.

By 1918, the Long-Bell Lumber Company was aware that, thanks to the dwindling supply of southern pine, it would have to decide whether to fold its tent and silently steal away or go some place else for timber. In October of that year, it bought 86,000 acres of land in southern Oregon. And this next figure is one worth pondering, for the 86,000 acres contained 1½ billion board feet of lumber, which the company figured was pretty good alongside of the amount they got from the same acreages in Missouri. The following year, the company bought another 70,000 acres in northern California.

But a thing Long-Bell had learned in 43 years of existence was that it was more profitable to cut good timber than poor in the first place. The company's timber scout kept hunting for bigger and better stands. And in 1919 he found what he considered the best piece of timberland he'd ever seen. It was within a few miles of a potentially important tidewater port.

This was one place where Weyerhaeuser missed the right turn in the dark . . . and, for whatever reason, sold its competitor Long-Bell a choice morsel of nearly 24,000 acres west of Castle Rock. This land yielded more timber than the 86,000 acres of land that Long-Bell had bought in Oregon, well over 5 times as much per acre, and resulted in the creation of Longview.

Weyerhaeuser had 30 billion board feet of timber in the area and 8 years later bought a mill site, including 2 miles of waterfront in Longview to erect it's biggest forest products complex. The company presently is spending close to $300,000,000 in modernizing that facility.

Uncommon shopping – Huson's Bakery, their specialty is "kitchen bread"; even on Sunday, doughnuts, pies, pastries. Appropriately, on site of the town's first school building . . . *Robins Roost Antiques*, exceptional antiques, Friday through Monday or "catch me if you can" . . . *The Cellar*, antiques, specializes in period furniture, glassware, jewelry, 7 days weekly.

A word about eating – *Gram's Confectionery*, homemade ice cream, hamburgers and — kids . . . *Village Pizza Parlor*, more kids.

Annual affairs – *Kon Tiki Raft Race*, 1st June Saturday, down the Cowlitz River to Kelso. Jaycees from all over participate. Some are goof-off rafts, carrying pumps, which have water fights. You can get wet on the banks just being a spectator . . . *National Champion Motorcycle Race*, in July. 30-lap national T.T. motorcycle event attended by 10 to 12 thousand . . . *Community Fair*, 1st week in August, county fair-style, queen's coronation, carnival.

Highway 504, which is called the "Gateway To Mount St. Helens," takes you past *Silver Lake*, which is the largest natural lake in the county. It's a highly popular recreational spot noted for it's bass fishing, waterlilies, bulrushes — and water skiing. Several islands dot the surface, the largest encompassing 55 acres. It's 6½ miles long — and only 10 feet deep. Across the road from the lake is very well-attended *Seaquest State Park*.

There's good rock-hounding for jasper and agate on the way up if you know what you're doing, but if you're our kind of traveler, you'll pause at a rock shop along the way, a procedure that's a little more expensive but surely saves time. You also will find bald eagles above the 3,000-foot elevation.

Mount St. Helens — (Elev. 9,671.) is the prettiest, youngest, smallest and feistiest volcano in the state. A single peak, it's sort of a miniature version of Mount Fujiyama (which is 3 times as high). Its origin dates back 10's of thousands of years instead of 100's of thousands. It's some 5,000 feet lower than Mt. Rainier, about 3,000 feet lower than Mt. Adams and 1,000 feet lower than Mt. Baker. But due to peculiarities of its lava formation and single crater, it periodically gets plugged up . . . and when she blows, she really blows. Ash from this mountain has been found as far away as Banff, Alberta. About 3,000 years ago, she dumped ash to depths of 5 feet at a distance of 50 miles and a mere 450 years ago she put 5 inches of the stuff on the ground at the same distance.

On November 22, 1842, she covered areas as far away as Portland with about half an inch of ash, and filled the immediate vicinity of Spirit Lake with pumice to depths ranging as high as 20 feet . . . burying virgin forests and burning the trees to create tree casts visible in and around the campground at Spirit Lake. (An interesting experiment is to put one of the pumice rocks in the water. It'll float as long as 5 minutes before sinking.) She's responsible for the longest lava caves in continental United States. Some years back a mudflow from the peak blocked the headwaters of the Toutle River, creating Spirit Lake . . . a lake that emits such strange sounds it frightened the Indians around and about. That's how the lake got its name. The Indians thought it was inhabited by supernatural beings with ventriloqual powers. The lake, shaped like a bent pin, is 1,300 feet deep in places . . . and there are other unmeasured areas deeper than that. The bottom is lined with white pumice.

As this is being written, the U.S. Bureau of Land Management has drawn for priority purposes the names of some 50 applicants who want to tap our mountains for geothermal power . . . and Mount St. Helens is the most popular of the bunch as a potential place to create electricity from steam.

Dr. Dwight R. Crandell of the U.S. Geological Survey, who was mentioned in connection with Mount Rainier, and Jack Hyde, geology instructor at Tacoma Community College, are in the process of becoming intimately acquainted with Mount St. Helens, and have some thoughts on the subject that may well fit in with the proposals to help this mountain let off steam. They note that while another eruption of volcanic ash might contaminate water and crops and perhaps cave in some roofs, the biggest danger would come from the possible collapse of the Ariel, Yale and Swift Dams on the Lewis River. Water in the reservoirs behind the dams could flood Portland.

Dr. Crandell opines firmly that one of the state's volcanoes could go tomorrow — or a thousand tomorrows from now.

Prowling Mount St. Helens

Spirit Lake — The U.S. Forest Service clocks about 200,000 visitor-days through Spirit Lake where there's a large campground and ranger information center during the summer months. This is great country for big wild blue huckleberries and small wild black blackberries (the ones with the real flavor). There are some 30 lakes within a day's hike of this ranger station. The timberline, lowest in the State, and advancing at a discernible rate, is about 4 miles away and 1,000 feet higher than the lake. It has picnic facilities and a geologic walk and view of the mountain.

A word about eating and sleeping – There are 3 private resorts, *Spirit Lake Lodge, Mt. St. Helens Lodge*, and *Harmony Lodge*, around the Lake. Simple accommodations, fare.

For further information – Write the Gifford Pinchot National Forest, P.O. Box 449, Vancouver, Washington 98660.

The return trip routes you through Toledo on Highway 505, past Vader and back down the west side of the Cowlitz to West Kelso.

Vancouver Tour 1 — In and Around the City (Map XVI)

What with cheaper cigarettes and laxer liquor laws in Oregon as a couple of lodestones over the years, what we have tended to forget about Vancouver is that she's the fountainhead of Washington history. You also have to admit that the frightful, glooped up traffic pattern in and among the garish motels and restaurants on old Highway 99, did little to create a favorable impression of this city.

And, let's face it, being the smaller of two cities at the bend in the Columbia here, did little to enhance Vancouver's image of herself. But here's a place where Interstate 5 performed a miracle. The freeway provided a new look at the tired old town. The resurgence of interest in history on the part of all of us has helped things along, together with a new appreciation of the environmental impact of the Mighty Columbia. Anyway this is the town where the United States and Great Britain had their last real nose-to-nose confrontation. This is where one lone man tried to stem the tide of American emigration in the West . . . which was a job much too big for any one man. And this is where the State of Washington began.

Vancouver — (Pop. 43,400. Elev. 115.) — If you view Vancouver without going back in your mind's eye to the tide of the empire as it swept through here, then you're not with the heartbeat of this city. And if you do open your eyes to its historical heritage, then a totally new concept is in store for you.

Let's face it, the federal government does not have the old Highway 99 motel strip in mind as it makes plans to spend something over $5,000,000 in the restoration of Fort Vancouver.

This is where the last decisive battle with Great Britain was fought — the fact that no shots were fired and the contretemps over the pig on San Juan Island something over a decade later to the contrary and notwithstanding.

By way of emotional entanglements, it must be remembered that Fort Vancouver was established a scant ten years after the British burned Washington, D.C. and the White House, during the War of 1812. Substantially more Americans were involved militarily in that war than in the Revolutionary War . . . nearly as many Americans had been killed in that one as in the Revolutionary War.

So the relations between the two countries were, at the very least, sensitive, until 1846 when the Oregon Territory question was settled.

Had that not been the case, it is more than likely that Vancouver would be the larger city instead of Portland along the banks of the Columbia River today.

In a nutshell, what happened was this: Great Britain decided that while the two countries had agreed on the present boundary at the 49th parallel as far west as the Rockies, the Columbia River would be the boundary west of the Rockies.

With this in mind, the Hudson's Bay Company was instructed to abandon Fort George at Astoria — on the stated grounds that the furs mildewed there — and establish Fort Vancouver in a commanding position down the

Columbia and Willamette and up the Cowlitz. And Dr. John McLoughlin, whose ulcerous stomach got him into petty quarrels with his superiors — was banished to the "sticks" with instructions to keep those Americans from settling north of the Columbia.

For the first few years when the fur trade was brisk and settlers stayed away in droves, things were all to the good with McLoughlin. He introduced the first farming . . . horticulture . . . dairying . . . wool-growing . . . saw and grist mills . . . library . . . school . . . hospital and government, to an area bigger than France and Spain. He was the progenitor of civilization in the Pacific Northwest.

In 1841, thirty settlers made it across the Oregon Trail to Vancouver, and with no sweat, McLoughlin ushered them into the Willamette Valley. But the next year the fantastic happened. A thousand people gathered themselves into one wagon train in Missouri and headed west. It was a dumb thing to do and they learned the hard way just how dumb it was. And there never was a wagon train that big again.

McLoughlin successfully steered them south of the Columbia.

But that was only the beginning.

In 1843, three thousand immigrants arrived in McLoughlin's domain. He lived up to his reputation as the "despot of the Rockies" when he herded all of those rugged individualists south of what Great Britain hoped was the border . . . and two years later, a couple of settlers decided to take advantage of all those potential customers McLoughlin was sending south by going into a real estate venture. They flipped a coin and called in Portland. That was the year that a man named James K. Polk, who had distinguished himself by losing the gubernatorial campaign in Tennessee for two elections in a row, got named President of the United States by 38,000 votes.

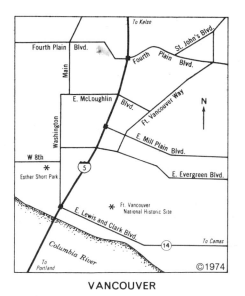

VANCOUVER

The campaign issue which the folks out West took seriously was "54-40 or fight!" They took note of the fact that McLoughlin had either conned or coerced them south of the big river, and started hollering for all of the western territory up to the bottom of Alaska.

Neither the United States, which was busy with those Mexicans at the time, nor Great Britain, which was looking at Russia with a jaundiced eye, wanted a repeat of the War of 1812. And in June of 1846 the two countries compromised on the present boundary between the United States and Canada.

As is the case in any big organization when things go wrong, the Hudson's Bay Company needed a goat and gladly selected McLoughlin for the role. By that time, he'd made enough enemies among the Americans with his big stop sign on the north bank of the river that they sailed an interesting law through the Congress of the United States: Any land that McLoughlin had sold to somebody else in Oregon was legally owned by them. But any he had retained for himself was confiscated.

If ever a guy was caught in the middle, McLoughlin was it. They got around to naming him "Father of Oregon" — but not until after he was dead.

Prowling Vancouver

If you're coming in from the north, go east on the Fourth Plain Boulevard exit past the Veterans Administration Hospital and take a right along Fort Vancouver Way for the most astonishing piece of property in the metropolitan area. Straddling the city limits to the east, it pays no attention whatsoever to the streets put together by civilian authorities. Bounded by East and West Reserve Streets, it cuts a grassy swath down the hill to the river. It's about a mile wide and two miles long diagonally down hill. Main roads which bend to cross it are McLoughlin, East Mill Plain and Evergreen Boulevards. This was the Reserve for Fort Vancouver, now turned over for the most part to civilian governmental units. It would be the equivalent in Seattle, for example, of taking out a huge chunk of downtown and saying, "Okay, fellas, here's a beautiful hunk of property which you can develop in line with our present-day thoughts on environmental impact. Let's see what you can do with it."

What they've done with it to date is very nice . . . and it looks like this is only the beginning.

The trick is to stop by the Washington State Information Booth on Interstate 5, or the Greater Vancouver Chamber of Commerce and pick up one of their "See and Do" sheets.

Presuming you have this in hand and are prepared to use it, the following background information should add zest to your tour.

Take the *Grant House Museum*, on the Post, for example. A log building presently covered with siding, it was built in 1849 and is the oldest building in the Vancouver Barracks. Today it's part of "Officers' Row," but in 1852-53, when he still was a brevet captain, President U.S. Grant had his office here . . .

And hated it.

After the Mexican War, Grant was married to Julia Dent and spent four years idyllically in posts at Sackets Harbor, N.Y. and Detroit, Michigan, but when his regiment was transferred to Fort Vancouver, Julia and their young family had to be left behind because they didn't have enough money for the long trip west.

Julia was the one woman of his life and he set about trying to improve his financial position so he could get her out here. He tried raising chickens, but they died. Then potatoes were commanding fabulous prices and he found some rich bottom land along the river. He borrowed some money from Lieut. Col. L. E. Bonneville at the usurious interest rate of 24% a year. And just as the plants were coming up nicely, the river rose and flooded him out.

San Francisco was a gung ho town with a gold rush at the time, but there was one essential ingredient they lacked — ice for their champagne buckets.

In desperation, at one point, a ship was commissioned specifically to go to Puget Sound for a load of the stuff which they were sure abounded in the lakes and streams in the winter and came back empty. So Grant got the bright idea of producing a cargo of ice from the ice caves upriver from Vancouver. But the ship became beclamed en route south and the cargo melted.

Adding fuel to the flames was Grant's superior officer, Col. Robert Buchanan, who rode him hard and a few years later helped precipitate Grant's decision to resign his commission.

In the meantime, he did the only logical thing.

He took to the booze to drown his troubles.

He got over raising chickens, and planting potatoes, and shipping melting ice, and his hatred for Buchanan, his separation from his family and his resignation from the army. But he surely didn't get over the drinking. And at one point during the Civil War a group of clergymen called on President Abraham Lincoln to protest Grant's drinking habits . . . giving rise to one of the great pieces of Americana.

When Lincoln asked the clergymen where Grant got his supply, they said they didn't know, and Lincoln said, "I'm sorry, for if you could tell me I would direct the Chief Quartermaster of the Army to lay in a large stock of the same kind of liquor, and would also direct him to furnish a supply to some of my generals who have never yet won a victory."

The City Cemetery, between 13th and East Mill Plain Boulevard, is a rich resource of memorabilia, if you like this sort of thing.

There is nothing richer than the story behind the headstone on the grave of Arthur Haine.

Haine, an Englishman, was studying for the priesthood in the 1850's but before he got very far, he fell in love with a chorus girl who jilted him.

That turned him into an atheist, which in turn zeroed him in on becoming the town's most colorful character. And the hunting season brought out his best characterization. Haine had an admirable hunting dog, a hunting cap of the two-billed variety Sherlock Holmes wore, knickers and a trusty fowling piece. When the hunting season started, he repaired to the nearest saloon completely equipped for the hunt — including the dog.

And he remained there until the hunting season was over.

When Arthur died, his friends followed his wishes by conveying his mortal remains to the cemetery in a beer wagon hauled by six white horses and preceded by a brass band.

His tombstone bears two words: "Haine H'ain't."

Esther Short Park, at 6th and Esther, is named after the "Mother" of Vancouver. *The Slocum House*, built in about 1867 by Charles W. and Laura Slocum, was moved to the Park in 1966. It's a magnificent Victorian structure that is now the Old Slocum House Theater, utilizing the former living room for seats, and dining room as stage. Plays written during or about the 19th Century are presented weekends year-round.

We'd be proud to live in a city which had so redoubtable a soul as Esther Short for its mother. Small wonder that the Pioneer Mother's Statue is located here, and with even further maternal perspicacity somebody saw to it that children's rest rooms also were installed at this historic site.

The headstone in the City Cemetery notes that Esther Short died at the age of "fifty-six years, six months and four days." She surmounted a lot of troubles in her day, most of them brought on by her husband, Amos, who would be referred to in these enlightened days as a "male chauvinist pig!"

In the 24 years they were married, for instance, she had to take a little time off every other year to bear one of Amos' children. No wonder they put the Pioneer *Mother's* Statue in Esther's Park. The total had reached 13 before Short's untimely death by drowning brought an end to this phase of her career. But the troubles he had initiated wouldn't be resolved in the courts until 18 years after Esther's death on June 27, 1862.

Among other things, Amos thought he was a hot-shot businessman although Clark County's delightful historian, Howard C. Burnham, said that Short never owned a piece of land in fee simple except the plot he was buried in. And Burnham ought to know. He ran a title insurance business in Vancouver for 30 years.

Amos and Dr. McLoughlin did not get along.

And in this instance, the evidence indicates that McLoughlin had the logical stance. In the beginning, a fellow named Henry Williamson hired a surveyor to lay out 500 lots in what would become the future city of Vancouver. When the area had been legally surveyed and mapped, it was legally recorded in the Recorder's Book in Oregon City.

Williamson went back east to marry his girl friend and bring her out here (only to find she had died). Amos jumped Williamson's claim. McLoughlin's men unceremoniously moved the Short family off the land and deposited them on the south side of the river, warning them not to come back.

Amos, of course, immediately returned and squatted on the land with his family. So McLoughlin, sent a tough crew of French Canadians to move them off again. Amos wasn't there when this crew showed up and started to lay hands to his fence. Esther, the Pioneer Mother, who was part Algonquin Indian, flattened the leader with a right hook that he still ruefully remembered when he was interviewed about it half a century later. He decided that if McLoughlin wanted the Shorts off that land, then McLoughlin could move them, and took his crew out of there.

It is possible to understand that the situation between the Shorts and the Hudson's Bay Company was relatively tense. Let's take it a step farther. The relationship between the United States and Great Britain was relatively tense.

And that's when Dr. David Gardner of the American Missionary Society came innocently down the pike. Dr. Gardner was new to the missionary business and his life expectancy in this line of endeavor was destined to be short. He had arrived in the area on December 28, 1849 to minister to the spiritual needs of benighted souls in the untamed West. In the four months he'd been there, he had come to the realization that he had his work cut out for him. But prior to April 5, 1850, when he went calling on the Short family, his ardor was undimmed. On the day in question, he approached the Short cabin with a trusted Kanaka (Hawaiian converted to Christianity) at his side. For purposes of the record in view of what ensued, it is necessary to note that both men were unarmed . . . and Esther wasn't home. Nevertheless, the two men were on God's mission.

As they approached the cabin, Amos shot and killed both of them.

The first word Esther got about the incident was this: The Congregational minister came calling and Amos murdered him.

By the time Esther arrived, the Hudson's Bay Company men had collared Amos and lodged him in the bastille. They had notions of doing unto him as he had done unto the Congregational minister. Esther moved in fast and got the Americans on the south side of the river to take Amos into protective custody. She successfully stalled a trial on the matter for the next three years, but justice did require that Amos ultimately would be called before the bench on the murder charge.

When Amos did appear before a jury, his was one of a dozen cases to be heard. The jurymen were busy with a lot of other things . . . and they intended to dispose of all of them in one day, which they did. Amos testified that a couple of tough Hudson's Bay Company men had come to drive him off his homestead. In the ensuing struggle they were killed. The jury dismissed the case against him and let him go . . . and that was the end of it.

No, not quite . . .

After that experience, Amos fell in love with the American System of Justice and decided it would be nice to be a judge. So he ran for the office of Probate Judge. To his surprise and delight, he was named chief justice of the 3-man Probate Court. What happened was the other two guys got only 22 votes apiece . . . and Amos got 23.

Meanwhile, the Roman Catholic Church had filed claim on the disputed property and it was a legal mess. But after Amos' death, Esther refused to recognize that anybody else had a claim to the land . . . built the first hotel . . . provided land for a park and more land for the Port . . . and in 1880 the courts agreed with her.

The "big" one in Vancouver is the *Fort Vancouver National Historic Site*, which commemorates the Hudson's Bay Company Fort, built in 1825. The site includes Officer's Row with the afore-mentioned historic buildings and a commanding view, a National Park Service Museum with exhibits and films, and the restoration of the Hudson's Bay Company Fort rising again on its original site. The north stockade is completed and the buildings are beginning to appear. The whole complex is on a long grassy slope ending at the Columbia River, and it's mighty mind-boggling to stand there and contemplate the colorful history of this scene. Plans are underway for an enormous, multi-million-dollar restoration.

The *Clark County Historical Museum*, at 16th and Main, has a pioneer doctor's office with complete drug display, one of the first printing presses, dioramas depicting the story of the area and an 1890 country store.

Now undergoing restoration to become a shopping mall is *Providence Academy*, built in 1873 by the area's first architect, Mother Joseph of the Sisters of Charity of Providence. The 1884 *St. James Church* with its Belgian hand-carved altar; the oldest house in the area, the *Covington House*, built in 1840, and the *Old Apple Tree*, planted from seed brought from London in 1825, are all worthy of a visit. Oh yes, and the *Kanaka Village Site*, with its marker for the Kanaka shot by Amos Short — the marker isn't much but there's a picnic table and one of the rare bits of good beach along the Columbia River adjacent.

A pleasant residential drive is out on McArthur Boulevard and jog south toward the river to Highland and Buena Vista Drives. Check with the Chamber of Commerce for industries you may visit.

Uncommon shopping – Not surprisingly in one of the State's oldest towns, Vancouver has a number of good antique shops, *Ted Hart's* and *Bob and Fran's* being two of the more interesting ones . . . For good "junkitiques," there's *Cochran's Second Hand Store* behind a typical Old West store front . . . For new things, the *Tower Mall*, a new shopping complex . . . if you're fond of good butcher shops, there's an excellent one in the *Tepee Market* on Columbia Street.

A word about eating – If you're in a more luxurious mood the *Inn of the Quay*, right over the river, or *Diamond Jim's*, Tower Mall, with a "Showboat" look . . . more moderate are two oldtimers, *Holland* and *Onslow's* as well as *The Stagecoach*, which features a soup course from a black kettle, *Chuckwagon* and *The Swain* . . . *The Hayloft*, Tower Mall, dressed up tavern, complete with old barn walls, serves beef stews, clams, steamed crab . . . *Alderbrook Haus*, in Orchards, authentic German food with beer garden and oompah band in summer. Garden complete with natural landscape, creek and colored lights . . . *Gram's*, for coffee and freshly made rolls . . . *Black Angus*, for good steaks and lounge entertainment . . . *Deli Shoppe*, turns out good sandwiches you might take on a picnic.

A word about sleeping – *Inn of the Quay*, on the river, is very comfortable and complete . . . Other good ones are *Travelodge, Riviera, Fort* and *Aloha*.

Annual affairs – *Art Fair*, 3 days in November, at Clark College, selective regional artists and craftsmen . . . *Flea Market*, in November and sponsored by St. Joseph's Hospital auxiliary. Popular annual event.

For further information – Greater Vancouver Chamber of Commerce; phone, 694-2588.

Vancouver Tour 2 — Ridgefield, Woodland, Ariel, Cougar, Battleground (Map XVI)

This is a tour that should challenge your instincts as an explorer, but it's worth it. It starts out along a ridge west of Interstate 5 into a town appropriately called Ridgefield. It follows a challenging maze of back-roads overlooking islands in the Columbia which from the standpoint of a real estate developer would be considered a real mess. On the other hand, they're a delightful location from the standpoint of a migratory bird and thanks to the Migratory Bird Hunting Stamp Act, a lot of it will become a refuge. Ridgefield is a "Tom Sawyer" type town.

Our favorite spot for prowling is in the area around Woodland where they grow beautiful vegetables and flower bulbs. It's the third most important area in the State for bulbs. You also can drive the dikes and get closeup views of huge ships towering above you in the river . . . in the fishing season, there are shoulder-to-shoulder fishermen along the dikes. This is "plains" country with an area of flatlands easily twice the size of those on the Portland side of the river. Climatically speaking, the region is considered an Interior Valley Zone and described as the warmest and driest west of the Cascades. Oak and pine trees are prevalent. The dairy industry is big on this tour and supplies the surrounding metropolitan areas on both sides of the river. Commercial berry farmers harvest strawberries, raspberries, blackberries and blueberries, a lot of nuts, and it's the leading filbert-growing area in the State. There also are grown here Italian prunes, Bartlett pears, cherries and some apples. Seed growers specialize in clover seed production. This is the most specialized cucumber acreage in the State and the second most important acreage in snap beans. Mint grown here also is a prime crop. Generally following the Lewis River, this tour includes the Ape Caves and the Old Grist Mill, as well as the 3 reservoirs that would flood Portland, should Mount St. Helens decide to erupt.

Going west on 78th in Vancouver, you eventually come to Lakeshore Boulevard, which goes north alongside Vancouver Lake. Following signs that direct you to Felida, Sara and Ridgefield, this route climbs to a ridge which has periodic views of the vast island area in the Columbia as the road jogs around property lines. You pass roadside stands selling corn, cukes, peas, berries. There are a lot of barns and silos and dairy cattle. It's that kind of country.

The best view of all is at a cemetery road junction shortly before you reach Ridgefield. The earlier in the day, the better the view.

Ridgefield — (Pop. 1,014, Elev. 60.) — It's the kind of town we visualize as the one Mark Twain had in mind when he wrote *Tom Sawyer*. It's a town of big square blocks rather than one long main street . . . along with a feeling of the early twentieth century with large old shade trees and wide streets. There's a pleasant city park with a stream bubbling through it and a grocery, hardware and *Nifty Thrifty Second Hand Store*. There is one small restaurant, the Ridgefield Cafe. Stop at the *Ridgefield National Wildlife Refuge* office in the bank building. A half-block walk will take you down to the Lake River that borders the Refuge, managed for migratory waterfowl, primarily to provide migrating and wintering habitat for the dusky Canada goose.

Other waterfowl that can be seen during the fall and winter include whistling swans, snow geese, mallard, pintail, widgeon, and wood ducks. Refuge land types vary from improved pasture protected by dike to tall stands of Douglas fir interspersed with flooded willow, brush and stands of oak. Livestock grazing is continued as an important management tool in maintaining the proper composition and condition of vegetation for waterfowl use.

Woodland — (Pop. 1,532. Elev. 33.) — We just love this little town, although you get almost no picture of it from the freeway. You can drive completely around it on dikes protecting a low, wide plain from the Lewis River on the south and east, and the Columbia River on the west. The 14 miles of dike create Woodland Bottoms, 6,000 acres of bulb, carrot, strawberry and dairy farms and lilac gardens. Located at the confluence of the 2 rivers, it is a small pocket protected from the weather in all directions. The road on the dike provides views of both the farms and the rivers. Driving along the Lewis, look sharply across by the railroad bridge to a handsome white colonial house and farm nestled by a hillside.

Prowling Woodland

Roads lead down to the Columbia for some of the most remarkable fishing in the world. Periodically, there are little three-sided lean-tos built of driftwood in the sand, and a lot of them are furnished with upholstered second-hand easy chairs. And the fishing is our kind. The poles are placed in patented pole holders, which are stuck in the sand. At the top of the pole is a bell. You can bring along your own deck chairs, build a small fire and wait until a biting fish rings the bell, while enormous freighters from the four corners of the earth parade in front of you. When the salmon and steelhead are running, poles line the bank about every 4 feet. Great place for kids and dogs.

The town isn't all that big, but there are some fine old buildings presently being restored with meticulous care. Not for visiting, but you can look as you drive by.

Uncommon shopping – *Woodland Shop*, in an old store, Jim Kemp, former Boeing employee and anthropologist, sells and repairs shoes, custommakes belts, bags, holsters, saddles, sandals and moccasins . . . *Dorwen* and *Cascade Products*, two small fishing pole factories.

A word about eating – *The Oak Tree*, reminiscent of the Nut Tree in California, does a brisk business in good food . . . *Woodland Bakery*, great coffee-n-rolls.

Annual affairs – *Planter's Day Celebration*, June at Horseshoe Lake; celebration of the first time the dike held, protecting Woodland bottom farms — includes water ski show, gem show, parade, logging demonstrations, bucking, climbing, log rolling, frog jumping contest, big barbecue.

The drive northeast from Woodland on Washington State 503 takes you up the Lewis River. No towns as such here, but the traveler will enjoy the lush Western Washington scenery of alder groves, heavily wooded second growth timber and beautiful views of lakes created by dams.

Ariel — Consists mostly of a combination country store and tavern owned by Germaine Tricola and husband, and is to the right of the road leading down to Merwin Park. Store building is old, wooden and a landmark in the area. Germaine says of her business "If the sun doesn't shine, people don't come, and the store people nitpick with the natives." It was a bit different for a while after D. B. Cooper hijacked a Northwest-Orient plane in 1972 and was dropped to disappear, presumably in this area. (Germaine was interviewed on the news one evening.) The "natives" are mostly loggers.

At the "Y" created by the road leaving State 503 leading to Lake Merwin is *Chief Lalooska's Potlatch House*, museum and studio workshop. Lalooska, a talented and industrious Indian woodcarver and master storyteller, has delved deeply into the cultural heritage of Northwest Coastal Indians.

His programs are scheduled through the Oregon Museum of Science and Industry (OMSI) in Portland and must be reserved in advance. There is always a program the fourth Saturday of each month (except December). The schools in this area use him as a resource and the kids love him.

The Pacific Power and Light Co. built the 3 dams — *Merwin, Yale,* and *Swift* on the Lewis River, which created 3 large lakes behind the dams. P. P. and L. has done a fine job creating parks and camps to encourage the use of the lakes and rivers. The campsites are semiprivate, not shoulder-to-shoulder, and all are attractively developed . . . Merwin Park on *Lake Merwin*, first and largest of the recreation areas, can accommodate 2,000 persons for picnics and swimming. Eleven miles up Lake Merwin is Speelyai Bay Park. On *Yale Lake* are Sadale Dam Park, Yale Park, and Cougar Park, all with picnicking, fishing and swimming (Cougar Camp is for "tent camping only" which is rather unique these days). On *Swift Creek Reservoir*, Eaglecliff Park is developed for benefit of bank fishermen.

The *H. L. Reese Store* east of Yale on Speelyai Creek is old and interesting. Mr. and Mrs. Reese came here in 1933 to stay 6 months and are still here and their store has a backwoods character, unpainted and brown weathered-looking with a sign-in spot on front porch for hikers. The Reeses' eyes dance when they tell their stories about "big foot" and display their huge plaster cast of a footprint. The father and his sons discovered the *Ape Cave* named so after a group of young men who explored this area and called themselves the Apes. (Not related to the apes mentioned by Mr. Wallace in Toledo.) North of Cougar are *Lava Tubes and Caves* created by the lava flows from Mount St. Helens. Ape Cave is 2.4 miles long under the ground (longest in world) and is featured by the State Department of Conservation as one to see on a self-guided tour. The entire lava tube area is oriental-looking on the surface with lava, moss and manzanita. To explore you need tough clothes, heavy shoes and flashlight. A map of Gifford Pinchot National Forest is handy to have here.

The road south from Yale to Amboy goes over a small pass and affords some dramatic views of Mount St. Helens to the north.

You might note *Nick's Tavern* in Amboy, because that's also a branch library. Part of a program to take the libraries to the loggers, the Ft. Vancouver Regional Library has branches in 5 taverns in rural Clark and Skamania Counties. The Vancouver director says loggers may feel they wouldn't be caught dead in a library, "but they do frequent taverns — so that's where we set up shop."

The *Old Cedar Creek Grist Mill*, built in 1874 and the only original structure of its kind, is located 8 miles west of Amboy on County Road 16, and now is recognized as an historic landmark.

North of *Battleground* on the east fork of the Lewis River is *Lewisville Park*, a day park offering picnicking, swimming, hiking and fishing capable of handling thousands of people. *Lucia Falls*, also on the east fork of the Lewis River is a scene of spectacular rocks, tall firs and deep pools. *Battleground Lake State Park* is a restful crater lake with fishing, boating, swimming, and a nearby small restaurant.

Annual affairs – *Silver Lake Bass Fishing Derby*, middle of April . . . *Amboy Territorial Days Celebration*, 2nd Saturday in July, parade . . . *Battleground Harvest Day*, 3rd Saturday in July, Harvest Day Queen coronation, carnival, parade, chicken barbecue, 4-H and FAA community fair.

—◆—

Vancouver Tour 3 — Camas, Washougal, North Bonneville, Skamania, Stevenson (Map XVI)

This tour takes you up the north bank of the Columbia River to the spot where the Cascade Crest Trail comes down out of the mountains. You can return via Oregon for a different look at the State of Washington if you're moved to. Highlights include a trip through the Zellerbach Paper Mill and its research department where you can learn how technology seeks to match our paper needs with our environmental desires . . . a trip through the Pendleton Woolen Mill and its outlet shop in Washougal . . . a visit to Beacon Rock and Bonneville Dam in the Columbia River Gorge . . . and a stop at Stevenson where with a little bit of luck and a certain amount of booze you may see the State's protected and official Monster, the Sasquatch.

Camas — (Pop. 5,825. Elev. 48.) — Named for Camassia Esculenta, a small wild plant with an edible bulb which was a favorite food of western Indians; once called La Camas (The Camas). Highway 14 out of Vancouver takes a direct route east slightly above the river to the two mill towns of Camas and Washougal. Rounding a small mountain into Camas, you pass its all-important Crown Zellerbach Mill. This town slopes down from a hillside residential area to the business district where Lackamas Creek flows into the Columbia, behind Lady Island. —◆—

The Crown Zellerbach Mill and research laboratory are not exactly the "beginning and end all" of Camas. They took a poll once and "breathing" nudged out the mill by just a little under two percentage points. A bit of an exaggeration, perhaps, but the importance is there all right, as some simple statistics will reveal.

In a town with a population of 5,790, the mill employs 3,000, not all living in Camas, of course. The annual payroll is $25,000,000 and the mill pays 75% of the school taxes. The money is important, naturally, but there's a matter of pride, too. The work done by the Research Department here looms large in all 12 of the Crown "Z" operations. And consider the problems that have been faced by the paper industry, in the last three-quarters of a century.

Since 1900, the population of the United States has increased less than 3 times, while the use of paper and paper products has gone up 47 times. Seventy-six million people used 30 pounds of paper apiece in 1899 and now 200 million use 530 pounds apiece. In the past quarter of a century pulp production in this State has tripled — without the cutting of a single extra tree. Those research guys are learning to use everything in the forest but the smell.

And speaking of the smell, the pulp mills have got two routes to go. In the sulfite process they create problems in the water. So they go the kraft process, but there they encounter trouble with the air. By chemical analysis, they can remove 98% of the sulfide. But getting rid of that last 2% is sheer murder, and, depending on the sensitivity of your olfactory nerves, you can pick it up.

We thought we detected a slight odor of sulphur when we were in town.

"Yeah," newspaper publisher Hal Zimmerman chuckled, "It's the sweet smell of money!"

Prowling Camas

This is a tidy little town with downtown mini-parks, plantings, and music piped outdoors. Call in advance for a 2 hour conducted tour of the *Crown Zellerbach Plant*, Tuesday through Thursday, 1 p.m., by appointment only — see pulp mill, paper products and research lab. One can picnic, fish, swim, at *Lackamas Park* half-a-mile northeast of town on Round Lake; fishing and boats at nearby *Lackamas Lake*. On the north shore of the lake is a startling *Victorian-style house*, painted bright red, and filled with beveled leaded glass windows. Drive up *Orune Hill* for a superb view both toward Portland and up the Columbia River.

Camas and Washougal are adjacent to each other — 2 miles, center to center — and used as one in many ways. One Chamber of Commerce serves both towns.

A word about eating – The Vancouver Quay people have a restaurant. *Parker's Landing*, right on the river with a fine overlook as you reach Washougal — intimate dining in a stylish building.

Washougal — (Pop. 3,394. Elev. 48.) — Indian for "rushing water." Town initially called Parker's Landing. Here is a town where Pendleton reigns. You may tour Pendleton Woolen Mills to see raw undyed wool become woven fabric, weekdays from 10 to 2.

Uncommon shopping – The outlet store for "seconds" at *Pendleton Woolen Mills* is a magnet for bargain hunters for miles around . . . *Gem Pit*, a lapidary shop for rockhounds.

We'll never know how much history has been changed by the casual spelling habits of the clerks who put things down on pieces of paper at the time, but there are a couple of instances connected with Clark County that are too good to be passed up.

For instance, until it was officially changed by the legislature in 1925, Clark County was spelled with an "e" on the end. And there still are a couple of venerable companies in the county like Clarke County Savings and Loan, and Clarke County Abstract and Title which carry the "e."

We are particularly charmed by an explanation for this spelling which appeared in *History of the Columbia River from the Dalles to the Sea* by Fred Lockley. Most people have heard of the Lewis and Clark Expedition. Perhaps a lesser number are aware that the two men involved spelled their names like this: "Merriwether Lewis" and "William Clark."

Mr. Lockley, however, did not have his facts on straight when he set about explaining in his history book how Clark County happened to be spelled with an "e" on the end. In his confusion, he also got the first names of the two men transposed. And this is how his explanation goes: ". . . in those days, Clark county was spelled with a final 'e' in honor of Captain Merri*weather* Clarke of the Lewis and *Clarke* expedition." (Italics ours.)

While, that distinctly belongs in the "how's that one again, please?" department, there's another rib-tickler in the official records about the founding of Washougal on a claim taken up by one "Dick Ough." Now, you must admit that "Ough" is an unusual spelling for anybody's name and the gentleman in question shared in the astonishment when he first saw it in print in the county records.

A cockney Englishman with accent to match, Dick started out life as Howe. When the clerk asked him his name, Howe left off the "H" and pronounced it "ow." The early-day clerk's method of spelling that kind of a sound was "ough."

Howe went by Ough from then on because it was easier to do than change the official records. And that's how it reads today.

A word about sleeping — *The Brass Lamp*, is a first-rate facility for both towns.

Annual affairs — *Heidelberg-Reed Island Marathon*, in May, power-boat races on the Columbia, with entrants from B.C. to California. Also at this time flower wreaths are set adrift on the river with a memorial service at Parker's Landing . . . *4th of July-Rodeo*, Washougal, fireworks, afternoon and evening in City Park.

The drive east from Washougal is most scenic. The road winds along a rock wall, climbing high above the river in some places, offering enchanting views. A good road, not too fast.

We'd surely hate to be a weatherman at *Cape Horn*, a jagged promontory about 8 miles east of Washougal, or anywhere along the dramatic Columbia River Gorge, for that matter. But at Cape Horn, weather fronts collide head-on.

During the winter, you periodically would find yourself coming up with weather reports like this: "Gale-force east-west winds . . ."

Sounds a little confusing if not downright conflicting, but this is the general area where westerly marine winds bearing rain come sweeping up the river to collide at the west end of the Gorge with cold continental air coming down from the Columbia River Plateau. Collision of the two systems results in blizzards, ice storms and freezing rain; and pretty confused vegetation that ends up with interesting and unusual deformations.

Beacon Rock State Park — offers an unequaled viewpoint from what locals call the second largest monolith in the world. From here the Columbia Gorge spreads before you — islands, river, bluffs and the huge Bonneville Dam. Beacon Rock rises in a great 900 ft. corrugated conical shape from the edge of the river, its summit covered with large blocks of red cinder and stunted trees. Adjacent is Little Beacon Rock and the two monoliths are the tough remnants from earlier times when early river floods plucked away loose lava. The Lewis and Clark Expedition camped here in 1805 going west and again the next year on their return trip. State Park facilities include picnic areas, campground, and about 4,000 acres to explore.

Beacon Rock is easily the outstanding visitor attraction between Vancouver and Bonneville Dam on the Columbia River. What with the park complex and all, it is visited annually by about 100,000 people. But that hasn't always been the case, and there's a tunnel 26 feet long at the bottom of the rock today that isn't part of the normal tour of the premises.

That hole was drilled there about three quarters of a century ago when the U.S. Army Engineers were engaged in the construction of a breakwater at the mouth of the Columbia about 150 miles on an easy haul downstream. The idea was to put 160 tons of dynamite in that hole and blow hell out of that rock. It would have reduced what today is quite a landmark to a pile of rubble that then could be hauled away in barges to protect the entrance of the river. Today, there'd be outraged cries in the public press over such a dastardly deed . . . and there were screams at the time — but not from the public.

The big blast got stopped in court by the railroad line along the north side of the Columbia — and even the railroad didn't object to the destruction of the rock. It was concerned that some of that stuff might fall across the track and interfere with the company's customer service policy.

And that one was mere child's play by comparison with episodes that took place during the 1920's.

◆

For years after the argument between the Army Engineers and the railroad, the status of Beacon Rock was clouded by court action, but in 1915, one Henry Biddle, a man with an enormous sense of proportions, bought the rock and blew $10,000 building a trail to the top. In the 2-year construction process, the only casualty was a donkey, which fell from the edifice and was killed. In later years, a Skamania County Commissioner opined that he could drive a motorcycle to the top of the rock. It was a somewhat precarious ride, but he made it. (And today, donkeys, Skamania County Commissioners and other people on motorcycles are prohibited from ascending the rock, although you can make the walk rather easily if you're up to climbing the equivalent of a structure nearly twice as high as the Space Needle.)

In the late 1920's, Mr. Biddle's heirs offered the rock to the State of Washington for $1 on the condition that the State turn it into a park. There were a lot of people who thought this was just about the nicest thing anybody had ever done for the State . . .

But Governor Roland Hartley, whom you will remember from the Great Cuspidor Caravan, was not among them. Hartley, who was about as budget-conscious as any governor we ever had, indignantly turned down the offer and hurled charges at the Biddle heirs that what they were trying to do was work some kind of a tax dodge . . . that's what they were trying to do . . . and as the protector of the peoples' pocketbook he wasn't going to hold still for it.

This wasn't the first time the irascible Hartley had gotten his nose out of joint on the question of a buck and the press declined to give the story much of a ride. The lethargy on the part of the public to Grandpa Biddle's favorite rock annoyed the Biddle heirs to pieces, but instead of nursing their wounds in private, they did something about it. They offered the rock to the State of Oregon on the theory the folks over there could at least look at the rock from their side of the river even if they couldn't come across the river to climb it.

They searched the law books and nobody could find any legal reason why one state couldn't own and operate a park in another state.

So Julius Meier, governor of Oregon, gladly accepted the offer and set about preparing the way for an Oregon State Park in the State of Washington . . .

Well, that woke everybody up!

The Seattle dailies went wild. Those cheap Oregon politicians were trying to come up to the State of Washington and steal this venerable and vital landmark for their own sneaky reasons. Let Oregon stay home and take care of Oregon.

E. C. Hamilton, acting secretary of the Cascade Pomona Grange, wrote a letter to Governor Meier saying in part that his Grange and the Stevenson Chamber of Commerce were "getting busy in this matter and would Governor Meier hold things up down there while we get going up here?"

Governor Meier, who must have had a very large cheek to put his tongue in, soberly informed the acting secretary of the Cascade Pomona Grange that he would do his best to hold up consummation of the Oregon park in the State of Washington until Mr. Hamilton and the others could settle the matter in a manner more satisfying to the residents of Skamania county.

By that time, Clarence D. Martin had succeeded Hartley as Governor of the State. A delegation from Skamania County waited upon him, pointing out that a dollar wasn't too much to spend for all that rock. After all, it had a $10,000 path on it leading to the top . . . and the Army Engineers could always use it for one of the jettys at the mouth of the Columbia. How could he lose?

Governor Martin agreed . . . and they skinned a dollar right off the top of the State budget and bought the rock.

On April 15, 1935, Rebecca Biddle Wood and Spencer Biddle, Henry's heirs, executed a deed of gift to the State of Washington conveying a tract of about 260 acres to use for park purposes.

The United States Bureau of Mines and Geology takes the rather dull position that this is not the second largest monolith in the world . . .

So, Gibraltar it ain't . . .

But the view from the top is great — and it's finally ours!

North Bonneville — (Pop. 534. Elev. 74.) — It's a town hanging by a thread. It will be flooded out when the new unit is added to the dam and doesn't know where it will go. Visit the fish counting station, fish ladder and the Dam.

North Bonneville Hot Springs has swimming, camping and picnicking and is open in summers. The town is named after the usurious Captain Benjamin Bonneville.

For a long time, there has been a definite tendency on the part of a lot of conservationists — especially the Save Our Salmon groups — to pick on the U.S. Army Corps of Engineers. The Corps is particularly damned for the dammed Columbia . . . and this is where it all began — with Bonneville . . . first big dam on the lower river.

Anthony Netboy, who knows about as much about salmon as just about anybody, covered the feeling on this front in his book *Salmon of the Pacific Northwest (Fish vs. Dams)*. Some of his copy went like this: "Naturally, there were widespread — almost hysterical — fears that Bonneville would spell the end of Columbia River salmon runs and confine the fishery to the lower river, thus wiping out part of an industry then valued at some $10 million annually. In an article in the *Saturday Evening Post* in November, 1937, when the dam was nearing completion, Richard L. Neuberger wrote: 'Prevalent throughout the principal salmon-producing region of the world today is the almost unshakable opinion that within a few years the fighting fish with the flaky flesh will be one and the same with the dodo bird — extinct . . . . ' "

You can see what they're doing here on the fish front, but there is further food for contemplation when you consider the events leading up to the "crime." We mentioned earlier about the fellows back in the 1920's who were predicting that within half a century this nation would be up to it's eyeballs in horse manure. And the congressmen from the Pacific Northwest, with plenty of approbation from the home folks, were screaming their eyes out that the world was robbing the Pacific Northwest of its natural resources, which were being shipped out of here raw. The processing plants and the jobs that went with them were someplace else. Here we had all this water running downhill that could be harnessed. And what we needed was electricity with a big "E!" Cheap electrical power meant jobs and prosperity and if we got them, we could care less about other details. So when the Corps of Engineers got its first assignment back in about 1925, Congress instructed the engineers to study all navigable streams and their tributaries showing promise of hydroelectric development. The studies were to include consideration of flood control, markets for power, competitive sources for power, hydrology, rainfall, run-off, silt content and municipal water supply . . .

But development of watersheds, fisheries, recreation and pollution were excluded from the scope of the river planning process. Then, the big Depression came along, together with a change of administration in Washington, D.C. and the country went gung ho for dams.

In the meantime, what about the fish?

Well, that story goes like this: We stopped swearing at those stinkin' salmon that putrefied on the banks of the rivers and started swearing by them when the first man figured out how to put them in cans and sell them at a profit in about the middle of the last century. We got awfully good at catching salmon . . . and learned the trade fast. By 1895, the mouth of the Columbia, to all practical purposes, was one big net when the salmon were running. The big question of the day was who would get the most fish, the Oregon fishermen or the guys from Washington?

On April 3, 1896, between 200 and 300 Oregon fishermen bent on destruction and armed to the teeth invaded the Washington side of the river. They wrecked property, set Washington fishermen adrift in the river and warned the Washingtonians to keep off of "their" river. Washington's Governor John McGraw called out the National Guard. And on April 9, also armed to the teeth, the National Guardsmen set out for the "border" where they would encamp on the shores of the Columbia for the next 3 months. Nobody shot anybody else, thanks in large measure to the diplomacy of one Captain Frank E. Adams who headed up the National Guard unit.

Hostilities came to a close when a Washington fisherman was arrested by an Oregon sheriff and succeeded in having his case heard in a Federal District Court. District judges from both Oregon and Washington heard the case and ruled that the lines of the two states extended to the river's center.

The thing that caused the big ruckus was the depletion of the salmon supply. They were fishing harder and enjoying it less for the simple reason they were catching fewer fish. The fact is that by 1896, the peak pack for all time from the Columbia River was 13 years behind them. That was 1883 — the year in which 30,200,000 pounds of Columbia River salmon (Compared with 5,000,000 today) were put in cans and sold to somebody.

Couldn't very well blame it on the dams, either.

Bonneville wouldn't even be started until half a century later.

◆

Uncommon shopping – In old interesting *Red Barn Trash and Treasures* one might find something.

A word about eating – Cakes and pies are good at the *Sportsman Cafe* . . . *Jerry's Cafe* advertises with "The Best By a Dam-site" sign.

Stevenson — (Pop. 926. Elev. 98.) — Seat of Skamania County, on low bluffs above the river, it spreads back against rolling hills. They do things better in Skamania County, perhaps because 80% of the county is made up of generally uninhabited forestland and civilization doesn't grind them down. Also the Cascade Mountains, east to west, are included in Skamania's span along the Columbia.

◆

Skamania County underwent an experience in 1864 — 10 years after it was created — that no other county in the State has attained.

The Legislature got mad at it and threw it out of the State. Then it split up the land, giving half each to Clark and Klickitat Counties.

The Legislators thought the folks at Skamania were playing footsie with the Oregon Navigation Company. Anyway, the county government found itself out on its ear and not likely to get back with the Legislature in the mood it was in. So the county commissioners took their case to Congress.

They finally got themselves, to coin a phrase, re-in "Stated."

◆

Skamania also is the only county in which the State's official Monster, the Sasquatch, has actually been seen. It was located near Beacon Rock by a scientific expedition that had casually been assembled at the local tavern one Saturday night.

Anyway, County Ordinance 69-01, passed on April 1, 1969 makes slaying a Sasquatch a felony with a fine of $10,000 or 5 years in jail. Also, by proclamation the State has made it our Official State Monster.

Prowling Stevenson

The Historical Museum and a famous *Rosary Chapel* is housed in the Stevenson Court House Annex. Given by Don Brown of North Bonneville to Skamania County, the rosaries number in the 3,000's and range from the simplest seeds to the most ornate and elaborate metals and jewels. Each rosary has a story and is carefully numbered and catalogued.

A *word about eating* – *Dari Freeze* has simple but attractively served food, modest prices, and a great view of the river. It's the "place" in Stevenson.

Annual *affair* – *Stevenson County Fair*, late August, stock judging, rodeo.

Carson — The St. Martins, an Indian family, have a *Mineral Hot Springs* near Carson with old hotel, family-style restuarant, and cabins. The best road into the *Gifford Pinchot National Forest* is through Carson which leads up into the Wind River Valley and to snowmobiling, jeeping, and scenic drives on logging roads. (To use the forest to best advantage, pick up a U.S. Department of Agriculture map at Vancouver's tourist bureau.) Just east of Carson is Wind Mountain and the Crest Trail which runs from Canada to Mexico. This is the only place for 1,000 miles where you can go through the Cascade Range virtually at sea level. (Elevations range from 51 to 98 feet, 1/80th as high as the mountain passes.)

Wind Mountain — The division point between the Wet Side and the Dry Side of the Mountains. A solitary, rounded hill, it looms in bold relief close to the river. On the east are wooded slopes and on the west jagged peaks. It has a peculiar slant caused by the river as it sawed its way through the rising mountain barrier and made two mountains out of one. The other one is Shell Rock in Oregon.

From here you can return to the Bridge of the Gods, a toll facility across the Columbia at approximately the location of what once was a natural bridge that collapsed some years ago — let's say before the automobile. It wasn't practical for automobiles anyway and the existing bridge will take you to the Oregon side where you have an opportunity to see the Cascade Locks and then speed back to Vancouver on an excellent four-lane, river-level highway with great views of the river and the State of Washington from the other side.

A *word about salmon* – No book of ours which involves the Columbia River would be complete without a mention of the best-tasting salmon on earth.

It's the early spring run of Columbia River Chinook.

Most people think the earliest spring run is in April or May. But don't you believe it. The one we're talking about comes somewhere between mid-February and mid-March. The Department of Fisheries limits the fishing to about 10 days during that period. The Japanese and the smoked-fish processors in Los Angeles, Chicago and New York will buy it all up if they can get their hands on it — if it isn't as outrageously expensive as it fortunately was in the winter of 1974. This, or some slightly inferior, is the smoked salmon you will pay more for than your main course in a fancy Paris restaurant. And we are the only people in the world who can get it fresh right out of the river.

The biological facts on the subject are these. In all of the Atlantic Ocean, there are about 3 million salmon running. In the Pacific Ocean, there are about 3 billion. Of all of these fish, about 30,000 pounds are caught during the first spring run in a sample year like 1972. All salmon spawn in the rivers at about the same time in the fall, but they don't eat once they enter the river for the final act of their lives. So Nature has to store enough fat in them to get them to the spawning grounds. The ones that enter the river the earliest, therefore, are the richest.

The thing to do is make the acquaintance of your favorite fishmonger, (ours is either City, or Pacific Fish). Keep in touch with him and tell him you want the early Columbia River Chinook run and only this run and you want fresh, not frozen salmon. Or plan a trip to this region at the proper time of the year.

On cooking it, our best suggestion is a word we got from Peter Canlis who said, "I'll tell you one thing. You don't put it on the stove and walk away from it!" We get a filet. This fish is so rich you don't have to have a piece up near the head. We salt it first and bake it in a hot oven or on top of the stove with the skin side down. When it starts bubbling on top, it's done . . .

And if it isn't removed immediately, it's ruined.

What do you cook it with? Nothing!

This may or may not be the best piece of information available to you in our book. But after reviewing everything in it, we can't think of anything it contains which is of greater importance.

A Word About Acknowledgements, Sources, Bibliography

My wife, Shirley, is totally responsible for what a lot of people will consider the better half of this book because she was the chief engineer of everything concerned with prowling. Her principal assist came from Genevieve Chambers who in many respects had the toughest job of anybody because she was the one to break the ice by visiting many of the communities involved as our advance scout. Some of the people who teamed up with Shirley in her prowling expeditions were Marilyn Thompson, Warrena Chapin, Julie Yarmouth, Pat Longhi, Betty Pennington, Liz Current and Charlotte Dille.

Other members of research teams that covered the territory were Tucker McHugh, Martha Shantry, Jean Ameluxen and Carol Barnard, who did a lot of the prowling in connection with the good cause.

Louise Dewey, who always takes on major assignments in our book projects, got involved in some of the major research projects, but also had the unenviable job of making the rest of us stick to the subject — which was not always that easy. Jo Addison, another stalwart daughter of our enterprises, did some of the original research and took on the tough assignment of indexing all this stuff. John Gilmore is responsible for the original idea of writing something about the Western Washington scene outside of Seattle.

There is no way of sufficiently thanking librarians everywhere for digging out those hard-to-find facts, but some of them must be singled out for special mention. And Hazel Mills and Nancy Pryor of the Washington State Library at Olympia tower above everybody else and must be commended. If the facts were there to be found, they found them, no matter how hard they had to dig. The pieces on Ezra Meeker and George B. McClellan are cases in point. Another old reliable from a previous picture yet is Phoebe Harris, head of the History Department of the Seattle Public Library. A couple of others who went away and above the normal call of duty were Rosalie Spellman of the Timberland Regional Library in Aberdeen and Kathy Patterson of the Kitsap County Library in Bremerton.

Howard W. Millan, forester for Weyerhaeuser, who took us on a forest tour, gave us a liberal education on clearcutting in particular and forestry practices in general. All of the people in the State Department of Fisheries were ready, willing and able to furnish the basic information, but to be singled out are Cedric Lindsay, Ron Westley and Clyde Sayce who have endured my questions for years, and Dick Noble who heard and nodded at some of the "fish" stories. Dr. Lauren Donaldson, of course, provided the basic information about salmon.

A special vote of thanks goes to the State Department of Commerce and Economic Development and most especially to Bill Shaw of that department for a huge supply of information about Western Washington and to the Automobile Club for an astonishing amount of knowledge about people, places and things you can drive to.

Dorothy Curran and Terry Wilkerson undertook a monumental rush typing job and Robert McCarthy took on the even more monumental job of

431

taking all this stuff and whipping it into a shape that could be encompassed by two book covers.

◆

BOOKS

AVERY, MARY W., *History and Government of the State of Washington;* BAGLEY, CLARENCE B., *History of King County and History of Seattle;* BANCROFT, HUBERT HOWE, *History of Washington, Idaho and Montana;* BEATON, WELFORD, *The City That Made Itself;* CANTWELL, ROBERT, *The Hidden Northwest;* CLARK, DONALD H., *18 Men and a Horse;* CLARK, NORMAN H., *Mill Town;* COCHRAN, THOMAS C., *Railroad Leaders 1845-1890;* COMAN, EDWIN T. JR. and GIBBS, HELEN M., *Time, Tide and Timber, A Century of Pope & Talbot;* CONOVER, C. T., *Mirrors of Seattle;* COOK, JIMMIE JEAN, *A Particular Friend, Penn's Cove;* CORLISS, MARGARET McKIBBEN, *Fall City in the Valley of the Moon;* DEMORO, HARRE, *The Evergreen Fleet;* DRYDEN, CECIL, *History of Washington;* EDSON, LELAH JACKSON, *The Fourth Corner;* EKMAN, LEONARD C., *Scenic Geology of the Pacific Northwest; Encyclopedia Americana; Encyclopedia Britannica;* FEDERAL WRITIERS' PROJECT, *Washington: A Guide to the Evergreen State;* FISH, BYRON, *Guidebook to Puget Sound;* FISH, EDWARDS R., *The Past At Present in Issaquah, Washington;* FREEMAN, MILLER, *The Memoirs of Miller Freeman;* FREEMAN, OTIS W. and MARTIN, HOWARD H., *The Pacific Northwest, An Over-All Appreciation;* GATES, CHARLES, *The First Century at the University of Washington;* GIBBS, JAMES A. JR., *Shipwrecks of the Pacific Coast;* GRANT, FREDERICK JAMES, *History of Seattle, Washington;* HANFORD, C. H., *Seattle and Evirons;* HAWLEY, ROBERT EMMETT, *Squee Mus or Pioneer Days on the Nooksack;* HIDY, RALPH W., HILL, FRANK ERNEST and NEVINS, ALLAN, *Timber and Men, The Weyerhaeuser Story;* HILL, ADA A., *A History of the Snoqualmie Valley;* HINES, REV. H. K., *An Illustrated History of the State of Washington; History of Skagit and Snohomish Counties;* HOLBROOK, STEWART H., *The Columbia;* HULT, RUBY EL, *Untamed Olumpics, Lost Mines and Treasures of the Pacific Northwest* and *Northwest Disaster;* HUNT, HERBERT, *Tacoma, Its History and Its Builders;* HUNT, HERBERT and KAYLOR, FLOYD C., *Washington West of the Cascades; Jimmy Come Lately, History of Clallam County;* JOHANSEN, DOROTHY O. and GATES, CHARLES M., *Empire of the Columbia;* JONES, SYLVIA CASE and CASADY, MYRA FREDERICKSON, *From Cabin to Cupola, County Courthouses of Washington;* KELLOG, GEORGE ALBERT, *A History of Whidbey's Island;* KIRK, RUTH, *The Olympic Seashore, Exploring the Olympic Peninsula* and *Exploring Mount Rainier;* KIRK, RUTH and NAMKUNG, JOHSEL, *The Olympic Rain Forest;* LOCKLEY, FREDERICK, *History of the Columbia from the Dalles to the Sea;* LYONS, CICELY, *Salmon, Our Heritage;* MARSHALL, LOUISE B., *100 Hikes in Western Washington;* McCALLUM, JOHN and ROSS, LORRAINE WILCOX, *Port Angeles, U.S.A.;* McCLELLAND, JOHN M. JR., *Longview, The Remarkable Beginnings of a Modern Western City;* McDONALD, LUCILE, *Coast Country;* McKINLEY, CHARLES, *Uncle Sam in the Pacific Northwest;* MEANY, EDMOND S., *History of the State of Washington;* MEEKER, EZRA, *The Busy Life of Eighty Five Years;* MORGAN, C. T., *The San Juan Story;* MORGAN, MURRAY CROMWELL, *Skid Road, The Last Wilderness,* and *Century 21, The Story of the Seattle World Fair, 1962;* NATIONAL CYCLOPEDIA OF AMERICAN BIOGRAPHY, *Leight Hunt;* NESBIT, ROBERT C., *He Built Seattle;* NETBOY, ANTHONY, *Salmon of the Pacific Northwest (Fish vs Dams);* NEWELL, GORDON R., *H. W. McCurdy Marine History of the Pacific Northwest;* OLSON, JOAN and GENE, *Washington Times and Trails;* PENINSULA ARTS ASSOCIATION, *An Informal Guide to Long Beach Peninsula and Nearby Area;* PHILLIPS, JAMES W., *Washington Place Names;* RIPLEY, THOMAS EMERSON, *Green Timber;* ROTH, LOTTIE ROEDER, *History of Whatcom County;* SPEIDEL, WILLIAM C., *The Sons of the Profits* and *You Still Can't Eat Mt. Rainier!;* STEELE, E. N., *Rise and Decline of the Olympia Oyster* and *The Immigrant (Pacific) Oyster;* STEVENS, HAZARD, *The Life of Isaac Ingalls Stevens;* STEVENS, JAMES, *Green Power, the Story of Public Law 273;* STEVENS, JOHN F., *An Engineer's Recollections;* SUNSET MAGAZINE, *Sunset Travel Guide to Washington and the Beautiful Northwest;* SWAN JAMES G., *The Northwest Coast or Thres Years Residence in Washington Territory;* VAN CLEVE, F. H., *Friday Harbor Then and Now;* VAN OLINDA, O.S., *History of Vashon-Maury Islands;* WILLIAMS, L. R., *Our Pacific County With Pride in*

Heritage, History of Jefferson County; WRIGHT, E. W., *Lewis and Dryden's Marine History of the Pacific Northwest.*

◆

GENERAL

AMERICAN AUTOMOBILE ASSOCIATION, most especially for its *Tour Maps,* which are the best in existence for tour purposes and for its *Tour Book;* APPELO, CARLTON E., *Pillar Rock* and *Brookfield, the Joe Megler Story;* ARNOLD, MARTIN H., Manager of Public Affairs, ITT Rayonier; ASSOCIATION OF WASHINGTON CITIES, *Officials of Washington Cities, 1972-73;* BROWNELL, FRANCIS H., *Reminiscences of the Monte Cristo Mine in the Cascades and of the Inception of Everett, Washington;* CARLSON, GLEN and MILDRED, *The Rosario Story;* CARSON, JOAN, *Tall Timber and the Tide;* CHITTENDEN MAJ. H.M., *Report of an Investigation by a Board of Engineers of the Means of Controlling Floods in the Duwamish-Puyallup Valleys and Their Tributaries;* DARVILL, FRED T. and MARSHALL, LOUISE B., *Winter Walks, a Pocket Guide to Lowland Trails in Whatcom, Skagit, San Juan and Island Counties;* FORT VANCOUVER HISTORICAL SOCIETY, *Clark County History;* GRAY, HENRY L., *The Gold of Monte Cristo;* GREATER BELLEVUE CHAMBER OF COMMERCE, *Bellevue, Washington; Guide to Fidalgo and the San Juan Islands;* HALL, ALFRED, *Wood Pulp and Paper, and People in the Northwest* and *The Pulp and Paper Industry and the Northwest;* HALLIDAY, WILLIAM R., *Caves of Washington;* HARRIS, LOUIS and ASSOCIATES, INC., *The Public's View of Environmental Problems in the State of Washington; Hood Canal Project Report, a Coordinated Study Program, Evergreen State College,* a class project; HUSSEY, JOHN, *Chinook Point, the Story of Fort Columbia;* McCORMICK, JOHN A., *Cruise of the Calcite;* McLACHLAN, EDITH, *They Named It Deer Harbor;* MORGAN, C. T., *The San Juan Story; Oyster Farming for Profit at Willapa Bay;* PACIFIC NORTHWEST BELL TELEPHONE COMPANY, *Telephone Directories* for the Wet Side of the Mountains; *Profile of the City of Aberdeen 1868-1968,* mimeographed study; QUALE, D. B., *Pacific Oyster Culture in British Columbia;* RANCK, HON. GLENN N., *Esther Short and the Redcoats;* RICHARDSON, DAVID, *Magic Islands;* SLAUSON, MORDA C., *100 Years on the Cedar;* SMITH, HERNDON, *Centralia, The First Fifty Years,* a high school class pamphlet; TACOMA AREA CHAMBER OF COMMERCE, *Editorial Copy for Tacoma Area, Washington* (Windsor Publications) and *Tacoma Statistics; The Westport Story;* THOMAS, ROBERT B., *Chuckanut Chronicles;* WARTMAN-ARLAND, FLORA E., *The Story of Montesano;* WELSH, WILLIAM D., *A Brief History of Camas, Washington, A Brief Historical Sketch of Port Townsend* and *A Brief History of Port Angeles;* WHATCOM COUNTY MUSEUM SOCIETY, *1972 Annual Report Whatcom Museum of History and Art.*

◆

GOVERNMENT SOURCES

CRANDELL, DWIGHT R., *The Geological Story of Mount Rainier;* CRANDELL, DWIGHT R. and MULLINEAUX, DONAL R., *Volcanic Hazards at Mount Rainier, Washington;* CRUTCHFIELD, JAMES A., *Socioeconomic Institutional and Legal Considerations in the Management of Puget Sound,* prepared for the Federal Water Pollution Control Administration; DEPARTMENT OF THE ARMY, CORPS OF ENGINEERS, *Navigation and Beach Erosion of Willapa River and Harbor and Naselle River;* DEPARTMENT OF THE ARMY, CORPS OF ENGINEERS, SEATTLE DISTRICT, *Ediz Hook Beach Erosion Control* and *Howard A. Hanson Dam, Eagle Gorge;* FARQUHARSON, F. B., *The Investigaiton of Models of the Original Tacoma Narrows Bridge Under the Action of Wind;* FISH AND WILDLIFE COMMITTEE, PACIFIC NORTHWEST RIVER BASINS COMMISSION, *Status of Columbia River Salmon and Steelhead Trout;* GRAYS HARBOR REGIONAL PLANNING COMMISION, *Annual Progress Report, 1971, Historical Sites in Grays Harbor County, Washington* and *Overall Economic Development Program for Grays Harbor;* MASON COUNTY PLANNING COMMISSION, *The Comprehensive Plan of Mason County;* PORT OF GRAYS HARBOR, *1971 Annual Report* and *1972 Annual Report;* PUGET SOUND GOVERNMENTAL CONFERENCE, *Agricultural Land Use in the Central Puget Sound Region, Unique Features Inventory for the Cedar River-Green River Drainage Basins;* ROBERTS, W. J., *Intercounty River Improvement on the White-Stuck and Puyallup*

Rivers; SEATTLE WATER DEPARTMENT, *Long Range Water Supply Plan for King County;* USDA, ENVIRONMENTAL STATEMENT, *The Skagit;* USDA FOREST SERVICE, *Snoqualmie Pass Wagon Road;* USDA PACIFIC NORTHWEST REGION FOREST SERVICE, *A Study of the Skagit River and Its Cascade, Sauk and Suiattle Tributaries;* USDA AND USDI, *The North Cascades;* USDI FISH AND WILDLIFE SERVICE, *Lower Columbia River National Wildlife Refuge;* USDI NATIONAL PARK SERVICE, *Master Plan, Olympic National Park and North Cascades Master Plan;* WASHINGTON STATE DEPARTMENT OF AGRICULTURE, *Washington Agricultural Statistics;* WASHINGTON STATE DEPARTMENT OF COMMERCE AND ECONOMIC DEVELOPMENT, TOURIST PROMOTION DIVISION, *Annual Attendance at State and National Parks and Other Major Tourist Attractions in Washington State and Tourist Resources and Investment Potential;* WASHINGTON STATE DEPARTMENT OF FISHERIES, *Columbia River Progress Report, 1968, Economic Valuations of the 1965-66 Salt Water Fisheries of Washington, 1968 Fisheries Statistical Report* and *1970 Salmon Sport Catch Report;* WASHINGTON STATE DEPARTMENT OF HIGHWAYS, *Biennial Reports, 1906-1920 and 1940, 1942, Washington Highway News* and *Washington Highways;* WASHINGTON STATE PARKS AND RECREATION COMMISSION, *Washington State Outdoor Recreational Guide;* WASHINGTON STATE SENATE SESSIONS OF 1959, *Proposed Puget Sound Bridge;* WASHINGTON STATE TRANSPORTATION AGENCIES, *1972 Annual Report.*

◆

NEWSPAPERS AND PERIODICALS

BEARDSLEY, ARTHUR S., "Washington Capital Location," *Pacific Northwest Quarterly;* BREWSTER, DAVID, "Our Least Developed Resource: The State Ferries," *The Argus;* CLEVINGER, WOODROW R., "Southern Appalachian Highlanders in Western Washington," *Pacific Northwest Quarterly;* COLLINS, CHAPIN, "The Circle That Works," *American Forests Magazine;* CONOVER, C.T., "When Leigh S. J. Hunt Was a Dominant Seattle Force," *Seattle Times;* COOPER, DAVID, "Beacon Rock Story," *Skamania County Pioneer;* DILGARD, DAVID, "Hewitt Tells Inside Story of Everett Founding," *Everett Herald;* DUNSIRE, CHARLES, "Witnesses Say, 'Don't Dynamite Mount Si,'" *Seattle Post-Intelligencer;* EIKUM, CAPT. A. F., "Puget Sound Super Ferries," *Journal of the Franklin Institute;* FINGER, JOHN R., "Henry Yesler's 'Grand Lottery' of Washington Territory," *Pacific Northwest Quarterly;* HAZELTINE, F. A., "Bruceport, the Ghostly City of Willapa Bay," *Sunday Oregonian;* HUSSEY, JOHN A., "Fort Casey — Garrison for Puget Sound," *Pacific Northwest Quarterly;* MASON, DAVID T., HENZE, KARL D., and BRIEGLEB, PHILIP A., "The Shelton Cooperative Sustained Yield Unit," *Journal of Forestry;* MONTCHALIN, YVONNE, "Beacon Rock in the Gorge," *Sunday Oregonian;* "Northwest Today" articles on the Wet Side, *Seattle Post-Intelligencer;* OVERMEYER, PHILIP HENRY, "George B. McClellan and the Pacific Northwest," *Pacific Northwest Quarterly;* "Resort Had to Dynamite. Stuck Valley Farmers Try to Blow Up White River Dam," *Seattle Post-Intelligencer, July 6, 1899;* SHERRARD, WILLIAM R., "The Kirkland Steel Mill," *Pacific Northwest Quarterly; South Bend Journal Souvenir Edition, 1891;* "Sunday Magazine Section" articles on the Wet Side, *Seattle Times;* "The Seed for a Nation on Wheels;" TYLER, ROBERT L., "Violence at Centralia, 1919," *Pacific Northwest Quarterly;* WALLACE, RAY, "Gateway to Mt. St. Helens and Spirit Lake," *Landing News;* WEGG, TALBOT, "The Sweet Seagoing Busses of Seattle," *City Magazine;* "Wild Water," (Vanport Flood), *Newsweek Magazine.*

A Word About Annual Affairs

January

None that we know of. Happy New Year.

February

1st Saturday — La Conner — *Smelt Derby*
Mount Vernon — *George Washington's Birthday Celebration*
Ocean Shores — *Fog Festival*
Poulsbo — *Annual Codfish Derby and Dance*

March

1st Sunday — Kelso — *Smelt Eating Contest*
Weekend after St. Patrick's Day — Westport — *Driftwood Show*
Centralia — *Lawn and Garden Show*
Port Angeles — *Skin Diving Meet and Octopus Grab*
March through May — *Puyallup, Sumner Daffodil Festival*
Mid May — San Juan Island — *Winter Salmon Derby*
March through May — Tacoma — *Daffodil Festival*
Tenino — *Old Time Music Festival*

April

13th — Westport — *Blessing of the Fleet*
Early — Raymond —*Willapa Bulb and Flower Society*
Middle — Silver Lake — *Bass Fishing Derby*
Last weekend — Oak Harbor — *Holland Happening and Northwest Tulip Festival*
Late — Auburn — *Old Fashioned Spring Festival*
Late — Redmond — *Marymoor Museum Open House*
Bothell — *Speedboat Races*
Bucoda — *Rebecca Annual Turkey Smorgasbord*
Cathlamet — *Little Theater*
Centralia — *Rabbit and Primrose Shows*
Everett — *"Ever on Sunday"*
Lynden — *International Plowing Match*
Rochester — *Strawberry Festival*
Aberdeen — *Rhododendron Annual Show*
Hoquiam — *Y.M.C.A. Book Sale*

May

1st weekend — Cathlamet — *Wahkiakum P.T.A. Smorgasbord*
1st Sunday — Friday Harbor — *Yacht Club Marine Parade*
14 — Cathlamet — *Norway Independence Day*
About 15th — Bay Center — *Methodist Church Seafood Dinner*
2nd weekend — Dungeness — *Irrigation Festival*
Middle — Bellevue — *Rhododendron Show*
Middle — Friday Harbor — *Family Festival*

Middle — Naselle — *Firemen's Smorgasbord*
3rd week — Skamokawa — *Firemen's Ball*
3rd weekend — Port Townsend — *Rhododendron Festival*
Last Wednesday — Olympia — *Silver Tea and Pound Party*
Late — Oakville — *Chehalis Indian Tribal Days*
Last weekend — Port Orchard — *Art and Historical Celebration*
Memorial Day — Friday Harbor — *Parade*
Memorial Day — Kent — *Fun Feast Festival*
Memorial Day — North Beach — *Indian Canoe Races up Quinault River*
Memorial Day — *Quinault Indian Reservation*
Anacortes — *Croatian Spring Festival*
Bainbridge Island — *Scotch Broom Festival*
Bellingham — *Blossomtime Festival*
Bremerton — *Rhododendron Forest Theater Productions*
Bremerton — *Armed Forces Day Parade*
Bremerton — *Annual Jazz Festival*
Olympia — *Homes of Interest Tour*
Poulsbo — *Viking Festival*
Rainier — *Rodeo*
Shelton — *Mason County Forest Festival*
Vashon Island — *Home Tours*
Washougal — *Heidelberg-Reed Island Marathon*

June

1 — Gig Harbor — *Harbor Holidays*
1st Saturday — Castle Rock — *Kon Tiki Raft Race*
1st week — Everett — *Salty Sea Days*
1st weekend — Roy — *Rodeo*
Early — Bellevue — *Miss Bellevue Pageant*
2nd weekend — Deming — *Logging Show*
2nd week — Grays River — *Not Quite White Water Run*
2nd weekend — Lummi Indian Reservation — *Lummi Indian Stommish*
3rd weekend — Edmonds — *Art Festival*
Father's Day — Rainier — *Team Pull*
Last weekend — Darrington — *Timberbown Rodeo*
Late — Burlington — *Dairy Berry Days*
Late — Montesano — *Farm Festival*
Aberdeen — *Rose Annual Show*
Bellingham — *Highland Games*
Cathlamet — *Kids Parade and Invitational Softball Tournament*
Centralia — *Appaloosa Horse Show*
Longview — *Lower Columbia Arts and Crafts Festival*
Lynden — *Farmer's Day Parade*
Maple Valley — *Cedar River Boat Race*
Olympia — *Maytown Flower Show*
Winlock — *Egg Day*
Woodland — *Planter's Day Celebration*

July

4th — Bainbridge Island — *Grand Old Fourth of July Celebration*
4th — Bellingham — *Dominion Day*

4th — Bothell — *Parade and Fireworks*
4th — Edmonds — *Fourth of July Celebration*
4th — Forks — *Old Fashioned Fourth of July*
4th — Long Beach — *Fireworks and Arts and Crafts Sale*
4th — Longview — *Fireworks*
4th — North Beach — *Annual Taholah Days*
4th — Oak Harbor — *Old Fashioned 4th*
4th — Oakville — *Fourth of July Celebration*
4th — Port Orchard — *Fathoms of Fun*
4th — Quinault Indian Reservation
4th — Renton — *Renton Aviation Festival*
4th — San Juan Island — *Fourth of July at American Camp*
4th — Sedro Woolley — *Loggerodeo*
4th — Washougal — *Rodeo*
Early — Steilacoom — *Salmon Bake*
About 4th — Swiss Park — *Schwingfest*
Weekend of 4th — Westport — *Fishing Derby*
2nd Saturday — Amboy — *Territorial Days Celebration*
2nd weekend — Olympia — *Capital Lakefair*
2nd weekend — Tumwater — *Outdoor Art Festival*
Mid — Kirkland — *Kirkland Summer Celebration*
Mid — McCleary — *Bear Festival*
Mid — Orcas Island — *San Juan County Horseman's Association Show*
    (alternated with San Juan Island)
3rd Saturday — Battleground — *Harvest Day*
3rd Saturday — Orcas Island — *Historical Society Parade*
3rd week — Cathlamet — *Summer Arts Festival*
3rd week — Port Angeles — *Arts in Action*
3rd weekend — Mt. Vernon — *Northwest Square Dance Festival*
Last week — Kalama — *Community Fair*
Last weekend — Anacortes — *Barbershop Quartet Show and Barbecue*
Last full weekend — Bellevue — *Pacific Northwest Arts and Crafts Fair*
Last weekend — Bucoda — *Annual Reunion*
Last Saturday — Orcas Island — *Episcopal Church White Elephant Sale*
    and Tea
Last — Fairground between Longview, Kelso — *Cowlitz County Fair*
Late — Bellevue — *Village Mall Festival*
Late — Oak Harbor — *North Whidbey Stampede*
Bothell — *Raft Races*
Castel Rock — *National Champion Motorcycle Race*
Centralia — *Arts and Crafts Fair*
Centralia — *Buck and Kids Goat Show*
Centralia — *Motorcycle Races*
Centralia — *Rose Show*
Kelso — *Highlander Summer Festival*
Kent — *Ezra Meeker Days*
Kirkland — *Lake Washington Saddle Club Horse Show*
Vashon Island — *The Festival*

August

Early — Yelm — *Prairie Days*
1st weekend — Anacortes — *Arts and Crafts Festival*

1st week — Castle Rock — *Community Fair*
1st week — Skykomish — *Tunnel or Skykomish Days*
2nd week — Cathlamet — *Annual Melodrama and Poster Art Exhibit*
2nd week — Orcas Island — *Library Board Fair*
2nd weekend — Coupeville — *Coupeville Festival Days*
2nd weekend — Mt. Vernon — *Skagit County Fair*
Mid — Elma — *Grays Harbor County Fair*
Mid — Morton — *Logger's Jubilee*
Mid — Skamokawa — *Wahkiakum County Fair*
3rd weekend — Aberdeen — *Rain Fair*
3rd week — Enumclaw — *King County Fair*
3rd weekend — San Juan Island — *San Juan County Fair*
3rd weekend — Stanwood — *Camano Community Fair*
Last weekend —Cape Flattery — *Makah Days*
Last Saturday — Medina — *Medina Day*
Late — Long Beach — *Art Show*
Late — Lynden — *Northwest Washington Fair*
Late — Lynden — *Threshing Bee*
Late — Monroe — *Evergreen State Fair*
Late — Stevenson — *County Fair*
Late — Westport — *Westport Charter Association Fishing Derby*
Darrington — *Grange Fair*
Darrington — *Stillaguamish Valley Frontier Days*
Enumclaw — *Folk Dance Festival*
Hoquiam — *Pet Show*
South of Littlerock — *Harness Races*
Menlo — *Pacific County Fair*
Moclips, Copalis, Ocean City and Ocean Shores — *Olympic North Beach
    Art Show*
Olympia — *Thurston County Fair*
Port Angeles — *Clallam County Fair*
Port Townsend — *Jefferson County Fair*
Redmond — *Bicycle Derby*
Suquamish — *Chief Seattle Days*

September

1st week — Everett — *Waterfront Art Show*
Labor Day weekend — Centralia — *Washington and Oregon Horse Game
    Finals*
Labor Day — Longview — *Festivities*
Labor Day — Port Angeles — *Derby Days*
Labor Day — Roy — *Rodeo*
Labor Day — South Bend
Labor Day — Tenino — *Oregon Trail Celebration*
Weekend after Labor Day — Port Angeles — *Junior Salmon Derby*
Early — Hoquiam — *Logger's Playday*
Early — Mt. Vernon — *Skagit County Rodeo*
Centralia — *Horseless Carriage Swap Meet*
Oak Harbor — *Naval Air Show (alternate years)*
Port Townsend — *Victorian Home Tour*
Puyallup — *Western Washington Fair*
Snohomish — *Tour of Historical Houses*

Fall

Aberdeen — *Annual Flea Market*
Auburn — *White River Buddhist Church Festival*

October

About 1st — San Juan Island — *One Day Fall Salmon Derby*
Early — Steilacoom — *Cider Squeeze*
Olympia — *Kiwanis Pancake Feed*
Port Townsend — *Victorian Home Tour*
Stanwood — *Lions' Lutefisk Dinner*
Tacoma — *McNeil Island Prison Art Show and Sale*

November

1st week — Kalama — *Amalak*
11 — Auburn — *Veterans' Day Parade*
Aberdeen — *A.A.U.W. Book Sale*
Hoquiam — *Y.M.C.A. Bazaar*
Kirkland — *Kirkland Creative Arts League's Annual Pot and Craft Show*
Olympia — *St. John's Antique Show*
Vancouver — *Art Fair*
Vancouver — *Flea Market*

December

1st Friday — Bothell — *Lighting Outdoor Christmas Tree*
1st Saturday — Bellingham — *Lutefisk Dinner*
1st Sunday — Kelso — *Annual Lutefisk Dinner*
1st weekend — Aberdeen — *Art Show*
1st week — Long Beach — *Annual Lutefisk and Meatball Dinner*
Centralia — *Boy Scout Show*
Centralia — *Indian Three-Feather Fair*
Centralia — *Northwest Pigeon Show*
Dungeness — *The Christmas House*
Kirkland — *Enchanted Castle*
Longview — *Tour of Homes*
San Juan Island — *Christmas Boat*

Index

441

*Weyerhaeuser Timber, Inc. formed in 1900. Became Weyerhaeuser Company in 1959.

A Word About Design

The text of this book is set in 9 point Mergenthaler VIP Caledonia Medium and the headings in **Caledonia Bold** and **Helvetica Bold.** The text is printed on Loyola Text, substance 60; the map section on Shasta Gloss, substance 60; the endpapers on Mountie Offset, substance 80. The volume is Smyth sewn and the four-color printed casing cloth is Corvon 120 with a nitrocellulose protective coating.

Cartography by Eugene Turner and Charles Ogrosky, in consultation with Dr. John C. Sherman, Department of Geography, University of Washington. Composition by Typeline, Seattle, Washington. Color separations by Color Control, Inc., Seattle, Washington. Typography, book design and production by Robert McCarthy.

A Word About This Book

This book is aimed primarily at the 80% of the population of this side of the mountains who live in and around Seattle, but never have seriously prowled the rest of the area west of the Cascade Mountains.

As anybody who lives in this country knows, the title "The Wet Side of the Mountains" is apropos on the weather front. However, there's a lot more wetness than that which falls out of the sky . . . like the lakes and streams and the general greenery that makes ours the Evergreen State. They also do a bit more drinkin' here than they do on the Dry Side. We selected the word "prowling" for the subtitle with due care. A tour is something somebody else explains to you. An exploration is sort of systematic. But prowling, ah, there's a word. The dictionary calls it "roaming in a predatory manner," and we like it. Your "finds" may include a unique peek at Mount Rainier or an "overheard" in the local tavern. But they add equally to the delight of life.

It's the people, however, who make the difference. Most of the stories in this book will cause the local people in the community to exclaim, "My word, I didn't know that!" At the very least, we hope we have hit the nail on the head enough so the locals will say, "well, he got *that* one straight." In all of the stories, we completely absolve all Chambers of Commerce of any blame for the contents. The librarians of Western Washington, will have to share some of the credit or blame as the case may be.

This is a changing world, so not everything we found in our prowling section will be the way it was when you show up. On the other hand, we make no pretense of being encyclopedic. We seek to stimulate your curiosity and sense of adventure. The book is designed for "car cushion travelers." You can get the picture of the Wet Side from an armchair in your living room. But for the *feel,* you'll have to get out and around. No specialized equipment is necessary to engage in the pursuits suggested. If there's an unusual bunch of birds like the eagles on the Skagit, they get a mention. But if you're a bird watcher, you'd better bring along your book.

Our tour maps have been superimposed upon the basic shaded relief map of the State of Washington published by the United States Geological Survey, which shows you where the mountains and valleys are and how the rivers flow, which in many instances will surprise you.

There's an American redundancy that goes like this: "Look and *see,*" and we hope that's what you will do.